Psychological Types

or

The Psychology of Individuation

By

C. G. JUNG

Dr Med. et Jur. of the University of Zürich
Author of "Psychology of the Unconscious"

.Translated by

H. GODWIN BAYNES, M.B., B.C. Cantab

ISBN: 979-8-89096-018-4

All Rights reserved. No part of this book maybe reproduced without written permission from the publishers, except by a reviewer who may quote brief passages in a review to be printed in a newspaper or magazine.

Printed: March 2023

Published and Distributed By:
Lushena Books
607 Country Club Drive, Unit E
Bensenville, IL 60106
www.lushenabks.com

ISBN: 979-8-89096-018-4

CONTENTS

TRANSLATOR'S PREFACE   i-xxii

FOREWORD   7

INTRODUCTION   9
   The Two Mechanisms: Extraversion and Introversion. The Four Psychological Basic Functions: Thinking, Feeling, Sensation, and Intuition, 9

CHAPTER I. THE PROBLEM OF TYPES IN THE HISTORY OF CLASSICAL AND MEDIEVAL THOUGHT   15

1. *Psychology in the Classical Age: the Gnostics, Tertullian, and Origen*   15
2. *The Theological Disputes of the Ancient Church*   30
3. *The Problem of Transubstantiation*   33
4. *Nominalism and Realism*   37
   (a) The Problem of the Universalia in the Classical Age, 38; (b) The Universalia Problem in Scholasticism, 52; (c) Abélard's Attempt at Conciliation, 62
5. *The Holy Communion Controversy between Luther and Zwingli*   84

CHAPTER II. SCHILLER'S IDEAS UPON THE TYPE PROBLEM

1. *Letters on the Æsthetic Education of Man*   87
   (a) The Superior and the Inferior Functions, 87; (b) Concerning the Basic Instincts, 123
2. *A Discussion on Naïve and Sentimental Poetry*   163
   (a) The Naïve Attitude, 165; (b) The Sentimental Attitude, 166; (c) The Idealist and the Realist, 168

CHAPTER III. THE APOLLONIAN AND THE DIONYSIAN 170

CHAPTER IV. THE TYPE PROBLEM IN THE DISCERNMENT OF HUMAN CHARACTER

1. *General Remarks upon Jordan's Types* 184
2. *Special Description and Criticism of the Jordan Types* 191
   (a) The Introverted Woman (the more-impassioned woman), 191; (b) The Extraverted Woman (the less-impassioned woman), 195; (c) The Extraverted Man, 200; (d) The Introverted Man, 204

CHAPTER V. THE PROBLEM OF TYPES IN POETRY
CARL SPITTELER'S *Prometheus and Epimetheus*

1. *Introductory Remarks on Spitteler's Characterization of Types* 207
2. *A Comparison of Spitteler's with Goethe's Prometheus* 215
3. *The Significance of the Reconciling Symbol* 234
   (a) The Brahmanic Conception of the Problem of the Opposites, 242; (b) Concerning the Brahmanic Conception of the Reconciling Symbol, 247; (c) The Reconciling Symbol as the Principle of Dynamic Regulation, 257; (d) The Reconciling Symbol in Chinese Philosophy, 264
4. *The Relativity of the Symbol* 272
   (a) The Service of Woman and the Service of the Soul, 272; (b) The Relativity of the Idea of God in Meister Eckehart, 297
5. *The Nature of the Reconciling Symbol in Spitteler* 320

CHAPTER VI. THE TYPE PROBLEM IN PSYCHIATRY 337

CHAPTER VII. THE PROBLEM OF TYPICAL ATTITUDES IN ÆSTHETICS 358

CONTENTS

CHAPTER VIII. THE PROBLEM OF TYPES IN MODERN PHILOSOPHY

1. *William James' Types* — 372
2. *The Characteristic Pairs of Opposites in James' Types* — 382

   (a) Rationalism v. Empiricism, 382; (b) Intellectualism v. Sensationalism, 387; (c) Idealism v. Materialism, 387; (d) Optimism v. Pessimism, 389; (e) Religiousness v. Irreligiousness, 391; (f) Indeterminism v. Determinism, 393; (g) Monism v. Pluralism, 396; (h) Dogmatism v. Scepticism, 396

3. *General Criticism of James' Conception* — 397

CHAPTER IX. THE TYPE PROBLEM IN BIOGRAPHY — 401

CHAPTER X. GENERAL DESCRIPTION OF THE TYPES

A. Introduction — 412

B. The Extraverted Type — 416

   (I) *The General Attitude of Consciousness* — 416

   (II) *The Attitude of the Unconscious* — 422

   (III) *The Peculiarities of Basic Psychological Functions in the Extraverted Attitude* — 428

   1. Thinking, 428; 2. The Extraverted Thinking Type, 434; 3. Feeling, 446; 4. The Extraverted Feeling Type, 448; 5. Recapitulation of Extraverted Rational Types, 452; 6. Sensation, 456; 7. The Extraverted Sensation Type, 457; 8. Intuition, 461; 9. The Extraverted Intuitive Type, 464; 10. Recapitulation of Extraverted Irrational Types, 468

C. The Introverted Type

   (I) *The General Attitude of Consciousness* — 471

   (II) *The Unconscious Attitude* — 477

   (III) *Peculiarities of the Basic Psychological Functions in the Introverted Attitude* — 480

1. Thinking, 480; 2. The Introverted Thinking Type, 484; 3. Feeling, 489; 4. The Introverted Feeling Type, 492; 5. Recapitulation of Introverted Rational Types, 495; 6. Sensation, 498; 7. The Introverted Sensation Type, 500; 8. Intuition, 505; 9. The Introverted Intuitive Type, 508; 10. Recapitulation of Introverted Irrational Types, 511; 11. The Principal and Auxiliary Functions, 513

CHAPTER XI. DEFINITIONS 518

1. Abstraction, 520; 2. Affect, 522; 3. Affectivity, 523; 4. Anima, 524; 5. Apperception, 524; 6. Archaism, 524; 7. Assimilation, 525; 8. Attitude, 526; 9. Collective, 530; 10. Compensation, 531; 11. Concretism, 533; 12. Consciousness, 535; 13. Constructive, 536; 14. Differentiation, 539; 15. Dissimilation, 540; 16. Ego, 540; 17. Emotion, 541; 18. Enantiodromia, 541; 19. Extraversion, 542; 20. Feeling, 543; 21. Feeling-into, 547; 22. Function, 547; 23. Idea, 547; 24. Identification, 551; 25. Identity, 552; 26. Image, 554; 27. Individual, 560; 28. Individuality, 561; 29. Individuation, 561; 30. Inferior Function, 563; 31. Instinct, 565; 32. Intellect, 566; 33. Introjection, 566; 34. Introversion, 567; 35. Intuition, 567; 36. Irrational, 569; 37. Libido, 571; 38. Objective Plane, 572; 39. Orientation, 572; 40. "Participation Mystique", 572; 41. Phantasy, 573; 42. Power-Complex, 582; 43. Projection, 582; 44. Rational, 583; 45. Reductive, 584; 46. Self, 585; 47. Sensation, 585; 48. Soul, 588; 49. Soul-Image, 596; 50. Subjective Plane, 599; 51. Symbol, 601; 52. Synthetic, 610; 53. Thinking, 611; 54. Transcendent Function, 612; 55. Type, 612; 56. Unconscious, 613; 57. Will, 616.

CONCLUSION 618

TRANSLATOR'S PREFACE

In presenting this, Jung's crowning work, to the English-speaking world, I would like to make a brief sketch of the curve of the author's thought; for, like everything that is rooted in reality, Jung's standpoint shows a definite line of development, and the following of this progression may add a historical sidelight to the understanding of the present work.

I would have preferred to avoid the troubled waters of controversy, but it does not seem possible to relate the history of Jung's standpoint without at the same time contrasting it with that of Freud. That this somewhat thankless task was necessary is proved by the still frequent coupling of the two schools of thought under a common denomination, suggesting that the general mind has, as yet, failed to make a clear distinction between the contrasting standpoints.

Freud undoubtedly is an analytical genius. One has only to read his early studies upon the ætiology of hysteria to be struck by the virtuosity of his subtle reasoning. It was an intuitive capacity of no ordinary shrewdness that revealed the hidden significance of the hysterical syndrome. For it opened the way to an entirely new conception of the unconscious, and led to a rediscovery of the dream as a significant and purposeful product of that same unconscious activity of which the hysterical manifestations were a somatic expression.

Freud was like a master-detective tracking down the incriminating complex in the unconscious, while Breuer, his colleague, contented himself with exorcizing the repressed elements from above by abreaction under hypnosis.

In medical science we can discern two main human types or attitudes whose behaviour towards the therapeutic problem presents a characteristic contrast. The chief interest of the one lies in the welfare of mankind and the healing of his patient; the other's interest is monopolized by the ætiological problem presented by the patient's condition, and is concerned in a less degree with its remedy. The one attempts to discover a remedy before understanding the problem; the other tends to become so completely immersed in the problem that the original objective, e.g. the healing of mankind, is often lost to view.

We do not find the greatest minds succumbing to either of these frailties, but it is not out of place to outline such typical predispositions, since the vague benevolence and imperfect understanding of the one are as far below the scientific desideratum, as are the other's exclusive ardours for the "scientific" chase a blemish upon the ideal of humanity.

While Breuer, therefore, seems to have been content with the therapeutic efficacy of hypnotic abreaction, Freud found in this procedure merely a starting-point for a further investigation of those avenues which the abreacted material opened out, and, as he rather naïvely admits, no one was more surprised than himself to observe that this further investigation of the patient's subterranean activities produced valuable therapeutic results. It is, of course, true that some of the most beneficent therapeutic measures have been discovered in precisely this way, as incidental by-products as it were, of the process of scientific investigation, but for the purpose of comparison it is important to stress the fact that Freud's approach was preeminently that of the empirical investigator, because it is in this attitude that we find both his strength and his limitation as a psychologist. We will return again to this point when the picture has been more fully outlined.

While Freud was enduring the obloquy of the psychological pioneer in Vienna, Jung was approaching similar conclusions from a very different angle in Zürich. By a further elaboration of the word-association experiments formerly employed by Galton and Wundt for other ends, he succeeded in the most delicate task of devising objective criteria for the recognition of unconscious complexes. The discovery of prolonged reaction time, perseveration, etc., associated with affect-toned presentations led to his invaluable formulation of the complex, from which he advanced to the same fundamental concept of repression which Freud had reached by the clinical route. This naturally brought the two pioneers together, and Jung found in Freud's masterly analytical technique the admitted highroad to the unconscious processes.

In so far as it was purely a question of method, Freud and Jung found themselves in harmony, but the study of psychological processes can never remain a mere question of method; sooner or later it must challenge the investigator to produce a philosophic standpoint. And here a basic psychological difference began to make itself felt. Freud the empiricist wanted to limit his psychological principles to empirically ascertainable matters of fact. On the lines of orthodox scientific determinism he preferred an exclusively causal and reductive account of the psyche. Jung, on the other hand, appreciated the fact that man was more than a variously disordered object—he was also a self-creating subject. He argued that the causal explanation cannot be regarded as exclusive in the psychological realm, since the final or purposive explanation finds equal justification in human experience. He began to feel that the inevitable sexual interpretations, however widely the term might be stretched, were too poor a rendering of the passionate and infinitely diverse aims of the human soul. In harmony, therefore, with Robert Mayer's conception in the realm of physics, he developed the energic conception of the libido, thus lifting the whole subject from a one-sided and purely empiricistic standpoint to the level of universal concepts, where science and philosophy are able to understand one another.

The actual point of divergence between the two standpoints occurred, significantly enough, over the question of the mother-imago. As is well known, Freud's interpretation of the mother-image in dreams is exclusively referred to the actual mother or mother-surrogate. Jung contended that the almost magical influence of the parent-imago with its supreme dynamic effect upon the whole course of a man's life, not only shaping his actions, thoughts, and relations to the world with secret and invisible determination, but also creating the figures of the father and mother deities in his religious and fantasy life, could find no final explanation in the actual events of infantile and adolescent experience. The difficulty was admitted by Freud, but the acceptance of inherited racial experience as an integral factor in psychic life opened such menacing vistas[1], involving frank disaster to the comprehensive system he had devised and was prepared to demonstrate to the world, that he resolutely shut his eyes to the possibility of this boundless and primeval continuity. He was only prepared to explain the discrete, individual psyche, and Jung's conception of the collective unconscious opened the door to unnamed things from the jungle and primeval forest: it introduced a world of unknown elemental forces which must be unconditionally excluded from a scientific system.

But, apart from the considerations above alluded to, Jung's argument was incontestable. The lungs of the new-born infant know how to breathe, the heart knows how to beat, the whole co-ordinated organic system knows how to function, only because the infant's body is the product of inherited functional experience. The whole story of man's struggle for adaptation to life, his whole phylogenetic history, are represented in that 'knowing how' of the infant's body. Is it then blindness or fear that urges us to deny to the infant psyche that same functional inheritance which is so mani-

[1] Cf. Jung's treatment of the "terrible mother" motif, in the *Psychology of the Unconscious*.

festly present in the other organs? What is this dark fear of our archaic past which prompts us to reject the possibility of any psychic experience other than that of our individual lives?

At all events it is clear that, once the existence of these inherited psychic structures is admitted as the basis of psychic activity, that conception of the unconscious and its contents which regards it as derived exclusively from objective experience in the single individual life must go by the board. Here, then, was the alternative which, from the historical standpoint, we must regard as crucial. Either Jung's conception of the collective unconscious must be admitted, and with it the whole inner world of the subject, wherein the inner images or archetypes are granted an equal determining power with the objects of the outer world, or the one-sided empirical system must be maintained with its somewhat arbitrary postulates, and the whole disturbing vision of the collective unconscious be rejected as a fantastic impossibility.

Jung's great work, *Psychology of the Unconscious*, was the final statement of his separation from and advance beyond the Freudian standpoint, and Freud's reaction to this work made it clear that he too recognized an insuperable opposition. For in this work Jung did not confine himself to a reduction of the Miller fantasies to their instinctive roots; he also identified the personal themes with universal religious and mythological conceptions, thus raising them to a level of general importance. But, in so doing, he also proved the necessity of the synthetic standpoint in analytical psychology—a demonstration that bore unavoidable implications unfavourable to the Freudian position.

That the divergence between Freud and Jung must sooner or later have become acute will, I think, be clear when we remember that between the two men there existed not only the difference of race but also a radical difference of type. An extravert, by his very nature, is bound to produce a psychology differing essentially from that of the introvert. For Freud the aims of empirical science, with its centripetal bias towards a minute and detailed analysis of observable facts, were absolute; whereas for Jung a purely objective psychology was not enough, in that it entirely omitted the undeniable reality and power of the idea.

This is not the place to enter into a discussion of the relative values of the extraverted empiricistic and the introverted abstracting attitudes in human thought; the struggle of these two elements, as Jung shows in the present work, is synonymous with the history of human culture. They are both essential as mutual correctives, and it is only when either tendency becomes a one-sided habitual attitude that commonsense steps in and makes its inscrutable judgment. In science these two general tendencies appear as the twin capacities of empirical observation of facts and of intellectual abstraction from the facts observed of generally valid principles, but only in the man of genius do we find both capacities fully and symmetrically developed.

In my view, criticism of Freud's achievement should be based not upon the fact that he failed to perceive the possibility of a general application of his ideas—this he apprehended only too clearly —but upon his inability to frame concepts of general validity.

He attempted to make the infinitely complex phenomena of the psyche harmonize with theories intuitively derived from clinical material; but he was unable to enlarge or reconstruct his theoretical system to embrace the wider aspects of human experience and culture. The normal was considered in terms of the pathological.

A gradual, but very definite, movement of intelligent opinion away from the Freudian standpoint at the present time is, in my view, a commonsense reaction to the damaging depreciation of essential human values involved in this reductive valuation of the psyche. For the reductive standpoint fails to see that every complex is Janus-faced, and that the energy invested in it is never purely regressive, but is rather a *reculer pour mieux sauter*. The extraordinary vitality of the infantile complex would be quite inexplicable on the supposition that it was a wholly regressive tendency. But it demands a synthetic standpoint to perceive that every dawning possibility in life is heralded by the image of the child, the symbol of eternal youth, and that the infantile complex with its simplicity and trust in life is also the growing point of the developing personality. Every child perceives, what the investigator may fail to see, that a living man in his most eager and productive moments exhibits certain essential characters of childhood. Creative activity demands the power and complexity of the man as well as the simple attitude of the child. But Jung himself deals so fully and so much more ably with the limitations of the purely reductive standpoint, that I need not elaborate this aspect of the subject here.

It has been argued that psycho-analysis does not claim to be more than a therapeutic technique and a method of research, and that it is irrelevant for the psychologist to concern himself with the question of human development or with the inevitable ancillary problems of morality, religion, and human relationship. In this very argument the essential limitations of this standpoint stand self-confessed, since a psychology that excludes the most vital problems of life from its sphere of responsibility requires no further criticism. It is already moribund. Actually, of course, a psychologic nihilism which broke down every individual form into its elements and put nothing in its place could not, conceivably, have anything but disastrous therapeutic results. But Freud does put something positive and definite in its place; for there always remains the transference to the analyst, which, in the case of a positive transference, involves a gradual assimilation by the patient to the analyst's general attitude to life, and in the alternative case a very definite rejection of the man and all his ways.

This unconscious identification with the analyst is quite outside the sphere of the latter's control. It is inherent in the analytical relationship. But for the analyst to wash his hands of this unconscious effect, with its far-reaching moral influence upon the patient's subsequent development, is as irresponsible as though a surgeon were to shut his eyes to the inevitable dangers of hæmorrhage and sepsis. The question of moral responsibility, therefore, is inherent in analytical practice, and, since this is so, we have every right to demand of a practical psychological system that it shall attempt to discover the fundamental laws of human development and, as far as possible, to formulate them.

We said at the beginning that Freud was an empirical investigator, and that this was both his strength and his limitation. It is his strength, because it required the empirical attitude to discover and establish the psycho-analytic technique; and it is his limitation, because the general attitude to life which is governed solely by objective facts and considerations is quite incapable of judging man as a subject. If, as Freud points out in *Totem and Taboo*, human morality can be traced back to the first primeval act of parricide, a derivative of some remote arboreal conflict between the parent's authority and the son's lust for his father's wives, then morality can exist only as a constituent of herd-psychology, and the individual moral law is as much a delusion as is free will to a determinist. It is obvious that a purely objective standpoint must similarly interpret all the realities of the inner world as mere derivatives or reflects of objective facts. Man is wholly determined, therefore, by things outside himself. He is nothing but a "*singe raté*", a mere mechanism that gets out of order, and, by an appropriate use of the correct method, can be put right again.

This standpoint is well illustrated by the Freudian interpretation of dreams, which always explains the dream-figures as carefully disguised ignoring the possibility that such images may also be symbols of subjective realities existing in their own right.

The Freudian standpoint, then, in attempting to explain all the phenomena of human psychology in terms of objective facts, remains one-sided, and the extent of its limitations may conceivably be measured by the intolerance with which it discusses or ignores every standpoint that ventures beyond its circumscribed terrain.

Since there have always been large numbers of men for whom the objects and experiences of the psychic life bear a more immediate sense of reality than the world of objective facts, it is clear that a purely objective account of the psychological processes could not win any considerable support beyond the specialized limit of its own peculiar faculty. But, however much the historical eye may regard the wider subjective valuation and synthetic method of Jung as the inevitable response of psychology to essential human demands, the greatest honour must none the less be given to Jung, for, not only was he the first psychologist to perceive these demands, but he also voiced them in principles whose universality could embrace the heights and the depths of the psyche and comprehend its manifold diversity.

In establishing the two typical mechanisms of introversion and extraversion together with the main categories of human types based upon this fundamental antithesis, Jung has demonstrated the impossibility of every attempt to formulate a generally valid theory of human psychology which ignores these typical differences. For a theory whose validity is incontestable for the psyche from which it originated proves itself worthless and even misleading for an individual of another type. From considerations such as these we must confess our inability to devise any rigid or dogmatic formula which can be authoritatively promulgated as a general system of psychological therapy. A physician once justly complained to Jung that he had made analysis so difficult. It is certainly true that the pronouncements of Freud relieve the analyst of a very considerable onus. He is not required to ask himself What is the individual way of this particular subject? He has merely to reduce his patient's psychological material to its elementary constituents according to prescribed 'orthodox' formulations, and if the patient is not satisfied he either proves himself psychologically inadequate to receive the truth, or so immersed in his morbid state that the analytical light serves only to reveal its impenetrable obscurities.

In his sub-title to this book Jung has called it the Psychology of Individuation, and therewith he affirms the essential principle of his philosophy; for to Jung the psyche is a world which contains all the elements of the greater world, with the same destructive and constructive forces—a pluralistic universe in which the individual either fulfils or neglects his essential rôle of creator.

The individuality is the central co-ordinating principle of this realm, analogous to the principle of royalty in the nation; and, in so far as this co-ordinating will achieves an effective command of the diverse and conflicting elements which constantly tend to disrupt his kingdom, are we justified in speaking of a differentiated individual.

The individuality is universally present, but as

a rule it exists mainly in the unconscious, often finding expression in dreams and fantasies in some royal or princely figure. It is a principle, therefore, which has to be created out of the unconscious by accepting individuation as a deliberate and conscious aim.

It may be asked what has individuation got to do with the treatment of nervous disorders? This question springs from the assumption that there is no fundamental relation between the realities of the psychic life and the symptomatic conditions of the body. And yet the lives of religious founders one and all bear witness to the fact that the healing of the body is not unconnected with the inner life.

If differentiation and co-ordination of function are admitted as the vital principles of organic life, it is difficult to see how one can regard psychic or functional disorders as anything else than a statement of the relative suppression of these principles in the individual in question. The psyche, therefore, has to be considered as a totality, and not as an ill-assorted collection of instincts and faculties. For, if man is not a mere passive mechanism to be shaped to the pattern of a chosen formula, he stands before us as a self-creating subject whose individual way may be directly opposed to the analyst's most cherished theories.

It has often been levelled against Jung that his is a pedagogic system, that he tries to teach people how they should live, how they should settle their problems, instead of merely indicating the unconscious state of affairs and leaving them to find their way out. We are told that the physician should confine himself to the purely medical aspect of the case, and that to voice any criticism which might suggest a definite moral or religious standpoint is to encroach upon other domains for which he has no qualifications. This point of view is very common and has a certain justification, supported as it is by the whole traditional constitution of society. But, in spite of an argument apparently so overwhelming, the individual psyche persistently over-rides the social categories, and, notwithstanding every rational attempt to regard it in terms of "mechanisms" and functions, its claim to be considered as a whole has never once abated.

Since this claim appears to have a socially subversive tendency and occasions very real fear in a great many minds, it might be well to examine its character. If we assume—and without this assumption no system of psycho-therapy has any reasonable basis—that a neurosis is an act of adaptation that has failed, we are faced, in an individual case, with the question: What is the nature of the reality to which this individual has failed to adapt? The materialist would fain have us believe that the only reality demanding psychic adaptation is represented by the sheer concrete facts of the physical environment. But, if concrete facts were the only reality, there would be no spiritual problem, and consequently no neurotics. The minimal adjustment to objective conditions demanded by social life could present no insuperable difficulty to anyone but an imbecile *unless* there were another reality of a very different nature always competing with the concrete world for prior claim upon our energy.

This other psychic or spiritual reality, which

comprises the whole inner life of the subject, is as constantly demanding new forms and expressions of its energy as is the world of external objects, even though it does not make the same compelling demand upon our attention. The fantastic hallucinations of the delirium tremens patient or the paranoic are equally strong evidence for the reality of these inner claims as are the ecstatic experiences of the religious mystic; only in the former case they are seen from the reverse side. For this reality the evidence is necessarily subjective. The snakes and frogs seen by the patient in his delirium, however delusional to an objective valuation, possess an indisputable reality to the man himself. Clearly, therefore, there are two quite different kinds of reality, both of which, while pressing their respective claims upon our capacity for adaptation, are nevertheless mutually dependent in the sense that neglect or disregard of either eventually destroys the validity of both.

Again, thousands of lives are fruitlessly spent in a neurotic attempt to escape an overpowering parental influence, just as there are innumerable lives seeking a release from the unconscious tyranny of collective authority. The need of the growing child to differentiate himself as an individual from the magical parental influence is essentially the same as the individuating impulse to distinguish oneself as a "single, separate person" from the collective "*en masse*". But the developing child who seeks to adventure beyond the magic circle of the family encounters not only the authority and conservatism of the older generation, but also the far more dangerous inertia and infantilism of his own psychology.

In either case it is essentially the same conflict between the individual and the collective elements, whether within or without, and what could prevail against the authority without or the inertia within, but an inner necessity or law whose incontestable superiority can stand firm against every attack.

The genuine rebel in his resistance against the law can win our sympathy in spite of ourselves. Notwithstanding every rational resistance, the inner superiority enforces our recognition of its power. The genuine neurotic (as opposed to the social deserter) is typically a man who cannot reconcile the claims of traditional forms and values with those of the obscure, but unbending, law within. For him, the inner and outer claims are contradictory and mutually exclusive. In answer to the persistent demands of the social tax-collector he can only guarantee the overdue payments to Cæsar when Cæsar shall first have recognized the paramount claims of God.

For such a man to be delivered over once again to the orthodox representatives of traditional values, whatever the formula may be, is merely to hand him over to his creditors. Before he can do justice to traditional forms or fulfil his social task, he must first submit himself unconditionally to the fundamental law of his own being. This is his stronghold, this his root in an enduring reality, and with this security he can go out into the world, not only to settle the old imperial demands, but also, perchance, to reanimate the forms that are with the vision of what is to be.

To the critic then who charges Jung with pedagogic interference, we would reply: Jung does not teach a man how he shall act or think or live, but he gives him a technique by which he can comprehend and finally submit to the laws of his own nature. The basic principles of human development are not vested in any faculty—they have no academic formula, for they embrace every function of human activity. They are commensurate with life. It is not surprising, therefore, that it is from just those quarters where authority reigns and where 'truth' is already congealed into a dogma, that this particular criticism usually springs. It is easier to teach and practise a formula than to try to interpret the meaning of life; but a rational formula is doomed from the outset, because it tends to seduce men to turn away from the enigma of life by offering them a formula in its stead: thus it opposes life, and its inherent destructiveness determines its own fate.

No psychological formula can ever explain life. At the best, it can only present the living process in a thinkable form to our reason. As soon as it claims to have explained a living process, its effect is destructive, since it interposes an authoritative, ready-made explanation between the individual and the real problems life presents, thus apparently relieving him of the need to seek his own individual solution.

This is what Jung describes as negative, in contrast to positive or creative, thinking; for what we call character is nothing but the measure of sincerity with which an individual creates a positive adaptation to the essential problems of life.

A formula is an artefact, a rigid and arbitrary frame into which the plastic and changing forms of life are impressed. The resistance of the unconscious to this imposition is perceptible in the impassioned dogmatism of the man who has accepted a formula as an explanation of life.

A principle, on the other hand, acquires its validity not from the authority of the man who lays it down, but from life itself, whose manifold processes it correlates and brings into abstract form. Formulæ live and die like their authors— one might almost say with their authors; whereas the validity of an abstract principle is just as durable as the processes it embraces and comprehends. It needs neither authority nor defence. It bears within it its own prerogative.

Jung's analytical interpretations are admittedly based upon the principles established in the present work, but practical application of them, i.e. their translation again into life, rests wholly with the individual subject.

The individuality is the alpha and omega of Jung's system, not, however, as an expression of personal power as the egoist would like to interpret it, but essentially as a function of the whole. This in itself sufficiently disposes of the pedagogic critics, for a system which aims at individual autonomy cannot justly be described as pedagogic. Naturally there could be no interpretation at all without a standpoint. In practice, therefore, the most that we can humanly demand is that the standpoint of the analyst should constantly be orientated towards the individual way, or "greatest ought" of the subject. It is, of course, true that, however genuinely an analyst may strive to realize this aim, his interpretation will, to a large extent, be subjectively conditioned. This is psychologically unavoidable, but the very sincerity with which he strives to interpret the fundamental needs of his patient from the material at his disposal must surely make for individual autonomy. Whereas the opposite standpoint that would reduce psychic experience into terms of arbitrary mechanisms must inevitably tend to standardize mankind; because, in this case, the main criterion of judgment is the relative measure of conformity with the orthodox formula.

From the point of view of social economy, there can surely be no two opinions that a psychological technique whose aim it is to create individuals is of greater value to society than a system which aims at conformity. For an individual who is at one with himself seeks a creative collective expression from inner necessity, while the dragooned neurotic is of as little service to society as an unwilling conscript.

But how, it may be asked, can a physician learn to forgo the customary collectivized view of his fellow-man and train himself to an unprejudiced view of his patient's individuality unobscured by his own unconscious projections?

It will, I think, be clear, that before a physician can fully recognize and respect the individuality of his patient, he must first have given allegiance to this principle in himself. This does not mean to say that only a differentiated individual is fitted to practise analysis—such a condition would disqualify every candidate—but it does demand that the analyst shall himself have been analysed and shall have made a sincere attempt to deal with his own life problems before undertaking to deal with those of his patients.

The aims of the individuality can never be fully apprehended by exclusive reference to the biological or instinctive life of the subject; in fact, just as little can they be explained in terms of instinct as a work-of-art in terms of energy. One might attempt to formulate the chief aim of the individuality as the effort to create out of oneself the most significant product of which one is capable. On the biological plane this is clearly the child but on the psychic level this must be interpreted more broadly as something that bears for the individual, in the fullest sense of the term, a significance at least analogous to that of the child. For the greatest individual value is always pregnant with value for mankind.

Hence the budding personality with its potentialities for good or ill is frequently represented in dreams in the form of a child.

The whole symbolism of rebirth is quite unintelligible from a purely biological standpoint; hence a system that is blinded by its preoccupation with purely instinctive interpretations presents a definite obstruction to the whole transforming or spiritualizing tendency of the libido. The obvious prospective significance of the rebirth symbolism in dreams is, to my mind, so apparent that one is tempted to accuse the reductive school of wilful blindness. But this would, of course, be quite absurd, and one has to remind oneself that the dream, like the lily of the field, is a natural product unassisted by human intention, and that it is quite as rational to regard the lily as a fortunate accidental grouping of basic organic elements as to conceive it as a symbol of purity. The standpoint, therefore, eventually decides the interpretation, as it also decides the manner in which the interpretation is employed.

I have now revealed the very practical motive which prompted me to bring this whole question of the underlying opposition of standpoint into the foreground of discussion. This attempt, although foredoomed to excite controversy, will, I hope, in spite of the obvious inadequacy of such a brief outline, help to clarify the situation in a way that a more cautious and non-committal statement would fail to do.

The great value of the present work lies in the fact that it is a mature and conscious survey of the psychological field, viewed by a mind of unique range and development whose astonishing wealth of psychological experience illumines the whole work. The range of Jung's thought has developed with his experience. The *Psychology of the Unconscious* was the shaft of the tree—this work is its ample spread.

For practical psychologists it must assuredly be regarded as the foundation of the science, for in no other work do we find basic psychological principles whose validity is commensurate with the undeniable facts of man's historic development and the realities of individual experience.

The actual translation of the work was a task of such difficulty that often I despaired of giving the book an adequate rendering into English. Fortunately I had exceptional opportunities of assistance from the author himself, for whose unstinted patience and generosity in listening to my translation week by week and offering invaluable suggestions I cannot be too grateful.

For most valued assistance in the various preparatory stages of the work I wish to tender my warmest acknowledgments to my wife, to Mrs

Lilian A. Clare, to Mr John M. Thorburn of Cardiff University, and finally, to Mr W. Swan Stallybrass (of Messrs Kegan Paul & Co. Ltd., my publishers) for whose friendly offices and indefatigable care in the matter of punctuation and typography throughout the book I offer my very cordial appreciation.

With regard to the use of italics in this book I wish to explain that, with the exception of titles of books, italics have been reserved to denote stress. Had all the numerous foreign words occurring in the text been printed in italic type, in accordance with English typographical convention, the special value of this type, from the point of view of the author's meaning, would have been lost. Our only other alternative was to use quotation-marks, but in many places foreign words occur so frequently that this would have served merely to blur the page and confuse the eye. There are a few exceptions to the above rule, the reasons for which will be obvious. Double quotation-marks are used for actual quotations; single marks for indicating philosophical terms used in special senses, *façons de parler*, etc.

For the fact that, with the exception of the quotations from Kant, I have nowhere availed myself of existing English translations either of the Oriental or the European authors quoted in the text, I must plead my residence in Zürich, where the various works were inaccessible.

H. G. BAYNES.

24 CAMPDEN HILL SQUARE,
LONDON, W.8.

FOREWORD

THIS book is the fruit of nearly twenty years' work in the domain of practical psychology. It is a gradual intellectual structure, equally compounded of numberless impressions and experiences in the practice of psychiatry and nervous maladies, and of intercourse with men of all social levels; it is a product, therefore, of my personal dealings with friend and with foe; and finally it has a further source in the criticism of my own psychological particularity.

I do not propose to burden the reader with casuistry; it is, however, incumbent upon me to link up the ideas, derived from experience, both historically and terminologically with already existing knowledge.

I have done this not so much from a sense of historical justice as from a desire to bring the experiences of the medical specialist out of narrow professional limits into more general relations; relations which will enable the educated lay mind to make use of the experiences of a specialized terrain. I would never have ventured to attempt this expansion, which might well be misunderstood as an encroachment upon other spheres, were I not convinced that the psychological points of view presented in this book are of wide significance and application, and are therefore better treated in a general connection than left in the form of a specialized scientific hypothesis.

With this aim in view I have confined myself to a discussion of the ideas of a few workers in the field of the problem under review, and have omitted to mention all that has already been said concerning our problem in general. Quite apart from the fact that to catalogue such a collection of correlated material and views with even bare adequacy would far exceed my powers, the inventory, when completed, could make no sort of fundamental contribution to the discussion and development of the problem. Without regret, therefore, I have omitted much that I have collected in the course of years, confining myself as far as possible to the main questions. A most valuable document, that afforded me great help, has also been sacrificed in this renunciation. This is a bulky correspondence which I exchanged with my friend, Dr H. Schmid of Basle, concerning the question of types. I owe a great deal to this interchange of ideas, and much of it, though of course in an altered and greatly revised form, has gone into my book. This correspondence belongs essentially to the stage of preparation, and its inclusion would create more confusion than clarity. But I owe it to the labours of my friend to express my thanks to him here.

C. G. JUNG.

Küsnacht, Zürich
Spring, 1920.

INTRODUCTION

"Plato and Aristotle! These are not merely two systems; they are also types of two distinct human natures, which from immemorial time, under every sort of cloak, stand more or less inimically opposed. But pre-eminently the whole medieval period was riven by this conflict, persisting even to the present day; moreover, this battle is the most essential content of the history of the Christian Church. Though under different names, always and essentially it is of Plato and Aristotle that we speak. Enthusiastic, mystical, Platonic natures reveal Christian ideas and their corresponding symbols from the bottomless depths of their souls. Practical, ordering, Aristotelian natures build up from these ideas and symbols a solid system, a dogma and a cult. The Church eventually embraces both natures—one of them sheltering among the clergy, while the other finds refuge in monasticism; yet both incessantly at feud."—H. HEINE, *Deutschland*, i.

IN my practical medical work with nervous patients I have long been struck by the fact that among the many individual differences in human psychology there exist also *typical distinctions*: *two types* especially became clear to me which I have termed the *Introversion* and the *Extraversion Types*.

When we reflect upon human history, we see how the destinies of one individual are conditioned more by the objects of his interest, while in another they are conditioned more by his own inner self, by his subject. Since, therefore, we all swerve rather more towards one side than the other, we are naturally disposed to understand everything in the sense of our own type.

I mention this circumstance at this point to prevent possible subsequent misunderstandings. As may well be understood, this basic condition considerably aggravates the difficulty of a general description of the types. I must presume a considerable benevolence on the part of the reader if I may hope to be rightly understood. It would be relatively simple if every reader himself knew to which category he belonged. But it is often a difficult matter to discover to which type an individual belongs, especially when oneself is in question. Judgment in relation to one's own personality is indeed always extraordinarily clouded. This subjective clouding of judgment is, therefore, a frequent if not constant factor, for in every pronounced type there exists a special *tendency towards compensation for the onesidedness of his type*, a tendency which is biologically expedient since it is a constant effort to maintain psychic equilibrium. Through compensation there arise secondary characters, or *types*, which present a picture that is extraordinarily hard to decipher, so difficult, indeed, that one is even inclined to deny the existence of types in general and to believe only in individual differences.

I must emphasize this difficulty in order to justify a certain peculiarity in my later presentation. For it might seem as though a simpler way would be to describe two concrete cases and to lay their dissections one beside the other. But every individual possesses both mechanisms—extraversion as well as introversion, and only the relative predominance of the one or the other determines the type. Hence, in order to bring out the necessary relief in the picture, one would have to re-touch it rather vigorously; which would certainly amount to a more or less pious fraud. Moreover, the psychological reaction of a human being is such a complicated matter, that my descriptive ability would indeed hardly suffice to give an absolutely correct picture of it.

From sheer necessity, therefore, I must confine myself to a presentation of principles which I have abstracted from an abundance of observed facts. In this there is no question of deductio a priori, as it might well appear: it is rather a deductive *presentation* of empirically gained understanding. It is my hope that this insight may prove a clarifying contribution to a dilemma which, not in analytical psychology alone but also in other provinces of science, and especially in the personal relations of human beings one to another, has led and still continues to lead to misunderstanding and division. For it explains how the existence of two distinct types is actually a fact that has long been known: a fact that in one form or another has dawned upon the observer of human nature or shed light upon the brooding reflection of the thinker; presenting itself, for example, to Goethe's intuition as the embracing principle of *systole* and *diastole*. The names and forms in which the mechanism of introversion and extraversion has been conceived are extremely diverse, and are, as a rule, adapted only to the standpoint of the individual observer. Notwithstanding the diversity of the formulations, the common basis or fundamental idea shines constantly through; namely, in the one case an outward movement of interest toward the object, and in the other a movement of interest away from the object, towards the subject and his own psychological processes. In the first case the object works like a magnet upon the tendencies of the subject; it is, therefore, an attraction that to a large extent determines the subject. It even alienates him from himself: his qualities may become so transformed, in the sense of assimilation to the object, that one could imagine the object to possess an extreme and even decisive significance for the subject. It might almost seem as though it were an absolute determination, a special purpose of life or fate that he should abandon himself wholly to the object.

But, in the latter case, the subject is and remains the centre of every interest. It looks, one might say, as though all the life-energy were ultimately seeking the subject, thus offering a constant hindrance to any overpowering influence on the part of the object. It is as though energy were flowing away from the object, as if the subject were a magnet which would draw the object to itself.

It is not easy to characterize this contrasting relationship to the object in a way that is lucid and intelligible; there is, in fact, a great danger of reaching quite paradoxical formulations which would create more confusion than clarity. Quite generally, one could describe the introverted standpoint as one that under all circumstances sets the self and the subjective psychological process above the object and the objective process, or at any rate holds its ground against the object. This attitude, therefore, gives the subject a higher value than the object. As a result, the object always possesses a lower value; it has secondary importance; occasionally it even represents merely an outward objective token of a subjective content, the embodiment of an idea in other words, in which, however, the idea is the essential factor; or it is the object of a feeling, where, however, the feeling experience is the chief thing, and not the object in its own individuality. The extraverted standpoint, on the contrary, sets the subject below the object, whereby the object receives the predominant value. The subject always has secondary importance; the subjective process appears at times merely as a disturbing or superfluous accessory to objective events. It is plain that the psychology resulting from these antagonistic standpoints must be distinguished as two totally different orientations. The one sees everything from the angle of his conception, the other from the view-point of the objective occurrence.

These opposite attitudes are merely opposite mechanisms—a diastolic going out and seizing of the object, and a systolic concentration and release of energy from the object seized. Every human being possesses both mechanisms as an expression of his natural life-rhythm—that rhythm which Goethe, surely not by chance, characterized with the physiological concepts of cardiac activity. A rhythmical alternation of both forms of psychic activity may correspond with the normal course of life. But the complicated external conditions under which we live, as well as the presumably even more complex conditions of our individual psychic disposition, seldom permit a completely undisturbed flow of our psychic activity. Outer circumstances and inner disposition frequently favour the one mechanism, and restrict or hinder the other; whereby a predominance of one mechanism naturally arises. If this condition becomes in any way chronic a *type* is produced, namely an habitual attitude, in which the one mechanism permanently dominates; not, of course, that the other can ever be completely suppressed, inasmuch as it also is an integral factor in psychic activity. Hence, there can never occur a pure type in the sense that he is entirely possessed of the one mechanism with a complete atrophy of the other. A typical attitude always signifies the merely relative predominance of one mechanism.

With the substantiation of introversion and extraversion an opportunity at once offered itself for the differentiation of two extensive groups of psychological individuals. But this grouping is of such a superficial and inclusive nature that it permits no more than a rather general discrimination. A more exact investigation of those individual psychologies which fall into either group at once yields great differences between individuals who none the less belong to the same group. If, therefore, we wish to determine wherein lie the differences of individuals belonging to a definite group, we must make a further step. My experience has taught me that individuals can quite generally be differentiated, not only by the universal difference of extra and introversion, but also according to individual basic psychological functions. For in the same measure as outer circumstances and inner disposition respectively promote a predominance of extraversion or introversion, they also favour the predominance of one definite basic function in the individual.

As basic functions, *i.e.* functions which are both genuinely as well as essentially differentiated from other functions, there exist *thinking, feeling, sensation*, and *intuition*. If one of these functions habitually prevails, a corresponding type results. I therefore discriminate thinking, feeling, sensation, and intuitive types. *Everyone of these types can moreover be introverted or extraverted* according to his relation to the object in the way described above.

In two former communications[1] concerning psychological types, I did not carry out the distinction outlined above, but identified the thinking type with the introvert and the feeling type with the extravert. A deeper elaboration of the problem proved this combination to be untenable. To avoid misunderstandings I would, therefore, ask the reader to bear in mind the distinction here developed. In order to ensure the clarity which is essential in such complicated things, I have devoted the last chapter of this book to the definitions of my psychological conceptions.

---

[1] Jung, *Contribution à l'étude des Types psychologiques* (*Arch. de Psychologie*, I, xiii, p. 289); *Psychological Types* (*Collected Papers on Analytical Psychology*, p. 287. London: Baillière 1916) *Psychologie der unbewussten Prozesse*, 2te Aufl. p. 65 (Zurich 1918).

CHAPTER I

THE PROBLEM OF TYPES IN THE HISTORY OF CLASSICAL AND MEDIEVAL THOUGHT

1. Psychology in the Classical Age: The Gnostics, Tertullian, and Origen

So long as the historical world has existed there has always been psychology; objective psychology, however, is of only recent growth. We might affirm of the science of former times that the lack of objective psychology corresponds with a proportionate yield of the subjective element. Hence the works of the ancients are full of psychology, but only little of it can be described as objective psychology. This may be conditioned in no small measure by the peculiarity of human relationship in classic and in medieval times. The ancients had, if one may so express it, an almost exclusively biological appreciation of their fellow-men; this is everywhere apparent in the habits of life and legal conditions of antiquity. In so far as a judgment of value found any general expression, the medieval world had a metaphysical valuation of its fellow-men; this had its source in the idea of the imperishable value of the human soul. This metaphysical valuation, which may be regarded as a compensation to the standpoint of antiquity, is just as unfavourable as the biological valuation, so far as that personal appraisement is concerned, which can alone be the groundwork of an objective psychology. There are indeed not a few who hold that a psychology can be written ex cathedra.

Nowadays, however, most of us are convinced that an objective psychology must above all be grounded upon observation and experience. This foundation would be ideal, if only it were possible. But the ideal and the purpose of science do not consist in giving the most exact possible description of facts—science cannot yet compete with kinematographic and phonographic records—it can fulfil its aim and purpose only in the establishment of law, which is merely an abbreviated expression for manifold and yet correlated processes. This purpose transcends the purely experimental by means of the *concept*, which, in spite of general and proved validity, will always be a product of the subjective psychological constellation of the investigator. In the making of scientific theory and concept much that is personal and incidental is involved. There is also a psychological personal equation, not merely a psycho-physical. We can see colours, but not wave-lengths. This well-known fact must nowhere be more seriously held in view than in psychology. The operation of the personal equation has already begun in the act of observation. *One sees what one can best see from oneself.* Thus, first and foremost, one sees the mote in one's brother's eye. No doubt the mote is there, but the beam sits in one's own, and—may somewhat hinder the act of seeing. I misdoubt the principle of 'pure observation' in so-called objective psychology, unless one confines oneself to the eye-pieces of the chronoscope, or to the ergograph and such-like "psychological" apparatus. With such methods one also ensures oneself against too great a yield of experimental psychological facts.

But the personal psychological equation becomes even more important in the presentation or the communication of observations, to say nothing of the interpretation and abstraction of the experimental material! Nowhere, as in psychology, is the basic requirement so indispensable that the observer and investigator should be adequate to his object, in the sense that he should be able to see not the subject only but also the object The demand that he should see *only* objectively is quite out of the question, for it is impossible. We may well be satisfied if we do not see *too* subjectively. That the subjective observation and interpretation agrees with the objective facts of the psychological object is evidence for the interpretation only in so far as the latter makes no pretence to be universal, but intends to be valid only for that field of the object that is under consideration. To this extent it is just the beam in one's own eye that enables one to detect the mote in the brother's eye. The beam in one's own eye, in this case, does not prove (as already said) that the brother has no mote in his. But the impairment of vision might easily give rise to a general theory that all motes are beams.

The recognition and taking to heart of the subjective limitation of knowledge in general, and of psychological knowledge in particular, is a basic condition for the scientific and accurate estimation of a psyche differing from that of the observing subject. This condition is fulfilled only when the observer is adequately informed concerning the compass and nature of his own personality. He can, however, be sufficiently informed only when he has in great measure freed himself from the compromising influence of collective opinion and feeling, and has thereby reached a clear conception of his own individuality.

The further we go back into history the more we see personality disappearing beneath the wrappings of collectivity. And, if we go right down to primitive psychology, we find absolutely no trace of the idea of the individual. In place of individuality we find only collective relationship, or "participation mystique" (Lévy - Bruhl). But the collective attitude prevents the understanding and estimation of a psychology which differs from that of the subject, because the mind that is collectively orientated is quite incapable of thinking and feeling in any other way than by projection. What we understand by the concept 'individual' is a relatively recent acquisition in the history of the human mind and human culture. It is no wonder, therefore, that the earlier all-powerful collective attitude almost entirely prevented an objective psychological estimation of individual differences, and forbade any general scientific objectification of individual psychological processes. It was owing to this very lack of psychological thinking that knowledge became 'psychologized', *i.e.* crowded with projected psychology. Striking instances of this are to be seen in the first attempts at a philosophical explanation of the universe. The development of individuality, with the resulting psychological differentiation of man, goes hand in hand with a de-psychologizing of objective science.

These reflections may explain why the springs of objective psychology have such a niggardly flow in the material handed down to us from antiquity. The description of the four temperaments gathered from antiquity is hardly a psychological typification, since the temperaments are scarcely more than psycho-physiological complexions. But this lack of information does not mean that we possess no trace in classical literature of the reality of the psychological antitheses in question.

Thus Gnostic philosophy established three types, corresponding perhaps with the three basic psychological functions: *thinking, feeling*, and *sensation*. The Pneumatici might correspond with thinking, the Psychici with feeling and the Hylici with sensation. The inferior estimation of the Psychici accorded with the spirit of the Gnosis, which in contrast with Christianity insisted upon the value of knowledge. But the Christian principle of love and faith did not favour knowledge. The Pneumaticist would accordingly suffer a decline in value within the Christian sphere, in so far as he distinguished himself merely by the possession of the Gnosis, *i.e.* knowledge.

Differences in type should also be remembered when we are considering the long and somewhat dangerous fight which from its earliest beginnings the Church conducted against the Gnosticism. In the practical tendency that undoubtedly prevailed in early Christianity, the intellectual, when, in obedience to his fighting instinct he did not lose himself in apologetic polemics, scarcely came into his own. The 'regula fidei' was too narrow and permitted no independent movement. Moreover, it was poor in positive intellectual content. It contained a few ideas, which, although of enormous practical value, were a definite obstacle to thought. The intellectual was much more hardly hit by the 'sacrificium intellectus' than the man of feeling. Hence it is easy to understand that the vastly superior intellectual content of the Gnosis, which in the light of our present intellectual development has not only not lost but has indeed considerably gained in value, must have made the greatest possible appeal to the intellectual within the Church. For him it was in very sooth the enticement of the world. *Docetism*, in particular, caused grave trouble to the Church, with its contention that Christ possessed only an apparent body and that his whole earthly existence and passion had been merely a semblance. In this contention the purely intellectual was given too prominent a part at the expense of human feeling. Perhaps the battle with the Gnosis is most clearly presented to us in two figures who were extremely influential, not only as Fathers of the Church but also as personalities. These are Tertullian and Origen, who lived about the end of the second century. Schultz says of them:

" One organism is able to take in nourishment well-nigh omnivorously and to assimilate it to its own nature; another with equal persistence rejects it again with every appearance of passionate refusal. Thus essentially opposed, Origen identified himself with one side, Tertullian with the other. Their reaction to the Gnosis is not only characteristic of the two personalities and their philosophy of life; it is also fundamentally significant of the position of the Gnosis in the mental life and religious tendencies of that time."—(*Dokumente der Gnosis*, Jena 1910.)

Tertullian was born in Carthage somewhere about 160 A.D. He was a pagan, and yielded himself to the lascivious life of his city until about his thirty-fifth year, when he became a Christian. He was the author of numerous writings, wherein his character, which is our especial interest, unmistakably shows itself. Clear and distinct are his unexampled, noble-hearted zeal, his fire, his passionate temperament, and the profound inwardness of his religious understanding. He is fanatical, ingeniously one-sided for the sake of an accepted truth, impatient, an incomparable fighting spirit, a merciless opponent, who sees victory only in the total annihilation of his adversary, and his speech is like a flashing steel wielded with inhuman mastery. He is the creator of the Church Latin which lasted for more than a thousand years. He it was who coined the terminology of the Early Church. " Had he seized upon a point of view, then must he follow it through to its every conclusion as though lashed by legions from hell, even when right had long since ceased to be on his side and all reasonable order lay mutilated before him." The passion of his thinking was so inexorable that again and again he alienated himself from the very thing for which he would have given his heart's blood. Accordingly his ethical code is bitter in its severity. Martyrdom he commanded to be sought and not shunned; he permitted no second marriage, and required the permanent veiling of persons of the female sex. The Gnosis, which in reality is a passion for thought and cognition, he attacked with unrelenting fanaticism, including both philosophy and science, which are so closely linked up with it. To him is ascribed the sublime confession: Credo quia absurdum est (I believe because it is against reason). This, however, does not altogether accord with historical fact; he merely said (*De Carne Christi*, 5): "Et mortuus est dei filius, prorsus credibile est, quia ineptum est. Et sepultus resurrexit; *certum est quia impossibile est*." (" And the Son of God died; this is therefore credible, just because it is absurd. And He rose again from the tomb; this is certain, because it is impossible".) By virtue of the acuteness of his mind he saw through the poverty of philosophic and of Gnostic learning, and contemptuously rejected it. He invoked against it the testimony of his own inner world, his own inner realities, which were one with his faith. In the shaping and development of these realities he became the creator of those abstract conceptions which still underlie the Catholic system of to-day. The irrational inner reality had for him an essentially dynamic nature; it was his principle, his consolidated position in face of the world and the collectively valid or rational science and philosophy. I translate his own words:

"I summon a new witness, or rather a witness more known than any written monument, more debated than any system of life, more published abroad than any promulgation, greater than the whole of man, yea that which constitutes the whole man. Approach then, O my soul, should'st thou be something Divine and eternal, as many philosophers believe—the less wilt thou lie—or not wholly Divine, because mortal, as forsooth Epicurus alone contends—then so much the less can'st thou lie—whether thou comest from heaven or art born of earth, whether compounded of numbers or atoms, whether thou hast thy beginning with the body or art later joined thereto; what matter indeed whence thou springest or how thou makest man what he is, namely a reasonable being, capable of perception and knowledge.

But I call thee not, O soul, as proclaiming wisdom, trained in the schools, conversant with libraries, fed and nourished in the academies and pillared halls of Attica. No, I would speak with thee, O soul, as wondrous simple and uneducated, awkward and inexperienced, such as thou art for those who have nothing else but thee, even just as thou comest from the alleys, from the street-corners and from the workshops. It is just thy ignorance I need."

The self-mutilation achieved by Tertullian in the sacrificium intellectus led him to the unreserved recognition of the irrational inner reality, the real ground of his faith. That necessity of the religious process which he sensed in himself he seized in the incomparable formula "*anima naturaliter Christiana*" ("the soul is naturally Christian"). With the sacrificium intellectus philosophy and science, hence the Gnosis also, had no more meaning for him.

In the further course of his life the qualities I have depicted stood out in bolder relief. While the Church was driven to compromise more and more with the masses, he revolted against it and became a follower of that Phrygian prophet Montanus, an ecstatic, who represented the principle of absolute denial of the world and complete spiritualization. In violent pamphlets he now began to assail the policy of Pope Calixtus I, and thus, together with Montanism, fell more or less extra ecclesiam. According to a statement of St Augustine he must later even have rejected Montanism and founded a sect of his own.

Tertullian is a classical representative of the introverted thinking type. His very considerable and keenly developed intellect is flanked by unmistakable sensuality. That psychological process of development which we term the *Christian* led him to the sacrifice, the amputation, of the most valuable function, a mythical idea which is also contained in the great and exemplary symbol of the sacrifice of the Son of God. His most valuable organ was the intellect, including that clear discernment of which it was the instrument. Through the sacrificium intellectus, the way of purely intellectual development was forbidden him; it forced him to recognize the irrational *dynamis* of his soul as the foundation of his being. The intellectuality of the Gnosis, its specifically rational coinage of the dynamic phenomena of the soul, must necessarily have been odious to him, for that was just the way he had to forsake, in order to recognize the principle of feeling.

In Origen we may recognize the absolute opposite of Tertullian. Origen was born in Alexandria about 185. His father was a Christian martyr. He himself grew up in that quite unique mental atmosphere wherein the ideas of East and West mingled. With an intense yearning for knowledge he eagerly absorbed all that was worth knowing, and accepted everything, whether Christian, Jewish, Grecian, or Egyptian, which at that time the teeming intellectual world of Alexandria offered him. He distinguished himself as a teacher in a school of catechists. The pagan philosopher Porphyrius, a pupil of Plotinus, said of him: " His outer life was that of a Christian and against the Law; but in his view of things phenomenal and divine he was a Hellenist, and substituted the conception of the Greeks for the foreign myths."

Already before A.D. 211 his self-castration had taken place; his inner motives for this may indeed be guessed, but historically they are not known to us. Personally he was of great influence, and had a winning speech. He was constantly surrounded by pupils and a whole host of stenographers who gathered up the precious words that fell from the revered master's lips. As an author he was extraordinarily fertile and he developed an amazing academic activity. In Antioch he even delivered lectures on theology to the Emperor's mother Mammæa. In Cæsarea he was the head of a school. His teaching activities were considerably interrupted by his extensive journeyings. He possessed extraordinary scholarship and had an astounding capacity for the investigation of things in general. He hunted up old Bible manuscripts and earned special merit for his textual criticism. "He was a great scholar, indeed the only true scholar the ancient Church possessed", says Harnack. In complete contrast to Tertullian, Origen did not bar the door against the influence of Gnosticism; in fact he even transferred it, in attenuated form, into the bosom of the Church; such at least was his aim. Indeed, judging by his thought and fundamental views, he was himself almost a Christian Gnostic. His position in regard to *faith* and *knowledge* is portrayed by Harnack in the following psychologically significant words:

"The Bible, in like wise, is needful to both: the believers receive from it the realities and commandments which they need, while the scholars decipher thoughts therein and gather from it that power which guideth them to the contemplation and love of God—whereby all material things, through spiritual interpretation (allegorical exegesis, hermeneutics), seem to be re-cast into a cosmos of ideas, until all is at last surmounted in the 'ascent' and left behind as stepping stones, while only this remaineth: the blessed abiding relationship of the God-created creature-soul to God (amor et visio)."

His theology as distinguished from Tertullian's was essentially philosophical; it was thoroughly pressed, so to speak, into the frame of a neo-Platonic philosophy. In Origen the two spheres of Grecian philosophy and the Gnosis on the one hand, and the world of Christian ideas on the other, peacefully and harmoniously intermingle. But this daring, intelligent tolerance and sense of justice also led Origen to the fate of condemnation by the Church. The final condemnation, to be sure, only took place posthumously, when Origen as an old man had been tortured in the persecution of the Christians by Decius, and had died not long after from the effects of the torture. In 399 Pope Anastasias I pronounced the condemnation, and in 543 his heresy was anathematized by a synod convoked by Justinian, which judgment was upheld by later Councils.

Origen is a classical example of the extraverted type. His basic orientation is towards the object; this shows itself in his conscientious consideration of objective facts and their conditions; it is also revealed in the formulation of that supreme principle: amor et visio Dei. The Christian process of development encountered in Origen a type whose bed-rock foundation is the relation to the object; a type that has ever symbolically expressed itself in sexuality; which also accounts for the fact that there even exist to-day certain theories which reduce every essential function of the soul down to sexuality. Castration is therefore the adequate expression of the sacrifice of the most valuable function. It is entirely characteristic that Tertullian should perform the sacrificium intellectus, whereas Origen is led to the sacrificium phalli, since the Christian process demands a complete abolition of the sensual hold upon the object, in other words: it demands the sacrifice of the hitherto most valued function, the dearest possession, the strongest instinct. Considered biologically, the sacrifice is brought into the service of domestication, but psychologically it opens a door for new possibilities of development to be inaugurated through the liberation from old ties.

Tertullian sacrificed the intellect, because it was that which most strongly bound him to worldliness. He battled with the Gnosis because for him it represented the side-track into the intellectual, which at the same time involves also sensuality. Parallel with this fact we find that in reality Gnosticism was also divided into two schools: one school striving after a spirituality that exceeded all bounds, the other losing itself in an ethical anarchism, an absolute libertinism that shrank from no lechery however atrocious and perverse. One must definitely distinguish between the Encratites (continent) and the Antitactes or Antinomians (opposed to order and law), who in obedience to certain doctrines sinned on principle and purposefully gave themselves to unbridled debauchery. To the latter school belong the Nicolaitans, the Archontici, etc., and the aptly named Borborites. How closely the apparent antitheses lay side by side is shewn by the example of the Archontici, for this same sect divided into an Encratitic and an Antinomian school, both of which remained logical and consistent. If anyone wants to know what are the ethical results of a bold intellectualism carried out on a large scale, let him study the history of Gnostic morals. He will thoroughly understand the sacrificium intellectus. These people were also practically consistent and lived what they had conceived even to absurd lengths. But Origen, in the mutilation of himself, sacrificed the *sensual* hold upon the world. For him, evidently, the intellect was not so much a specific danger as feeling and sensation with their enchainment to the object. Through castration he freed himself from the sensuality that was coupled with Gnosticism; he could then yield himself unafraid to the riches of Gnostic thought, while Tertullian through his sacrifice of intellect turned away from the Gnosis, but thereby reached a depth of religious feeling that we miss in Origen. "In one way he was superior to Origen", says *Schultz*, "because in his deepest soul he lived every one of his words; it was not reason that carried him away, like the other, but the heart. But in another respect he stands far behind him, inasmuch as he, the most passionate of all *thinkers*, was on the verge of rejecting knowledge altogether, for his battle against the Gnosis was tantamount to a complete denial of human thought."

We see here how, in the Christian process, the original

type has actually become reversed: Tertullian, the acute thinker, becomes the man of feeling, while Origen becomes the scholar and loses himself in the intellect. Logically, of course, it is quite easy to reverse the state of affairs and to say that Tertullian had always been the man of feeling and Origen the intellectual. Disregarding the fact that the difference of type is not done away with by this procedure, but exists as before, the reversed point of view has still to be explained; how comes it that Tertullian saw his most dangerous enemy in the intellect, while Origen in sexuality? One could say they were both deceived, and one could advance the fatal result of both lives by way of argument. One must assume, if that were the case, that both had sacrificed the less important thing, and thus to a certain extent both had made a bargain with fate. That is also a view which contains a principle of recognizable validity. Are there not just such sly-boots among the primitives who approach their fetish with a black hen under the arm, saying: "See, here is thy sacrifice, a beautiful black pig." I am, however, of opinion that the depreciatory method of explanation, notwithstanding the unmistakable relief which the ordinary human being feels in dragging down something great, is not under all circumstances the correct one, even though it may appear to be very 'biological.' But from what we can personally know of these two great ones in the realm of the mind, we must say that their whole nature and quality had such sincerity that their Christian conversion was neither a fraudulent enterprise nor mere deceit, but had both reality and truthfulness.

We shall not lose ourselves upon a by-path if we take this opportunity of trying to grasp what is the psychological meaning of this breaking of the natural instinctive course (which is what the Christian process of sacrifice seems to be). From what has been said above it follows that conversion signifies also a transition to another attitude. It is further clear whence the impelling motive towards conversion arises, and how far Tertullian was right in conceiving the soul as "naturaliter Christiana." The natural, instinctive course, like everything in nature, follows the principle of least resistance. One man is rather more gifted here, another there; or, again, adaptation to the early environment of childhood may demand either relatively more restraint and reflection or relatively more sympathy and participation, according to the nature of the parents and other circumstances. Thereby a certain preferential attitude is automatically moulded, which results in different types. In so far then as every man, as a relatively stable being, possesses all the basic psychological functions, it would be a psychological necessity with a view to perfect adaptation that he should also employ them in equal measure. For there must be a reason why there are different ways of psychological adaptation: evidently one alone is not sufficient, since the object seems to be only partially comprehended when, for example, it is either merely thought or merely felt. Through a one-sided (typical) attitude there remains a deficit in the resulting psychological adaptation, which accumulates during the course of life; from this deficiency a derangement of adaptation develops, which forces the subject towards a compensation. But the compensation can be obtained only by means of *amputation* (sacrifice) of the hitherto one-sided attitude. Thereby a temporary heaping up of energy results and an overflow into channels hitherto not consciously used though already existing unconsciously. The adaptation deficit, which is the causa efficiens of the process of conversion, becomes subjectively perceived as a vague sense of dissatisfaction. Such an atmosphere prevailed at the turning-point of our era. A quite astonishing need of redemption came over mankind, and brought about that unheard-of efflorescence of every sort of possible and impossible cult in ancient Rome. Moreover, representatives of the 'living the full life,' theory were not wanting, who, albeit innocent of 'biology,' operated with similar arguments founded on the science of that day. They, too, could never be done with speculations as to why it is that mankind is in such a poor way; only the causalism of that day, as compared with the science of ours, was somewhat less restricted; their 'harking back' reached far beyond childhood to cosmogony, and many systems were devised that pointed to all sorts of events in remote antiquity as being the source of insufferable consequences for mankind.

The sacrifice that Tertullian and Origen carried out is drastic—too drastic for our taste—but it corresponded with the spirit of that time, which was thoroughly concretistic. In harmony with this spirit the Gnosis simply took its visions as real, or at least as bearing directly upon reality, hence for Tertullian there was an objective validity in the realities of his feeling. Gnosticism projected the subjective inner perception of the attitude-changing process into the form of a cosmogonic system, and believed in the reality of its psychological figures.

In my book *Psychology of the Unconscious*[1] I left the whole question open as to the origin of the libido course peculiar to the Christian process. I spoke of a splitting of the libido into halves, each directed against the other. The explanation for this is to be found in the one-sidedness of the psychological attitude growing so extreme that the need for compensation became urgent on the side of the unconscious. It is precisely the Gnostic movement in the early Christian centuries which most clearly demon-

[1] Translated by Dr B. M. Hinkle (London: Kegan Paul & Co 1919; new edn. 1921).

strates the outbreak of unconscious contents in the moment of compensation. Christianity itself signified the demolition and sacrifice of the cultural values of antiquity, *i.e.* of the classical attitude. As regards the problem of the present, it need hardly be said that it is quite indifferent whether we speak of to-day or of that age two thousand years ago.

2. The Theological Disputes of the Ancient Church

It is more than probable that the contrast of types would also appear in the history of those schisms and heresies so frequent in the disputes of the early Christian Church. The Ebionites or Jewish Christians, who in this respect were probably identical with the primitive Christians generally, believed in the exclusive humanity of Christ and held him to be the son of Mary and Joseph, only subsequently receiving his consecration through the Holy Ghost. The Ebionites are, therefore, upon this point diametrically opposed to the Docetists. The effects of this opposition endured long after. The conflict came to light again in an altered form—which, though essentially attenuated, had in reality an even graver effect upon Church politics—about the year 320 in the heresy of Arius. Arius denied the formula propounded by the orthodox church Τῷ Πατρὶ ὁμοούσιος (like unto the Father). When we examine more closely the history of the great Arian controversy concerning Homoousia and Homoiousia (the complete identity as against the essential similarity of Christ with God), it certainly seems to us that the formula of Homoiousia definitely lays the accent upon the sensuous and humanly perceptible, in contrast to the purely conceptual and abstract standpoint of Homoousia. In the same way it would appear to us, as though the revolt of the Monophysites (who upheld the absolute one-ness of the nature of Christ) against the Dyophysitic formula of the Council of Chalcedon (which upheld the inseparable duality of Christ, namely his *human* and *divine* nature fashioned in one body) once more asserted the standpoint of the abstract and unimaginable as opposed to the sensuous and natural viewpoint of the Dyophysitic formula. At the same time the fact becomes overwhelmingly clear to us that alike in the Arian movement as in the Monophysite dispute, the subtle dogmatic question, though indeed the main issue for those minds where it originally came to light, had no hold upon the vast majority who took part in the quarrel of dogmas. So subtle a question had even at that time no motive force with the mass, stirred as it was by problems and claims of political power that had nothing to do with differences of theological opinion. If the difference of types had any significance at all here, it was merely because it provided catch-words that gave a flattering label to the crude instincts of the mass. But in no way should this blind one to the fact that, for those who had kindled the quarrel, Homoousia and Homoiousia were a very serious matter. For concealed therein, both historically and psychologically, lay the Ebionitic creed of a purely human Christ with only a relative ("apparent") divinity, and the Docetist creed of a purely divine Christ with only apparent corporeality. And beneath this level again lies the great psychological schism. The one position holds that supreme value and importance lie in the sensuously perceptible, where the subject, though indeed not always human and personal, is nevertheless always a projected human sensation; while the other maintains that the chief value lies in the abstract and extra-human, of which the subject is the function; in other words in the objective process of Nature, that runs its course determined by impersonal law, beyond human sensation, of which it is the actual foundation. The former standpoint overlooks the function in favour of the function-complex, if man can be so regarded; the latter standpoint overlooks the individual as the indispensable controlling vehicle in favour of the function. Both standpoints mutually deny each other their chief value. The more resolutely the representatives of either standpoint identify themselves with their own point of view, the more do they mutually strive, with the best intentions perhaps, to obtrude their own standpoint and thereby violate the other's chief value.

Another aspect of the type-antithesis appears on the scene in the *Pelagian* controversy in the beginning of the fifth century. The experience so profoundly sensed by Tertullian, that man cannot avoid sin even after baptism, grew with St Augustine—who in many respects is not unlike Tertullian—into that thoroughly characteristic pessimistical doctrine of original sin, whose essence consists in the *concupiscentia*[1] inherited from Adam. Over against the fact of original sin there stood, according to St Augustine, the redeeming grace of God, with the institution of the church ordained by His grace to administer the means of salvation. In this conception the value of man stands very low. He is really nothing but a miserable rejected creature, who is delivered over to the devil under all circumstances, unless through the medium of the church, the sole means of salvation, he is made a participator of the divine grace. Therewith, to a greater or less degree, not only man's value but also his moral freedom and self-government crumbled away; as a result, the value and importance of the church as an *idea* was so much the more enhanced, corresponding to the expressed programme in the Augustinian civitas Dei.

Against such a stifling conception, springing ever anew,

---

[1] Cupidity. We would rather say: untamed libido, which as εἱμαρμένη (rule of the stars, or fate) led man into wrong-doing and destruction.

rises the feeling of the freedom and moral value of man; it is a feeling that will not long endure suppression whether by inspection however searching, or logic however keen. The justice of the feeling of human value found its advocates in Pelagius, a British monk, and Cælestius, his pupil. Their teaching was grounded upon the moral freedom of man as a given fact. It is significant of the psychological kinship existing between the Pelagian standpoint and the Dyophysitic view that the persecuted Pelagians found asylum with Nestorius, the Metropolitan of Constantinople. Nestorius emphasized the separation of the two natures of Christ in contrast to the Cyrillian doctrine of the φυσικὴ ἕνωσις, the physical one-ness of Christ as God-man. Also, Nestorius definitely did not wish Mary to be understood as θεοτόκος (Mother of God), but only as χριστοτόκος (Mother of Christ). With some justification he even called the idea that Mary was Mother of God heathenish. From him originated the Nestorian controversy, which finally ended with the secession of the Nestorian church.

3. The Problem of Transubstantiation

With those immense political upheavals, the collapse of the Roman Empire and the sinking of antique civilization, these controversies lapsed likewise into oblivion. But, as in the course of many centuries a certain stability was again reached, psychological differences also reappeared, tentatively at first but becoming ever more intense with advancing civilisation. No longer indeed was it those problems which had brought the ancient church into confusion; new forms had come to light, under which however the same psychology was concealed.

About the middle of the ninth century the Abbot Paschasius Radbertus appeared with a writing upon the Holy Communion, in which he advanced the doctrine of transubstantiation, *i.e.* the view that the wine and holy wafer become transformed in the Communion into the actual blood and body of Christ. As is well-known, this conception became a dogma, according to which the transformation is accomplished "vere, realiter, substantialiter" ("in truth, in reality, in substance"); although the 'accidentals' preserve their outer aspect of bread and wine, they are substantially the flesh and the blood of Christ. Against this extreme concretization of a symbol Ratramnus, a monk of the same monastery in which Radbertus was abbot, dared to raise a certain opposition. Radbertus, however, found a more resolute adversary in Scotus Erigena, one of the great philosophers and daring thinkers of the early Middle Ages; who, as Hase says in his *History of the Church*, stood so high and solitary above his time that the anathema of the Church reached him only after centuries. As Abbot of Malmesbury, he was butchered by his own monks about the year 889. Scotus Erigena, to whom true philosophy was also true religion, was no blind follower of authority and the 'once accepted'; because, unlike the majority of his age, he could himself think. He set reason above authority, very unseasonably perhaps but in a way that assured him of the recognition of the later centuries. Even the Fathers of the Church, who were considered to be above discussion, he held as authorities only in so far as their writings contained treasures of human reason. Thus he also held that the Communion is merely a commemoration of that Last Supper which Jesus celebrated with his disciples; a view in which the reasonable man of every age will, moreover, participate. But Scotus Erigena, although clear and humanly simple in his thoughts and little disposed to detract from the meaning and value of the sacred ceremony, was not at one with the spirit of his time and the desires of the world around him; a fact that might, indeed, be inferred from his betrayal and assassination by his own comrades of the cloister. Because he could think reasonably and consistently success did not come to him; instead, it fell to Radbertus, who assuredly could not think, but who 'transubstantiated' the symbolical and meaningful, making it coarse and sensuous: in so doing he clearly chimed in with the spirit of his time, which craved for the concretizing of religious occurrences.

Again, in this controversy one can easily recognise those basic elements which we have already met with in the disputes commented upon earlier, namely, the abstract standpoint that is averse from any intercourse with the concrete object and the concretistic, that is, turned to the object.

Far be it from us to pronounce, from the intellectual view-point, a one-sided, depreciatory judgment upon Radbertus and his achievement. Although to the modern mind this dogma must appear simply absurd, we must not be misled on that account into regarding it as historically worthless. It is, indeed, a showpiece for every collection of human errors, but its worthlessness is not therefore eo ipso established; before passing judgment, we must minutely investigate what this dogma effected in the religious life of those centuries, and what our age still indirectly owes to its operation. It must, for instance not be overlooked, that it is precisely the belief in the reality of this miracle that demanded a release of the psychic process from the purely sensuous; and this cannot remain without influence upon the nature of the psychic process. The process of directed thinking, for instance, becomes absolutely impossible when the sensuous holds too high a threshold value. By virtue of too high a value it constantly invades the psyche, where it disintegrates and destroys the function of directed thinking based as this is precisely upon the exclusion of the unsuitable.

From this elementary consideration there immediately follows the practical importance of those rites and dogmas which hold their ground both from this standpoint as well as from a purely opportunist, biological way of thinking; to say nothing of the direct specific religious impressions which came to individuals from belief in this dogma. Highly as we esteem Scotus Erigena, the less is it permitted to despise the achievement of Radbertus. We may, however, learn from this example, that the thought of the introvert is incommensurable with the thought of the extravert, since the two thought-forms, as regards their determinants, are wholly and fundamentally different. One might perhaps say: the thinking of the introvert is *rational*, while that of the extravert is *programmatical*.

These arguments—and this I wish particularly to emphasize—do not pretend to be in any way decisive with regard to the individual psychology of the two authors. What we know of Scotus Erigena personally—it is little enough—is not sufficient to enable us to make any sure diagnosis of his type. What we do know speaks in favour of the introversion type. Of Radbertus we know next to nothing. We know only that he said something that ran counter to common human thought, but with surer feeling-logic he divined what his age was prepared to accept as suitable. This fact would speak in favour of the extraversion type. We must, however, through our insufficient knowledge, suspend judgment upon both personalities, since, especially with Radbertus, the matter might quite well be decided differently. Equally might he have been an introvert, but with a level of intelligence that altogether failed to rise above the conceptions of his milieu, and with a logic so lacking in originality that it merely sufficed to draw an obvious conclusion from already prepared premises in the writings of the Fathers. And, vice versa, Scotus Erigena might as well have been an extravert, if it could be shown that he was carried by a milieu which in any case was distinguished by common sense and which felt a corresponding expression to be suitable and desirable. The latter is in no sort of way proved concerning Scotus Erigena. But on the other hand we do know how great was the yearning of that time for the reality of the religious miracle. To this character of that age the view of Scotus Erigena must have seemed cold and deadening, whilst the assertion of Radbertus must have been alive with a sense of promise, since it concretized what every man desired.

4. Nominalism and Realism

The Holy Communion controversy of the ninth century was merely the anacrusis of a much greater strife that for centuries severed the minds of men and embraced immeasurable consequences. This was the opposition between *nominalism* and *realism*.

By nominalism one understands that school which asserted that the so-called universalia, namely the generic or universal concepts, such as beauty, goodness, animal, man, etc., are nothing but nomina (names) or words, derisively called "flatus vocis". Anatole France says: "Et qu'est-ce que penser? Et comment pense-t-on? Nous pensons avec des *mots*—songez-y, un métaphysicien n'a, pour constituer le système du monde, que le cri perfectionné des singes et des chiens." This is extreme nominalism; so with Nietzsche when he conceives reason as "speech metaphysics".

Realism, on the contrary, affirms the existence of the universalia ante rem, namely, that the universal concepts have existence in themselves after the manner of the Platonic ideas. Despite its ecclesiastical association, nominalism is a sceptical current which denies that separate existence which is characteristic of the abstract. It is a kind of scientific scepticism within a quite rigid dogmatism. Its concept of reality necessarily coincides with the sensuous reality of things; it is the individuality of things which represents the real as opposed to the abstract idea. Strict realism, on the contrary, transfers the accent of reality to the abstract, the idea, the universal, which it places ante rem (before the thing).

(a) *The Problem of the Universalia in the Classical Age*

As is shown by the reference to the Platonic ideology, we are discussing a conflict that reaches very far back. Certain venomous remarks in Plato concerning "greybeards and belated scholars" and "the poor in spirit' hint at the representatives of two allied schools of philosophy which agreed ill with the Platonic spirit, namely the Cynics and the Megarians. Antisthenes, the representative of the former school, although by no means remote from the Socratic mental atmosphere and even a friend of Xenophon, was nevertheless avowedly ill-disposed to Plato's beautiful world of ideas. He even wrote a pamphlet against Plato, in which he offensively converted Plato's name to Σάθων. Σάθων means boy or man, but from the sexual aspect, since σάθων comes from σάθη, penis; whereby Antisthenes, in the well-known manner of projection, delicately suggests to us upon what matters he has a grudge against Plato. As we have seen, this was also for Origen, the Christian, the 'other'—prime-cause (Auch-Urgrund), that very devil whom he sought to lay hold of by means of self-castration, in order to pass over without impediment into the richly embellished world of ideas. But Antisthenes was a pre-Christian pagan, to whom that thing was still of profound interest for which the phallus since earliest times has stood as the acknowledged symbol, namely sensation in its most liberal sense; not that he was alone in this interest, for as we well know it concerned the whole Cynic school, whose Leitmotiv was: back to nature! The reasons which might push Antisthenes' concrete feeling and sensation into the foreground were by no means few; he was before everything a proletarian, who made a virtue of his envy. He was no ἰθαγενής, no thorough-bred Greek: he was of the periphery; moreover, his teaching was carried on outside, before the gates of Athens, where he devoted himself to the study of proletarian behaviour, a model of Cynic philosophy. Furthermore, the whole school was composed of proletarians, or at least "peripheral" people, all of whom were in themselves a demolishing criticism of traditional values. After Antisthenes one of the most outstanding representatives of the school was Diogenes, who conferred upon himself the title Κύων (Dog); his tomb was also adorned by a dog in Parian marble. Despite his warm love of man, for his whole nature irradiated a wealth of human understanding, he none the less ruthlessly satirized everything that men of his time held sacred. He ridiculed the horror that gripped the spectators in the theatre at sight of the Thyestian repast[1], or the incest tragedy of Œdipus; anthropophagy was not so bad, since human flesh can lay no claim to an exceptional position as against other flesh, and furthermore the misfortune of an incestuous relationship was by no means such a grave evil, as the illuminating example of our domestic animals proves to us. In various respects the Megarian school was allied to the Cynics. Was not Megara the unhappy rival of Athens? After a most promising start, in which Megara had risen to prominence through the founding of Byzantium and the Hyblaeaic Megara in Sicily, internal squabbles broke out, from which

[1] Thyestes, son of Pelops, in the course of a struggle for the kingdom with his brother Atreus, was given—unknown to himself—the flesh of his own children to eat. [Translator]

Megara soon wasted and fell away, and in every respect became outstripped by Athens. Loutish peasant wit was called in Athens: 'Megarian jesting'. From this envy, which in a defeated race is imbibed with the mother's milk, not a little might be explained that is characteristic of Megarian philosophy. Like the Cynic, this philosophy was thoroughly nominalistic and directly opposed to the realism of Plato's ideology.

A prominent representative of this school was Stilpon of Megara, about whom the following characteristic anecdote is related: Stilpon came one day to Athens and saw upon the Acropolis the wondrous statue of Pallas Athene made by Phidias. A true Megarian, he observed, it is *not the daughter of Zeus, but of Phidias*. In this jest the whole of the Megarian thought is expressed, for Stilpon taught that generic concepts are without reality or objective validity; who, therefore, speaks of man speaks of nobody, because he designates "οὔτε τόνδε οὔτε τόνδε" ("neither this nor that"). Plutarch ascribes to him the statement "ἕτερον ἑτέρου μὴ κατηγορεῖσθαι" ("one thing can affirm nothing concerning [the nature of] another"). Antisthenes' teaching was very similar. The most ancient representative of this manner of thought seems to have been Antiphon of Rhamnus, a Sophist and contemporary of Socrates. One statement handed down from him runs: "Whoso perceiveth just some long objects, neither seeth length with the eyes nor discerneth it with the mind." The denial of the substantiality of the generic concept follows directly from this statement. Naturally the whole position of the Platonic ideas is undermined by this characteristic sort of judgment, for with Plato it is precisely ideas that receive an eternal and immutable validity, while the "actual" and the "multiple" are merely a fugitive reflection. The Cynic-Megarian criticism, on the contrary, from the standpoint of the actual, resolves these generic concepts into purely casuistic and descriptive nomina, without any substantiality. The accent is laid upon the individual thing.

This manifest and fundamental opposition was lucidly apprehended by Gomperz as the problem of *inherency* and *predication*. When, for instance, we speak of 'warm' and 'cold', we speak of 'warm' and 'cold' things, to which 'warm' and 'cold' as attributes, predicates, or assertions respectively belong. The statement refers to something perceived and actually existing, namely to a warm or a cold body. From a plurality of similar cases we abstract the concepts of 'warmth' and 'coldness', with which also we immediately connect or associate something concrete. Thus 'warmth' and 'coldness', etc., are to us something real, because of the perseveration of perception in the abstraction. It is extremely difficult for us to strip off that which pertains to things from the abstraction, since there naturally clings to every abstraction its corresponding derivation. In this sense the 'thing-ness' of the predicate is essentially a priori. If now, we pass over to a higher grade generic concept 'temperature', its 'thingness' (das Dinghafte) is still readily perceptible to us, so that, in spite of a certain diminution in its sensuous definiteness, it has renounced none of its representability. But representability also adheres closely to sensual perception. If we further ascend to a still higher generic concept, viz. *energy*, the character of 'thingness' quite disappears, and with it, to a certain degree, goes the quality of representability. At this point the conflict about the "nature" of energy appears: whether energy is purely conceptual and abstract, or whether something real. Assuredly the learned nominalist of our day is quite convinced that 'energy' is merely a nomen, a 'counter' of our mental calcule; yet, in spite of this, our every-day speech refers to 'energy' as though it were something quite tangible; thus constantly sowing among devoted heads the greatest confusion from the standpoint of the theory of cognition.

The reality of the purely conceptual, which thus naturally creeps into our process of abstraction, and evokes the "reality" either of the predicate or the abstract idea, is no artificial product, no arbitrary hypostasizing of a concept, but necessary by nature. For it is not the case that the abstract idea is arbitrarily hypostasized and transplanted into another world of equally artificial origin: the actual historical process is just the reverse. With the primitive, for instance, the imago, the psychic reverberation of the sense-impression, is so strong and so avowedly sensuous in hue and texture, that, when it appears reproduced, *i.e.* as a spontaneous memory-image, it sometimes even has the quality of hallucination. Thus when the memory-image of his dead mother suddenly reappears to a primitive, it is as if it were her ghost that he sees and hears. We only 'think' of the dead, the primitive perceives them, just because of the extraordinary sensuousness of his mental images. Hence arises the primitive belief in ghosts. The ghosts are what we quite simply call 'thoughts'. When the primitive 'thinks', he literally has visions, whose reality is so great that he is constantly mistaking the psychic for the real. Powell says: "The primary and fundamental confusion in the thought of uncivilized peoples is the confusion of the objective and the subjective." Spencer and Gillen observe: "What a savage experiences during a dream is just as real to him as what he sees when he is awake." What I myself have seen of the psychology of the negro completely endorses that finding. From this basic fact of the sensuous realism of the image, in presence of the autonomy of the sense impression, springs the belief in spirits, and not from any need of explanation on the part of the savage, which is merely a European imputation. For the primitive, thought is visionary and auditory—

hence it also has the character of revelation. Thus the magician, *i.e.* the visionary, is always the thinker of the tribe who brings to pass the manifestation of spirits or gods. This is the source of the magical effect of thought; it is as good as action, just because it is real. In the same way the word, the outer covering of thought, has 'real' effect, because the word calls up 'real' memory images. Primitive superstition surprises us only because we have very largely succeeded in de-sensualizing the psychic image, *i.e.* we have learnt to think 'abstractly', always, of course, with the above-mentioned limitations.

Whoever is engaged in the practice of analytical psychology grows constantly more aware of the fact that a frequent reminder is necessary, even for his 'educated' European patients, that 'thinking' is not 'action'; this one needs it, may be, because he believes that to think something is enough, and that one, because he feels he must not think something, else must he go and do it. The dream of the normal individual, and the hallucination that accompanies mental disorientation, show how easily the primitive reality of the psychic image once more emerges. Mystical practice endeavours, even by use of artificial introversion, to re-establish the primitive reality of the imago, in order to increase the counter-weight against extraversion. We find a speaking example of this in the initiation of the Mohammedan mystic, Tewekkul-Beg, by Molla-Shâh[1]. Tewekkul-Beg relates:

"After these words he (Molla-Shâh) called me to seat myself opposite to him, while still my senses were as though bemused, and commanded me to create his own image in my inner self; and after he had bound mine eyes, he bade me assemble all the forces of the soul into my heart. I obeyed, and in the twinkling of an eye, by divine favour and with the spiritual succour of the Sheikh, my heart was opened. I beheld there in my innermost heart something resembling an overturned bowl; when this

---

[1] Buber, *Ekstatische Konfessionen*, 1909, p. 31 ff.

vessel was righted, a feeling of boundless joy flooded my whole being. I said to the Master: 'From this cell, in which I am seated before thee, I behold within me a true vision, and it is as though another Tewekkul-Beg were seated before another Molla-Shâh.'"

The Master explained this to him as the first phenomena of his initiation. Other visions soon followed, when once the way to the primitive real images had been opened up.

The reality of the predicate is granted a priori, since it has always existed in the human mind. Only by subsequent criticism is the abstraction deprived of the character of reality. Even in the time of Plato the belief in the magical reality of the word-idea was so great that it was actually worth the philosopher's while to devise traps or fallacies by which he was able, with the aid of the absolute verbal significance, to extort an absurd reply. A simple example is the Enkekalymmenos (the veiled man) fallacy, called after the Megarian Eubulides. It is worded as follows: "Canst thou recognize thy father? Yes. Canst thou recognise this veiled man? No. Thou contradictest thyself; for this veiled man is thy father. Thus thou canst recognize thy father and yet at the same time not recognize him." The fallacy lies merely in this, that the one questioned naïvely assumes that the word 'recognize' designates in all cases one and the same objective matter of fact, while in reality its validity is limited only to certain definite cases. The fallacy of the Keratines (the horned one) rests upon the same principle: it runs as follows: "What thou hast not lost, thou still hast; thou hast not lost horns, therefore thou hast horns." Here also the fallacy lies in the naïveté of the questioned one, who accepts in the premise a definite matter of fact. It could be convincingly proved by this method that absolute verbal significance was a delusion. As a consequence, the reality of the generic concept, which in the form of the

Platonic idea [1] had a metaphysical existence and exclusive validity, was also in jeopardy. Gomperz says: "Men were not yet filled with that distrust of speech which inspires us and makes us perceive in words a frequently quite inadequate expression of the actual facts. Instead, there prevailed the naïve belief that the orbit of the meaning and the orbit of application of the word on the whole corresponding with it must in every respect coincide." In presence of this absolute magical verbal significance, which pre-supposes that in the word there is also given the objective behaviour of things, the Sophist criticism is thoroughly in place. It convincingly proves the impotence of language. In so far as ideas are only nomina—a supposition that has to be proved—the attack upon Plato is justified. But generic concepts cease to be merely nomina when similarities or conformities of things are designated by them. Then the question at issue is, whether or not these conformities are objective realities. Such conformities actually exist, hence the generic concept also corresponds with reality. As a container of the reality of a thing, it is as good as the exact description of a thing. The generic concept is distinguished from the latter only in the fact that it is the description or designation of the conformities of things. The discrepancy, therefore, lies neither in the concept nor in the idea but in its verbal expression, which obviously under no circumstances renders either the thing adequately or the conformity of things. The nominalist attack upon the doctrine of ideas is therefore, in principle, an encroachment without justification. Thus Plato's irritated parry was altogether justified.

According to Antisthenes, the inherency-principle

[1] The unities which lie at the basis of the visible and changeable, and which can be reached only by pure thinking, were *ideas* in Plato's sense. He included under the term everything stable amidst changing phenomena, e.g. the ideas of genus, species, and the laws and ends of Nature. [Translator]

consists in this, that not only not many predicates, but that no predicate at all, can be affirmed of a subject which differs from it. Antisthenes granted as valid only those predicates that were identical with the subject. Apart from the circumstance that such statements of identity (as 'the sweet is sweet') affirm nothing at all and are, therefore, without meaning, the weakness of the inherency principle lies in this: that a judgment of identity has also nothing to do with the thing; the word 'grass' has literally nothing to do with the thing 'grass.' The principle of inherency suffers then in much the same degree as the ancient word-fetichism, which naïvely assumes that the word coincides also with the thing. When, therefore, the nominalist calls to the realist: "You are dreaming—you think you are dealing with things, but in reality you are only fighting verbal chimeras", the realist can answer the nominalist in precisely the same words; for neither is the nominalist concerned with things in themselves but with words, which he sets in the place of things. Even when for every separate thing he sets a separate word, yet they are always only words and not things themselves.

Although indeed, the idea of "energy" is admittedly a verbal concept, it is nevertheless so extraordinarily real that the electrical Company pays dividends out of it. The board of directors would certainly allow no metaphysical argument to convince them of the unreality of energy. 'Energy' simply designates the undeniable conformity of the phenomena of force, which in the most telling ways daily proves its existence. In so far as the thing is real, and a word conventionally designates the thing, the word also receives 'reality-significance'. In so far as the conformity of things is real, the generic concept designating the conformity of things also receives 'reality-significance'; furthermore, it is a significance that is neither greater nor less than that of the word which designates the individual thing. The shifting of the accent of value from one side to the other is a matter of individual attitude and contemporary psychology. Gomperz also felt this psychological foundation in Antisthenes, and brings out the following points : . . . " a sturdy commonsense, a resistance to all enthusiasm, perchance also a strength of individual feeling, which stamp the personality and therefore the whole individual character as a type of complete reality." We might further add, the envy of a man without the full rights of citizenship, a proletarian, a man whom fate had sparingly endowed with beauty, and who could at the best, only climb to the heights by demolishing the values of others. Especially was this characteristic of the Cynic, who must ever be carping at others, and to whom nothing was sacred when it chanced to belong to another; he even made no scruples at destroying the peace of the home, if he might thereby seize an occasion to impose upon mankind his invaluable counsel.

To this essentially critical attitude of mind Plato's world of ideas with its eternal reality stands diametrically opposed. It is plain that the psychology of the man who fashioned that world had an orientation that was altogether foreign to the critical, disintegrating judgments portrayed above. Plato's thinking, abstracted and created from the plurality of things synthetic constructive concepts, which designate and express the universal conformities of things as the essentially existing. Their invisible and suprahuman quality is directly opposed to the concretism of the inherency principle, which would reduce the material of thought to the category of the unique, individual, and objective. This attempt is, however, just as impossible as the exclusive acceptance of the principle of predication, which would exalt what has been affirmed concerning many isolated things to an eternally existing substance above all decay. Both forms of judgment are justifiable, as both are also naturally present in every man. This is best seen, according to my view, in the fact that the very founder of the Megarian school, Euclid of Megara, established an "All-unity" principle that stands immeasurably above the individual and casuistic. For he linked together the Eleatic principle[1] of the "existing" with the "good", so that for him the "existing" and the "good" were identical. Against which there stood only the "non-existing evil". This optimistic 'all-oneness', is, of course nothing but a generic concept of the highest order, one that directly embraces the existing, but at the same time contravenes all evidence, and this in a much higher degree than the Platonic ideas. With this concept Euclid created a compensation to the critical disintegration of the constructive judgment into mere word things. This all-in-one principle is so remote and so vague that it utterly fails to express the conformity of things; it is no type at all, but rather the product of a desire for a unity that shall' comprehend the disordered multitude of individual things. The desire for such a unity urges itself upon all who pay allegiance to an extreme nominalism, in so far as there is an effort to emerge from the negatively critical attitude. Hence, not at all infrequently we find in people of this sort an idea of fundamental homogeneity that is manifestly improbable and arbitrary. For the inherency principle as an exclusive basis is an impossibility. Gomperz pertinently observes:

"That such an attempt will prove abortive in every age can be foreseen. Its success was absolutely out of the question in an age that was destitute in historical understanding, and in which any deep insight into the soul was almost completely

---

[1] The Eleatic was a Greek school of philosophy founded by Xenophanes of Elea about 460 B.C. Its fundamental doctrine was that the One, Absolute, pure Being is the only real existence; that the world of phenomena, or the many, is merely an appearance. All attempts to explain it, therefore, are useless. [Translator]

disregarded. The danger that the more obvious and transparent, but taken all in all the less important, forms of usefulness should force the more concealed, but in reality the more solid, potentialities into the background, was in such conditions not only menacing—it was inevitable. In taking the animal kingdom and primitive man for a model, and in the attempt to prune back the outgrowths of civilization to this standard, a destroying hand was laid upon much that was the fruit of a more or less ascending development through countless myriads of years."

Constructive judgment—which, as opposed to inherency, is based upon the conformity of things—has created universal ideas which belong to the greatest values of civilization. Even if these ideas belong only to the dead, yet threads still bind us to them, which, as Gomperz says, have gained an almost unbreakable strength. He continues: "The inanimate thing can merit a claim to honour, consideration, and even self-sacrificing devotion, in the same way as the human dead; one need only mention the statues, graves, and colours of the soldier. But, though I do violence to myself and succeed in my efforts to tear down those threads, I will assuredly relapse into brutality; for I suffer grave damage to all those feelings that clothe the hard rock-bottom of naked reality as with a rich covering of living bloom. Upon the high valuation of this covering growth, upon the estimation of all that one might call inherited values, depends every refinement, every grace and delicacy of life, every cultivation of animal instinct, as well as every enjoyment and pursuit of art—in fact, all those things which the Cynics without scruple or compassion would have striven to uproot. Certainly—and one may readily concede this to them and their not inconsiderable modern following—there is a limit beyond which we may not suffer the sway of the principle of association to extend, without ourselves being equally guilty of that same folly and superstition which quite certainly grew out of the unlimited sway of that principle."

We have entered thus minutely into the problem of inherency and predication, not merely because this problem was revived once more in the nominalism and realism of the scholastics, but because it has never yet been finally set at rest, and, presumably, it never will. For here again the question at issue is the typical opposition between the abstract standpoint—in which the decisive value lies in the thought process itself—and the specific thinking and feeling upon which, whether consciously or unconsciously, the objective orientation is based. In the latter case, the mental process is a means which has the development of the personality for its end. It is little wonder that it was precisely the proletarian philosophy that adopted the inherency principle. Wherever sufficient reasons exist for the shifting of emphasis upon individual feeling, thinking and feeling become negatively critical, through a poverty of positive creative energy (which is diverted to personal ends); thinking declines to a mere analytical organ that reduces down to the concrete and the singular. Over the resulting accumulation of disordered individual things a vague all-in-oneness whose wish character is more or less transparent will, at best, supervene. But when the emphasis is laid upon the mental processes, the result of the mental activity is superordinated over the multiplicity as *idea*. The idea is as far as possible de-personalized; but the personal apprehension goes over almost completely into the mental process which it hypostasizes.

Before passing on we might perhaps enquire whether the psychology of the Platonic ideology justifies us in the supposition that Plato may personally belong to the introverted type, and whether the psychology of the Cynics and the Megarians allows us to reckon such figures as Antisthenes, Diogenes, or Stilpon as extraverted? A decision of the question put in this form is *quite impossible.*

A really careful and minute examination of Plato's authentic writings considered as his 'documents humains' might possibly allow one to conclude to which type he personally belonged. For my own part, I would not venture to pronounce any positive judgment. If someone were to furnish evidence that Plato belonged to the extraverted type, it would not surprise me. What has been transmitted concerning the others is so very fragmentary that a decision is, in my opinion, an impossibility.

Since the two kinds of thinking under review depend upon a displacement of the accent of value, it is of course equally possible in the case of the introvert that personal apprehension may, for various reasons, be pushed into the foreground and will supersede thinking, so that his thinking becomes negatively critical. For the extravert, the accent of value is laid upon the relation to the object simply, and not necessarily upon his personal relationship to it. If the relation to the object stands in the foreground, the mental process is already subordinate; but, in so far as it is exclusively occupied with the nature of the object and avoids the admixture of personal apprehension, it does not possess a destructive character. We have, therefore, to note the particular conflict between the principles of inherency and of predication as a *special case*, which in the further course of our investigation will be given a more thorough examination. The special nature of this case lies in the positive and negative parts played by personal apprehension. When the type (generic concept) suppresses the individual thing to a shadow, then the type, the idea, has won to reality. When the value of the individual thing abolishes the type (generic concept), anarchic disintegration is at work. Both positions are extreme and unfair, but they make a contrasting picture whose clear outlines leave nothing to be desired, and whose very exaggeration brings into relief certain traits, which, albeit in milder and therefore more concealed forms, also adhere to the nature of the introverted and extraverted type, even when personalities are concerned in whom personal apprehension is not pushed into the foreground. It makes, for instance, a considerable difference whether the intellectual function is master or servant. The master thinks and feels differently from the servant. Even the most far-reaching abstraction of the personal in favour of the general value never renders a complete elimination of personal admixture possible. Yet, in so far as this exists, thought and feeling contain also those destructive tendencies which proceed from the self-assertion of the person in face of the inclemency of social conditions. But it would surely be a great folly if, for the sake of personal tendencies, we were to reduce values of universal reality down to mere personal undercurrents. That would be pseudo-psychology. Such, however, exists.

(*b*) *The Universalia Problem in Scholasticism*

The problem of the two forms of judgment remained unsolved because—tertium non datur. Porphyrius handed down the problem to the Middle Ages thus: " Mox de generibus et speciebus illud quidem sive subsistant sive in nudis intellectibus posita sint, sive subsistentia corporalia sint an incorporalia, et utrum seperata a sensibilibus an in sensibilibus posita et circa haec consistentia, dicere recusabo.". ("As regards the universal and generic concepts, the real question is whether they are substantial or merely intellectual, whether material or immaterial, whether apart from things perceived or in and around them"). Somewhat in this form the Middle Ages resumed the discussion: they distinguished the Platonic view, the universalia ante rem, the universal or the idea as a standard or example above all individual things and altogether detached from them, existing ἐν οὐρανίῳ τόπῳ (in a heavenly place), as the wise Diotima says to Socrates in the dialogue upon Beauty:

"This *beauty* will not reveal itself to him as a face or as hands or whatever else belongeth to the body, nor yet as an abstract statement or knowledge, nor as anything at all that belongeth to another, whether it be an individual being on the earth or in heaven or in any other place, but it is *in and for itself, and is itself eternally the same;* for every other beauty only partly revealeth its beauty, so that itself, through the dawning and passing hence of other beauty, is neither increased nor diminished, nor yet suffereth any ill." (*Symposium*, 211 B).

The Platonic form, as we saw, stood opposed to the critical assumption that generic concepts are merely words. In this case the real is prius, the ideal posterius. To this view the label was attached: universalia post rem.

Between both conceptions stands the temperate realistic conception of Aristotle, which can be called the "universalia in re", namely, that form (εἶδος) and matter co-exist. The Aristotelian standpoint is a concretistic attempt at a settlement fully corresponding with Aristotle's nature. In contrast to the transcendentalism of his teacher Plato, whose school then relapsed into a Pythagorean mysticism, Aristotle was entirely a man of reality—of his classical reality one should add—which contained much in concrete form which was subtracted by later epochs and added to the inventory of the human mind. His solution corresponds with the concretism of classical common sense.

These three forms also show the structure of medieval opinions in the great universalia dispute, which was the real essence of the scholastic controversy. It cannot be my task—even were I competent—to probe deeply into the particular points of the great controversy. I must content myself with a mere survey of the orientating allusions.

The dispute began with the views of Johannes Roscellinus about the end of the eleventh century. The universalia were for him nothing but nomina rerum, names of things, or, as tradition says "flatus vocis". For him there were only individual things. He was, as Taylor aptly observes, "strongly held by the reality of individuals". To think of God also as only individual was the next obvious conclusion, thereby dissolving the Trinity into three persons; so that Roscellinus actually arrived at tritheism. That, the prevailing realism of that time, could not stand; in 1092 the views of Roscellinus were anathematized by a synod at Soissons. Upon the other side stood Guillaume von Champeaux, the teacher of Abélard, an extreme realist but of Aristotelian complexion. According to Abélard, he taught that one and the same thing existed both in its totality and in different individual things at the same time. There were no essential differences at all between individual things, but merely a multiplicity of 'accidentals'. In the latter concept the actual differences of things are explained as fortuitous, just as in the dogma of transubstantiation, bread and wine, as such, are only "accidentals".

Upon the side of realism also stood Anselm of Canterbury, the father of the Scholastics. A genuine Platonist, the universalia were for him part of the divine Logos. From this position, the psychologically important *proof of God* which Anselm established, and which is called the *ontological proof*, can also be understood. This proof demonstrates the existence of God as contingent upon the idea of God. Fichte (*Psychologie*, ii, 120) formulated this proof concisely as follows: "The existence of the idea of an absolute in our consciousness proves the real existence of this absolute." Anselm's view is that the concept of a Supreme Being present in the intellect involves also the quality of existence (non potest esse in intellectu solo). He continues thus: "Vero ergo est aliquid, quo majus cogitari non potest, ut nec cogitari posset non esse, et hoc es tu, Deus noster." ("In sooth there exists something than which nothing greater can be thought, as also it cannot be thought that it exists not, and this, our God, art Thou"). The logical weakness of the ontological argument is so obvious that it even requires psychological explanation to show how a mind like Anselm's could advance such an argument. The immediate ground can be sought in the general psychological disposition of realism, namely in the fact that there were not only a class of men, but, in keeping with the current of the age, also certain groups of men who laid their accent of value upon the idea, so that the idea represented for them a higher reality or life-value than the reality of individual things. Hence it seemed simply impossible to concede that what to them was most valuable and significant should not also *really* exist. Indeed, they had the most striking proof of its efficacy to their very hands, since it is evident that their lives, thoughts, and feelings were wholly orientated to this point of view. The invisibility of the idea matters little by the side of its extraordinary *efficacy*, which in fact is a *reality*. They had an ideal and not a sensational concept of reality.

A contemporary opponent of Anselm, Gaunilo, objected, it is true, that the oft-recurring idea of the Islands of the Blessed (after the manner of Phæacia; Homer, *Od.* viii) does not necessarily prove their actual existence. This objection is palpably reasonable. Not a few objections of this nature were raised in the course of centuries, which, however, in no way hindered the survival of the ontological argument even down to quite recent times; for it still found representatives in the nineteenth century in Hegel, Fichte, and Lotze. Contradictions of this kind are not to be ascribed to some peculiar defect in logic or to an even greater infatuation for one side or the other. That would be absurd. Rather is it a matter of deep-seated psychological differences, which must be recognized and upheld. The assumption that there exists only one psychology or only one fundamental psychological principle is an intolerable tyranny, belonging to the pseudo-scientific prejudice of the normal man. People are always speaking of *the* man and of his 'psychology', which is invariably traced back to the 'nothing else but'. In the same way one always talks of *the* reality, as though there were only one. Reality is that which works in a human soul and not that which certain people assume to be operative, and about which prejudiced generalizations are wont to be made. Moreover, however scientifically such generalizations may be advanced, it must not be forgotten that science is not the *summa* of life, that it is indeed only one of the psychological attitudes, only one of the forms of human thought.

The ontological argument is neither argument nor proof, but merely the psychological verification of the fact that there is a class of men for whom a definite idea has efficacy and reality—a reality which practically rivals the world of perception. The sensationalist relies upon the certainty of his 'reality', and the man of the idea adheres to his psychological reality. Psychology has to recognize the existence of these two (or more) types, and must under all circumstances avoid thinking of one as a misconception of the other; and it should never seriously try to reduce one type to the other, as though everything essentially 'other' were only a function of the one. This does not mean that the trustworthy scientific principle— principia explicandi præter necessitatem non sunt multiplicanda—should be abrogated. But the necessity for a plurality of psychological principles still remains. But, quite apart from the foregoing arguments in favour of this assumption, our eyes should be opened by the remarkable fact that, notwithstanding the apparently final despatch of the ontological argument by Kant, there are still not a few post-Kantian philosophers who have again resumed it. And we are to-day just as far or perhaps even further from an understanding of the pairs of opposites—idealism : realism, spiritualism: materialism, and all the subsidiary questions involved therein—than were the men of the early Middle Ages, who at least had a common world-philosophy.

In favour of the ontological proof there is surely no logical argument that appeals to the modern intellect. The ontological argument in itself had really nothing to do with logic, but in the form in which Anselm bequeathed it to history there arises a supplementary intellectualized or rationalized *psychological fact*, which, naturally, without petitio principii or other sophistries could never have occurred. But it is just in this that the unassailable validity of the argument reveals itself; namely, that it exists, and that the consensus gentium proves it to be universally existing. It is the fact that has to be reckoned with, not the sophistry of its proof; for the impotence of the ontological argument consists simply and solely in this: that it will argue logically, while in reality it is much more than a purely logical proof. For the real issue is a psychological fact whose occurrence and effectiveness are so overwhelmingly clear that no sort of argumentation is needed. The consensus gentium proves that, in the statement "God *is*, because he is thought", Anselm is right. It is an obvious truth, indeed nothing but a statement of identity. The 'logical' argumentation about it is quite superfluous, and is moreover wrong, inasmuch as Anselm wished to establish his idea of God as a concrete reality. He says: "Existit ergo procul dubio aliquid, quo majus cogitari non volet, et in intellectu et in re." Beyond all doubt there exists something than which nothing greater can be thought, and moreover it

c*

exists as much in the intellect as in the thing (*Dinglichkeit*, 'reality'). The concept "res" was, however, to the Scholastics something that stood upon the same level as thought. Thus Dionysius the Areopagite, whose writings exercised a considerable influence upon early medieval philosophy, distinguishes in neighbouring categories "entia rationalia, intellectualia, sensibilia, simpliciter existentia" (rational, intellectual, perceptible, simply existing things). Thomas Aquinas calls that which is in the soul "res" (quod est in anima), as also that which is outside the soul (quod est extra animam). This noteworthy juxtaposition still enables us to discern the primitive objectivity of the idea in the thought of that time. From this mental attitude the psychology of the ontological proof becomes easily intelligible. The hypostasizing of the idea was not at all an essential step; but, rather, as an echo of the primitive concreteness of thought, it was taken for granted. The counter-argument of Gaunilo is psychologically insufficient, for although, as the consensus gentium proves, the idea of an Island of the Blessed frequently occurs, yet it is indubitably less effective than the idea of God, which consequently receives a higher "reality-value".

Later writers who resumed the ontological argument all fell, at least in principle, into Anselm's error. Kant's reasoning should be final. We will therefore briefly outline it. He says:

"The concept of an absolutely necessary Being is a pure concept of reason, i.e. an idea only, whose objective reality is not by any means proved because the reason has need of it."
"The unconditioned necessity of a judgment, however, is not an absolute necessity of the thing. For the absolute necessity of a judgment is only a conditioned necessity of the thing or of the predicate in the judgment."

Immediately prior to this Kant gives, as an example of a necessary judgment, that a triangle must have three angles. He is referring to this statement when he continues:

"The proposition just cited does not say that three angles are absolutely necessary, but only that, if a triangle exists, it must contain three angles. But this mere logical necessity has given evidence of such a great power of illusion that people have framed a priori the conception of a thing that seems to include existence within its content, and have then assumed that because existence belongs necessarily to the object as conceived, it must also belong necessarily to the thing itself. Thus it is inferred that there is an absolutely necessary being, because the existence of that being is thought in a conception that has been arbitrarily assumed, and assumed under the supposition that there is an actual object corresponding to it."

The power of illusion to which Kant here alludes, is nothing else but the primitive *magical power of the word*, which likewise mysteriously inhabits the idea. It needed a long process of development before man once fundamentally realized that the word, the flatus vocis, does not in every case also signify or effect a reality. But that certain men have understood this, has not by any means sufficed to uproot from every mind that superstitious power which dwells within the formulated concept. There is evidently something in this 'instinctive' superstition that will not be uprooted: it exhibits, therefore, some right to existence, which till now has not been sufficiently appreciated. The paralogism (false conclusion) is in like manner introduced into the ontological argument, namely through an illusion which Kant elucidates as follows. He is now speaking of the assertion of "absolutely necessary subjects" the conception of which is simply inherent in the idea of existence, and, therefore, without intrinsic contradiction cannot be dismissed. This conception would be that of the "most real being for all".

"This being, it is said, possesses all reality, and such a being, as I am willing to admit, we are justified in assuming to be possible. Now that which really comprehends all reality must comprehend also existence. Hence existence is involved in the conception of a thing as possible. If, therefore, the thing is denied existence, even its internal possibility is denied, and this is self-contradictory. Either the thought in you must itself be the thing, or you have simply assumed existence to be implied in mere possibility, which is nothing but a wretched tautology."

"*Being* is evidently no real predicate, i.e. a conception of something that is capable of being added to the conception of a thing. It is merely the ungrounded assertion of a thing or of certain determinations as an object of thought. In logic, *being* is simply the copula of a judgment. The proposition: ' God is omnipotent' contains two conceptions, the objects of which are respectively ' God ' and ' omnipotence ', and the word *is* adds no new predicate but is merely a sign that the predicate omnipotent is asserted in relation to the subject God. If, then, I take the term God, which is the subject, to comprehend the whole of the predicates, including the predicate omnipotent, and say : ' God is ', or ' There is a God ', I do not enlarge the conception of God by a new predicate, but I merely bring the subject in itself with all its predicates, in other words, the object, into relation with my conception. The content of the object and of my conception must be exactly the same, and hence I add nothing to my conception, which expresses merely the possibility of the object by simply placing its object before me in thought and saying that it *is*. The real contains no more than the possible. A hundred real dollars do not contain a cent more than a hundred possible dollars. No doubt there are in my purse a hundred dollars more if I actually possess them than if I have merely the conception—that is, have merely the possibility of them."

" Our conception of an object may thus contain whatever and how much it will; nevertheless we must ourselves stand away from the conception, in order to bestow existence upon it. This happens with sense-objects through the connection with any one of our perceptions in accordance with empirical laws ; but for objects of pure thought there is no sort of means for perceiving their existence because it is wholly a priori that they can be known ; our consciousness of all existence, however, belongs altogether to a unity of experience and an existence outside this field cannot absolutely be explained away as impossible. But it is a supposition that we have no means of justifying."

This detailed reminder of the fundamental exposition of Kant seems to me necessary, since it is precisely here that we find the sharpest division between the esse in intellectu and the esse in re. Hegel cast the reproach at

Kant that one could not compare the idea of God with the phantasy of a hundred dollars. But, as Kant rightly pointed out, logic must be abstracted from all content; there would certainly be no more logic if content were to prevail. Seen from the standpoint of logic, there exists, as ever, no third—between the logical "either . . . or." But between "intellectus" and "res" there is still "anima," and this "esse in anima" makes the entire ontological argument superfluous. Kant himself in his *Critique of Practical Reason* (Eng. transl., p. 298) attempted on a large scale to make a philosophical estimate of the "esse in anima". There he introduces God as a postulate of practical reasoning proceeding from the a priori recognition of "respect for moral law necessarily directed towards the highest good, and the supposition or inference therefrom of the objective reality of the same."

The "esse in anima" then is a matter of psychological fact, concerning which it is only necessary to decide whether it appears once, often, or universally in human psychology. The fact which is called God and is formulated as "the highest good" signifies, as the term already reveals, the supreme psychic value, or in other words the idea which either confers or actually receives the highest and most general significance in respect of the determination of our action and thought. In the language of analytical psychology the concept of God coincides with that complex which, in accordance with the foregoing definition, combines within itself the highest sum of libido (psychic energy). Accordingly the actual God-concept of the anima differs completely in different men—a fact which also corresponds with experience. Even in the idea, God is not one constant Being, still less is He so in reality. For, as we well know, the highest operative value of a human soul is variously located. There are men ὧν ὁ θεὸς ἡ κοιλία(whose God is their belly.—*Phil.*, 3, 19); similarly there are men whose God is money, science, power, sexuality, &c. The whole psychology of the individual, at least in its principal tendencies, is displaced in accordance with the respective localization of the 'highest good', so that a psychological theory which is exclusively based upon any one basic instinct, as for example power or sexuality, can adequately explain features of only secondary significance, when applied to an individual of another orientation.

(c) *Abélard's Attempt at Conciliation*

It is not without interest to investigate how Scholasticism itself attempted to settle the universalia dispute, how it tried to create an equipoise between the typical opposites which the tertium non datur divided. This attempt at settlement was the work of Abélard, that unhappy man who burned with love for Héloise and who paid for his passion with the loss of his manhood. Whoever is acquainted with the life of Abélard will know how intensely his own soul housed those severed opposites whose philosophical reconciliation was for him such a vital issue. De Rémusat[1] characterizes Abélard as an eclectic, who criticized and rejected every accepted theory concerning the universalia, but who none the less freely borrowed from them what was true and tenable. Abélard's writings, so far as they relate to the universalia dispute, are confusing and difficult, because the author is constantly engaged in weighing every argument and aspect of the case. It is precisely because he acknowledged no truth in the avowed standpoint, but always sought to comprehend and reconcile the contrary view, which is responsible for the fact that he was never once thoroughly understood even by his own pupils. Some understood him as a nominalist, others as a realist. This misunderstanding is characteristic: it is much easier to think from one definite type—for within it one

---

[1] Charles de Rémusat, *Abélard* (Paris 1845)

can remain logical and consistent—than it is to remain consistent with both types, since the intermediate standpoint is lacking. Realism as well as nominalism if pursued consistently leads to finality, clarity, and uniformity. But the weighing and adjustment of the opposites leads to confusion and to an unsatisfactory issue for the types, since to neither is the solution completely satisfying.

De Rémusat has collected from Abélard's writings a whole series of almost contradictory assertions relating to our subject. He exclaims: "Faut-il admettre en effet, ce vaste et incohérent ensemble de doctrines dans la tête d'un seul homme et la philosophie d'Abélard est elle le chaos?"

From nominalism Abélard takes the truth that the universalia are words, in the sense that they are intellectual conventions expressed by language; furthermore, he takes from it the truth that a thing in reality is not universal but always something particular, and that substance in reality is never a universal but an individual fact. From Realism Abélard takes the truth that 'genera' and 'species' are combinations of individual facts and things on the ground of their indubitable similarity. *Conceptualism* is for him the mediatory standpoint; this is to be understood as a function which comprises the individual objects perceived, classifies them into genera and species upon the basis of their similarity, and thus reduces their absolute multiplicity to a relative unity. However unquestionable multiplicity and diversity may be, the existence of similarities, which by means of the concept makes fusion possible, is equally beyond dispute. For whoever is psychologically so adapted as to perceive mainly the similarity of things the collective or constellating concept is, so to speak, taken for granted, *i.e.* it frankly obtrudes itself with the undeniable actuality of the sense-perception. But, for the man who is psychologically so adjusted as to perceive mainly the diversity of things, the similarity of things is not exclusively assumed; what he sees is their difference, which indeed forces itself upon him with just as much actuality as similarity does to the other.

It seems as though "*feeling-into*" (Einfühlung) the object were the psychological process which brought the distinctiveness of the object into an especially bright light, and as though *abstraction* from the object were the process most calculated to blind one's eyes to the actual distinctiveness of individual things in favour of their general similarity, which is the very foundation of the idea. Feeling-into and abstraction combined produce that function which underlies the idea of conceptualism. It is founded, therefore, upon the only psychological function which has any real possibility of uniting the divergence between nominalism and realism and bringing them upon a common way.

Although the Middle Ages knew how to speak great words of the soul, psychology they had none, which is one of the youngest of all sciences. If at that time a psychology had existed, Abélard would have framed the esse in anima as his mediatory formula. De Rémusat clearly discerned this, for he says:

"Dans la logique pure les universalia ne sont que les termes d'un langage de convention. Dans la physique, qui est pour lui plus transcendante qu'expérimentale, qui est sa véritable ontologie, les genres et les espèces se fondent sur la manière dont les êtres sont réellement produits et constitués. Enfin, entre la logique pure et la physique, il y a un milieu et comme une science mitoyenne, qu'on peut appeler une psychologie, où Abélard recherche comment s'engendrent nos concepts et retrace tout cette généalogie intellectuelle des êtres, tableau ou symbole de leur hiérarchie et de leur existence réelle." (Tome ii, p. 112)

The universalia ante rem and post rem have remained a matter of dispute for every ensuing century, even though they cast aside their scholastic robe and appeared under a new disguise. Fundamentally it was the old problem.

At one time the attempt at solution inclined towards the realistic side, at another towards the nominalistic. The scientific character of the nineteenth century gave the problem a push once more towards the side of nominalism, after the philosophy of the beginning of the nineteenth century had first done full justice to realism. But the opposites are no longer so widely sundered as in Abélard's time. We have a psychology, a mediatory science; which alone is capable of uniting idea and thing, without doing violence either to the one or to the other. This capacity abides in the very nature of psychology, but no one could contend that psychology has hitherto accomplished this task. One must, in this connection, acquiesce in the words of De Rémusat:

"Abélard a donc triomphé; car, malgré les graves restrictions qu'une critique clairvoyante découvre dans le nominalisme ou le conceptualisme qu'on lui impute, son esprit est bien l'esprit moderne à son origine. Il l'annonce, il le dévance, il le promet. La lumière qui blanchit au matin l'horizon est déjà celle de l'astre encore invisible qui doit éclairer le monde."

If one overlooks the existence of psychological types, as also the contingent circumstance that the truth of the one is the error of the other, then Abélard's labour will mean nothing but one Scholastic sophistry the more. But in so far as we recognize the existence of the two types, the effort of Abélard must appear to us of the greatest importance. He seeks the mediatory standpoint in the "sermo," by which he understood not so much a "discourse" as a formed sentence joined to a definite meaning; a definition, in fact, only requiring additional words for the consolidation of its meaning. He does not speak of "verbum," for to nominalism this is nothing more than a "vox," a "flatus vocis." Indeed, it is the great psychological achievement of both the classic and medieval nominalism that it completely abolished the primitive, magical, or mystical identity of the word with the objective matter of fact; too completely, indeed, for the type of man who has his foundation not in the foothold offered by things but in the abstraction of the idea from things. Abélard was too wide in his outlook to have been able to overlook this value of nominalism. For him the word was indeed a "vox," but the statement (or in his language the "sermo") was something more, for it carried with it solid meaning, it described the common factor, the idea, what in fact has been thought and understood about things. In the sermo the universale lived, and there alone. It is, therefore, intelligible that Abélard was also counted among the nominalists; incorrectly however, for the universale was to him a greater reality than a vox.

The expression of his Conceptualism must have been difficult enough for Abélard, for he had necessarily to construct it out of contradictions. An epitaph contained in an Oxford manuscript gives us, I think, a searching insight into the paradox of his teaching:

> Hic docuit voces cum rebus significare,
> Et docuit voces res significando notare;
> Errores generum correxit, ita specierum.
> Hic genus et species in sola voce locavit,
> Et genus et species sermones esse notavit.
>
> . . . . . .
>
> Sic animal nullumque animal genus esse probatur.
> Sic et homo et nullus homo species vocitatur.

In so far as an expression is striven for, that is based in principle upon one standpoint, viz. the intellectual in the case in point, the antagonism can hardly be bridged except by paradox. We must not forget that the radical difference between nominalism and realism is not purely a logical and intellectual distinction but also a psychological one, which in the last resort amounts to a typical difference of psychological attitude to the object as well as to the idea. Whoever is orientated to the idea, apprehends and reacts from the angle of vision governed by the idea. But the man who is orientated to the object, apprehends and reacts from the standpoint of his sensation. For him the abstract is of secondary importance, since what must be thought about things seems to him relatively inessential, while with the former it is just the reverse. The man who is orientated to the object is naturally nominalistic: "the name is sound and smoke" (Goethe's *Faust*) in so far as he has not yet learnt to compensate his objective attitude. Should this latter event take place, he will become, if he has the necessary ability, an over-nice logician, one who is constantly on the lookout for a meticulousness, a method and a dullness that can equal his own. The man who is orientated to the idea is naturally logical; that is why, when all is said and done, he can neither understand nor appreciate text-book logic. The development towards a compensation of his type makes him, as we saw in Tertullian, a man of passionate feeling, whose feelings, however, remain within the magic circle of his ideas. But the man who is a logician by compensation remains with his world of ideas within the magic circle of his object.

With these reflections we come to the shaded side of Abélard's thought. His attempt at solution is one-sided. If in the opposition between nominalism and realism it were merely a question of logical-intellectual arrangement, it would be incomprehensible why no terminal conclusion other than a paradox is possible. But since it is a question of a psychological opposition, a one-sided intellectual formulation must end in paradox. "Sic et homo et nullus homo species vocitatur". ("Thus both man and not-man are called species"). The logico-intellectual expression is absolutely incapable, even in the form of the sermo, of providing that mediatory formula which can do justice to the real natures of the two opposing psychological attitudes, for it is wholly derived from the side of the abstract and is completely lacking in the recognition of concrete reality.

Every logico-intellectual formulation, however embracing it may be, divests the objective impression of its living and immediate quality. It must do this in order to reach any formulation whatsoever. But, in so doing, just that is lost which to the extraverted attitude seems absolutely essential, namely the relationship to the real object. No possibility exists, therefore, that we shall find upon the line of either attitude any satisfactory and reconciling formula. And yet man cannot remain in this division—even if his mind could—for this discussion is not merely a matter of remote philosophy; it is the daily repeated problem of the relations of man to himself and to the world. And, because this at bottom is the problem at issue, the division cannot be resolved by a discussion of nominalist and realist arguments. For its solution a third intermediate standpoint is needed. To the "esse in intellectu" tangible reality is lacking; to the "esse in re" the mind.

Idea and thing come together, however, in the psyche of man which holds the balance between them. What would the idea amount to if the psyche did not provide its living value? What would the objective thing be worth if the psyche withheld from it the determining force of the sense impression? What indeed is reality if it is not a reality in ourselves, an "esse in anima"? Living reality is the exclusive product neither of the actual, objective behaviour of things, nor of the formulated idea; rather does it come through the gathering up of both in the living psychological process, through the "esse in anima." Only through the specific vital activity of the psyche does the sense-perception attain that intensity, and the idea that effective force, which are the two indispensable constituents of living reality.

This peculiar activity of the psyche, which can be explained neither as a reflexive reaction to sense-stimuli nor as an executive organ of eternal ideas is, like every vital process, a perpetually creative act. Each new day reality is created by the psyche. The only expression I can use for this activity is *phantasy*. Phantasy is just as much feeling as thought; it is intuitive just as much as sensational. There are no psychic functions which in phantasy are not inextricably inter-related with the other psychic functions. At one time it appears primordial, at another as the latest and most daring product of gathered knowledge. Phantasy, therefore, appears to me as the clearest expression of the specific psychic activity. Before everything it is the creative activity whence issue the solutions to all answerable questions; it is the mother of all possibilities, in which too the inner and the outer worlds, like all psychological antitheses, are joined in living union. Phantasy it was and ever is which fashions the bridge between the irreconcilable claims of object and subject, of extraversion and introversion.

In phantasy alone are both mechanisms united.

If Abélard had gone deep enough to recognize the psychological difference between the two standpoints, he would logically have had to enlist phantasy for the formulation of the reconciling expression. But in the world of science phantasy is just as much taboo as is feeling. If, however, we appreciate the underlying opposition as a psychological one, it will be seen that psychology is not only obliged to recognize the standpoint of feeling; it must also acknowledge the intermediate standpoint of phantasy. Here, however, comes the great difficulty: phantasy for the most part is a product of the unconscious. It doubtless includes conscious elements, but none the less it is an especial characteristic of phantasy that it is essentially involuntary and stands inherently opposed to conscious contents. It has this quality in common with the dream, though the latter has of course strangeness and spontaneity in a much higher degree.

The relation of the individual to his phantasy is very largely conditioned by his relation to the unconscious in general, and this in its turn is peculiarly influenced by the spirit of the age. In inverse ratio to the degree of prevailing rationalism will the individual be more or less disposed to have dealings with the unconscious and its products. The Christian sphere, like every completed religious form, undoubtedly tends to suppress the unconscious in the individual to the fullest limit, thus paralysing his phantasy activity. In its stead, religion offers stereotyped symbolical ideas which replace the individual unconscious. The symbolical presentations of all religions are stages of unconscious processes in a typical and universally binding form. Religious teaching gives, as it were, conclusive information concerning the 'Last Things' and the 'other world' of human consciousness. Wherever we can observe a religion at its birth, we see how even the figures of his doctrine flow into the founder as revelations, *i.e.* as concretizations of his unconscious phantasy. The forms arising out of his unconscious are interpreted as universally valid and thus in a measure replace the individual phantasies of others. The evangelist Matthew has preserved for us a fragment of this process from the life of Christ: in the story of the Temptations we see how the idea of kingship emerges from the Founder's unconscious in the form of the devil who offers him power over the kingdoms of the earth. Had Christ misunderstood the phantasy and taken it concretely, there would have been one madman the more in the world. But he refused the concretism of his phantasy and entered the world as a King, unto whom the Kingdoms of *Heaven* are subject. He was therefore no paranoiac, as indeed the result also proved. The views advanced from time to time from the psychiatric side concerning the morbidity of Christ's psychology are nothing but ludicrous rationalistic twaddle, altogether remote from any sort of comprehension of the meaning of such processes in the history of man.

The forms in which Christ presented the content of his unconscious to the world became accepted and interpreted as universally binding. Therewith all individual phantasy lapsed; it became not only invalid and worthless but it was actually persecuted as heretical, as the fate of the Gnostic movement, and of all later heresies testifies. The prophet Jeremiah speaks in a similar sense when he says (*Jeremiah*, xxiii):

> 16. " Thus saith the Lord of Hosts,
>   Hearken not unto the words of the prophets that
>   prophesy unto you :
>   They make you vain :
>   They speak a *vision of their own hear.,*
>   And not out of the mouth of the Lord.
>
> 26. I have heard what the prophets said,
>   That prophesy lies in My name, saying :—
>   ' *I have dreamed*, I have dreamed.'
>
> 26. How long shall this be in the heart of the prophets that
>   prophesy lies ?
>   Yea, they are prophets of the deceit of their own heart ;
>
> 27. ' Which think to cause My people to forget My name
>   By their dreams which they tell every man to his
>   neighbour,
>   As their fathers have forgotten My name through Baal.
>
> 28. The prophet that hath a dream,
>   Let him tell a dream ;
>   And he that hath My word,
>   Let him speak My word faithfully.
>   What is the chaff to the wheat ? saith the Lord.'"

We see also in early Christianity how, for example, the Bishops zealously strove to root out the efficacy of the individual unconscious among the monks. The Archbishop Athanasius of Alexandria in his biography of St Anthony offers us a particularly valuable insight into this activity[1]. In this document he describes, by way of instruction to his monks, the apparitions and visions, the perils of the soul, which befall those that pray and fast in solitude. He warns them how cleverly the devil disguises himself in order to bring saintly men to their fall. The devil is, of course, the voice of the anchorite's own unconscious, which revolts against the violent suppression of the individual nature. I give a group of exact quotations from this rather inaccessible book. Very clearly they show how the unconscious was systematically suppressed and depreciated.

"There is a time when we see no man and yet the sound of the working of the devils is heard by us, and it is like the singing of a song in a loud voice; and there are times when the words of the Scriptures are heard by us, just as if a living man were repeating them, and they are exactly like the words which we should hear if a man were reading the Book. And it also happeneth that they (the devils) rouse us up to the night prayer, and incite us to stand upon our feet, and they make us to see also the similitudes of monks and the forms of those who mourn (i.e. the anchorites); and they draw nigh unto us as if they had come from a long journey, that they may make lax the understanding of those who are feeble of soul, and they begin to utter words like unto these: 'Are we condemned throughout all creation to love places of desolation. Were we not able when we came to our houses, to fear God and to do fair deeds?' And when they are unable to work their will by means of a scheme of this kind, they cease from this kind of deceit and turn unto another and say: 'How is it possible for thee to live? For thou hast sinned and committed iniquity in many things. Thinkest thou, that the Spirit hath not revealed unto me what hath been done by thee, or that I know not that thou hast done such and such a thing?' If therefore a simple brother hear these things, and feel within himself that he hath done evil as the Evil One hath said, and he be not acquainted with his craftiness, his mind will be troubled straightway, and he shall fall into despair and turn backwards.

---

[1] *Lady Meux' Manuscript, no. 6: The Book of Paradise*, by Palladius, Hieronymus, etc., edited by E. A. Wallis Budge (London 1904)

It is then, O my beloved, unnecessary for us to be terrified at these things, and we have need to fear only when the devils multiply the speaking of the things *which are true* and then we must rebuke them severely ... Therefore let us be on our guard ... We must not then even appear to incline our hearing to their words, even though they be words of truth which they utter; for it would be a disgrace unto us that those who have rebelled against God should become our teachers. And let us, O my brethren, arm ourselves with the armour of righteousness, and let us put on the helmet of·redemption, and in the time of contending let us shoot out from a believing mind spiritual arrows as from a bow which is stretched. For they (the devils) are nothing at all, and even if they were, their strength hath in it nothing which would enable it to resist the might of the Cross."

St Anthony relates:

" Once there appeared unto me a devil of an exceedingly haughty and insolent appearance, and he stood up before me with the tumultuous noise of many people, and he dared to say unto me : ' I, even I, am the power of God ', and ' I, even I, am the Lord of the worlds.' And he said unto me : ' What dost thou wish me to give thee ? Ask, and thou shalt receive.' Then I blew a puff of wind at him, and I rebuked him in the name of Christ....

And on another occasion, when I was fasting, the crafty one appeared to me in the form of a brother monk carrying bread, and he began to speak unto me words of counsel, saying ' Rise up, and stay thy heart with bread and water, and rest a little from thine excessive labours, for thou art a man, and howsoever greatly thou mayest be exalted thou art clothed with a mortal body and thou shouldest fear sickness and tribulations.' Then I regarded his words, and I held my peace and refrained from giving an answer. And I bowed myself down in quietness, and I began to make supplications in prayer, and I said : ' O Lord, make Thou an end of him, even as Thou hast been wont to do him away at all times ' ; and as I concluded my words he came to an end and vanished like dust, and went forth from the door like smoke.

Now on one occasion Satan approached the house one night and knocked at the door, and I went out to see who was knocking, and I lifted up mine eyes and saw the form of an exceedingly tall and strong man ; and, having asked him ' Who art thou ? ', he answered and said unto me : ' I am Satan.' And after this I said unto him : ' What seekest thou ? ' and he answered unto me : ' Why do the monks and the anchorites, and the other Christians revile me, and why do they at all times heap curses upon me ? ' And having clasped my head firmly in wonder at his mad folly, I said unto him: 'Wherefore dost thou give them trouble?' Then he answered and said unto me: 'It is not I who trouble them, but it is they who trouble themselves. For there happened to me on a certain occasion that which did happen to me, and had I not cried out to them that I was the Enemy, his slaughters would have come to an end for ever I have therefore no place to dwell in, and not one glittering sword, and not even people who are really subject unto me, for those who are in service to me hold me wholly in contempt; and moreover, I have to keep them in fetters, for they do not cleave to me because they esteem it right to do so, and they are ever ready to escape from me in every place. The Christians have filled the whole world, and behold, even the desert is filled full with their monasteries and habitations. Let them then take good heed to themselves when they heap abuse upon me.'

Then, wondering at the grace of our Lord, I said unto him: 'How doth it happen that whilst thou hast been a liar on every other occasion, at this present the truth is spoken by thee? And how is it that thou speakest the truth now when thou art wont to utter lies? It is indeed true that when Christ came into this world, thou wast brought down to the lowest depths, and that the root of thine error was plucked up from the earth.' And when Satan heard the name of Christ, his form vanished and his words came to an end."

These quotations show how, with the aid of the universal belief, the unconscious of the individual was rejected notwithstanding the fact that it transparently spoke the truth. There are in the history of the mind especial reasons for this rejection. It does not behove us at this point to elucidate these reasons further. We must content ourselves with the actual fact that it was suppressed. Speaking psychologically, this suppression consists in a withdrawal of libido (psychic energy). The libido thus acquired, promotes the synthesis and development of the conscious attitude, whereby a new conception of the world is gradually built up. The undoubted advantages gained by this process naturally consolidate this attitude. It is, therefore, not surprising that the psychology of our time is characterized by a prevailingly unfavourable attitude towards the unconscious.

It is not only intelligible, but absolutely necessary, that all sciences have excluded both the standpoints of feeling and of phantasy. They are sciences for that very reason. But how does it stand with psychology? If it is to be regarded as a science, it must do the same. But will it then do justice to its material? Every science ultimately seeks to formulate and express its material in abstractions; thus psychology could, and indeed does, lay hold of the processes of feeling, sensation, and phantasy in the form of intellectual abstractions. This treatment certainly establishes the right of the intellectual-abstract standpoint, but not the claims of other quite possible psychological points of view. These other possible standpoints can obtain only a bare mention in a scientific psychology; they cannot emerge as the independent principles of a science. Science, under all circumstances, is an affair of the intellect, and the other psychological functions are submitted to it in the form of objects. The intellect is sovereign of the scientific realm. But it is another matter when science steps across into the realm of practical application. The intellect, which was formerly king, is now merely a resource, a scientifically perfected instrument it is true, but still only an implement—no more the aim itself, but merely a condition. The intellect, and with it science, is now placed at the service of creative power and purpose. Yet this is still "psychology" although no longer science: it is a psychology in a wider meaning of the word, a psychological activity of a creative nature, in which creative phantasy is given priority. Instead of using the term "creative phantasy", it would be just as true to say that in a practical psychology of this kind the leading rôle is given to *life*, for on the one hand, it is undoubtedly phantasy, procreating and productive, which uses science as a resource, but on the other, it is the manifold demands of external reality which prompt the activity of creative phantasy. Science as an end in itself is assuredly a high ideal, but its accomplishment brings about as many "ends in themselves" as there are sciences and arts. Naturally this leads to a high differentiation and specialization of the particular functions concerned, but it also leads to their aloofness from the world and from life, and an inevitable multiplication of specialized terrains, which gradually lose all connection with each other. The result of this is an impoverishment and stagnation that is not merely confined to the specialized terrains, but also invades the psyche of the man, who is thus differentiated up or reduced down to the specialist level. By this token must science prove her value to life; it is not enough that she be mistress—she must also be the maid. By so doing she in no way dishonours herself. Although science has already led us to recognize the disproportions and disorders of the psyche, thus deserving our profound respect for her intrinsic intellectual gifts, it is nevertheless a grave mistake to concede her an absolute aim which would incapacitate her for her métier as an instrument of life. For when we approach the province of actual living with the intellect and its science, we realize at once we are in a confined space that shuts us out from other, equally real provinces of life. We are, therefore, compelled to acknowledge the universality of our ideal as a limitation, and to look around us for a spiritus rector which from the standpoint and claims of a complete life, can offer us a greater guarantee of psychological universality than the intellect alone can compass.

When Faust exclaims "feeling is everything", he is expressing merely the antithesis to the intellect, and therefore only reaches the other extreme; he does not achieve that totality of life and of his own psyche in which feeling and thought are joined in a third and higher principle. This higher third, as I have already indicated, can be understood either as a practical goal or as the phantasy which creates the goal. This aim of totality can be recognized neither by the science, whose end is in itself, nor by feeling, which lacks the faculty of vision belonging to thought. The one must lend itself as auxiliary to the other, yet the contrast between them is so great that we need a bridge. This bridge is already given us in creative phantasy. It is not born of either, for it is the mother of both—nay, further, it is pregnant with the child, that final aim which reconciles the opposites. If psychology remains only a science, we do not reach life—we merely serve the absolute aim of science. It leads us, certainly, to a knowledge of the actual state of affairs, but it always resists every other aim but its own. The intellect remains imprisoned in itself just so long as it does not willingly sacrifice its supremacy through its recognition of the value of other aims. It recoils from the step which takes it out of itself, and which denies its universal validity; since from the standpoint of intellect everything else is *nothing but phantasy*. But what great thing ever came into existence that was not first phantasy? Just in so far as the intellect rigidly adheres to the absolute aim of science is it insulated from the springs of life. It interprets phantasy as nothing but a wish-dream, wherein is expressed that depreciation of phantasy which for science is both welcome and necessary. It is inevitable that science should be regarded as an absolute aim so long as the development of science is the sole question at issue. But this at once becomes an evil when it is a question of life itself demanding development. Thus it was an historical necessity in the Christian process of culture that unfettered phantasy activity should be kept under; and, similarly, though for different reasons, it was also a necessity that phantasy should be suppressed in our age of natural science. It must not be forgotten that creative phantasy, if not restrained within just bounds, can also degenerate into a most pernicious luxuriance. But these bounds are never those artificial limitations set by the intellect or by reasonable feeling; they are boundaries governed by necessity and incontestable reality.

The tasks of every age differ, and it is only in retrospect that we can discern with certainty what had to be and what should not have been. In the momentary present the conflict of convictions always predominates, for "war is the father of all". History alone decides. Truth is not eternal—it is a programme. The more "eternal" a truth, the more is it lifeless and worthless; it tells us nothing more, because it is self-evident.

How phantasy is assessed by psychology, so long as this remains merely a science, is beautifully exemplified in the well-known views of Freud and of Adler. The Freudian interpretation reduces it to causal, primitive, instinctive processes. Adler's conception reduces it to the final, elementary aims of the self. The former is an instinctive psychology, the latter an ego-psychology. Instinct is an impersonal biological phenomenon. A psychology which is founded upon instinct must by its nature neglect the ego, since the ego owes its existence to the principium individuationis, *i.e.* to individual differentiation whose sporadic and individual character at once removes it from the category of general biological phenomena. Although general biological instinct-forces make the moulding of personality possible, individuality is nevertheless essentially different from general instincts; indeed, it stands in the most direct opposition to them, just as the individual is as a personality always distinct from the collective. Its essence consists precisely in this distinction. What every ego-psychology must therefore exclude and ignore is just the collective element that is essential to instinct-psychology, for it is describing that very ego-process which is differentiated from collective instincts. The characteristic animosity between the representatives of the two standpoints arises from the fact that either standpoint necessarily involves a depreciation and lowering of the other. For so long as the radical difference between instinct and ego-psychology is not realized, either side must naturally hold its respective theory to be universally valid. This does not mean to say that instinct-psychology, for example, could not put up a theory of the ego-process. It can do so very ably, but in a form and manner which to the ego-psychologist looks too much like the negative of his theory. Hence we find that with Freud the "ego-instincts" do indeed occasionally emerge, but in the main they support a very modest existence. With Adler, on the other hand, it would seem as though sexuality were the merest vehicle, which in one way or another serves the elementary aims of power. The Adlerian principle is the safe-guarding of personal power, which is superimposed upon the general instincts. With Freud it is instinct that makes the ego serve its purposes, so that the ego appears as a mere function of instinct.

Within both types the scientific tendency prevails to reduce everything to its own principle; from which their deductions again proceed. With phantasies this operation is accomplished with particular ease; since these, unlike the functions of consciousness, which are adapted to reality and have therefore an objectively orientated character, express both instinctive as well as ego-tendencies. It is not difficult for the man who adopts the standpoint of instinct to discover in them the "wish-fulfilment", the "infantile wish", and "repressed sexuality". But the man who judges from the standpoint of the ego can just as easily discover those elementary aims concerned with the safeguarding and differentiation of the ego, since phantasies are intermediary products between the ego and the general instinct. They accordingly contain elements of both sides.

Interpretation from either side is always, therefore, somewhat forced and arbitrary, because one character is always suppressed. Nevertheless, a demonstrable truth does on the whole appear; but it is only a partial truth, which can make no claim to general validity. Its validity extends just so far as the range of its principle. But in the province of other principles it is invalid. The Freudian psychology is characterized by one central idea, namely the *repression* of incompatible wish-tendencies. Man appears as a bundle of wishes which are only partially adaptable to the object. His neurotic difficulties consist in the fact that milieu-influences, educational and objective conditions, are a considerable check upon a free expression of instinct. Influences are derived from father and mother, either morally hindering or infantile, which tend to produce fixations that compromise later life. The original instinctive constitution is an unalterable quantity which suffers disturbing modifications mainly through objective influences; hence the most untrammelled possible expression of instinct towards the suitably chosen object would appear to be the needful remedy. Conversely, Adler's psychology is characterized by the central idea of ego-superiority. The individual appears pre-eminently as an ego-point which must under no circumstances be subjected to the object. While with Freud the craving for the object, the fixation to the object, and the impossible nature of certain desires towards the object play an important rôle, with Adler everything aims at the superiority of the subject. Freud's repression of instinct towards the object becomes with Adler the safe-guarding of the subject. With him the healing remedy is the removal of the isolating safe-guard; with Freud it is the removal of the repression that renders the object inaccessible. Hence with Freud the basic formula is *sexuality*, which expresses the strongest relation between subject and object; with Adler it is that *power* of the subject which most effectively ensures him against the object, and gives to the subject an unassailable isolation which amputates every relation. Freud would vouchsafe the instincts an unfettered excursion towards their objects. But Adler would break through the inimical spell of the object, in order to deliver the ego from suffocation in its own defensive armour. The former view must therefore be essentially extraverted, while the latter is introverted. The extraverted theory holds good for the extraverted type, while the introverted theory is valid only for the introverted type. In so far as the pure type is a quite one-sided product of development, it is also necessarily unbalanced. Over-emphasis upon the one function is synonymous with repression of the other.

Psycho-analysis fails to resolve this repression just in so far as the particular method applied is orientated according to the theory of its own type. Thus the extravert, in accordance with his theory, will reduce his phantasies, as they emerge from the unconscious, to their instinct content. But the introvert will reduce them to his power-tendency. The gain accruing from such analysis goes to the already existing predominance. This kind of analysis, therefore, merely intensifies the already existing type, and by such means no mutual understanding or mediation between the types is made possible. On the contrary, the gap is widened, both without and within. An inner dissociation arises, because fragments of other functions, occasionally arising to the surface in unconscious phantasies (dreams, etc.) are depreciated and again repressed. On these grounds a certain critic was in a measure justified when he described Freud's as a neurotic theory; but the truth of the statement cannot justify a certain malevolence in expression which only serves to absolve one from the duty of serious concentration upon the problems raised. The standpoints both of Freud and of Adler are equally one-sided and are, therefore, characteristic of only one type.

Both theories reject the principle of imagination, since they reduce phantasies and treat them as a merely semiotic[1] expression. But in reality phantasies mean more than that, for they represent also the other mechanism. Thus with the introverted type they represent repressed extraversion, and with the extraverted repressed introversion. But the repressed function is unconscious, hence, undeveloped, embryonic, and archaic. In this condition it is not to be reconciled with the higher niveau of the conscious function. The inacceptable nature of phantasy is principally derived from this peculiarity of the unrecognised function-root.

Imagination, for everyone to whom adaptation to external reality is the leading principle, is for these reasons something objectionable and useless. And yet we know that every good idea and all creative work is the offspring of the imagination, and has its source in what one is pleased to term infantile phantasy. It is not the artist alone, but every creative individual whatsoever who owes all that is greatest in his life to phantasy. The dynamic principle of phantasy is '*play*,' which belongs also to the child, and as such it appears to be inconsistent with the principle of serious work. But without this playing with phantasy no creative work has ever yet come to birth. The debt we owe to the play of imagination is incalculable. It is therefore short-sighted to treat phantasy, on account of its daring or inacceptable character, as of small account. It must not be forgotten that it is just in the imagination that the most valuable promise of a man may

---

[1] I say "semiotic" in contradistinction to "symbolic". What Freud terms symbols are no more than *signs* for elementary instinctive processes. But a symbol is the best possible expression for an actual matter of fact, which nevertheless cannot be expressed except by a more or less close analogy.

lie. I say *may* advisedly, because on the other hand phantasies are also valueless, since in the form of raw material they possess no sort of realizable worth. In order to unearth the valuable treasure they contain, a development is needed. But this development is not achieved by a simple analysis of the phantasy material; a synthetic treatment is also needed by means of a constructive method[1].

It remains an open question whether the opposition between the two standpoints can ever be satisfactorily adjusted intellectually. Although in one sense Abélard's attempt must be profoundly respected, yet practically no consequences worth mentioning have matured from it; for he was able to establish no mediatory psychological function beyond conceptualism or sermonism, which is merely a revised edition, altogether one-sided and intellectual, of the ancient Logos conception. The Logos, as a mediator, had of course this advantage over the sermo, inasmuch as in His[2] human manifestation He also did justice to non-intellectual aspirations.

I cannot, however, rid myself of the impression that Abélard's brilliant mind, which so fully grasped the great Yea and Nay, would never have remained satisfied with his paradoxical conceptualism, thus renouncing all claim to creative effort, if the impelling force of passion had not been lost to him through the tragedy of fate. In confirmation of this idea we need only compare conceptualism with the way in which the great Chinese philosophers Lao-Tse and Tschuang-Tse, as also the poet Schiller, confronted this problem.

---

[1] Cf. Jung, *Collected Papers: Content of the Psychoses.* Idem, *Psychology of Unconscious Processes.*
[2] Logos appearing in human form as Christ the Son of God.

5. The Holy Communion Controversy between Luther and Zwingli

Of the later antagonisms which stirred men's minds Protestantism and the Reformation movement should really receive our first consideration. Only this phenomenon is of such complexity that it must first be resolved into many separate psychological processes before it can become an object for analytical elucidation. But that lies outside my province. I must therefore content myself by selecting a single case from that great arena, namely the Holy Communion controversy between Luther and Zwingli. The transubstantiation dogma, already mentioned, was sanctioned by the Lateran Council of 1215, and from that time formed an established article of faith; in which form Luther himself grew up. Although the notion that a ceremony and its concrete practice can have an objective redeeming value is really quite unevangelical, since the evangelical movement was actually directed against Catholic institutions, Luther was nevertheless unable to free himself from the immediately effective sensuous impression in the taking of bread and wine. He perceived in it not merely a token, but the actual sensuous reality with its contingent and immediate experience; these were for him an indispensable religious necessity. He therefore claimed the actual presence of the body and blood of Christ in the Communion. "In and beneath" bread and wine he received the body and the blood of Christ. For him the religious meaning of the immediate objective experience was so great that his imagination was spell-bound by the concretism of the material presence of the sacred body. All his attempts at explanation are, therefore, under the spell of this fact: the body of Christ is present, albeit 'non-spatially'. According to the so-called doctrine of consubstantiation the actual substance of the sacred body was also really present beside the substance of the bread and wine. The ubiquity of Christ's body, which this assumption postulated, an idea involving considerable distress to human intelligence, was indeed substituted by the concept of volipresence, which means that God is everywhere present, where He wills to be. But Luther, untroubled by all these difficulties, held unflinchingly to the immediate experience of the sensuous impression and preferred to assuage all the scruples of human reason with explanations which were either absurd or at the best quite unsatisfying.

It is hardly credible that it was merely the power of tradition which determined Luther to cling to this dogma, for he assuredly gave abundant proof of his ability to throw aside traditional forms of belief. Indeed we should not go far wrong in assuming that it was rather the actual contact with the 'real' and material in the Communion, and the feeling-significance of this contact for Luther himself, that prevailed over the evangelical principle, which maintained that the word was the sole vehicle of grace and not the ceremony. With Luther the word certainly had redeeming power, but the partaking of the Communion was also a transmitter of grace. This, I repeat, must have been only an apparent concession to the institutions of the Catholic Church; for in reality it was the acknowledgment, demanded by Luther's psychology, of the fact of feeling, grounded upon the immediate sense-experience.

As against the Lutheran standpoint Zwingli represented the purely symbolic conception. What really concerned him was a 'spiritual' partaking of the body and blood of Christ. This standpoint has the character of reason; it is a conceptual attitude to the ceremony. It has the merit that it offers no violence to the evangelical principle, and at the same time it avoids all hypotheses that run counter to reason. This conception, however, does little justice to the thing which Luther wished to preserve, namely the reality of the sense-impression and its peculiar feeling-value. Zwingli, it is true, also administered the Communion, and with Luther also partook of bread and wine—nevertheless his conception contained no formula which could have adequately rendered the unique sensational and feeling value of the object. Luther gave a formula for this, but it was opposed to reason and the evangelical principle. To the standpoint of sensation and feeling this matters little, and indeed rightly, for the idea, the 'principle', is just as little concerned about the sensation of the object. Both points of view are in the last resort mutually exclusive.

The Lutheran formulation favours the extraverted conception of things, while Zwingli has the conceptual standpoint. Although Zwingli's formula does no violence to feeling and sensation, but merely gives a conceptual formulation, and appears furthermore to have left room for the efficacy of the object, yet it seems as though the extraverted standpoint is not content with an open space, but demands also a formulation in which the conceptual follows the sensuous value, exactly as the conceptual formulation requires the subservience of feeling and sensation.

At this point, with the consciousness of having given merely a statement of the problem, I close this chapter on the principle of types in the history of classic and medieval thought. I am not sufficiently competent to be able to treat so difficult and voluminous a problem in any way exhaustively. If I have been successful in conveying to the reader an impression of the existence of typical differences of standpoint, my purpose has been achieved. I need scarcely add that I am aware that none of the material here touched upon has been conclusively dealt with. I must bequeath this task to those who command a fuller knowledge of this province than myself.

CHAPTER II

SCHILLER'S IDEAS UPON THE TYPE PROBLEM

1. Letters on the Æsthetic Education of Man

(a) *The superior and the inferior functions*

So far as my somewhat limited range extends, Friedrich Schiller seems to have been the first to have made any considerable attempt at a conscious discrimination of typical attitudes, and to have developed a fairly complete presentation of their singularities. This important endeavour to represent the two mechanisms in question, and at the same time to discover a possibility of their reconciliation, is to be found in his treatise first published in 1795: *Über die ästhetische Erziehung des Menschen*[1]. The paper consists of a number of letters which Schiller addressed to the Duke of Holstein-Augustenburg.

Schiller's essay, by the depth of its thought, the psychological penetration of its material, and its wide vision of the possibility of a psychological solution of the conflict, prompts me to a somewhat extensive presentation and appreciation of his ideas, for never yet has it fallen to their lot to be treated in such a connection.

The merit due to Schiller from our psychological viewpoint, as will become clear in our further discussion, is by no means inconsiderable; for he gives us developed points-of-view which we, as psychologists, are just beginning to appreciate. My responsibility will, of course, not be light,

[1] Cotta'sche Ausgabe, 1826, Bd. xviii. The English translation is in many ways unsatisfactory and even incorrect: the references therefore are to the German edition.

for it may well happen that I shall be accused of giving a construction to Schiller's ideas which his actual words do not warrant. For, although I shall take considerable pains, at every essential point, to quote the actual words of the author, yet it may not be altogether possible to introduce his ideas in the connection I intend to establish here without giving them certain interpretations or constructions. I am obliged not to overlook this possibility, but, on the other hand, we must bear in mind the fact that Schiller himself belongs to a definite type, and is therefore constrained, even in spite of himself, to deliver a one-sided characterization.

The limitation of our conceptions and cognition becomes nowhere so apparent as in psychological presentations, where it is almost impossible for us to trace any other picture than that whose main outlines are already marked out in our own psyche. From various characteristics I conclude that Schiller belongs to the introverted type, while Goethe inclines more to the extraverted side.

We can easily trace Schiller's own image in his description of the idealistic type. An inevitable limitation is imposed upon his formulation through this identification, a fact which must never be lost sight of in our effort to gain a fuller understanding. This limitation is to be ascribed to the fact that the one mechanism is presented by Schiller in richer outline than the other, for the latter is still imperfectly developed in the introvert, and just because of its imperfect development it must necessarily have certain inferior characters clinging to it. In such cases the presentation of the author demands our criticism and correction. It is clear, too, that this limitation of Schiller's has also prompted him to use a terminology which fails in general applicability. As an introvert Schiller has a better relation to ideas than to things of the world. The relation to ideas can be relatively more emotional or reflective according to whether the individual belongs more to the feeling or the thinking type. At this point I would request the reader, who perhaps may have been led by my earlier publications to identify feeling with extraversion and thinking with introversion, to be good enough to bear in mind the definitions furnished in the last chapter. With the introverted and extraverted types I have there distinguished two general classes of men, which can be further sub-divided into function-types, *e.g* thinking, feeling, sensational, and intuitive. Hence an introvert can be a thinking or a feeling type, since feeling as well as thinking can come under the supremacy of the idea, just as both in given cases can be ruled by the object.

If then I consider that Schiller, both in his nature and particularly in his characteristic opposition to Goethe, corresponds with the introvert, the question next arises as to which subdivision he belongs. This question is hard to answer. Without doubt the factor of intuition plays a considerable rôle with him; we might on this account, or if we were regarding him exclusively as a poet, count him as an intuitive type. But in the *Über die ästhet. Erziehung* it is undoubtedly Schiller the thinker who confronts us. Not only from these, but also from his own repeated admissions, we know how strong the reflective element was in Schiller. Consequently we must shift his intuitiveness over towards the side of thinking, so that we may also approach him from this other angle, *i.e.* from our understanding of the psychological viewpoint of an *introverted thinking* type. It will, I hope, be sufficiently proved hereafter that this conception coincides with reality, for there are not a few passages in Schiller's writings that speak distinctly in its favour. I would, therefore, request the reader to bear in mind that the hypothesis I have just outlined underlies my whole argument. This is, in my opinion, necessary, because Schiller handles the problem from the angle of his own inner experience. In view of the fact that another psychology, *i.e.* another type, would have apprehended the problem in quite another form, the highly general formulation which Schiller gives to it might be regarded in the nature of an encroachment, or as an ill-considered generalization. But such a judgment would be incorrect, since there is actually a large class of men for whom the problem of the differentiated functions is precisely the same as it was for Schiller. If, therefore, in the ensuing argument I occasionally emphasize Schiller's one-sidedness and subjectivity, I do not wish to detract from the importance and validity of the problem he has raised, but rather to make room for other formulations. Such criticisms as I may occasionally offer, therefore, are intended rather as a *transcription* into a form of expression, which disembarrasses Schiller's formulation of its subjective limitations. My argument, nevertheless, clings very closely to Schiller's, since it is concerned much less with the general question of introversion and extraversion —which in Chapter I exclusively engaged our attention— than with the *typical conflict of the introverted thinking type*.

Schiller concerns himself at the very outset with the question of the cause and origin of the bifurcation of the two mechanisms. With sure instinct he hits upon the differentiation of the individual as the basic motive. "It was culture itself, which dealt this wound to the modern man" (p. 22). This one sentence at once shows Schiller's embracing understanding of our problem. The breaking up of the harmonious co-operation of the psychic forces that exists in instinctive life is like an ever open and never healing wound, a veritable Amfortas' wound; since the differentiation of one function among several inevitably leads to overgrowth of the one and to neglect and crippling of the rest.

"I do not ignore the advantages", says Schiller, "which the present generation, regarded as a whole, and measured by reason, may boast over what was best in the bygone world; but it must enter the contest as a compact phalanx and measure itself as whole against whole. What individual modern could enter the lists, man against man, and contest the prize of manhood with an individual Athenian? Whence then arises this unfavourable individual comparison in the face of every advantage from the standpoint of the race?" (p. 22).

Schiller places the responsibility for this decline of the modern individual upon culture, *i.e.* upon the differentiation of functions. He next points out how, in art and scholarship, the intuitive and the speculative minds have become estranged, and how each has zealously excluded the other from its respective field of application.

"And with the sphere into which man confines his operation, he has also made unto himself a ruler; which fact not infrequently results in the suppression of his other faculties. Whereas, in the case of the former, the luxuriating power of imagination makes a wilderness of the laborious plantations of the mind, in the latter the spirit of abstraction consumes the fire that should have warmed the heart and kindled phantasy" (p. 23).

And further:

"When the commonwealth makes the office or function the measure of the man, when of its citizens it does homage only to memory in one, to a tabulating intelligence in another, and to a mechanical capacity in a third; when here, regardless of character, it urges only towards knowledge, while there it encourages a spirit of order and law-abiding behaviour with the profoundest intellectual obscurantism—when, at the same time, it wishes these single accomplishments of the subject to be carried to just as great an intensity as it absolves him of extensity—is it to be wondered at that the remaining faculties of the mind are neglected, in order to bestow every care upon the special one which it honours and rewards?"

In these thoughts of Schiller there lies much weight. It is understandable that Schiller's age, whose imperfect knowledge of the Grecian world appraised the man of Greece by the greatness of his bequeathed works, should thereby over-estimate him beyond all bounds, inasmuch as the peculiar beauty of Grecian art owed its existence in no small measure to its contrast with the milieu from which it arose. The advantage of the Greek consisted in the fact that he was less differentiated than the modern, if indeed one is disposed to regard that as an advantage; for the disadvantage of such a condition must at least be equally obvious. The differentiation of functions is assuredly no product of human caprice; its origin, like that of everything in nature, was necessity. Could one of these modern admirers of the Grecian heaven and Arcadian bliss have visited the earth as an Attic helot, he might well have surveyed the beauties of the land of Greece with rather different eyes. Even were it the fact that the primitive conditions of the fifth century before Christ yielded the individual a greater possibility for an all-round unfolding of his qualities and capacities, this nevertheless was possible only because thousands of his fellow-men were admittedly cramped and crippled in wretched circumstances. A high level of individual culture was undoubtedly reached by certain figures, but a collective culture was quite unknown to the ancient world. This achievement was reserved for Christianity. Hence it comes about that, as a mass, the moderns can not only rival the Greeks, but by every standard of collective culture they easily surpass them. Schiller, on the other hand, is perfectly right in his contention that our individual has not kept pace with our collective culture; and it has certainly not improved during the hundred and twenty years that have passed since Schiller wrote—rather the reverse; for, if we had not wandered even farther into the collective atmosphere to the prejudice of individual development, the violent reactions which took shape in the mind of a Stirner or a Nietzsche would scarcely have been required. Still to-day, therefore, Schiller's words must remain both timely and valid.

Like the ancients, who with a view to individual development catered for the claims of an upper class by an almost total suppression of the great majority of the common people (helots and slaves), the subsequent Christian world reached a condition of collective culture through an identical process, albeit translated as far as possible into the individual sphere (or, raised to the subjective level, as we prefer to express it). While the value of the individual was proclaimed to be an imperishable soul by the Christian dogma, it became no longer possible for the inferior majority of the people to be suppressed for the freedom of a superior minority, but now the superior function was preferred over the inferior functions in the *individual*. In this way the chief importance was transferred to the one valued function, to the prejudice of all the rest. Psychologically this meant that the external form of society in antique civilization was translated into the subject, whereby in individual psychology, an inner condition was produced which had been external in the older civilization, namely, a dominating, preferred function, which became developed and differentiated at the expense of an inferior majority. By means of this psychological process a collective culture gradually came into existence, in which "*les droits de l'homme*" certainly had an immeasurably greater guarantee than with the ancients. But it had this disadvantage, that it depended upon a subjective slave-culture, *i.e.* upon a transfer of the antique majority enslavement into the psychological sphere, whereby collective culture was undoubtedly enhanced, while individual culture depreciated.

Just as the enslavement of the mass was the open wound of the antique world, the enslavement of the inferior function is an ever-bleeding wound in the soul of man to-day. "One-sidedness in the exercise of his powers leads in the individual infallibly to error, but in the race to truth" (p. 29) says Schiller. The favouritism of the superior function is just as serviceable to society as it is prejudicial to the individuality. This prejudicial effect has reached such a pitch that the great organizations of our present day civilization actually strive for the complete disintegration of the individual, since their very existence depends upon a mechanical application of the preferred individual functions of men. It is not man that counts, but his one differentiated function. Man no longer appears as man in collective civilization: he is merely represented by a function—nay, further, he is even exclusively identified with this function and denies any responsible membership to the other inferior functions. Thus the modern individual sinks to the level of a mere function, because this it is that represents a collective value and alone affords a possibility of livelihood. But, as Schiller clearly discerns, differentiation of function could have come about in no other way: "There was no other means to develop man's manifold capacities than to set them one against another. This antagonism of human qualities is the great instrument of culture; it is only the instrument, however, for so long as it endures man is only upon the way to culture" (p. 28).

According to this conception the present state of warring capacities could not yet be a state of culture, but only a stage on the way. Opinion will, of course, be divided about this, for by culture one man will understand a state of collective culture, while another will merely regard this as *civilization* and will ascribe to culture the sterner demands of individual development. Schiller is, of course, mistaken when he exclusively allies himself with the second stand-point and contrasts our collective culture with that of the individual Greek, since he overlooks the defectiveness of the civilization of that time, which renders the absolute validity of that culture very questionable. Hence no culture is ever really complete that swings towards a one-sided orientation, *i.e.* when at one time the cultural ideal is extraverted, the chief value being given to the *object* and the objective relation, while at another the ideal is introverted when the supreme importance lies with the individual or *subject* and his relation to the idea. In the former case, culture takes on a collective character, while in the latter an individual. One can easily understand, therefore, that it was through the operation of the Christian sphere, whose principle is Christian love (and also through contrast-association with its counterpart, viz. the violation of the individuality) that a collective culture came about in which the individual threatens to be swallowed up, and individual values are depreciated on principle. Hence there arose in the time of the German 'classics', that extraordinary yearning for the antique which was for them a symbol of individual culture, and on that account was for the most part very much overvalued and often grossly idealized. Not a few attempts were even made to imitate or recapture the spirit of Greece; attempts which now-a-days appear to us somewhat silly, but which none the less must be valued as the forerunners of an individual culture. In the hundred and twenty years which have passed since Schiller's time, conditions in respect to individual culture have become not better but worse, since individual interest is to-day engrossed to a far greater extent in collective preoccupations, and therefore much less leisure is available for the development of individual culture. Hence we possess to-day a highly developed collective culture, which in organization far exceeds anything that ever existed, but which for that very reason has become increasingly injurious to individual culture. There exists a deep gulf between what a man is and what he represents, *i.e.* between the man as an individual and his function-capacity as a collective being. His function is developed at the expense of his individuality. Should he excel, he is merely identical with his collective function; but should he not, then, although certainly esteemed as a function in society, he is as an individuality wholly on the side of his inferior, undeveloped functions, and therefore simply barbarous, whereas the former has more fortunately deceived himself concerning his actually existing barbarism. This one-sidedness has undoubtedly yielded not inconsiderable advantages to society, which has thereby gained acquisitions that could have been won in no other way; as Schiller finely observes: "Only by focussing the whole energy of our mind and knitting together our entire nature in one unique faculty, do we, as it were, give wings to this individual gift and bring it by artifice far beyond the limits which nature seems to have laid down for it" (p. 29).

But this onesided development must inevitably lead to a reaction, since the repressed inferior functions cannot be indefinitely excluded from common life and development. The time will come when "the cleavage in the inner man must again be resolved", that the undeveloped may be granted an opportunity to live.

I have already alluded to the fact that the differentiation of function in civilized development ultimately effects a dissociation of the basic functions of the psyche, thus in a certain measure transcending the differentiation of capacity, and even encroaching upon the province of the psychological attitude in general, which governs the whole manner and character of the application of capacity. By this means culture effects a differentiation of that function which already enjoys a better development through heredity. In one man it is the function of thought, in another feeling, which is especially accessible to further development. Thus it happens that the urge of cultural demands engages the individual's special concern with the development of that capacity which Nature has already intended as his most favourable line. But this capacity for development does not mean that the function has an a priori claim to any particular fitness; it merely pre-supposes—one might almost say, on the contrary—a certain functional delicacy, lability, and plasticity. On this account the highest individual value is not by any means always to be sought or found in this function; but just in so far as it is developed for a collective end, it may possibly yield the highest collective value. But it may well be the case, as already observed, that far higher individual values lie hidden among the neglected functions, which, although of small importance for the collective life, are of the very greatest value to individual development. These, therefore, represent a living value which can endow the life of the individual with an intensity and beauty that he will vainly seek in his collective function. The differentiated function certainly procures for him the possibility of collective existence, but not that satisfaction and joy of life which the development of individual values alone can give. Their absence is often sensed as something deeply lacking, and the severance from them is like an inner division which, with Schiller, one might compare with a painful wound.

" Thus, however much may be gained for the world at large by the separate development of human capacities, it cannot be denied that the individuals affected by it suffer under the curse of this general aim. Athletic bodies are certainly built up by means of gymnastic exercises, but beauty is won only through the free and uniform play of the limbs. In the same way the tension of individual mental powers can produce extraordinary men, but it is only the uniform temperature of the same that can give man happiness and fulfilment. And in what sort of relation should we stand to past and coming ages, if the development of human nature compelled us to such a sacrifice? We would become the thralls of mankind; thousands of years long for humanity's sake we should be doing *slave labour*, and have imprinted upon our crippled nature the shameful brand of this servitude only that some later generation might nurse its moral health in blissful leisure, and unfold the ample spread of its humanity! But can it be that man is destined, for any aim whatsoever, to neglect himself? Can Nature with her aims rob us of that perfection which the aims of reason prescribe for us? It must, therefore, be false, that the development of individual capacities necessitates the sacrifice of their totality; or, even if the law of nature still pressed towards such a goal, *we must never relinquish that totality in our nature which cunning art has demolished, but which a still higher art may re-establish.*" (p. 30)[1]

It is evident that Schiller in his personal life had a profound sense of this conflict, and that it was just this antagonism in himself which begat a longing to seek that coherence and uniformity which should bring deliverance to the wasting and enslaved functions and a restoration of harmonious life. This is also the impelling motive in Wagner's *Parsifal*, where it receives symbolical expression in the restitution of the missing spear and the healing of the wound. What Wagner attempted to say in artistic, symbolical expression Schiller laboured to formulate in philosophical thought. Although it is nowhere frankly stated, the implication is clear enough that his problem revolves around the possibility of *resuming the classical manner and conception of life*; from which one is obliged to conclude that he either overlooks the Christian solution of his problem or deliberately ignores it. In any case his mind is focussed more upon classic beauty than upon the Christian doctrine of redemption, which, nevertheless, has no other aim but the solution of that selfsame problem in which Schiller himself travailed, viz. the *deliverance from*

[1] The italics in the text are mine.

evil. The heart of man is "filled with raging battle", says Julian the Apostate in his discourse upon King Helios: and these words significantly mark his insight not only into his own problem but into that of his whole time, namely that inner laceration of the later classical epoch which found its outward expression in an unexampled, chaotic confusion of hearts and minds, and from which the Christian doctrine promised deliverance. What Christianity gave was, of course, not a *solution* but a *redemption*, a detachment of one valuable function from all the other functions which, at that time, made an equally peremptory claim for a share in government. Christianity gave *one* definite direction, to the exclusion of every other possible direction. This may have been the essential reason why the possibility of salvation that Christianity offered was passed by Schiller in silence.

The pagan's near contact with Nature seemed to promise just that possibility which Christianity did not offer.

"Nature, in her physical creation, shows us the way which man has to travel in the moral world. Not until the battle of elemental forces is spent in the lower organizations, does she mount to the noble form of physical man. In the same way this elemental strife in the ethical man, this conflict of blind instincts, must first be assuaged; man must end the crude antagonism in himself before he can venture to unfold his own diversity. Upon the other hand, the independence of his character must be assured, and submissiveness to strange despotic forms have given place to a decent freedom before man may subject the diversity in himself to the unity of the ideal." (p. 32)

Thus it is not to be a detachment or redemption of the inferior function, but an acknowledgment of it, a coming to terms with it, as it were, which reconciles the opposites upon the natural way. But Schiller feels that the acceptance of the inferior function might lead to a "conflict of blind instincts", just as—only vice versa—the unity of the ideal might re-establish that priority of the superior over the inferior function, and thereby once again precipitate the original state of affairs. The inferior functions are opposed to the superior, not so much in their essential nature but as a result of their actual momentary form. They were originally neglected and repressed, because they hindered civilized man in the attainment of his aims; but these correspond with one-sided interests, and are by no means synonymous with a consummation of human individuality. If this were the aim, these unacknowledged functions would be indispensable, and as a matter of fact their nature does not contradict such an end. But, so long as the goal of culture does not coincide with the ideal of individuality, these functions are also subjected to a depreciation which means a decline into relative repression. The conscious acceptance of the repressed functions is synonymous with civil war, or with the unlocking of previously coupled antitheses, whereby "independence of character" is immediately abolished. This independence can be reached only by a settlement of this conflict, which appears to be impossible without despotic jurisdiction over the antagonizing forces. But thereby freedom is compromised, without which the constitution of a morally free personality is inconceivable. But if one preserves freedom, one is delivered over to the conflict of instincts.

"Upon the one hand, in his recoil from liberty, who in her first essays ever wears the semblance of an enemy, man will throw himself into the arms of a comfortable servitude, while upon the other, reduced to despair by a pedantic tutelage, he will escape into the wild unrestraint of the state of nature. Usurpation will evoke the weakness of human nature, while insurrection its dignity, until finally blind force, the great sovereign of all human affairs, will intervene, and like a common pugilist decide the ostensible battle of principles." (p. 33)

The contemporary revolution in France gave to this statement a living, albeit a bloody background; begun in the name of philosophy and reason, with loftily soaring idealism, it ended in a bloodthirsty chaos, from which arose the despotic genius of Napoleon. The goddess of reason proved herself powerless against the might of the unchained beast. Schiller feels the defeat of reason and truth and therefore has to postulate that truth itself shall become a *force*.

" If she has hitherto evinced so little of her conquering power, the fault lies not so much with the intellect that knew not how to unveil her, as with the heart that shut her out, and with the instinct that did not work for her. Then whence this still prevailing prejudice, this intellectual darkness, beside all the light enthroned by philosophy and experience ? *The age is enlightened*, knowledge has been found and is publicly accessible ; this should at least suffice to correct our practical principles. The spirit of free research has destroyed the illusions which so long barred the approach to truth ; it has undermined the ground upon which fanaticism and fraud had built their thrones. Reason has purged herself of sense-delusion and false sophistries ; even philosophy, which at first made us desert her, calls us with loud insistence back to the bosom of nature—whence comes it then that we are still barbarians ? " (p. 35)

In these words of Schiller we can feel the nearness of the French enlightenment and the phantastic intellectualism of the Revolution. "The age is enlightened"—what a strange over-valuation of the intellect! "The spirit of free research has destroyed the illusions"—what rationalism! One is vividly reminded of the words of the Proktophantasmists: "Vanish! we have enlightened!"[1] If, on the one hand, men of that time were too fain to over-estimate the importance and efficacy of reason, quite forgetting that if reason really possessed such a power, she had long had the amplest opportunity to manifest it; on the other hand, the fact must not be overlooked that not all the authoritative minds of that time held this view; consequently this soaring of a rationalistic intellectualism may well have sprung from an especially strong subjective development of this element in Schiller himself. In him we have to

[1] *Faust*, Part I : *Walpurgis-Nacht*.

reckon with a predominance of the intellect, not at the expense of his poetic intuition, but at the cost of feeling. To Schiller himself it seemed as though there were a perpetual conflict between imagination and abstraction, *i.e.* between intuition and intellect. Thus he writes to Goethe (31st August 1794): "This it is which gave me, especially in early years, a certain awkwardness both in speculation and in the realm of poetry; as a rule the poet would overtake me when I would be the philosopher, and the philosophic spirit hold me when I would be the poet. Even yet it happens often enough that imaginative power disturbs my abstraction, and cold reasoning my poetry." His extraordinary admiration of Goethe's mind, and his almost feminine appreciation of his friend's intuition, to which he so often gives expression in his Letters, rests upon a penetrating perception of this conflict, which must have seemed redoubled in himself in contrast to the almost completely synthetic nature of Goethe. This conflict was due to the psychological circumstance that the energy of feeling gave itself in equal measure both to the intellect and the creative imagination. Schiller seems to have appreciated this fact, for in the same letter to Goethe he makes the observation that no sooner has he begun "to know and to use" his moral forces, which should apportion reasonable limits to the rival claims of imagination and intellect, than a physical illness threatens to shatter them. For it is the characteristic (already frequently alluded to) of an imperfectly developed function, that it withdraws itself from conscious disposition and with its own impetus, *i.e.* with a certain autonomy, becomes unconsciously implicated with other functions. Whereby, without any sort of differentiated choice, it behaves as a purely dynamic factor; it might well be described as an impetus or reinforcement which lends the conscious differentiated function the character of being carried away or coerced. So that, in one case, the conscious function is seduced beyond the limits set by purpose and decision ; in another, it is held up before the attainment of its goal and led away upon a by-path ; while, in a third case, it is brought into conflict with the other conscious functions, a conflict which remains unresolved so long as the unconsciously implicated and disturbing instinctive force is not differentiated in its own right and subjected as such to a certain conscious disposition. Thus one is almost driven to assume that the cry : 'Whence comes it then that we are still barbarians?' is no mere reflexion of the spirit of that age, but also springs from Schiller's subjective psychology. Like other men of his time, he too sought the root of the evil in the wrong place, for at no time did barbarism consist in a state where reason or truth have an insufficient effect; it appears only when man expects such an effect from them, or, we might even say, it is because man provides reason with too much efficacy from a superstitious over-valuation of 'truth'. Barbarism is onesidedness, lack of moderation—bad proportion generally.

In the impressive example of the French Revolution, which had just then reached the culminating point of terror, Schiller could see to what extent the goddess of reason held sway in man, and how far the unreasoning beast was triumphant. It was doubtless these events of Schiller's epoch which urged the problem upon him with especial force, for it frequently happens that, when a problem that is at bottom personal, and therefore apparently subjective, impinges upon outer events which contain the same psychological elements as the personal conflict it is suddenly transformed into a general question that embraces the whole of society. In this way, the personal problem gains a dignity that was hitherto wanting ; since a state of inner discord has an almost mortifying and degrading quality, so that one sinks into a humiliated condition both without and within, like a State dishonoured by civil war. It is this that makes one shrink from displaying before a larger public a purely personal conflict, provided, of course, that one does not suffer from an over-daring self-esteem. But when it happens that the connection between the personal problem and the larger contemporary events is discerned and understood, a relativity is established that promises release from the isolation of the purely personal; in other words, the subjective problem is amplified to the dimensions of a general question of our society. This is no small gain as regards the possibility of a solution. For, whereas the rather meagre energy of conscious interest in one's own person was hitherto the only source available for the personal problem, there is now assembled the combined forces of collective instinct, which flow in and unite with the interests of the ego; thus a new situation is brought about which offers new possibilities of a solution. For what would never have been possible to personal will or courage is made possible by the force of collective instinct; it bears a man over obstacles which his own personal energy could never overcome.

We are therefore prompted to conjecture that it was largely the impressions of contemporary events that gave Schiller the courage to undertake this attempt to solve the conflict between the individual and the social function.

The same antagonism was also deeply sensed by Rousseau—indeed it was the starting point of his work *Emile, ou de l'éducation* (1762). Several passages are to be found in it which have interest for our problem.

"L'homme civil n'est qu'une unité fractionnaire qui tient au dénominateur, et dont la valeur est dans son rapport avec l'entier, qui est le corps social. Les bonnes institutions sociales sont celles qui savent le mieux dénaturer l'homme, lui ôter son existence absolue pour lui en donner une relative, et transporter le moi dans l'unité commune.

"Celui qui dans l'ordre civil veut conserver la primauté des sentiments de la nature ne sait ce qu'il veut. Toujours en contradiction avec lui-même, toujours flottant entre ses penchants et ses devoirs, il ne sera jamais ni homme ni citoyen ; il ne sera bon ni pour lui ni pour les autres."[1]

Rousseau opens his work with the famous sentence: "Tout est bien, sortant des mains de l'Auteur des choses ; tout dégénère entre les mains de l'homme."[2] This statement is characteristic not for Rousseau alone but for that whole epoch.

Schiller also turns back, not of course to Rousseau's natural man—and here lies an essential difference—but to the man who lived "under a Grecian heaven". But the *retrospective orientation* that is common to both is inextricably bound up with an idealization and over-valuation of the past. Schiller in the wonder of pagan art forgets the actual everyday Greek; Rousseau mounts to dizzy heights, losing himself in phrases such as: " l'homme naturel est tout pour lui ; il est l'unité numérique, l'entier absolu."[3] Whereby he overlooks the fact that the natural man is wholly collective, *i.e.* just as much in others as in himself, and is everything else besides a mere unity. In another passage Rousseau says:

" Nous tenons à tout, nous nous accrochons à tout, les temps, les lieux, les hommes, les choses, tout ce qui est, tout ce qui

---

[1] *Emile*, livre i: " Man as a citizen is only a fractional unity dependent upon a denominator, and his value lies in his relation with the whole, which is society. Those institutions are good which best understand how to change the nature of man, how to take from him his absolute existence unto himself and give him a relative one, how, in short, to translate the ego into a common unity.
" He who wishes to preserve in his life as a citizen the supremacy of natural feelings knows not what he wants. Ever in contradiction with himself, ever hovering between his inclinations and his duties, he will become neither man nor citizen ; he will be useless both to himself and others."

[2] " Everything as it leaves the hands of the Author of things is good ; everything degenerates under the hands of man."

[3] *Emile*, livre ii: " Natural man is wholly himself ; he is an integral unity, an absolute whole."

sera, importe à chacun de nous, notre individu n'est plus que la moindre partie de nous-mêmes. Chacun s'étend, pour ainsi dire, sur la terre entière, et devient sensible sur toute cette grande surface."

"Est-ce la nature qui porte ainsi les hommes si loin d'eux-mêmes?"[1]

Rousseau deceives himself; he believes this state to be a recent development. But this is not so. Granted it has only recently become conscious to us, it none the less always existed, and it reveals itself all the more vividly the further we descend into the origins. For what Rousseau depicts is nothing but that primitive collective mentality which Lévy-Bruhl has aptly termed "participation mystique".[2] This state of suppression of the individuality is no new acquisition, but a residue of that archaic time when there was no individuality whatsoever.

What we are dealing with is not, therefore, a recent suppression, but merely a new sense and awareness of the overwhelming power of the collective. One naturally projects this power into political and ecclesiastical institutions, as though there were not already ways and means enough for the evasion of even moral commands when occasion suited! In no way have these institutions that presumed omnipotence for which they are from time to time assailed by innovators of every sort; the suppressing power lies unconsciously in ourselves, namely in our own barbarian element with its primitive collective mentality. To the collective psyche every individual development is obnoxious which does not directly serve the ends of collectivity. Hence the differentiation of the one function mentioned

[1] "We cling to everything, we clutch on to all times, places, men, things; all that is, and all that will be, matters to each of us; our individual self is only the least part of ourselves. Each extends, as it were, over the whole earth, and becomes sensitive to this whole vast surface.

"Is it nature which thus bears men so far from themselves?"

[2] Lévy-Bruhl, *Les Fonctions mentales dans les sociétés inférieures*.

above, although certainly a development of an individual value is still so largely conditioned by the view-point of collectivity, that the individual himself, as we have already seen, actually suffers from this development.

Both authors have to thank their imperfect acquaintance with earlier conditions of human psychology for their lapse into false judgments upon the values of the past. The result of this false judgment is a belief in the illusory picture of an earlier, more perfect type of man, who somehow fell from his high estate. Backward orientation is in itself a relic of pagan thinking, for it is a well-known characteristic of the whole classic and barbaric mentality that it imagined a paradisiacal age as a golden forerunner of the present evil time.

It was the great social and educational act of Christianity which first gave man a future hope, assuring him of a future possibility for the realization of his ideals[1]. The stronger note of this retro-orientation in the more recent intellectual movements may be connected with the appearance of that general regression towards the pagan which with the Renaissance made itself increasingly manifest.

It seems to me certain that this retrogressive orientation must also have a definite influence upon the means selected for human education. For a mind thus orientated is ever seeking support in some phantasmagoria in the past. We could make light of this, if the knowledge of the conflict between the types and the typical mechanisms were not also constantly urging us to seek for that which could re-establish their unity. As we may see in the following passages, this goal had also a profound interest for Schiller. His fundamental idea about it is expressed in the following words, which indeed actually sum up what has just been said:

"Let a benevolent deity snatch in time the suckling from his mother's breast, nourish him with the milk of a better age,

---

[1] Indications of this are already to be found in the Grecian mysteries.

and let him ripen to maturity under that far Grecian heaven. Then, when he is become a man, let him return, a strange figure, into his own century: but not that he may delight it with his appearance, but terrible, like Agamemnon's son, to purify it."
—*Erziehung d. Menschen*, p. 39

The leaning towards the Grecian model could scarcely be more clearly expressed. But in this narrow formulation one can also glimpse a limitation, which in the following paragraph urges him to a very essential amplification, for he continues: "His material will he indeed take from the present, but his form he will borrow from an older age. *Yea, from beyond all ages, from the absolute, unchangeable unity of his being.*" Schiller clearly felt that he must go back still further, into some primeval heroic age, where men were still half-divine. He therefore continues: "Here from the pure æther of his dæmonic nature wells forth the source of beauty, untainted by the depravity of the generations and epochs, which whirl in troubled eddies far below." Here is ushered in the lovely phantom of a Golden Age, when men were still gods and were constantly refreshed with the vision of eternal beauty. But here, too, the poet has overtaken the thinker in Schiller. A few pages further on the thinker again gets the upper hand. "The fact", says Schiller (p. 47), "must cause one to reflect that in almost every epoch of history, when the arts blossomed and taste ruled, one finds that humanity declined; furthermore *not one single example can be shown* of a people where a high level and a wide universality of æsthetic culture went hand in hand with political freedom and civic virtue, or where beautiful manners went with good morals, or polished behaviour with truth."

According to this familiar and in every way undeniable experience, those heroes of olden days must have pursued a none too scrupulous conduct of life, which, moreover, no single myth, either Grecian or otherwise, maintains.

Beauty could still delight in her existence, for as yet there was neither penal code nor guardian of public morals.

With the recognition of the psychological fact that living beauty unfolds her golden splendour only when soaring above a reality of gloom, torment, and squalor, Schiller's particular aim is undermined; for he had undertaken to prove that what was separated would be reconciled by the vision, enjoyment, and creation of the beautiful. Beauty was to be the mediator which should restore the primal unity of human nature. But, nevertheless, all experience goes to show that beauty needs her opposite as a necessary condition of her existence.

As before it was the poet, it is now the thinker that possesses Schiller; he *mistrusts* beauty, he even holds it possible, arguing from experience, that she may exercise an unfavourable influence: " Wherever we turn our eyes into the world of the past, we find taste and freedom fleeing one another, and *beauty establishing her sovereignty only upon the ruins of the heroic virtues.*" This insight, which is the product of experience, can hardly sustain the claim that Schiller makes for beauty. In the further pursuit of his theme he even reaches a point where he abstracts the reverse of beauty with an all too enviable clarity: " Thus, if one's view about the effect of beauty is entirely influenced by what one learns from all bygone experience, one cannot be greatly encouraged in the work of *educating feelings which prove to be so dangerous to the true culture of man;* and, in spite of the danger of crudity and hardness, man is wiser to forego the softening power of beauty than, with every advantage of refinement, to be delivered over to her enervating influence."

The matter between the poet and the thinker would surely allow of adjustment if the thinker took the words of the poet not literally but *symbolically*, which is how the tongue of the poet desires to be understood. Can

Schiller have misunderstood himself? It would almost seem so—otherwise he could not argue thus against himself. The poet sings of a spring of unsullied beauty which flows beneath every age and generation, and is constantly swelling in every human heart. It is not the man of ancient Greece, the poet means, but the old pagan in ourselves; that piece of eternal, unspoiled nature and natural beauty which lies unconscious but living within us, whose reflected splendour transfigures the shapes of former days, and for whose sake we even embrace the error that those distant men actually possessed the beauty which we are seeking. It is the archaic man in ourselves, who, rejected by our collectively orientated consciousness, appears to us as hideous and inacceptable, but who is nevertheless the bearer of that beauty which we elsewhere unavailingly seek. This is the man the poet Schiller means, but the thinker Schiller mistakes him for his Grecian prototype. But what the thinker cannot logically deduce from all his massed material, and at which he labours in vain, the poet in symbolical language reveals to him as a promised land.

It is now sufficiently clear from all that has been said that every attempt at an adjustment of the one-sided differentiation of the human being of our times has to reckon with the serious acceptance of the inferior, because undifferentiated, functions. No attempt at mediation will succeed which does not understand how to release the energies of the inferior functions and to lead them over into differentiation. This process can take place only in accordance with the laws of energetics, *i.e.* a potential must be created which offers the latent energies a possibility of coming into play.

It would be a hopeless task—which nevertheless has been often undertaken and as often foundered—to transform an inferior function directly into a superior one.

It would be as easy to make a perpetuum mobile. No inferior form of energy can be simply converted into a superior form unless at the same time a source of higher value lends its support, *i.e.* the conversion can be accomplished only at the expense of the superior function. But under no circumstances can the initial value of the superior energy-form be attained by the inferior function or resumed once more by the superior function; a levelling at some intermediate temperature must inevitably result. But for every individual who identifies himself with his one differentiated function, this entails a descent to a condition that is certainly balanced, but of a definitely lower value as compared with the apparent initial value. This conclusion is unavoidable. Every education of man which aspires after the unity and harmony of his nature has to deal with this fact. After his own manner, Schiller also draws this conclusion, but he struggles against accepting his results, even to the point where he has to renounce beauty. But when the thinker has uttered his ruthless judgment, the poet speaks again: "But it may be that *experience* is no tribunal before which a question like this shall be decided, and before we give weight to its testimony, let all doubt be set at rest that the beauty we speak of, and that against which these examples testify, is one and the same." (p. 50). One sees that Schiller here attempts to take his stand above experience; in other words he bestows upon beauty a quality which experience does not grant her. He believes that "*Beauty must be proven a necessary condition of mankind*", *i.e.* a necessary, compelling category. He even speaks of a purely intellectual concept of beauty, and a "transcendental way" which shall take us out of the "round of appearances and away from the living presence of things". "Who durst not go beyond reality will never vanquish truth." A subjective resistance to the experimental, inevitable, downward way prompts Schiller to suborn the logical intellect in the service of feeling, thus forcing it to construct a formula which would ultimately make possible the attainment of the original aim, notwithstanding the fact that its impossibility is already sufficiently exposed. A similar violence is committed by Rousseau in his assumption that, whereas dependence upon nature does not involve depravity, it does if one is dependent upon man; from which he arrives at the following conclusion:

"Si les lois des nations pouvaient avoir comme celles de la nature, une inflexibilité que jamais aucune force humaine ne pût vaincre, la dépendance des hommes redeviendrait alors celle des choses ; on réunirait dans la république tous les avantages de l'état naturel à ceux de l'état civil ; on joindrait à la liberté qui maintient l'homme exempt de vice la moralité qui l'élève à la vertu".[1]

Arising out of these reflections he gives the following advice:

"Maintenez l'enfant dans la seule dépendance des choses, vous aurez suivi l'ordre de la nature dans le progrès de son éducation. . . Il ne faut point contraindre un enfant de rester quand il veut aller, ni d'aller quand il veut rester en place. Quand la volonté des enfants n'est point gâtée par notre faute, ils ne veulent rien inutilement.[2]"

But the misfortune lies in this: that never, under any circumstances, do "les lois des nations" possess that admirable accord with the laws of nature which could enable the civilized to be at the same time a natural state.

[1] "If the laws of nations, like those of nature, could have an inflexibility that no human force could ever vanquish, the dependence of men would become once more like that of things ; one could combine in the republic all the advantages of the natural state with those of citizenship ; one could add to the liberty which exempts man from vice the morality which raises him to virtue."

[2] *Emile*, livre ii: "Keep the child dependent solely upon things, you will have followed the order of nature in the progress of his education. . . Do not force a child to stay when it wants to go, or to go when it wants to stay quiet. When the will of our children is not spoiled by our own fault, they desire nothing that is useless."

If such a settlement could be regarded as at all possible, it could be conceived only as a compromise wherein neither of the two conditions would attain its own ideal but both would remain far below it. Whoever wishes to attain the ideal of either state will have to rest with the statement that Rousseau himself formulated: "Il faut opter entre faire un homme ou un citoyen: car on ne peut faire à la fois l'un et l'autre." ("One must choose whether to make a man or a citizen; for at the same time one cannot make both.")

Both these necessities exist in ourselves: Nature and culture. We cannot only be ourselves, we must also be related to others. Hence a way must be found that is not a mere rational compromise; it must also be a state or process that wholly corresponds with the living being, it must be a "semita et via sancta" as the prophet says, a "via directa ita ut stulti non errent per eam." ("A highway and the way of holiness." "A straight way so that fools shall not err therein.") (*Isaiah*, xxxv. 8). I am therefore disposed to give the poet in Schiller his just due, although in this case he has encroached somewhat outrageously upon the province of the thinker; since rational truths are not the last word, there are also irrational truths. In human affairs, what appears impossible upon the way of the intellect has very often become true upon the way of the irrational. Indeed, all the greatest changes that have ever affected mankind have come not by the way of intellectual calculation, but by ways which contemporary minds either ignored or rejected as absurd, and which only long afterwards became fully recognised through their intrinsic necessity. More often than not they are never perceived at all, for the all-important laws of mental development are still to us a seven-sealed book.

I am, however, little disposed to grant any considerable

E

value to the philosophical demeanour of the poet, for the intellect is a deceptive instrument in his hands. What the intellect can achieve, it has in this case already done; for it disclosed the contradiction between desire and experience. To persist, then, in demanding a solution of this contradiction from philosophical thinking would be quite useless. And, even if a solution could finally be thought out, the real obstacle would still confront us, for the solution does not lie in the possibility of thinking it or in the discovery of a rational truth, but in the revealing of a way which real life can accept. Propositions and wise precepts have indeed never been wanting. If it were only a question of these, even in the remote days of Pythagoras, man had the finest opportunity of reaching the heights from every direction. Therefore what Schiller proposes must not be taken in a literal sense, but rather as a *symbol*, which, in harmony with Schiller's philosophical temperament, assumes the character of a philosophical concept. Similarly the "transcendental way" which Schiller sets out to tread must not be understood as a cognitional raisonnement, but symbolically as that way which a man always follows when he encounters an obstacle immediately inaccessible to his reason—in a word, an insoluble task. But, before he is able to discover and follow this way, he must first abide a long time with the opposites into which his former way divided. The obstacle dams up the river of his life. Whenever such a damming up of libido occurs, the opposites, formerly united in the steady flow of life, fall apart and henceforth oppose one another like antagonists eager for battle. In a prolonged conflict, the upshot and duration of which cannot be foretold, the opposites become exhausted, and from the energy which goes out of them is that third element created which is the beginning of the new way.

In accordance with this law, Schiller now devotes

himself to a profound research of the actual opposites at work. Whatever the nature of the obstacle we may strike —provided only it be difficult—the cleavage between our own purpose and the contending object at once becomes a conflict in ourselves. For, inasmuch as I am striving to subordinate the contending object to my will, my whole being is gradually placed into relationship with it, corresponding, in fact, with the strong libido application, which as it were transveys a part of my being into the object. The result of this is a partial identification between certain portions of my personality and similar qualities in the nature of the object. As soon as this identification has taken place, the conflict is transferred into my own psyche. This 'introjection' into myself of the conflict with the object creates an inner discord, which gives rise to a certain impotence vis-à-vis the object, and also releases affects, which are always symptomatic of inner disharmony. But the affects prove that I am perceiving myself and am therefore in a situation—if I am not blind—to apply my observation upon myself, and to follow up the play of opposites in my own psyche.

This is the way that Schiller takes. The division that he finds is not between the State and the individual, but, in the beginning of the eleventh Letter (p. 51), he conceives it as the duality of "person and condition", namely as the self or ego and its changing affectedness[1]. Whereas the ego has a relative constancy, its relatedness (or affectedness) is variable. Schiller thus intends to seize the discord at the root. Actually, the one side is also the conscious ego-function, while the other is the collective relationship. Both determinants belong to human psychology. But the various types will respectively see these basic facts in quite a different light. For the introvert, the idea of the self is doubtless the abiding and dominant note of consciousness,

[1] Affectedness is used to denote the state of being affected.

and its antithesis for him is relatedness or affectedness. For the extravert, on the contrary, much more stress is laid upon the continuity of the relation with the object, and less upon the idea of the self. Hence for him the problem is differently situated. We must hold this point in view and consider it more fully as we follow Schiller's further reflections. When, for instance, he says the person reveals itself "in the eternally constant self and in this alone", this is viewed from the standpoint of the introvert. From the standpoint of the extravert, on the other hand, we should say that the person reveals itself simply and solely in its relationship, *i.e.* in the function of relation to the object. For only with the introvert is the "person" exclusively the ego; with the extravert the person lies in his affectedness and not in the affected self. His self is, as it were, of less importance than his affection, *i.e.* his relation. The extravert finds himself in the fluctuating and changeable, the introvert in the constant. The self is not "eternally constant", least of all with the extravert, for whom, as an object, it is a matter of small moment. To the introvert, on the other hand, it has too much importance: he therefore shrinks from every change that is at all liable to affect his ego. For him affectedness can mean something directly painful, while to the extravert it must on no account be missed. The following formulation immediately reveals the introvert: " In every change to remain himself constant, referring every perception to experience, *i.e.* to the unity of knowledge, and relating each of its varying aspects in his own time to the law of all times; this is the command given him by his reasoning nature" (p. 54). The abstracting, self-contained attitude is evident; it is even made a supreme rule of conduct. Every occurrence must at once be raised to the level of experience, and from the sum of experience a law for the future must also immediately emerge; whereas the other attitude, in which no experience shall be made from the occurrence lest laws might transpire which would hamper the future, is equally human.

It is altogether in keeping with this attitude that Schiller cannot think of God as *becoming*, but only as eternally *being* (p. 54); hence with unerring intuition he also recognizes the "God-likeness" of the introverted attitude towards the idea: "Man, presented in his perfection would be the constant unit, remaining eternally the same amid the floods of change." "Man carries the divine disposition incontestably within his personality" (p. 54).

This view of the nature of God agrees ill with His Christian incarnation and with those similar neo-Platonic views of the mother of the Gods and of her son, who descends into creation as Demiurgos.[1] But it is clear from this view to which function Schiller attributes the highest value, the divinity, viz. the constancy of the idea of the self. The self that is abstracted from affectedness is for him the most important thing, and hence, as is the case with every introvert, this is the idea which he has chiefly developed. His God, his highest value, is the abstraction and conservation of the self. To the extravert, on the contrary, God is the experience of the object, the fullest expansion into reality: hence a God who became human is to him more sympathetic than an eternal, immutable law-giver. Here I must observe in anticipation that these points-of-view should be regarded only as valid for the conscious psychology of the types. In the unconscious the relations are reversed. Schiller seems to have had an inkling of this: although indeed his consciousness believes in an unchangingly existing God, yet the way to God-hood is revealed to him by the senses, hence in affectedness, in the changing and living process. But this is for him the function of secondary importance,

[1] Cf. the discourse of Julian upon the mother of the Gods.

and, to the extent that he identifies himself with his ego and abstracts it from the "changing" process, his conscious attitude also becomes quite abstracted; whereby the function of affectedness or relatedness to the object perforce relapses into the unconscious. From this state of affairs noteworthy consequences ensue:

I. From the conscious attitude of abstraction, which in pursuit of its ideal makes an experience from every occurrence, and from the sum of experience a law, a certain constriction and poverty results, which is indeed characteristic of the introvert. Schiller clearly feels this in his relationship with Goethe, for he sensed Goethe's more extraverted nature as something objectively opposed to himself[1]. Significantly Goethe says of himself: "As a contemplative man I am an arrant realist. I find that among all the things which confront me I am in the position of desiring nothing from them or added to them, and I make no sort of discrimination among objects beyond their interest for myself."[2] Concerning Schiller's effect upon him, Goethe very characteristically says: "If I have served you as the representative of many objects, you have led me from a *too intense observation of outer things and their relationships back into myself. You have taught me to view the many-sidedness of the inner man with finer equity*" etc.[3] Whereas in Goethe Schiller finds an oft-times accentuated complement or fulfilment of his own nature, at the same time sensing his difference, which he indicates in the following way:

"Expect of me no great material wealth of ideas, for that is what I find in you. My need and endeavour is to make much out of little, and, if ever you should realize my poverty in all that men call acquired knowledge, you will perhaps find that in many ways my aspiration has succeeded. Because my circle of ideas is smaller I traverse it more quickly and oftener. I may,

---

[1] *Letter to Goethe*, January 5th 1798. [2] *Letter to Schiller*, April 1798.
[3] *Letter to Schiller*, January 6th 1798.

SCHILLER AND THE TYPE-PROBLEM 119

therefore, even make a better use of what small ready cash I own, creating a diversity through form which the contents lack. You strive to simplify your great world of ideas, while I seek variety for my small possessions. You have a kingdom to rule, and I only a somewhat numerous family of ideas which I would fain expand to a small universe."—*Letter to Goethe*, Aug. 31st 1794.

If we subtract from this utterance a certain feeling of inferiority characteristic of the introvert, and add to it the fact that the extravert's "great world of ideas" is not so much under his rule as he himself is subject to it, then Schiller's presentation gives a striking picture of the poverty which tends to develop as a result of an essentially abstract attitude.

II. A further result of the abstracting, conscious attitude, and one whose significance will become more apparent in the further course of our investigation, is that the unconscious develops a compensating attitude. For the more the relation to the object is restricted by the abstraction of consciousness (because too many 'experiences' and 'laws' are made), all the more insistently does a craving for the object develop in the unconscious. This finally declares itself in consciousness as *a compulsive sensuous hold upon the object;* whereupon the sensuous tie takes the place of a *feeling-relation* to the object, which is lacking, or rather suppressed, through abstraction. Characteristically, therefore Schiller regards the *senses*, and not the *feelings*, as the way to God-hood. His ego lies with thinking, but his affectedness, his feelings, with sensation. Thus with him the schism is between spirituality as thinking, and sensuousness as affectedness or feeling. With the extravert, however, matters are reversed: his relation to the object is developed, but his world of ideas is sensational and concrete.

Sensuous feeling, or to put it better, the feeling that exists in the state of sensation, is *collective*, i.e. it begets a state of relation or affectedness, which at the same time always translates the individual into the condition of "participation mystique", hence into a state of partial identity with the sensed object. This identity declares itself in a compulsory dependence upon the sensed object, and it is this which again prompts the introvert, after the manner of the circulus vitiosus, to an intensification of that abstraction which shall abolish both the burdensome relation and the compulsion it evokes. Schiller recognized this peculiarity of the sensuous feeling: "So long as he merely senses, craves, and works from desire, *man is still nothing more than world*." (p. 55). But since, in order to escape affectedness, the introvert cannot abstract indefinitely, he ultimately sees himself forced to shape the external world. "That he may not be merely world, he must impart form to matter" says Schiller (*ibid.*); "he shall externalize all within, and shape everything without." Both tasks, in their highest achievement, lead back to the idea of divinity from which I started out.

This connection is important. Let us suppose the sensuously felt object to be a man—will he accept this prescription? Will he, in fact, permit himself to take shape as though the man to whom he is related were his creator? To play the god on a small scale is certainly man's vocation, but ultimately even inanimate things have a divine right to their own existence and the world long ago ceased to be chaos when the first man-apes began to sharpen stones. It would, indeed, be a serious business if every introvert wished to externalize his narrow world of ideas and to shape the external world accordingly. Such experiments happen daily, but the individual ego suffers, and very justly, from this "God-likeness".

For the extravert, this formula should run: "to internalize all that is without and shape everything within".

Goethe. Goethe gives a telling parallel to this. He writes to Schiller: "In every sort of activity I, on the other hand, am—one might almost say—completely *idealistic: I ask nothing at all from objects; but instead I demand that everything shall conform to my conceptions.*" (April 1798). This means that when the extravert thinks, things go just as autocratically as when the introvert operates externally[1]. This formula therefore can hold good only where an almost complete stage has already been reached; when in fact the introvert has attained a world of ideas so rich and flexible and capable of expression that the object no longer forces him upon a Procrustean bed; and the extravert such an ample knowledge of and consideration for the object that a caricature of it can no longer arise when he operates with it in his thinking. Thus we see that Schiller bases his formula upon the highest possible, and therefore makes an almost prohibitive demand upon the psychological development of the individual—assuming also that he is thoroughly clear in his own mind what his formula involves in every particular. Be that as it may, it is at least fairly clear that this formula: "To externalize all that is within and shape everything without" is the ideal of the conscious attitude of the introvert. It is based, on the one hand, upon the hypothesis of an ideal range of his inner world of concepts and formal principles, and, on the other, upon the possibility of an ideal application of the sensuous principle, which in that case no longer appears as affectedness, but rather as an active power. So long as man is "sensuous" he is "nothing but world"; that he may be "not merely world he must impart form to matter". Herein lies a reversal of the

[1] I wish it to be clearly understood that all my observations upon the extravert and introvert in this chapter hold valid only for the special types here dealt with, viz. the intuitive, feeling extravert represented by Goethe, and the intuitive, thinking introvert represented by Schiller.

passive, enduring, sensuous principle. Yet how can such a reversal come to pass? That is the whole question. It can scarcely be assumed that a man can give to his world of ideas that extraordinary range which would be necessary in order to impose a congenial form upon the material world, and at the same time convert his affectedness, his sensuous nature, from a passive to an active condition, thus bringing it to the heights of his world of ideas. Somewhere or other man must be related, *subjected* as it were, else would he be really God-like. One is forced to conclude that Schiller would let it reach a point at which violence was done to the object. But in so doing he would concede to the archaic inferior function an unlimited right to existence, which as we know Nietzsche has actually done—at least theoretically. This assumption, however, is by no means conclusive with regard to Schiller, since, so far as I am aware, he has nowhere consciously expressed himself to this effect. His formula has instead a thoroughly naïve and idealistic character, a character withal quite consistent with the spirit of his time, which was not yet infected by that deep mistrust of human nature and human truth which haunted the epoch of psychological criticism inaugurated by Nietzsche.

The Schiller formula could be carried out only by a power standpoint, applied without ruth or consideration: a standpoint with never a scruple about equity and reasonableness towards the object nor any conscientious examination of its own competence. Only under such conditions, which Schiller certainly never contemplated, could the inferior function also win to a share in life. In this way, archaic, naïve, and unconscious elements, though decked out in a glamour of mighty words and lovely gestures, ever came crowding through, and assisted in the moulding of our present 'civilisation,' concerning the nature of which humanity is at this moment in some measure of disagreement. The archaic power instinct, which hitherto had hidden itself behind the gesture of culture, finally came to the surface in its true colours, and proved beyond question that we "are still barbarians." For it should not be forgotten that, in the same measure as the conscious attitude has a real claim to a certain God-likeness by reason of its lofty and absolute standpoint, an unconscious attitude also develops, whose God-likeness is orientated downwards towards an archaic god whose nature is sensual and brutal. The enantiodromia of Heraclitus forebodes the time when this deus absconditus shall also rise to the surface and press the God of our ideals to the wall. It is as though men at the close of the eighteenth century had not really seen what that was which was taking place in Paris, but persisted in a certain æsthetical, enthusiastic, or trifling attitude, that they might perchance delude themselves concerning the real meaning of that glimpse into the abysses of human nature.

" But in that netherworld is terror,
And man tempteth not the gods,
Craving only that he may never, never see
What they in pity veil with night and horror."
Schiller's *Der Taucher*.

When Schiller lived, the time for dealing with the underworld was not yet come. Neitzsche at heart was much nearer to it, for to him it was certain that we were approaching an epoch of great struggle. He it was, the only true pupil of Schopenhauer, who tore through the veil of naïvete and in his *Zarathustra* conjured up from that lower region ideas that were destined to be the most vital content of the coming age.

(*b*) *Concerning the basic instincts*

In the twelfth Letter Schiller deals with the two basic instincts, to which at this point he devotes a somewhat fuller description. The "sensuous" instinct is that which is concerned with the "placing of man within the confines of time, and making him material." This instinct demands that "there be change, and that time should have a content. This state, which is merely filled time, is called *sensation*" (p. 56). "In this state man is nothing but a unit of magnitude, a filled moment of time or—more correctly—he is not even that, for his personality is dissolved so long as sensation rules him and time carries him along" (p. 57). "With unbreakable bonds this instinct chains the upward-striving mind to the world of sense, and calls abstraction from unfettered wandering in the infinite, back into the confines of the present."

It is entirely characteristic of Schiller's psychology that he should conceive the expression of this instinct as "sensation", and not as active, sensuous *desire*. This shows that for him sensuousness has the character of *reaction*, of affectedness, which is altogether characteristic of the introvert. An extravert would undoubtedly first lay stress upon the character of *desire*. There is further significance in the statement that it is this instinct which demands change. The idea wants changelessness and eternity. Whoever lives under the supremacy of the idea, strives for permanence; hence everything that pushes towards change must be against it. In Schiller's case it is feeling and sensation that oppose the idea, since by natural law they are fused together as a result of their undeveloped state. Schiller did not even sufficiently discriminate in thought between *feeling* and *sensation*, as the following passage demonstrates: "Feeling can only say: This is true for this subject at this moment; but another moment or another subject may come and revoke the statement of this present sensation" (p. 59). This passage clearly shows that, with Schiller, sensation and feeling are actually interchangeable terms, and its content reveals an inadequate valuation and differentiation of feeling as opposed to sensation. Differentiated feeling can also establish *universal validity*; it is not purely casuistical. But it is certainly true, that the "*feeling-sensation*" of the introverted thinking type is, by reason of its passive and reactive character, purely casuistical. For it can never mount above the individual case, by which it is alone stimulated, to an abstract comparison of all cases; because with the introverted thinking type this office is allotted not to feeling but to thinking. But matters are reversed with the introverted feeling type, whose feeling reaches an abstract and universal character and can establish permanent values.

From a further analysis of Schiller's description we find that "feeling-sensation" (by which term I mean the characteristic fusion of feeling and sensation in the introverted thinking type) is that function with which the ego is not definitely identified. It has the character of something inimical and foreign, that "destroys" the personality; it draws it away with it as it were, setting the man outside himself and alienating him from himself. Hence Schiller likens it to the affect that sets a man "beside himself"[1]. When one has collected oneself, this is termed with equal justice "being oneself again,[2] *i.e.* returning once more to the self, restoring one's personality". The conclusion, therefore, is unmistakable that to Schiller it seems as though "feeling-sensation" does not really belong to the person, but is merely a more or less precarious accessory, to which on occasion "a robust will is victoriously opposed". But to the extravert it is just this side of him which seems to constitute his real nature; it is as if he were actually with himself only when he is affected by the object—a circumstance we can well understand, when we consider

[1] i.e. extraverted. [2] i.e. introverted.

that the relation to the object is his superior, differentiated function to which abstract thinking and feeling are just as much opposed as they are indispensable to the introvert. The thinking of the extraverted feeling type is just as prejudicially affected by the sensuous instinct as is the feeling of the introverted thinking type. For both it means extreme "limitation" to the material and casuistical. Living through the object has also its "unfettered wandering in the infinite", and not abstraction alone, as Schiller thinks.

By means of this exclusion of sensuousness from the idea and range of the 'person', Schiller is able to arrive at the view that the person is "absolute and indivisible unity, which can never be in contradiction with itself." This unity is a desideratum of the intellect, which would fain maintain its subject in the most ideal integrity; hence as the superior function it must exclude the sensuous or relatively inferior function. But the final result of this is that crippling of the human being which is the very motive and starting-point of Schiller's quest.

Since, for Schiller, feeling has the quality of "feeling-sensation" and is therefore merely casuistical, the supreme value, a really eternal value, is given to formative thought, the so-called "formative instinct"[1], as Schiller calls it: "But when thought has once affirmed *This is, it is decided for all time*, and the validity of its pronouncement is vouched for by the *personality* itself, which *offers defiance to all change*" (p. 59). But one cannot refrain from asking: Does the meaning and value of personality really reside only in what is constant and permanent? Can it not be that change, becoming and development, represent even higher values than sheer "defiance" against change?[2]

---

[1] "Formative instinct" is equivalent to "thinking faculty" for Schiller.

[2] Schiller himself criticizes this point later.

"When the formative instinct becomes the guiding power and the pure object works in us, then is the supreme unfolding of being, then do all barriers dissolve, then, from a unit of magnitude, to which needy sense confined him, has man arisen to a unit of idea embracing the entire realm of phenomena. No longer are we individuals, but the race: through our mind is the judgment of all minds pronounced, and by our deed is the choice of every heart represented."

It is unquestionable that the thought of the introvert aspires towards this Hyperion; it is only a pity that the unit of idea is the ideal of such a very limited class of men. Thinking is merely a function which, when fully developed and exclusively obeying its own laws, naturally sets up a claim to general validity. Only one part of the world, therefore, can be comprehended through thinking, another part only through feeling, a third only through sensation, etc. There are, in fact, various psychic functions; for, biologically, the psychic system can be understood only as an adaptation system; eyes exist presumably because there is light. Thinking, therefore, under all circumstances commands only a third or a fourth of the total significance, although in its own sphere it possesses exclusive validity—just as vision is the exclusively valid function for the reception of light-waves, and hearing for sound-waves. Hence a man who sets the unit of idea on a pinnacle, and senses " feeling-sensation " as something antithetic to his personality, can be compared with a man who has good eyes but is nevertheless quite deaf and anæsthetic.

" No longer are we individuals, but the race ": certainly, if we exclusively identify ourselves with thinking, or with any *one* function whatsoever; for then are we collective and generally valid beings, although quite estranged from ourselves. Outside this quarter-psyche, the other three quarters are in the darkness of repression and inferiority. "Est-ce la nature, qui porte ainsi les hommes si loin d'eux-mêmes?" we might here ask with Rousseau—is it indeed Nature, or is it not rather our own psychology, which so barbarously overprizes the one function and allows itself to be swept away by it? This impetus is of course a piece of Nature, namely that untamed, instinctive energy, before which the differentiated type recoils if ever it should 'accidentally' reveal itself in an inferior and despised function, instead of in the ideal function, where it is prized and honoured as divine enthusiasm. Schiller truly says: "But thy individuality and thy present need change will bear away, and what to-day thou ardently craveth in days to come she will make the object of thy loathing." [*Letter* xii] Whether the untamed, extravagant, and disproportionate energy shows itself in sensuality — in abjectissimo loco — or in an overestimation and deification of the most highly developed function, it is at bottom the same, viz. *barbarism*. But naturally no insight of this state can be gained while one is still hypnotized by the *object* of action so that one ignores the How of the acting.

Identification with the one differentiated function means that one is in a collective state; not, of course, that one is *identical with the collective* as is the primitive, but *collectively adapted;* for "the judgment of all minds is expressed by our own", in so far as our thought and speech exactly conform to the general expectation of those whose thinking is similarly differentiated and adapted. Furthermore, "the choice of every heart is represented by our act," just in so far as we think and do, as all desire it to be thought and done. There is certainly a universal belief and desire that that value is the best and most worth while wherein an identity with the one differentiated function is as fully achieved as possible; for that brings the most obvious social advantages, albeit the greatest disadvantages to those minorities of our nature, which often constitute a great portion of the individuality.

"As soon as one affirms", says Schiller, "a primordial, therefore necessary, antagonism of the two instincts, there is of course no other means of preserving unity in man than for him *unconditionally to subordinate* the sensuous to the reasoning instinct. Mere uniformity can only result from this, not harmony, and man still remains eternally divided." (pp. 61 ff.)

" Because it costs much to remain true to one's principles through every fluctuation of feeling, one seizes upon the more comfortable expedient of *consolidating the character through the blunting of feeling ;* for in sooth it is infinitely easier to obtain peace from a disarmed adversary than to command a daring and robust enemy. Very largely also this operation includes that process which we call ' forming the man ' and this in the best sense of the word, where it embraces the idea of an inner cultivation and not merely outer form. A man thus formed will indeed be safeguarded from being mere crude nature or from appearing as such ; but he will also be armoured by principle against every sensation of nature, so that humanity will reach him as little from without as from within." (pp. 67 ff.)

Schiller was also aware that the two functions, thinking and affectedness (feeling-sensation), can *substitute one another* (which happens, as we saw, when one function is preferred).

" He may shift the intensity which the active function demands upon the passive one (affectedness), he can substitute the formative instinct by the instinct for material, and convert the receiving into a determining function. He can assign to the active function (positive thinking) the extensity which belongs to the passive one, he can entrench upon the instinct for material to the benefit of the formative instinct and substitute the determining for the receiving function. In the first instance, never will he be himself; in the second, he will never be anything else." (pp. 64 ff.)

In this very remarkable passage much is contained which we have already discussed. When the energy belonging to positive thinking is bestowed upon "feeling-sensation", which would be equivalent to a reversal of the introverted type, the qualities of the undifferentiated, archaic "feeling-sensation" become paramount, *i.e.* the individual relapses into an extreme relatedness, or identification with the sensed object. This state corresponds with a so-called *inferior extraversion*, i.e. an extraversion which, as it were, detaches the individual entirely from his ego and dissolves him into archaic, collective ties and identifications. He is then no longer "himself", but a mere relatedness; he is identical with his object and consequently without a standpoint. Against this condition the introvert instinctively feels the greatest resistance, which, however, is no sort of guarantee against his repeated and unwitting lapse into it. Under no circumstances should this state be confused with the extraversion of an extraverted type, although the introvert is continually prone to make this mistake and to show towards the true extraversion that same contempt which, at bottom, he always feels for his own extraverted relation[1]. The second instance, on the other hand, corresponds with a pure presentation of the introverted thinking type, who through amputation of the inferior feeling-sensation condemns himself to sterility, *i.e.* he enters that state in which "humanity will reach him as little from without as from within".

Here also, it is obvious that Schiller continues to write purely from the standpoint of the introvert, because the extravert, who possesses his ego not in thinking, but rather in the feeling relation to the object, really finds himself through the object, while the introvert loses himself in it. But when the extravert, proceeds to introvert, he comes to his inferior relationship with collective ideas, *i.e.* to an identity with collective thinking of an archaic, concretistic quality, which one might describe as *sensation-presentation*. He loses himself in this inferior function just as much as the introvert in his inferior extraversion. Hence the extravert has the same repugnance, fear, or silent scorn for introversion as the introvert for extraversion.

Schiller senses this opposition between the two mechanisms—thus in his own case between sensation and thinking,

---

[1] To avoid misconception, I would here like to observe that this contempt does not concern the object, not at least as a rule, but merely the relation to it.

or, as he also says, between "material and form", or again "passivity and activity" (affectedness and active thinking)[1] —as *unbridgeable*. "The distance between sensation and thinking" is "infinite" and "any sort of mediation is absolutely inconceivable". The two "conditions are opposed to each other, and can never be joined."[2] But both instincts are insistent, and as "energies"—as Schiller himself in very modern fashion regards them[3]—they need, and in fact, demand effective "discharge". "The demands of both the material and the formative instincts are a serious matter; for the one is related in cognition to the *reality* while the other to the *necessity* of things."[4] "But the discharge of energy of the sensuous instinct must, in no way, have the effect of a physical disability or a blunting of sensation, which only deserves universal contempt—it must be an act of freedom, an activity of the person, tempering everything sensual by its moral intensity."[5] "Only to the mind may sense give place." It must follow, then, that the mind may give place only in favour of sense. Schiller, it is true, does not say this directly, but it is surely implied where he says:

" Just as little should this discharge of the formative instinct have the effect of a spiritual disablement and a loosening of the powers of thought and of will; for this would mean a lowering of mankind. Abundance of sensations must be its honourable source; sensuousness itself must maintain her province with conquering power and resist the despotism which the mind with its encroaching activity would willingly inflict upon her."

In these words a recognition of the equal rights of "sensuousness"[6] and spirituality is expressed. Schiller

[1] In contrast to the *reactive* thinking previously referred to.
[2] *Letter XXIII*, pp. 90 ff.   [3] *XIII*, p. 68.   [4] *XV*, p. 76.
[5] *XIII*, pp. 68 ff.
[6] "Sensuousness" unfortunately does not carry the ambivalence that is contained in the German *Sinnlichkeit*, which has equally the meaning of sensuality. It is, therefore, important to point out that in all these latter quotations from Schiller the ambivalent significance is definitely intended. [Translator]

therefore concedes to sensation the right to its own existence. But, at the same time, we can also see in this passage allusions to a still deeper thought, namely the idea of a "reciprocity" between the two instincts, a community of interest, or *symbiosis*, as we should perhaps prefer to call it, in which the waste-products of the one would be the food-supply of the other. Schiller himself says that "the reciprocity of the two instincts consists in this, that the effectiveness of the one both *establishes* and *restricts* the effectiveness of the other, and that each in its own separate sphere can reach its highest manifestation only through the activity of the other." Hence, if we follow out this idea, their opposition must in no way be conceived as something to be done away with, but must, on the contrary, be regarded as something useful and life-promoting, which should be preserved and strengthened. But this is a direct attack against the predominance of the one differentiated and socially valuable function, since it is the primary cause of the repression and absorption of the inferior functions. This would signify a slave-rebellion against the heroic ideal which compels us, for the sake of *one*, to sacrifice the *remaining all*.

If this principle, which as we know, was first especially developed by Christianity for the spiritualizing of man—subsequently becoming equally effective in furthering his materialization—were once finally broken, the inferior functions would find a natural release and would demand, rightly or wrongly, the same recognition as the differentiated function. The complete opposition between sensuousness and spirituality, or between the "feeling-sensation" and thinking of the introverted thinking type would therewith be openly revealed. This complete opposition, as Schiller also allows, entails a reciprocal limitation, equivalent psychologically to an abolition of the power principle i.e. to a renunciation of the claim to a generally valid standpoint on the strength of one differentiated and generally adapted, collective function.

The direct outcome of this renunciation is *individualism*, i.e. the necessity for a realization of individuality, a realization of man as he *is*. Let us hear how Schiller tries to approach the problem. " This reciprocity of the two instincts is indeed merely a problem of the reason; it is a task which man is able wholly to solve only through the perfecting of his being. It is the idea of his humanity in the truest meaning of the word; hence it is an absolute to which in the issue of time he can constantly approach without ever attaining."[1] It is a pity that Schiller is so conditioned by his type; if it were not so, it could never have occurred to him to look upon the co-operation of the two instincts as a " problem of the reason", since opposites are not to be united rationally: tertium non datur—that is the very basis of their opposition. Then it must be that Schiller understands by reason something else than ratio, namely a higher and almost mystical faculty. Opposites can be reconciled practically only in the form of compromise, i.e. *irrationally*, wherein a *novum* arises between them, which, though different from both, has the power to take up their energies in equal measure as an expression of both and of neither. Such an expression cannot be contrived; it can only be created through living. As a matter of fact, Schiller also means this latter possibility, as we see in the following sentence:

" But should instances occur when he (man) proved at the same time this double experience, wherein he was not only conscious of his freedom but also sensed his own existence ; when feeling himself to be matter, he, at the same time, knew himself to be spirit ; in this unique state and in no other would he gain a complete vision of his humanity, and the object which evoked this vision would serve as the symbol of his accomplished destiny."[2]

---

[1] *Letter XIV*, p. 69. [2] *Letter XIV*, p. 70.

Thus, if the individual were able to live both faculties or instincts at the same time, *i.e.* thinking by sensing and sensing by thinking, out of that experience (which Schiller calls the object) a *symbol* would arise which would express his accomplished destiny, *i.e.* his way upon which his Yea and his Nay are reconciled.

Before we take a nearer survey of this idea, it would be well for us to ascertain how Schiller conceives the nature and origin of the symbol: "The object of the sensuous instinct is *Life* in its widest meaning; a concept that signifies all material being, and all things directly present to the senses. The object of the formative instinct is *Form*, a concept that embraces all formal qualities of things and all relations of the same to the thinking function."[1] The object of the mediating function is, therefore, "living form" according to Schiller; for this would be precisely that symbol which unites the opposites: "a concept which serves to describe all æsthetic qualities of phenomena, which embraces in a single word the thing called beauty in its fullest significance". But the symbol also presupposes a function which creates symbols and, while creating them, is an indispensable agent for their apprehension. This function Schiller calls a third instinct, the *play instinct*; it has no similarity with the two opposing functions; it none the less stands between them and does justice to both natures, always provided (which Schiller does not mention) that sensation and thinking are recognised as *serious* functions. But there are many with whom neither sensation nor thinking is wholly serious; in which case seriousness must hold the middle place instead of play. Although in another place Schiller denies the existence of a third mediating instinct (p. 61), we will nevertheless assume, though his conclusion is somewhat at fault, his intuition to be all the more accurate. For, as a matter

[1] *Letter XV*, p. 73.

of fact, something does stand between the opposites, though it has become invisible in the differentiated type. In the introvert it lies in what I have termed "feeling-sensation". On account of its relative repression, the inferior function is only partly attached to consciousness; its other part is dependent upon the unconscious. The differentiated function is most fully adapted to outer reality; it is essentially the reality-function; hence it is as much as possible shut off from any admixture of phantastic elements. These elements, therefore, become linked up with the inferior functions, which are similarly repressed. For this reason the sensation of the introvert, which is usually sentimental, has a very strong tinge of unconscious phantasy. The third element, in which the opposites merge, is on the one hand creative, and on the other receptive, *phantasy-activity*. It is this function which Schiller terms the play-instinct, by which he means more than he actually says. He exclaims: "For, let us admit once and for all, man only plays when he is a man in the fullest meaning of the word, and he is only completely man when he is playing."[1] For him the object of the play instinct is beauty. "Man shall only play with *beauty*, and only with beauty shall he *play*."

Schiller was actually aware what it might mean to assign the chief position to the 'play-instinct'. The release of repression, as we have already seen, effects a recoil of the opposites upon each other plus a compensation, which necessarily results in a depreciation of the hitherto highest value. For culture, as we understand it to-day, it is certainly a catastrophe when the barbaric side of the European comes uppermost, for who can guarantee that such a man, when he begins to play, shall forthwith take the æsthetic motive and the enjoyment of pure beauty as his goal? That would be an entirely unjustifiable

[1] *Letter XV*, p. 79.

anticipation. As a result of the inevitable debasement of cultural achievement a very different result must first be expected. Therefore with justice Schiller observes: "The æsthetic play instinct will, therefore, in its first essays be scarcely recognizable, because the sensual instinct with its capricious temper and savage lusts ceaselessly intervenes. Thus we see crude taste avidly seizing upon the new and startling, the motley, adventurous, and bizarre, even upon the violent and savage, and fleeing nothing so eagerly as simplicity and calm."[1] From this passage we must conclude that Schiller was aware of the danger of this conversion. It also follows that he cannot himself acquiesce in the solution found, but feels a compelling need to give man a more substantial foundation for his manhood than the somewhat insecure basis which an æsthetic-playful attitude can offer him. That must indeed be so. For the opposition between the two functions, or function-groups, is so great and so inveterate that play alone could hardly suffice to counterbalance all the difficulty and seriousness of this conflict — similia similibus curantur: a third factor is needed, which at the least can equal the other two in seriousness. With the attitude of play all seriousness must vanish, whereby the possibility of an absolute determinability presents itself. At one time the instinct is pleased to be allured by sensation, at another by thinking; now it will play with objects, and now with ideas. But in any case it will not play exclusively with beauty, for in that case man would be no longer a barbarian but already æsthetically educated, whereas the actual question at issue is: How is he to emerge from the state of barbarism? Above all else, therefore, it must be definitely established where man actually stands in his innermost being. A priori he is as much sensation as he is thinking; he is in opposition to

[1] *Letter* XXVII, p. 156.

himself—hence must he stand somewhere in between. In his deepest essence, he must be a being who partakes of both instincts, yet may he also differentiate himself from them in such a way that, although he must suffer the instincts and in given cases submit to them, he can also apply them. But first he must differentiate himself from them, as from natural forces to which he is subject but with which he does not regard himself identical. Concerning this Schiller expresses himself as follows: " This inherency of the two root-instincts in no way contradicts the absolute unity of the mind, provided only that man distinguishes himself from both instincts. Both certainly exist and work in him, but in himself he is neither substance nor form, neither sensuousness nor reason."[1]

Here, it seems to me, Schiller refers to something very important, viz. the *separability of an individual nucleus*, which can be at one time the subject and at another the object of the opposing functions, though ever remaining distinguishable from them. This discrimination is itself as much an intellectual as a moral judgment. In the one case it happens through thinking, in the other through feeling. If the separation does not succeed, or if it is not even attempted, a dissolution of the individuality into the pairs of opposites inevitably follows, since it becomes identical with them. The further consequence is an estrangement with oneself, or an arbitrary decision in favour of one or the other side, together with a violent suppression of its opposite. This train of thought belongs to a very ancient argument, which, so far as my knowledge goes, received its most interesting formulation, psychologically, at the hands of Synesius, the Christian bishop of Ptolemais and pupil of Hypatia. In his book *De Somniis*[2] he assigns to the " spiritus phantasticus " practically the

[1] *Letter XIX*, p. 99.
[2] I quote from the Latin translation of Marsilius Ficinus, 1497.

same psychological rôle as Schiller to the play-instinct, and I to creative phantasy; only his mode of expression is *metaphysical* rather than psychological, which, being an ancient form of speech, is hardly suitable for our purpose. Synesius speaks of it thus: "Spiritus phantasticus inter aeterna et temporalia medius est, quo et plurimum vivimus." ("The phantastic spirit comes between the eternal and the temporal, in which [spirit] are we also most alive".) The "spiritus phantasticus" combines the opposites in itself; hence it also participates in instinctive nature upon the animal plane, where it becomes instinct and incites to dæmoniac desires:

"Vendicat enim sibi spiritus hic aliquid velut proprium, tanquam ex vicinis quibusdam ab extremis utrisque, et quae tam longe disjuncta sunt, occurrunt in una natura. Atqui essentiae phantasticae latitudinem natura per multas rerum sortes extendit, descendit utique usque ad animalia, quibus non adest ulterius intellectus... Atque est animalis ipsius ratio, multaque per phantasticam hanc essentiam sapit animal, &c... Tota genera daemonum ex ejusmodi vita suam sortiuntur essentiam. Illa enim ex toto suo esse imaginaria sunt, et iis quae fiunt intus, imaginata."[1]

Psychologically, demons are interferences from the unconscious, *i.e.* spontaneous irruptions into the continuity of the conscious process on the part of unconscious complexes. Complexes are comparable to demons which fitfully harass our thoughts and actions, hence antiquity and the Middle Ages conceived acute neurotic disturbances as possession. When, therefore, the individual stands consistently upon one side, the unconscious ranges itself

[1] ("For this spirit borrows of both extremes and makes of them something of its own, so that they which formerly lay far apart, now appear in one nature. In many parts of the existing order has Nature extended the realm of the power of phantasy. It even descends to the creatures who do not yet possess reason... In truth, it represents the intelligence of the creature, and the creature understands much by means of this power of phantasy... All sorts of demons derive their essence from this kind of life. For they are in their whole nature imaginary and in their origin are inwardly fashioned.")

squarely upon the other, and rebels—which in all probability was what must have befallen the neo-Platonic or Christian philosophers, in so far as they represented the standpoint of exclusive spirituality. Particularly valuable is the allusion to the phantastic nature of the demons. It is, as I have previously discussed, precisely the phantastic element which becomes associated in the unconscious with the repressed functions. Hence, if the individuality (a term which more briefly expresses the individual nucleus) is not differentiated from the opposites, it becomes identified with them, and is thereby inwardly rent, *i.e.* a tormenting disunion takes place. Synesius expressed this as follows : " Proinde spiritus hic animalis, quem beati spiritualem quoque animam vocaverunt, fit deus et dæmon omniformis et idolum. In hoc etiam anima pœnas exhibet." (" This spiritual essence, which devout men have also called the vital flame, is both God and idol and demon of every shape. Herein also doth the soul receive her chastisement.") Through participation in the instinctive forces the spirit becomes " a God and a demon of many shapes ". This strange idea becomes immediately intelligible when we recollect that in themselves sensation and thinking are collective functions, in which through non-differentiation the individuality (the spirit, according to Schiller) has become dispersed. Thus the individuality becomes a collective being, *i.e.* god-like, since God is a collective idea of an all-pervading nature. " In this state ", says Synesius, "the soul suffereth torment". But deliverance is won through differentiation; because the spirit, when it has become " humidus et crassus " (" wet and fat ") sinks into the depths, *i.e.* becomes entangled in the object; but when purged through pain it becomes dry and hot and again ascends; for it is just this fiery quality which distinguishes it from the humid nature of its subterranean abode.

Here the question naturally arises, by virtue of what

power can the indivisible, *i.e.* the individuality, maintain itself against the separative instincts? That it can do so upon the line of the play-instinct even Schiller, at this point, no longer believes; for here we are dealing with something serious, some considerable power which can effectively detach the individuality from the opposites. From the one side comes the call, of the highest value, the highest ideal; while from the other comes the enchantment of the strongest desire: "Each of these two root-instincts", says Schiller, "as soon as it reaches a state of development, must of necessity strive towards the satisfaction of its own nature; but, because both are necessary and since both must pursue antagonistic objects, this two-fold urgency is mutually suspended, and between the two the *will* asserts a complete freedom. Thus it is the will which behaves as a power towards both instincts, but neither of the two can, of itself, behave as a power towards the other. There is in man no other power but his will, and only that which abolishes man, death and every destroyer of consciousness, can abolish this inner freedom."[1]

That the opposites must cancel each other is *logically* correct, but *practically* it is not so, for the instincts stand in mutual and active opposition, causing, temporarily, insoluble conflicts. The will could indeed decide, but only if we anticipate that condition which must first be reached. But the problem how man may emerge out of barbarism is not yet solved; neither is that condition established which alone could lend the will such efficacy as would reconcile the two root-instincts. It is in fact the sign of the barbarous state that the will has a one-sided determination through one function; yet the will must none the less have a content, an aim. And how is this aim to be reached? How else than through a

[1] *Letter XIX*, pp. 99, 100.

preliminary psychic process by which either an intellectual or an emotional judgment, or a sensuous desire, shall provide the will with its content and its goal? If we allow sensuous desire as a motive of will, we act in harmony with the one instinct against our rational judgment. Yet, if we transfer the adjustment of the dispute to the rational judgment, then even the fairest and most considerate allotment must always be based upon rational grounds, whereby the rational instinct is conceded a prerogative over the sensuous.

The will, in any case, is determined more from this side or from that, just so long as it is dependent for its content upon one side or the other. But, to be really able to decide the matter, it must be grounded on a mediate state or process, which shall give it a content that is neither too near nor too remote from either side. According to Schiller's definition, this must be a *symbolical* content, since the intermediate position between the opposites can be reached only by the symbol. The reality presupposed by the one instinct differs from the reality of the other. To the other it would be quite *unreal* or *apparent* and vice versa. But this dual character of real and unreal is inherent in the symbol. If only real, it would not be a symbol, since it would then be a real phenomenon and therefore removed from the nature of the symbol. Only that can be symbolical which embraces both. If altogether unreal, it would be mere empty imagining, which, being related to nothing real, would be no symbol.

The rational functions are, by their nature, incapable of creating symbols, since they produce only a rational product necessarily restricted to a single meaning, which forbids it from also embracing its opposite. The sensuous functions are equally unfitted to create symbols, because, from the very nature of the object, they are also confined to single meanings which comprehend only themselves and neglect the other. To discover, therefore, that impartial basis for the will, we must appeal to another element, where the opposites are not yet definitely divorced but still preserve their original unity. Manifestly this is not the case with consciousness, since the whole nature of consciousness is *discrimination*, distinguishing ego from non-ego, subject from object, yes from no, and so forth. The separation into pairs of opposites is entirely due to conscious differentiation; only consciousness can recognize the suitable and distinguish it from the unsuitable and worthless. It alone can declare one function valuable and another worthless, thus favouring one with the power of the will while suppressing the claims of the other. But, where no consciousness exists, where the still unconscious instinctive process prevails, there is no reflection, no pro et contra, no disunion, but simple happening, regulated instinctiveness, proportion of life. (Provided, of course, that instinct does not encounter situations to which it is still unadapted. In which case damming up, affect, confusion, and panic arise).

It would, therefore, be unavailing to appeal to consciousness for a decision of the conflict between the instincts. A conscious decree would be quite arbitrary, and could never give the will that symbolic content which alone can create an irrational settlement of a logical antithesis. For this we must go deeper; we must descend into those foundations of consciousness which have still preserved their primordial instinctiveness; namely into the unconscious, where all psychic functions are indistinguishably merged in the original and fundamental activity of the psyche. The lack of differentiation in the unconscious arises in the first place from the almost direct association of the brain centres among themselves, and in the second from the relatively weak energic value of unconscious elements[1]. It may be concluded that they possess relatively little energy from the fact that an unconscious element at once ceases to remain subliminal as soon as it receives a stronger accent of value; this enables it to rise above the threshold of consciousness, which it can achieve only by virtue of a specific informing energy. Therewith it becomes an "irruption", a "spontaneously arising presentation" (Herbart). The strong energic value of the conscious contents has an effect like intensive illumination, whereby distinctions become clearly perceptible and mistakes eliminated. In the unconscious, on the contrary, the most heterogeneous elements, in so far as they possess only a vague analogy, may become mutually substituted for each other, just by virtue of their relative obscurity and frail energic value. Even heterogeneous sense-impressions coalesce, as we see in the "photisms" (Bleuler) of "audition colorée". Language also contains not a few of these unconscious blendings, as I have shown for example with sound, light, and emotional states.[2]

The unconscious, therefore, might be that neutral region of the psyche where everything that is divided and antagonistic in consciousness flows together into groupings and formations. These, when examined in the light of consciousness, reveal a nature that exhibits the constituents of the one side as much as the other; they nevertheless belong to neither side, but occupy an independent middle station. This mediate position, constitutes for consciousness both their value and their worthlessness; worthless in so far as nothing clearly distinguishable emerges instantaneously from their formation, thus leaving consciousness embarrassed as to its purpose; but valuable in so far as their undifferentiated

[1] Cf. H. Nunberg's work: *On the Physical Accompaniments of Association Processes* (in Jung's *Studies in Word-Association*, p. 531)
[2] *Psychology of the Unconscious*, pp. 179 ff.

state gives them that symbolic character which is essential to the content of a mediatory will.

Besides the will, which is entirely dependent upon its content, man gains a further resource, then, in the unconscious, that maternal womb of creative phantasy, which is constantly potent to fashion symbols in the natural process of elemental psychic activity, symbols which *can* serve in the determination of the mediating will. I say "can" advisedly, because the symbol does not eo ipso step into the breach, but remains in the unconscious just so long as the energic value of the conscious content exceeds the value of the unconscious symbol. Under normal conditions this is, moreover, always the case; while under abnormal conditions a reversal of value takes place, whereby the unconscious receives a higher value than the conscious. In such a case the symbol penetrates the surface of consciousness, without however being taken up by the conscious will and the executive conscious functions, since these, on account of the reversal of values, have now become *subliminal*. The unconscious has become *superliminal*, and an abnormal mental state, a mental disorder, has declared itself.

Under normal conditions, therefore, energy must be artificially added to the unconscious symbol, in order to increase its value and thus bring it to consciousness. This occurs (and here we return again to the idea of differentiation provoked by Schiller) through a differentiation of the *Self* from the opposites. This differentiation is equivalent to a detachment of the libido from both sides, in such measure as the *libido is disposable*. For the libido invested in the instinct is only to a certain degree disposable, just so far in fact as the power of the will extends. This is represented by that quantity of energy which is under the "free" disposition of the ego. In such a case the will has the Self as a possible aim. In such measure as further development is arrested by the conflict is this goal the more possible. In this case, the will does not decide between the opposites, *but merely for the Self*, i.e. the disposable energy is withdrawn into the Self—in other words it is *introverted*. This introversion simply means that the libido is held with the Self and is prevented from participation in the conflicting opposites. Since the outward way is barred to it, it turns naturally towards thought, whereby it is again in danger of becoming entangled in the conflict. The act of differentiation and introversion involves the detachment of disposable libido, not merely from the outer object alone but also from the inner object, namely ideas. It becomes wholly objectless; it is no longer related to anything that could be a conscious content; it therefore sinks into the unconscious, where it automatically takes possession of the waiting phantasy material, which it activates and urges towards consciousness.

Schiller's expression for the symbol, viz. " living form " is happily chosen, because the phantasy material thus animated contains images of the psychological development of the individuality in its successive states, thus providing a sort of model or representation of the further way between the opposites. Although it may frequently happen that the discriminating conscious activity cannot find much in these images that can be immediately understood, such intuitions nevertheless contain a living power, which may have a determining effect upon the will. For the content of the will receives determinants from both sides; as a result the opposites after a certain time recuperate. But the resumed conflict again demands the same process, whereby a further stage is continually made possible. This function of mediation between the opposites I have termed the *transcendent function*, by which I mean nothing mysterious, but merely a combined function of conscious and unconscious elements, or, as in mathematics, a common function of real and imaginary factors [1].

Besides the will—whose importance must not be thereby denied—we have also creative phantasy, an irrational, instinctive function, which alone has the power of yielding the will a content of such a character as can unite the opposites. It is this function which Schiller intuitively apprehended as the source of symbols; but he termed it 'play-instinct', and therefore could make no further use of it for the motivation of the will. In order to obtain this content of the will he went back to the intellect and in doing so allied himself to one side. But he is surprisingly near to our problem when he says:

" The power of sensation must, therefore, be destroyed before law (i.e. rational will) can be established. It is not forthwith accomplished when something has a beginning which before had none. Man cannot immediately pass from sensation to thinking; he must take a step backwards, since only when one determinant is abolished can its opposite take its place. He must be momentarily free from every determinant and pass through a condition of pure determinability. Accordingly he must in some way return to that negative state of pure non-determination which he enjoyed before ever any sort of impression was made upon his senses. But that was a state entirely empty of content, whereas now our chief concern is to harmonize an equal non-determination and an unlimited determinability with the greatest possible fullness; because forthwith from this condition must something positive result. The determination, which he receives through sensation, must therefore be maintained, since he must not lose reality; but at the same time, in so far as it is a restriction, it should be abolished, because an unlimited determinability must be permitted."—*Letter* XX, p. 104.

With the help of what has been said above, this difficult passage can easily be understood, if only we bear in mind

[1] I must emphasize the point that I am here presenting only this function in principle. Further contributions to this very complex problem, for which, in particular, the manner of accepting unconscious material into consciousness has a fundamental importance, will be found in my work: *La structure de l'inconscient* (*Archives de Psychologie*, Dec. 1916): also in my paper: *The Psychology of Unconscious Processes* (*Collected Papers*, ch. xiv)

the fact that Schiller has a constant inclination to seek the solution with the rational will. This factor must be allowed for. What he says is then perfectly clear. The step backwards is the differentiation from the antagonistic instincts, the detachment and withdrawal of the libido both from the inner and outer object. Here, of course, above all, Schiller has the sensuous object in mind, since, as already explained, his constant aim is to reach over towards the side of rational thinking; for to him this seems quite indispensable for the determination of the contents of the will. But, in spite of this, the necessity to abolish every determinant still urges itself upon him. In this necessity the detachment from the inner object, the idea, is implied; otherwise it would be impossible to achieve a complete absence of content and determinant together with that original state of unconsciousness, where a discriminating consciousness has not yet distinguished subject from object. It is obvious that Schiller had in mind that same process which I have described as *introversion into the unconscious*.

"Unlimited determinability" clearly means something very like the unconscious, a state in which everything can have effect upon everything else without distinction. This empty state of consciousness must correspond with the "greatest possible fullness". This fullness, as the counterpart of conscious emptiness, can only be the content of the unconscious, since no other content is given. In this way Schiller expresses the union of the unconscious with the conscious, and "from this state something positive" must result. This "positive" something is for us the *symbolic determinant of the will*. For Schiller it is a mediate condition, through which the reconciliation of sensation and thinking is brought about. He calls it a "middle disposition", in which sensuousness and reason are equally active; but for this very reason their determining power is mutually cancelled; their opposion effects a negation.

This suspension of the opposites produces an emptiness, which we call the unconscious. Because it is not determind by the opposites this condition is susceptible to every determinant. Schiller calls it an "*æsthetic*" condition [Letter xx., p. 105]. It is worth noting that he thereby overlooks the fact that sensuousness and reason cannot both be "active" in this condition, since, as Schiller himself says, they are already suspended through mutual negation. But, since something must be active and Schiller has no other function at his disposal, the pairs of opposites must, according to him, again become active. Their activity naturally persists, but since consciousness is "empty" they must necessarily be in the unconscious[1]. But this concept Schiller lacks—accordingly he becomes contradictory at this point. His mediating æsthetic function would thus be equivalent to our symbol-forming activity (creative phantasy). Schiller defines the "æsthetic disposition" as the relation of a thing "to the totality of our various faculties (mental functions), without its being a definite object for any one individual faculty". He would here perhaps have done better, instead of this vague definition, to return to his earlier concept of the symbol, since the symbol has this quality, that it is related to all the psychic functions without being a definite object of any single one. Having now reached this mediating disposition, Schiller perceives that "it is henceforth possible for man, in the way of nature, to make what he will of himself—that the freedom to be what he ought to be is wholly restored to him."

Because by preference Schiller proceeds intellectually and rationally he falls a victim to his own conclusion. This is already revealed in his choice of the expression "æsthetic". If he had been acquainted with Indian

---

[1] As Schiller rightly says, in the æsthetic state man is nothing. *Letter XX*, p. 108.

literature, he would have seen that the *primordial image* which floated before his inner mind had a very different meaning from the "æsthetic" one. His intuition found the unconscious model which from oldest times has exercized its living force in our unwitting minds. Yet he interprets it as "æsthetic", although he himself had previously emphasized its symbolic character. The primordial image to which I refer is revealed in that growth of oriental thought which centres around the *Brahman-Atman teaching* in India, and in China found its philosophical representative in Lao-Tze.

The Indian conception teaches liberation from the opposites, by which every sort of affective state and emotional hold to the object is understood. The liberation succeeds a detachment of the libido from all contents, whereby a state of complete introversion results. This psychological process is characteristically called *tapas*, a term which can best be rendered as self-brooding. This expression clearly pictures the state of meditation without content in which the libido is supplied to the Self somewhat in the manner of incubating heat. As a result of the complete detachment of every function from the object, there necessarily arises in the inner man (the Self) an equivalent of objective reality, a state of complete identity of inner and outer which may be technically described as the *tat twam asi* (that art thou). Through the fusion of the Self with the relations to the object there proceeds the identity of the Self (Atman)[1] with the essence of the world (*i.e.* with the relations of the subject to the object,) so that the identity of the inner with the outer Atman becomes recognized. The concept of Brahman differs only slightly from the concept of Atman, since in Brahman the idea of the Self is not explicitly given : it is, as it were,

[1] Atman has been defined as the soul of Self-hood—the highest principle of life in the universe—the Divine germ in man. [Translator]

a more general, almost indefinable, state of identity between the inner and the outer.

Parallel, in a certain sense, with tapas is the concept *yoga*; by which, not so much a state of meditation as a conscious technique for the attainment of the tapas state, is to be understood. Yoga is a method by which the libido is systematically 'drawn in' and thereby released from the bondage of the opposites. The aim of tapas and yoga is the establishing of a mediate condition from which the creative and redeeming element emerges. For the individual, the psychological result is the attainment of Brahman, the "supreme light," or "*ânanda*" (bliss). This is the final aim of the redeeming practice. But at the same time this process is also interpreted in terms of cosmogony, since from Brahman-Atman as the foundation of the world all creation proceeds. The cosmogonic myth, like every myth, is a projection of unconscious processes. The existence of this myth proves, therefore, that in the unconscious of the tapas practitioner creative processes take place, which can be interpreted as new adjustments towards the object. Schiller says: "So soon as it is *light* in man, it is no longer night without. So soon as it is still in him, lulled is the storm in the universe: the contending forces of nature find rest within lasting bounds. Little wonder then that the immemorial poems speak of this great event in the inner man as of a revolution in the outer world, etc." [*Letter* XXV, p. 135].

Through yoga the relations to the object become introverted, *i.e.* through a deprivation of energic value they sink into the unconscious, where, as described above, they can engage in new associations with other unconscious contents, and, thus transformed, they rise again, when the tapas practice is completed, towards the object. Through the transformation of the relation to the object, the object now acquires a new aspect. It is as though newly-created; hence the cosmogonic myth is a speaking symbol for the final result of the tapas exercise. In the almost exclusively introverted direction of the Indian religious exercise the new adaptation to the object has, of course, no significance, but it persists as unconsciously projected cosmogonic myth doctrine, without achieving any practical reorganization of life. In this respect the Indian religious attitude stands, as it were, diametrically opposed to the Christian attitude of Western lands; since the Christian principle of love is extraverted and absolutely demands the outer object. The former principle gains the riches of knowledge, the latter the fullness of works.

In the concept of Brahman there is also contained the concept of *Rita* (right course), the regulated order of the world. In Brahman, as the creative essence and foundation of the world, things come upon the right way, since in It they are eternally dissolved and recreated; out of Brahman proceeds all development upon the ordered way. The concept of Rita leads us on to that of *Tao* in Lao-Tze. Tao is the right way, law-abiding ordinance, a middle road between the opposites, freed from them and yet uniting them in itself. The purpose of life is to travel this middle path and never to deviate towards the opposites.

The ecstatic factor is entirely absent with Lao-Tze; it is replaced by a superior philosophic clarity, an intellectual and intuitive wisdom obscured by no mystical haze; a wisdom which presents what is simply the highest attainable to spiritual superiority, and therefore also lacks the chaotic element in so far as the air it breathes is distant as the stars from the disorder of this actual world. It tames all that is wild, without purifying and transforming it into something higher.

One could easily object that the analogy between Schiller's train of thought and these apparently remote ideas is rather far-fetched. But it must not be forgotten that not so long after Schiller's time, these very ideas found a powerful utterance in the genius of Schopenhauer and became so intimately wedded to the Western Germanic mind that they have persisted and thriven even to the present day. In my view it is of small importance that the Latin translation of the Upanishads by Anquetil du Perron (1802) was accessible to Schopenhauer, whilst Schiller with the very sparing information of his time had at least no conscious connection with these sources[1]. I have seen enough in my own practical experience to become convinced that direct communication is not essential in the formation of such relationships. Indeed, something very similar is to be seen in the fundamental ideas of Meister Eckehart, as also in a measure in the thought of Kant, where we find a quite astonishing similarity with the ideas of the Upanishads, without the faintest trace of influence either direct or indirect. It is the same here as with myths and symbols, which can arise autochthonously in every corner of the earth and are none the less identical, just because they are fashioned out of the same world-wide human unconscious, whose contents are infinitely less variable than are races and individuals.

There is another reason urging me to draw a parallel between Schiller's ideas and those of the East; and this is, that the thoughts of Schiller might be rescued from the too narrow cloak of æsthetism[2]. Æsthetism is not fitted to solve the exceedingly serious and difficult problem of the education of man; for it always presupposes the very thing it should create, namely the capacity for the love of

[1] Schiller died in 1805.
[2] I employ the word 'æsthetism' as an abbreviated expression for 'æsthetic world-philosophy'. Hence, I do not mean that æsthetism with the evil accompaniment of æsthetic action and sentimentality which might perhaps be described as æstheticism.

beauty. It actually prevents a deeper searching of the problem, since it always looks away from the evil, the ugly, and the difficult, and aims at enjoyment, even though it be of a noble kind. Æsthetism, therefore, lacks all moral motive power, because au fond it is still only refined hedonism. Schiller is indeed at some pains to introduce an unconditional moral motive, but without any convincing success; since, just because of his æsthetic attitude, it is impossible for him to perceive the kind of consequences which a recognition of the other side of human nature would entail. For the conflict which thereby arises involves such a confusion and suffering for the individual, that, although in the most favourable cases his vision of the beautiful may enable him persistently to repress its opposite, he does not thereby escape from it; so that, even at the best, the old condition is once more established. In order to help a man out of this conflict, an attitude other than the aesthetic is needed. This is revealed nowhere more clearly than in this parallel with the ideas of the East. The Indian religious philosophy has apprehended this problem to its very depth and has demonstrated what category of remedies is needed to render a solution of the conflict possible. For its achievement the highest moral effort, the greatest self-denial and sacrifice, the most intense religious earnestness and saintliness, are needed.

Schopenhauer, with every regard for the æsthetic, has most definitely brought out just this aspect of the problem. We must not, however, imagine that the words 'æsthetic,' 'beauty,' etc., called up the same associations for Schiller as they do for us. Indeed, I am not putting it too stongly when I affirm that for Schiller 'beauty' was a *religious ideal*. Beauty was his religion. His "æsthetic disposition" might equally well be rendered "religious devotion." Without definitely expressing anything of the sort, and without explicitly describing his central problem as a religious one,

Schiller's intuition none the less arrived at the religious problem; it was, however, the religious problem of the primitive, which he even discusses at some length in his investigation, without ever pressing along this line to the end.

It is worth noting that in the further pursuit of his ideas the question of the 'play-instinct' fell quite into the background in favour of the idea of the æsthetic disposition, which apparently reached an almost mystical valuation This, I believe, is not accidental, but has a quite definite foundation. Oftentimes it is just the best and most profound ideas in a work which most stubbornly resist a clear apprehension and formulation, even though they are suggested in various places and presumably, therefore, should be sufficiently ripe for a lucid and characteristic synthesis. It seems to me that here there is a difficulty of this sort. Into the concept of the "æsthetic disposition" as a mediatory creative state, Schiller himself instils ideas which at once reveal the depth and the seriousness of this concept. And yet, quite as clearly, he discerned the "play-instinct" as that long-sought mediating activity. Now one cannot deny that these two conceptions stand in a certain opposition to each other, for play and seriousness are scarcely compatibles. Seriousness comes through deep inner necessity, but play is its more external expression, that aspect of it which is turned toward consciousness. It is not a question, of course, of a *will to play*, but of *having to play*, a playful manifestation of phantasy through *inner* necessity, without the compulsion of circumstances, without even the compulsion of will. *It is a serious play*[1]. And

---

[1] Compare what Schiller says: *On the Necessary Limitations in the Use of Beautiful Form* [Essays, p. 241]. "For since, in the man of æsthetic refinement, the imaginative faculty, even in its free play, is directed according to laws, and sense approves of enjoyment only with the consent of reason, the reciprocal favour is easily required of reason, that it shall be directed, in the earnestness of its law-giving, in accordance with the interests of the imagination and not command the will, without the concurrence of the sensuous instincts."

yet it is certainly play in its outer aspect, seen from the view-point of consciousness, *i.e.* from the standpoint of collective judgment. But it is play from inner necessity. That is the ambiguous quality which clings to everything creative.

If the play expires in itself without creating anything durable and living, it is only play; but in the alternative event it is called creative work. Out of a playful movement of elements, whose associations are not immediately established, there arise groupings which an observant and critical intellect can only subsequently appraise. The creation of something new is not accomplished by the intellect, but by the play-instinct from inner necessity. The creative mind plays with the objects it loves.

Hence one can easily regard every creative activity whose potentialities remain hidden from the many as play. There are, indeed, very few creative men at whom the reproach of playing has not been cast. For the man of genius, and Schiller certainly was this, one is inclined to approve of this point of view. But he himself wished to go beyond the exceptional man and his kind, and to reach the common man, that he too might share that help and deliverance which the creator from sternest inner necessity cannot in any case avoid. The possibility of extending such a point of view to the education of man in general is not, however, guaranteed as a matter of course; at least it would seem not to be.

For a decision of this question we must appeal, as in all such cases, to the testimony of the history of human thought. But before doing so we should again realize from what basis we are attacking the question. We have seen how Schiller demands a release from the opposites even to the point of a complete emptying of consciousness, in which neither sensations, feelings, ideas, nor purposes play any sort of rôle. The condition thus striven for is a state of undifferentiated consciousness, or a conscious state, where, from a depotentiation of energic values, all contents have forfeited their distinctiveness. But a real consciousness is possible only where values effect a discrimination of contents. Where discrimination is wanting, no real consciousness can exist. Accordingly, such a state might be called "unconscious", although the possibility of consciousness is at all times present. It is a question therefore of an "abaissement du niveau mental" (Janet) of an artificial nature; hence also a certain resemblance to yoga and to states of hypnotic "engourdissement".

So far as I know, Schiller has nowhere expressed himself as to his actual view concerning the technique— if one may use the word—for the induction of the æsthetic mood. The example of Juno Ludovisi that he mentions incidentally in his letters [p. 81] shows us a state of "æsthetic devotion" whose character consists in a complete surrender to and "feeling-into" the object of contemplation. But such a state of devotion lacks the essential characteristic of being without content and determinant. Nevertheless, in conjunction with other passages, this example shows that the idea of "devotion" was constantly present in Schiller's mind[1]. Which brings us once more to the province of the religious phenomenon; but at the same time we are permitted a glimpse of the actual possibility of extending such a view-point to the common man. *The state of religious devotion is a collective phenomenon, which does not depend upon individual endowment.*

There are, however, yet other possibilities. We have seen that the empty state of consciousness, *i.e.* the unconscious condition, is brought about by a submersion of the libido into the unconscious. Dormant in the unconscious there lie relatively accentuated contents, namely remini-

---

[1] "Whereas the feminine God demands our adoration, the god-like woman also kindles our love."—*l.c.*, p. 81.

scence-complexes of the individual past; above all the parent-complex, which is identical with the childhood-complex· in general. Through devotion, *i.e.* through the sinking of the libido into the unconscious, the childhood-complex is reactivated, whereby the reminiscences of childhood, especially the relations to the parents, are again infused with life. From the phantasies proceeding out of this reactivation there dawns the birth of the Father and Mother divinities, and there awakens the religious child-like relations to God with the corresponding child-like feeling. Characteristically, it is the symbols of the parents that become conscious and by no means always the images of the actual parents; a fact which Freud explains as the repression of the parent *imago* through resistance to incest. I am of the same mind upon this interpretation, and yet I believe it is not exhaustive, since it overlooks the *extraordinary significance of this symbolical replacement*. Symbolization in the shape of the God-image means an immense step forward from the concretism, the sensuousness, of reminiscence; inasmuch as the regression to the parent, through the acceptance of the "symbol" as a real symbol, is straight-way transformed into a progression; it would remain a regression if the so-called symbol were to be finally interpreted merely as a sign of the actual parents and were thus robbed of its independent character[1].

Humanity came to its gods through accepting the reality of the symbol, *i.e.* it came to *the reality of the idea*, which alone has made man lord of the earth. Devotion, as Schiller correctly conceived it, is a regressive movement of the libido towards the primordial, a diving down into the source of first beginnings. Emerging as an image of the commencing progressive movement there rises the

[1] I have discussed this point at length in my book *Psychology of the Unconscious*.

symbol, which represents a comprehensive resultant of all the unconscious factors. It is "*living form*", as Schiller calls the symbol, a God-image as history unfolds it. It is not, therefore, an accident that our author has straightway chosen a divine image, the Juno Ludovisi, as a paradigm. Goethe makes the divine images of Paris and Helen float up from the tripod of the mothers—on the one hand the rejuvenated pair, but on the other the symbol of a process of inner union which is precisely what Faust passionately craves for himself as the supreme inner atonement. This is clearly shown in the subsequent scene, and it is equally manifest in the further course of the Second Part. As we can see in this very example of Faust, the vision of the symbol is a significant indication as to the further course of life, an alluring of the libido towards a still distant aim, but which henceforth operates unquenchably within him, so that his life, kindled like a flame, moves steadily onwards to the far goal. This is the specific life-promoting significance of the symbol. This is the value and meaning of the religious symbol. I am speaking, of course, not of symbols that are dead and stiffened by dogma, but of living symbols that rise from the creative unconscious of living man.

The immense significance of such symbols can be denied only by the man whose history of the world begins at the present day. It ought to be superfluous to speak of the significance of symbols, but unfortunately this is not so, for the spirit of our time believes itself superior to its own psychology. The moral and hygienic standpoint of our day must always know whether such and such a thing is harmful or useful, right or wrong. A real psychology cannot concern itself with such queries: to recognize how things are in themselves is enough.

The forming of symbols arising out of the state of

devotion is, again, one of those collective religious phenomena which are not bound up with individual endowment. Hence, also in this respect the possibility of extending the view-point, mentioned above, to the ordinary man may be assumed. I think I have now sufficiently demonstrated at least the theoretical possibility of Schiller's point-of-view for general human psychology. For the sake of completeness and clarity I might add here that the question of the relation of the symbol to consciousness and the conscious conduct of life has long engaged my mind. I have reached the conclusion that, in view of its great significance as a representative of the unconscious, too slight a value should not be given to the symbol. We know from daily experience in the treatment of nervous subjects what an eminently practical significance unconscious interventions possess. The greater the dissociation, *i.e.* the more the conscious attitude becomes aloof from the individual and collective contents of the unconscious, the more powerful are the harmful and even dangerous inhibitions or reinforcements of conscious contents from the side of the unconscious. From practical considerations, therefore, the symbol must be conceded a not inconsiderable value. But if we grant the symbol a value, whether great or small, the symbol thereby obtains conscious motive power, *i.e.* it is perceived, and its unconscious libido-charge is therewith given opportunity for development in the conscious conduct of life. Herein —according to my view—a not inessential practical advantage is gained: namely, the *co-operation of the unconscious*, its participation in the conscious psychic activities and therewith the elimination of disturbing influences from the unconscious.

This common function, the relation to the symbol, I have termed the *transcendent function*. I cannot undertake, at this stage, to elucidate this problem at all adequately. To do so, it would be absolutely necessary to produce all the material that comes up as the result of unconscious activity. The phantasies hitherto described in the special literature give no conception of the symbolic creations we are here dealing with. There exist, however, not a few examples of these phantasies in the literature of belles-lettres; but these of course are not "purely" observed and presented—they have undergone an intensive "aesthetic" elaboration. Among all these examples I would single out two works of Meyrink for special attention, viz. *Der Golem* and *Das grüne Gesicht*. But the treatment of this side of the problem I must reserve for a later investigation.

Although these conclusions concerning the mediatory state were, so to speak evoked by Schiller, we have already gone far beyond his conceptions. In spite of the fact that he discerned the opposites in human nature with keenness and depth, he remained stuck at an early stage in his attempt at solution. For this failure his terminus "æsthetic disposition" is in my opinion, not without blame. For Schiller makes the "æsthetic disposition" practically identical with the beautiful, thus transveying the feeling into the mood[1]. Therewith not only does he take cause and effect together, but he also gives to the state of indeterminability, quite against his own definition, a single-meaning definiteness, since he makes it equivalent with the beautiful. Moreover, from the very outset the edge is taken off the mediating function, since beauty immediately prevails over ugliness, whereas it is equally a question of ugliness. Schiller defines as the "æsthetic quality" of a thing that it should be related "to the totality of our various faculties". Consequently "beautiful" cannot coincide with "æsthetic", since our different faculties also vary æsthetically: some are ugly, some beautiful, and

[1] *Letter XXIII*, p. 108.

only an incorrigible idealist and optimist could conceive the "totality" of human nature as simply "beautiful". To be quite accurate, human nature is just real; it has its light and its dark sides. The sum of all colours is grey —light upon a dark background or dark upon light.

From this conceptual immaturity and inadequacy we may also explain the circumstance that it is not at all clear how this mediatory state shall be established. There are numerous passages containing the unequivocal meaning that in the "enjoyment of pure beauty", the mediatory state is brought about. Thus Schiller says:

"Whatever flatters our senses with immediate sensation opens our yielding and shifting emotion to every impression, while it also makes us in equal measure less fitted for effort. Whatever strains our power of thought and invites us to abstract ideas strengthens our mind to every sort of resistance, but it also hardens it and robs us of susceptibility in the same degree as it helps us to a greater spontaneity. For this reason the one just as much as the other leads necessarily, in the last resort, to exhaustion . . . . If, on the contrary, we have surrendered ourselves to the enjoyment of pure beauty, we are, in such a moment, master of our passive and active faculties in equal measure and we can apply ourselves to seriousness and to play, to rest and to motion, to yielding and to resistance, to abstract thought and to perception with the same ease."

This presentation stands in abrupt opposition to the provisions of the "æsthetic state" previously laid down, where the man was to be "naught", undetermined, whilst here he is in the highest degree determined by beauty ("surrendered to it"). It would not repay us to pursue this question further with Schiller. Here he meets a boundary common both to himself and his time, which it was impossible for him to overstep, for everywhere he encounters the invisible "ugliest man", whose unveiling was reserved for our age in the person of Nietzsche.

Schiller was intent on making the sensuous into a rational being, because from the outset he makes man æsthetic. He himself says [Letter xiii, p. 118]: "We must change the nature of the sensuous man" (p. 120); again he says: "Man must submit the physical life to form", he must "carry out his physical destiny according to the laws of beauty" (p. 121), "upon the indifferent plane of the physical life man must begin his moral being" (p. 123), he must "though still confined within his sensuous bounds, begin his rational freedom", "upon his inclinations he must impose the law of his will", "he must learn to desire nobly" (p. 124).

That "must" of which our author speaks is the familiar 'ought', which is always invoked when one can see no other way. Here again we meet inevitable barriers. It would be unjust to expect one individual mind, were he never so great, to vanquish this gigantic problem, a problem which only times and peoples can resolve; and even so by no conscious purpose, but as only fate can solve it.

The greatness of Schiller's thought lies in his psychological observation, and his intuitive apprehension of the things observed. There is yet another of his trains of thought I would like to mention, which abundantly deserves consideration. We have seen above that the middle state is characterized by effecting a "positive" something, viz. the *symbol*. The symbol combines antithetic elements within its nature; hence it also reconciles the real-unreal antithesis, because on the one hand it is certainly a psychological reality (on account of its effectiveness), while on the other it corresponds with no physical reality. It is a fact and yet a *semblance*. This circumstance is brought out clearly by Schiller, in order to append to it an apologia for *semblance*[1], which in every respect is significant.

"The greatest stupidity and the highest understanding have herein a certain affinity with each other, that they both

---
[1] *Letter XXVI*, p. 111.

seek the *real* and are both quite insensitive to mere semblance. Only by the immediate presence of an object in sensation is the former torn from its apathy, and only through the relating of its ideas to the facts of experience is the latter brought to rest; in a word, foolishness cannot soar above reality and intelligence cannot remain below truth. Inasmuch, then, as need for reality and devotion to the real are merely the products of a human defect, indifference to reality and interest in semblance represent a true progress for humanity and a decisive step towards culture." [1]

When speaking just now about an appraisement of the symbol's value, I showed the practical advantage that an appreciation of the unconscious possesses: namely, we exclude the unconscious disturbance of conscious functions when, from the first, we have taken the unconscious into account through a consideration of the symbol. It is familiar that the unconscious, when not realized, is ever at work casting a false glamour over everything: it *appears to us always upon objects*, because everything unconscious is projected. Hence, when we are able to understand the unconscious as such, we strip away the false appearance from objects, and this can only promote truth. Schiller says:

" This human right to rule man exercises in the *mastery of semblance*, and the more rigidly he severs mine from thine, the more scrupulously he separates form from essence, and the more independence he learns to give to the same, the more does he not merely enlarge the kingdom of beauty—he is actually establishing the boundaries of truth, for he cannot cleanse away appearance from the face of reality without at the same time delivering reality from semblance."—*Letter* xxvi, p. 146.

" The effort to achieve this independence of semblance demands a greater power of abstraction, a greater freedom of heart and more energy of will than is required of man in the effort to confine himself in reality, and already must he have left this behind him if he would achieve that."—*ibid.*, p. 151.

2. A Discussion on Naïve and Sentimental Poetry

For a long time it seemed to me as though Schiller's division of poets into *naïve* and *sentimental* [2] were a classi-

[1] *Letter XXVI*, p. 142.
[2] Schiller, *Ueber naive und sentimentalische Dichtung*.

fication that harmonized with the points of view here expounded. After mature reflection, however, I have come to the conclusion that this is not so. Schiller's definition is very simple: "*the naïve poet is Nature, the sentimental poet seeks her*". This easy formula is enticing, since it affirms two different kinds of relation to the object. It might also be put like this: He who seeks or desires Nature as an object does not possess her; such a man would be the introvert, and, vice versa, he who already is Nature herself, standing therefore in the most intimate relation with the object, would be the extravert. But a rather arbitrary interpretation such as this would have little in common with Schiller's point of view. His division into naïve and sentimental is one which, in contrast to our type-division, is not merely concerned with the individual mentality of the poet, but rather with the character of his creative activity, that is, with its product. The same poet can be sentimental in one poem, naïve in another. Homer certainly is naïve throughout, but how many of the moderns are not, for the most part, sentimental? Evidently Schiller feels this difficulty, and therefore asserts that the poet is conditioned by his time, not as an individual but as a poet. Thus he says: "All poets, who are really such, will respectively belong to the naïve or sentimental to the degree in which the quality of the age in which they flower, or mere accidental circumstances exert an influence upon their general make-up and upon their passing emotional mood". Consequently it is not a question of fundamental types for Schiller, but rather of certain characteristics or qualities of the individual product. Hence it is at once obvious that an introverted poet, on occasion, can be just as naïve as he is sentimental. It therefore follows that to identify respectively naïve and sentimental with extravert and introvert would be quite beside the point, in so far as the problem of *types* is concerned.

Not so, however, in so far as it is a question of *typical mechanisms*.

(a) The naïve attitude

I will first present the definitions which Schiller gives of this attitude. It has already been mentioned that the naïve poet is "Nature". He simply "follows Nature and sensation and confines himself to the mere copying of reality" (*l.c.*, p. 248). "With naïve representations we delight in the living presence of objects in our imagination" (p. 250) "Naïve poetry is a boon of Nature. It is a happy throw, needing no bettering when it succeeds, but fit for nothing when it has failed" (p. 303). "The naïve genius must do everything through his nature: he can do little through his freedom; he will accomplish his idea, only when Nature works in him as an inner necessity" (p. 304). Naïve poetry "is the child of life and unto life it returns" (p. 303). The naïve genius depends wholly upon "experience", upon the world, with which he is in "direct touch". He "needs succour from without" (p. 305). To the naïve poet the "common nature" of his surroundings can "become dangerous", since "sensibility is always more or less dependent upon the external impression, and only a constant activity of the productive faculty, which is not to be expected of human nature, would be able to prevent mere material from committing him, at times, to a blind receptivity. But whenever this is the case, the poetic feeling will be commonplace" (pp. 307 ff.). "The naïve genius allows Nature unlimited sway in him" (p. 314). From this definition the dependence of the naïve poet upon the object is especially clear. His relation to the object has a compelling character, because he introjects the object, *i.e.* unconsciously identifies himself with it, or has, as it were, a priori identity with it. Lévy-Bruhl describes this relation to the object as "participation mystique".[1] This

[1] *Les fonctions mentales dans les sociétés inférieures.*

identity is always derived from an analogy between the object and an unconscious content. One could also say that the identity comes about through the projection of an unconscious analogy-association upon the object. An identity of this nature has always a compelling character, because it is concerned with a certain libido-sum, which, like every libido-discharge working from the unconscious, has a compelling character in relation to the conscious, *i.e.* it is not disposable to consciousness. The naïve attitude is, therefore, in a high degree conditioned by the object; the object operates independently in him, as it were; it fulfils itself in him because he himself is identical with it. To a certain extent, therefore, he gives his function of expression to the object, and presents it in a certain way, not in the least actively or intentionally, but because it is represented in him. He is himself Nature: Nature creates in him the product. He allows Nature to hold absolute sway in him. Supremacy is given to the object. To this extent is the naïve attitude extraverted.

(b) *The sentimental attitude*

We mentioned above that the sentimental poet *seeks* Nature. He "reflects upon the impression objects make upon him, and upon that reflection alone is the emotion based with which he himself is exalted, and which likewise affects us. Here the object is related to an idea, and from this relation alone his poetic power is derived" (*l.c.*, p. 249). He "is always involved with two opposing presentations and sensations, with reality as a finite boundary, and with his idea as an infinite: the mixed feeling that he provokes will always bear witness to this dual origin" (p. 250). "The sentimental mood is the result of the effort to reproduce the naïve sensation, in accordance with its content, *under the conditions of reflection*" (p. 301). "Sentimental poetry is the product of abstraction"

(p. 303). "As a result of his effort to remove every limitation from human nature the sentimental genius is exposed to the danger of abolishing human nature altogether; not merely mounting, as he must and should, above every sort of defined and restricted reality to the farthest possibility—to idealize in short—but even transcending possibility itself; in other words, to *become phantastical.*" "The sentimental genius forsakes reality, in order to rise to the world of ideas and command his material with greater freedom" (p. 314).

It is easy to see that the sentimental poet, in contrast with the naïve, is characterized by a reflective and abstract attitude towards the object. He "reflects" about the object, because he is abstracted from it. Thus he is, as it were, severed from the object a priori as soon as his production begins; it is not the object that works in him, but he himself is operative. He does not, however, work inwardly into himself, but outwardly beyond the object. He is distinct from the object, not identical with it; he seeks to establish *his* relation to it, "to command his material." Proceeding from this, his separateness from the object, there comes that impression of duality which Schiller refers to; for the sentimental poet creates from two sources, namely from the object or from his perception of it, and from himself. The external impression of the object is, for him, not something unconditioned but material which he handles in accordance with his own contents. Hence he stands above the object, and yet has a relation to it; it is not, however, the relation of impressionability, but of his own free choice he bestows a value or quality upon the object. His is therefore an introverted attitude.

With the designation of these two attitudes as introverted and extraverted we have not, however, exhausted Schiller's idea. Our two mechanisms are basic phenomena of a rather general nature, which only vaguely outline the specific. For the understanding of the naïve and sentimental types we must call two further principles to our aid, namely the elements *sensation* and *intuition*. I shall discuss these functions in greater detail at a later stage. I only wish to say at this point that the naïve is characterized by a preponderance of the sensational element, the sentimental by the intuitive. Sensation fastens to the object, it even draws the subject into the object; hence for the naïve type the "danger" consists in his subjection to the object. Intuition, being a perception of one's own unconscious processes, withdraws from the object; it mounts above it, ever seeking to command its material, and to shape it, even violently, in accordance with the subjective view-point, though without awareness of the fact. The danger for the sentimental type, therefore, is a complete severance from reality, and a going-under into the fluid phantasy world of the unconscious.

(c) *The Idealist and the Realist*

In the same essay Schiller's reflections lead him to a conception of two psychological human types. He says:

" This brings me to a very remarkable psychological antagonism among men in an age of progressive civilization, an antagonism which, because it is radical and rooted in the innate emotional constitution, is the cause of a sharper cleavage among men than the accidental quarrel of interests could ever bring about; an antagonism which robs the poet and artist of all hope of making a universal appeal—although this is his task; which makes it impossible for the philosopher, in spite of every effort, to be universally convincing; yet, none the less, this is involved in the very idea of a philosophy—and which, finally, will never permit a man in practical life to see his mode of action universally applauded: in short, an opposition which is responsible for the fact that no work of the mind and no deed of the heart can make a decisive success with one class, without thereby drawing upon it a condemnation from the other. This opposition is, without doubt, as old as the beginning of culture, and to the end it can hardly be otherwise, save in rare individual subjects, such as have always existed and, it is to be hoped, will always exist. But although this lies in the very nature of its operation, that it frustrates every attempt at an adjustment, because no section can be brought to see either a deficiency upon its own side, or a reality upon the other; it is nevertheless always a sufficient gain to follow up such an important division to its final source, and thus, at least, to bring the actual point at issue to a simpler formulation"

It follows conclusively from this passage that through the observation of antagonistic mechanisms Schiller arrived at the conception of two psychological types, which claim the same significance in his presentation as I ascribe to the introvert and extravert. With regard to the mutual relation between the two types established by myself, I can endorse almost word for word what Schiller says of his. Schiller, in harmony with what I pointed out earlier, reaches the type from the mechanism, since he "severs alike from the naïve and sentimental character a poetic quality that is common to both". If we carry out this operation we shall have to subtract the gifted, creative character; then to the naïve poet there remains the hold to the object and its autonomy in the subject, while to the sentimental there remains the superiority over the object, which is expressed in a more or less arbitrary judgment or treatment of the object. Schiller says:

"After this there remains of the former (the naïve) nothing else, theoretically, but a dispassionate spirit of observation and a solid dependence upon the equable testimony of the senses; and, practically, a resigned submission to the necessity of Nature. ... Of the sentimental character there remains nothing but a restless spirit of speculation which insists upon the unconditioned in all cognitions; and, in practice, a moral severity which insists upon the absolute in every act of will. Whoever counts himself among the former class can be called a *realist*, and whoever numbers himself with the latter an *idealist*."

Schiller's further elaborations concerning his two types refer almost exclusively to the familiar phenomena of the realistic and idealistic attitudes, and are therefore without interest for our investigation.

CHAPTER III

THE APOLLONIAN AND THE DIONYSIAN

THE problem discerned, and indeed partially worked out, by Schiller was resumed in a fresh and original way by Nietzsche in his work: *Die Geburt der Tragödie*, dating from 1871. This early work is more nearly related to Schopenhauer and Goethe than to Schiller. But it at least appears to share æsthetism and Hellenism with Schiller, pessimism and the motive of deliverance with Schopenhauer, and unlimited points of contact with Goethe's *Faust*. Among these connections, those with Schiller are naturally the most significant for our purpose. Yet we cannot leave Schopenhauer without paying tribute to the way in which he achieved reality for those dawning rays of Eastern knowledge which in Schiller only emerge as insubstantial wraiths. If we disregard the pessimism that springs from a contrast with the Christian joy in faith, and certainty of redemption, Schopenhauer's doctrine of deliverance is seen to be essentially Buddhistic. He was captured by the East. This step was undoubtedly a contrast reaction to our occidental atmosphere. It is, as we know, a reaction that still persists to a very considerable extent in various movements more or less completely orientated towards India. This pull towards the East caused Nietzsche to halt in Greece. He, too, felt Greece to be the middle point between East and West. To this extent he is in touch with Schiller—but how utterly different is his conception of the Grecian character! He sees the dark foil upon which the serene and golden world of Olympus is painted. "In order to make life possible, the Greeks from sheer necessity had to make these Gods". "The Greek knew and felt the terror and awfulness of existence: to be able to live at all he had to interpose the shining, dream-borne Olympian world between himself and that dread. That monstrous mistrust of the titanic powers of Nature, the *Moira* pitilessly enthroned above all knowledge, the vulture of Prometheus the great lover of man, the awful fate of the wise Oedipus, the family curse of the Atridæ which drove Orestes to matricide— this dread was ever being conquered anew through that artist's middle world of Olympus, or was at least veiled and withdrawn from sight."[1] The Greek "serenity," that smiling Heaven of Hellas, seen as a glamourous illusion hiding a forbidding background—this discernment was reserved for the moderns; a weighty argument against moral æsthetism!

Nietzsche here takes up a standpoint differing significantly from Schiller's. What one might have guessed in Schiller, namely that his letters on æsthetic education were also an attempt to deal with his own problems, becomes a complete certainty in this work of Nietzsche: it is a "profoundly personal" book. Whereas Schiller, almost timidly and with faint colours, begins to paint light and shade, apprehending the opposition in his own psyche as "naïve" versus "sentimental," while excluding everything that belongs to the background and abysmal profundities of human nature, Nietzsche's apprehension takes a deeper grasp and spans an opposition, whose one aspect yields in nothing to the dazzling beauty of the Schiller vision; while its other side reveals infinitely darker tones, which certainly enhance the effect of the light, but allow still blacker depths to be divined.

[1] Nietzsche, *The Birth of Tragedy*, transl. by W. H. Haussmann, p. 35 (Edinburgh 1909).

Nietzsche calls his fundamental pair of opposites: the *Apollonian-Dionysian*. We must first try to picture to ourselves the nature of this opposite pair. To this end I shall select a group of citations by means of which the reader—even though unacquainted with Nietzsche's work—will be in a position to form his own judgment about it, and at the same time to criticize mine.

1. " We shall have gained much for the science of æsthetics, when the view is once finally reached—not merely the logical insight, but the immediate certainty—that the continuous development of art is bound up with the duality of the *Apollonian* and the *Dionysian*: in much the same way as generation depends upon the duality of the sexes, involving perpetual conflicts with only periodically intervening reconciliation." (p. 21)

2. " From their two art-deities, Apollo and Dionysos, we derive our knowledge that an *immense opposition* existed in the Grecian world, both as to origin and aim, between the art of the shaper, the Apollonian, and the Dionysian non-plastic art of music. These two so different tendencies run side by side, for the most part in open conflict with each other, ever mutually rousing the other to new and mightier births in which to perpetuate the warring antagonism that is only seemingly bridged by their common term ' art ' ; until, finally, by a metaphysical miracle of the Hellenic ' will ', they appear *paired one with the other* and in this mating the equally Dionysian and Apollonian creation of Attic tragedy is at last brought to birth." (p. 22)

For the purpose of fuller characterization Nietzsche compares the two " tendencies " by means of the peculiar psychological states they give rise to, namely *dreaming* and *frenzy*. The Apollonian impulse produces a state that may be compared with the *dream*, while the Dionysian creates a condition that is akin to *frenzy*. By dreaming, as Nietzsche himself explains, he essentially understands the "inner vision", the "lovely semblance of the dream world ". Apollo "governs the beauteous illusion of the inner world of phantasy "; he is "the god of all shaping faculties ". He is measure, number, limitation, the mastery of everything savage and untamed. "One might almost describe Apollo as the splendid divine image of the *principii individuationis.*" (p. 26).

The Dionysian, on the contrary, is the freeing of unmeasured instinct, the breaking loose of the unbridled *dynamis* of the animal and the divine nature; hence in the Dionysian choir man appears as *satyr*, god above and goat below. It represents horror at the annihilation of the principle of individuation, and at the same time "rapturous delight" at its destruction. The Dionysian is, therefore, comparable to frenzy, which dissolves the individual into collective instincts and contents, a disruption of the secluded ego by the world. In the Dionysian, therefore, man again finds man; "estranged, hostile, subjugated Nature celebrates once more her feast of reconciliation with her lost son, man." (p. 26). Every man feels himself "one" with his neighbour ("not merely united, reconciled, and merged "). His individuality must therefore, be entirely suspended. " Man is no longer the artist—he has become the work of art ". " All the artistry of Nature here reveals itself in the ecstasies of frenzy". (p. 27.) Which means that the creative *dynamis*, the libido in instinctive form, takes possession of the individual as an object and uses him as a tool, or expression of itself. If one might conceive the natural being as a "product of art", then of course a man in the Dionysian state has become a natural work of art; but, inasmuch as the natural being is also emphatically not a work of art in the ordinary meaning of the word, he is nothing but sheer Nature, unbridled, a raging torrent, not even an animal that is restricted to itself and its own laws. I must emphasize this point both in the interests of clarity and of subsequent discussion, since, for some reason Nietzsche has omitted to make this clear, and has thereby shed over the problem a deceptive æsthetic veiling, which at certain places he himself has instinctively to draw aside.

Thus, for instance, where he speaks of the Dionysian orgies: "In almost every case, the essence of these festivals lay in an exuberant sexual licence, whose waves inundated every family hearth with its venerable traditions; the most savage beasts of nature were here unchained, even to the point of that disgusting alloy of lust and cruelty", etc. (p. 30).

Nietzsche considers the reconciliation of the Delphic Apollo with Dionysos as a symbol of the reconciliation of this antagonism within the breast of the civilized Greek. But here he forgets his own compensatory formula, according to which the Gods of Olympus owe their splendour to the darkness of the Grecian soul. The reconciliation of Apollo with Dionysos would, according to this, be a "beauteous illusion", a desideratum, evoked by the need of the civilized half of the Greek in the war with his barbaric side, that very element which broke out unchecked in the Dionysian state.

Between the religion of a people and its actual mode of life there always exists a compensatory relation; if this were not so, religion would have no practical significance at all. Beginning with the sublime moral religion of the Persians co-existing with the notorious dubiousness— even in antiquity—of the Persian manner of life, right down to our 'Christian' epoch, where the religion of love assisted in the greatest butchery of the world's history: wherever we turn we find evidence of this rule. We may, therefore, conclude from this very symbol of the Delphic reconciliation an especially violent cleavage in the Grecian character. This would also explain that craving for deliverance which gave the mysteries their immense meaning for the social life of Greece, and which, moreover, was completely overlooked by earlier admirers of the Grecian world. They contented themselves with naïvely attributing to the Greeks what they themselves lacked.

Thus in the Dionysian state the Greek was anything but a 'work of art'; on the contrary, he was gripped by his own barbaric nature, robbed of his individuality, dissolved into all his collective constituents, made one with the collective unconscious (through the surrender of his individual goal), identified with "the genius of the race, even with Nature herself". To the Apollonian side which had already achieved a substantial domestication of Nature, this frenzied state that made a man forget both himself and his manhood and turned him into a mere creature of instinct, must have been altogether despicable; for this reason a violent conflict between the two instincts was inevitable. Supposing the instincts of civilized man were let loose! The culture-enthusiast imagines that only beauty would stream forth. Such a notion proceeds from a profound lack of psychological knowledge. The dammed-up instinct-forces in civilized man are immensely more destructive, and hence more dangerous, than the instincts of the primitive, who in a modest degree is constantly living his negative instincts. Consequently no war of the historical past can rival a war between civilized nations in its colossal scale of horror. It will not have been otherwise with the Greeks. It was precisely from a living sense of the gruesome that the Dionysian-Apollonian reconciliation gradually came to them—"through a metaphysical miracle", as Nietzsche says at the beginning. This utterance, as well as that other where he says that the opposition in question "is only seemingly bridged by their common term 'art'" must be kept clearly in mind. It is well to remember this sentence in particular, because Nietzsche, like Schiller, has a pronounced inclination to ascribe to art the mediating and redeeming rôle. The result is that the problem remains stuck in the æsthetic—the ugly is also "beautiful"; even the evil and atrocious may wear a desirable brilliance in the false glamour of the æsthetically beautiful. Both in Schiller and in Nietzsche, the artist nature, with its specific faculty for creation and expression is claiming the redeeming significance for itself. And so Nietzsche quite forgets that in this battle between Apollo and Dionysos, and in their ultimate reconciliation, the problem for the Greeks was never an æsthetic but a *religious question*. The Dionysian satyr-feasts, according to every analogy, were a sort of totem-feast with an identification backward to a mythical ancestry or directly to the totem animal. The cult of Dionysos had in many ways a mystical and speculative tendency, and in any case exercised a very strong religious influence. The fact that Greek tragedy arose out of the original religious ceremony is at least as significant as the connection of our modern theatre with the medieval passion-play with its exclusively religious roots; such a consideration, therefore, scarcely permits the problem to be judged on its purely æsthetic aspect. Æsthetism is a modern glass, through which the psychological mysteries of the cult of Dionysos are seen in a light in which they were certainly never seen or experienced by the ancients. With Nietzsche, as with Schiller, the religious point-of-view is entirely overlooked, and its place is taken by the æsthetic. These things have their obvious æsthetic side, which one cannot neglect.[1] Yet if one gives medieval Christianity a purely æsthetic appreciation, its true character is debased and falsified, just as much, indeed, as if it were viewed exclusively from the historical standpoint. A true understanding can emerge only when equal weight is given to all sides; no one would

---

[1] Æsthetism can, of course, replace the religious function. But how many things are there which could not do the same? What have we not all come across at one time or another as a surrogate for a lacking religion? Even though æsthetism may be a very noble surrogate, it is none the less only a compensatory structure in place of the real thing that is wanting. Moreover, Nietzsche's later "conversion" to Dionysos shows very clearly that the æsthetic surrogate did not stand the test of time.

wish to maintain that the nature of a railway-bridge is adequately comprehended from a purely æsthetic angle. In adopting the view, therefore, that the conflict between Apollo and Dionysos is purely a question of antagonistic art-tendencies, the problem is shifted onto æsthetic grounds in a way that is both historically and materially unjustifiable; whereby it is submitted to a partial consideration which can never do justice to its real content.

This shifting of the problem must doubtless have its psychological cause and purpose. One need not seek far for the advantages of this procedure: the æsthetic estimation immediately converts the problem into a picture which the spectator considers at his ease, admiring both its beauty and its ugliness, merely reflecting the passion of the picture, and safely removed from any actual participation in its feeling and life. The æsthetic attitude shields one from being really concerned, from being personally implicated, which the religious understanding of the problem would entail. The same advantage is ensured to the historical manner of approach, which Nietzsche himself criticizes in a series of unique passages [1].

The possibility of taking such a prodigious problem "a problem with horns," as he calls it, merely æsthetically is of course very tempting, since its religious understanding, which in this case is the only adequate one, presupposes an experience either now or in the past to which the modern man can indeed rarely pretend. Dionysos, however, seems to have taken vengeance upon Nietzsche. Let us compare his *Attempt at a Self-criticism*, which bears the date 1886 and prefaces *The Birth of Tragedy*: "What indeed is Dionysian? In this book there lies the answer, a 'knowing one' speaks there, the *initiate and disciple of his God*". But that was not the Nietzsche

[1] Nietzsche, *On the Utility and Advantage of History for Life*, Part ii: *Occasional Papers*.

who wrote *The Birth of Tragedy*; at that time he was moved æsthetically, while he became Dionysian only at the time of writing *Zarathustra*, not forgetting that memorable passage with which he concludes his *Attempt at a Self-criticism;* "Lift up your hearts, my brother, high, higher! And neither forget the legs! Lift up also your legs, ye good dancers, and better still: let ye also stand on your heads!"

In spite of his æsthetic self-protection, the singular depth with which Nietzsche grasped the problem was already so close to the reality that his later Dionysian experience seems an almost inevitable consequence. His attack upon Socrates in *The Birth of Tragedy* is aimed at the rationalist, who proves himself impervious to Dionysian orgiastics. This reaction corresponds with the analogous error into which the æsthetic standpoint always falls, i.e *it holds itself aloof from the problem.* But even at that time, in spite of the æsthetic viewpoint, Nietzsche had an intuition of the real solution of the problem; as, for instance, when he wrote that the antagonism was not bridged by art, but by a "metaphysical miracle of the Hellenic 'will'". He writes "will" in inverted commas, which, considering how strongly he was at that time influenced by Schopenhauer, we might well interpret as referring to the concept of the metaphysical will. "Metaphysical" has for us the psychological significance of "unconscious". If, then, we replace "metaphysical" in Nietzsche's formula by "unconscious", the desired key to this problem would be an unconscious "miracle". A "miracle" is irrational; the act itself therefore is an unconscious irrational happening, a shaping out of itself without the intervention of reason and conscious purpose; it just happens, it grows, like a phenomenon of creative Nature, and not as a result of the deep probing of human wits; it is the fruit of yearning expectation, faith and hope.

THE APOLLONIAN AND THE DIONYSIAN 179

At this point I will leave this problem for the time being, as we shall have occasion to discuss it in fuller detail in the further course of our inquiry. Let us proceed instead to a closer examination of the Apollonian and Dionysian conceptions with regard to their psychological attributes. First we will consider the Dionysian. The presentation of Nietzsche at once reveals it as an unfolding, a streaming upward and outward, a "diastole", as Goethe called it; it is a motion embracing the world, as Schiller also presents it in his ode *An die Freude*:

" Seid umschlungen, Millionen.
  Diesen Kuss der ganzen Welt." [1]

and further:

" Freude trinken alle Wesen
  An den Brüsten der Natur ;
  Alle Guten, alle Bösen
  Folgen ihrer Rosenspur.
  Küsse gab sie uns und Reben,
  Einen Freund geprüft im Tod ;
  Wollust war dem Wurm gegeben
  Und der Cherub steht vor Gott." [2]

That is Dionysian expansion. It is a flood of mightiest universal feeling, which bursts forth irresistibly, intoxicating the senses like strong wine. It is a drunkenness in the highest sense.

In this state the psychological element *sensation*, whether it be sensation of sense or of affect, participates in the highest degree. It is a question, therefore, of an extraversion of those feelings which are inextricably bound up

[1] (" Be embraced, oh ye millions.
     Be this kiss for all the world.")
[2] (" Joy doth every creature drink,
     At Nature's flowing bosom ;
     Neither good nor evil shrink,
     To tread her path of blossom.
     Kisses and the wine she gave,
     A friend when Death commandeth.
     Lust was for the worm to have,
     'Fore God the Cherub standeth.")

with the element of sensation; for this reason we define it as feeling-sensation. What breaks forth in this state has more the character of pure affect, something instinctive and blindly compelling, finding specific expression in an affection of the bodily sphere.

In contrast to this, the Apollonian is a perception of the inner image of beauty, of measure, of controlled and proportioned feelings. The comparison with the dream clearly indicates the character of the Apollonian attitude: it is a state of introspection, of inner contemplation towards the dream world of eternal ideas: it is therefore a state of *introversion*.

So far the analogy with our mechanisms is indeed unarguable. But, if we were to content ourselves with the analogy, we should acquiesce in a limitation of outlook that does violence to Nietzsche's ideas; we should have laid them in a Procrustean bed.

We shall in the course of our investigation see that the state of introversion, in so far as it becomes habitual, always involves a differentiated relation to the world of ideas, while habitual extraversion entails a similar relation to the object. We see nothing of this differentiation in Nietzsche's ideas. The Dionysian feeling has the thoroughly archaic character of affective sensation. It is not therefore pure feeling, abstracted and differentiated from the instinctive into that mobile element, which in the extraverted type is obedient to the commands of reason, lending itself as her willing instrument. Similarly Nietzsche's conception of introversion is not concerned with that pure, differentiated relation to ideas which is abstracted from perception — whether sensuously determined or creatively achieved — into abstract and pure form. The Apollonian is an inner perception, an intuition of the world of ideas. The parallel with the dream clearly shows that Nietzsche regarded this state as a merely perceptive condition on the one hand and as a merely pictorial one on the other.

These characteristics are individual peculiarities, which we must not include in our concept of the introverted or extraverted attitude. In a man whose prevailing attitude is reflective this Apollonian state of perception of inner images produces an elaboration of the material perceived in accordance with the character of the individual thought. Hence proceed ideas. In a man of a predominantly feeling attitude a similar process results: a searching feeling into the images and an elaboration of a feeling-idea which may essentially correspond with the idea produced by thinking. Ideas, therefore, are just as much feeling as thought: for example, the idea of the fatherland, of freedom, of God, of immortality, etc. In both elaborations the principle is rational and logical. But there is also a quite different standpoint, from which the logical-rational elaboration is not valid. This *other standpoint is the æsthetic*. In introversion it stays with the *perception* of ideas, it develops intuition, the inner perception; in extraversion it stays with *sensation* and develops the senses, instinct, affectedness. Thinking, for such a standpoint, is in no case the principle of inner perception of ideas, and feeling just as little; instead, thinking and feeling are mere derivatives of inner perception or outer sensation.

Nietzsche's ideas, therefore, lead us on to the principles of a third and a fourth psychological type, which one might term the æsthetic, as opposed to the rational types (thinking and feeling). These are the *intuitive* and the *sensation* types. Both these types have the mechanisms of introversion and extraversion in common with the rational types, but they do not—like the thinking type on the one hand—differentiate the perception and contemplation of the inner images into thought, nor—like the feeling type on the other—differentiate the affective experience of instinct and sensation into feeling. On the contrary, the intuitive raises unconscious perception to the level of a differentiated function, by which he also becomes adapted to the world. He adapts himself by means of unconscious indications, which he receives through an especially fine and sharpened perception and interpretation of faintly conscious stimuli. How such a function appears is naturally hard to describe, on account of its irrational, and, so to speak, unconscious character. In a sense one might compare it with the dæmon of Socrates: with this qualification, however, that the strongly rationalistic attitude of Socrates repressed the intuitive function to the fullest limit; it had then to become effective in concrete hallucination, since it had no direct psychological access to consciousness. But with the intuitive type this latter is precisely the case.

The sensation-type is in all respects a converse of the intuitive. He bases himself almost exclusively upon the element of external sensation. His psychology is orientated in respect to instinct and sensation. Hence he is wholly dependent upon actual stimulation.

The fact that it is just the psychological functions of intuition on the one hand, and of sensation and instinct on the other, that Nietzsche brings into relief, must be characteristic of his own personal psychology. He must surely be reckoned as an intuitive type with an inclination towards the side of introversion. As evidence of the former we have his pre-eminently intuitive, artistic manner of production, of which this very work *The Birth of Tragedy* is highly characteristic, while his master work *Thus Spake Zarathustra* is even more so. His aphoristic writings are expressive of his introverted intellectual side. These, in spite of a strong admixture of feeling, exhibit a pronounced critical intellectualism in the manner of the French intellectuals of the eighteenth century. His lack of rational moderation and conciseness argues for the intuitive type in general. Under these circumstances it is not surprising that in his initial work he unwittingly sets the facts of his own personal psychology in the foreground. This is all quite in harmony with the intuitive attitude, which characteristically perceives the outer through the medium of the inner, sometimes even at the expense of reality. By means of this attitude he also gained deep insight into the Dionysian qualities of his unconscious, the crude forms of which, so far as we know, reached the surface of consciousness only at the outbreak of his illness, although they had already revealed their presence in various erotic allusions. It is therefore extremely regrettable, from the standpoint of psychology, that the fragments—so significant in this respect—which were found in Turin after the onset of his malady, should have met with destruction at the hands of moral and æsthetic scruples.

CHAPTER IV

THE TYPE-PROBLEM IN THE DISCERNMENT OF HUMAN
CHARACTER

1. General Remarks upon Jordan's Types

IN my chronological survey of previous contributions to this interesting problem of psychological types, I now come to a small and rather odd work (my acquaintance with which I owe to my esteemed colleague Dr Constance Long, of London): *Character as seen in Body and Parentage* by Furneaux Jordan, F.R.C.S. (3rd edn., London 1896).

In his little book of one hundred and twenty-six pages, Jordan's main description refers to two types or characters, whose definition interests us in more than one respect. Although—to anticipate slightly—the author is really concerned with only one half of our types, the point of view of the other half, namely the intuitive and sensation types, is none the less included and confused with the types he describes.

I will first let the author speak for himself, presenting his introductory definition. On p. 5 he says:

"There are two generic fundamental biases in character . . . two conspicuous types of character (with a third, an intermediate one) . . . one in which the tendency to action is extreme and the tendency to reflection slight, and another in which the proneness to reflection greatly predominates and the impulse for action is feebler. Between the two extremes are innumerable gradations ; it is sufficient to point only to a third type . . . in which the powers of reflection and action tend to meet in more or less equal degree. . . In an intermediate class may also be placed the characters which tend to eccentricity, or in which other possibly abnormal tendencies predominate over the emotional and non-emotional."

It can be clearly seen from this definition that Jordan contrasts reflection, or thinking, with activity. It is thoroughly understandable that an observer of men, not probing too deeply, would first be struck by the contrast between the reflective and the active natures, and would therefore be inclined to define the observed antithesis from this angle. The simple reflection, however, that the active nature does not necessarily proceed from impulse, but can also originate in thought, would make it seem necessary to carry the definition somewhat deeper. Jordan himself reaches this conclusion, for on p. 6 he introduces a further element into his survey, which has for us a particular value, namely the element of feeling. He states here that the active type is less passionate, while the reflective temperament is distinguished by its passionate feelings. Hence Jordan calls his types "the less impassioned" and "the more impassioned". Thus the element which he overlooked in his introductory definition he subsequently raises to the constant factor. But what mainly distinguishes his conception from ours is the fact that he also makes the "less impassioned" type "active" and the other "inactive".

This combination seems to me unfortunate, since highly passionate and profound natures exist which are also energetic and active, and, conversely, there are less impassioned and superficial natures which are in no way distinguished by activity, not even by the low form of activity that consists in being busy. In my view, his otherwise valuable conception would have gained much in clarity if he had left the factors of activity and inactivity altogether out of account, as belonging to a quite different point-of-view, although in themselves important characterological determinants.

It will be seen from the arguments which follow that with the "less impassioned and more active" type Jordan is describing the extravert, and that his "more impassioned and less active" type corresponds with the introvert. Either can be active or inactive without thereby changing its type; for this reason the factor of activity should, in my opinion, be ruled out as an index character. As a determinant of secondary importance, however, it still plays a rôle, since the whole nature of the extravert appears more mobile, more full of life and activity than that of the introvert. But this quality depends upon the phase which the individual temporarily occupies vis-à-vis the outer world. An introvert in an extraverted phase appears active, while an extravert in an introverted phase appears passive. Activity itself, as a fundamental trait of character, can sometimes be introverted; it is then wholly directed within, developing a lively activity of thought or feeling behind an outer mask of profound repose; or at times it can be extraverted, showing itself in vigorous and lively action whilst behind the scenes there stands a firm dispassionate thought or untroubled feeling.

Before we make a more narrow examination of Jordan's train of ideas, I must, for greater clarity, stress yet another point which, if not borne in mind, might give rise to confusion. I remarked at the beginning that in earlier publications I had identified the introvert with the thinking and the extravert with the feeling type. As I said before, it became clear to me only later that introversion and extraversion are to be distinguished from the function-types as general basic attitudes. These two attitudes may be recognized with the greatest ease while a sound discrimination of the function types requires a very wide experience. At times it is uncommonly difficult to discover which function holds the premier place. The fact that the introvert naturally has a reflective and contemplative air, as a result of his abstracting attitude, has a misleading effect. This leads us to assume in him a priority of thinking. The extravert, on the contrary, naturally displays many immediate reactions, which easily allow us to conclude a predominance of the feeling-element. But these suppositions are deceptive, since the extravert may well be a thinking, and the introvert a feeling, type. Jordan merely describes the introvert and the extravert in general. But, where he goes into individual qualities, his description becomes misleading, because traits of different function-types are confused together, which a more adequate examination of the material would have kept apart. In general outlines, however, the picture of the introverted and extraverted attitude is unmistakable, so that the nature of the two basic attitudes can be plainly discerned.

The characterization of the types from the standpoint of affectivity appears to me as the really important aspect of Jordan's work. We have already seen that the "reflective" and contemplative nature of the introvert finds compensation in an unconscious, archaic life with regard to instinct and sensation. We might even say that that is why he is introverted, since he has to rise above an archaic, impulsive, passionate nature to the safer heights of abstraction, in order to dominate his insubordinate and turbulent affects. This statement of the case is in many instances not at all beside the mark. Conversely, we might say of the extravert that his less deeply rooted emotional life is more readily adapted to differentiation and domestication than his unconscious, archaic thought and feeling, and it is this deep phantasy activity which may have such a dangerous influence upon his personality. Hence he is always the one who seeks life and experience as busily and abundantly as possible, that he may never come to himself and confront his evil thoughts and feelings. From observations such as these, which are very easily verified, we may explain an otherwise paradoxical passage in Jordan, where he says (p. 6), that in the "less impassioned" (extraverted) temperament the intellect predominates with an unusually large share in the shaping of life, whereas the affects claim the greater importance with the "reflective" or introverted temperament.

At first glance, this interpretation would seem to contradict my assertion that the "less impassioned" corresponds with my extraverted type. But a nearer scrutiny proves that this is not the case, since the reflective character, though certainly *trying* to deal with his unruly affects, is in reality more influenced by passion than the man who takes for the conscious guidance of his life those desires which are orientated to objects. The latter, namely the extravert, attempts to make this principle all inclusive, but he has none the less to experience the fact that it is his subjective thoughts and feelings which everywhere harass him on his way. He is influenced by his inner psychic world to a far greater extent than he is aware of. He cannot see it himself, but an observant entourage always discerns the personal *purposiveness* of his striving. Hence his golden rule should always be to ask himself: "What is my actual wish and secret purpose?"

The other, the introvert, with his conscious, thought-out aims, always tends to overlook what his circle perceives only too clearly, namely that his aims are really in the service of powerful impulses, to whose influence, though lacking both purpose and object, they are very largely subject. The observer and critic of the extravert is liable to take the parade of feeling and thought as a thin covering, that only partially conceals a cold and calculated personal aim. Whereas the man who tries to understand the introvert might readily conclude that vehement passion is only with difficulty held in check by apparent sophistries.

Either judgment is both true and false. The conclusion is *false* when the conscious standpoint, *i.e.* consciousness in general, is strong enough to offer resistance to the unconscious; but it is true when a weaker conscious standpoint encounters a strong unconscious, to which it eventually has to give way. In this latter case the motive that was kept in the background now breaks forth; the egotistical aim in the one case, and the unsubdued passion, the elemental affect, that throws aside every consideration in the other.

These observations allow us to see how Jordan observes: he is evidently preoccupied with the affectivity of the observed type, hence his nomenclature: "less emotional" and "more impassioned". If, therefore, from the emotional aspect he conceives the introvert as the passionate, and from the same standpoint he sees the extravert as the less impassioned and even as the intellectual, type, he thereby reveals a peculiar kind of discernment which one must describe as *intuitive*. This is why I previously drew attention to the fact that Jordan confuses the rational with the perceptional point of view. When he characterizes the introvert as the passionate and the extravert as the intellectual, he is clearly seeing the two types from the side of the *unconscious, i.e. he perceives them through the medium of his unconscious*. He observes and recognizes *intuitively*: this must always be more or less the case with the practical observer of men. However true and profound such an apprehension may sometimes be, it is subject to a most essential limitation: it overlooks the living reality of the observed man, since it always judges him from his unconscious reflexion instead of his actual presence. This error of judgment is inseparable from intuition, and reason has always been at loggerheads with it on this account, only grudgingly acknowledging its right to existence, in spite of the fact that it must often be convinced of the objective accuracy of the intuitive finding. On the whole, then, Jordan's formulations accord with reality, though not with reality as it is understood by the rational types, but with the reality which is for them unconscious. Naturally, this is a circumstance than which nothing is more calculated to confuse all judgment upon the observed persons, and to enhance the difficulty of interpretation of the facts observed. In these questions, therefore, one ought never to quarrel over nomenclature, but should hold exclusively to the actual facts of observable, contrasting differences. Although my own manner of expression is altogether different from that of Jordan, we are nevertheless at one, with certain divergences, upon the classification of the observed phenomena.

Before going on to comment upon the way Jordan reduces his observed material into types, I should like briefly to return to his postulated third or "intermediate" type. Jordan, as we saw, ranged under this heading the wholly balanced on one side, and the unbalanced on the other. It will not be superfluous at this point to call to mind the classification of the Valentinian school[1], in which the *Hylic* man is subordinated to the psychic and pneumatic. The hylic man, according to his definition, corresponds with the sensation type, *i.e.* with the man whose prevailing determinants are supplied in and through the senses. The sensation type has neither a differentiated thinking nor a differentiated feeling, but his sensuousness is well developed. This, as we know, is also the case with the primitive. But the instinctive sensuality of the primitive has a counterweight in the spontaneity of the psychic processes. His mental product, his thoughts, practically confront him. He does not make or devise

[1] The name given to the adherents of Valentinus, an Egyptian theologian who flourished circa A.D. 150 and founded a Gnostic sect. The Hylici suffered themselves to be so captivated by the inferior world as to live only a hylic or material life. (*New English Dictionary*)

them—he is not capable of that: they make themselves, they happen to him, even confronting him like hallucinations. Such a mentality must be termed intuitive, since intuition is the instinctive perception of an emerging psychic content. Although the principal psychological function of the primitive is as a rule sensation, the less prominent compensating function is intuition. Upon the higher levels of civilization, where one man has thinking more or less differentiated and another feeling, there are also quite a number of individuals who have developed intuition to a high level and employ it as the essentially determining function. From these we get the intuitive type. It is my belief, therefore, that Jordan's middle group may be resolved into the sensation and intuitive types.

2. Special Description and Criticism of the Jordan Types

With regard to the general appearance of the two types Jordan emphasizes the fact (p. 17) that the less emotional yields far more prominent and striking personalities than the emotional type. This notion springs from the fact that Jordan identifies the active type of man with the less emotional, which in my opinion is inadmissible. Leaving this mistake on one side, it is certainly true that the behaviour of the "less emotional", or let us say the extravert, makes him more conspicuous than the emotional or introvert.

(*a*) *The Introverted Woman* (The more-impassioned woman)

The first character that Jordan discusses is that of the *introverted woman*. Let me summarize the chief points of his description (pp. 17 ff.):

" She has quiet manners, and a character not easy to read: she is occasionally critical even sarcastic . . . but though bad temper is sometimes noticeable, she is neither fitful nor restless, nor captious, nor censorious, nor is she a "nagging" woman. She diffuses an atmosphere of repose, and unconsciously she comforts and heals, but under the surface emotions and passions lie dormant. Her emotional nature matures slowly As she grows older the charm of her character increases. She is "sympathetic", i.e. she brings insight and experience to bear on the problems of others. The very worst characters are found among the more impassioned women. They are the cruellest stepmothers. They make the most affectionate wives and mothers, but their passions and emotions are so strong that these frequently hold reason in subjection or carry it away with them. They love too much, but they also hate too much. Jealousy can make wild beasts of them. Stepchildren, if hated by them, may even be done to death.

"If evil is not in the ascendant, morality itself is associated with deep feeling, and may take a profoundly reasoned and independent course which will not always fit itself to conventional standards. It will not be an imitation or a submission: not a bid for a reward here or hereafter. It is only in intimate relations that the excellences and drawbacks of the impassioned woman are seen. Here she unfolds herself; here are her joys and sorrows . . . here her faults and weaknesses are seen, perhaps slowness to forgive, implacability, sullenness, anger, jealousy, or even . . . uncontrolled passions. . . She is charmed with the moment . . . and less apt to think of the comfort and welfare of the absent . . . . she is disposed to forget others and forget time. If she is affected, her affectation is less an imitation than a pronounced change of manners and speech with changing shades of thought and especially of feeling. . . . In social life she tends to be the same in all circles. . . . In both domestic and social life she is as a rule not difficult to please, she spontaneously appreciates, congratulates, and praises. She can soothe the mentally bruised and encourage the unsuccessful. In her there is compassion for all weak things, two-footed or four. . . . She rises to the high and stoops to the low, she is the sister and playmate of all nature. Her judgment is mild and lenient. When she reads she tries to grasp the inmost thought and deepest feeling of the book; she reads and re-reads the book, marks it freely, and turns down its corners."

From this description it is not difficult to recognize the introverted character. But the description is, in a certain sense, one-sided, because the chief stress is laid upon the side of feeling, without emphasizing the one characteristic to which I give special value, viz. the *conscious inner life*. He mentions, it is true, that the introverted woman is "contemplative," but he does not pursue the matter further. His description, however, seems to me a confirmation of my comments upon the manner of his observation; in the main it is the outward demeanour constellated by feeling, and the manifestations of passions which strike him; he does not probe into the nature of the conscious life of this type. Hence he never mentions that the inner life plays an altogether decisive rôle in the introvert's conscious psychology. Why, for example, does the introverted woman read so attentively? Because above everything she loves to understand and comprehend ideas. Why is she restful and soothing? Because she usually keeps her feelings to herself, living them inwardly, instead of unloading them upon others. Her unconventional morality is based upon deep reflection and convincing inner feelings. The charm of her calm and intelligent character depends not merely upon a peaceful attitude, but derives from the fact that one can talk with her reasonably and coherently, and because she is able to estimate the value of her companion's argument. She does not interrupt him with impulsive demonstrations, but accompanies his meaning with her thoughts and feelings, which none the less remain steadfast, never yielding to opposing arguments.

This compact and well-developed ordering of conscious psychic contents is a stout defence against a chaotic and passionate emotional life, of which the introvert is very often aware, at least in its personal aspect: she fears it because it is present to her. She meditates about herself: she is therefore outwardly equable and can recognize and appreciate another, without loading him with either blame or approbation. But because her emotional life would devastate these good qualities, she as far as possible rejects her instincts and affects, but without thereby mastering them. In contrast, therefore, to her logical and consolidated consciousness, her affect is proportionally elemental, confused and ungovernable. It lacks the true human note; it is disproportionate and irrational; it is a *phenomenon of Nature*, which breaks through the human order. It lacks any tangible arrière pensée or purpose: at times, therefore, it is quite destructive—a wild torrent, that neither contemplates destruction nor avoids it, profoundly indifferent and necessary, obedient only to its own laws, a process that accomplishes itself. Her good qualities depend upon her thinking, which by a tolerant or benevolent comprehension has succeeded in influencing or restraining one element of her instinctive life, though lacking the power to embrace and transform the whole. Her affectivity is far less clearly conscious to the introverted woman in its whole range than are her rational thoughts and feelings. She is incapable of comprehending her whole affectivity, although her way of looking at life is well adapted. Her affectivity is much less mobile than her intellectual contents: it is, as it were, tough and curiously inert, therefore hard to change; it is perseverant, hence also her self-will and her occasional unreasonable inflexibility in things that touch her emotions.

These considerations may explain why a judgment of the introverted woman, taken exclusively from the angle of affectivity, is incomplete and unfair in whatever sense it is taken. If Jordan finds the vilest feminine characters among the introverts, this, in my opinion, is due to the fact that he lays too great a stress upon affectivity, as if passion alone were the mother of all evil. We can torture children to death in other ways than the merely physical. And, from the other point-of-view, that wondrous wealth of love of the introverted woman is not always by any means her own possession;

she is more often possessed by it and cannot choose but love, until one day a favourable opportunity occurs, when suddenly, to the amazement of her partner, she displays an inexplicable coldness. The emotional life of the introvert is generally his weak side; it is not absolutely trustworthy. He deceives himself about it; others also are deceived and disappointed in him, when they rely too exclusively upon his affectivity. His mind is more reliable, because more adapted. His affect is too close to sheer untamed nature.

(b) *The Extraverted Woman* (The less-impassioned woman)

Let us now turn to Jordan's delineation of the "less impassioned woman". Here too I must reject everything which the author has confused by the introduction of activity, since this admixture is only calculated to render the typical character less recognizable. Thus, when we speak of a certain quickness of the extravert, this does not mean the element of energy and activity, but merely the mobility of active processes.

Of the extraverted woman Jordan says :[1]

"She is marked by a certain quickness and opportuneness rather than by persistence or consistency... Her life is almost wholly occupied with little things. She goes even further than Lord Beaconsfield in the belief that unimportant things are not very unimportant, and important things not very important. She likes to dwell on the way her grandmother did things, and how her grandchildren will do them, and on the universal degeneracy of human beings and affairs. Her daily wonder is how things would go on if she were not there to look after them. She is frequently invaluable in social movements. She expends her energies in household cleanliness, which is the end and aim of existence to not a few women. Frequently she is 'idea-less, emotionless, restless and spotless'. Her emotional development is usually precocious, and at eighteen she is little less wise than at twenty-eight or forty-eight. Her mental outlook usually lacks

---

[1] p. 9 ff.

range and depth, but it is clear from the first. When intelligent, she is capable of taking a leading position. In society she is kindly, generous and hospitable. She judges her neighbours and friends, forgetful that she is herself being judged, but she is active in helping them in misfortune. Deep passion is absent in her, love is simply preference, hatred merely dislike, and jealousy only injured pride. Her enthusiasm is not sustained, and she is more alive to the beauty of poetry than she is to its passion and pathos. . . . Her beliefs and disbeliefs are complete rather than strong. She has no convictions, but she has no misgivings. She does not believe, she adopts, she does not disbelieve, she ignores. She never enquires and never doubts. . . . In large affairs she defers to authority; in small affairs she jumps to conclusions. In the detail of her own little world, whatever is, is wrong : in the larger world outside . . . whatever is, is right. . . . She instinctively rebels against carrying the conclusions of reason into practice.

" At home she shows quite a different character from the one seen in society. With her, marriage is much influenced by ambition, love of change or obedience to well-recognized custom, and a desire to be 'settled in life', or from a sincere wish to enter a greater sphere of usefulness. If her husband belongs to the impassioned type, he will love children more than she does.

" In the domestic circle her least pleasing characteristics are evident. Here she indulges in disconnected, disapproving comment, and none can foresee when there will be a gleam of sunshine through the cloud. The unemotional woman has little or no self-analysis. If she is plainly accused of habitual disapproval she is surprised and offended, and intimates . . . that she only desires the general good ' but some people do not know what is good for them '. She has one way of doing good to her family, and quite another way where society is concerned. The household must always be . . . ready for social inspection. Society must be encouraged and propitiated. . . . Its upper section must be impressed and its lower section kept in order. . . . Home is her winter, society her summer. If the door but opens and a visitor is announced, the transformation is instant.

" The less emotional woman is by no means given to asceticism ; respectability . . . does not demand it of her. She is fond of movement, recreation, change. . . . Her busy day may open with a religious service, and close with a comic opera. . . . She delights . . . to entertain her friends and to be entertained by them. In society she finds not only her work and her happiness, but her rewards and her consolations. . . She believes in society, and society believes in her. Her feelings are little influenced by prejudice, and as a rule she is ' reasonable '. She is very imitative and usually selects good models, but is only dimly conscious of her imitations. The books she reads must deal with life and action."

This familiar type of woman, which Jordan terms the "less impassioned", is extraverted beyond a doubt. The whole demeanour sets forth that character which from its very nature must be called extraverted. The continual criticizing, that is never founded upon real reflection, is an extraversion of a fleeting impression, which has nothing to do with true thinking. I remember a witty aphorism I once read somewhere or other: "Thinking is so difficult—therefore most of us prefer *to pass judgments*".[1] Reflection demands time above everything: therefore the man who reflects has no opportunity for continual criticism. Incoherent and inconsequent criticism, with its dependence upon tradition and authority, reveals the absence of any independent reflection; similarly the lack of self-criticism and the dearth of independent ideas betrays a defect of the function of judgment. The absence of inner mental life in this type is expressed much more distinctly than is its presence in the introverted type depicted above. From this sketch one might readily conclude that there is here just as great or even a greater defect of affectivity, for it is obviously superficial, shallow, almost spurious; because the aim always involved in it or discernible behind it, makes the emotional effort practically worthless. I am, however, inclined to assume that the author is here undervaluing just as much as he overvalued in the former case. Notwithstanding an occasional recognition of good qualities, the type, on the whole, comes out of it very indifferently. I must assume in this case a certain bias on the part of the author. It is usually enough to have tasted a bitter experience, either with one or more representatives of a certain type, for one's taste to be spoiled

[1] "*Denken ist so schwer—darum urteilen die Meisten.*"

for every similar case. One must not forget that, just as the good sense of the introverted woman depends upon a scrupulous accommodation of her mental contents to the general thought, the affectivity of the extraverted woman possesses a certain mobility and lack of depth, on account of her adaptation to the general life of human society. In this case, it is a question of a socially differentiated affectivity of incontestable general validity, which compares more than favourably with the heavy, sticky, passionate affect of the introvert. The differentiated affectivity has cut away the chaotic affect, and has become a disposable function of adaptation, though at the expense of the inner mental life, which is remarkable by its absence. It none the less exists in the unconscious, and moreover in a form which corresponds with the passion of the introvert, *i.e.* in an undeveloped state. The character of this state is infantile and archaic. The undeveloped mind, working from the unconscious, provides the affective struggle with contents and hidden motives, which can not fail to make a bad impression upon the critical observer, although unperceived by the uncritical eye. The disagreeable impression that the constant perception of thinly veiled egoistic motives has upon the beholder makes one only too prone to forget the actual reality and adapted usefulness of the efforts thus displayed. All that is easy, unforced, moderate, unconcerned and superficial in life would disappear, if there were no differentiated affects. One would either be stifled in continuously manifested pathos, or be engulfed in the yawning void of repressed passion. If the social function of the introvert mainly perceives individuals, the extravert certainly promotes the life of the community, which also has a claim to existence. That is why he needs extraversion because first and foremost it is the bridge to one's neighbour.

As we all know, the expression of emotion works suggestively, while the mind can only unfold its effectiveness indirectly, by arduous translation. The affects required by the social function must not be at all deep, or they beget passion in others. And passion disturbs the life and prosperity of society. Similarly the adapted, differentiated mind of the introvert has extensity rather than depth; hence it is not disturbing and provocative but reasonable and sedative. But, just as the introvert is troublesome through the violence of his passion, the extravert is irritating through an incoherent and abrupt application of his half unconscious thoughts and feelings in the form of tactless and unsparing judgments upon his fellow-men. If we were to make a collection of such judgments and were to try synthetically to construct a psychology out of them, we should arrive at an utterly brutal conception, which in cheerless savagery, crudity, and stupidity, would be a fitting rival to the murderous affect-nature of the introvert. Hence I cannot subscribe to Jordan's view that the worst characters are to be found among the passionate introverted natures. Among the extraverts there is just as much and just as basic wickedness. Whereas introverted passionateness reveals itself in coarse actions, the vulgarity of the extravert's unconscious thinking and feeling commits infamous deeds upon the soul of the victim. I know not which is worse. The drawback in the former case is that the deed is visible, while the latter's vulgarity of mind is concealed behind the veil of an acceptable demeanour. I would like to lay stress upon the social thoughtfulness of this type, his active concern for the general welfare, as well as a most definite tendency to provide pleasure for others. The introvert as a rule has these qualities only in phantasy.

Differentiated affects have the further advantage of charm and beautiful form. They diffuse an æsthetic, beneficent atmosphere. There are a surprising number of extraverts who practise an art (chiefly music) not so much because they are specially qualified in that direction as from a desire to be generally serviceable in social life. Extraverted fault-finding, moreover, is not always unpleasant or wholly worthless in character. It very often confines itself to an adapted, educational tendency, which does a great deal of good. Similarly, his dependence of judgment is not necessarily evil under all circumstances, for it often conduces to the suppression of extravagant and pernicious out-growths, which in no way further the life and welfare of society. It would be altogether unjustifiable to try to maintain that one type is in any respect more valuable than the other. The types are mutually complementary, and from their distinctiveness there proceeds just that measure of tension which both the individual and society need for the maintenance of life.

(c) *The Extraverted Man*

Of the extraverted man Jordan says (pp. 26 ff.):

" He is fitful and uncertain in temper and behaviour, given . . . to petulance, fuss, discontent and censoriousness. He makes depreciatory judgments on all and sundry, but is ever well satisfied with himself. His judgment is often at fault and his projects often fail, but he never ceases to place unbounded confidence in both. Sidney Smith, speaking of a conspicuous statesman of his time, said he was ready at any moment to command the Channel Fleet or amputate a limb. . . . He has an incisive formula for everything that is put before him : . . . either the thing is not true—or everybody knows it already. . . . In his sky there is not room for two suns. . . . If other suns insist on shining, he has a curious sense of martyrdom. . . .

" He matures early : he is fond of administration, . . . and is often an admirable public servant. . . . At the committee of his charity he is as much interested in the selection of its washerwoman as in the selection of its chairman. In company he is usually alert, to the point, witty, and apt at retort. He resolutely, confidently, and constantly shows himself. Experience helps him and he insists on getting experience. He would rather be the *known* chairman of a committee of three than the *unknown* benefactor of a nation. When he is less gifted he is probably no less self-important. Is he busy? He believes himself to be energetic. Is he loquacious? He believes himself to be eloquent.

"He rarely puts forth new ideas, or opens new paths . . . but he is quick to follow, to seize, to apply, to carry out. . . . His natural tendency is to ancient, or at least accepted forms of belief and policy. Special circumstances may sometimes lead him to contemplate with admiration the audacity of his own heresy. . . . Not rarely the less emotional intellect is so lofty and commanding, that no disturbing influence can hinder the formation of broad and just views in all the provinces of life. His life is usually characterized by morality, truthfulness, and high principle; but sometimes his desire for immediate effect leads him into difficulties.

"If, in public assembly, adverse fates have given him nothing to do, nothing to propose, or second, or support, or amend, or oppose, he will rise and ask for some window to be closed to keep out a draught, or, which is more likely, that one be opened to let in more air; for physiologically, he commonly needs much air as well as much notice. . . . He is especially prone to do what he is not asked to do. . . He constantly believes that the public sees him as he wishes it to see him . . . a sleepless seeker of the public good. . . . He puts others in his debt, and he cannot go unrewarded. He may, by well-chosen language, move his audience although he is not moved himself. He is probably quick to understand his time or at least his party . . . he warns it of impending evil, organizes its forces, deals smartly with its opponents. He is full of projects and bustling activity. Society must be pleased if possible, if it will not be pleased it must be astonished; if it will neither be pleased nor astonished it must be pestered and shocked. He is a saviour by profession and as an acknowledged saviour is not ill pleased with himself. We can of ourselves do nothing right—but we can believe in him, dream of him, thank God for him, and ask him to address us.

"He is unhappy in repose, and rests nowhere long. After a busy day he must have a pungent evening. He is found in the theatre, or concert, or church, or the bazaar, at the dinner, or conversazione or club, or all these, turn and turn about. . . . If he misses a meeting, a telegram announces a more ostentatious call."

From this description the type is easily recognized. But, even more perhaps than in the description of the extraverted woman, there emerges notwithstanding individual evidences of appreciation, an element of caricaturing depreciation. This is partly due to the fact that this method of description cannot be just to the extraverted nature in general, because with the intellectual medium it is well-nigh impossible to set the specific value of the extravert in a fair light: while with the introvert this is much more possible, since his conscious motivation and goodsense permit of expression through the intellectual medium as readily as do the facts of his passion and its inevitable consequences. With the extravert, on the other hand, the chief value lies in his relation to the object. To me it seems that only life itself can concede the extravert that justice which intellectual criticism fails to give him. Life alone reveals and appreciates his values. We can, of course, state the fact that the extravert is socially useful, that he deserves great merit for the progress of human society, and so on. But an analysis of his means and motivations will always give a negative result, since the chief value of the extravert lies not in himself but in the reciprocal relation to the object. The relation to the object belongs to those imponderabilia, which the intellectual formulation can never seize.

Intellectual criticism cannot abstain from proceeding analytically: it must constantly seek evidence concerning motivation and aims, in order to bring the observed type to complete definition. But from this process a picture emerges which is no better than a caricature for the psychology of the extravert, and the man who is fain to believe he has found the extravert's real attitude upon the basis of such a description will be astonished to find the actual personality turning his description to ridicule. Such a one-sided conception entirely prevents any adaptation to the extravert. In order to do him justice, thinking about him must be altogether excluded; similarly the extravert can adjust himself correctly to the introvert only when he is prepared to accept his mental contents in themselves quite apart from their possible practical application. Intellectual analysis cannot help charging the extravert with every possible design, subtle aim, mental reservation, and so forth, which have no actual existence, but at the most are only shadowy effects leaking in from the unconscious background.

It is certainly true that the extravert, if he has nothing else to say, may find it necessary for a window to be opened or shut. But who has remarked it? Who is essentially struck by it? Only the man who is trying to give an account of the possible grounds and intentions of such an action, one therefore who reflects, dissects, and reconstructs, while for everyone else this little stir is altogether dissolved in the general bustle of life, without offering an invitation to any ulterior deduction. But it is just in this way that the psychology of the extravert reveals itself: it belongs to the occurrences of daily human life, and it signifies nothing more, either above or below. But the man who reflects, sees further and—as far as the actual life is concerned—sees crooked, although his vision is sound enough as regards the unconscious background. He does not see the positive man, but only his *shadow*. And the shadow admits the justice of the criticism, to the prejudice of the conscious, positive human being. For the sake of understanding, it is, I think, a good thing to detach the man from his shadow, the unconscious; otherwise the discussion is threatened with an unparalleled confusion of ideas. One sees much in another man which does not belong to his conscious psychology, but which gleams out from his unconscious, and one is rather tempted to regard the observed quality as belonging to the conscious ego. Life and fate may do this, but the psychologist, to whom the knowledge of the structure of the psyche and the dawning possibility of a better understanding of man is of the deepest concern, must not. A clean discrimination of the conscious man from his unconscious is imperative, since only by the assimilation of conscious standpoints will clarity and understanding be gained, and never through a process of reduction to the unconscious backgrounds, side-lights, and quarter-tones.

(d) *The Introverted Man*

Of the character of the introverted man (the more impassioned and reflective man), Jordan says (p. 35):

"His pleasures do not change from hour to hour, his love of pleasure is of a more genuine nature, and he does not seek it from mere restlessness. If he takes part in public work he is probably invited to do so from some special fitness; or it may be that he has at heart some movement . . . which he wishes to promote. When his work is done he willingly retires. He is able to see what others can do better than he; and he would rather that his cause should prosper in other hands than fail in his own. He has a hearty word of praise for his fellow-workers. Probably he errs in estimating too generously the merits of those around him. . . . He is never, and indeed cannot be, an habitual scold. Such men develop slowly, are liable to hesitate, never become the leaders of religious movements, are never so supremely confident as to what is error that they burn their neighbours for it; never so confident that they possess infallible truth that, although not wanting in courage, they are prepared to be burnt in its behalf. If they are especially endowed, they will be thrust into the front rank by their environment, while men of the other type place themselves there."

To me it seems significant that the author in his chapter on the introverted man, with whom we are now concerned, actually says no more than I have substantially given above. A description of the passion on which account he is termed the "impassioned" type is for the most part omitted. One must, of course, be cautious in making diagnostic conjectures—but this case seems to invite the supposition that the section on the introverted man has received such niggardly treatment from subjective causes. One might have expected, after the searching and unfair delineation of the extraverted type, a similar thoroughness of description for the introvert. Why is it not forthcoming?

Let us suppose that Jordan himself is upon the side of the introverts. It would then be intelligible that a description like the one he gives to his opposite type with such pitiless severity, would scarcely be acceptable. I would not say because of a lack of objectivity, but rather for lack of discernment of his own shadow. How he appears to his counter-type, the introvert cannot possibly know or imagine, unless he allows the extravert a privileged recital of it, at the risk of being obliged to challenge him to a duel. Just as little as the extravert is disposed to accept the above characteristics without more ado, as a benevolent and striking picture of his character, is the introvert willing to receive his characteristics from an extraverted observer and critic. For it would be just as depreciatory. As the introvert, who tries to get hold of the nature of the extravert, invariably goes wide of the mark, so the extravert who tries to understand the other's inner mental life from the standpoint of externality is equally at sea. The introvert makes the mistake of always wanting to relate action to the subjective psychology of the extravert, while the extravert can only conceive the inner mental life as a product of external circumstances. For the extravert an abstract train of thought must be a phantasy, a sort of chimera, when an objective relation is not in evidence. And as a matter of fact introverted brain-weavings are often nothing more. At all events a lot could be said of the introverted man, and one could draw a shadow portrait of him neither less complete nor unfavourable than that which Jordan in his earlier section drew of the extravert.

Jordan's observation that the pleasure of the introvert

is of a "more genuine nature" seems to me important. This appears to be a peculiarity of the introverted feeling in general: it is genuine; it is because it just is; it is rooted in the man's deeper nature; it wells up out of itself as it were, having itself as its own aim; it will serve no other ends, lending itself to none, and is content to accomplish itself. This coincides with the spontaneity of the archaic and natural phenomenon, which has never yet bowed the head to the ends and aims of civilization. Whether rightly or wrongly, or at least without consideration of right or wrong, of suitability or unsuitability, the affective state manifests itself, forcing itself upon the subject even against his will and expectation. It contains nothing from which one might conclude a thought-out motivation.

I. do not wish to enlarge upon the further sections of Jordan's book. He cites historical personalities as examples, whereby numerous distorted points of view appear which derive from the fallacy already referred to: *i.e.* the author introduces the criterion of active and passive, and mixes it up with other criteria. From this medley the conclusion is frequently drawn that an active personality must also be counted as a passion-less type, and, *vice versa*, a passionate nature must likewise always be passive. My standpoint seeks to avoid this error by altogether excluding the factor of activity as a point-of-view.

To Jordan, however, the credit belongs of being the first, so far as I know, to give a relatively appropriate character-sketch of the emotional types.

CHAPTER V

THE PROBLEM OF TYPES IN POETRY
CARL SPITTELER'S PROMETHEUS AND EPIMETHEUS

1. Introductory Remarks on Spitteler's Characterization of Types

IF, among the themes offered to the poet by the intricacies of emotional life, the problem of types did not play a significant rôle, it would practically prove that such a problem did not exist. But we have already seen how in Schiller this problem stirred the poet in him as deeply as the thinker. In this chapter we shall turn our attention to a poetic work which is almost exclusively based upon the motif of the type-problem. I refer to Carl Spitteler's *Prometheus and Epimetheus*, which first appeared in 1881.

I have no wish to explain at the outset that Prometheus, the forethinker, stands for the introvert, while Epimetheus, the man of action and after-thinker, signifies the extravert. In the conflict of these two figures the principal issue is the battle of the introverted with the extraverted line of development in one and the same individual, though the poetic presentation has embodied the conflict in two independent figures with their typical destinies.

It is self-evident that Prometheus exhibits introverted character traits. He presents the picture of a man faithfully introverted to his inner world, true to his soul. His reply to the angel is a telling expression of his nature[1]: "Yet it is not mine to judge my soul's appearance, for behold, my mistress she is, my god in joy and sorrow,

---
[1] *Prometheus und Epimetheus*. Diedrich's Edition, 1920, p. 9.

and whatsoever I am, I have from her alone. And so, with her, will I share my glory, and if need be boldly will I renounce it."

In this act Prometheus surrenders himself unconditionally to his own soul, *i.e.* to the function of relation to the inner world. Hence the soul has also a mysterious metaphysical character, precisely on account of its relation to the unconscious. Prometheus concedes it absolute significance, as mistress and guide, in the same unconditional manner in which Epimetheus yields himself to the world. He sacrifices his individual ego to the soul, to the relation with the unconscious, as the mother-womb of eternal images and meanings; he thereby surrenders the Self, since he loses the counterweight of the persona[1], *i.e.* the relation to the external object. With this surrender to his soul Prometheus drops away from every connection with the surrounding world, thus escaping the indispensable correction gained through external reality. But this loss is irreconcilable with the nature of this world. Therefore an angel appears to Prometheus, clearly a representative of world-government: expressed psychologically, he is the projected image of a tendency directed towards reality-adaptation. The angel accordingly says to Prometheus:

"It shall come to pass, if thou dost not prevail and free thyself from thy soul's unrighteous way, that the great reward of many years and thy heart's content and all the fruits of thy subtle mind shall be lost unto thee."

And in another place:

"Rejected shalt thou be on the day of glory for the sake of thy soul, who knoweth no God and heedeth no law, for to her arrogance nothing is holy, neither in heaven nor upon earth."

Because Prometheus has a one-sided orientation to his soul; every impulse towards adaptation to the outer world

---

[1] Cf. Jung: *La structure de l'inconscient* (*Arch. de Psych.*, vol. xvi), and *Analytical Psychology*, ch. XV.

tends to be repressed and to sink into the unconscious. Consequently, if perceived at all, they appear as separate from the individuality, hence as projections. In this connection it would seem that there is a certain contradiction in the fact that the soul, whose cause Prometheus has espoused and which he as it were accepted in full consciousness, appears as a projection. Since the soul, like the persona, is a function of relationship, it must consist in a certain sense of two parts, one part belonging to the individuality and the other adhering to the object of relationship, in this case the unconscious. One is indeed generally inclined—unless one is a frank adherent of the Hartmann philosophy—to grant the unconscious only the relative existence of a psychological factor. On the grounds of the theory of cognition, we are as yet quite unable to make any valid statement with regard to an objective reality of the phenomenal psychological complex which we term the unconscious, just as we are equally powerless to determine anything valid about the nature of real things which lie beyond our psychological capacity. On the ground of experience, I must, however, point out that in relation to our conscious activity the contents of the unconscious make the same claim to reality by virtue of their obstinacy and persistence, as do the real things of the outer world, even when this challenge appears very improbable to a mentality with a preferential bias towards external reality. It must not be forgotten that there have always been many for whom the contents of the unconscious possessed a greater reality than the things of the outer world. The history of human thought bears witness to both realities. A more searching investigation of the human psyche shows unquestionably that there is, on the whole, an equally strong influence from both sides upon conscious activity; so that, psychologically, we have a right on purely empirical grounds to treat the contents of the unconscious as just as *real* as the things of the outer world, albeit these two realities may be mutually contradictory and appear entirely different in their natures. But to superordinate one reality over the other would be an altogether unjustifiable presumption. Theosophy and spiritualism are no better than materialism in their outrageous encroachments upon reality. We have, in fact, to resign ourselves to the sphere of our psychological possibilities.

The peculiar reality of unconscious contents, therefore, gives us the same right to describe these as *objects* as the things of the outer world. Whereas the persona, considered as a relation, is always conditioned by the outer object, and hence is as firmly anchored in the outer object as it is in the subject; the soul, as the relation to the inner object, is similarly represented by the inner object; in a sense, therefore, it is always distinct from the subject, and is actually perceptible as something distinct. Hence it appears to Prometheus as something quite separate from his individual ego. In the same way as a man who yields himself entirely to the outer world still has the world as an object distinct from himself, so the unconscious world of images remains as an object distinct from the subject, even when a man is wholly surrendered to it.

Just as the unconscious world of mythological images speaks indirectly, through the experience of external things, to the man who abandons himself to the outer world, so the real world and its claims find their way indirectly to the man who has surrendered himself to the soul; for no man can escape both realities. If a man is fixed upon the outer reality, he must live his myth; if he is turned towards the inner reality, then must he dream his outer, his so-called real life. Thus the soul says to Prometheus:

" A God of crime am I who leadeth thee astray upon untrodden paths. But thou would'st not hearken unto me, and now hath it come to pass according to my words; for my sake have they robbed thee of the glory of thy name and stolen from thee thy life's content." [1]

Prometheus refuses the kingdom the angel offers him; which means that he refuses adaptation to things as they are because his soul is demanded from him in exchange.

While the subject, *i.e.* Prometheus, is essentially human, the soul is of quite a different character. It is dæmonic, because the inner object, namely the supra-personal collective unconscious to which it is attached as the function of relation, gleams through it. The unconscious, regarded as the historical background of the psyche, contains in a concentrated form the entire succession of engrams (imprints), which from time immemorial have determined the psychic structure as it now exists. These engrams may be regarded as function-traces which typify, on the average, the most frequently and intensely used functions of the human soul. These function-engrams present themselves in the form of mythological themes and images, appearing often in identical form and always with striking similarity among all races; they can also be easily verified in the unconscious material of modern man. It is intelligible, therefore, that avowedly animal traits or elements should also appear among the unconscious contents by the side of those sublime figures which from oldest times have accompanied man on the road of life. The unconscious disposes of a whole world of images, whose boundless range yields in nothing to the claims of the world of "real" things. To the one who personally surrenders himself wholly to the outer world the unconscious comes in the form of some intimate and beloved being, in whom, should his destiny lie in extreme devotion to the personal object, he will experience the duality of the world and his own nature; in

[1] *Prometheus and Epimetheus*, pp. 24 ff.

like manner there comes to the other a dæmonic personification of the unconscious embodying the totality, the extreme oppositeness and duality of the world of images. These are border-line phenomena which overstep the normal; hence the normal mind knows nothing of these cruel enigmas. They do not exist for him. It is always only the few who reach the rim of the world, where its mirage begins. For the man who stands always upon the normal path the soul has a human, and not a dubious, dæmonic character; neither do his fellow-men appear to him in the least problematical. Only complete abandonment either to one world or to the other evokes their duality. Spitteler's intuition caught that picture of the soul which in a less profound nature would at most have found utterance in dreams.

Accordingly we read (*ibid.*, p. 25):

"And, while he thus demeaned himself in the fury of his passion, there played a strange quiver about her mouth and face, and ever and again her eyelids flickered, shutting and opening hastily, and behind the soft, delicate fringe of her lashes there lurked something which threatened and crept about *like the fire* which glideth stealthily through the house, or *like the tiger* stealing among the bushes while from the dark foliage, in broken flashes, gleameth ever and anon his yellow mottled flanks."

The line of life which Prometheus chooses is thus unmistakably introverted. He sacrifices all connection with the present, in order to create in anticipation the distant future.

It is very different with *Epimetheus*; he realizes that his aim is the world, and what the world values.

Hence he says to the angel: "Yet now I long for truth, and my soul lieth in thy hand; an it please thee, therefore, give me a conscience that will teach me '-tion' and '-ness' and every just precept."

Epimetheus cannot resist the temptation to fulfil his own destiny and submit himself to the "soulless" point of view. This junction with the world is immediately rewarded.

"And it came to pass, as Epimetheus rose up, that he felt his stature was increased and his courage more steadfast; he was at one with all his being, and his whole feeling was sound and mightily at ease. And thus he strode with bold steps through the valley, on a straight course, as one who feareth no man; and with a bold glance like a man inspired by the contemplation of his own riches."

He has, as Prometheus says, bartered his free soul for "-tion" and "-ness". The soul is lost to him in favour of his brother. He has followed his extraversion, and because this orientates him towards the external object, he is caught up in the desires and expectations of the world seemingly at first to his great advantage. He has become an extravert, after having lived many solitary years under the influence of his brother as an extravert *falsified* through imitation of the introvert.

Such involuntary "simulation dans le caractère" (Paulhan) occurs not infrequently. His conversion to true extraversion is, therefore, a step towards 'truth', and deservedly brings him a partial reward.

Whilst Prometheus, through the tyrannical claims of his soul, is hampered in every relation to the external object and has to make the cruellest sacrifices in the service of the soul, Epimetheus receives an immediately effective shield against the danger that most threatens the extravert, viz. a complete surrender to the external object. This protection consists in the conscience which is based upon traditional "right ideas"; and which, therefore, possesses that not-to-be-despised treasure of inherited worldly wisdom which is employed by public opinion in much the same fashion as the judge uses the penal code. This provides Epimetheus with a circumscribed code which restrains him from abandoning himself to objects in the same degree as Prometheus does to his soul. This is forbidden him by the conscience, which stands in the place of his soul. When Prometheus turns his back upon the world of men and its codified conscience, he falls into the hands of his cruel soul-mistress with her arbitrary power, and only through endless suffering does he make expiation for his neglect of the world.

The prudent restraint of a blameless conscience sets such a bandage over Epimetheus' eyes that he must blindly live his myth, but ever with the sense of doing right, since he dwells in constant harmony with general expectation, with success ever at his side since he fulfils the wishes of all. Thus men desire to see the King, and thus Epimetheus plays his part to the inglorious end, never forsaken by the strong backing of public approval. His self-assurance and self-righteousness, his unshakable confidence in his general worth, his unquestionable right-doing and good conscience, present an easily recognizable portrait of that extraverted character which Jordan depicted. Compare p. 102 and the following pages, describing the visit of Epimetheus to the sick Prometheus, where King Epimetheus is anxious to heal his suffering brother:

"And when all was duly accomplished the king stepped forth, and, supported by a friend on the left hand and on the right, he lifted up his voice in greeting and spake these *well-intentioned* words: 'My heart grieveth me on thy account, Prometheus, my beloved brother. But now take heart, for behold I have here a salve of virtue for every ill. Wond'rous is its healing power both in heat and in frost, and thou mayest use it alike to comfort or chastize thyself.'

"And speaking thus he took his staff, and bound the salve fast and proffered it him all warily with *weighty mien*. But hardly had Prometheus perceived the odour and aspect of the ointment than he turned his head away with disgust. Whereupon the King changed the tones of his voice, and began to cry aloud and to prophesy with great heat: 'Of a truth it seemeth thou hast need of greater punishment, since thy present fate doth not suffice to teach thee.' And, speaking thus, he drew a mirror from his cloak, and declared unto him all things from the beginning, and became very eloquent and knew all his faults."

The words of Jordan are speakingly illustrated in this scene: "Society must be pleased if possible; if it will not be pleased, it must be astonished; if it will neither be pleased nor astonished, it must be pestered and shocked."

In the above scene we find almost the same climax. In the Orient a rich man makes known his rank by never showing himself in public unless supported by two slaves. Epimetheus affects this pose in order to make an impression. Well-doing must at the same time be combined with admonition and moral discourse. And, as that does not produce an effect, the other must at least be horrified by the picture of his own baseness. Thus everything is aimed towards making an impression.

There is an American saying which runs: "In America, two sorts of men make good—the man who can *do* something, and the man who can *bluff* well." Which means that pretence is sometimes just as successful as actual performance. An extravert of this kind preferably makes his effect by *appearance*. The introvert tries to *force* the situation and to this end may even *abuse* his work.

If we fuse Prometheus and Epimetheus into one personality, we should have a man outwardly Epimethean and inwardly Promethean—an individual constantly torn by both tendencies, each seeking to enlist the ego finally on its side.

2. A Comparison of Spitteler's with Goethe's Prometheus

Considerable interest is to be found in comparing this Prometheus conception with that presented by Goethe. I believe I am justified in the conjecture that Goethe belongs more to the extraverted than the introverted type, while Spitteler would seem to belong to the latter. Only an exhaustive examination and analysis of Goethe's biography could succeed in establishing the justice of this assumption. My conjecture is based upon divers impressions, which I will refrain from discussing owing to my inability to furnish sufficient explanations.

The introverted attitude need not necessarily coincide with the Prometheus figure, by which I mean that the traditional Prometheus figure can also be interpreted quite differently. This other version is found, for instance, in Plato's Protagoras, where the distributer of vital powers to the creature fashioned by the gods in equal measure out of earth and fire is Epimetheus and not Prometheus. Prometheus (conforming with classical taste both in this situation and throughout the myth) is principally the cunning and inventive genius.

With Goethe two conceptions are presented. In the *Prometheus Fragment* of 1773 Prometheus is the defiant, self-sufficing, godlike, god-disdaining creator and artist. His soul is Minerva, daughter of Zeus. Prometheus' relation with Minerva has a clear similarity with the relation of Spitteler's Prometheus with his soul. Thus Prometheus says to Minerva:

> " From the beginning thy words have been celestial light to me;
> *Ever as tho' my soul spake unto herself,*
> She revealed herself;
> And in her of their own accord sister harmonies rang out,
> And when I deemed it was myself,
> A deity gave utterance;
> And did I dream a god was speaking,
> Lo ! 'twas mine own voice.
> And thus with thee and me,
> So one, so closely-knit are we,
> My love is thine eternally ! "

and further:

> " As the twilight glory of the departed sun
> Hovereth over the gloomy Caucasus,
> And encompasseth my soul with holy peace;
> Parting, yet ever present with me,
> So have my powers waxed strong,
> With every breath drawn from thy celestial air."

Thus Goethe's Prometheus is also dependent upon his soul. There is a strong resemblance to the relationship of Spitteler's Prometheus with his soul. Thus the latter says to his soul:

"And though I be stripped of all, yet am I rich beyond all measure so long as thou alone remainest with me, while 'my friend' falleth from thy sweet lips, and the light of thy proud and gracious countenance goeth not from me."

In spite of the similarity of the two figures and their relations with the soul, there remains, however, an essential difference. Goethe's Prometheus is a creator and artist; Minerva inspires his clay-images with life. Spitteler's Prometheus is suffering rather than creative; only his soul creates and her creating is secret and mysterious. She says to him in farewell:

"And now I depart from thee, for lo! a great work awaiteth me; 'tis a mighty deed, and I must hasten to accomplish it."

It would seem that, with Spitteler, the Promethean creativeness is allotted to the soul, while Prometheus himself merely suffers the pangs of a creative soul. But Goethe's Prometheus is self-active; he is essentially and exclusively creative, defying the gods out of the strength of his own creative power:

> "Who helped me
> Against the insolence of the Titans?
> Who rescued me from death?
> From slavery?
> Didst thou not thyself accomplish all
> O sacred, glowing heart?"

Epimetheus in this fragment is only sparingly sketched; he is throughout inferior to Prometheus; an advocate of collective feeling, who can only understand the service of the soul as obstinacy. Thus he says to Prometheus:

"Thou standest alone! Thy obstinacy knoweth not that bliss, when the gods and thou and all thou hast, thy world, thy heaven, are enfolded in one embracing unity."

Such indications as are to be found in the *Prometheus fragment* are too sparse to enable us to discern the character of Epimetheus. But the delineation of Goethe's Prometheus reveals a typical distinction from the Prometheus of Spitteler.

Goethe's Prometheus creates and works outwardly in the world; he peoples space with the figures he has fashioned and his soul has animated; he fills the earth with the offspring of his creation; he is both master and educator of man. But with the Prometheus of Spitteler everything goes to the world within and vanishes in the darkness of the soul's depths; just as he himself disappears from the world of men, even wandering from the narrow confines of his home, that he may become the more invisible. In accordance with the principle of compensation (a basic principle in our analytical psychology) the soul, *i.e.* the personification of the unconscious, must be especially active in such a case, preparing a work which, however, is as yet invisible.

Besides the passages already quoted, Spitteler gives us a complete description of this anticipated compensation-process. This we find in the *Pandora* interlude.

Pandora, that enigmatical figure in the Prometheus myth, is in Spitteler's creation the divine maid who lacks every relation with Prometheus but the very deepest. This conception is founded upon the version of the myth in which the woman who figures in the Prometheus relation is either Pandora or Athene.

The Prometheus of mythology has his soul-relation with Pandora or Athene, as in Goethe. But, in Spitteler, a noteworthy departure is introduced which, however, is already indicated in the historical myth, where the Prometheus-Pandora relation is contaminated with the Hephaestus-Athene analogy. With Goethe, the version Prometheus-Athene is preferred. But, in Spitteler,

Prometheus is removed from the divine sphere and is given a soul of his own. But his divinity and his original relation with Pandora in the myth are preserved as a cosmic counterplot, enacted independently in the celestial sphere. The happenings of the other world are the things that take place on the further side of our consciousness, that is in the unconscious. The Pandora interlude, therefore, is a presentation of what goes on in the unconscious during the suffering of Prometheus. When Prometheus vanishes from the world, destroying every link that binds him to mankind, he sinks into the depths of himself, into his walled-in isolation—his only object himself. And 'godlike' withal, for God, according to his definition, is the Being who is universally self-contained, who by virtue of his omnipresence has Himself as universal object. Naturally Prometheus does not feel in the least godlike— he is supremely wretched. After Epimetheus has come to spit upon his misery, the interlude in the other world begins, in that moment, naturally, when all Prometheus' relations to the world are suppressed to the extreme limit.

Experience shows that it is such moments that yield the unconscious contents the likeliest possibility of gaining independence and vitality, even to the point of overpowering consciousness [1].

Prometheus' condition in the unconscious is reflected in the following scene:

"And on the clouded morning of the same day, in a still and solitary meadow above all the worlds, wandered God, the creator of all life, pursuing the accursed round in obedience to the strange nature of his mysterious and sore sickness. For by reason of this sickness he could never make an end of his revolving task, might never find rest for his feet upon the weary path; but ever with measured stride day after day, and year after year, with heavy gait, and bowed head, with furrowed brow and distorted countenance, must he make the round of

---

[1] Cf. Jung, *The Content of the Psychoses* (*Collected Papers*, ch. xii); Idem, *Psychology of the Unconscious*.

the still meadow; whilst ever towards the mid-point of the circle sped his darkling eye. And as to-day he performed the daily inevitable round, while the more sorrowfully he sunk his head, and the more he dragged his heavy steps for weariness, as though the grievous vigils of the night had spent the very fountain of his life, there came to him through the night and the dim dawn, Pandora, his youngest daughter, who approached with uncertain steps, honouring the hallowed ground, and stood there humbly at his side, greeting him with modest glance, and questioned him with lips that held a reverential silence."

It is at once evident that God has the malady of Prometheus. Just as Prometheus allows all his passion, his whole libido to flow inwards to the soul, to his innermost depths, in complete dedication to his soul's service, his God also pursues his course round and round the pivot of the world, thus spending himself like Prometheus, whose whole being comes near to extinction. Which means that his libido has entirely passed over into the unconscious, where an equivalent must be prepared; for libido is energy which cannot disappear without a trace— it must always create an equivalent. The equivalent is Pandora and the gift she brings the father, for she brings him a precious jewel which she intends for the easing of men's woes.

If we translate this process into Prometheus' human sphere, it would mean that while Prometheus is suffering his 'godlike' state, his soul is preparing a work destined to alleviate the sufferings of mankind. His soul wants to get to men. Yet the work which his soul actually plans and carries out is not identical with the work of Pandora. Pandora's jewel is an unconsciously mirrored image which *symbolically* represents the actual work of Prometheus' soul. The text shows unmistakably what the jewel is. It is a God-deliverer, a renewal of the sun[1]. This longing expresses itself in the sickness of the God: he longs for

---

[1] Respecting this theme of the treasure and rebirth, I must refer the reader to my book *Psychology of the Unconscious*.

rebirth, and to this end his whole life-force flows back into the centre of the self, *i.e.* into the depths of the unconscious, out of which life is born anew. This may explain why the appearance of the jewel in the world is depicted in such curious assonance with the scene of the birth of Buddha in the Lalitavistara[1].

Pandora lays the jewel beneath a walnut tree (just as Maya bears her child under a fig-tree):—

" In the midnight shades beneath the tree it glows and sparkles and flames, and, like the morning star in the dark heavens, its diamond lightning flashes afar. Then sped on eager wing the bees and butterflies, which danced above the flower garden to play and sport around the *wonder child* . . . and out of the heavens came larks in steep descent, eager to pay homage to the *new and lovelier sun-countenance*, and as they drew near and beheld the bright radiance, their hearts swooned. . . . And, enthroned over all, fatherly and benign, *the chosen tree* with his giant crown and heavy mantle of green, held his kingly hands protectingly over the faces of his children. And all his ample branches bowed themselves lovingly down and leaned towards the earth as though they wished to screen and ward off curious eyes, jealous that they alone might enjoy the gift's unmerited favour; while all the myriads of gently-moving leaves fluttered and trembled with rapture, murmuring in joyous exultation a soft, clear-toned chorus in whispered accord : ' Who could know what lies hidden beneath this lowly roof, or guess the treasure reposing in our midst.' "

So with Maya, who, when her hour was come, bore her child beneath the Plaksa fig-tree, which drooped its sheltering crown to earth.

From the incarnate Bodhisattva unimaginable radiance extended over the world; Gods and Nature alike took part in the birth. As Bodhisattva treads the earth there grows at his feet an immense lotus, and standing in the lotus he views the world. Hence the Thibetan prayer: " *Om mani padme hum* " (" Oh! behold the jewel in the lotus ").

The moment of re-birth finds Bodhisattva beneath

[1] Spitteler, *l.c.*, p. 126.

the chosen bodhi-tree, where he becomes Buddha (the Enlightened One). This re-birth, or renewing, is accompanied by the same dazzling light, the same prodigies and apparitions of gods, as at the birth.

But in the kingdom of Epimetheus, where in place of the soul conscience reigns, the inestimable treasure gets lost. The angel raging over the stupidity of Epimetheus, reviles him:—" And hadst thou no soul, that like the wild and unreasoning beasts thou should'st hide thyself from the *wondrous Godhead?* "[1]

We see that Pandora's jewel is a renewal of the god, a new god; but this takes place in the heavenly sphere, *i.e.* in the unconscious. Such intimations of the process as penetrate consciousness are not understood by the Epimethean element, which dominates the relation to the world. This is elaborately presented by Spitteler in the following passages [*l.c.*, pp. 132 ff.], in which we see how the world, *i.e.* the conscious, with its rational attitude and objective orientation, is unfitted to make a true estimate of the value and significance of the jewel. For which reason the jewel is irretrievably lost.

The renewed god signifies a renewed attitude, *i.e.* a renewed possibility of intense life, a recovery of life; because, psychologically, God always signifies the greatest value, hence the greatest sum of libido, the greatest intensity of life, the *optimum* of psychological activity. Accordingly with Spitteler the Promethean, just as much as the Epimethean, adaptation proves to be inadequate.

The two tendencies are dissociated: the Epimethean attitude harmonizes with the actual conditions of the world; the Promethean, on the contrary, does not, which means that the latter must work out a renewal of life. This tendency creates also a new attitude to the world

[1] Spitteler depicts the famous "conscience" of Epimetheus as a little animal. It corresponds to the opportunist instinct of animals.

(the world to which the jewel is given), but of course without the consent of Epimetheus. Nevertheless, in the Pandora gift, as represented by Spitteler, it is not difficult to recognize a symbolic attempt to solve that same problem we discussed in the chapter on the Schiller *Letters*, viz. the problem of the reconciliation of the differentiated and undifferentiated functions.

Before we proceed further with this problem, however, we must turn back to Goethe's Prometheus. As we have already seen, there are unmistakable differences between the creative Prometheus of Goethe and the suffering figure of Spitteler. A further and more important distinction lies in the relation with Pandora. With Spitteler, Pandora is a being of the other world, a duplicate of the soul of Prometheus belonging to the divine sphere; but, with Goethe, she is altogether the creature and daughter of the Titan, and therefore in absolute dependence upon him. The relation of Goethe's Prometheus with Minerva puts him in the place of Vulcan, and the fact that Pandora is wholly his creature, and does not figure as a being of divine origin, makes him a creative deity, thus removing him altogether from the human sphere. Hence Prometheus says:

> " And when I deemed it was myself,
> A deity gave utterance.
> And did I dream a god was speaking,
> Lo ! 'twas mine own voice !"

With Spitteler, on the other hand, Prometheus is stripped of all divinity, even his soul is only an unofficial dæmon; his divinity becomes a law unto itself, quite severed from the human. Goethe's conception is classical to this extent: it emphasizes the divinity of the Titan. Accordingly Epimetheus, by contrast, must also be very inferior, whilst with Spitteler, he appears as a much more positive character. In Goethe's *Pandora*, we are fortunate in possessing a work which conveys a far more complete portrait of Epimetheus than the fragment so far discussed. There, Epimetheus introduces himself as follows :—

> " For me day and night are as one,
> And ever I bear with me the old evil of my name,
> For my progenitors named me Epimetheus.
> Thinking on the past, hasty-actioned ;
> Backward-turning, with troubled phantasies,
> To the melancholy opportunities of past days ;
> Such bitter toil was laid upon my youth,
> That turning impatiently towards life,
> I seized the present heedlessly,
> But only won tormenting burdens of fresh care."

With these words Epimetheus reveals his nature; he broods over the past, and can never free himself from Pandora, whom (according to the classical myth) he has taken to wife, *i.e.* he cannot rid himself of her imaged memory, although she herself has long since deserted him, leaving him her daughter Epimeleia (Anxiety), but taking with her Elpore (Hope).

Epimetheus is here so clearly figured that we are at once able to recognize which psychological function he represents. While Prometheus is still the same creator and modeller, who daily rises early from his couch with the same unconquerable urgency to create and to influence the world, Epimetheus is entirely given up to phantasies, dreams, and memories, full of anxious misgivings and troubled deliberations. Pandora appears as the creature of Hephæstus, rejected by Prometheus but chosen by Epimetheus for a wife. He says of her: " Even the pains which *such a treasure* brings are pleasure."

Pandora is to him a precious treasure, in fact the supreme value:

> " And forever is she mine, the glorious one !
> Supreme delight hath she revealed to me !
> I possessed Beauty, and Beauty hath enfolded me.
> In the wake of spring splendidly she came.

I knew her, I caught her, and there was it done.
Clouding thoughts vanished like a mist,
She lifted me from earth to Heaven.
Seek'st thou for words worthily to praise her?
Would'st thou extol her, she is already beyond thee.
Set thy best beside her, 'tis at once worthless.
Her words bewilder thee, but lo! she is right.
Thou mayest oppose her, the fight she doth win.
Thou faltereth in serving her, but yet art her thrall.
Goodness and love would she ever repay.
High esteem helpeth not, she bringeth it low.
She setteth her goal, and taketh her flight.
If she barreth thy way, at once she doth hold thee.
Would'st thou make her an offer, she'll raise thee thy bid.
Till thou givest riches and wisdom and all in the bargain.
She descendeth to earth in myriad forms,
She hovereth o'er waters, she strideth the plains,
In divine proportions she shineth, proclaimeth,
With form ennobling the inner meaning.
When giving, she lendeth him power supreme.
Radiant with youth she came, in womanly form."

For Epimetheus, as these verses clearly show, Pandora has the significance of a soul-image—she represents his soul; hence her divine power, her unshakable superiority. Wherever such attributes are conferred upon certain personalities we may with certainty conclude that such personalities are *symbol-bearers;* in other words *imagines* of projected unconscious contents. For it is the contents of the unconscious which operate with the supreme power above described, and especially in the way incomparably seized by Goethe in the line:

" Would'st thou make her an offer, she'll raise thee thy bid."

In this line the characteristic affective reinforcement of certain conscious contents through association with analogous unconscious contents is beautifully pictured.

This reinforcement has in it something dæmonic and compelling, and thus has a 'divine' or 'devilish'-effect.

We have already described Goethe's Prometheus figure as extraverted. It is still the same in his *Pandora*, although here, the relation of Prometheus with the soul, the unconscious feminine principle is lacking. Instead, however, Epimetheus appears as the introvert, directed towards his inner world. He broods, he recalls memories out of the grave of the past, he "reflects". He differs absolutely from Spitteler's Epimetheus. We might say, therefore, that here (in Goethe's Pandora) the position indicated earlier—where Prometheus becomes the extraverted man of affairs, and Epimetheus the brooding introvert—has actually transpired. This Prometheus has somewhat the same quality in extraverted form as Spitteler's in the form of the introvert. In the 'Pandora', on the contrary, Prometheus is definitely creative for collective ends; he has set up a regular manufactory in his mountain, where necessary articles for the whole world are produced. Hence, he is cut off from his inner world, which relation now devolves upon Epimetheus, namely that secondary and purely reactive thinking and feeling of the extravert which possess all the characteristics of the relatively undifferentiated function. Thus it comes about that Epimetheus is unconditionally pledged to Pandora, because in every respect she is superior to him. Psychologically, this means that the conscious Epimethean function of the extravert, namely that phantastic, brooding, ruminating fancy, becomes intensified by the intervention of the soul. If the soul is coupled with the relatively undifferentiated function, we must draw the conclusion that the superior, *i.e.* the differentiated, function is too collective. It is in the service of the collective conscience[1], and not in the service of freedom. Wherever such a case occurs (and it happens very frequently), the less differentiated function, *i.e.* the "other side", is reinforced by a pathological egocentricity. The extravert fills up his spare time with melancholic or hypochondriacal musing; he

[1] Spitteler's "*-heit*" und "*-keit*" ("-tion" and "-ness").

may even have hysterical phantasies and other symptoms[1]; while the introvert wraps himself about with compulsive feelings of inferiority, which take him unawares and put him into a no less dismal plight[2].

The resemblance between the Prometheus of the "Pandora" and the Prometheus of Spitteler goes no further. He is merely the collective 'itch for action', which in its onesidedness signifies a repression of the erotic. His son Phileros ("he whom Eros loves") is simply erotic passion; for, as the son of his father, he must, as is often the case with children, retrieve under unconscious compulsion the unlived lives of his parents.

The daughter of Epimetheus, the unreflecting, the type that acts heedlessly after first deliberating, is significantly Epimeleia (Anxiety). Phileros loves Epimeleia, Pandora's daughter, and thus the guilt of Prometheus, who has rejected Pandora, is expiated. Prometheus and Epimetheus become simultaneously reconciled, whereby the Promethean industry turns out to be unrecognized erotism, while Epimetheus' persistent reference to the past is shown to be rational misgivings, which might well check the equally persistent productiveness of Prometheus and restrain it within reasonable bounds.

This effort of Goethe to find a solution, which appears to be evolved from an extraverted psychology, brings us back to Spitteler's attempt, which we left for the time being in order to discuss Goethe's Prometheus figure.

Spitteler's Prometheus, like his God, turns away from the world, the periphery, and gazes inwards to the middle point, that "narrow passage" of re-birth. This concentration, or introversion, brings the libido gradually into the

[1] In place of these, a compensatory outburst of sociability may appear and a more intense impulse to social claims; in the eager pursuit of which forgetfulness is sought.
[2] As compensation, a morbid and feverish activity may appear, which also serves the purposes of repression.

unconscious, whereby the activity of the unconscious contents is increased—the soul begins to "work," and creates a product which tends to emerge from the unconscious into consciousness. The conscious, however, has two attitudes—the Promethean, which withdraws the libido from the world, introverting without giving out, and the Epimethean, which is constantly responding in a soulless fashion, held by the claims of external objects. When Pandora makes her gift to the world it means, psychologically, that an unconscious product of great value is on the point of reaching extraverted consciousness, *i.e.* it is seeking a relation to the real world. Although the Promethean side, *i.e.* the artist intuitively apprehends the great value of the work, his personal relations to the world are so subordinated to the tyranny of tradition that the work is merely appreciated as a work of art and not at its real significance, viz. as a symbol that promises a renewal of life. In order to convert it from a purely æsthetic interest into a living reality, it must also reach life, and be accepted and lived in the sphere of reality. But if the attitude is mainly introverted and given to abstraction, the extraverted function is inferior, and is therefore under the spell of collective restrictiveness. This restrictiveness prevents the soul-created symbol from living. Thus the jewel gets lost; but one cannot really live if "God", *i.e.* the highest symbolic expression of living value, cannot also become a living fact. Hence the loss of the jewel also signifies the beginning of Epimetheus' downfall.

And now the enantiodromia begins. Instead of taking for granted, as every rationalist and optimist is inclined to do, that a good state will be followed by a better, since everything tends towards "upward development", the man of blameless conscience and universally acknowledged moral principles makes a compact with Behemoth and his evil host, and even the divine children entrusted to his care are bartered to the devil.

Psychologically, this means that the collective, undifferentiated attitude to the world stifles man's highest values; it thus becomes a destructive power, whose influence multiplies until a point is reached when the Promethean side, namely the ideal and abstract attitude, places itself at the service of the soul, and, like a true Prometheus, kindles for the world a new fire. Spitteler's Prometheus has to come out of his solitude and tell men, even at the risk of his life, that they are in error, and where they err. He must acknowledge the relentlessness of truth, just as Goethe's Prometheus, in Phileros, has to experience the relentlessness of love.

That the destructive element in the Epimethean attitude is actually this traditional and collective restrictiveness is clearly shown in Epimetheus' raging fury against the "lamb", an obvious caricature of traditional Christianity. In this affect something gleams through which is already familiar to us in the approximately contemporary Asses' Feast of Zarathustra. It is the expression of a contemporary tendency.

Mankind is constantly inclined to forget that what was once good does not remain good eternally. He goes along the old ways that once were good, long after they have become injurious to him; only through the greatest sacrifices and with untold suffering can he rid himself of this delusion, and discern that what was good once is now perhaps grown old and is good no longer. This is so in the little things as in the big. The ways and customs of his childhood, once so sublimely good, he can barely lay aside even when their harmfulness has long since been proved. The same, only on a gigantic scale, is the case with historical changes of attitude. A general attitude corresponds with a religion, and changes of religion belong to the most painful moments in the world's history. In this respect our age has a blindness without parallel. We think we have only to declare an acknowledged form of faith to be incorrect or invalid, to become psychologically free of all the traditional effects of the Christian or Judaic religion. We believe in enlightenment, as if an intellectual change of opinion had somehow a deeper influence on emotional processes, or indeed upon the unconscious! We entirely forget that the religion of the last two thousand years is a psychological attitude, a definite form and manner of adaptation to inner and outer experience, which moulds a definite form of civilization; it has, thereby, created an atmosphere which remains wholly uninfluenced by any intellectual disavowal. The intellectual change is, of course, symptomatically important as a hint of coming possibilities, but the deeper levels of the psyche continue for a long time to operate in the former attitude, in accordance with psychic inertia. In this way the unconscious has preserved paganism alive. The ease with which the classic spirit springs again into life can be observed in the Renaissance. The readiness with which the vastly older primitive spirit reappears can be seen in our own time, even better perhaps than in any other historically known epoch.

The more deeply rooted the attitude, the more effective must be the means that shall set it free. "Écrasez l'infame", the cry of the age of enlightenment, heralded the religious upheaval within the French revolution, which, viewed psychologically, meant nothing but an essential readjustment of attitude, which, however, was lacking in universality. The problem of a general change of attitude has never slept since that time; it leaped to the surface again in many prominent minds of the nineteenth century. We have seen how Schiller sought to master the problem. In Goethe's treatment of the Prometheus and

Epimetheus problem we again recognize the attempt to make some sort of reconciliation between the more highly differentiated function, corresponding with the Christian ideal of favouring the good, and the relatively undifferentiated function whose repression and non-recognition corresponds with the Christian ideal of rejecting the evil [1]. In the symbols of Prometheus and Epimetheus, the difficulty which Schiller endeavoured to master philosophically and æsthetically, is shrouded in the garment of the classical myth. Therewith something happens which, as I pointed out earlier, is altogether typical and regular: namely, when a man meets a difficult task which he cannot master with the means at his command, a retrograde movement of the libido automatically begins, *i.e.* a regression occurs. The libido draws away from the problem of the moment, becomes introverted, and activates a more or less primitive analogy of the conscious situation in the unconscious together with an earlier mode of adaptation. This law determines Goethe's choice of a symbol: Prometheus was the saviour who brought life and fire to mankind languishing in darkness. Goethe's deep scholarship could easily have found another saviour; the actual form of the determinant, therefore, is not sufficiently explained. The explanation must lie rather in the classical spirit, which was felt to contain an absolutely compensatory value for that particular time (the turning point of the eighteenth century); it was expressed in every possible way, in æsthetics, philosophy, morals, even politics (philhellenism). It was the Paganism of antiquity, glorified as "freedom", "naïveté", "beauty", and so on, which responded to the yearnings of that time. This yearning, as Schiller so clearly shows, arose from

[1] Cf. Goethe's *Geheimnisse*. There the Rosicrucian solution is attempted, namely the reconciliation of the rose and the cross, Dionysos and Christ. The poem leaves us cold. One cannot pour new wine into old bottles.

a feeling of incompleteness, of spiritual barbarism, of moral servitude, of ugliness. These feelings proceeded collectively and individually from a one-sided valuation, whose inevitable consequences enabled the psychological dissociation between the more highly and the less differentiated functions to become manifest. The Christian dismemberment of mankind into a valuable and worthless portion was unbearable to that age, which, compared with earlier times, was much more highly sensitized. Sinfulness had stumbled upon the idea of an everlasting, natural beauty, a conception which was already possible for that age; it reached backwards, therefore, to an older time when the idea of sinfulness had not yet disrupted the unity of mankind, when both the higher and lower in human nature could still live together in complete naïveté without offending moral or æsthetic susceptibilities.

But the effort towards a regressive renaissance shared the fate of the *Prometheus Fragment* and the *Pandora*; it was still-born. The classical solution would no longer do, for the intervening centuries of Christianity, with their profound tides of spiritual experience, could not be denied. Hence the penchant for the antique had to content itself with a gradual attenuation into the medieval form. This process becomes manifest in Goethe's *Faust*, where the problem is seized by the horns. The divine wager between good and evil is accepted. Faust, the medieval Prometheus, enters the lists with Mephistopheles, the medieval Epimetheus, and makes a pact with him. And here the problem is already so well focussed that we can see that Faust and Mephisto are one and the same individual. The Epimethean element which refers all things to the retrospective angle, and leads them back into the original chaos of "fluid shapes of possibilities," is sharpened into the form of the devil whose evil power opposes every living thing with "the cold devil's fist" and who would force the light back into the maternal darkness from which it was born. The devil has throughout a true Epimethean thinking, the "nothing but" intellectual attitude, which reduces everything living to original nothingness. The naïve passion of Epimetheus for the Pandora of Prometheus becomes Mephistopheles' devil's plot for the soul of Faust. And the cunning foresight of Prometheus in declining the divine Pandora is expiated in the tragedy of the Gretchen episode and the yearning for Helen, with its belated fulfilment, and in the endless ascent to the heavenly Mothers ("The eternal feminine draws us upwards").

We have the Promethean defiance of the accepted gods in the figure of the medieval magician. The magician has preserved a trace of primitive paganism[1]; in himself there is an element still untouched by the Christian cleavage, *i.e.* he has access to the unconscious that is still pagan, where the opposites still lie together in their primeval naïveté, beyond the reach of "sinfulness," but liable, when accepted into conscious life, to beget evil as well as good with the same primeval and therefore dæmonic force. ("A part of that power which ever willeth evil while ever creating the good")[2].

He is, therefore, a destroyer as well as a deliverer. Hence this figure is pre-eminently fitted to become the bearer of the reconciling symbol. Moreover, the medieval magician has laid aside the antique naïveté which is no longer possible, and through stern experience has thoroughly absorbed the Christian atmosphere. His pagan element immediately urges him to a complete Christian denial and mortification of self; his craving for deliverance is so imperative that every possible means

[1] We frequently find that it is the representatives of older nationalities who possess magical powers. In India it is the Nepaulese, in Europe the gipsies, and in Protestant regions the Capuchin friars.
[2] *Faust*, Part I, Sc. i: Studierzimmer.

must be seized. But in the end the Christian attempt at solution also fails, and then it is seen that it is precisely the longing for deliverance, the obstinacy and self-confidence of the heathen element, which offers the real possibility for deliverance, because the anti-christian symbol affords a possibility for the acceptance of evil. Goethe's intuition, therefore, has apprehended the problem with enviable clarity. It is certainly characteristic that the other more superficial attempts at solution—the *Prometheus Fragment*, the *Pandora*, and the Rosicrucian compromise[1] with its attempt at a syncretism of Dionysian joyousness with Christian self-sacrifice — remained uncompleted.

Faust's redemption begins with his death. His life sustains the Promethean divine character which only falls from him in death, *i.e.* with his re-birth. Psychologically, this means that the Faust attitude must cease before the unity of the individual can be accomplished. The figure which first appeared as Gretchen and then on a higher level as Helen, and finally became exalted into the Mater Gloriosa, is a symbol that I cannot now exhaust of its manifold meanings. I will merely point out that it deals with the same archaic image with which the Gnosis was so profoundly concerned, viz. the idea of the divine harlot, Eve, Helen, Mary, and Sophia-Achamoth.

3. The Significance of the Reconciling Symbol

If from the standpoint now gained we glance once more at the unconscious elaboration of the problem by Spitteler, we appreciate at once that the compact with evil originates, not in the *aim* of Prometheus, but in the thoughtlessness of Epimetheus, who only possesses a collective conscience and no power of discrimination for the

[1] *Die Geheimnisse.*

things of the inner world. As invariably happens with the collective standpoint that is orientated to the object, he allows himself to be determined exclusively by collective values, and consequently overlooks what is new and original.

Current collective values are certainly mensurable by the objective standard, but only a free and unfettered valuation—a matter of living feeling—can yield a true estimate of the thing that is newly created. But such an appreciation belongs to the man possessing a soul, and not merely relations to external objects.

The downfall of Epimetheus begins with the loss of the new-born, divine image. His incontestably moral thinking, feeling, and acting in no way hinder the evil, hollow, and destructive from creeping in. This invasion of evil signifies a conversion of something previously good into something definitely harmful. In this fashion Spitteler expresses the idea that the moral principle hitherto prevailing, although excellent to begin with, loses with the lapse of time its essential connection with life, since it no longer embraces the abundance and variety of life. The rationally correct is too meagre a concept upon which to found a hope for an adequate and permanent expression of life in its totality. But the irrational occurrence of the divine birth stands beyond the frontiers of the rational kingdom. Psychologically, the divine birth heralds the fact that a new symbol, a new expression of supreme vital intensity, is being created. Every Epimethean element in man and every Epimethean man is incapable of comprehending this event. Yet from this moment the supreme intensity of life is to be found only upon the new line. Every other direction falls gradually away, dissolving into oblivion.

The new symbol, the bestower of life, springs from Prometheus' love for his soul, a figure pregnant with dæmonic characters. One may be sure, therefore, that, interwoven in the new symbol with its living beauty, there is also the element of evil, for, if not, it would lack the glow of life as well as beauty since life and beauty are naturally indifferent to morality. For this reason, Epimethean collectivity finds no value in it. For it is quite blinded by its one-sided moral standpoint, which is identical with the "lamb", *i.e.* the traditional Christian standpoint. The raging of Epimetheus against the "lamb" is therefore merely "Écrasez l'infame" in a new form, a revolt against the established Christianity which was unable to comprehend the new symbol wherewith to guide life upon a new way.

Such a reaction, however, might remain entirely unproductive were there no poets who could fathom and read the collective unconscious. They are the first in their time to divine the darkly moving mysterious currents, and to express them according to the limits of their capacity in more or less speaking symbols.

They make known, like true prophets, the deep motions of the collective unconscious, "the will of God" in the language of the Old Testament, which, in the course of time, must inevitably come to the surface as a general phenomenon. The redemptive significance of the deed of Prometheus, the downfall of Epimetheus, his reconciliation with his soul-serving brother, and the vengeance Epimetheus wreaks upon the "lamb"—recalling in its note of cruelty the scene (Dante, *Inferno* xxxii.) between Ugolino and the Archbishop Ruggieri—prepares a solution of the conflict that involves a deadly revolt against traditional collective morality.

We may assume in a poet of modest limits that the summit of his work does not overtop the height of his personal joys, sorrows, and aspirations. But with Spitteler his work quite transcends personal destiny. For this reason his solution of the problem does not stand alone.

From here to Zarathustra, the breaker of the tables, is only a step. Stirner also joined the company after Schopenhauer had first conceived the idea of denial. He spoke of the denial of the world. Psychologically, 'the world' means how I see the world, my attitude to the world; thus the world can be regarded as 'my will' and 'my presentation.' In itself the world is indifferent. It is my Yes and No that create the differences.

The idea of negation, therefore, is concerned with an attitude to the world, and particularly Schopenhauer's attitude to it, which on the one hand is purely intellectual and rational, while on the other it is a mystical identity with the world in his most individual feeling. This attitude is introverted; it suffers therefore from its typological antithesis. But Schopenhauer's work in many ways transcends his personality. It voices what was obscurely thought and felt by many thousands. Similarly with Nietzsche: preëminently his *Zarathustra* brings to light the contents of the collective unconscious of our time; in him, therefore, we also find the same distinguishing features: iconoclastic revolt against the conventional moral atmosphere, and the acceptance of the "ugliest man", which in Nietzsche leads to that shattering unconscious tragedy presented in *Zarathustra*. But what creative minds bring up out of the collective unconscious also actually exists, and sooner or later must make its appearance in collective psychology. Anarchy, regicide, the constant increase and splitting off of an anarchistic element upon the extreme socialist left, with an avowed programme that is absolutely hostile to culture—these are phenomena of mass-psychology, which were long adumbrated by poets and creative thinkers.

We cannot, therefore, afford to be indifferent to the poets, since in their principal works and deepest inspirations they create from the very depths of the collective unconscious, voicing aloud what others only dream. But what the poets proclaim is only the symbol in which they sense æsthetic pleasure, without any consciousness of its true meaning.

That poets and thinkers have an educational influence upon their own and succeeding epochs I would be the last to dispute; but it seems to me that their influence essentially consists in the fact that they voice rather more clearly and resoundingly what all know, and, only in so far as they express this universal unconscious "knowledge", have they any considerable effect, whether educational or seductive. The greatest and most immediately suggestive effect is gained by the poet who knows how to express the most superficial levels of the unconscious in a successful form. Should the vision of the creative mind search more deeply, it becomes all the more strange to mankind in the mass, and provokes an even greater resistance in all those who occupy conspicuous positions in the eyes of the mass. The mass does not understand it although unconsciously living what it expresses; not because the poet proclaims it, but because its life issues from the collective unconscious into which he has peered. The more thoughtful of the nation certainly comprehend something of his message, but, because his utterance corresponds with events already developing among the mass and also because he anticipates their own aspirations, they hate the creator of such thoughts, not at all viciously, but merely from the instinct of self-protection. When apprehension of the collective unconscious reaches a depth where conscious expression can no longer grasp its content, it cannot be decided at once whether it is a morbid product we have to deal with, or whether something quite incomprehensible because of its extraordinary depth. An imperfectly understood yet deeply significant content has usually a somewhat morbid character. And morbid products are as a rule significant. But in both cases the approach is difficult. If it ever arrives at all, the fame of these creators is posthumous, and often delayed for several centuries. Ostwald's opinion that, at the most, a highly gifted mind of to-day would obtain recognition within a decade or so was not, I hope, intended to reach beyond the realm of technical discoveries; for, if so, such an assertion would be extremely ludicrous.

There is another point of particular importance to which I feel I ought to refer. The solution of the problem in *Faust*, in the *Parsifal* of Wagner, in Schopenhauer, even in Nietzsche's *Zarathustra*, is *religious*. That Spitteler is also drawn towards a religious setting is therefore not to be wondered at. When a problem is accepted as religious, it gains a psychological significance of immense importance; a value is involved which relates to the whole of man, hence also the unconscious (the realm of the gods, the other world, etc.). With Spitteler the religious form possesses such an exuberant wealth that its specially religious quality loses in depth, although it certainly gains in mythological richness, in archaic as well as prospective symbolism. The luxuriating mythological web makes the work difficult of approach, as it also tends to shroud the problem from comprehension and a possible solution. The abstruse, grotesque, and uncouth quality that always clings to mythological exuberance hinders the flow of sympathy, alienates one's sensibility from the work, and gives the whole work a rather disagreeable suggestion of a certain type of originality which can only successfully escape the charge of psychic abnormality by a painstaking and scrupulous adaptation in other directions. However fatiguing and unpalatable such mythological exuberance may be, it has the advantage of allowing the symbol to expand and develop in a relatively unconscious unfolding, whereby the conscious wits of the poet are quite at a loss as to how to assist in the expression of the meaning. Thus he labours with single mind in the husbandry of the mythological yield and its plastic development. Spitteler's poem differs, in this respect, both from *Faust* and from *Zarathustra*, for in these works there is a greater conscious participation on the part of the poet in the meaning of the symbol; accordingly the mythological luxuriance in *Faust* and the intellectual exuberance in *Zarathustra* are pruned down to the advantage of the desired solution. Both *Faust* and *Zarathustra* are, for this reason, far more *beautiful* than Spitteler's *Prometheus*. But the latter, as a more or less faithful image of the actual processes of the collective unconscious, has deeper *truth*.

Faust and *Zarathustra* are of the very greatest assistance in the individual mastery of the problem in question; but Spitteler's *Prometheus and Epimetheus*, thanks to its abundant harvest of mythological material, provides not only a more general appreciation of the problem, but also its manner of appearance in collective life. The principal revelation of the unconscious religious contents in Spitteler's work, is the symbol of the *God-renewal*, which is subsequently more fully expanded in the *Olympian Spring*. This symbol appears in the most intimate connection with the type and function antithesis, and manifestly bears the significance of an effort to find the solution in a renewal of the general attitude, which in the language of the unconscious is expressed as a renewal of God. The God-renewal is a familiar archetypal image, that is quite universal; I need only mention the whole complex of the dying and rejuvenating God with all its mythological precursors, down to the re-charging of fetishes and churingas with magical force. The image affirms a transformation of attitude by which a new potential of energy, a new manifestation of life, a new fruitfulness have come into being. This latter analogy explains the connection — for which there is abundant proof—

THE TYPE-PROBLEM IN POETRY 241

between the God-renewal and seasonal and vegetational phenomena.

There is a natural inclination to confine astral or lunar myths to these seasonal and vegetational analogies. In so doing, however, we entirely lose sight of the fact that a myth, like everything psychic, cannot be solely conditioned by outer events. The psychic product brings with it its own inner conditions, so that one might assert with equal right that the myth is purely psychological and merely uses the facts of meteorological or astronomical processes as material for expression. The arbitrariness and absurdity of so many of the primitive mythical assertions make the latter version appear more frequently applicable than any other.

The psychological point of departure for the god-renewal corresponds with an increasing divergence in the manner of application of psychic energy or libido. One half of the libido moves towards a Promethean, while the other towards an Epimethean, manner of application. Such an opposition is, of course, a very great hindrance not only in society but also in the individual. Hence the optimum of life recedes more and more from the opposing extremes, and seeks out a middle way, which must necessarily be irrational and unconscious, just because the opposites are rational and conscious.

Since the middle position, as a function of mediation between the opposites, possesses an irrational character, it appears projected in the form of a reconciling God, a Messiah or Mediator. To our Western forms of religion, which are still too primitive in matters of discernment or understanding, the new possibility of life appears in the figure of a God or Saviour, who, in his fatherly care and love and from his own inner resolve, puts an end to the division, in his own time and season, for reasons we are not fitted to understand. The childishness of this con-

T

ception is self-evident. The East has for thousands of years been familiar with this process, and has founded thereon a psychological doctrine of salvation which brings the way of deliverance within the compass of human intention. Thus both the Indian and the Chinese religions, as also Buddhism which combines the spheres of both, possess the idea of a redeeming middle path of magical efficacy which is attainable through a conscious attitude. The Vedic conception is a conscious attempt to find release from the pairs of opposites in order to gain the path of redemption.

(a) The Brahmanic Conception of the Problem of the Opposites

The Sanskrit term for the pair of opposites in the psychological sense is *Dvandva*. Besides the meaning of pair (particularly man and woman), it denotes strife, quarrel, combat, doubt, etc. The pairs of opposites were ordained by the Creator of the world:

"Moreover, in order to distinguish actions, he separated merit from demerit, and he caused the creature to be affected by the *pairs of opposites*, such as pain and pleasure." [1]

As further pairs of opposites, the commentator Kulluka names desire and anger, love and hate, hunger and thirst, care and folly, honour and disgrace. "Beneath the pairs of opposites must this world suffer without ceasing." [2]

Not to allow oneself to be influenced by the pairs of opposites (*nirdvandva*—free, untouched by the opposites), but to raise oneself above them, is then an essentially ethical task, since freedom from the opposites leads to redemption. In the following passages I give a series of examples:

1. From the book of Manu: [3] "He who becometh indifferent towards all objects by the disposition of his feelings attaineth

---

[1] *Mānava-Dharmaçāstra*, i, 26 *Sacred Books of the East*, xxv (p. 13).
[2] *Rāmāyana*, ii, 84, 20.
[3] *Mānava-Dharmaçāstra*, vi, 80 ff., pp. 212-3.

eternal blessedness, as much in this world as after death. Whosoever in this wise hath gradually surrendered all bonds and freed himself from all the opposites, reposeth in Brahman." [1]

2. The famous exhortation of Krishna [2]: " The Vedas speak of the three Gunas [3]: nevertheless, O Arjuna be thou indifferent concerning the three Gunas, indifferent towards the opposites (*nirdvandva*), ever steadfast in courage ".

3. In the *Yogasutra* of Patanjali we find [4]: " Then (in deepest contemplation, *samadhi*) cometh that state which is untroubled by the opposites." [5]

4. Concerning the wise one: [6] " Both good and evil deeds doth he shake off in that place; they who are known unto him and are his friends take upon them his good deeds, but they who are not his friends, his evil works: and like one who faring fast in a chariot looketh down upon the chariot wheels, so upon day and night, upon good and evil deeds and upon all opposites, doth he look down; but he, freed from good and evil deeds, as knower of Brahman, entereth into Brahman."

5. (To the one who is called to meditation). " Whosoever overcometh desire and anger, the cleaving to the world and the lust of the senses; whoso maketh himself free from the opposites, and relinquisheth the feeling of self (above all self-seeking), that one is released from expectation." [7]

6. Pandu, who desires to be a hermit, says: " Clothed with dust, housed under the open sky, I will take my lodging at the root of a tree, surrendering all things loved as well as unloved, tasting neither grief nor pleasure, forfeiting blame and praise alike, neither cherishing hope, nor offering respect, free from the opposites (*nirdvandva*), with neither fortune nor belongings." [8]

7. " Whosoever remaineth the same in living as in dying, in fortune as in misfortune, whether gaining or losing, in love and in hatred, will be redeemed. Whoso nothing pursueth and regardeth nothing of small account, whoso is free from the opposites (*nirdvandva*), whose soul knoweth no passion—he is wholly delivered. Whosoever doeth neither right nor wrong, renouncing

---

[1] Brahman is the designation generally applied to the Supreme Soul (*paramātman*), or impersonal, all-embracing, divine essence, the original source and ultimate goal of all that exists. (*Encyclo. Brit.*)

[2] *Bhagavadgītā*, ii.

[3] Qualities or factors or constituents of the world.

[4] Deussen, *Allgemeine Geschichte d. Philosophie*, i, 3, pp. 511 ff.

[5] Yoga is well-known as a system of training for the attainment of the higher states of redemption.

[6] *Kaushītakī-Upanishad*, 1-4.

[7] *Tejovindu-Upanishad*, 3.   [8] *Mahābhārata*, 1-119, 8 ff.

the treasure of (good and evil) deeds heaped up in former lives, whose soul is tranquil when the bodily elements vanish away, whoso holdeth himself free from the opposites, that one is redeemed."[1]

8. "Full thousand years have I enjoyed the things of sense, while still the craving for them springeth up unceasingly. These, therefore, will I renounce and direct my mind upon Brahma; indifferent towards the opposites (*nirdvandva*) and, freed from the feeling of self-will, I will roam with the wild (creatures)."[2]

9. "Through forbearance to all creatures, through the ascetic life, through self-discipline and freedom from desire, through the vow and the blameless life, through equanimity and endurance of the opposites, will man share the bliss in Brahma, who is without qualities."[3]

10. "Whosoever is free from overweening vanity and delusion and hath overcome the frailty of dependence, whoso remaineth faithful to the highest Atman, whose desires are extinguished, who remaineth untouched by the opposites of pleasure and pain—that one released from delusion shall attain that imperishable state."[4]

It follows from these quotations[5] that it is external opposites, such as heat and cold, which must first be denied psychic participation in order that extreme affective fluctuations like love and hatred, etc., may also be avoided.

Affective fluctuations are the natural and constant accompaniments of every psychic antithesis—hence of every antagonism of ideas, whether moral or otherwise. Such affects, as we know by experience, are proportionately greater, the more the exciting factor affects the totality of the individual. The meaning of the Indian aim is therefore clear: its purpose is to redeem human nature altogether from the opposites, to attain a new life in Brahman, to win a state of deliverance, and at the same

[1] *Mahābhārata*, xiv, 19-4 ff.
[2] *Bhāgavata-Purāna*, ix, 19, 18 ff. "After he hath put off silence and non-silence, thus will he become a Brahmana." *Brihadāranyaka-Upanishad*, 3, 5.
[3] *Bhāgavata-Purāna*, iv, 22, 24.
[4] *Garuda-Purāna*, 16, 110.
[5] I am indebted to the kind help of Dr Abegg of Zürich, the Sanskrit specialist, for these, to me somewhat inaccessible, citations (Nos. 193, 201-5)

time God. Brahman, therefore, must signify the irrational union of the opposites—hence their final overcoming. Although Brahman, as the cause and creator of the world, has created the opposites, they must again be resolved in Him, if He is to signify the state of redemption. In the following passages I give a group of examples:

1. "Brahman is *sat* and *asat*, the existing and non-existing, *satyam* and *asatyam*, reality and unreality." [1]
2. "In truth, there are two forms of Brahman; the formed and the formless, the mortal and the immortal, the solid and the fluid, the definite and the indefinite." [2]
3. "God, the creator of all things, the great Self, who dwelleth eternally in the hearts of men, is discernible by the heart, by the soul, by the mind; who knoweth that, gaineth immortality. When the light hath dawned, then is there neither day nor night, neither being nor not-being." [3]
4. "Two things are eternal, in the infinite supreme Brahman contained, *knowing* and *not-knowing*. Perishable is not-knowing, eternal knowing, yet He who as lord controlleth them is the Other." [4]
5. "In the heart of this creature is concealed the Self, smaller than the small, greater than the great. By the grace of the Creator a man freed from desires and released from affliction beholdeth the majesty of the Self. Though sitting still, he wandereth far; he extendeth over all, yet lieth in one place. Who is there, beside myself, able to know this God, who rejoiceth yet rejoiceth not?" [5]
6. "One there is—without stirring and yet swift as thought—
   Speeding hence, not even o'ertaken by the gods—
   Standing still, it surpasseth all the runners—the wind-god
   Wove among the strands of its being the primordial water.
   Resting, it is yet ever restless:
   It is distant and yet so near.
   It is indwelling in all things,
   Yet is it outside everything." [6]

---

[1] Deussen, i, 2, p. 117, *l.c.*
[2] *Brihadāranyaka-Upanishad*, 2, 3 (*Sacred Books* xv) (Definite —" *sat* ", lit. being or this, and indefinite—" *tya* ", lit. that or hereafter).
[3] *Svetāsvatara-Upanishad*, 4, 17 ff. [4] *Svetāsvatara-Upanishad*, 5, 1.
[5] Deussen here translates: "He sitteth, yet wandereth further. He lieth, yet everywhere hovereth. Concerning the swaying hither and thither of God, who understandeth it save myself?" *Katha-Upanishad*, 1, 2, 20 ff.
[6] *Iça-Upanishad*, 4-5 (Deussen)

7. "Like as a falcon or an eagle tiring after wide circuits in the windy spaces of heaven foldeth his wings and droppeth to quiet cover, so urgeth the spirit toward that state whose repose no desire troubleth nor delusion entereth.

"That is its true being, from yearnings, from evil, and from fear delivered. Like unto a man in the embrace of a beloved wife, unaware of things without or things within, is the spirit that is embraced by the all-discerning self." (Brahman).[1]

"This one second is an ocean, free from duality: this, O King! is the world of Brahman. Thus Yajnavalkya taught him. This is his highest goal, this his dearest success, this his greatest world and this his supreme rapture."[2]

8. "What is agile, flying and yet standing still.
What breatheth yet draweth no breath, what closeth the eyes,
What beareth the whole manifold Earth,
And bringeth all together in unity."[3]

These quotations show, that Brahman is the reconciliation and dissolution of the opposites—hence standing beyond them as an irrational factor.[4] It is a divine essence as well as the Self (in a lesser degree, of course, than the analogous Atman-concept); it is also a definite psychological state, characterized by detachment from emotional fluctuations. Since suffering is an affect, the release from affects means deliverance. Release from the fluctuations of affects, which means from the tension of opposites, is synonymous with the way of redemption that gradually leads to the state of Brahman. In a certain sense, therefore, Brahman is not only a state, but also a process, a "durée créatrice". It is, therefore, not surprising that the symbolical expression of this Brahman concept in the Upanishads makes use of all those symbols which I have termed libido symbols[5]. The following are a few appropriate examples:

[1] This describes the resolution of the subject-object antithesis.
[2] *Brihadâranyaka-Upanishad*, 4, 3.
[3] *Atharvaveda*, 10, 8, 11. (Deussen)
[4] Hence Brahman is quite beyond knowledge and comprehension.
[5] Jung, *Psychology of the Unconscious*.

(b) Concerning the Brahmanic Conception of the Reconciling Symbol

1. " When it is said: Brahman first in the East was born, it meaneth, each new day like yonder sun Brahman is reborn in the East." [1]
2. " Yonder man in the sun is Parameshtin, Brahman, Atman." [2]
3. " Yonder man, whom they point out in the sun, that is Indra, Prajapati, Brahman." [3]
4. " Brahman is a light like unto the sun." [4]
5. " What is this Brahman but that which gloweth yonder as the sun's disc." [5]
6. " *Brahman first in the East was born :*
From the horizon the Gracious One appeareth in splendour;
The forms of this world, the deepest, the highest,
He lighteth ; the cradle He is, of what is and is not.
Father of the shining ones, *Creator* of the treasure,
Many-formed he appeareth in the spaces of the air :
They glorify Him in hymns of praise ; *The Eternal Youth Which Brahman is increaseth ever through Brahman's* (*decree*)
Brahman brought forth the deities, Brahman created the world." [6]

· I have emphasized certain specially characteristic passages with italics; from these it would appear that Brahman is not only the producing one but also that which is produced, the ever-becoming. The epithet "Gracious One" (*Vena*), here bestowed upon the sun, is in other places given to the *seer* who is endowed with the divine light, for, like the Brahman-sun, the mind of the seer also traverses "earth and heaven contemplating Brahman".[7] This intimate relation, identity even, of the divine being with the Self (Atman) of mankind, is

[1] *Çatap. Brāhm.*, 14, 1, 3, 3. (Deussen).
[2] *Taitt. Ar.*, 10, 63, 15. (Deussen).
[3] *Çankh. Br.*, 8, 3. (Deussen).
[4] *Vaj. Samh.*, 23, 48. (Deussen).
[5] *Çatap. Br.*, 8, 5, 3, 7. (Deussen).
[6] *Taitt. Br.*, 2, 8, 8, 8. ff. (Deussen).
[7] *Atharvaveda*, 2, 1, 4, 1, 11, 5.

generally recognised. I mention the following example from the *Atharvaveda*:

" The disciple of Brahman advanceth, reanimating both worlds.
In him all the gods are unanimous.
He containeth and upholdeth the earth and the heavens,
He even feedeth the master with his tapas.[1]
To the Brahman disciple there come, to visit him,
Fathers and Gods, singly and in multitudes :
And he nourisheth all the Gods by tapas."

The Brahman disciple is himself an incarnation of Brahman, from which the identity of the Brahman-essence with a definite psychological state is clearly established.

7. " Prompted by the Gods, the *sun* burneth there in splendour unsurpassed ;
From him proceedeth Brahman-force, supreme Brahman.
Yea, even all the Gods ; and what he maketh dieth not.
The Brahman disciple upholdeth Brahman resplendent,
Interwoven in him are the hosts of the Gods." [2]

Brahman is also Prana—breath of life and the cosmic life-principle; Brahman is also Vayu—Wind, which is referred to in the *Brihadāranyaka-Upanishad* (3, 7) as the cosmic and psychic life-principle.[3]

8. " He who is this (Brahman) in man, and the One who is that (Brahman) in the sun, are both one." [4]

9. (Prayer of one dying) : " The countenance of truth (of Brahman) is covered by a golden disc. Open this, O Pushan (Savitir, sun), that we may behold the nature of truth. Unfold and assemble thy holy rays, O Pushan, thou only seer, Yama, Surya (sun), son of Prajapati. I behold the light, thy loveliest semblance. What he is, I am (i.e. the man in the sun).[5]

10. " And this light, which spreadeth above this heaven higher than all, higher even than those in the highest world, above and beyond which there are no more worlds, this is the same light that burneth in the inner world of man. Whereof we have this visible token; only to feel warmth and perceive bodies."[6]

---

[1] The practice of self-brooding. Cf. Jung, *Psychology of the Unconscious*.
[2] *Atharvaveda*, 11, 5, 23 ff. (Deussen). [3] Deussen, *Allg. Gesch. d. Phil.*, I, 2, pp. 93 ff. [4] *Taitt.-Up.*, 2, 8, 5. (Max Müller). [5] *Brihadār.-Up.*, 5, 15, 1 ff. (Max Müller). [6] *Khandogya-Up.*, 3, 13, 7 ff. (Max Müller).

THE TYPE-PROBLEM IN POETRY 249

11. " As a grain of rice, or barley, or millet, yea like even unto the kernel of a millet-seed is this spirit in the inner Self, golden, like a flame without smoke ; and greater is it than the heavens, vaster than space, greater than this earth, surpassing all beings.
It is the soul of life, it is my own soul : departing hence, into this soul shall I enter."[1]

13. In the *Atharvaveda*, 10, 2, Brahman is conceived as the vitalistic principle, the life-force, which fashions all the organs and their respective instincts.

" Who planted the seed within him, that he might ever spin the thread of generation, who assembled within him the powers of mind, gave him voice and play of features ? "

Even the power of man originates in Brahman. From these examples, whose number could be multiplied indefinitely, it clearly follows that, by virtue of all its attributes and symbols, the Brahman concept is in full harmony with that idea of a dynamic or creative element, which I have named 'libido'. The word Brahman means: 1, prayer; 2, incantation; 3, sacred speech; 4, sacred knowledge (*Veda*); 5, holy life; 6, the absolute; 7, the sacred caste (the Brahmans). Deussen stresses the prayer-significance as being especially characteristic[2]. Brahman is derived from *barh*, farcire, 'swelling'[3], *i.e.* 'prayer' conceived of as "the upward-urging will of man striving towards the holy, the divine".

A certain psychological state is indicated in this derivation, namely a specific concentration of libido which through overflowing innervations produces a general state of tension, and hence is associated with the feeling of swelling. Thus in colloquial references to such a state, images of overflowing, *e.g.* 'one cannot restrain oneself', 'bursting', etc. are frequently used. ("What filleth the heart, goeth out by the mouth").

[1] *Çatap. Brāhm.*, 10, 6, 3. (Deussen)
[2] *Allg. Gesch. d. Phil.*, 1, 1, pp. 240 ff.
[3] This is confirmed by the reference to *Brahman-prana*. Matriçvan (" he who swelleth within the mother "). *Atharvaveda*, 11, 4, 15.

I*

Indian practice seeks to accomplish this state of damming or heaping-up of libido by systematically withdrawing the attention (libido) alike from objects, and from psychic states, in a word from the 'opposites'. This elimination of sense-perception and blotting-out of conscious contents leads inevitably to a lowering of consciousness in general (just as in hypnosis), whereby the unconscious contents, *i.e.* the primordial images, which possess a cosmic and superhuman character on account of their universality and immense antiquity, become activated.

Those age-old allegories of sun, fire, flame, wind, breath, etc., which from earliest time have symbolized the begetting, world-moving, creative power, have all come about in this way. Since I have made a special study of these libido-images in another work [1], I will not further expand this theme here. The idea of a creative world principle is a projected perception of the living essence in man himself.

In order to preclude all vitalistic misunderstandings, one is well advised to make an abstract conception of this essence as *energy*. But, on the other hand, that hypostasizing of the energy-concept in the fashion of modern energetics must, of course, be firmly rejected.

Since an energic current necessarily presupposes the existence of an opposition, *i.e.* of two states of differing potential, without which no current can take place, the concept of opposition is also associated with the energy-concept. Every energic phenomenon (and there are no phenomena that are not energic) manifests both beginning and end, upper and lower, hot and cold, earlier and later, cause and effect, etc., *i.e.* pairs of opposites. This inseparability of the energy-concept from the concept of opposition also involves the libido-concept. Hence libido-

[1] Jung, *Psychology of the Unconscious.*

symbols of a mythological or philosophic-speculative character, are either represented by a direct antithesis or become immediately broken up into opposites. In a former work I have already referred to this inner splitting of the libido, thereby provoking a certain opposition, though not justifiably, so it seems to me, since the immediate association of a libido-symbol with the concept of opposition is sufficient justification. We also find this association in the Brahman concept or symbol. The character of Brahman as prayer, and at the same time as primordial creative force, the latter being resolved into the opposition of sexes, is very remarkably presented in a hymn of *Rigveda*:[1]

" And ever unfolding, this prayer of the singer
Became a cow, which was before the world existed ;
Dwelling together in this womb of God,
Fledgelings of the same brood are the Gods.
What hath been the wood, and what was the tree,
Out of which Earth and Heaven were hewn,
The twain, changeless and eternally helpful,
When days vanished and the dawn's first flush came not.
Greater than He nothing existeth ;
He is the bull, upholding earth and heaven
The cloud sieve he girdleth like a fleece ;
When He, the Lord, driveth like Surya His cream horses.
As an arrow of the sun He irradiateth the wide earth,
As the wind scattereth the mist, He stormeth through creatures,
When he cometh as *Mitra*, as *Varuna* chasing around.
As *Agni* in the forest, he distributeth *glowing light*.
When driven to him, the cow brought forth,
Moved, freely-pasturing, the unmoved thing she created.
She bore the son, the one who was older than the parents—"

That the idea of opposition is closely bound up with the world creator is presented in another form in *Çatapatha-Brahmanam*, 2, 2, 4 :

" In the beginning was Prajapati alone ; he meditated : How can I propagate myself ? So he travailed and practised

[1] *Rigveda*, 10, 31, 6. (Deussen).
[2] Cosmic creative principle—libido. *Taitt. Samh.*, 5, 5, 2, 1 : " When he had created them, he instilled love into all his creatures."

tapas :[1] then he begat Agni (fire) out of his mouth; because he begat him out of his mouth,[2] therefore is Agni food-devourer. Prajapati reflected : As food-devourer have I created this Agni out of myself ; *but there existeth here nothing else beside myself* that he may devour, for at that time the earth was quite barren ; neither herbs nor trees were there : and this thought was heavy upon him. *Then turned upon him Agni with gaping maw.* Thus spake unto him his own greatness : *Sacrifice!* Then knew Prajapati : This, my own greatness hath spoken unto me ; and he sacrificed. Thereupon he ascended, he burneth yonder (the sun) ; thereupon he rose up, he that purifieth here (the wind). Because Prajapati sacrificed in this wise, he propagated himself, and, because death in the form of Agni would have devoured him, he also saved himself from death."

The sacrifice is always the renunciation of the valuable part; the sacrificer thus avoids being eaten up; this does not mean a transformation into the opposite, but a unification and adjustment, from which there arises a new libido-direction or attitude to life; sun and wind are generated. It is stated in another place in the *Çatapatha-Brahmanam*, that one half of Prajapati is mortal, the other immortal[3].

Similar to the way Prajapati divides himself into bull and cow is his division into the two principles *Manas* (mind) and *Vac* (speech). "This world was Prajapati alone, Vac was his Self, and Vac his second Self (his alter ego); thus he meditated : This Vac will I send forth, and she shall go hence and pervade all things. Then he sent forth Vac, and she went and filled this universe."[4] This passage is of especial interest, inasmuch as speech is here conceived as a creative, extraverted libido-movement, as a diastole in Goethe's sense. There is a further parallel in the following passage : "In truth Prajapati was this world, with him was Vac his second Self: with her did he

[1] Solitary meditation, asceticism, introversion.
[2] The begetting of fire from the mouth has a noteworthy relation to speech. Cf. Jung, *Psychology of the Unconscious.*
[3] Cf. Dioscuri motive in *Psychology of the Unconscious* (Jung).
[4] Deussen, *Allg. Gesch. d. Phil.*, I, 1, p. 206 ; *Pancav. Br.*, 20, 14, 12.

beget life: she conceived: whereupon she went forth out of him, and made these creatures, and once again entered into Prajapati."[1] In the Çatapatha-Br., 8, 1, 2, 9, the share attributed to Vac is a prodigious one: "Truly Vac is the wise Viçvakarman, for through Vac was this whole world made." However, in Çatap. Br., 1, 4, 5, 8, the question of precedence between Manas and Vac is decided differently:

"Upon a time it came to pass that Mind and Speech strove for priority one with the other. Mind said: ' I am better than thou, for thou speakest nothing that I have not first discerned.' Then said Speech: ' I am better than thou, since I announce what thou hast discerned and make it known.' To Prajapati they went, for the question to be judged. Prajapati decreed for Mind saying: ' Truly is Mind better than thou ; for thou dost copy what Mind doeth and runnest in his tracks : moreover, it is the inferior who is wont to imitate his betters.' " [2]

These passages show that the World-creator can also divide himself into Manas and Vac, who are themselves mutually opposed. As Deussen points out, both principles are first contained within Prajapati, the world-creator. This appears in the following text: "Prajapati yearned: 'I wish to be many, I will multiply myself.' Then silently he meditated in his *manas;* what was in his manas fashioned Crihat[3]; then he pondered 'This lieth in me as the fruit of my body, through *vac* will I bring it to birth.' Thereupon made he *vac*" etc.[4]

This passage shows the two principles in their character of psychological functions ; namely, manas as introversion of the libido with the creation of an inner product ; vac as the divesting function or extraversion. With this explanation we can now understand a further text[5] relating to Brahman:

[1] Weber, *Indische Studien*, 9, 477.
[2] Quoted from Deussen, *Allg. Gesch. d. Phil.*, 1, 1, p. 206.
[3] The name of a *saman*—Song.
[4] Deussen, *l.c.*, 1, 1, 205. *Pancav. Br.*, 7, 6.
[5] *Çatap. Br*, 11, 2, 3. (Deussen).

"Brahman made two worlds. When he had come into this other world, he pondered: 'How can I reach again into the world?' *Twofold did he extend himself into this world*, through *Form* and through *Name. These twain are the two great monsters of Brahman ; whosoever knoweth these two great monsters of Brahman becometh like unto them ;· these twain are the two mighty aspects of Brahman.*"

A little later "form" is explained as manas ("manas is form, for man knoweth through manas what this form is"), and "name" is shown to be vac ("for through vac man seizeth the name"). Thus the two "monsters" of Brahman emerge as manas and vac, hence as two psychic functions, with which Brahman can 'extend himself' into two worlds, clearly signifying the function of 'relation.' The form of things is 'conceived' or 'taken in' by introverting through manas; names are given to things by extraverting through vac. Both are bound up with the relations and adaptations or assimilations of things. The two monsters are also evidently regarded as personifications; an indication of this lies in their other title "aspects"=*yaksha*, since yaksha is an equivalent of dæmon, or superhuman being. Psychologically, personification always signifies a relative independence (autonomy) of the personified contents, *i.e.* a relative splitting-off from the psychic hierarchy. A content of this kind is not obedient to voluntary reproduction, but either reproduces itself spontaneously or in some similar way becomes insulated from consciousness.[1] For instance, when an incompatibility exists between the ego and a certain complex, such a cleavage is produced. As is well known, one frequently observes this dissociation between the ego and the sexual complex. But other complexes may also become split-off, the power-complex, for instance, corresponding with the sum of all those aspirations and ideas. which aim at the acquisition of personal power.

[1] Cf. Jung, *Dementia Præcox* (1907)

There is, however, another sort of cleavage, namely *the splitting-off of the conscious ego, together with a selected function from the remaining components of the personality* This cleavage may be defined as an *identification of the ego with a certain function* or group of functions. A dissociation of this kind is very often seen in men who are too deeply immersed in one of their psychic functions, thereby differentiating it as their only conscious function of adaptation.

A good literary example of such a man is provided by Faust at the beginning of the tragedy. The remaining elements of the personality approach in the form of the poodle, and later as Mephistopheles. According to my view, we should not be justified in interpreting Mephistopheles as a split-off complex, as repressed sexuality for instance, in spite of the fact, which is undoubtedly borne out by many associations, that Mephistopheles also represents the sexual complex.

This explanation is too limited, for Mephistopheles is more than mere sexuality—he is also power; with the exception of thinking and research he is practically the whole life of Faust. The result of the pact with the devil shows this most distinctly. What undreamed-of possibilities do not unfold themselves to the rejuvenated Faust! The correct view, therefore, would seem to be that Faust identifies himself with the one function and therewith becomes split off from the personality as a whole. Subsequently, the thinker in the form of Wagner also becomes split off from Faust.

Conscious capacity for one-sidedness is a sign of the highest culture. But involuntary one-sidedness, *i.e.* inability to be anything but one-sided, is a sign of barbarism. Hence we find among half-savage peoples the most one-sided differentiations, as, for instance, certain aspects of Christian asceticism which are an affront to good taste, and parallel phenomena among the Yogis and Tibetan Buddhists.

For the barbarian, this tendency to fall a victim to one-sidedness in one way or another, thereby losing sight of his whole personality, is a great and constant danger. The Gilgamesh epic, for example, begins with this conflict. In the barbarian the one-sided libido movement breaks out with dæmoniacal compulsion; it possesses the character of Berserker rage and "running amok". The barbaric one-sidedness presupposes a certain stunting of instinct; this is lacking in the primitive, because in general he is still free from the one-sidedness of the semi-civilized barbarian.

Identification with one definite function at once produces a tension between the opposites. The more compulsive the one-sidedness, *i.e.* the more untamed the libido which urges to one side, the more dæmoniacal is its quality. When a man is carried away by his uncontrolled, undomesticated libido, he speaks of dæmoniac possession or of magical effect. In this way manas and vac are indeed potent dæmons, since they can work mightily upon men. All things that exercise powerful effects were regarded either as gods or dæmons. Thus, in the Gnosis, manas became personified as the serpent-like *nous*, vac as Logos. Vac bears the same relation to Prajapati as Logos to God. The sort of dæmons that introversion and extraversion may become is for us an everyday experience. With what irresistible persuasion and force the libido streams within or without, with what unshakable tenacity an introverted or extraverted attitude can take root, we see in our patients and can feel in ourselves. The description of manas and vac as monsters of Brahman is in complete harmony with the psychological fact that at the instant of its appearance the libido divides into two streams, which as a rule alternate periodically but at times may also appear simultaneously in the form of a conflict, namely an outward stream opposing an inward stream. The dæmonic quality of the two movements lies in their ungovernable nature and superior power. These qualities are, of course, in evidence only when the instinct of the primitive is already so curtailed that a natural and appropriate counter-movement against his one-sidedness is prevented; and where that culture which might assist him so far to tame his libido as to be able voluntarily and deliberately to participate in its introverting and extraverting tides is not yet sufficiently advanced.

(c) The Reconciling Symbol as the Principle of Dynamic Regulation

In the foregoing passages from Indian sources we have followed the development of the redeeming principle from the pairs of opposites, and have traced the origin of the pairs of opposites to the same creative principle, thereby gaining an insight into a law-determined psychological occurrence which is found to be easily reconcilable with the concepts of our modern psychology.

This impression of a law-determined event is also conveyed to us from Indian sources, since they identify Brahman with Rita. What then is Rita? Rita signifies: established order, regulation, direction, determination, sacred custom, statute, divine law, right, truth. According to etymological evidence its root-meaning is: ordinance, (right) way, direction, course (to be followed). That which is ordained by Rita fills the whole world, but the particular manifestations of Rita are in those Nature-processes which always remain constant, and inevitably arouse the idea of regulated recurrence: " By Rita's ordinance the heaven-born dawn was lighted." " In obedience to Rita " the Ancient Ones who order the world " made *the sun* to mount the heavens", who himself "is the burning countenance of Rita". Around the heavens circles the year, that twelve-spoked wheel of Rita which never ages. Agni is called the offspring of Rita. In the doings of man, Rita operates as the moral law, which enjoins truth and the straight way. " *Whosoever followeth Rita, findeth a thornless path and fair to walk in.*"

In so far as they represent a magical repetition or reproduction of cosmic events, Rita also appears in religious rites. As the streams flow in obedience to Rita and the crimson dawn is set ablaze, so "under the harness[1] of Rita" is the sacrifice kindled; upon the path of Rita, Agni brings the sacrifice to the gods. "Pure of magic, I invoke the gods; with Rita I do my work, and shape my thought", are the words of the sacrificer. Although the Rita concept does not appear personified in the Veda, yet, according to Bergaigne a certain tinge of *concrete being* undoubtedly clings to it. Since Rita expresses an ordering of events, we find "paths of Rita", "charioteers"[2] and "ships of Rita"; on occasion the gods appear as parallels. The same attribute, for instance, is given to Rita as to Varuna. Mitra also, the ancient sun-god, is brought into relation with Rita (as above). Concerning Agni we read: "Thou shalt become Varuna, if thou strivest after Rita"[3]. The gods are the guardians of Rita[4]. I have selected a group of essential references:

1. " Rita is Mitra, for Mitra is Brahman and Rita is Brahman."[5]

---

[1] Suggesting the horse, which indicates the *dynamic* nature of the Rita concept.
[2] Agni is called the charioteer of Rita. *Vedic Hymns* (Sacred Books, xlvi) p. 158; 7, p. 160; 3, p. 229; 8.
[3] Cf. Oldenburg, *Nachr. d. Gött. Ges. d. Wiss.*, 1915, p. 167 ff. *Religion des Veda*, p. 194. For this reference I am indebted to the kindness of Dr Abegg of Zürich.
[4] Deussen, *Allg. Gesch. d. Phil.*, I, 1, p. 92
[5] Çatapatha-Brāhmanam, 4, 1, 4, 10. (Eggeling).

2. " Giving the cow to the Brahmans man gaineth all the worlds, for in her is Brahman contained in Rita, and Tapas also." [1]

3. " Prajapati is called the first-born of Rita." [2]

4. " The gods followed the laws of Rita." [3]

5. " He who saw the hidden one (Agni), and drew nigh to the streams of Rita." [4]

6. " O wise one of Rita, know Rita ! Bore and release Rita's many streams." [5]

The boring refers to the worship of Agni, to whom this hymn is dedicated. (Agni is here called the "red bull of Rita "). In the worship of Agni, fire obtained by boring is used as a magic symbol of the regeneration of life. Here clearly the "boring" of the streams of Rita bears the same significance, namely the streams of life rise again to the surface, libido is freed from its bonds[6]. The effect produced by the ritual fire-boring, or through the recital of hymns, is naturally regarded by the believers as the magical effect of the object; in reality, however, it is an 'enchantment' of the subject, namely an intensification of vital feeling, a release and propagation of life-force, a restoration of psychic potential.

7. Thus we find : " Though he (Agni) creepeth away, yet unto him straightway goeth the prayer. They (the prayers) have led forth the flowing streams of Rita." [7]

The revival of living feeling, of this sense of streaming energy, is very generally likened to a spring gushing from its source, to the melting of the iron-bound ice of winter

---

[1] *Atharvaveda*, 10, 10 ,33. (Deussen). [2] *Atharvaveda*, 10, 12, 1, 61. (Bloomfield). [3] *Vedic Hymns* (*Sacred Books*, xlvi), p. 54. [4] *Vedic Hymns*, p. 61. [5] *Vedic Hymns*, p. 393.

[6] Release of libido is obtained through *ritual* work. The release brings the libido to the disposal of consciousness. It becomes domesticated. From an instinctive, undomesticated state it is converted into a state of disposability. This is depicted in a verse which runs : " When the rulers, the bountiful lords, brought Him forth (Agni) by their power from *the depths, they released Him from the form of the bull*." *Vedic Hymns*, p. 147.

[7] *Vedic Hymns*, p. 174.

in springtime, or to the breaking of long drought by rain[1].

8. The following passage is in harmony with this theme: " With full udders the lowing milch cows of Rita were overflowing. The streams which implored the favour (of the gods) from afar, have broken through the mountain rocks with their floods."[2]

This imagery clearly suggests a tension of energy, a damming up of libido, and its release. Rita here appears as the possessor of blessing, of "lowing milch cows" and as the ultimate source of the released energy.

9. Corresponding with the image of rain as a symbol of the release of libido, we find the following passage: " The mists fly, the clouds thunder. When he who is swollen with the milk of Rita, is led upon the straightest path of Rita; then Aryaman, Mitra and Varuna, (He who transformeth the earth) fill the leathern sack (the clouds) in the womb of the lower (atmosphere)."[3]

It is Agni who, swollen with the milk of Rita, is likened here to the force of lightning, that bursts forth from massed clouds heavy with rain. Here Rita appears again as the actual source of energy, whence Agni also is born; this is explicitly mentioned in the *Vedic Hymns*, p. 161, 7. Rita is also path, *i.e.* regulated process.

10. " With acclamations have they greeted the stream of Rita, which lay hidden by the birth-place of God, nigh unto His throne. There did He drink, when, still divided, He dwelt in the womb of the waters."[4]

This passage confirms what was just said about Rita as the source of libido, in which God dwells and whence He is brought forth in the sacred ceremonies. Agni is the positive appearance of hitherto latent libido; He is the accomplisher or fulfiller of Rita, its "charioteer" (see above); He harnesses the two long-maned red mares of Rita.[5] He even holds Rita like a horse, by the bridle.

[1] Cf. the *Tishtrya Lied.* Jung, *Psychology of the Unconscious.*
[2] *Vedic Hymns*, p. 88.   [3] *Vedic Hymns*, p. 103.
[4] *Vedic Hymns*, p. 160, 2.   [5] *Vedic Hymns*, p. 244, 6, and p. 316, 3.

(*Vedic Hymns*, p. 382). He brings the gods to mankind, *i.e.* He brings their force and their blessing; they represent definite psychological states, in which the feeling and energy of life flow with greater freedom and joy, where the pent ice is broken. Nietzsche catches this state in that wonderful verse:

> " Thou who with spear of flame
> Dissolveth the ice of my soul !
> Storming now she hasteneth
> Toward the sea of her highest hopes."

11. The following invocations are in harmony with this theme : " Let the divine gates, the multipliers of Rita, be flung wide. Open the much desired gates, that the gods may come forth. Let night and morning—the young mothers of Rita, be seated together upon the ritual grass, etc." [1]

The analogy with the rising sun is unmistakable. Rita appears as the sun, since out of night and twilight is the new sun born.

12. " Open ye for our succour, O divine doors easy of access. Ever more and more fill the sacrifice with blessedness : (with prayers) we draw nigh unto night and morning—*the multipliers of living power, the two young mothers of Rita.*"

There is no need, I think, for further examples to show that the concept of Rita, like sun and wind etc., is a libido-symbol. Only the Rita concept is less concretistic, and contains the abstract element of established direction and lawfulness, *i.e.* the determined and ordered path or process.

Already, therefore, it is a philosophical libido-symbol which can be directly compared with the Stoic concept εἱμαρμένη. With the Stoics εἱμαρμένη had, of course, the significance of a creative primordial heat, and at the same time a determined, regulated process (hence also its meaning—"compulsion by the stars"). It is self-evident that libido as a psychological energy concept corresponds with

[1] *Vedic Hymns*, p. 153 and p. 8.

these attributes; since a process always proceeds from a higher potential to a lower, the energy-concept includes the idea of a determined, directed process eo ipso. It is the same with the libido-concept, which merely signifies the energy of the process of life. Its laws are the laws of vital energy. Libido as an energy concept is a quantitative formula for the phenomena of life, which are naturally of varying intensity.

Like physical energy, libido passes through every conceivable transformation; we find ample evidence of this in the phantasies of the unconscious and in the myths. These phantasies are primarily self-representations of the energic transformation processes, which follow their natural and established laws, their determined "way" of evolution. This way signifies both the line or curve of the optimum of energic discharge as well as the corresponding result in work. Hence this "way" is simply the expression of flowing and self-manifesting energy. The way is Rita, the "*right way*", the flow of vital energy or libido, the determined course upon which the ever-renewing process is possible. This way is also destiny, in so far as destiny is dependent upon our psychology. It is the way of our vocation and our law.

It would be quite wrong to assert that such an aim is merely *naturalism*, by which one means a complete surrender to one's instincts. An assumption is herewith involved that the instincts have a constant "downward" tendency, and that naturalism is a non-ethical rechute upon an inclined plane. I have nothing against such an interpretation of naturalism, but I am bound to observe that the man who is left to his own devices, and has therefore every opportunity for backsliding, as for instance the primitive, not only has a morality and a legislation but one which in the severity of its demands is often considerably more exacting than our civilized morality

Whether, for the primitive good and evil have a value which differs from ours, has nothing to do with the case; his naturalism leads to legislation—that is the chief point. Morality is no misconception, conceived by an ambitious Moses upon Sinai, but something inherent in the laws of life and fashioned like a house or a ship or any other cultural instrument in the normal process of life. The natural flow of libido, this very middle path, involves a complete obedience to the fundamental laws of human nature, and there can positively be no higher moral principle than that harmony with natural laws whose accord gives the libido the direction in which life's optimum lies. The optimum of life is not to be found upon the line of crude egoism, since man, whose fundamental make-up discerns an absolutely indispensable meaning in the happiness he brings to his neighbour, can never win his life's optimum upon the line of egoism. An unbridled craving for individual pre-eminence is equally unfitted to achieve this optimum, since the collective element is so strongly rooted in man that his yearning for fellowship destroys all pleasure in naked egoism. The optimum of life can be gained only by obedience to the tidal laws of the libido, by which systole alternates with diastole, laws which provide happiness and the necessary limitations, even setting the life-tasks of the individual nature, without whose accomplishment life's optimum can never be achieved. If the attainment of this way consisted in a mere surrender to instinct, which is what is really meant by the bewailer of "naturalism", the profoundest philosophical speculation and the whole history of the human mind would have no sort of raison d'être. Yet, as we study the Upanishad philosophy, the impression grows on us that the attainment of the path is not just the simplest of tasks. Our western air of superiority in the presence of Indian understanding is a part of our essential barbarism, for which any true perception of the quite extraordinary depth of those ideas and their amazing psychological accuracy is still but a remote possibility. In fact, we are still so uneducated that we actually need laws from without, and a task-master or Father above, to show us what is good and the right thing to do. It is because we are still so barbarous that faith in the laws of human nature and the human path appears as a dangerous and non-ethical naturalism. Why is this? Because under the barbarian's thin skin of culture the wild-beast lurks in readiness, amply justifying his fear. But the beast that is caged is not thereby conquered. *There is no morality without freedom.* When a barbarian loosens the animal within him, he is not free, but bound. Barbarism must first be vanquished, before freedom can be won. Theoretically this takes place when an individual perceives and feels the basic root and motive power of his own morality as an inherent element of his own nature, and not as external prohibitions. But how else is man to attain this realization and insight but through the conflict of the opposites?

(d) *The Reconciling Symbol in Chinese Philosophy*

The idea of a middle path that lies between the opposites is also to be found in China, in the form of *Tao*. The idea of *Tao* is usually associated with the name of the philosopher Lao-Tsze, born B.C. 604. But this concept is older than the philosophy of Lao-Tsze, since it is bound up with certain ideas belonging to the ancient national religion of the Tao, the celestial "way". This concept corresponds with the Vedic Rita. The meanings of Tao are as follows: (1) way, (2) method, (3) principle, (4) Nature-force or life-force, (5) the regulated processes of Nature, (6) the idea of the world, (7) the primal cause of all phenomena, (8) the right, (9) the good, (10) the eternal moral law. Some translators even translate Tao as God, not without a certain right, since Tao, like Rita, has a certain admixture of concrete substantiality.

I will first give a few illustrations from the *Tao-te-king*, the classical book of Lao-tsze:

1. " I do not know whose son it (Tao) is; it seems to have existed before God." (ch. iv)
2. " A being there is, indefinable, perfected, that existed before heaven and earth. How still it was how formless, alone, unchanging, embracing all and inexhaustible! It would seem to be the *mother of all things*. I know not its name, but I call it Tao." (ch. xxv)
3. In order to characterize its essential quality, Lao-tsze likens it to water: " The blessing of water is shown in this, it doeth good to all and seeketh at once the lowliest place, which all men shun. It hath in it something of Tao."

The idea of the energic process could not surely be better expressed.

4. " Dwelling without desire, one perceiveth its essence; clinging to desire, one seeth only its outer form." (ch. i)

The kinship with the basic Brahmanic ideas is unmistakable—which does not necessarily imply direct contact. Lao-tsze is an entirely original thinker, and the primordial image underlying both the Rita-Brahman-Atman and Tao conceptions is as universal as man, appearing in every age and among all peoples, whether as a primitive energy concept, as "soul force" or however else it may be designated.

5. " He who knoweth the eternal is comprehensive; comprehensive, therefore just; just, therefore a king; a king, therefore celestial; celestial, therefore in Tao; in Tao, therefore enduring; without hurt he suffereth the loss of the body." (ch. xvi)

The knowledge of Tao has therefore the same redeeming and uplifting effect as the "knowing" of Brahman. Man becomes one with Tao, with the unending "durée créatrice"; thus to range this latest philosophical concept appropriately by the side of its older kindred, since Tao is also the stream of time.

6. " Tao is an irrational, hence a wholly inconceivable fact: Tao is essence, but unseizable, incomprehensible." (ch. xxi)

7. Tao also is non-existing: "From it the existing, all things under Heaven have their source, but the being of this existing one arose in its turn from it as the non-existing." (ch. xl). "Tao is hidden, nameless." (ch. xli)

Clearly Tao is an irrational union of the opposites, therefore a *symbol* which is and is not.

8. "The spirit of the valley is immortal, it is called the deep feminine. The gate-way of the deep feminine is called root of heaven and earth."

Tao is the creative essence, as father begetting and as mother bringing forth. It is the beginning and end of all creatures.

9. "He whose actions are in harmony with Tao becometh one with Tao."

Therefore the complete one is freed from the opposites whose intimate connection and alternating appearance he is aware of. Thus in Chapter ix he says: "to withdraw oneself is the celestial way".

10. "Therefore is he (the complete one) inaccessible to intimacy, inaccessible to estrangement, inaccessible to profit, inaccessible to injury, inaccessible to honour, inaccessible to disgrace." (ch. lvi)

11. "Being one with Tao resembles the spiritual condition of a *child*." (ch. x, xxviii, lv)

This is, admittedly, the psychological attitude which is an essential condition of the inheritance of the Christian Kingdom of Heaven, and this—in spite of all rational interpretations—is the central, irrational essence, the basic image and symbol whence proceeds the redeeming effect. The Christian symbol merely has a more social (civil) character than the allied Eastern conceptions. These latter are more directly rooted in eternally existing *dynamistic* conceptions, such as the image of magical power, issuing from things and men, and on a higher level from gods, or a principle.

12. According to the ideas of the Taoistic religion, *Tao* is divided into a *principle pair of opposites*, *Yang* and *Yin*. Yang is warmth, light, masculinity. Yin is cold, darkness, femininity. Yang is also heaven, Yin earth. From the Yang force arises *Schen*, the celestial portion of the human soul; and from the Yin force arises *Kwei*, the earthly part. As a microcosm, man is also in some degree a reconciler of the pairs of opposites. Heaven, man, and earth, form the three chief elements of the world, the *San-tsai*.

This image is an altogether primordial idea, which we find elsewhere in similar forms; as for instance in the West African myth where Obatala and Odudua, the first parents (heaven and earth) lie together in a calabash, until a son, man, arises between them. Hence as a microcosm, uniting in himself the world-opposites, man corresponds with the irrational *symbol* which reconciles psychological antitheses. This root-image of man clearly accords with Schiller, when he calls the symbol "living form".

The division of the human soul into a Schen or Hwun soul, and a Kwei or Poh soul, is a great psychological truth. This Chinese presentation also suggests the familiar passage in Faust:

" Two souls, alas ! within my bosom dwell—
One would from the other sever :
The one in full delight of love
Clings with clutching organs to the world :
The other, mightily, from earthly dust
Would mount on high to the ancestral fields."

The existence of two mutually contending tendencies, both striving to drag man into extreme attitudes and entangle him in the world—whether upon the spiritual or material side—thereby setting him at variance with himself, demands the existence of a counter-weight, which is just this irrational fact, Tao. Hence the believer's anxious effort to live in harmony with Tao, lest he fall into the conflict of the opposites. Since Tao is an irrational fact, it cannot be deliberately achieved; a fact which Lao-Tsze frequently emphasizes. *Wuwei*, another specifically Chinese concept, owes its particular significance to this condition. It signifies "doing nothing", but, as Ular pertinently explains, it should be rendered: "not-doing, and not doing nothing". The rational "desire to bring it about", which is the greatness and the evil of our own epoch, does not lead to Tao.

Thus the aim of the Taoistic ethic sets out to find deliverance from that tension of the opposites which is an inherent property of the universe, by a return to Tao.

In this connection we must also remember the "Sage of Omi" Nakae Toju[1], that distinguished Japanese philosopher of the seventeenth century. Based upon the teaching of the Chu-Hi school which had migrated from China, he established two principles, *Ri* and *Ki*. Ri is the world-soul, Ki the world-matter. Ri and Ki are however one and the same, inasmuch as they are attributes of God, hence only existing in and through Him. God is their union. Similarly the *soul* embraces Ri and Ki. Concerning God, Toju says: "As the essence of the world, God enfoldeth the world, but at the same time He is also in our midst and even in our own bodies." For him God is a *universal Self*, while the *individual Self* is "heaven in us", an immaterial, divine essence that is called *Ryochi*. Ryochi is "God in us", and dwells in each individual. It is the *true* Self. For Toju distinguishes a true from a false self. The false self is an acquired personality arising from perverted beliefs. We might freely describe this false self as persona, *i.e.* that general idea of our nature which we have built up from experiencing our effect upon the world around and its effect upon us.

The persona expresses the personality as it *appears* to oneself and one's world; but not what one *is*, to use

[1] Cf. Tetsujiro Inouye, *Japanese Philosophy* (In *Kultur der Gegenwart* 1913)

the words of Schopenhauer. What one is, is one's individual Self, according to Toju, one's true Self or Ryochi. Ryochi is also called "alone being", or "alone knowing", clearly because it is a condition related to the essence of the Self, a state existing beyond all personal judgments that are determined by outer experience. Toju conceives Ryochi as the summum bonum, as 'bliss' (Brahman is *Ananda*—bliss). Ryochi is the light which pervades the world; a further parallel with Brahman, according to Inouye. Ryochi is human love, immortal, all-knowing good. Evil comes from willing (Schopenhauer!). It is the self-regulating function, the mediator and reconciler of the pairs of opposites, Ri and Ki: it is in fullest harmony with the Indian idea of the "ancient Wise One who dwelleth in thy heart". Or as Wang-Yang-Ming, the Chinese father of the Japanese philosophy, says: "In every heart there dwelleth a Sejin (Sage). Only man will not steadfastly believe it—therefore hath the whole remained buried."

From the point we have now reached, the primordial image which contributed to the solution of the problem in Wagner's *Parsifal* is no longer hard to understand; the suffering proceeds from the tension of the opposites represented by the Grail and the power of Klingsor, the latter consisting in the possession of the holy spear. Beneath the spell of Klingsor is Kundry, the instinctive, nature-cleaving life-force which Amfortas lacks. Parsifal delivers the libido from the state of restless compulsion, because in the first place he does not succumb to her power, but in the second because he himself is detached from the Grail. Amfortas is with the Grail; whereby he suffers, because he lacks the other. Parsifal possesses naught of either; he is '*nirdvandva*', free from the opposites; hence he is also the deliverer, the bestower of healing and renewed life-force, the reconciler of the opposites, *i.e.* the light, celestial, feminine, of the Grail, and the dark, earthly, masculine, of the spear. The death of Kundry may be freely interpreted as the release of the libido from the nature-clinging, undomesticated form (the "form of the bull": compare above), which falls from her as a lifeless mould, while energy bursts forth as newly-streaming life in the glowing of the Grail.

Through his partly involuntary abstention from the opposites, Parsifal causes the damming up by which the new 'fall', *i.e.* the new manifestation of energy is made possible. One might easily be misled by the unmistakably sexual language into a one-sided interpretation, by which the union of the spear and the vessel of the Grail would merely signify a liberation of sexuality. That it is not merely a question of sexuality, the fate of Amfortas makes clear, since it was precisely his rechute to a nature-bound, brutish attitude, which was the cause of his suffering and brought about the loss of his power. His seduction by Kundry has the value of a symbolic act, which would signify that it is not sexuality that deals such wounds so much as an attitude of nature-clinging compulsion, an irresolute yielding to biological temptation. This attitude is equivalent to the supremacy of the animal part of our psyche.

The sacrificial wound that is destined for the beast strikes the man who is overcome by the beast (for the sake of man's further development). The fundamental problem, as I have already pointed out in my book *Psychology of the Unconscious*, is not sexuality per se, but the domestication of the libido, which concerns sexuality only in so far as it is one of the most important and most dangerous forms of libido expression.

If, in the case of Amfortas and the union of spear and Grail, only the sexual problem is discerned, we reach an insoluble contradiction, since the thing that harms is also the remedy that heals. But only when we see the opposites as reconciled upon a higher plane is such a paradox either true or permissible; a realization, namely, that it is not a question of sexuality, either in this form or that, but purely a question of the attitude by which every activity, including the sexual, is regulated.

Once again I must stress my view that the practical problem of analytical psychology lies deeper than sexuality and its repression. Such a view-point is doubtless valuable in explaining that infantile and therefore morbid *part* of the soul, but, as a principle of interpretation for the totality of the human soul, it is inadequate.

What stands behind sexuality or the instinct to power is the *attitude to sexuality and power*. In so far as attitude is not merely an intuitive phenomenon (*i.e.* unconscious and spontaneous) but also a conscious function, it is, in the main, *one's view of life*. Our views in regard to all problematical things are enormously influenced, sometimes consciously but more often unconsciously, by certain collective ideas which mould our mental atmosphere. These collective ideas are intimately bound up with the view of life or world-philosophy of the past hundred or thousand years. Whether or no we are conscious of this dependence has nothing to do with the case, since we are influenced by these ideas through the very atmosphere we breathe. Such collective ideas have always a religious character, and a philosophical idea acquires a religious character only when it expresses a primordial image, *i.e.* a collective root-image. The religious character of these ideas proceeds from the fact that they express the realities of the collective unconscious; hence they also have the power of releasing the latent energies of the unconscious. The great problems of life—sexuality, of course among others —are always related to the primordial images of the collective unconscious. These images are really balancing or compensating factors which correspond with the problems life presents in actuality.

This is not to be marvelled at, since these images are deposits, representing the accumulated experience of thousands of years of struggle for adaptation and existence. Every great experience in life, every profound conflict, evokes the treasured wealth of these images and brings them to inner perception; as such, they become accessible to consciousness only in the presence of that degree of self-awareness and power of understanding which enables a man also to think what he experiences instead of just living it blindly. In the latter case he actually lives the myth and the symbol without knowing it.

4. The Relativity of the Symbol

(a) *The Service of Woman and the Service of the Soul*

The Service of God is the Christian principle which reconciles the opposites; with Buddhism it is *service of the Self* (self-development); while the principle of solution suggested by Goethe and Spitteler is *service of the soul*, symbolized in the *service of woman*.

Contained herein is the principle of modern individualism on the one hand, and on the other a primitive polydæmonism which assigns, not merely to every race but to every tribe, every family, even to every individual, its own religious principle.

The medieval material in *Faust* possesses its quite extraordinary importance, because it is actually a medieval element which stands at the cradle of modern individualism. Individualism seems to have begun with the service of woman, thereby effecting a most important reinforcement of man's soul as a psychological factor; since service of woman means service of the soul. This is nowhere more beautifully and perfectly expressed than in Dante's *Divina Commedia*.

Dante is the spiritual knight of his lady; he undertakes the adventure of the upper and nether worlds for her sake. And in this heroic labour her image is exalted into that heavenly, mystical figure of the Mother of God—a figure which in its complete detachment from the object has become a personification of a purely psychological entity, *i.e.* that unconscious content whose personification I have termed the anima or soul. Canto xxxiii of the *Paradiso* contains this crowning of Dante's spiritual development in the prayer of St Bernard:

" Oh Virgin Mother, daughter of thy Son,
More lovely, more sublime than any creature !
Of the Lord of the eternal throne the chosen goal,
Thou hast so ennobled the nature of man
That He who created the highest good
Hath chosen in thee to become creature."

Concerning Dante's development we have verses 22 *ff.*

" He who appeared from the deepest gorge
Of the Universe, who with ghostly art and being,
From realm to realm probing and inquiring, passed ;
He entreateth with thee for thy strength,
That he may lift up his eyes
And consecrate his vision to the highest grace."

Verses 31 ff.

" May every cloud of his mortality
Be banished through thy prayer ! Unfolded
Now for him the highest bliss and joy eternal."

Verses 37 ff.

" Let him withstand the earthly motions.
Behold, Beatrice ! so many glorious ones
Intercede for me, with folded hands."

The fact that Dante here speaks through the mouth of St Bernard points to the transformation and exaltation of his own being. The same successive transformation is also seen in Faust, who ascends from Margaret to Helen, from Helen to the Mother of God; his nature is altered through repeated figurative deaths until he finally attains the highest goal as Doctor Marianus. As such Faust utters his prayer to the Virgin Mother:

" Supreme and sovereign Mistress of the world !
In the azure outstretched dome of Heaven
Let me behold thy secret.
The strong and tender motions of man's breast
That with holy passion of love ascend to Thee
Graciously approve.
Unconquerable our courage burns,
Under Thy celestial guidance
Suddenly our passions cool
In Thine assuaging calm.
Oh Virgin, in highest sense most pure,
Oh Mother, worthy of all worship,
Our chosen Queen, equal with the Gods."

And:

"Gaze upon her saving glance,
All ye frail and penitent,
With grace accept your holy Fate,
For when ye thank, ye prosper.
Better seemeth every wish
To her service given.
Virgin Mother, Sovereign Queen,
Goddess, ever gracious !"

In this connection, the significant symbol-attributes of the Virgin in the Litany of Loretto must also be mentioned:

Mater amabilis	Thou beloved Mother
Mater admirabilis	Thou wonderful Mother
Mater boni consilii	Thou Mother of good counsel
Speculum justitiæ	Thou Mirror of justice
Sedes sapientiæ	Thou Seat of wisdom
Causa nostræ laetitiæ	Thou Source of our joy
Vas spirituale	Thou spiritual Vessel
Vas honorabile	Thou venerable Vessel
Vas insigne devotionis	Thou surpassing Vessel of devotion
Rosa mystica	Thou mystical Rose
Turris Davidica	Thou Tower of David
Turris eburnea	Thou Tower of ivory
Domus aurea	Thou House of gold
Fœderis arca	Thou Ark of the Covenant
Janua coeli	Thou Gate of Heaven
Stella matutina	Thou Star of the morning

(*Missale Romanum*)

These attributes show the functional importance of the image of the Virgin Mother; they demonstrate how the soul-image affects the conscious attitude, namely as vessel of devotion, as solid form, as source of wisdom and renewed life.

In a most concise and comprehensive form we find this characteristic transition from the service of woman to the service of the soul in an Early Christian writing: *The Shepherd* of Hermas, who wrote about A.D. 140. This book, written in Greek, consists of a number of visions and revelations, which symbolically represent the consolidation of the new faith. The book, long regarded as canonical, was nevertheless rejected by the Muratorian Canon. It begins as follows:

"The man who reared me, sold me to a certain Rhoda in Rome. After many years, I met with her again and began to love her like a sister. On a day a little while after, I saw her bathing in the Tiber, and gave her my hand and helped her out of the river. As I beheld her beauty, I had this thought in my heart: 'Happy would I be, had I a wife of such beauty and such distinction.' That was my sole wish and nothing more (ἕτερον δὲ οὐδὲ ἕν)."

This experience was the starting-point for the visionary episode that followed. Hermas had apparently served Rhoda as slave; then, as often happened, he obtained his freedom, and subsequently encountered her again, when, probably as much from gratitude as from pleasure, a feeling of love was stirred in his heart; which, however, so far as he was aware, had merely the character of brotherly love. Hermas was a Christian, and moreover, as the text subsequently reveals, he was at that time already the father of a family; circumstances which render the repression of the erotic element easily understandable.

Yet the peculiar situation, doubtless provocative of many problems, was all the more favourable for bringing the erotic wish to consciousness. It is, in fact, quite clearly expressed in the thought that he would have liked Rhoda for a wife, although it is definitely confined to this unqualified appreciation as Hermas is at pains to emphasize, since naturally the implied and more direct issue at once incurred a moral prohibition. It is abundantly clear from what follows that this repressed libido evoked a powerful transformation in his unconscious, for it imbued the soul image with life, thus bringing it to spontaneous efficacy.

Let us now follow the text further:

"After a certain time, as I journeyed unto Cumæ, praising God's creation in its immensity, beauty, and power, in my going I grew heavy with sleep. And a spirit caught me up, and led me away through a pathless region where a man may not go. For it was a place full of crevices and torn by water-courses. I made my passage over the river and came upon even ground, where I threw myself upon my knees, and prayed to God, confessing my sins. While I thus prayed, the heavens opened and I beheld that lady for whom I yearned, who greeted me from heaven and said: 'Hail to thee, Hermas!' While my eyes dwelt upon her, I spake and said: 'Mistress, what doest thou there?' And she answered: 'I was taken up, in order to charge thee with thy sins before the Lord.' I said unto her: 'Dost thou now accuse me?' 'No', said she, 'yet hearken now unto the words which I shall speak unto thee. For God, who dwelleth in heaven, and hath created the existing out of the non-existing, and hath magnified it and brought it to increase for the sake of His Holy Church, is wroth with thee, because thou hast sinned against me.' I answered and spake unto her: 'How have I sinned against thee? When and where spake I ever an evil word unto thee? Have I not looked upon thee as a goddess? Have I not ever treated thee like a sister? Wherefore, O lady, dost thou falsely charge me with such evil and unclean things?' She smiled and said unto me: 'The desire of sin arose in thy heart. Or is it not indeed a sin in thine eyes for a just man to cherish a sinful desire in his heart? Verily is it a sin', said she, 'and a great one. For the just man striveth after what is just.'"

Solitary wanderings are, as we know, conducive to day-dreaming and reverie. Probably Hermas, on his way to Cumæ was pondering on his mistress; while thus engaged, the repressed erotic phantasy gradually withdrew

THE TYPE-PROBLEM IN POETRY 277

his libido into the unconscious. Sleep overcame him, as a result of this lowering of the intensity of consciousness, and he fell into a somnambulent or ecstatic state, which is merely a phantasy of great intensity that altogether captivates the conscious. It is significant that what comes to him is no erotic phantasy, but he is transported as it were to another land, represented in phantasy as the crossing of a river and a journey through a pathless country. The unconscious appears to him as an opposite or over-world, in which events take place and men move about as in reality.

His mistress appears before him, not in an erotic phantasy, but in "divine" form, seeming to him like a goddess in the heavens. This fact indicates that the repressed erotic impression in the unconscious has activated the latent primordial image of the goddess, which is in fact the archetypal soul-image. The erotic impression has evidently become united in the collective unconscious with those archaic residues which from primordial time have held the imprints of vivid impressions of woman's nature; woman as mother, and woman as desirable maid. Such impressions have immense power, since they release forces, both in the child and the man, which, in their irresistible and absolutely compelling nature, merit the attribute divine. The recognition of these forces as dæmonic powers can scarcely be due to moral repression, but rather to a self-regulation of the psychic organism which seeks by this orientation to protect itself from loss of equilibrium. For if, against the wholly overwhelming power of passion, which casts a man unconditionally in the path of another, the psyche succeeds in erecting a counterposition, whereby at the summit of passion it severs the idol from the utterly desired object and forces the man to his knees before the divine image, it has thereby delivered him from the curse of the object's spell. He is restored again to himself; he is even forced upon himself; thus coming once more into his own way between gods and men, and subject to his own laws. The awful dread which haunts the primitive, that dread of every impressive phenomenon which he at once senses as magic, as though things were charged with magical power, preserves him in a practical way against that most dreaded possibility, the loss of the soul, with its inevitable sequel of disease or death.

The loss of a soul corresponds with the tearing loose of an essential part of one's nature; it is the disappearance and emancipation of a complex, which therewith becomes a tyrannical usurper of consciousness, oppressing the whole man; it throws him out of his course, and constrains him to actions whose blind one-sidedness has self-destruction as its inevitable issue. The primitives are notoriously subject to such phenomena as running amok, Berserker rage, possessions, and the like. An intuitive knowledge of the dæmonic character of this power supplies an effective guard, for such an insight at once deprives the object of its strongest spell, shifting its source to the world of dæmons, *i.e.* to the unconscious, whence the force of passion actually springs. Exorcising rites, whose aim is to bring back the soul and release the enchantment also effects this backflow of libido into the unconscious.

This mechanism is clearly effective in the case of Hermas. The transformation of Rhoda into the divine mistress deprives the actual object of her provocative and destructive power, and brings Hermas under the law of his own soul and its collective determinants.

By virtue of his ability, he doubtless took an important share in the spiritual movements of his age. At that very time his brother Pius occupied the episcopal see at Rome. Hermas, therefore, was called to collaborate in the great tasks of his time, in a higher degree than he, as a former slave, may have consciously realized. No able mind of that time could for long have withstood the contemporary task of spreading Christianity, unless the limitations and conditions of race naturally assigned to him another function in the great process of spiritual transformation.

Just as external conditions of life constrain a man to social functions, the soul also contains collective determinants which constrain him to the socializing of opinions and convictions. Through the conversion of a possible social trespass and a probable passional self-injury to the service of the soul, Hermas is guided to the accomplishment of a social task of a spiritual nature, which for that time was, assuredly, of no small importance.

In order to fit him for this task, it is clearly necessary that his soul shall destroy the last possibility of an erotic bondage to the object. For this last possibility means dishonesty towards himself. That he may consciously forswear the erotic desire, Hermas merely demonstrates that it would be more agreeable to him if the erotic desire did not exist, but he gives no kind of evidence that he actually has no erotic intentions and phantasies. Therefore his sovereign lady, the soul, mercilessly reveals to him the existence of his sin, thus releasing him from his secret bondage to the object. As a "vessel of devotion" she therewith receives that passion which was on the point of being fruitlessly lavished upon the object. The last vestige of this passion had to be eradicated in order that the contemporary task might be accomplished; this lay in the crying need of mankind for a severance from sensual bondage, *i.e.* the state of primitive "participation mystique". To the man of that age this subjection had become intolerable. Clearly a differentiation of the spiritual function had to take place, in order to re-establish psychic equilibrium. Every one of those philosophical attempts to restore psychic poise or equanimity, which largely emanated from the Stoic teaching, foundered upon their rationalism. Reason can provide this desired equilibrium only to the man whose reason is already an organ of balance. But for how many individuals and at what period of history has this actually been the case? As a general rule, a man must also acquire the opposite of his own condition before he finds himself, willy-nilly, in the middle way. For the sake of mere reason he can never forgo the appealing sensuousness of the immediate situation. Against the power and temptation of the temporal, therefore, he must set the joy of the eternal, and against the passion of the sensual, the ecstasy of the spiritual. As real as the one is for him, must the other be compellingly effective.

Through insight into the actual existence of his erotic desire it is possible for Hermas to reach a realization of this metaphysical reality; which means that the soul-image also acquires that sensual libido which has hitherto adhered to the concrete object. Henceforth this libido bestows upon the image, the idol, that reality which from all time the sense object has exclusively claimed as its own. Thus the soul is able to speak with effect, and successfully enforce her claims.

After the talk with Rhoda recorded above, her image vanishes, and the heavens close. In her stead there now appears an "old woman in shining garments", who informs Hermas that his erotic desire is a sinful and foolish undertaking against a venerable spirit, but that God is wroth with him, not so much on that account but because he, Hermas, tolerates the sins of his family. In this adroit way the libido is entirely withdrawn from the erotic wish and is directed in its next swing into the social task. An especial refinement lies in the fact that the soul has discarded the image of Rhoda and has taken on the aspect of an old woman, thus allowing the erotic element to recede as far as possible into the background.

It is later revealed to Hermas that this old woman is the *Church*, whereby the concrete and personal is dissolved into an abstraction and the ideal gains an actuality and a reality which it had never before possessed. Thereupon the old woman reads to him from a mysterious book directed in general against the heathen and apostates, but whose exact meaning he is unable to seize. Subsequently we learn that the book contains a mission. Thus the sovereign lady presents him with his task, which as her knight he needs must accomplish.

The trial of virtue is also not lacking. For, not long after, Hermas has a vision, in which the old lady appears, promising to return about the fifth hour, in order to explain the revelation. Whereupon Hermas betook himself into the country to the appointed place, where he found a couch of ivory, set with a pillow and a cover of fine linen.

" As I beheld these things lying there", writes Hermas, " I was sore amazed, and a quaking fell upon me and my hair stood on end, and a dreadful fear befell me, because I was alone in that place. But when I came once more to myself, I remembered the glory of God and took new courage ; I knelt down and again confessed my sins unto God, as I had done before. Then she drew near with six young men, the which also I had seen before, and stood beside me and listened while I prayed and confessed my sins unto God. And she touched me and said: ' Hermas, have done with all thy prayers and the reciting of thy sins. Pray also for righteousness, whereby thou mayest bear some of it with thee to thy house.' And she raised me up by the hand and led me to the couch, and said unto the young men: ' Go and build !' And when the youths were gone and we were alone, she said unto me : ' Sit thee here !' I said unto her : ' Mistress, let the aged first be seated.' She said : ' Do as I said unto thee and be thou seated.' But, when I made as though to seat myself upon her right hand, she motioned me with a gesture of the hand to be seated upon her left.

" As I wondered thereat, and was troubled, that I might not sit upon the right side, she said unto me : ' Why art thou grieved, Hermas ? The seat upon the right is for those who are already well-pleasing to God and have suffered for the Name. But to thee there lacketh much before thou canst sit with them. Yet remain as heretofore in thy simplicity, and thou shalt surely sit with them, and thus shall it be for all who shall have accomplished the work which those wrought, and endured what they suffered.'"

The erotic misunderstanding of the situation was indeed very possible for Hermas. The rendez-vous has at once the feeling of a trysting-place in "a beautiful and sequestered spot" (as he puts it). The rich couch waiting there is a fatal reminder of Eros, and makes the fear which overcomes Hermas at this spectacle seem very intelligible. Clearly he must vigorously combat the erotic association, lest he fall into a profane mood. He certainly does not appear to have recognized the temptation, unless perhaps this recognition is taken as self-evident in the description of his dread, an honesty which was far more possible to a man of that time than to a man of to-day. For in that age man was more nearly in touch with his whole nature than are we—hence he was all the more likely to have a direct perception of his natural reactions and to appreciate them correctly. In this case his confession of sin may have aroused forthwith the perception of a profane feeling. In any case the question arising at this juncture, as to whether he shall sit on the right hand or the left, leads to a moral reprimand at the hands of his mistress.

In spite of the fact that signs coming from the left were regarded as favourable in the Roman auguries, the left side, both with the Greeks and the Romans was on the whole inauspicious; allusion to this is found in the double meaning of the word 'sinister'. But the question here raised of right and left, as an immediately ensuing passage shows, has nothing to do with popular superstitions; it is clearly of Biblical origin, referring to *Math.*, xxv, 33: "He shall set the sheep on His right hand, but the goats on the left". Sheep by virtue of their harmless and gentle nature, are an allegory for the good, while the unruly and salacious character of goats provides a suitable image of evil. His mistress, therefore, by assigning to him the seat on the left, figuratively reveals to him her understanding of his psychology.

When Hermas has taken his seat upon the left, rather sadly, as he records, his soul-mistress further reveals to him a visionary scene, which unrolls itself before his eyes: he beholds how the youths, assisted by ten thousand other men, build a mighty tower whose stones fit one into the other without joints. This jointless tower (hence by its very nature of indestructible solidity) symbolizes the Church, so Hermas understands. *The mistress is the Church, and so is the tower.* In the attributes of the Lorettian Litany we have already seen how the Virgin is characterized as Turris Davidica and Turris eburnea (tower of ivory). It would seem as though an identical or similar association were concerned here. The tower undoubtedly has the meaning of something steadfast and secure suggesting the reference in the *Psalms*, lvi, 4:

"For Thou hast been a shelter for me
And a strong tower from the enemy".

A certain resemblance to the Tower of Babel can, I think, be excluded from our interpretation, on the strength of strong internal counter-evidence. None the less it may have chimed in, since Hermas, in company with every other thinking mind of that epoch, must have suffered much from the depressing spectacle of the ceaseless schisms and heretical strifes of the Early Church. Such an impression may also have provided the essential motive for the writing of this book; an inference to which we are all the more entitled by the fact that the revealed book is directed against heathens and apostates. That same confusion of tongues which frustrated the Tower of Babel almost completely dominated the Christian Church in the first century, demanding desperate exertions on the part of the faithful to overcome the confusion.

Since Christendom at that time was far from being one flock under one shepherd, it was only natural that Hermas longed to find the mighty "shepherd", the *Poimen*, as well as that firm and stable form which should unite in one inviolable whole the elements gathered from all the four winds, the mountains and the seas.

Chthonic craving, sensuality in all its manifold forms, with its eager hold upon the enticements of the world and its incessant dissipation of psychic energy in the world's prodigal variety, is a crowning hindrance to the development of a coherent and purposive attitude. Hence the elimination of this obstacle must have been the most important task of that time. It is therefore not surprising that in the *Poimen* of Hermas, it is the vanquishing of this very obstacle that is unfolded before our eyes. We have already seen how the original erotic stimulus and the energy thereby released became translated into the personification of the unconscious complex, *i.e* the figure of Ecclesia as the old woman, who in her visionary appearances demonstrates the spontaneity of the underlying complex. We learn, moreover, at this point that the old woman, the Church, becomes the Tower, as it were, since the Tower is also the Church. This transition is unexpected, for the connection between the Tower and the old woman is not immediately evident. The attributes of the Virgin in the Lorettian Litany, however, will help us upon the right track, because there we find, as already mentioned, the attribute "tower" associated with the Virgin Mother.

This attribute has its source in *The Song of Songs*, IV, 4:

"Sicut turris David collum tuum, quæ ædificata est cum propugnaculis." ("Thy neck is like the tower of David, builded for an armoury").

VII, 4: "Collum tuum sicut turris eburnea." ("Thy neck is as a tower of ivory"). Similarly VIII, 10: "Ego murus, et ubera mea sicut turris." ("I am a wall, and my breasts like towers.")

The Song of Songs, as is well known, was originally a secular love-poem, perhaps a wedding-song which was actually denied canonical recognition by Jewish scholars till quite recently. Mystical interpretation, however, always loved to conceive the bride as Israel and the bridegroom as Jehovah, and, indeed, from a right instinct; since the aim of this conception is a translation of the erotic emotion into a national relationship with God. From the same motives Christianity also possessed itself of *The Song of Songs*, in order to conceive the bridegroom as Christ and the bride as the Church. To the psychology of the Middle Ages this analogy had an extraordinary appeal, and it inspired the perfectly frank Christian erotism of medieval mysticism, of which Mechtild von Magdeburg is one of the most shining examples. In this spirit was the Lorettian Litany conceived. It derives certain attributes of the Virgin directly from *The Song of Songs*. We have already shown this in connection with the tower symbol.

The rose is already employed by the Greek fathers as an attribute of Mary; so too is the lily; these are also related to *The Song of Songs*, 2, 1:

"Ego flos campi et lilium convallium.
Sicut lilium inter spinas, sic amica mea inter filias."

"I am the rose of Sharon,
And the lily of the valleys.
As the lily among thorns,
So is my love among the daughters."

An image much used in the medieval hymns to Mary is the "enclosed garden" from *The Song of Songs*, 4, 12: "Hortus conclusus, soror mea sponsa" ("A garden enclosed is my sister, my spouse") and the "sealed fountain". (*Song of Songs*, 4, 12 : "fons signatus" "A spring shut up, a fountain sealed"). The unmistakably erotic nature of this simile in *The Song of Songs* is explicitly accepted as such by the Fathers. Thus, for example, St Ambrosius interprets the hortus conclusus as Virginity (*De Instit. Virg.*, c. 10). In the same way St Ambrosius compares (*Comm. in Apoc.*, c. 6) Mary with Moses' basket of rushes :

"per fiscellam scirpeam, beata virgo designata est. Mater ergo fiscellam scirpeam, in qua Moses ponebatur ; praeparavit, quia sapientia dei, quae est filius dei, beatam Mariam Virginem elegit, in cuius utero hominem, cui per unitatem personae conjungeretur, formavit." ("Like a basket of rushes is the blessed Virgin designated. Therefore the mother prepared the basket in which Moses was laid ; because the wisdom of God, which is the Son of God, chose the blessed Virgin Mary, in whose womb he fashioned himself man, and with whom by unity of person he became united.")

St Augustine employs the simile (frequently used later) of the thalamus (bridal chamber) for Mary, again with an express implication of the anatomical meaning: "elegit sibi thalamum castum, ubi conjungeretur sponsus sponsae" (*Serm.*, 192) ("He chose for himself the chaste bridal chamber, where as spouse he could be joined to spouse"), and "processit de thalamo suo, id est, de utero virginali" (*Serm.*, 124) ("He issued forth out of the bridal chamber, *i.e.* from the virginal womb").

The interpretation of vas as uterus may accordingly be taken as certain, when parallel with the just quoted passage from St Augustine, we have St Ambrosius saying: "non de terra, sed de coelo *vas* sibi hoc, per quod descenderet, elegit, et sacravit *templum pudoris*" (*De Instit. Virg.*, c. 5) ("Not of earth but of Heaven did He choose this *vessel* for Himself, through which He should descend and sanctify the *temple of shame*"). Similarly with the Greek Fathers the designation σκεῦος (vessel) is not infrequent. Here, too, the derivation from the erotic allegory of *The Song of*

Songs is not improbable, for, although the designation vas does not appear in the Vulgate text, we come upon the image of the goblet and of drinking: "Umbilicus tuus crater tornatilis nunquam indigens poculis. Venter tuus sicut acervus tritici, vallatus liliis."

> " Thy navel is like a round goblet,
> Wherein no mingled wine is wanting:
> Thy belly is like an heap of wheat
> Set about with lilies."
> Song of Songs, VII, 2)

Parallel with the meaning of the first sentence, we find Mary compared with the cruse of oil of the widow of Sarepta in the *Meisterlieder* of the Colmar manuscript (Bartsch, Stuttgart 1862).

".Sarepta in Sydonien lant dar Helyas wart gesant zuo einer witwen diu in solte neren, der glîcht mîn lîp wol wirdeclich, dô den propheten sant in mich got und uns wolt die tiurunge verkêren." ("Sarepta in the Sidonian land, whither Elias was sent to a widow who should nourish him; my body is meetly compared with hers, for God sent the prophet unto me, to change for us our time of famine.")

Parallel with the second sentence St Ambrosius says: "In quo Virginis utero simul acervus tritici et lilii flores gratia germinabat: quoniam et granum tritici generabat et lilium, etc." ("In the womb of the Virgin grace increased like a heap of wheat and the flowers of the lily, just as it also generated the grain of wheat and the lily"). Very remote passages are enlisted by Catholic authorities (Salzer, *Sinnbilder und Beinamen Mariens*) in the quest of this vessel-symbolism, as for instance *Song of Songs*, I, I :

" Osculetur me osculo oris sui: quia meliora sunt ubera tua vino."
" Let him kiss me with the kisses of his mouth :
For thy love is better than wine." (love : lit. breasts)

and even from the book of *Exodus XVI*, 33 : "And Moses said unto Aaron: 'Take a *pot*, and put an omer full of manna therein, and lay it up before the Lord, to be kept for your generations.'"

These artificial associations tell against, rather than for, the Biblical origin of the vessel-symbolism. In favour of the possibility of an extra-Biblical origin, we have the undeniable fact that the medieval hymn to Mary boldly borrows its similes from everywhere, and practically everything that is in any way precious is associated with the Virgin. The fact that the vessel-symbol is certainly very ancient[1]—it springs from the period of the third and fourth centuries—does not argue against its worldly origin, since even the Fathers inclined towards extra-Biblical, "heathenish" similes; as for instance Tertullian[2], St Augustine[3], and others, who compared the Virgin with the earth still undefiled and the unploughed field, certainly not without an obvious side glance towards Kore[4] of the mysteries. Such comparisons were moulded upon pagan models just as Cumont has shown in the early medieval ecclesiastical book-illustration in the case of Elijah's ascension into Heaven, which holds closely to an antique Mithraic prototype. In usages innumerable, of which not

[1] The magic cauldron of the Celtic mythology is further evidence of the vigorous pagan root that contributed to the vessel symbolism. Dagda, one of the benevolent gods of ancient Ireland, has such a cauldron, which fills everybody with food according to his needs or merits. The Celtic god Bran also possesses the cauldron of renovation. It has even been suggested that the name Brons, one of the figures of the Grail legend, is really a development of this Bran. Alfred Nutt considers that Bran, lord of the cauldron, and Brons, are steps in the transformation of the Celtic Peredur Saga into the quest of the Holy Grail. It would seem, therefore, that the Grail motives already existed in Celtic mythology. I am indebted to Dr Maurice Nicoll, of London, for the above allusions.

[2] "Illa terra virgo nondum pluviis rigata nec imbribus foecundata, &c." ("This virgin land has not been watered by rain nor fertilized by showers ").

[3] "Veritas de terra orta est, quia Christus de Virgine natus est." (" Truth is born of the earth, because Christ was born of the Virgin ".)

[4] Kore—Virgin-goddess, identical with Sophia of the Gnosis. Cf. W. Bousset, *Hauptprobleme der Gnosis*. 1907.

the least is the translation of Christ's birth to the 'natalis solis invicti' (birthday of the invincible sun), the Church followed the pagan model. Thus St Hieronymus compares the Virgin with the sun as the mother of light.

These designations of an extra-Biblical nature can have had their source only in the pagan conceptions still current at that time. It is therefore only just, when considering the vessel-symbol, to call to mind the well-known and widely spread Gnostic vessel-symbolism of that time. A great number of contemporary gems have been preserved which bear the symbol of a vessel, or cruse, with remarkable winged bands, at once recalling the uterus with the ligamenta lata. This vessel, according to Matter, is termed the "Vase of Sin", in contrast with the hymn to Mary, in which the Virgin is extolled as 'vas virtutum'. King (*The Gnostics and their Remains*, p. 111) rejects such an idea as arbitrary, and agrees with Köhler's view that the cameo-image (principally Egyptian) refers to the pitcher of the Persian wheel, which pumps the Nile water over the fields, and that this also explains the peculiar bands which clearly served for fastening the pitcher to the wheel.

The fertilizing activity of the pitcher was, as King notes, expressed in antique phraseology as the "impregnation of Isis by the seed of Osiris". One frequently finds upon the vessel a winnowing-basket, probably with reference to the "mystica vannus Jacchi" ("the mystical winnowing basket of Iakchos"), or λίκνον, the figurative birth-place of the grain of wheat and symbol of the god of fertility (Cf. Jung, *Psychology of the Unconscious*, p. 374). There used to be a Greek marriage-ceremony in which a winnowing-basket filled with fruit was laid upon the head of the bride, a manifest fertility charm.

This conception approaches the ancient Egyptian idea that everything originated from the primeval water, Nu or Nut, which is identified either with the Nile or the Ocean. Nu is written with *three pots*, three *water marks*, and the sign of heaven. In a hymn to Ptah-Tenen we find: "Maker of grain, which cometh forth from Him in His name Nu the Aged, who maketh the water appear on the mountains, to give life unto man and woman."[1] Sir Wallis Budge drew my attention to the fact that the uterus symbolism also exists to-day in the Southern Egyptian hinterland in the form of rain and fertility charms. Occasionally it still happens that the natives in the bush kill a woman and take out her uterus, in order to make use of this organ in magical rites. (Cf. P. Amaury Talbot, "*In the Shadow of the Bush*", pp. 67, 74 ff.)

When one bears in mind how powerfully the Fathers of the Church were influenced by Gnostic ideas, in spite of the strongest resistance to such heresies, it is not unthinkable that in this very symbolism of the vessel a pagan relic which proved adaptable to Christianity should have crept in; all the more easily, in fact, since the Virgin worship is itself a vestige of paganism, by which the Christian Church secured the entail of the Magna Mater, Isis, and others. The image of the *Vas sapientiæ* also recalls a Gnostic prototype, viz. Sophia, an immensely significant symbol for the Gnosis.

I have lingered rather longer upon the vessel symbolism than my readers might have expected. I have done this, however, for a definite reason, because, to my mind, this legend of the Grail, so essentially characteristic of the early Middle Ages, contains considerable psychological enlightenment in its relation to the service of woman.

The central religious idea of this infinitely varied legendary material is the holy vessel, which, as everyone must see, is a thoroughly non-Christian image, whose origin is to be sought in other than canonical sources. On the

[1] Budge, *The Gods of the Egyptians*, i, 511 (1904)

strength of the foregoing arguments, I believe it to be a genuine piece of the Gnosis, which either survived the rooting out of heresies by means of secret tradition, or owed its resurrection to an unconscious reaction against the dominion of official Christianity. The survival, or unconscious revivification, of the vessel-symbol indicates a strengthening of the feminine principle in the masculine psychology of that time. This symbolization by means of a mysterious image must be interpreted as a spiritualizing of the erotic motive evoked by the service of woman. But spiritual transformation always means the holding back of a sum of libido, which would otherwise be immediately squandered in sexuality. Experience shows that, when a sum of libido is thus retained, one part of it flows into the spiritualized expression, while the remainder sinks into the unconscious, where it effects a certain activation of corresponding images of which this vessel symbolism is the expression. The symbol lives through the holding back of certain libido forms, and then in its turn becomes an effective control of these libido tendencies.

The dissolution of the symbol is synonymous with a dispersal of libido along the immediate path, or at least with an almost irresistible urge towards direct application. But the living symbol exorcises this peril. A symbol loses its magical, or, if one prefers it, its redeeming power, as soon as its dissolubility is recognised. An effective symbol, therefore, must have a nature that is unimpeachable. It must be the best possible expression of the existing world-philosophy, a container of meaning which cannot be surpassed; its form must also be sufficiently remote from comprehension as to frustrate every attempt of the critical intellect to give any satisfactory account of it; and, finally, its æsthetic appearance must have such a convincing appeal to feeling that no sort of argument can be raised against it on that score.

For a certain period the Grail symbol clearly fulfilled these demands, and to this circumstance its living efficacy was due, which, as the example of Wagner shows, is even to-day not exhausted, although our age and our psychology are urgent for its solution.

Official Christianity, therefore, absorbed certain Gnostic elements which were manifesting themselves in the psychology of the service of woman, and found a place for them in an intensified worship of Mary. From an abundance of equally interesting material I have selected the Lorettian Litany as a familiar example of this assimilation process. This assimilation into the general Christian symbol dealt a death-blow to the service of woman, which was really a swelling bud in the process of soul-culture for man. His soul, which expressed itself in the image of the chosen mistress, lost its individual expression in this translation into the general symbol. Consequently the possibility of an individual differentiation was also lost; it was inevitably repressed by the collective expression. Such deprivations always tend to have bad results, and in this case they soon became apparent. For, in so far as the soul relation to woman was expressed in the collective Virgin worship, the image of woman lost a value to which human nature has a certain natural claim. This value, for which only individual choice can provide a natural expression, relapses into the unconscious when the individual is replaced by a collective expression. In the unconscious the image of woman now receives an energic value which in its turn activates certain infantile archaic dominants[1].

The relative depreciation of the real woman is thus compensated by dæmonic impulses, since all unconscious contents, in so far as they are activated by split off sums

---

[1] For further references to this process cf. Jung, *Psychology of Unconscious Processes*, ch. xiv (*Collected Papers*, 1917).

of libido, appear projected upon the object. In a certain sense man loves woman less as a result of this relative depreciation—hence she appears as a persecutor, *i.e.* a witch. Thus the delusion about witches, that ineradicable blot upon the Later Middle Ages, developed along with, and indeed as a result of, the intensified worship of the Virgin. But this was not the only consequence.

Through the splitting-off and repression of an important progressive tendency a certain general activation of the unconscious came about. This activation could find no satisfying outlet in the general Christian symbol, since adequate expression at once demands individual forms of expression. Thus the way was paved for heresies and schisms, against which a conscious Christian orientation must fanatically defend itself. The frenzy of the Inquisition was the product of over-compensated doubt which came crowding up from the unconscious, and its final result was one of the greatest schisms of the Church, viz. the Reformation.

From this rather lengthy discussion the following insight is gained. We set out from that vision of Hermas in which he was shown how a *tower* was to be built. The old woman, who had at first been interpreted as the Church, now explains that the tower is the symbol of the Church; whereby her significance is transferred to the tower, with which the further text of the *Poimen* is wholly taken up. Henceforth his principal concern is with the tower, no longer with the old woman, and least of all with the real Rhoda. The detachment of the libido from the real object, its translation into the symbol and conversion into a symbolic function, is thus completed. Henceforth the idea of a universal and undivided Church, expressed in the symbol of a jointless and immovable tower, becomes an unshakable reality in the mind of Hermas.

There is a displacement of libido away from the object

into the subject, whereby the unconscious images are activated. These images are archaic forms of expression, which become symbols, and appear in their turn as equivalents for relatively depreciated objects.

This process is in any case as old as mankind; symbols appear among the relics of prehistoric man, just as they abound among the lowest living types of to-day. Clearly, therefore, a biological function of supreme importance must also be concerned in this symbol-forming process. Since the symbol can come to life only at the expense of a relative depreciation of the object, it follows that its purpose is also concerned with object depreciation. If the object had an unconditional value, it would also be absolutely determining for the subject, thereby entirely prohibiting all subjective freedom of action, since even a relative freedom could no longer exist in the presence of unconditional determination by the object. The condition of absolute relatedness to the object is synonymous with a complete externalization of the process of consciousness, *i.e.* with an identification of subject and object, whereby every possibility of cognition is destroyed. In attenuated form this condition still exists to-day among the primitives. The so-called *projections* that are familiar enough in our analytical practice are also mere residua of this original identity of subject and object.

The prohibition and exclusion of all cognition and conscious experience which results from such a state means a considerable sacrifice of the power of adaptation, and this weights the scales heavily against man, who is already handicapped by his natural defencelessness and by a progeny which for many years has a relative inferiority to that of other animals. But the cognitionless state also means a dangerous inferiority, from the standpoint of affectivity, because an identity of feeling with the object possesses the following disadvantages. Firstly, any object whatsoever can affect the subject to any degree, and, secondly, any sort of affect on the part of the subject also immediately compromises and violates the object. An episode from the life of a bushman may illustrate what I mean : A bushman had a little son, upon whom he lavished the characteristic doting fondness of the primitives. It is obvious that, psychologically, such a love is wholly auto-erotic, *i.e.* the subject loves himself in the object. In a sense the object serves as an erotic mirror. One day the bushman came home in a rage: he had been fishing, and had caught nothing. As usual the little fellow ran eagerly to meet him. But the father seized him and wrung his neck upon the spot. Subsequently, of course, he mourned for the dead boy with the same abandon and lack of comprehension as had before made him strangle him.

This case is a good example of the identity of the object with the affect of the moment. Clearly such a mentality is a very serious hindrance to every protective organization of the tribe. From the standpoint of the propagation and extension of the species, it is an unfavourable factor ; hence in a species with strong vitality it must be repressed and transformed. This is the purpose the symbol serves, and for this end it came into being, since it withdraws a certain sum of libido from the object, which is thereby relatively depreciated, bestowing the libido surplus upon the subject. But this surplus operates within the unconscious of the subject, who now finds himself between an inner and an outer determinant, whence arises the possibility of choice and a relative subjective freedom.

The symbol is always derived from archaic residues, or imprints engraven in the very stem of the race, about whose age and origin one can speculate much although nothing definite can be determined. It would certainly be quite wrong to look to personal sources for the source of the symbol, as for instance repressed sexuality. At best, such a repression could only furnish the libido-sum which activates the archaic imprint. The imprint (engram) corresponds with a functional inheritance whose existence is not contingent upon ordinary sexual repression but proceeds from instinct differentiation in general. Differentiation of instinct is an essential biological measure; it is not something peculiar to the human species, for it finds an even more drastic manifestation in the sexual deprivation of the working bee.

In the foregoing instances of the vessel-symbol, I have demonstrated the source of the symbol in archaic ideas. Since we find the primitive notion of the uterus at the root of this symbol, a similar origin might be surmised in connection with the tower symbol. The tower may well belong to that category of symbols, fundamentally phallic, in which the history of symbols is so rich. It is hardly to be wondered at that the moment which reveals to Hermas the alluring couch, thus demanding the repression of the erotic phantasy, should also evoke a phallic symbol, which presumably corresponds with erection. We saw that other symbolic attributes of the Virgin Church have also an undoubted erotic origin, already confirmed as such by their derivation from *The Song of Songs*, and moreover expressly so interpreted by the Fathers. The tower symbol of the Lorettian Litany springs from the same source and may, therefore, have a similar root-meaning. The attribute "ivory" given to the tower is doubtless of an erotic nature, since it refers to the tint and texture of skin (*Song of Songs*, 5, 14: "His belly is as bright ivory"). But the tower itself is also found in an unmistakably erotic connection in *The Song of Songs*, 8, 10 : " I am a wall, and my breasts like towers", which surely refers to the prominence of the breasts with their full and elastic consistency, as in the similar passage: "His legs are as pillars of marble" (5, 15). In further unison we find: "Thy neck is as a tower of ivory", and "Thy nose is as the tower of Lebanon" (7, 5), an obvious allusion to something slender and projecting. These attributes originate in tactile and organic sensations, which are transferred into the object. Just as a gloomy mood seems gray, and a joyous one bright and coloured, the sense of touch is likewise under the influence of subjective sexual sensations (in this case the sensation of erection), whose quality is transferred to the object. The erotic psychology of *The Song of Songs* effects an enhancement of value in the object by directing upon it the images awakened in the subject. Ecclesiastical psychology employs these same images in order to pilot the libido upon the figurative object, while the psychology of Hermas raised the unconsciously awakened image to an aim in itself wherein to embody ideas which held a supreme importance for the mentality of that time, namely the consolidation and organization of the newly won Christian attitude and view of life.

(*b*) *The Relativity of the Idea of God in Meister Eckehart*

The process which Hermas passed through, represents on a small scale what took place in early medieval psychology, namely, a new revelation of woman and the flowering of the feminine Grail symbol. Hermas saw Rhoda in a new light, while the sum of libido thereby released became unconsciously transformed into the accomplishments of the social task of his time.

It is, I think, characteristic of our psychology that the present epoch was, as it were, ushered in by two minds who were destined to have immense influence upon the hearts and minds of the younger generation:

Wagner, the advocate of love, who in his music sounds the whole scale of feeling from Tristan down to incestuous passion, and from Tristan up to the loftiest spirituality of the Grail, and Nietzsche, the advocate of power and of the victorious will of the individuality. In his last and loftiest utterance Wagner took hold of the Grail legend, as Goethe selected Dante, while Nietzsche chose the image of a lordly caste and a lordly morality, an image which had found its embodiment in many a fair-haired heroic and knightly figure of the Middle Ages. Wagner breaks the bonds that stifle love, while Nietzsche shatters the "tables of value" that cramp the individuality. They both strive after similar goals, while at the same time creating irremediable discord, for, where love is, individual power can never prevail, while the dominating power of the individual precludes the reign of love.

The fact that three of the greatest of German minds should fasten upon early medieval psychology in their most important works, is, in my view, proof enough that there is still an unanswered problem surviving from that age.

It may be well, therefore, to try and gain a nearer view of this question. For I have a strong impression that the mysterious something which sprang to life in certain knightly orders of that time (the Templars for instance), and which seems to have found its expression in the legend of the Grail, may possibly contain a shoot or bud of a new orientation to life, in other words a new symbol. The non-Christian or Gnostic character of the Grail symbol takes us back to those Early Christian heresies, those almost grandiose foundations, which conceal so great an abundance of daring and brilliant ideas. Now the Gnosis displays unconscious psychology in full flower, perhaps in almost perverse luxuriance; it reveals, therefore, that very element which most stoutly resists the 'regula fidei', that Promethean and creative spirit which will submit only to the soul and to no collective ruling. Although in a crude form, we find in the Gnosis that belief in the power of individual revelation and of individual discernment which was absent in the later centuries. This belief had its source in that proud feeling of individual relationship with God which is subject to no human statute, and which may even constrain the gods by the sheer might of understanding. Within the Gnosis lay the beginning of that way which led to the intuitions of German mysticism (with their immense psychological significance) which was actually in its flower at the time of which we are speaking.

The focussing of the question now before us immediately brings to our mind the greatest thinker of that time, Meister Eckehart.[1] Just as signs of a new orientation became perceptible in chivalry, so in Eckehart new thoughts confront us ; thoughts belonging to that same *psychic* orientation which prompted Dante to follow the image of Beatrice into the underworld of the unconscious, and which inspired the singers who sang the rune of the Grail.

Nothing is known, unfortunately, of Eckehart's personal life which could shed light upon the way which led him to his knowledge of the soul. But it is with a sense of deep contemplation that he observes in his discourse upon repentance: " ouch noch erfrâget man selten, daz die liute koment ze grôzen dingen, sie sîen zu dem êrsten etwaz vertreten ". ("And still to-day one findeth rarely, that people come to great things without they first go somewhat astray.") This permits us to conclude that he wrote from personal experience. Strangely appealing is Eckehart's feeling of the inner relation with God, when contrasted with the Christian feeling of sinfulness. We feel ourselves transported into

[1] Johannes (or Heinrich) Eckehart, German Dominican monk, born about 1250 and died about 1328. [Translator].

the atmosphere of the Upanishads. A quite extraordinary enhancement of the soul's value must have taken place in Eckehart, *i.e.* a magnified sense of his own inner being, that enabled him to rise to a, so to speak, purely psychological, hence relative, conception of God and of His relation with man.

The discovery and circumstantial formulation of the relativity of God to man and his soul, is, in my view, one of the most important steps upon the way to a psychological understanding of the religious phenomenon; it is the dawning possibility of a liberation of the religious function from the stifling limitations of intellectual criticism, though this criticism has, of course, an equal right to existence.

We now come to the real task of this chapter, namely the discussion of the relativity of the symbol. To my mind the *relativity of God* denotes a point of view which ceases to regard God as an "absolute", *i.e.* removed from the human subject and existing outside all human conditions, but as, in a certain sense, dependent upon the human subject; it also involves the existence of a reciprocal and indispensable relation between man and God, whereby man is not merely regarded as a function of God, but God also becomes a psychological function of man.

To our analytical psychology, which from the human standpoint must be regarded as an empirical science, the image of God is the symbolic expression of a certain psychological state, or function, which has the character of absolute superiority to the conscious will of the subject; hence it can enforce or bring about a standard of accomplishment that would be unattainable to conscious effort. This overwhelming impulse—in so far as the divine function is manifested in action—or this inspiration that transcends all conscious understanding, proceeds from a heaping-up of energy in the unconscious. This libido accumulation animates images which the collective unconscious contains as latent possibilities. Here is the source of the God-*imago*, that imprint which from the beginning of time has been the collective expression of the most powerful and absolute operation of unconscious libido-concentration upon consciousness.

Hence, for our psychology, which as a science must confine itself to the empirical within the limits set by our cognition, God is not even relative, but a function of the unconscious, namely the manifestation of a split-off sum of libido, which has activated the God-*imago*. To the orthodox view God is, of course, absolute, *i.e.* existing in Himself. Such a conception implies a complete severance from the unconscious, which means, psychologically, a complete unawareness of the fact that the divine effect springs from one's own inner self. But the standpoint of the relativity of God signifies that a not inconsiderable part of the unconscious processes is discerned, at least by inference, as a psychological content. Such an insight, of course, can only take place when the soul is granted a more than ordinary attention, when in fact the unconscious contents are withdrawn from their projections into objects, and a certain awareness is granted them (the contents), so that they now appear as belonging to and conditioned by the subject. This was the case with the mystics. Not that this was the first appearance of the idea of the relativity of God in general, for there exists both naturally and fundamentally a relativity of God among the primitives. Almost universally on the lower human levels the idea of God has a purely dynamic character, *i.e.* God is a *Divine force*, related to health, to the soul, to medicine, to riches, to the chief—a force which certain procedures can procure, and turn to the making of things essential to the life and health of man, as also upon occasion to the production of magical and malevolent effects. The primitive feels this force as much outside him as within, *i.e.* it is just as much his own life-force as it is the "medicine" in his amulet, or the influence emanating from his chief. This is the first demonstrable conception of a permeating and imbuing spiritual force. Psychologically, the power of the fetich, or the prestige of the medicine-man, is an unconscious subjective evaluation of these objects. Fundamentally, therefore, it is a question of the libido, which is present in the subject's unconscious and is perceived in the object, because whenever unconscious contents are activated they appear projected. The relativity of God of medieval mysticism is, therefore, a harking-back to a primitive condition. Whereas the kindred Eastern conceptions of the individual and supra-individual Atman are not so much a regression to the primitive as a constantly unfolding development away from the primitive, in harmony with the Eastern way, though still retaining principles already clearly present and effective among the primitives. This harking-back to the primitive is not at all surprising, in view of the fact that every vital form of religion, either in its ceremonials or its ethics, embodies one or more primitive tendency, whence indeed proceed those mysterious instinctive forces which promote the perfecting of human nature in the religious process.[1] This recourse to, or interrupted connection with, the primitive (as in the Indian) means a contact with mother-Earth, the original source of all power. Every point-of-view which is differentiated to rational or ethical standards must sense these instinctive forces as 'impure'. But life itself flows from clear and muddy springs. Hence every too great 'purity' also lacks vitality. Every renewal of life emerges through the muddy towards the clear. A constant effort towards clarity and differentiation involves a proportionate lack of

[1] There are numerous examples of this. I have mentioned a few in *Psychology of the Unconscious*.

vital intensity, because of the very exclusion of muddy elements. The process of development needs the muddy as well as the clear. This was clearly perceived by the great relativist Meister Eckehart when he says:

" Dar umbe lîdet got gerne den schaden der sünden unde hât dicke gelitten und aller dickest verhenget über die menschen, die er hat versehen, daz er sie ze grôzen dingen ziehen welle. Nim war ! Wer was unserm herren ie lieber unde heimlicher denne die aposteln wâren ? Der beleip nie keiner, er viele in tôtsünden, alle wâren sie tôtsünder gewesen. Daz hât er in der alten unde niuwen ê dicke bewîset von den, die ime verre die liebsten darnâch mâles wurden, und ouch noch erfraget man selten, daz die liute koment ze grôzen dingen, sie sîen ze dem êrsten *etwas vertreten.*" (" Therefore suffereth God willingly the mischief of sins and much hath He suffered ; moreover, those hath he burdened most whom he chose to lead to great things. Behold ! who were more near and dear to our Lord than the apostles ? None there was who fell not into deadly sins ; all were mortal sinners. This hath he shown in the old and new covenants (which he made) with those who afterwards he loved the most ; and still to-day one rarely findeth people coming to great things who first go not *somewhat astray.*")—Pfeiffer, *Deutsche Mystiker*, vol. ii

Both on account of his psychological penetration and of his religious feeling and thought, Meister Eckehart is the most brilliant representative of that critical movement in the Church at the close of the thirteenth century. I would like therefore to cite a few of his sayings, which throw light upon his relativistic conception of God[1]:

(1) " For man is truly God, and God truly man "
(2) " Whereas who holdeth not God as such an inner possession, *but with every means must fetch Him from without*, either in this thing or in that, where he seeketh Him insufficiently, with every manner of deeds, people or places ; verily such a man hath Him not, and easily something cometh to trouble him. And it is not only evil company which troubleth him, but also the good, not only the street, but also the church, not only evil words and deeds, but even the good. For the hinderance lieth within him-

---

[1] *Von den Hindernissen an wahrer Geistlichkeit.* H. Büttner, *Meister Eckehart's Schriften und Predigten*, vol. ii, 185. (Diederichs, Jena 1909)

self : in him God hath not yet become the world. Were He that to him, then would he feel at ease in all places, and secure with all people, always possessing God." [1]

This passage is of especial psychological interest, for it shows a trait of the primitive idea of God which we sketched above. "With every means fetching God from without" is synonymous with the primitive view that the *tondi*[2] is to be procured from without. With Eckehart, of course, it may be merely a figure of speech, through which the original meaning still glimmers. In any case Eckehart clearly understands God as a psychological value. This is proved by the following sentence : "Who fetcheth God from without, troubled is he by objects." For, when God is without, He is necessarily projected into the object, whereby the object acquires an excessive valuation. But whenever this is the case, the object also gains a supreme influence over the subject, holding him in a certain slavish dependence. Eckehart is evidently referring to this familiar subjection to the object, which makes the world appear in the rôle of God, *i.e.* as an absolutely determining factor. Hence for such a one "God has not yet become the world", says Eckehart, since for him the world has taken the place of God. Such a man has not succeeded in detaching and introverting the surplus value from the object, thus converting it into an inner possession. Were he to possess it in himself he would have God (this same value) continually as object or world, whereby God would become the world. In the same portion Eckehart says : "Whosoever is right in his feeling findeth things fitting in all places and with all people, whereas he that is wrong findeth nothing right wherever or with whom he may be. For a man of right feeling hath God with him." A

[1] *Geistliche Unterweisung*, 4. (Büttner, vol. ii, p. 8)
[2] The libido-concept of the Bataks. Warnecke, *Die Religion der Batak* (Leipzig 1909). *Tondi* is the name for the magic force around which everything turns, as it were.

man who has this value in himself is everywhere well-disposed; he is not dependent upon objects, *i.e.* he is not for ever needing and hoping from the object, what he himself lacks.

It should be sufficiently evident from these considerations that, for Eckehart, God is a psychological, or more accurately a *psycho-dynamic, state.*

(3) " Again must ye understand the *soul* as the Kingdom of God. For the *soul is of like nature with Divinity*. All that was here spoken of God's Kingdom, so far as God Himself is this Kingdom, may be truly said in like manner of the soul. *All things came to pass through Him*, saith St John. *This must be understood of the soul, since the soul is the All.* Such it is, as an image of God. But as such is it also the Kingdom of God. So deeply, saith one master, is God in the soul, that His whole Divine nature resteth upon it. That God is in the soul is an higher estate than that the soul is in God : when the soul is in God, it is not blessed therein, but blessed indeed is the soul which God inhabits. Of this be ye certain : *God is Himself blessed in the soul !*"

The soul, that ambiguous and variously-interpreted concept, corresponds historically with a psychological content to which a certain independence must belong within the limits of consciousness. For, if this were not the case, man would never have arrived at the notion of ascribing an independent nature to the soul, as though it were an objectively discernible thing. Like every autonomous complex, it must be a content to which spontaneity, and hence a partial unconsciousness, necessarily belongs. The primitive, as we know, usually possesses several souls, *i.e.* several autonomous complexes with a considerable degree of independence, which gives them the appearance of having a separate existence (as in certain mental disorders.) Ascending to the higher human levels, we find the number of souls decreasing, until the highest level of culture shows us the soul quite dispersed in the consciousness of all psychic activities, and only granted a further existence as a term for the totality of psychic processes. This absorption of the soul into consciousness is just as much a characteristic of Eastern as it is of Western culture. In Buddhism everything is dissolved into consciousness; even the *Samskaras*, the unconscious constructive forces, must be possessed and transformed through religious self-development. To this quite universal historic development of the soul-concept the view of analytical psychology stands definitely opposed, since the analytical idea of the soul does not coincide with the totality of the psychic functions. On the one hand, we define the soul as the relation to the unconscious; while, on the other, it is a personification of unconscious contents. From the standpoint of culture, it may seem deplorable that personifications of unconscious contents still exist, just as an educated and differentiated consciousness might well lament the existence of contents that are still unconscious. Since, however, analytical psychology is concerned with man as he is, and not with the hypothetical man which certain views would like to make him, we have to admit that those same phenomena which persuade the primitive to speak of 'souls', are in fact constantly happening, just as there are still innumerable people among civilized European nations who believe in ghosts. In spite of our carefully wrought theory affirming the 'unity of the self', according to which autonomous complexes cannot exist, Nature does not appear in the least concerned about such intelligent notions.

If we regard the 'soul' as a personification of unconscious contents, so God, according to our previous definition, is also an unconscious content—a personification, in so far as He is personally conceived, an image or expression, when regarded as purely or chiefly dynamic. God, therefore, is essentially the same as the soul, in so far as it is regarded as the personification of unconscious contents.

Hence Meister Eckehart's conception is purely psychological. So long as the soul, as he says, is only in God, it is not blessed. If by 'blessedness' one understands an especially intense and harmonious vital condition, such a state, according to Eckehart, cannot exist, so long as the *dynamis* which is termed God, *i.e.* the libido, is concealed in objects. For, as long as the chief value or God (after Eckehart) does not reside in the soul, power is without, and therefore in objects. God, *i.e.* the chief value, must be withdrawn from objects and brought into the soul, which signifies a 'higher estate' and for God 'blessedness'. Psychologically, this means: that the libido appertaining to God, *i.e.* the projected over-value, becomes recognized as projection;[1] through such recognition objects fade in significance, whereby the surplus value is accredited to the individuality, giving rise to an intensified vital feeling, *i.e.* a new potential. God, *i.e.* the highest intensity of life, then resides in the soul, in the unconscious. But this does not mean that God becomes completely unconscious, in the sense that the idea of Him also vanishes from consciousness. It is as though the chief value were shifted elsewhere, so that it is now found within and not without. Objects are no longer autonomous factors, but God has become an autonomous psychological complex. But an autonomous complex is always only partially *conscious*, since it is only conditionally associated with the ego, *i.e.* never to such an extent that the ego could wholly embrace it, in which case it would no longer be autonomous. From this moment the over-valued object is no longer the determining factor, but the unconscious. The determining influ-

[1] The recognition of something as a projection must never be understood as a purely intellectual process. Intellectual cognition dissolves a projection only when it is already ripe for dissolution. To withdraw libido from a projection that is not matured is not possible by means of intellectual judgment and will.

ences now proceed from the unconscious, *i.e.* one feels and knows them as coming from the unconscious, a knowledge which produces a "unity of being" (Eckehart), *i.e.* a relation between conscious and unconscious, in which of course the unconscious predominates.

We should now ask ourselves, whence comes this "blessedness" or wonder of love[1]? (*ânanda*, as the Indians call the state of Brahman). In this State the superior value lies in the unconscious, involving a fall of potential in the conscious, which means to say that the unconscious appears as the determining factor, while the self of the reality-consciousness practically disappears. This state is strongly reminiscent of the state of the *child* on the one hand, and of the *primitive* on the other, who likewise is immensely under the influence of the unconscious One might conclusively say that the restoration of the earlier paradisiacal state is the cause of this blessedness. But we have still to understand why this original state is so peculiarly blissful. The feeling of bliss accompanies all those moments which have the character of flowing life, moments, therefore, or states, when what was dammed up can freely flow, when we have longer to satisfy this or that condition or seek around with conscious effort in order to find a way or effect a result. We have all known situations or moods 'when it goes of itself', when there is no longer any need to manufacture all sorts of wearisome conditions by which joy or pleasure might be stimulated.

The age of childhood is the unforgettable token of this joy, which, undismayed by things without, streams all-embracing from within. 'Childlikeness' is therefore a symbol for the unique inner condition which accompanies blessedness. To be 'like unto a child' means to possess a treasury of constantly accessible libido. The

---

[1] William Blake, the English mystic, says: "Energy is eternal delight". *Poetical Works*, Vol. i, p. 240. (London 1906)

libido of the child flows into things; in this way he gains the world, then by degrees loses himself in the world (to use the language of religion) through a gradual overvaluation of things. Whence arises the dependence upon things, entailing the necessity of sacrifice, *i.e.* the drawing away of libido, the severance of ties. This is the way by which the intuitive doctrine of the religious system attempts to re-assemble the wasted energy; indeed, this harvesting-process is actually represented in its symbols. The overvaluation of the object, as contrasted with the inferiority of the subject, results in a retrogressive current which would bring the libido quite naturally back to the subject, were it not for the obstructing power of consciousness.

Everywhere with the primitives we find religious practice harmonizing with Nature, since the primitive is able to follow his instinct without difficulty, first in one direction and then in another. The practice of religion enables him to recreate the needful magic force, or to recover the soul that was lost during the night.

The objective of the great religions is contained in the injunction 'not of this world', which suggests the inward subjective movement of the libido into the unconscious. The general withdrawing and introversion of the libido creates an unconscious libido-concentration, which is symbolized as a 'treasure', as in the Parables of the "costly pearl" and the "treasure in the field". Eckehart also uses the latter allegory, which he interprets in the following way: "The Kingdom of Heaven is like unto a treasure which is hid in a field, saith Christ. This field is the soul—wherein the treasure of the Kingdom of God lieth hidden. In the soul, therefore, are God and all creatures blessed."[1] This interpretation agrees with our psychological principles. The soul is the personifica-

[1] Büttner, *l.c.*, vol. ii, p. 195.

tion of the unconscious, where lies the treasure, *i.e.* the libido which is submerged or absorbed in introversion. It is this sum of libido which is described as 'the Kingdom of God'. This signifies a constant unity or reconciliation with God, a living in His Kingdom, *i.e.* in that state in which a paramount libido accumulation lies in the unconscious, by which the conscious life is determined. The libido concentrated in the unconscious comes from objects, from the world, whose former ascendancy it conditioned. God was then 'without', whereas now He works from 'within', as that hidden treasure which is conceived as 'God's Kingdom'. This clearly contains the idea that the libido assembled in the soul represents a relation to God (God's Kingdom). Now when Meister Eckehart reaches the conclusion that the soul is itself the Kingdom of God, he conceives it as a relation to God, and God as the power working within the soul and perceived by it. Eckehart even calls the soul the *image of God*. Ethnological and historical ways of regarding the soul make it abundantly evident that it represents a content which belongs partly to the subject, but partly also to the world of spirits, *i.e.* to the unconscious. Hence the soul has always an earthly as well as a rather ghostly quality. It is the same with the magic power, the divine force of the primitives, whereas the point of view of the higher cultural levels definitely severs God from man, finally exalting Him to the heights of pure ideality. But the soul never forgoes its middle station. Hence its claim to be regarded as a function between the conscious subject and these (to the subject) inaccessible depths of the unconscious. The determining force (God) which operates from these depths is reflected by the soul, *i.e.* it creates symbols and images, and is itself only an image. Through these images it transveys the forces of the unconscious into the conscious; so that it is both receiver and transmitter, a perceptive organ, in fact, for unconscious contents. What it perceives are symbols. But symbols are shaped energies, or forces, *i.e.* determining ideas whose spiritual value is just as great as their affective power. As Eckehart says, when the soul is in God, it is not yet blessed, *i.e.* when this function of perception is entirely flooded by the *dynamis*, it is by no means a happy state. But when God is in the soul, *i.e.* when the soul, as perception, comprehends the unconscious and takes on the imaged form or symbol of it, this is a truly happy state. We perceive and realize that the happy state is a *creative state*.

(4) Meister Eckehart utters these noble words:

" If one asketh me ' Wherefore do we pray, wherefore fast, wherefore do we perform all manner of good works, wherefore are we baptized, wherefore did God become Man ?', I would answer ' For that God might be born in the soul and the soul again in God. Therefore is the Holy Script written. Therefore hath God created the whole world, that God might be born in the soul and the soul again in God. *The innermost nature of all corn meaneth wheat, and of all metal, gold, and of all birth, man!*'"

Here Eckehart frankly affirms that God's existence is dependent upon the soul, and, in the same breath, that the soul is the birthplace of God. This latter sentence can readily be understood in the light of our previous reflections. The function of perception (the soul) apprehends the contents of the unconscious, and as a creative function brings the *dynamis* to birth in symbolic form[1]. In the psychological sense the soul brings to birth images which the general rational consciousness assumes to be worthless. Such images are certainly worthless, in the sense that they cannot immediately be turned to account in the objective world. The *artistic* is the foremost possibility for their application, in so far as such a means of expression lies in

[1] According to Eckehart the soul is just as much the comprehender, as the comprehended. Büttner, *l.c.*, vol. i, p. 186.

one's power[1]; a second possibility is *philosophical speculation*[2]; a third is the *quasi-religious*, which leads to heresies and the founding of sects; there remains the fourth possibility of employing the forces contained in the images in every form of licentiousness.

The two latter forms were manifested in an especially marked form in the Encratitic (abstinent, ascetic) and the Antitactic (anarchical) schools of the Gnostics. As regards reality-adaptation, there is, however, a certain indirect value in raising these images to consciousness, since the relation to the real world is thereby cleared of an admixture of phantasy. But the images possess their chief value in assuring subjective happiness and well-being, irrespective of the changing aspects of outer conditions. To be adapted is certainly an ideal. Yet adaptation is not always possible; there are situations in which the only correct adaptation is patient endurance. A passive adaptation of this kind is made possible and easy through a development of the phantasy-images. I used the word "development", because at first the phantasies are merely raw material of doubtful value. In order to reach that form which is likely to yield the maximum value, they must be submitted to treatment. This treatment is a matter of technique, which it is hardly appropriate to discuss here. For the sake of clearness I need only say that there are two possibilities of treatment: (1) the reductive, and (2) the synthetic, method. The former traces everything back to primitive instincts; the latter develops a process from the given material which aims at the differentiation of the personality.

The reductive and synthetic methods are mutually complementary, for reduction to instinct leads to reality,

[1] Literary examples of this are: E. T. A. Hoffman, Meyrink, Barlach (*Der tote Tag*): on the higher levels, Spitteler, Goethe (Faust), Wagner.

[2] Nietzsche in *Zarathustra*.

in fact to the overvaluation of reality, and hence to the necessity of sacrifice. The synthetic method develops the symbolic phantasies resulting from the libido which is introverted through sacrifice. Out of this development a new attitude towards the world arises, whose very difference guarantees a new potential. This transition to a new attitude I have termed *transcendent function*[1]. In the regenerated attitude, the libido that was formerly submerged in the unconscious emerges in the form of positive achievement. It corresponds with a newly-won and visible life, whose image is the symbol of the Divine birth. Conversely, when the libido is withdrawn from the outer object and sinks into the unconscious, the 'soul is born in God'. But because it is, essentially, a negative act as regards daily living, and a symbolic descent to the 'deus absconditus' (concealed God), who possesses very different qualities from the God that shines by day, this is not a happy state (as Eckehart rightly observes)[2].

Eckehart speaks of the Divine birth as of an oft-recurring process. Actually the thing we are dealing with here is a psychological process, which unconsciously repeats itself almost continually, but of which we are only relatively conscious in its most extensive fluctuations. Goethe's idea of systole and diastole certainly hit the mark intuitively. It may have to do with a vital rhythm, or with fluctuations of vital forces, which as a rule take place unconsciously. This may also explain why the existing terminology for this process is either prevailingly religious or mythological, since such expressions or formulæ are primarily related to unconscious psychological

---

[1] Compare a previous handling of this theme in *Psychology of Unconscious Processes* (Jung).
[2] Eckehart says: "Therefore do I turn back once more unto myself, there do I find the deepest places, deeper than hell itself; but again my wretchedness urgeth me hence: Lo, I cannot escape myself! Herein will I plant myself and here will I remain." Büttner, *l.c.*, i, 180.

facts and not—as scientific myth interpretation often asserts—to phases of the moon and other planetary events. And because it is pre-eminently a question of unconscious processes, we have, scientifically, the greatest possible difficulty so far to extricate ourselves from the language of metaphor, as at least to attain the level of the figurative speech of other sciences. Veneration for the great natural mysteries, which religious language endeavours to express in symbols consecrated by their antiquity, significance, and beauty, will suffer no injury from the extension of psychology upon this terrain, to which science has hitherto found no access. We only shift the symbols back a little, thus shedding light upon a portion of their realm, but without embracing the error that by so doing we have created anything more than a new symbol for that same enigma which confronted all the ages before us. Our science is also a language of metaphor, but from the practical standpoint it succeeds better than the old mythological hypothesis, which expresses itself by concrete presentations, instead of, as we do, by conceptions.

5. The soul " through its being a creature first made God, so that formerly, until the soul was made something, there was none (God). A little while since I declared ' that God is God, of whom I am a cause.' That God is, He hath from the soul : that He is Godhead, hath He from Himself." (Büttner, vol. i, p. 198)

6. " But God also becometh and passeth away." (Büttner, vol. i, p. 147)

7. " Because all creatures proclaim Him, God becometh. While I still abode in the ground and bottom of the Godhead, in its flood and source, no man questioned me, whither I went or what I did : none was there who could have questioned me. In the moment I flowed forth all creatures proclaimed God.— And why speak they not of the Godhead ?—All that is in the Godhead, is *One*, and nothing can one say of it. *Only God doeth something ;* the Godhead doeth nothing, it hath nothing to do, and never hath it looked about for aught to do. God and Godhead are different as doing and doing nothing." . . . " When I again come home into God, I make nothing more in myself ; so this my breaking-through is much more excellent than my first

THE TYPE-PROBLEM IN POETRY 315

issue. For I—the one—verily *raise all creatures out of their own, into my perception,* so that in me they also become the One ! When I then go back into the ground and bottom of the Godhead, into its flood and source, none asketh me whence do I come, or whither have I been : for none hath missed me. . . . Which meaneth *God passeth away."* (Büttner, vol. i, p. 148)

As we see from these citations, Eckehart distinguishes between God and the Godhead; the Godhead is the All; neither knowing nor possessing Itself, whereas *God appears as a function of the soul,* just as the soul appears as a function of the Godhead. The Godhead is clearly the all-pervading creative power; psychologically, it is the generating, producing instinct, that neither knows nor possesses itself, comparable with Schopenhauer's conception of the *will.* But God appears as issuing forth from the Godhead and the soul. The soul as creature "expresses" Him. He exists, in so far as the soul is distinguished from the unconscious, and in so far as it perceives the forces and contents of the unconscious; he passes away, as soon as the soul is immersed in the "flood and source" of unconscious energy. Thus Eckehart says in another place :

" As I came forth out of God, all things said ' There is a God ! " That cannot now make me blessed, for therewith I conceive myself as creature. But in the breaking-through, when I will to stand free in the will of God, and also free of God's will, and all His works, *even of God Himself*—then am I more than all creatures, *then* am I neither God nor creature : I am, what I was, and what I shall remain, now and evermore ! *Then* do I receive a push which brings me up above all the angels. In this push I am become so rich that God cannot be enough for me, even in all which as God He is, and in all His Divine works : for in this breaking-through I receive what I and God have in common. *Then* I am what I was, *then* I neither increase nor diminish, for I am something unmoved which moveth all things. Here God findeth no more place in man, for here hath man conquered again through his poverty what eternally he hath been and ever will remain. Here is God taken into the spirit."

The "coming forth" signifies a becoming aware of the unconscious contents, and of unconscious energy in the form of an *idea* born of the soul. This is an act of conscious discrimination from the unconscious *dynamis*, a severance of the ego as subject, from God (*i.e.* the unconscious *dynamis*) as object. In this way God "becometh". When, through the "breaking-through", *i.e.* through a "cutting off" of the ego from the world, and through an identification of the ego with the motivating *dynamis* of the unconscious, this severance is once more resolved, God disappears as object and becomes the subject which is no longer distinguished from the ego, *i.e.* the ego as a relatively late product of differentiation, becomes once more united with the mystic, dynamic, universal participation ("participation mystique" of the primitives). This is the immersion in the "flood and source". The numerous analogies with the ideas of the East are at once evident. Writers more competent than myself have already fully elaborated them. But in the absence of direct influence this parallelism proves that Eckehart thinks from the depth of the collective psyche which is common to East and West. This common basis, for which no common historical background can be made answerable, is the primordial foundation of primitive mentality, with its primitive energic notion of God, in which the impelling *dynamis* has not yet crystallized into the abstract idea of God.

This harking-back to primeval nature, this religiously organized regression to psychic conditions of early times, is common to all religions which are in the deepest sense living; commencing with the identification backward of the totem ceremonies of the Australian negro[1], continuing down to the ecstasies of the Christian mystics of our own age and civilization. This retrogressive process re-

[1] Spencer and Gillen, *The Northern Tribes of Central Australia.*

establishes an original state or attitude, viz. the improbability of the identity with God, and, by virtue of this improbability, which has nevertheless become a supremely important experience, a new potential is produced—the world is created anew, because the individual's attitude to the object has been regenerated.

When speaking of the relativity of the symbol of God, it is a duty of the historical conscience also to mention that solitary poet who, as a tragic fate willed it, could find no relation to his own vision: Angelus Silesius[1]. What Meister Eckehart laboured to express with great effort of mind, and often in hardly intelligible language, Silesius sings in brief, touching, intimate verses, which reveal in their naïve simplicity the same relativity of God that Meister Eckehart had already conceived. The few verses I quote will speak for themselves:

I know that without me
God can no moment live;
Were I to die, then He
No longer could survive.

God cannot without me
A single worm create;
Did I not share with Him
Destruction were its fate.

I am as great as God,
And He is small like me;
He cannot be above,
Nor I below Him be.

In me is God a fire
And I in Him its glow;
In common is our life,
Apart we cannot grow.

God loves me more than Self
My love doth give His weight,
Whate'er He gives to me
I must reciprocate.

He's God and man to me,
To Him I'm both indeed;
His thirst I satisfy,
He helps me in my need.

This God, who feels for us,
Is to us what we will;
And woe to us, if we
Our part do not fulfil.

God is whate'er He is,
I am what I must be;
If you know one, in sooth,
You know both Him and me.

I am not outside God,
Nor leave I Him afar;
I am His grace and light,
And He my guiding star.

I am the vine, which He
Doth plant and cherish most;
The fruit which grows from me
Is God, the Holy Ghost.

[1] Johann Scheffler, mystic and doctor, 1624-77.

I am God's child, His son,	To illuminate my God
And He too is my child;	The sunshine I must be;
We are the two in one,	My beams must radiate
Both son and father mild.	His calm and boundless sea.

It would be ludicrous to assume that such thoughts as these, and those of Meister Eckehart, are nothing but the vain products of conscious speculation. Such thoughts are always significant historical phenomena, the yield of unconscious tides in the collective psyche. Thousands of other nameless ones are behind, standing with similar thoughts and feelings below the threshold of consciousness, ready to open the gates of a new age. In the boldness of these ideas speaks the imperturbable and immovable certainty of the unconscious mind, which will bring about with the finality of a natural law a spiritual transformation and renewal. With the Reformation the current reached the general surface of conscious life. The Reformation in a great measure did away with the Church as the intermediary and dispenser of salvation, and established once again the personal relation with God. This was the culminating point in the objectification of the idea of God, and from this point the concept of God again became increasingly subjective. The logical result of this subjectifying process is a splitting-up into sects, and its most extreme outcome is individualism, representing a new form of 'remoteness', whose immediate danger is submersion in the unconscious *dynamis*. The cult of the 'blonde beast' springs from this development, besides much else that distinguishes ours from other ages. But, whenever this rechute into instinct takes place, an ever growing resistance against the purely shapeless and chaotic character of sheer *dynamis* inevitably appears, the unquenchable need for form and law. The soul, which dives into the stream, must also create the symbol, which embraces, maintains, and expresses this energy. It is this process in the collective psyche which is either felt or intuitively sensed by those poets and artists whose chief creative source is the collective unconscious (*i.e.* perceptions of unconscious contents), and whose intellectual horizon is sufficiently wide to apprehend the main problems of the age, at least in their outer aspects.

Spitteler's *Prometheus* marks a psychological turning-point: he depicts the falling asunder of the pairs of opposites which were formerly together. Prometheus the artist, the soul-server, disappears from human ken; while human society in obedience to a soul-less moral routine is delivered over to Behemoth, the antagonistic, destructive outcome of an outlived ideal. At the right moment Pandora (the soul) creates the saving jewel in the unconscious, which, however, does not reach mankind because men fail to understand it. The change for the better takes place only through the intervention of the Promethean tendency, which by virtue of its insight and understanding brings first a few, and then many, individuals to their senses. It can hardly be doubted that this work of Spitteler has its roots in the intimate life of its creator. But, if it consisted only in a poetic elaboration of this purely personal experience, it would to a large extent lack general validity and permanence. Yet, because it is not merely personal but is largely concerned with the presentation of the collective problems of our time as personally experienced, it achieves universal validity. Its first appearance was none the less certain to encounter the apathy of contemporaries, for contemporaries are in the great majority only fitted to maintain and appraise the immediate present, thus helping to bring about that same fatal issue whose confusion the divining, creative mind had already sought to unravel.

5. The Nature of the Reconciling Symbol in Spitteler

There still remains an important question to discuss: namely the character of this jewel or symbol of renewed life, which the poet divines as the vessel of joy and deliverance. We have compared a number of excerpts, which substantiate the "Divine" nature of the jewel. We find it more or less clearly stated that the symbol contains possibilities for new energic deliveries, *i.e.* the release of libido unconsciously bound. The symbol always says: In some such form as this will a new manifestation of life, a deliverance from the bondage and weariness of life, be found. The libido which is freed from the unconscious by means of the symbol is symbolized as a young or rejuvenated God; in Christianity, for instance, Jehovah achieved a transformation into the loving Father, embracing an altogether higher and more spiritual morality. The motif of the God-renewal[1] is universal, and therefore presumably familiar. Referring to the redeeming power of the jewel, Pandora says: "But lo! I have heard of a race of men, full of sorrow and deserving of pity; therefore have I conceived a gift, with which, perchance, an thou grantest my petition, I may soothe and solace their many woes."[2] The leaves of the tree which shelter the birth sing: "For here abideth presence, blessedness and grace."[3]

Love and joy is the message of the "wonderchild", the new symbol; hence a sort of paradisiacal state. This is parallel with the message that heralded the birth of Christ, while the greeting by the Sun-goddess[4] and the miracle, wherein men at remote distances became 'good' and blessed at the moment of the birth,[5] are attributes of the birth of Buddha. Concerning the 'Divine blessing' I wish to emphasize only this one significant passage:

[1] Cf. Jung, *Psychology of the Unconscious*.
[2] Spitteler, *Prometheus and Epimetheus*, p. 108.   [3] *Ibid.*, p. 127.
[4] *Ibid.*, p. 132.   [5] *Ibid.*, p. 129.

"Those images return again to every man, whose rainbow tinted, dream-like fabric once painted his childhood's future"[1]. This is clearly a statement that childhood's phantasies tend to go to fulfilment, *i.e.* that these images are not lost, but come again in ripe manhood and should be fulfilled. Old Kule in Barlach's *Der tote Tag*[2] says:

"When I lay o' nights, and the pillows of darkness weigh me down, at times there presses about me a light that resounds, visible to mine eyes and audible to mine ears; and there about my bed stand the lovely forms of a better future. Stiff are they yet, but of radiant beauty, still sleeping—*but he who shall awaken them would make for the world a fairer face. A hero would he be who could do it.*" "What would those hearts be like which then might beat! Quite other hearts, thrilling so differently from those that beat to-day."—(Of the images) "They stand not in the sun and nowhere are they lit by the sun. *But they shall and must (come) once out of the night.* That would be the master-work, to bring them up into the Sun; there would they live."

Epimetheus also yearns for the image, the jewel; in his speech on the statue of Heracles (the hero!) he says: "This is the meaning of the image, and with the understanding of it our sole achievement shall be, that we seize and experience the opportunity *so that a jewel shall ripen above our head, a jewel that we must win.*"[3] So too when the jewel, declined by Epimetheus, is brought to the priests, these sing in just the same strain as did Epimetheus in his former craving for the jewel: "Oh come, oh God with Thy grace", only to repudiate and revile in the very next instant the heavenly jewel that is offered them. The beginning of the hymn sung by the priests is not difficult to recognize as the Protestant hymn:

> "*Living Spirit* once again
> Come *Thou true eternal God!*
> Nor Thy *power* descend in vain,
> Make us ever Thine abode;
> So shall *spirit, joy and light*
> Dwell in us, where all was night.

---

[1] Spitteler, *l.c.*, p. 128. [3] Paul Cassirer, Berlin 1912, pp. 16 ff.
[2] Spitteler, *l.c.*, p. 138.

> *Spirit Thou of strength and power*
> Thou *new Spirit* God hath given
> Aid us in temptation's hour
> Train and perfect us for heaven" etc.

This hymn is a perfect parallel with our foregoing argument. It wholly corresponds with the rationalistic nature of Epimethean creatures that the same priests that sing this hymn should reject the new spirit of life, the newly-created symbol. Reason must always seek the solution upon rational, sequential, logical ways, in which it is certainly justified in all normal situations and problems; but in the greatest and really decisive questions the reason proves inadequate. It is incapable of creating the image, the symbol; for the symbol is irrational. When the rational way has become a cul de sac—which is its inevitable and constant tendency—then, from the side where one least expects it, the solution comes. ("What good thing cometh out of Nazareth?") Such, for instance, is the psychological law underlying the Messianic prophecies. The prophecies themselves are projections of the unconscious, which always foreshadows the future event. Because the solution is irrational, the appearance of the Redeemer is associated with an impossible, *i.e.* irrational condition, the pregnancy of the Virgin (*Isaiah*, 7, 14). This prophecy, like many another, has impossible conditions attaching to it; as for instance:

> " Macbeth shall never vanquished be *until*
> Great Birnam wood to high Dunsinane hill
> Shall come against him." (*Macbeth*, IV, i)

The birth of the Saviour, *i.e.* the rise of the symbol, happens in that very place where one is least expecting it, whence indeed a solution is of all things the most improbable. Thus Isaiah says (53, 1):

> " Who hath believed our report?
> And to whom is the arm of the Lord revealed?
> For he grew up before Him as a tender plant,
> And as a root out of the dry ground:

He hath no form nor comeliness;
And when we shall see him,
There is no beauty that we should desire him.
He is despised and rejected of men;
A man of sorrows and acquainted with grief:
And we hid as it were our faces from him;
He was despised and we esteemed him not."

Not only does the redeeming power spring where nothing is expected, but it also reveals itself, as this passage shows, in a form which to the Epimethean judgment contains no special value. In Spitteler's description of the symbol's rejection there can hardly have been any conscious reference to the Biblical model, or one would certainly be able to trace it in his words. It is much more likely that he too created from those same depths, whence prophets and creative minds call up the redeeming symbol.

The appearance of the Saviour signifies a reconciliation of the opposites:

" The wolf also shall dwell with the lamb,
And the leopard shall lie down with the kid;
And the calf and the young lion and the fatling together,
And a little child shall lead them.
And the cow and the bear shall feed;
Their young ones shall lie down together:
And the lion shall eat straw like the ox.
And the sucking child shall play on the hole of the asp,
And the weaned child shall put his hand on the cockatrice' den."—*Isaiah*, 11, 6 ff.

The nature of the redeeming symbol is that of a child (the "wonderchild" of Spitteler), *i.e.* child-likeness or an attitude which assumes nothing is of the very nature of the symbol and its function. This "childlike" attitude carries with it the condition eo ipso that, in place of self-will and rational purposiveness, another guiding principle shall have effect whose Divinity is synonymous with 'superior power'. The guiding principle is of an irrational nature, wherefore it appears in a miraculous guise. Isaiah gives this character very beautifully:

" For unto us a child is born,
Unto us a son is given;
And the government shall be upon his shoulder:
And his name shall be called Wonderful,
Counsellor, The mighty God.
The everlasting Father, The Prince of Peace."
—*Isaiah*, 9, 5.

These conditions give the essential qualities of the redeeming symbol, which we have already established above. The criterion of the "Divine" effect is the irresistible force of the unconscious impulse. The hero is always the figure endowed with magical power, who makes the impossible possible. The symbol is the middle way, upon which the opposites unite towards a new movement, a water-course that pours forth fertility after long drought. The tension that precedes the release is likened to a pregnancy:

" Like as a woman with child,
That draweth near the time of her delivery,
Is in pain, and crieth out in her pangs;
So have we been in Thy sight, O Lord.
We have been with child, we have been in pain,
We have as it were brought forth wind;
We have not wrought any deliverance in the earth;
Neither have the inhabitants of the world fallen.
Thy dead shall live, my dead bodies shall arise."
—*Isaiah*, 26, 17 ff.

In the act of redemption, what was inanimate and dead comes to life, *i.e.* psychologically, those functions which have lain fallow and unfertile, psychic elements that were unused, repressed, despised, under-valued, etc., suddenly burst forth and begin to live. It is precisely the less-valued function, whose life was threatened with extinction by the differentiated function, that continues[1]. This motif recurs in the New Testament idea of the ἀποκατάστασις

[1] Compare my discussion on the Schiller letters.

THE TYPE-PROBLEM IN POETRY 325

πάντων (restoration for all), or reintegration[1], which is a higher evolutionary form of that world-wide version of the hero-myth in which the hero, on his exit from the belly of the whale, brings with him not only his parents but the whole company of those previously swallowed by the monster—what Frobenius calls the "universal hatching out"[2]. This association with the hero-myth is also confirmed by Isaiah in the two verses:

" In that day the Lord
With His sore and great and strong sword
Shall punish leviathan the piercing serpent,
Even leviathan that crooked serpent;
And *He shall slay the dragon that is in the sea.*"—*Isaiah*, 27, 1.

With the birth of the symbol, the regression of the libido into the unconscious ceases. Regression is converted into progression, damming-up gives place to flowing; whereupon the absorbing power of the primeval is broken. Thus Kule says in Barlach's drama *Der tote Tag*:

" And there about my bed stand the lovely forms of a better future. Stiff are they yet, but of radiant beauty, still sleeping—but he who shall awaken them would make for the world a fairer face. A hero would he be who could do it.

Mother: An heroic life in misery and dire need !
Kule: But perchance there might be one !
Mother: *He first must bury his mother.*"

I have abundantly illustrated the motif of the "mother-dragon" in an earlier work[3], so I may spare myself a repetition of it here. The dawn of new life and fruitfulness in the direction where nothing could be expected is also sung by Isaiah:

" Then the eyes of the blind shall be opened,
And the ears of the deaf shall be unstopped,
Then shall the lame man leap as an hart,
And the tongue of the dumb sing :

---

[1] *Epistle to the Romans*, 8, 19.
[2] Frobenius, *Das Zeitalter des Sonnengottes*.
[3] *Psychology of the Unconscious*. We find in Spitteler a parallel with the slaughter of Leviathan in the overpowering of Behemoth.

> For in the wilderness shall waters break out,
> And streams in the desert.
> And the parched ground shall become a pool,
> And the thirsty land springs of water:
> In the habitation of jackals, where each lay,
> Shall be grass with reeds and rushes.
> *And an highway shall be there, and a way,*
> *And it shall be called The way of holiness:*
> The unclean shall not pass over it;
> But it shall be for those:
> The wayfaring men, yea fools,
> Shall not go astray therein."—*Isaiah*, 35, 5 ff.

The redeeming symbol is a highway, a way upon which life can move forward without torment and compulsion.

Hölderlin says in *Patmos*:

> " Near is God and hard to seize.
> But wherever danger lurks
> Groweth the thing that saves."

That sounds as though the nearness of God were a danger, *i.e.* as though the concentration of libido in the unconscious were a danger to the conscious life. And this is actually the case; for the more the libido is invested—or, more accurately, invests itself—in the unconscious, the greater becomes the influence, or effective potentiality, of the unconscious; which means that all the rejected, thrown aside, outlived function possibilities which for generations have been entirely lost, become reanimated and begin to exercise an increasing influence upon consciousness, notwithstanding often desperate resistance on the part of conscious insight. The saving factor is the symbol, which is able to reconcile the conscious with the unconscious and embrace them both.

While the consciously disposable libido becomes gradually used up in the differentiated function, and is only restored again with constantly increasing difficulty, and while the symptoms of inner discord multiply, there is an ever growing danger of a flooding and disintegration by unconscious contents; but all the time the symbol is developing which is fitted to resolve the conflict. But the symbol is so intimately bound up with the dangerous and threatening that it may either be confounded with it, or its appearance may actually call forth the evil and destructive. In every instance the appearance of the redeeming factor is closely linked up with ruin and devastation. If the old were not ripe for death, nothing new would appear; and, if the old were not injuriously blocking the way for the new, it could not and need not be rooted out. This natural psychological association of the opposites is also found in *Isaiah* where (7, 16 ff.; 7, 14) we find that a virgin is to bear a son, who shall be called Immanuel. Immanuel significantly means 'God with us', *i.e.* union with the latent *dynamis* of the unconscious, which is assured in the redeeming symbol. In the verses which immediately follow, we see what this reconciliation portends.

"For before the child shall know to refuse the evil and choose the good,
The land whose two kings thou abhorrest shall be forsaken."

8, 1: "Moreover the Lord said unto me: 'Take thee a great roll, and write in it with a man's pen, Concerning *Maher-shalal-hash-baz.*' ('Rob soon. Hasten booty')."

8, 3: "And I went unto the prophetess; and she conceived, and bare a son. Then said the Lord to me: 'Call his name *Maher-shalal-hash-baz.* For before the child shall have knowledge to cry My father, and My mother, the riches of Damascus and the spoil of Samaria shall be taken away before the king of Assyria.'"

8, 6: "Forasmuch as this people refuseth the waters of Shiloah that go softly—Behold, the Lord bringeth up upon them the waters of the River, strong and many, even the king of Assyria and all his glory; and he shall come up over all his channels, and go over all his banks; and he shall pass through Judah; he shall overflow and go over, he shall reach even to the neck; and the stretching out of his wings shall fill the breadth of thy land, O Immanuel."

I have already pointed out in my book *Psychology of the Unconscious* that the birth of the God is threatened by the dragon, the danger of inundation, and child-murder. Psychologically, this means that the latent *dynamis* may burst forth and overwhelm consciousness. For Isaiah this peril is the enemy-king, who rules a hostile and powerful realm. The problem for Isaiah, of course, is not psychological, but concrete, on account of his complete projection.

With Spitteler, on the contrary, the problem is already very psychological, and, therefore, detached from the concrete object; it is nevertheless expressed in forms that closely resemble those in *Isaiah*, although it is hardly necessary to assume a conscious derivation.

The birth of the deliverer is equivalent to a great catastrophe, since a new and powerful life issues forth just where no life or force or new development was anticipated. It streams forth out of the unconscious, *i.e.* from that part of the psyche which, whether we desire it or not, is unknown and therefore treated as nothing by all rationalists. From this discredited and rejected region comes the new tributary of energy, the revivification of life. But what is this discredited and despised region? It is the sum of all those psychic contents which are repressed on account of their incompatibility with conscious values, hence the ugly, immoral, wrong, irrelevant, useless, etc.; which means everything that at one time appeared so to the individual in question. Now herein lies the danger that the very force with which these things reappear, as well as their new and wonderful brilliance, may so intrigue the individual that he either forgets or repudiates all former values. What he formerly despised is now a supreme principle, and what was formerly truth now becomes error. This reversal of values is tantamount to a destruction of previously accepted values; hence it resembles the devastation of a country by floods.

Thus, with Spitteler, Pandora's heavenly gift brings evil both to the country and to man. Just as, in the classical saga, diseases streamed from Pandora's box, to flood and ravage the land, a similar evil is caused by the jewel. To grasp this, we must first probe into the nature of this symbol. The first to find the symbol are the peasants, as the shepherds are the first to greet the Saviour. They turn it about in their hands, first this way then that, "until at length they are quite dumbfounded by its strange, immoral unlawful appearance". When they brought it to the king, and he, to prove it, showed it to the conscience, demanding its Yea or Nay about it, stricken with terror it sprang pell-mell from the wardrobe to the floor, where it ran and hid itself under the bed with "impossible suspicions". Like a fleeing crab "staring with venomous eyes and malevolently brandishing its twisted claws, the conscience peered from under the bed, and it came to pass that whenever Epimetheus nearer pushed the image, the further did the other recoil with gesticulations of disgust. And thus all silent it crouched, and never a word, nay not a syllable, did it utter, however much the king might beg and entreat and cajole with every manner of speech."

To the conscience evidently the new symbol was acutely unsympathetic. The king, therefore, bade the peasants bear the jewel to the priests.

"But hardly had Hiphil-Hophal (the high-priest) glanced at the face of the image than he began to shudder and sicken, and, raising his arms as though to guard his forehead from a blow, he cried and shouted: 'Away with this mockery, for in it is something *opposed to God;* moreover carnal is its heart and insolence flashes from its eyes.'"

Thereupon the peasants brought the jewel to the academy; but the professors of the university found that the image lacked "feeling and soul"; moreover, "it wanted in sincerity, and had in general no guiding thought".

Finally the goldsmith found the jewel to be spurious and of common metal. On the market-place, where the peasants wished to get rid of the image, the police descended upon it. At sight of the image the guardians of the law exclaimed:

"Dwells there no heart in your body and shelters no conscience in your soul, that ye dare thus openly before all eyes to expose this sheer, wanton, shameless nakedness? ... And now away with ye in haste ! and woe upon you if by any chance the sight of it hath polluted our stainless children and unsullied wives."

The symbol is characterized as strange, immoral, unlawful, opposed to moral sense, antagonizing our feeling and idea of the spiritual, as well as our conception of the 'Divine'; it appeals to sensuality, is shameless and liable to become a serious danger to public morality by the stimulation of sexual phantasies. Such attributes define an essence which is in frank opposition to our moral values; but it is also opposed to our æsthetic judgment, since it lacks the higher feeling-values; and finally the absence of a "guiding thought" suggests an irrationality of its intellectual content. The verdict "opposed to God" might also be rendered 'anti-Christian', since this history is localized neither in remote antiquity nor in China. This symbol, then, by reason of all its attributes, is a representative of the inferior function, hence of unrecognized psychic contents. It is obvious that the image represents—though it is nowhere stated—a naked human figure, in fact, 'living form'. This form expresses complete freedom, which means to be just as one is—as also the duty, to be just as one is: it accordingly stands for the highest possible attainment of æsthetic as well as moral beauty. It signifies man as he might be through

Nature and not through some artificially-prepared, ideal form. Such an image, presented to the eyes of a man as he is at present, can have no other effect than to release in him all that has lain bound in slumber and has not shared in life. If by chance he be only partly civilized, and still more than half barbarian, all his barbarism will be aroused at such a vision. For a man's hatred is always concentrated upon that which makes him conscious of his bad qualities. Hence the jewel's fate was sealed at the moment of its appearance in the world. The dumb shepherd-lad who first found it is half cudgelled to death by the enraged peasants; then the peasants "hurl" the jewel upon the road. Thus the redeeming symbol ends its brief but typical course. The association with the Christian passion-theme is unmistakable. The redeeming nature of the jewel is also revealed in the fact that it appears only once in a thousand years; it is a rare occurrence, this "flowering of the treasure", this appearance of a Saviour, a Saoshyant, or a Buddha.

The end of the jewel's career is mysterious: it falls into the hands of a wandering Jew. "No Jew of this world was it, and strange to us beyond measure seemed his raiment"[1]. This peculiar Jew can only be Ahasuerus, who did not accept the actual Redeemer, and here again steals, as it were, the redeeming-image. The Ahasuerus legend is a medieval Christian saga, in which form it cannot be dated back earlier than the beginning of the thirteenth century[2]. Psychologically, it springs from an element of the personality or a sum of libido which finds no application in the Christian attitude to life and the world, and is accordingly repressed. The Jews were always a symbol for this repressed portion, which accounts for the medieval delirium of persecution against the Jews. The ritual-

[1] Spitteler, *l.c.*, p. 163.
[2] E. König, *Ahasver* (1907)

murder notion contains the idea of the rejection of the Redeemer in an acute form, for one sees the mote in one's own eye as a beam in the eye of one's brother. The ritual-murder idea also plays a part in the Spitteler story, since the Jew steals the wonder-child sent from Heaven. This idea is a mythological projection of the unconscious perception that the redeeming effect is constantly being frustrated by the presence of an unredeemed element in the unconscious. This unredeemed, undomesticated, untrained, or barbaric portion, which can only be held on a chain and not yet allowed to run free, is projected upon those who have never accepted Christianity. In reality, of course, it is an element in ourselves, which has always contrived to escape the Christian process of domestication.

An unconscious perception of this resistant element, whose existence one would like to disavow, is certainly present—hence the projection. Restlessness is a concrete expression of this unredeemed state. The unredeemed element at once monopolizes the new light and the energy of the new symbol. This is another way of expressing the same thing that we have already indicated above when describing the effect of the symbol upon the collective psyche. The symbol intrigues all the repressed and unrecognised contents, as instanced by the 'guardians of the market-place'; similarly with Hiphil-Hophal, who, because of his unconscious resistance against his own religion, immediately brings out and emphasizes the ungodliness and sensuality of the new symbol. The affect displayed in the rejection corresponds with the amount of repressed libido. It is in the moral degradation of the pure gift of heaven in the sultry phantasy-loom of these minds that the ritual-murder is accomplished. The appearance of the symbol has, nevertheless, had its benign effect. Although not accepted in its pure form, it was greedily devoured by the archaic, undifferentiated forces, wherein conscious morality and æsthetic values continued to co-operate. Here the enantiodromia begins, the conversion of the hitherto valued into the worthless, the changing of the former good into the bad.

The realm of the good, whose king is Epimetheus, had lived in age-long enmity with the kingdom of Behemoth.

Behemoth and Leviathan [1] are the two familiar *monsters of God* from the book of Job; they are the symbolical expression of His force and power. As crude animal symbols they portray psychologically allied forces in human nature [2]. Thus Jehovah says: (*Job*, XI., 15 ff.)

"Behold now Behemoth, which I made with thee;
Lo now, his strength is in his loins,
And his force is in the muscles of his belly.
He moveth his tail like a cedar:
And the sinews of his stones are wrapped together.[3]
He is the beginning of the ways of God."

One must read these words attentively: this force is "the beginning of the ways of God", *i.e.* of Jehovah, the Jewish God, who in the New Testament lays aside this form. There He is no longer the Nature-God. This means, psychologically, that this crude instinctive side of the libido accumulated in the unconscious is permanently held under in the Christian attitude; thus the divine half of the libido is repressed, or written down to man's debit account, and in the last resort is assigned to the domain of the devil. Hence, when the unconscious force begins to well up, when "the ways of God" begin, God comes in the shape of Behemoth [4].

One might say with equal truth that God presents

[1] Spittaler, *l.c.*, p. 179.
[2] Cf. *Psych. of the Unconscious*, p. 70.
[3] The Vulgate actually reads: nervi testiculorum ejus perplexi sunt. Spitteler makes Astarte the daughter of Behemoth—significantly enough.
[4] One may compare this with Flournoy: *Une mystique moderne* (*Arch. de Psych.*, xv, 1915).

himself in the Devil's shape. But these moral valuations are optical delusions: the force of life is beyond the moral judgment. Meister Eckehart says:

"Said I therefore God is good : it is not true, I am good, God is not good ! I go still further: I am better than God ! For only what is good can be better, and only what can become better can become the best. God is not good—therefore can He not be better; and, because not better, neither can He be best. Far away from God are these three conditions ' good ', ' better ', ' best '. He standeth above them all."—Büttner, vol. i, p. 165

The immediate effect of the redeeming symbol is the reconciliation of the pairs of opposites: thus the ideal realm of Epimetheus becomes reconciled with the kingdom of Behemoth, *i.e.* moral consciousness enters into a dangerous alliance with the unconscious contents, together with the libido belonging to, or identical with these contents.

Now the children of God have been entrusted to the care of Epimetheus, namely those highest Goods of mankind, without which man is a mere animal. Through the reconciliation with his own unconscious opposite, the menace of disaster, flooding and devastation descend upon him, *i.e.* the values of the conscious are liable to become swamped in the energic values of the unconscious. If that image of natural beauty and morality had been really accepted and valued, instead of serving, merely by virtue of its innocent naturalness, as an incitement to all the filthiness hiding in the background of our "moral" civilization, then, notwithstanding the pact with Behemoth, the Divine children would never have been jeopardized, for Epimetheus would always have been able to discriminate between the valuable and the worthless. But, because the symbol appears inacceptable to our one-sided, rationalistic and therefore deformed, mentality, every standard of value fails. When, in spite of all, the reconciliation of the pairs of opposites transpires as a force majeure, the danger of inundation and disintegration necessarily follows, and in a peculiarly characteristic way, since the dangerous counter-tendencies get smuggled in under the cloak of 'correct ideas'. Even the evil and pernicious can be rationalized and made æsthetic. Thus, one after another, the Divine children are handed over to Behemoth, *i.e.* conscious values are exchanged for sheer impulsiveness and stupidity. Conscious values are greedily devoured by crude and barbarous tendencies which were hitherto unconscious; thus Behemoth and Leviathan erect an *invisible whale* (the unconscious) as symbolizing their principle, while the corresponding symbol of the Epimethean kingdom is the *bird*. The whale, as denizen of the sea, is the universal symbol of the devouring unconscious[1]. The bird, as a citizen of the luminous kingdom of the air, is a symbol of conscious thought; it also symbolizes the ideal (wings) and the Holy Spirit.

The final extinction of Good is prevented by the intervention of Prometheus. He rescues Messias, the last of the sons of God, out of the power of his enemy. Messias becomes the heir to the Divine kingdom, while Prometheus and Epimetheus, the personifications of the severed opposites, become united in the seclusion of their "native valley". Both are relieved of sovereignty — Epimetheus, because he was forced to forgo it, and Prometheus, because he never strove for it. Which means, in psychological terms, that introversion and extraversion cease to dominate as one-sided lines of direction, and consequently the psychic dissociation also ceases. In their stead a new function appears, symbolically represented by a child named Messias, who had long lain asleep. Messias is the mediator, the symbol of the new attitude that shall reconcile the opposites. He is a child, a boy,

[1] Abundant examples of this are to be found in *Psychology of the Unconscious*

the 'puer aeternus' of the immemorial prototype, heralding by his youth the resurrection and rebirth of what was lost (Apokatastasis). That which Pandora brought to earth as an image, and being rejected by men became the cause of their undoing, is fulfilled in Messias. This association of symbols corresponds with a frequent experience in the practice of analytical psychology: a symbol emerging in dreams is rejected for the very reasons detailed above, and even affects a counter-reaction, which corresponds with the invasion of Behemoth. The result of this conflict is a simplification of the personality, based upon individual characteristics which have been present since birth; this reintegration ensures the connection of the matured personality with the energy-sources of childhood. In this transition, as Spitteler shows, there is a great danger that, instead of the symbol, the archaic instincts thereby awakened shall become rationalistically accepted and sheltered among established views.

The English mystic William Blake says[1]: "There are two classes of men: the *prolific*[2] and the *devouring*[3]. Religion is an endeavour to reconcile the two."

With these words of Blake, which are a simple epitome of the fundamental ideas of Spitteler and my elaborations thereon, I would like to close this chapter. If I have unduly expanded it, this came about, as in the discussion of the Schiller letters, through a wish to do justice to the profusion of ideas Spitteler awakens in his *Prometheus and Epimetheus*. I have, as far as possible, confined myself to the essentials; indeed, I have deliberately omitted a whole group of problems which would claim attention in a full elaboration of this material.

[1] *Poetical Works*, i, p. 249.
[2] The prolific=the fruitful, who brings forth out of himself.
[3] The devouring=the man who swallows up and takes into himself.

CHAPTER VI

THE TYPE-PROBLEM IN PSYCHIATRY

WE now come to the work of a psychiatrist who from the bewildering multiplicity of so-called *psychopathic states* attempted to bring two definite types into relief. This very extensive group embraces all those psychopathic border-line states which can no longer be included under the heading of the psychoses proper—hence all the neuroses and degenerative states, *e.g.* intellectual, moral, affective, and such like psychic inferiorities.

This attempt was made in 1902 by Otto Gross, who published a theoretical study entitled *Die zerebrale Sekundärfunktion*, and it was the basic hypothesis of this work that prompted him to the conception of two psychological types[1]. Although the empirical material treated by Gross is taken from the domain of psychic inferiority, this is no reason why the points of view thus obtained should not be transferred to the wider regions of normal psychology; since the unbalanced psychic state affords the investigator a very favourable opportunity of gaining an almost exaggeratedly distinct view of certain psychic phenomena, which are often only dimly perceptible within the boundaries of the normal. Occasionally the abnormal condition has the effect of a magnifying glass. As we shall soon see, Gross himself, in his final chapter, also extends his conclusions to the wider terrain.

By "secondary function" Gross understands a cerebral

[1] Gross also gives a revised though essentially unaltered presentation of the types in his book *Ueber psychopathologische Minderwertigkeiten*, pp. 27 ff. (Braumüller, Vienna 1909)

cell-process that comes into action after the "primary function" has already taken place. The primary function would correspond to the actual performance of the cells, viz. the production of a positive psychic process, let us say, a representation. This performance represents an energic process, presumably, the release of a chemical tension, *i.e.* a chemical decomposition. In the wake of this sudden discharge, termed by Gross the primary function, the secondary function begins. It represents, therefore, a restitution, a rebuilding by means of assimilation. This function will occupy a shorter or longer interval in proportion to the intensity of the preceding expenditure of energy. During such time the cell, as compared with its former condition, is in an altered state; viz. a state of stimulation, which cannot be without influence upon the further psychic process. Processes that are especially *highly-toned* and *loaded with affect* must entail an increased expenditure of energy, hence a definitely prolonged period of restitution or secondary function. The effect of the secondary function upon the psychic process is considered by Gross to be a specific and demonstrable influencing of the subsequent association sequence, with the particular effect of restricting the choice of associations to the 'thema' represented in the primary function, the so-called 'leading idea'. Not long after, as a matter of fact, I was able to show in my own experimental work (as likewise several of my pupils in corresponding investigations) *phenomena of perseveration*[1] following ideas with a high feeling-tone. These phenomena are accessible to mathematical proof. My pupil Dr Eberschweiler, in an investigation of speech-phenomena, has demonstrated this same phenomenon in assonances and agglutinations[2]. Furthermore, we know

[1] Jung, *Studies in Word-Association.*
[2] Eberschweiler, *Untersuchungen ueber die sprachliche Komponente der Association* (Inaug. Diss. Zürich) 1908 (*Allg. Zeitschr. f. Psychiatrie*, 1908)

from pathological experience how frequently perseverations occur in severe brain-lesions, *e.g.* apoplexies, tumours, atrophic and other degenerative conditions. These may well be ascribed to this impeded restitution-process. Thus Gross' hypothesis has a good share of probability. It is only natural, therefore, to raise the question whether there may not be individuals, or even types, in whom the restitution period, the secondary function, persists longer than in others, and, if so, whether certain peculiar psychologies may not eventually be traceable to this. A brief secondary function, clearly, influences fewer consecutive associations in a given length of time than a long one. Hence, in the former case, the primary function can occur much more frequently. The psychological picture, in such a case, would show a constant and rapidly renewed readiness for action and reaction, hence a kind of *capacity for deviation*, a tendency to a superficiality of associative connections, and a lack of the deeper, more integrated connections, a certain incoherence, therefore, in so far as significance is expected of the association. On the other hand many new themata crowd up in the unit of time, though not at all deeply engaged or clearly focussed; so that heterogeneous ideas of varying values appear, as it were, on the same niveau, thus giving an impression of a "levelling of ideas" (Wernicke). This rapid succession of ideas in the primary function excludes any real experience of the affective value of the thema per se; hence the affectivity cannot be anything but superficial. But, at the same time, rapid adaptations and changes of attitude are thereby rendered possible. The real intellectual process—or, better still, abstraction—naturally suffers from the abbreviation of the secondary function, since the process of abstraction demands a sustained contemplation of several initial ideas plus their after-effects, and therefore a longer secondary function. Without this, no intensification and abstraction of an idea or of a group of ideas can take place.

The more rapid recovery of the primary function produces a higher '*réagibilité*,' not of course in the intensive, but in the extensive, sense; hence it provides a prompt grasp of the immediate present, though only of its surface, not of its deeper meaning. From this circumstance we may easily gain the impression of an uncritical or open-minded disposition, as the case may be; we are struck by a certain compliancy and understanding, or we may find an unintelligible inconsiderateness, a crude tactlessness, or even brutality. That too facile gliding over the deeper meanings gives the impression of a certain blindness for everything not immediately transparent or superficial. The quick 'réagibilité' also has the appearance of so-called presence of mind, of audacity even to the point of foolhardiness; thus, besides a lack of criticism, it also suggests an inability to realize danger. His rapidity of action looks like decisiveness; it is more often blind impulse. His encroachment upon another's province is almost a matter of course; this is facilitated by his ignorance of the emotional value of an idea or action, and its effect upon his fellow-men. As a result of the rapid restoration of the state of readiness, the elaboration of perceptions and experiences is disturbed; accordingly *memory* is seriously handicapped, since, as a rule, only those associations are accessible to immediate reproduction, with which abundant connections are engaged. Relatively isolated contents are quickly submerged; for which reason it is infinitely more difficult to retain a series of meaningless (incoherent) words than a poem. Quick inflammability, rapidly fading enthusiasms, are further characteristics of this type. There is also a certain want of taste, which arises from the too rapid succession of heterogeneous contents with a non-realization of their different emotional values. His thinking has a representative character; it tends more towards a quick presentation and orderly arrangement of contents than towards abstraction and synthesis.

In this outline of the type with the shorter secondary function I have substantially followed Gross, with the addition of a few transcriptions into the normal. Gross calls this type: *inferiority with shallow consciousness*. But, if the too unmitigated traits are toned down to a normal level, we get a general picture, in which the reader will again easily recognize the less emotional type of Jordan, in other words, *the extravert*. Full acknowledgment is due to Gross, since he was the first to establish a uniform and simple hypothesis for the production of this type.

The type opposed to it is termed by Gross: *inferiority with contracted consciousness*. In this type the secondary function is particularly intensive and prolonged. By its prolongation, consecutive association is influenced to a greater extent than in the type mentioned above. Obviously, we may also assume an accentuated primary function in this case, and, therefore, a more extensive and complete cell performance than with the extravert. A prolonged and reinforced secondary function would be the natural consequence of this. The prolonged secondary function causes a longer duration of the effect stimulated by the initial idea. From this we get what Gross terms a "contractive effect," namely a specially directed choice (in the sense of the initial idea) of consecutive associations. An extensive realization, or 'approfondissement', of the 'thema', is thereby obtained. The idea has an enduring effect; the impression goes deep. One disadvantage of this is a certain limitation within a narrow range, whereby thinking suffers both in variety and abundance. Synthesis, notwithstanding, is essentially assisted, since the elements to be composed remain constellated long enough to render their abstraction possible. Moreover, this restriction to one thema undoubtedly effects an enrichment of the relevant associations and a firm inner cohesion and integration of the complex; at the same time, however, the complex is shut off from all extraneous material and thus attains an associative isolation, a phenomenon which Gross (in support of Wernicke's concept) terms "sejunction." A result of the sejunction of the complex is an accumulation of groups of ideas (or complexes), which have no mutual connection or only quite a loose one. Outwardly such a condition reveals itself as a disharmonious, or, as Gross [1] calls it, a "*sejunctive*" personality.

The isolated complexes exist side by side without any reciprocal influence: accordingly they do not interpenetrate, mutually levelling and correcting each other. In themselves, they are strictly and logically integrated, but they are deprived of the correcting influence of differently orientated complexes. Hence it may easily come about that an especially strong, and therefore particularly shut-off and uninfluenced complex, becomes an "excessively valued idea," *i.e.* it becomes a dominant, defying every criticism and enjoying complete autonomy, until finally it comes to be an uncontrollable factor, in other words, 'spleen.' In pathological cases we find it as a compulsive or paranoic idea, *i.e.* it becomes an absolutely insurmountable factor, coercing the whole life of the individual into its service. As a result, the entire mentality becomes differently orientated, the standpoint becomes 'deranged.' From this conception of the genesis of a paranoic idea the fact might also be explained that, in certain incipient

[1] In another place (*Psychopath. Minderw.*, p. 41) Gross draws a distinction, rightly in my view, between the "overvalued idea" and the so-called "complex with commanding value". For the latter is characteristic not only of this type, as Gross thinks, but also of the other. The "conflict" complex has always considerable value by virtue of its accentuated feeling tone, no matter in which type it may appear.

conditions, the paranoic idea can be corrected by means of an appropriate psychotherapeutic procedure; namely, when the latter succeeds in combining it with other broadening and therefore correcting complexes.[1] There is also an undoubted wariness, even anxiety, connected with the re-integration of severed complexes. The things must remain cleanly sundered, the bridges between the complexes must be, as far as possible, broken down by a strict and rigid formulation of the complex content. Gross calls this tendency "association fear"[2].

The strict inner seclusiveness of such a complex hampers every attempt at external influence. Such an attempt has a prospect of success only when it succeeds in combining either the premises or the conclusion of the complex, just as strictly and logically with another complex as they are themselves mutually bound. The accumulation of insufficiently connected complexes naturally effects a rigid seclusion from the outer world, and, as we would say, a powerful heaping-up of libido within. Hence, we regularly find an extraordinary concentration upon the inner processes, directed, in accordance with the nature of the subject, either upon physical sensations in one preferentially orientated by sensation, or upon mental processes in the more intellectual subject. The personality seems arrested, absorbed, dispersed, 'sunk in thought', intellectually one-sided, or hypochondriacal. In every case there is only a meagre participation in external life, and a distinct inclination to an unsociable and solitary existence, which often finds compensation in a special love for plants or animals.

The inner processes enjoy a heightened activity, because from time to time complexes which hitherto had only a

---

[1] Cf. P. Bjerre: *Zur Radikalbehandlung der chronischen Paranoia.* (*Jahrbuch für psychoanal. Forschungen*, Bd. iii, pp. 795 ff.)
[2] *Psychopath. Minderw.*, p. 40.

slight connection, or even none at all, suddenly collide; this again gives rise to an intensive primary function which, in its turn, releases a long secondary function that amalgamates the two complexes. One might imagine that all the complexes would at some time or other collide in this way, thus producing a general uniformity and integration of psychic contents. Naturally, this wholesome result could take place only if in the meantime one were to arrest all change in the external life. But, since this is impossible, fresh stimuli are continually arriving and making new secondary functions, which intersect and confuse the inner lines. Consequently this type has a decided tendency to hold external stimuli at a distance, to keep out of the path of change, to maintain life when possible, in its constant daily stream, until· every interior amalgamation shall have been effected. In a diseased subject, this tendency is also clearly in evidence; he gets away from people as far as possible and endeavours to lead the life of a recluse. Only in slight cases, however, will the remedy be found in this way. In all the more severe cases there is nothing for it but to reduce the intensity of the primary function; which problem, however is a chapter in itself, and one which we have already attacked in the discussion of the Schiller letters.

It is now clear that this type is distinguished by quite definite *affect-phenomena*. We have already seen how the subject realizes the associations belonging to the initial presentation. He carries out a full and coherent association of the material relevant to the thema, in so far, that is, as there is no question of material already linked up with another complex. When a stimulus hits upon such material, *i.e.* upon a complex, the result is either a violent reaction and an affective explosion, or, when the isolation of the complex precludes all contact, entirely negative. But, when realization takes place, all the affective values are released; a powerful emotional reaction occurs, which leaves a long after-effect. Frequently this remains outwardly unobserved, but actually it bores in all the deeper. These reverberations of the affect engross the individual's attention, incapacitating him from receiving new stimuli until the affect has faded away. An accumulation of stimuli becomes unbearable, whence violent defence-reactions appear. Wherever a strong complex accumulation occurs, a chronic attitude of defence usually develops, which may proceed to general distrust, and in pathological cases to delusions of persecution.

Sudden affective explosions, alternating with taciturnity and defence, often give such a bizarre appearance to the personality that these persons become quite enigmatic to their entourage. Their impaired readiness, due to inner absorption, leaves them deficient whenever presence of mind or promptness of action is demanded. Accordingly, embarrassing situations frequently occur for which no remedy is at hand—one reason the more for a further seclusion from company. Through the occasional explosions confusion is created in one's relations to others, and the very presence of this perplexity and embarrassment incapacitates one from restoring one's relations upon the right lines.

This faulty adaptation leads to a series of untoward experiences, which unfailingly beget a feeling of inferiority or bitterness, if not of actual animosity, that is readily directed against those who were actually or ostensibly the originators of one's misfortune. The affective inner life is very intense, and the manifold emotional reverberations develop an extremely fine gradation and perception of feeling tones; there is a peculiar emotional sensibility, revealing itself to the outer world in a peculiar timidity and uneasiness in the presence of emotional stimuli, or before every situation where such impressions might be possible. This touchiness, or irritation, is specifically directed against the emotional conditions of the environment. Hence, from brusque expressions of opinion, assertions charged with affect, attempts to influence feeling etc., there is an immediate and instinctive defence, proceeding, of course, from this very fear of the subject's own emotion, which might again release a reverberating impression whose force might overmaster him.

From such sensitiveness time may well develop a certain melancholy, due to a sense of being shut off from life. In another place[1] "melancholy" is mentioned by Gross as a special characteristic of this type. In the same passage he also points out that the realization of the affective value easily leads to excessive emotional valuation, or to '*taking things too seriously*'.

The strong relief given in this picture to the inner processes and the emotional life at once reveals the introvert. The description given by Gross is much fuller than Jordan's outline of the "impassioned type", which must, however, in its main characters be identical with the type pictured by Gross.

In Chapter V of his work Gross observes that, within normal limits both the inferiority types he describes present *physiological differences of individuality*. The shallow extensive or the narrow intensive consciousness is, therefore, distinctive of the whole character[2]. According to Gross, the type of extensive consciousness is preferably practical, because of his quick adaptation to the environment. The inner life does not predominate, since it has no great part to play in the formation of great idea-complexes. "They are energetic propagandists for their own personality, and, on a higher level, they also work for the great ideas already handed down."[3] Gross asserts

---
[1] Gross, *Ueber psychopathologische Minderwertigkeiten*.
[2] *l.c.*, p. 59.   [3] Cf. the similar testimony of Jordan.

that the feeling life of this type is primitive; though in the higher representatives it becomes organized "through the taking over of ready-made ideals from without." His activity, therefore, with respect to the feeling life can (as Gross says) become heroic. "Yet it is always banal". "Heroic" and "banal" scarcely seem compatible attributes. But Gross shows us at once what he means: in this type there is not a sufficiently rich or developed connection between the erotic complex and the remaining conscious content, *i.e.* with the remaining complexes, æsthetical, ethical, philosophical, and religious. At this point Freud would speak of the repression of the erotic element. The distinct presence of this connection is regarded by Gross as a "true sign of the superior nature" (p. 61). For the sound formation of this connection a prolonged secondary function is indispensable, since only through the "approfondissement" and prolonged consciousness of the necessary elements can such a synthesis be brought about. Sexuality can certainly be pressed into the paths of social utility, through the agency of accepted ideals, but it "never mounts above the limits of triviality". This somewhat harsh judgment relates to a circumstance rendered easily intelligible in the light of the extraverted character: the extravert is exclusively orientated by external data, and it is always his pre-occupation with these wherein the principal bias of his psychic activity lies. Hence he has nothing at his command for the ordering of his inner affairs. They have to be subordinated, as a matter of course, to determinants accepted from without. Under such circumstances, no true connection between the more highly and the less developed functions can take place, for this demands a great expense of time and trouble; it is a lengthy and difficult labour of self-education which cannot possibly be achieved without introversion. But for this, the extravert lacks both time and inclination;

moreover, were he so inclined, he is hampered by that same avowed distrust with which he envisages his inner world, or the introvert the outer world.

One should not imagine, however, that the introvert, thanks to his greater synthetic capacity and his greater ability for the realization of affective values, is thereby immediately fitted to carry out the synthesis of his own individuality, *i.e.* to establish once and for all a harmonious association between the higher and lower functions. I prefer this formulation to Gross' conception, which holds that the sole question is one of sexuality; since, in my view, it is not purely a question of sexuality, but of other instincts as well. Sexuality is, of course, a very frequent form of expression for undomesticated, raw instincts; but the struggle for power in all its manifold aspects is an equally crude instinctive expression.

Gross has invented the expression "sejunctive personality" for the introvert, by which, he singles out the peculiar difficulty with which this type obtains any cohesion or connection between his severed complexes. The synthetic capacity of the introvert merely serves to build complexes, as far as possible, isolated from each other. But such complexes are a direct hindrance to the development of a higher unity. Thus, in the introvert also, the complex of sexuality, or the egotistical striving for power, or the search for enjoyment, remains as far as possible isolated and sharply divorced from other complexes. For example, I remember an introverted and highly intellectual neurotic, who wasted his time alternating between the loftiest flights of transcendental idealism and the most squalid suburban brothels, without any conscious admission of the existence of a moral or æsthetic conflict. The two things were utterly distinct as though belonging to different spheres. The result, naturally, was an acute compulsion neurosis.

We must bear this criticism in mind when following Gross' elaboration of the type with intensive consciousness. Deepened consciousness is, as Gross says, "the basis for the deepening of individuality". As a consequence of the strong contractive effect, external stimuli are always regarded from the standpoint of an idea. In place of the instinct for practical life in so called reality, there is an impelling tendency to 'approfondissement'. "Things are not conceived as individual phenomena, but as partial ideas or constituents of the great idea-complex". This conception of Gross accurately coincides with our former reflection à propos the discussion of the nominalistic and realistic standpoints with their antecedent representatives in the Platonic, Megaric, and Cynic schools. In the light of Gross' conception one may easily discern wherein the difference between the two standpoints exists: the man with the short secondary function has in a unit of time many, and only loosely connected, primary functions; hence, he is especially held by the individual phenomenon and the individual case. For such a man the universalia are only nomina and are deprived of reality; whereas for the man with a long secondary function the inner facts, abstracta, ideas, or universalia, are always in the foreground; they are to him the real and actual, to which he must relate all individual phenomena. He is, therefore, by nature a realist (in the scholastic sense). Since, for the introvert, manner of thinking always takes precedence over perception of externals, he is inclined to be a relativist (Gross, p. 63). Harmony in his surroundings gives him especial pleasure (p. 64): it corresponds with his inner pressure towards the harmonizing of his isolated complexes. He shuns every sort of "unrestrained demeanour", for it might easily lead to disturbing stimuli (cases of affect explosion must, of course, be excepted). Social consideration, as a result of his absorption by inner processes, is rather meagre. The strong predominance of his own ideas does not favour an acceptance of the ideas or ideals of others. The intense inner elaboration of the complexes gives them a pronounced individual character. "The feeling-life is frequently unserviceable socially, but is always individual" (p. 65).

This statement of the author must be submitted to searching criticism, for it contains a problem which, in my experience, always gives occasion for the greatest misunderstandings between the types. The introverted intellectual, whom Gross clearly has here in mind, though outwardly showing as little feeling as possible, manifests logically correct views and actions, not least because in the first place he has a natural distaste for any parade of feeling, and secondly because he is fearful lest by incorrect behaviour he should excite disturbing stimuli, i.e. the affects of his fellow-men. He is fearful of disagreeable affects in others, because he credits others with his own sensitiveness; furthermore, he has always been distressed by the quickness and apparent fitfulness of the extravert. He represses his feeling; hence in his inner depths it occasionally swells to passion, when only too clearly he perceives it. His tormenting emotions are well known to him. He compares them with the feelings shown by others, principally, of course, with those of the extraverted feeling type, and he finds that his "feelings" are quite different from those of other men. Hence he embraces the idea that his "feelings" (or, more correctly, emotions) are unique, i.e. individual.

It is natural that they should differ from the feelings of the extraverted feeling type, since the latter are a differentiated instrument of adaptation, and are wanting, therefore in the "genuine passionateness" which characterizes the deeper feelings of the introverted thinking type. But passion, as an elemental, instinctive force, possesses little that is individual—rather is it common to all men. Only what is differentiated can be individual. Hence, in the deepest affects, the distinctions of type are at once obliterated in favour of the universal "all too human". In my view, the extraverted feeling type has really the chief claim to individualized feeling, because his feelings are differentiated; but where his thinking is concerned, he falls into a similar delusion. He has thoughts which torment him. He compares them with the ideas expressed in the world about him, *i.e.* ideas largely derived in the first place from the introverted thinking type. He discovers his thoughts have little in common with these ideas; he may therefore regard them as individual and himself, perhaps, as an original thinker, or he may repress his thoughts altogether, since no-one else thinks the same. In reality, however, his thoughts are common to all the world, although but seldom uttered. In my view, therefore, Gross' statement mentioned above springs from a subjective deception, which, however, is also the general rule.

"The increased contractive power enables an absorption in things, to which an immediate vital interest is no longer attached". (Gross, p. 65). Here Gross lights upon an essential trait of the introverted mentality: the introvert delights in developing ideas for their own sake, quite apart from all external reality. Herein lies both a superiority and a danger. It is a great advantage to be able to develop an idea in an abstract sphere, where sense no longer intervenes. But there is a danger lest the train of thought should become removed from every practical application, and its value for life be proportionately diminished. Hence the introvert is always somewhat in danger of getting too remote from life, and of viewing things too much from their symbolical aspect. Gross also lays stress upon this character. The extravert, however, is in no better plight, only for him matters are rather different. He has the capacity so to curtail his secondary function that he experiences almost nothing but the positive primary function, *i.e.* he no longer remains anchored to anything, but flies above reality in a sort of frenzy; things are no longer seen and realized, but are merely used as stimulants. This capacity has a great advantage, for it enables one to manœuvre oneself out of many difficult situations ("Lost art thou, when thou thinkest of danger", Nietzsche); but it is also a great disadvantage, and catastrophe is its almost inevitable outcome, so often does it lead one into inextricable chaos.

From the extraverted type Gross produces the so-called civilizing genius, and the so-called *cultural* genius from the introverted. The former corresponds with "practical achievement", the latter with "abstract invention". In conclusion Gross expresses his conviction "that our age stands in especial need of the contracted, intensified consciousness, in contrast to former ages where consciousness was shallower and more extensive" (pp. 68 ff.) "We delight in the ideal, the profound, the symbolical. Through simplicity to harmony, this is the art of the highest culture".

Gross wrote this, to be sure, in the year 1902. And how is it now? If we were to express any opinion at all; we must confess that we manifestly need both civilization *and* culture, a shortening of the secondary function for the one, and a prolongation for the other. For we cannot create the one without the other, and we are, unhappily, bound to admit that in humanity to-day there is a lack on either side. Or, let us say, where one is in excess, the other is deficient; thus to express ourselves more guardedly; for the continual harping upon progress has become untrustworthy and is under suspicion.

In summing up, I would observe that the views of Gross

coincide substantially with my own. Even my terms extraversion and introversion are justified from the standpoint of Gross' conception. It only remains for us to make a critical examination of Gross' basic hypothesis, the concept of the secondary function.

It is always a delicate matter, this framing of physiological or 'organic' hypotheses in connection with psychological processes. It will be familiar that, at the time of the great successes of brain research, a kind of mania prevailed for fabricating physiological hypotheses for psychological processes; among these, the hypothesis that the cell-processes withdrew during sleep is by no means the most absurd which received serious appreciation and "scientific" discussion. One was justified in speaking of a veritable brain-mythology; but I have no desire to treat Gross' hypothesis as a "brain myth",—its working value is too important for that. It is an excellent working hypothesis, which has received repeated and well deserved acknowledgment from other quarters.

The idea of the secondary function is as simple as it is ingenious. This simple concept enables one to bring a very large number of complex psychic phenomena into a satisfying formula; it deals, moreover, with phenomena whose diverse nature would have successfully withstood a simple reduction and classification by any other single hypothesis. With such a fortunate hypothesis one is always tempted to overestimate its range and application. Such a possibility might well apply in this case, although in fact, this hypothesis has unfortunately but limited range. Let us entirely disregard the fact that in itself the hypothesis is only a postulate, since no one has ever seen the secondary function of the brain-cells, and no one could ever demonstrate why, theoretically, the secondary function should, qualitatively have the same contractive effect upon the next associations as the primary function, which, according to its definition, is essentially different from the secondary function. There is a further circumstance which in my opinion carries even greater weight: viz. in one and the same individual the habits of the psychological attitude can alter in a very short space of time. If the duration of the secondary function is of a physiological or organic character, it must surely be regarded as more or less permanent. It is not to be expected, then, that the duration of the secondary function should suddenly change; such changes are never found in a physiological or organic character, pathological changes, of course, excepted. But, as I have already emphasized more than once, introversion and extraversion are not *characters* at all, but *mechanisms*, which can, as it were, be inserted or disconnected at will. Only from their habitual predominance do the corresponding characters develop. There is an undoubted predilection depending upon a certain inborn disposition, which, however, is not always absolutely decisive for one or other mechanism. I have frequently found milieu influences to be almost equally important. On one occasion a case actually came within my own experience, in which a man who had presented a marked extraverted demeanour, while living in the closest proximity to an introvert, changed his attitude and became quite introverted when subsequently closely involved with a pronounced extraverted personality.

I have repeatedly observed in what a short space of time certain personal influences effect an *essential alteration* in the duration of the secondary function, even in a well-defined type, and how the former condition becomes re-established with the disappearance of the foreign influence. With such experiences in view, we should, I think, direct our interest more to the constitution of the primary function. Gross himself lays stress upon the special prolongation of the secondary function after strong affects[1], thus bringing the secondary function into a dependent relation upon the primary function.

There exists, in fact, no sort of plausible ground why the theory of types should be based upon the duration of the secondary function; it might conceivably be grounded equally well upon the *intensity of the primary function*, since the duration of the secondary function is obviously dependent upon the intensity of energy-consumption and cell-performance. We might naturally rejoin that the duration of the secondary function depends upon the rapidity of restoration, and that there may be individuals with a specially prompt cerebral assimilation, as opposed to others who are less favoured. If this were the case, the brain of the extravert must possess a higher restitution capacity than that of the introvert. To such a very improbable assumption every basis of proof is lacking. What is known to us of the actual causes of the prolonged secondary function is limited to the fact that, leaving pathological conditions on one side, the special intensity of the primary function effects, quite logically, a prolongation of the secondary function. Hence, in accordance with this fact, the real problem would lie with the primary function and might be resolved into the question, whence comes it that in one the primary function is as a rule intensive, while in another it is weak? If we must shift the problem upon the primary function, we have undertaken to explain the varying intensity, and the manifestly rapid alteration of intensity of the primary function. It is my belief that this is an energic phenomenon, dependent upon a general *attitude*.

The intensity of the primary function seems to be directly related to the degree of tension involved in the

[1] *l.c.*, p. 12. Also in Gross' book: *Ueber pathologische Minderwertigkeiten*, p. 30, and p. 37.

state of readiness. Where a large amount of psychic tension is present, the primary function will also have a special intensity, with corresponding results. When with increasing fatigue tension diminishes, a tendency to deviation and a superficiality of association appear, proceeding to 'flight of ideas'; a condition, in fact, which is characterized by a weak primary and short secondary function. The general psychic tension (apart from physiological causes, such as relaxation, etc.) is dependent upon extremely complex factors, such as mood, attention, expectation, etc., *i.e.* upon judgments of value, which in their turn are again resultants of all the antecedent psychic processes. By these, of course, I do not understand logical judgments only, but also feeling judgments. Technically, we should express the general tension in the *energic* sense as *libido*, while, in the *psychological sense relating to consciousness, we should refer to it as value*. The intensive process is 'charged with libido'; in other words, it is a manifestation of libido, a high-tension energic process. The intensive process is a psychological *value*, hence the associative combinations proceeding from it are termed *valuable*, as opposed to those which are the result of slight contractive effect—these we describe as worthless or superficial.

The *tense* attitude is essentially characteristic only for the introvert, while the *relaxed*, easy attitude denotes the extravert[1], apart, of course, from exceptional conditions. Exceptions, however, are frequent even in one and the same individual. Give the introvert a thoroughly congenial, harmonious milieu, and he relaxes and expands to complete extraversion, until one begins to wonder whether one may not be dealing with an extravert. But transfer the extravert into a dark and silent chamber, where every repressed

[1] This tension or relaxation can occasionally be demonstrated even in the tone of the musculature. Usually one can see it expressed in the face.

complex can gnaw at him, and he will be reduced to a state of tension, in which the faintest stimulus becomes a poignant realization. The changing situations of life can have a similar effect momentarily reversing the type; but the preferential attitude is not, as a rule, permanently altered, *i.e.* in spite of occasional extraversion the introvert remains what he was before, and the extravert likewise.

To sum up: the primary function is, in my view, more important than the secondary. The intensity of the primary function is the decisive factor. It depends upon the general psychic tension, *i.e.* upon the sum of accumulated and disposable libido. The factor that is conditioned by this accumulation is a complex matter, and is the resultant of all the antecedent psychic states. It may be characterized as mood, attention, emotional state, expectation, etc. Introversion is distinguished by general tension, intensive primary function and a correspondingly long secondary function. Extraversion is characterized by general relaxation, weak primary function, and a correspondingly short secondary function.

CHAPTER VII

THE PROBLEM OF TYPICAL ATTITUDES IN ÆSTHETICS

IT is, as it were, self-evident that every province of the human mind that is either directly or indirectly concerned with psychology should yield its contribution to the question we are here discussing. Now that we have listened to the philosopher, the poet, the physician, and the observer of men, let us hear what the representative of æsthetics has to say.

Æsthetics has to deal, not only with the æsthetic nature of things, but also—and in perhaps even higher degree—with the psychological question of the æsthetic attitude. Not for long could such a fundamental phenomenon as the opposition of introversion and extraversion escape the æsthetic standpoint, since the form and manner in which art and beauty are sensed and regarded by different individuals differ so widely that one could not but be struck by this opposition. Disregarding the many, more or less, sporadic and unique individual peculiarities of attitude, there exist two contrasting basic forms, which Worringer has described as '*feeling-into*' ('empathy')[1] and '*abstraction*'[2]. His definition of 'feeling-into' is derived principally from Lipps. For Lipps, feeling-into is "the objectification of my quality into an object distinct from myself, whether the quality objectified merits the

---

[1] There exists, unfortunately, no English equivalent for *Einfühlung*. Notwithstanding a certain unavoidable clumsiness such a term involves, I have preferred the literal 'feeling-into' to a more manageable, though inadequate rendering such as 'empathy'. [Translator]

[2] Worringer, *Abstraktion und Einfühlung*, 3rd ed., Munich 1911.

term 'feeling' or not". "While I am in the act of apperceiving an object, I experience, as though in it or issuing from it, as something apperceived and present in it, an impetus towards a definite manner of inner behaviour. This appears as given through it, as though imparted to me by it.[1]" Jodl[2] interprets it as follows: "The sensuous appearance given by the artist is not merely an inducement which brings to our mind kindred experiences by the laws of association; but, since it is subordinated to the universal laws of externalization,[3] and appears as something outside of ourselves, we also project into it those inner processes which it reproduces in our minds. We thereby give it *æsthetic animation*—an expression which may be preferred to the term 'feeling-into'—because, in this introjection of one's own inner state into the picture, it is not feeling alone that is concerned, but every sort of inner process." By Wundt feeling-into is reckoned among the elementary *assimilation processes*.[4]

Feeling-into, therefore, is a kind of perception process, distinguished by the fact that it transveys, through the agency of feeling, an essential psychic content into the object; whereby the object is introjected. This content, by virtue of its intimate relation with the subject, assimilates the object to the subject, and so links it up with the subject that the latter senses himself, so to speak, in the object. The subject, however, does not feel himself into the object, but the object felt into appears rather as though it were animated and expressing itself of its own accord. This peculiarity depends upon the fact that the

[1] Lipps, *Leitfaden der Psychologie*, 2nd ed. 1906, p. 193.
[2] Jodl, *Lehrbuch der Psychologie* (1908), vol. ii, p. 436.
[3] By externalization Jodl understands the localizing of the sense-perception in space. We neither hear tones in the ear nor do we see colours in the eye, but in the spatially localized object. (*l.c.*, vol. ii, p. 247).
[4] Wundt, *Grundzüge der physiologischen Psychologie*, 5th ed., vol. iii. p. 191.

projection transfers an unconscious content into the object, whence also the feeling-into process is termed *transference* (Freud) in analytical psychology. *Feeling-into, therefore, is an extraversion.* Worringer defines the æsthetic experience in feeling-into as follows: " *Æsthetic enjoyment is objectified pleasure in oneself*" (*l.c.*, p. 4). Consequently, only that form is *beautiful into* which one can *feel* oneself. Lipps says: "Only so far as this feeling-into extends are forms beautiful. Their beauty is simply: this my ideal freely living itself out in them" (*Æsthetik*, p. 247). The form into which one cannot feel oneself is, accordingly, *ugly*. Herein is also involved the limitation of the feeling-into theory, since there exist art-forms, as Worringer points out, whose products do not correspond with the attitude of feeling-into.

Specifically one might mention the oriental and exotic art-forms as being of this nature. But, with us in the west, long tradition has established 'natural beauty and truth to Nature' as the criterion of beauty in art, since it is also the criterion and essential character of Græco-Roman and occidental art in general. (With the exception, however, of certain medieval forms.)

For ages past our general attitude to art has been one of feeling-into, and we can describe as beautiful only a thing into which we can feel ourselves. If the artistic form of the object is opposed to life, inorganic or abstract, we cannot feel our life into it; whereas this naturally always takes place when we have a feeling-into relationship with the object. ("What I feel myself into is life in general", Lipps). We can feel ourselves only into organic form—form that is true to Nature and has the will to live. And yet another art-principle certainly exists, a style that is opposed to life, that denies the will to live, that is distinct from life, and yet makes a claim to beauty. When artistic energy creates forms whose abstract inorganic quality is opposed to life, there can no longer be any question of a creative will arising from the feeling-into need; rather is it a need to which feeling-into is directly opposed—in other words, a tendency to suppress life. "*The impulse to abstraction* would seem to be this counter-urge to the feeling-into need." (Worringer, *l.c.*, p. 16).

Concerning the psychology of this impulse to abstraction, Worringer says: "What psychic suppositions are there for the impulse to abstraction? Among those peoples where it exists we must look for them in their feeling towards the world, in their psychic behaviour vis-à-vis the cosmos. Whereas the feeling-into impulse is conditioned by a happy, pantheistic, trustful relationship between man and the phenomena of the outer world, the impulse to abstraction is the result of a great inner uneasiness or fear of these phenomena, and in the religious connection corresponds with a strong transcendental colouring of every idea. Such a state might be called an immense spiritual agoraphobia. When Tibullus says 'primum in mundo fecit deus timorem' ('The first thing God made in the world was fear'), this very feeling of dread is admitted as the primal root of artistic energy."

This is literally true; feeling-into does presuppose a subjective attitude of readiness, or trustfulness vis-à-vis the object. It is a free movement of response, transveying a subjective content into the object; thus producing a subjective assimilation, which brings about a good understanding between subject and object, or at least simulates it. A passive object allows itself to be assimilated subjectively, but in doing so its real qualities are in no way altered; although through the transference they may become veiled or even, conceivably, violated. Through the feeling-into process similarities and apparently common qualities may be created which have no real existence in themselves. It is quite understandable, therefore, that the possibility of another kind of æsthetic relation to the object must also exist—an attitude, namely, that neither responds nor advances to the object, but, on the contrary, seeks to withdraw from it, and to ensure itself against any influence on the part of the object by creating a subjective psychic activity whose function it is to paralyse the effect of the object.

To a certain extent the feeling-into attitude presupposes an emptiness of the object, which can thereupon be imbued with its own life. Abstraction, on the other hand, presupposes a certain living and operating force on the part of the object; hence it seeks to remove itself from the object's influence. Thus the abstracting attitude is centripetal, *i.e.* introverted. Worringer's concept of abstraction, therefore, corresponds with the introverted attitude. It is significant that Worringer describes the influence of the object in terms of fear or dread. Thus, the abstracting attitude would have a posture vis-à-vis the object, suggesting that the latter had a threatening quality, *i.e.* an injurious or dangerous influence, against which it must defend itself. Doubtless this apparently a priori quality of the object is also a projection or transference, but a transference of a negative kind. We must, therefore, assume that the act of abstraction is preceded by an unconscious act of projection, in which negatively stressed contents are transveyed to the object.

Since feeling-into, like abstraction, is a conscious act, and since the latter is preceded by an unconscious projection, we may reasonably ask whether feeling-into may not also be preceded by an unconscious act. Since the nature of feeling-into is a projection of subjective contents, the antecedent unconscious act must be the opposite—viz. a neutralizing of the object, *i.e.* making it inoperative. For by this means the object is, as it were, emptied, robbed of spontaneity, and thereby made a suitable receptacle for the subjective contents of the feeling-into individual. The feeling-into subject seeks to feel his life into the object, to experience in and through the object; hence it is essential that the independence of the object and the difference between it and the subject be not too manifest. Through the unconscious act preceding the feeling-into process, the independent power of the object is thus depotentiated or over-compensated, because the subject forthwith unconsciously superordinates himself to the object. But this act of superordination can happen only unconsciously, through an intensification of the importance of the subject. This may happen through an unconscious phantasy, which either deprives the object forthwith of its value and force, or enhances the value of the subject placing him above the object. Only by such means can that difference of potential arise which the act of feeling-into demands for the subjective contents to be transveyed into the object.

The man with the abstracting attitude finds himself in a terribly animated world, which seeks to overpower and smother him; he therefore retires himself, so that in himself he may contrive that redeeming formula which can be relied upon to enhance his subjective value to a point where at least it shall be a match for the influence of the object. The man with the feeling-into attitude finds himself, on the contrary, in a world that needs his subjective feeling to give it life and soul. Confidingly he bestows his animation upon it, while the abstracting individual retreats mistrustingly before the dæmons of objects, and builds up a protective counterworld with abstract creations.

If we recall our argument of the preceding chapter, we shall easily recognize the mechanism of extraversion in the feeling-into attitude, and that of introversion in the abstracting. "The great inner uneasiness occasioned by the phenomena of the outer world" is nothing but the stimulus-fear of the introvert, who, as a result of his deeper sensibility and realization, has a real dread of too rapid or too powerful changes of stimuli. Through the agency of the general concept his abstractions also serve a most definite aim; viz. to confine the changing and irregular within law-abiding limits. It is self-evident that this, at bottom magical, procedure is to be found in fullest flower among the primitives, whose geometrical signs are less valuable from the standpoint of beauty than for their magical properties.

Of the orientals, Worringer rightly says: "Tormented by the confused combination and changing play of external phenomena, such people were overtaken by an immense need of repose. The possibility of happiness which they sought in art consisted not so much in immersing themselves in the things of the outer world and seeking pleasure therein as in the raising of the individual thing out of its arbitrary and seemingly accidental existence, with a view to immortalizing it within the sphere of abstract form: wherein to find a point of rest amid the ceaseless stream of phenomena" (*l.c.*, p. 18).

"These abstract, law-determined forms, therefore, are not merely the highest, but indeed the only, forms wherein man may find repose in face of the monstrous confusion of the world spectacle" (*l.c.*, p. 21).

As Worringer says, it is precisely the oriental religious and art-forms which exhibit this abstracting attitude to the world. To the oriental, therefore, the world in general must appear very different from what it does to the occidental, who animates his object with the feeling-into attitude. To the oriental, the object is imbued with life a priori and always tends to overwhelm him; thus he withdraws himself, in order to abstract his impressions from it. An illuminating insight into the oriental attitude is offered by Buddha in the *Fire-sermon*, where he says:

"All is in flames. The eye and all the senses stand in flames, kindled by the fire of love, by the fire of hate, by the fire of delusion; through birth, ageing and death, through pain and lamentations, through sorrow, suffering, and despair is the fire kindled.—The whole world standeth in flames; the whole world is wrapt and shadowed in smoke; the whole world is devoured by fire; the whole world quaketh."

It is this fearful and sorrowful vision of the world that forces the Buddhist into his abstracting attitude, as, indeed, according to legend, Buddha also was brought to his life's quest through a similar impression of the world. The dynamic animation of the object as the fons et origo of abstraction is strikingly expressed in Buddha's symbolic language. This animation is not dependent upon feeling-into, but corresponds rather with an a priori unconscious projection—a projection actually existing from the beginning. The term 'projection' hardly seems qualified to carry the real meaning of this phenomenon. Projection is really an act that transpires, and not a condition existing from the beginning, which is clearly what we are dealing with here. It seems to me that Lévy-Bruhl's concept "participation mystique" is more descriptive of this condition, seeking, as it does, to formulate the primordial relationship of the primitive to his object. For the primitive, objects have a dynamic animation, charged, as it were, with soul-stuff or soul-force (not absolutely soul-endowed as is assumed by the animistic hypothesis), so that they have an immediate psychic effect upon the man, producing what is practically a dynamic identification with the object. Thus in certain primitive languages objects of personal use have a gender denoting 'alive' (the suffix of the 'thing living'). With the abstracting attitude it is much the same, for here also the object has an a priori animation and independence; far from needing any feeling-into on the part of the subject, the object commands so strong an influence that introversion is almost forced upon one. The powerful unconscious libido charge of the object is dependent upon its "participation mystique" with the unconscious of the introverting subject. This is clearly implied in the words of Buddha; the world-fire is identical with the subject's libido-fire, the expression of his burning passion, which, however, appears objective to him, because it is not yet differentiated into a subjectively disposable function.

Abstraction, then, seems to be a function which is at war with the original state of "participation mystique". Its effort is to part from the object, thus to put an end to the object's tyrannical hold. Its effect is either to lead to the creation of art forms, or to the cognition of the object. Similarly, the function of feeling-into is just as effective as an organ of artistic creation as it is of cognition. But it can take place only upon a very different basis from that of abstraction. For, just as the latter is grounded upon the magical importance and power of the object, feeling-into is rooted in the magical importance of the subject, whereby the object is secured by means of *mystical identification*. It is similar with the primitive, who, on the one hand, is magically influenced by the power of the fetish and at the same time, is also the magician, the accumulator of magical power who dispenses potency to the fetish. (Cf. the churinga rites of the Australians)[1].

The unconscious depotentiation of the object, which results from the act of feeling into means also a permanent more moderate valuation of the object. For in this case the unconscious contents of the feeling into subject are identical with the object, thus making it appear inanimate[2]. For this reason feeling-into is necessary for the cognition of the nature of the object. One might speak in this case, of a continually existing, unconscious abstraction which

[1] Spencer and Gillen, *The Northern Tribes of Central Australia* (London, 1904)
[2] Because the unconscious contents of the feeling-into subject are themselves relatively inanimate.

presents the object as inanimate. For abstraction has always this effect: it kills the independent activity of the object, in so far as this is magically related to the psyche of the subject. The abstracting attitude performs this consciously, in order to protect itself from the magical influence of the object. From the a priori inanimateness of the object there likewise proceeds that relation of trust which the feeling-into subject has towards the world; there is nothing there that could inimically affect or oppress him, since he alone dispenses life and soul to the object, although to his conscious appreciation the converse would seem to be true. But, to the man with the abstracting attitude, the world is filled with powerfully operating and therefore dangerous objects; these inspire him with fear, and with a consciousness of his own impotence: he withdraws himself from a too close contact with the world, thus to create those ideas and formulæ with which he hopes to gain the upper hand. His, therefore, is the psychology of the oppressed, whilst the feeling-into subject confronts the object with an a priori confidence—its inanimateness has no dangers for him.

This characterization is naturally schematic, and makes no pretence to be a complete portrait of the extraverted or introverted attitude; it merely emphasizes certain nuances, which, nevertheless, have a not inconsiderable importance.

Just as the feeling-into subject is really taking unconscious delight in himself by way of the object, so the abstracting subject unwittingly sees himself while meditating upon the impression that reaches him from the object. For what the feeling-into subject transveys into the object is himself, *i.e.* his own unconscious content, and what the abstracting man thinks concerning his impression of the object is really thoughts about his own feelings, which appear to him as though belonging to the object. It follows, therefore, that both functions are involved in a real understanding of the object, as indeed they are also essential to a real creativeness in art. Both functions are also constantly present in the individual, although for the most part unequally differentiated.

In Worringer's view the common root of these two basic forms of æsthetic experience is the need for self-divestiture. In abstraction the effort of the subject "is to be wholly delivered from the fortuitous in human affairs, the apparently arbitrary power of general organic existence, in the contemplation of something immovable and necessary". In face of the bewildering and impressive profusion of animated objects, the individual creates an abstraction, *i.e.* an abstract and general image, which conjures impressions into a law-abiding form. This image has the magical importance of a defence against the chaotic change of experience. He becomes so lost and submerged in this image that finally its abstract truth is set above the reality of life; and therewith life, which might disturb the enjoyment of abstract beauty, is wholly suppressed. He raises himself to an abstraction; he identifies himself with the eternal validity of his image and therein congeals, since it practically amounts to a redeeming formula. In this way he divests himself of his real self and transfers his life into his abstraction, in which it is, so to speak, crystallized.

But since the feeling-into subject *feels* his activity, his life, *into* the object, he therewith also yields himself to the object, in so far as the felt-into content represents an essential part of the subject. He becomes the object; he identifies himself with it, and in this way gets rid of himself. Because he objectifies himself he, therefore, de-subjectifies himself. Worringer says:

" But since we *feel* this will to activity *into* another object, we *are* in the other object. We are released from our own individual being, just in so far as our urge for experience engrosses us in an outer object or an extrinsic form. In contrast to the limitless diversity of individual consciousness, we feel our individuality flowing, as it were, within fixed bounds. In this self-objectification there lies a self-divestiture. At the same time, this affirmation of our individual need for activity represents a restriction of its illimitable possibilities, a negation of its irreconcilable diversities. We needs must rest, with our inner urgings towards activity, within the limits of this objectification." (*l.c.*, p. 27)

As in the case of the abstracting individual, the abstract image represents a comprehensive formula, a bulwark against the disintegrating effects of the unconsciously animated object[1], so for the feeling-into subject, the transference to the object is a defence against the disintegration caused by inner subjective factors, which consist in boundless phantasy possibilities and corresponding impulses to activity. Although, according to Adler, the introverted neurotic, is held fast to a "fictitious guiding line", the extraverted neurotic clings no less tenaciously to his transference to the object. The introvert has abstracted his "guiding line" from his good and evil experiences with objects, and he trusts himself to his formula as a means of defence against the unlimited possibilities of life.

Feeling-into and abstraction, extraversion and introversion, are mechanisms of adaptation and defence. In so far as they make adaptation possible, they protect man from external dangers. In so far as they are *directed functions*[2] they liberate him from fortuitous impulses; moreover, they actually protect him, since they render *self-divestiture* possible for him.

As our daily psychological experience testifies, there

[1] Fr. Th. Vischer, in his novel *Auch Einer* gives an excellent picture of "animated" objects.
[2] Cf. directed thinking: Jung, *Psychology of the Unconscious* ch. i, pp. 13 ff.

are numbers of men who are wholly identified with their directed function (the "valuable" function), and among them are those very types we are here discussing. Identification with the directed function has the incontestable advantage that by so doing a man can best adapt himself to collective claims and expectations; moreover, it also enables him to avoid his inferior, undifferentiated, and undirected functions through self-divestiture. Besides, from the standpoint of social morality, unselfishness is always considered a particular virtue. But, upon the other side, we have to weigh the great disadvantage that inevitably accompanies this identification with the directed function, viz. the *degeneration of the individual*. Man, doubtless, is capable of a very extensive reduction to the mechanical level, although never to the point of complete surrender, without suffering gravest injury. For the more he is identified with the one function, the more does its over-charge of libido withdraw libido from the other functions. For a long period, maybe, they will endure even an extreme deprivation of libido, but in time they will inevitably react. The draining of libido involves their gradual relapse below the threshold of consciousness, their associative connection with consciousness gets loosened, until they sink by degrees into the unconscious. This is synonymous with a regressive development; namely, a recession of the relatively developed function to an infantile and eventually archaic level But, since man has spent relatively only a few thousand years in a cultivated state, as opposed to many hundred thousand years in a state of savagery, the archaic function-ways are correspondingly extraordinarily vigorous and easily reanimated. Hence, when certain functions become disintegrated through deprivation of libido, their archaic foundations begin to operate in the unconscious.

This condition involves a dissociation of the personality; for, the archaic functions having no direct relation with consciousness, no practicable bridges exist between the conscious and the unconscious. It follows, therefore, that the further self-divestiture goes, the further do the atonic functions decline towards the archaic. Therewith the importance of the unconscious also increases. It begins to provoke symptomatic disturbances of the directed function, thus producing that characteristic circulus vitiosus, which we encounter in so many neuroses: the patient seeks to compensate the unconsciously disturbing influence by means of special performances of the directed function; and so the chase continues, even, on occasion, to the point of nervous collapse.

Conceivably, this possibility of self-divestiture through identification with the directed function depends not only upon a one-sided restriction to the one function, but also upon the fact that the nature of the directed function is a principle which actually demands self-divestiture. Thus every directed function demands the strict exclusion of everything not suited to its nature; thinking excludes every harassing feeling, just as feeling excludes each disturbing thought. Without the repression of everything that differs from itself, the directed function cannot operate at all. But, on the other hand, the self-regulation of the living organism makes such a strong, natural demand for the harmonizing of human nature that the consideration of the less favoured functions forces itself to the front as a necessity of life, and an unavoidable task in the education of the human race.

CHAPTER VIII

THE PROBLEM OF TYPES IN MODERN PHILOSOPHY

1. William James' Types

THE existence of two types has also been revealed in modern pragmatic philosophy, particularly in the philosophy of *William James*[1]. He says:

" The history of philosophy is, to a great extent, that of a certain clash of human *temperaments* (characterological dispositions) " (p. 6.) " Of whatever temperament a professional philosopher is, he tries, when philosophizing, to sink the fact of his temperament. . . . Yet his temperament really gives him a stronger bias than any of his more strictly objective premises. It loads the evidence for him one way or the other, making for a more sentimental or a more hard-hearted view of the universe, just as this fact or that principle would. He *trusts* his temperament. Wanting a universe that suits it, he believes in any representation of the universe that does suit it. He feels men of opposite temper to be out of key with the world's character, and in his heart considers them incompetent and ' not in it,' in the philosophic business, even though they may far excel him in dialectical ability.

" Yet in the forum he can make no claim, on the bare ground of his temperament, to superior discernment or authority. There arises thus a certain insincerity in our philosophic discussions: the potentest of all our premises is never mentioned."[2]

Whereupon James proceeds to the characterization of the two temperaments. Just as in the province of manners and customs we find formalists and free-and-easy persons, in the political world authoritarians and anarchists, in literature purists or academicals and realists,

[1] W. James, *Pragmatism : a new name for some old ways of thinking.* (London : Longmans 1911)
[2] pp. 7 ff.

in art classics and romantics, so in philosophy, according to James, there are also to be found two types, viz. the "rationalist" and the "empiricist". The rationalist is "your devotee to abstract and eternal principles". The empiricist is the "lover of facts in all their crude variety".[1] Although no man can dispense either with facts or with principles, yet entirely distinct points of view develop which correspond with the value given to either side.

James makes "rationalism" synonymous with "intellectualism" and "empiricism" with "sensationalism". Although, in my opinion, this comparison is not sound, we will continue with James' line of thought, reserving our criticism for the time being. According to his view, an idealistic and optimistic tendency is associated with intellectualism, whilst empiricism inclines to materialism and a purely conditional and precarious optimism. Rationalism (intellectualism) is always *monistic*. It begins with the "whole" and the universal and unites things; whereas empiricism begins with the part and converts the whole into a *collection*. The latter therefore, may be termed *pluralistic*. The rationalist is a man of feeling, while the empiricist is a hard-headed creature. The former is naturally disposed to a firm belief in free will, the latter to fatalism. The rationalist is readily dogmatic in his statements, while the empiricist is sceptical (pp. 10 ff.) James describes the rationalist as *tender-minded*, the empiricist as *tough-minded*. His aim, clearly, is to characterize the peculiar quality of the two mentalities. We must take a further opportunity of examining this characterization rather more closely. It is interesting to hear what James has to say concerning the prejudices which are mutually cherished by the two types. "They have a low opinion of each other. Their antagonism, whenever as individuals their temperaments have been

[1] p. 9.

intense, has formed in all ages a part of the philosophic atmosphere of the time. It forms a part of the philosophical atmosphere of to-day. The tough think of the tender as sentimentalists and soft-heads. The tender feel the tough to be unrefined, callous, or brutal. . . Each type believes the other to be inferior to itself." (pp. 12 ff.)

James catalogues the qualities of both types in two contrasting columns thus:

Tender-minded	*Tough-minded*
Rationalistic (going by principles)	Empiricist (going by facts)
Intellectualistic	Sensationalistic
Idealistic	Materialistic
Optimistic	Pessimistic
Religious	Irreligious
Free-willist	Fatalistic
Monistic	Pluralistic
Dogmatical	Sceptical

This comparison touches upon various problems we have met with already in the chapter upon nominalism and realism. The tender-minded has certain traits in common with the realist, and the tough-minded with the nominalist. As I have already pointed out, realism corresponds with the principle of introversion, nominalism with extraversion. Without doubt the *universalia* controversy also belongs, in the first place, to that historical "clash of temperaments" in philosophy to which James alludes. These associations prompt us to regard the tender-minded as introverted, and the tough-minded as extraverted. It devolves upon us, however, to redouble our scrutiny before deciding whether or no this combination is valid.

From my naturally somewhat limited knowledge of James' writings, I have not succeeded in discovering any more detailed definitions or descriptions of the two types, although he frequently refers to these two kinds of thinking, and incidentally describes them as "thin" and "thick". Flournoy[1] interprets "thin" as "mince, ténu, maigre, chétif" and "thick" as "épais, solide, massif, cossu". James, on one occasion, also uses the expression "soft-headed" for the tender-minded. Both "soft" and "tender" suggest something delicate, mild, gentle, light; hence weak, subdued, and rather powerless, in contrast to "thick" and "tough", which are resistant qualities, solid and hard to change, recalling the nature of matter and substance. Flournoy accordingly elucidates the two kinds of thinking as follows: "It is the opposition between the *abstractionist* manner of thinking—in other words, the purely logical and dialectical fashion so dear to philosophers, which fails, however, to inspire James with any confidence, appearing to him as fragile, hollow "chétive", because too withdrawn from the contact of individual things—and the *concrete* manner of thinking, which is nourished on the facts of experience and never quits the earthy region of tortoise-shells or other positive facts." (p. 32).

We should not, of course, conclude from this commentary that James has a one-sided approval of concrete thinking. He appreciates both standpoints: "Facts are good, of course . . . give us lots of facts. Principles are good . . . give us plenty of principles." Admittedly, a fact never exists only as it is in itself, but also as we view it. If, therefore, James describes concrete thinking as "thick" or "tough", he thereby demonstrates that for him this kind of thinking has something substantial and resistant, while abstract thinking appears as something weak, thin, and pallid, perhaps even (if we interpret with Flournoy) rather sickly and decrepit. Naturally, such a view is possible only for one who has made an a priori, connection between substantiality and the concrete fact,

[1] Th. Flournoy, *La philosophie de W. James*, p. 32 (Saint Blaise, 1911)

and that, as we have already said, is just where the question of temperament comes in. If the "empirical" thinker attributes a resistant substantiality to his concrete thinking, from the abstract standpoint he is deceiving himself, because substantiality, or "hardness", belongs to the external fact and not to his "empirical" thinking. In fact, the latter turns out to be particularly weak and decrepit; for, so little does it know how to maintain itself in the presence of the external fact, that it must always be running after, even depending upon, sense-given facts, and, in consequence, can hardly be said to rise above the level of a mere classifying or presenting activity.

From the thinking standpoint, therefore, there is something very frail and dependent about concrete thinking, because, instead of having stability in itself, it depends upon outer objects, which are superordinated to thought as determining values. Hence this kind of thinking is characterized by a succession of sense-bound representations, which are set in motion, not so much by an inner thought-activity, as by the changing stream of sense perceptions. A succession of concrete representations conditioned by sensuous perceptions is not precisely what the abstract thinker would term thinking, but at best only a passive apperception.

The temperament that prefers concrete thinking, and grants it substantiality, is distinguished, therefore, by a preponderance of sense-conditioned representations, as against active apperception, which springs from a subjective act of will, whose aim it is to command the sense-determined representations in accordance with the tendencies of an *idea*. To put it more briefly: more weight is given to the object in such a temperament; the object is felt-into; it maintains a quasi-independent behaviour in the idea-world of the subject, and carries comprehension along in its train. This is therefore an extraverting temperament. The thinking of the extravert is concretistic. His soundness and stability do not lie in himself, but very largely outside himself in the felt-into facts of experience, whence also James' qualification "tough" is derived. To the man who is always ranged upon the side of concrete thinking, *i.e.* upon the side of representations of facts, abstraction appears as something feeble and decrepit, something he is well able to dispense with, in face of the solidity of concrete, sense-established facts. But, for the man who is on the side of abstraction, it is not the sense-conditioned representation, but the *abstract idea*, which is the decisive factor.

According to the current conception, an idea is nothing but an abstraction of a sum of experiences. With such a notion the human mind is readily conceived as a sort of tabula rasa, that gradually gets covered with the perceptions and experiences of life. From this standpoint, which in the widest sense is the standpoint of our empirical science, the idea can be nothing at all, but an epiphenomenal, a posteriori abstraction from experiences—hence feebler and more colourless than these. But we know that the mind cannot be a tabula rasa, since we have only to criticize our principles of thought to perceive that certain categories of our thinking are given *a priori*, i.e. antecedent to all experience, and make a simultaneous appearance with the first act of thought, being, in fact, its preformed conditions. For what Kant proved for logical thinking holds good for the psyche over a still wider range. At the beginning, the psyche is no more a tabula rasa than is the mind (the province of thought). To be sure the concrete contents are lacking, but the contents - possibilities are given a priori through the inherited and preformed functional disposition. The psyche is simply the product of brain-functioning throughout our whole ancestral line, a precipitate of the adaptation-efforts and experiences of the phylogenetic succession. Hence the newly-born brain or function-system is an ancient instrument, prepared for quite definite ends; it is not merely a passive, apperceptive instrument, but is also in active command of experience outside itself, forcing certain conclusions or judgments. These adjustments are not merely accidental or arbitrary happenings, but adhere to strictly preformed conditions, which are not transmitted, as are perception-contents, through experience, but are a priori conditions of apprehension. They are ideas ante rem, form-determinants, basic lines engraven a priori, assigning a definite formation to the stuff of experience; so that we may regard them as *images* (as Plato also conceived them), as schemata as it were, or inherited function - possibilities, which, moreover, exclude other possibilities, or, at all events, restrict them to a great extent. This explains why even phantasy, the freest activity of the mind, can never roam in the infinite (albeit, so the poet senses it), but remains bound to the preformed possibilities, the *primordial images or archetypes*. In the similarity of their motives, the fairy-tales of the most remote peoples show this binding connection to certain root-images. The very images which underlie scientific theories reveal this inherent restrictiveness; for example, ether, energy, its transformations and its constancy, the atomic theory, affinity, and so forth.

Just as the sense-given representation prevails in, and gives direction to, the concretely thinking mind, so the contentless, and therefore unrepresentable, archetype is paramount in the mind that thinks abstractly. It remains relatively inactive, so long as the object is felt-into and thus raised to the determining factor of thought. But, when the object is not felt-into, and thus deprived of its priority in the mental process, the energy thus denied to it returns again into the subject. The subject is unconsciously felt-into; whereupon the preformed images are awakened from their slumber, emerging as effective factors in the mental process, although in unrepresentable form, rather like invisible stage managers behind the scenes. Being merely activated function possibilities, they are without contents, therefore unimaginable; accordingly, they strive towards realization. They draw the stuff of experience into their shape, presenting themselves in facts rather than presenting facts. They clothe themselves in facts, as it were. Hence they are not a known starting-point, like the empirical fact in concrete thinking, but only become experienceable through their unconscious shaping of the stuff of experience. Even the empiricist can arrange and shape the material of his experience; he, nevertheless, forms it, as far as possible, after a concrete idea which he has built up on the basis of past experience. The abstractionist, on the other hand, shapes after an unconscious model, only gaining an a posteriori experience of the *idea*, which was his model, by a consideration of the phenomenon he has formed. The empiricist, working from his own psychology, is always inclined to assume that the abstractionist shapes the material of experience in a quite arbitrary fashion from certain pale, feeble, and inadequate premises, measuring as he does the mental process of the abstractionist by his own modus procedendi. The actual premise, *i.e.* the idea or root-image, is, however, just as unknown to the abstractionist as, in the case of the empiricist, is that theory which, after such and such experiments, he will subsequently build up out of experience. As was explained in an earlier chapter, the one sees the individual object and interests himself in its individual behaviour, while the other has mainly in view the relations of similarity between objects, and disregards the individuality of the fact. Amidst the disintegration of multiplicity he finds more peace and comfort in what is uniform and coherent. To the former, however, the relation of similarity is frankly burdensome and harassing, something that may even hinder him from seizing the perception of the object's particularity. The further he is able to feel himself into the individual object, the more he discerns its peculiarity, and the more the reality of a relation of similarity with another object vanishes from his view. But, if he also knew how to feel himself into another object, he would be in a position to sense and understand the similarity of both objects to a far higher degree than the man who viewed them simply and solely from without.

It is because he first feels himself into one object and then into another that the concrete thinker comes only very slowly to the discernment of the connecting similarities, and for this reason his thinking appears torpid and sluggish. But his feeling-into flows readily. The abstract thinker quickly seizes the similarity, replaces the individual object by general, distinguishing marks, and shapes this material with his own inner thought activity, which, however, is just as powerfully influenced by the 'shadowy' archetype as is the concrete thinker by the object. The greater the influence the object has upon thinking, the more are its characters stamped upon the thought-image. But the less the object operates in the mind, with all the more power will the a priori idea set its impress upon experience.

Through the exaggerated importance of the empirical object there has arisen in science a certain sort of specialist theory, as, for instance, that familiar 'brain-mythology' which appeared in psychiatry, wherein an attempt was made to explain a very large domain of experience from principles, which, although pertinent for the elucidation of certain constellations of facts within narrow limits, are wholly inadequate for every other application. But, on the other hand, abstract thinking, which accepts one individual fact only because of its similarity with another, creates a universal hypothesis which, while bringing the idea to a more or less clear presentation, has just as much or as little to do with the nature of concrete facts as a myth.

Both thought-forms, therefore, in their extreme expressions, create a mythology, the one expressing it concretely with cells, atoms, vibrations, and so forth, the other with "eternal" ideas. Extreme empiricism has, at least, this advantage: it brings facts to the clearest possible presentation. But the advantage of extreme ideologism is that it reflects back the a priori forms, the ideas or archetypes, with the utmost purity. The theoretical results of the former are exhausted with their material; the practical results of the latter are confined to the presentation of the psychological idea.

Because our present scientific mind adopts a one-sided, concrete, and purely empirical, attitude, it has no standard by which to value the man who presents the idea; since, in the estimation of the empiricist, facts rank higher than the knowledge of those primordial forms in which human intelligence conceives them. This tacking toward the side of concretism is, as we know, a relatively recent acquisition, a relict from the epoch of enlightenment. The results of this development are astonishing, but they have led to an accumulation of empirical material whose very immensity gradually produces more confusion than clarity. It inevitably leads to a scientific separatism, and therewith to a specialist mythology, which spells death to universality. But the preponderance of empiricism not only means a smothering of active thinking, it also involves a danger to the laying down of sound theories within any branch of science. The absence of a general view-point favours mythical theory-building, just as much as does the absence of an empirical point of view.

In my view, therefore, James' "tender-minded" and 'tough-minded" are manifestly but a one-sided terminology, and at bottom conceal a certain prejudice. But it should, at least, have become evident from this discussion that James' characterization deals with those same types which I have termed the introverted and the extraverted.

2. The Characteristic Pairs of Opposites in James' Types

(*a*) The first pair of opposites instanced by James as a distinguishing feature of the types is *Rationalism* versus *Empiricism*.

As the reader will have remarked, I have already dealt with this antithesis in a previous chapter, conceiving it as the opposition between ideologism and empiricism. I have avoided the expression "rationalism", because concrete, empirical thinking is just as "rational" as active, ideological thinking. The *ratio* governs both forms. There exists, moreover, not merely a logical rationalism but also a feeling rationalism; for rationalism is nothing but a general psychological attitude towards reasonableness of thought and feeling. With this understanding of the concept "rationalism", I find myself in definite and conscious opposition to the historical philosophical conception, which understands "rationalistic" in the sense of "ideological", thus conceiving rationalism as the supremacy of the idea. With the modern philosophers, however, the *ratio* has been stripped of its purely ideal character; it is even described as a capacity, instinct, intention, as a feeling even, or, again, a method. At all events—considered psychologically—it is a certain attitude governed, as Lipps says, by the "feeling of objectivity". Baldwin [1] regards it as the "constitutive, regulative principle of the mind".

[1] Baldwin, *Handbook of Psychology*, i, p. 312.

Herbart interprets it as "the capacity of reflection"[1]. Schopenhauer says of the reason, that it has only *one* function, namely "the shaping of the idea; and from this unique function all those above-mentioned manifestations, which distinguish the life of man from that of the animal, are very easily and completely explained, and in the application or non-application of that function, positively everything is meant which men in all places and of all times have called reasonable or unreasonable"[2]. The "above-mentioned manifestations" refer to certain properties of reason, instanced by Schopenhauer by way of example, namely "the command of affects and passions, the capacity for drawing conclusions and constructing general principles, ... the concerted action of several individuals ... civilization, the state; also science and the preservation of previous experience, etc." If reason, as Schopenhauer asserts, has the function of forming ideas, it must also possess the character of that psychic attitude which is fitted to shape ideas through the activity of thought. It is entirely in this sense of an attitude that Jerusalem[3] also conceives the reason, namely as a *disposition of the will* which enables us, in our decisions, to make use of our reason and control our passions.

Reason, therefore, is the capacity to be reasonable, a definite attitude which enables thought, feeling, and action to correspond with objective values. From the standpoint of empiricism this "objective" value is the yield of experience, but from the ideological standpoint it is the result of a positive act of valuation on the part of the reason, which in the Kantian sense would be a "faculty of judgment and action in accordance with basic principles". For, with Kant, the reason is the source of the *idea*, which

---

[1] Herbart, *Psychologie als Wissenschaft*, sect. 117.
[2] Schopenhauer, *The World as Will and Idea*, vol. i, par. 8.
[3] Jerusalem, *Lehrbuch der Psychologie*, p. 195.

is a "reasoning concept whose object can positively not be encountered in experience", and which "contains the primordial image of the use of the mind—as a regulative principle for the purpose of gaining general coherence in our empirical mental practice" (*Logik*, pp. 140 ff.). This is a genuinely introverted view. In vivid contrast to this is the empiricistic view of Wundt, who declares that the reason belongs to a group of complex intellectual functions, knit together into one general expression, together with "their antecedent phases, which yield them an indispensable sensuous substratum".[1]

" It is self-evident that this concept ' intellectual ' is a survival of the faculty-psychology, and suffers, possibly even more than such old concepts as memory, mind, phantasy etc., from *confusion with logical points of view which have nothing to do with psychology*. What is more natural, therefore, than that it should become all the more indefinite, and at the same time more arbitrary, the more manifold the psychic contents it embraces?" "If, to the standpoint of scientific psychology, there exists no memory, no mind, and no phantasy, *but merely certain elementary psychic processes and their relations*, which, with rather arbitrary discrimination one includes under those names, still less, of course, can there exist an ' intelligence ' or ' an intellectual function ', but merely a uniform, permanently restricted concept corresponding with matter of fact. Nevertheless certain cases remain where it is useful to avail oneself of these borrowed concepts from the old inventory of the faculty psychology, even though one uses them in a sense modified by their psychological acceptation. Such cases arise whenever we encounter complex phenomena of very variously mingled constituents, which, on account of the regularity of their combination, and above all on practical grounds, demand our consideration; or when individual consciousness affords us definite tendencies of design and formation, and when, once again, the regularity of the combination challenges an analysis of such complex mental capacities. *But in all these cases it is naturally the task of psychological research not to remain rigidly adherent to the general concepts thus formed, but to reduce them, whenever possible, to their simple factors.*"

This view is thoroughly extraverted. I have italicized the specially characteristic passages. Whereas to the

[1] Wundt, *Grundzüge der phys. Psychol.*, 5th edn., vol. iii, pp. 582 ff.

introverted point of view 'general concepts' such as reason, intellect, etc., are 'faculties', *i.e.* simple basic functions, which embrace in a uniform sense the multiplicity of the psychic processes governed by them, to the standpoint of the extraverted empiricist they are nothing but secondary, derived concepts, elaborations of those elementary processes upon which the holders of this view lay the chief value. According to this standpoint, it is better that we should have no dealings with such concepts, but should, on principle, "constantly reduce them to their simple factors". Obviously for the empiricist any other than reductive thinking in connection with general concepts is simply out of the question, since for him concepts are mere derivatives of experience. He can have no sort of knowledge of 'rational concepts', or a priori ideas, since his passive, apperceptive thinking is orientated by sense-conditioned experience. As a result of this attitude, the object is always accentuated: it is, as it were, active, necessitating perceptions and complicated reasonings; but these demand the existence of general concepts, which, however, serve only to comprise certain groups of phenomena under one collective designation. Thus the general concept is, naturally, a mere secondary factor, which, apart from language, has no real existence.

Science, therefore, can concede to reason, phantasy, etc., no right to independent existence, so long as it supports the view that only what is present as sense-accredited matter of fact ('elementary factors') has any real existence. But when thinking, as in the case of the introvert, is orientated by active apperception, reason, intellect, phantasy, etc., have the value of basic functions, or faculties, *i.e.* powers or activities operating externally from within: this is because the accent of value for this standpoint is given to the concept, and not to the elementary processes covered and comprised by the concept. Such a thinking is fundamentally synthetic. It is regulated in accordance with the schema of the concept, and employs the material of experience for the fulfilment of its ideas. The concept appears as the active principle just by reason of its own inner force, which seizes and shapes the material of experience.

The extravert assumes that the source of this force is mere arbitrary choice, or else an ill-considered generalization from limited experience. The introvert, who is unconscious of his own thought-psychology, and may even have adopted the empiricism in vogue as his guiding principle, finds himself defenceless against this reproach. But the reproach itself is merely a projection of extraverted psychology. For the active thinking type derives the energy of his thought-activity neither from arbitrary choice nor from experience, but from the idea, *i.e.* from the innate functional form which is activated through his introverted attitude. To him, this source is unconscious, since by reason of its a priori lack of content he can only become aware of the idea in an a posteriori formation, namely, in the form which the material of experience assumes through its elaboration by thought. But, to the extravert, the object and the elementary process are important and indispensable, because he has unconsciously projected the idea into the object; hence he is able to mount to the concept, and therewith to the idea, only through empirical accumulation and comparison. The two ways of thinking are mutually opposed in a remarkable way: the one shapes the material out of his own unconscious idea, and thus comes to experience; the other lets himself be guided by the material which contains his unconsciously projected ideas, and thus reaches the idea. There is something intrinsically irritating in this conflict of attitude, and at bottom, this is the cause of the most heated and futile scientific discussions.

I trust that this discussion sufficiently illustrates my view, that the *ratio* and its one-sided elevation to a principle, viz. rationalism, applies equally well both to empiricism and to ideologism. Instead of ideologism, we might have used the term 'idealism'. But to this application of the word, its antithesis 'materialism' stands opposed, and it would have been impossible to use 'ideological' as opposed to 'materialistic', since the materialist, as the history of philosophy testifies, may be, and often is, just as much an ideologist, *e.g.* when he is not an empiricist but thinks actively from the universal concept of matter.

(*b*) The second pair of opposites advanced by James is *Intellectualism* versus *Sensationalism*.

Sensationalism is the expression that characterizes the nature of extreme empiricism. It postulates sense-experience as the unique and exclusive source of cognition. The sensationalistic attitude is entirely orientated by the sense-given object; its orientation, therefore, is outward. James evidently means an intellectual rather than an æsthetic sensationalism, but "intellectualism" even then scarcely seems its appropriate antithesis. Psychologically, intellectualism is an attitude that is distinguished by the fact that it gives the principal determining value to the intellect, *i.e.* to cognition upon a conceptual level. But with such an attitude I can also be a sensationalist, viz. I may engage my thinking with concrete concepts wholly derived from sense experience. Hence the empiricist may also be intellectual. In philosophy, intellectualism and rationalism are employed almost promiscuously; hence ideologism must again be used as the antithesis to sensationalism, since, in its essence, sensationalism is only an extreme empiricism.

(*c*) James' third pair of opposites is Idealism versus Materialism.

One may already have begun to wonder whether by "sensationalism" James merely intended an intensified empiricism, *i.e.* an intellectual sensationalism, or whether, in using the expression "sensationalistic", he may conceivably have wished to bring out the quality pertaining to sensation as a function quite apart from the intellect. By 'pertaining to sensation' I mean true *sensuousness* (Sinnlichkeit), not of course as voluptas in the vulgar sense, but as a psychological attitude in which the orientating and determining factor is not so much the felt-into object as the mere fact of sense-stimulation and sense-perception. This might also be described as a reflexive attitude (*i.e.* an attitude based on reflex phenomena), since the whole mentality depends upon and culminates in sense-perception. The object is neither realized abstractly nor felt-into, but operates through its natural form and manner of existence, the subject being exclusively orientated by sense-impressions stimulated by contact with the object. This attitude would correspond with a primitive mentality. Its essential antithesis is the *intuitive attitude*, which is distinguished by an immediate sensing or apprehension that is neither intellectual nor feeling, but contains both in inseparable combination. Just as the sensuous object *appears* in perception, so the psychic content also *appears* in intuition, hence as quasi-illusionary or hallucinatory.

That James should describe the tough-minded as both "sensationalistic" and "materialistic" (and further still as "irreligious") encourages the doubt as to whether, in his description of types, he has really in view the same type antithesis as I have. Materialism, as commonly understood, is an attitude whose orientation corresponds with "material" values—in other words, a kind of moral sensationalism. Hence James' characterization would yield a very unfavourable portrait, if we were to misconstrue these expressions in the sense of their common significance. But this must not be imputed to James, whose observations upon the types, quoted above, should prevent any such misunderstanding. We are almost justified, therefore, in assuming that James is principally concerned with the philosophical significance of the terms in question. Materialism, then, means an attitude naturally orientated by material values, not, however, by "sensuous" so much as fact values, wherein "fact" signifies something external and, in a sense, concrete. Its antithesis is "idealism", in the philosophical sense of a supreme valuation of the *idea*. It cannot be a moral idealism that is meant here, for in that case we should have to assume, contrary to James' intention, that his "materialism" means a moral sensationalism. But, if we assume that by materialism he means an attitude wherein the principal orientating value is given to actual reality, we are again in a position to trace an *extraverted* peculiarity in this attribute, whereat our original doubts vanish. We have already seen that philosophical idealism corresponds with *introverted* ideologism. A moral idealism would in no way be characteristic for the introvert, for the materialist can also be morally idealistic.

(*d*) The fourth pair of opposites is Optimism versus Pessimism.

I am extremely doubtful whether this familiar antithesis, by which, indeed, human temperaments can be differentiated, is really applicable to James' types. Is, for instance, the empiricism of Darwin also pessimistic? It is undoubtedly true of the man who, with an ideologistical view of the world, sees the other human types through the glasses of an unconscious feeling projection. But even the empiricist is by no means wont to conceive his view as pessimistic on that account. Or take the thinker Schopenhauer, for instance, whose world-philosophy is purely ideologistic (in all respects like the pure ideologism of the Upanishads); is he somewhat of an optimist according to the James classification? Kant himself, a very pure introverted type, stands as remote from either optimism or pessimism as do the great empiricists.

It seems to me, therefore, that this antithesis has nothing to do with James' types. Just as there are optimistic introverts, there are also optimistic extraverts and vice versa. It would, however, be quite possible for James to have fallen into this mistake as a result of the subjective projection previously referred to. A materialistic or purely empiricistic or positivistic world-philosophy seems utterly cheerless from the standpoint of the ideologist. He must, therefore, sense it as pessimistic. But, to the man who puts his faith in the god 'Matter', the materialistic view of the world seems optimistic. From the ideological standpoint the materialistic conception seems to sever the vital nerve, since its chief power, active apperception and the realization of the archetypes, is thereby paralysed. To the ideologist, therefore, such a view must appear completely pessimistic, for it robs him of all hope of ever again beholding the eternal idea embodied and realized upon the phenomenal plane. A world of real facts would mean banishment and perpetual homelessness. When, therefore, James draws a parallel between the materialistic and the pessimistic points of view, we are entitled to infer that he personally may belong to the ideologistical side —an assumption that might easily be subtantiated by numerous other characteristics from the life of this philosopher. This circumstance might also explain why the tough-minded has been saddled with the three somewhat dubious epithets—sensationalistic, materialistic, and irreligious. This inference is further corroborated by that passage in *Pragmatism* where James compares the mutual aversion between the types with a rencontre between

Bostonian tourists and the inhabitants of Cripple Creek[1]. This comparison is hardly flattering to the other type, and allows one to infer an emotional aversion against which even a strong desire for justice does not wholly prevail. This little human document seems to me a most valuable witness to the existence of an irritating disparity between the two types. It may, perhaps, seem trivial that I should make rather a point of such incompatibilities of feeling. But numerous experiences have convinced me that it is just such feelings as these, lying unobserved in the background of consciousness, that occasionally deflect even the most impartial reasoning, colouring it with prejudice and wholly thwarting understanding. It is, indeed, conceivable that the Cripple Creek inhabitants might also eye the Boston tourists in their own particular way.

(e) The fifth pair of opposites is Religiousness versus Irreligiousness.

Naturally, the validity of this antithesis for James' type-psychology depends essentially upon the definition he gives to religiousness. If he conceives its nature wholly from the ideologistical standpoint, as an attitude in which the religious idea plays the dominant rôle (in contrast to feeling), he is certainly justified in describing the tough-minded as also irreligious. But James' thought is so wide and so essentially human that he can hardly have omitted to see that the religious attitude can also be determined by religious *feeling*. In fact, he himself says: "But our esteem for facts has not neutralized in us all religiousness. *It is itself almost religious.* Our scientific temper is devout."[2]

[1] James, *Pragmatism*, p. 13. The Bostonians are notorious on account of their "spiritualized" æstheticism. Cripple Creek is a well-known mining district in Colorado. The contrast can be easily imagined. "Each type believes the other to be inferior to itself; but disdain in the one case is mingled with amusement, in the other it has a dash of fear."

[2] James, *l.c.*, p. 15.

The empiricist replaces a lack of respect for "eternal" ideas by an almost religious belief in the actual fact. If a man's attitude is orientated by the idea of God, it would be psychologically the same, were he orientated by the idea of matter, or were he to exalt real facts to the determining factor of his attitude. Only in so far as this orientation takes place *unconditionally* does it deserve the epithet "religious". But, considered from a high standpoint, the real fact has the value of an unconditional factor equally with the idea, the archetype, which is the age-long product of the reactions and repercussions of man and his inner determinants with the hard facts of external reality. At all events, from the psychological standpoint, absolute surrender to real facts can never be described as irreligious. The tough-minded has his empiricistic, just as the tender-minded has his ideologistic, religion. It is, however, also a fact of our present cultural epoch that science is governed by the object, religion by the subject, *i.e.* ideologism, for the primordial, self-operative idea must take refuge somewhere, when, as in science, it has been ousted from its place by the object. If religion is thus understood as the present day phenomenon of culture, James is so far justified in describing the empiricist as irreligious—but only thus far. For philosophers are not an absolutely isolated class of men, and their types also will reach to common humanity, far beyond the province of philosophic men, perchance extending even to civilized humanity in general. On this general ground, therefore, it is surely not permitted to class as irreligious the half of civilized mankind. From the psychology of the primitive we know that the religious function belongs simply to the constitution of the psyche, and is constantly and everywhere present, however undifferentiated it may be.

If we are not to assume a limitation of James' concept

of "religion" such as we have just alluded to, then again it must be a question of an affective derailment, which, as we have already seen, can happen only too easily.

(*f*) The sixth pair of opposites is Indeterminism versus Determinism.

This antithesis is, psychologically, of great interest. It is obvious that empiricism thinks *causally*, whereby the necessary connection between cause and effect is axiomatically assumed. The empiricistic attitude is orientated by the felt-into object; it is, as it were, 'impressed' by the external fact with a sense of the inevitability of effect following cause. It is quite natural that the impression of the unalterableness of the causal connection should, psychologically, obtrude itself upon such an attitude. The identification of the inner psychic processes with the course of external facts is already granted by the fact that a considerable sum of one's own activity and life is unconsciously bestowed upon the object in the act of feeling-into. The subject is thereby assimilated to the object, although the feeling-into subject believes that it is the object which is assimilated. But, whenever a strong accent of value is laid upon the object, it at once assumes an importance which, in its turn, also influences the subject, forcing him to a dissimilation from himself. Human psychology is, admittedly, chameleon-like. This is a fact of daily experience in the work of the practical psychologist. Where the object is constantly paramount, an assimilation to the nature of the object takes place in the subject. Thus, for example, identification with the loved object plays no small part in analytical therapy. Furthermore, the psychology of the primitive provides us with abundant examples of dissimilation in favour of the object, as, for instance, the frequent assimilation to the totem animal or ancestral spirits. The stigmatizing of Saints in medieval, and even in recent times, belongs also to this connection.

In the *Imitatio Christi* dissimilation is actually exalted to a principle.

In view of this unquestionable aptitude of the human psyche for dissimilation, the translation of the objective causal connections into the subject can be easily understood. The psyche, accordingly, labours under an impression of the unique validity of the causal principle, and the whole armoury of the theory of cognition is required to ward off the overmastering power of this impression. This is further aggravated by the fact that the very nature of the empiricistic attitude prevents one from believing in the inner freedom; since every proof, indeed every possibility of proof, is lacking. Of what consequence is that frail, indefinite feeling of freedom in face of the overwhelming mass of objective proofs to the contrary?

The determinism of the empiricist, therefore, is almost inevitable, assuming that the empiricist carries his thinking to its logical conclusion, and does not prefer—as not infrequently happens—to possess two compartments, one for science and the other for the religion he has acquired from his parents and from society.

As we have already seen, the essence of ideologism consists in the unconscious activation of the idea. This activation can result from an aversion to feeling-into acquired later in life, or it can exist from birth as an a priori attitude, fashioned and favoured by Nature. (I have, in my practical experience, seen many such cases.) In this latter case the idea has an a priori activity, without, however, appearing in consciousness, which is accounted for by its emptiness and unrepresentability. As a paramount, inner, though unrepresentable, fact, it is superordinated to "objective" external facts, and yields, at least, a sense of its independence and freedom to the subject, who, as a result of this inner assimilation to the idea, feels himself independent and free vis-à-vis the object. When the idea is the principal orientating factor, it assimilates the subject to its own quality just as completely as the subject tries to assimilate the idea to himself through the shaping of the material of experience. Thus, as in the above-mentioned attitude to the object, there takes place a dissimilation of the subject from himself, in the reversed sense, however, viz. in favour of the idea.

The inherited archetype survives all ages; it is a factor superordinated to every change upon the phenomenal plane, preceding and superseding all individual experience. Hence the idea acquires a particular force. Its activation transveys a pronounced feeling of power into the subject, since it assimilates the subject to itself by means of inner unconscious identification. There dawns within the subject a feeling of power, independence, freedom, and eternity. (Cf. Kant's postulate of God, freedom, and immortality.) When the subject senses the free activity of his idea exalted above the reality of facts, the idea of freedom makes its natural claim upon him. If his ideologism is pure, he must certainly arrive at a conviction of free-will.

The antithesis here reviewed is highly characteristic for our types. The extravert is distinguished by his striving towards the object, his feeling into and identification with the object, and his willed dependence upon the object. He is influenced by the object in the same degree as he strives to assimilate it. The introvert, on the other hand, is distinguished by his apparent self-assertion in presence of the object. He struggles against every dependence upon the object; he repels every influence from the object; on occasion he even fears the object. All the more, however, is he dependent upon the idea which shields him from outer reality and yields him this feeling of inner freedom; albeit, in return, it also gives him a pronounced power psychology.

(*g*) James' seventh antithesis is Monism versus Pluralism.

It is at once intelligible from the foregoing argument that the attitude orientated by the idea must tend towards monism. The idea has always a hierarchical character, whether it be gained by abstraction from representations and concrete concepts, or whether it has an a priori existence as unconscious form. In the former case it is the highest point of the building which, in a sense, rounds off and comprises everything subordinated to it; in the latter, it is the unconscious law-giver, regulating the possibilities and necessities of thought. The idea in both instances has a ruling quality. Although a plurality of ideas may be present, yet for a longer or shorter period one idea gains the upper hand, constellating the majority of the psychic elements in a monarchical fashion.

Conversely, it is equally clear that the attitude orientated by the object must always incline to a majority of principles (pluralism), since the multiplicity of objective qualities entails also a plurality of concepts and principles without which a suitable interpretation of the nature of the object cannot be gained.

The monistic tendency belongs to the introverted attitude, the pluralistic to the extraverted.

(*h*) The eighth antithesis is Dogmatism versus Scepticism.

It is also easy to see in this case that dogmatism is the attitude par excellence that follows and clings to the idea, although an unconscious realization of the idea is not *eo ipso* dogmatic. It is none the less true that the way in which an unconscious idea is almost violently embodied inevitably persuades one to believe that the man in whom the idea is paramount starts out from a dogma in whose rigid folds the material of experience is impressed. It is self-evident that the attitude governed by the object must have an a priori scepticism in relation to all ideas, since its chief desire is that objective experience in general should be allowed its say, undisturbed by universa concepts. In this sense scepticism is an actually indispensable pre-condition of all empiricism.

This pair of opposites also confirms the essential similarity between James' types and my own.

3. General Criticism of James' Conception

In criticizing James' conception, I must first lay stress upon the fact that it is almost exclusively concerned with the thinking qualities of the types. In a philosophical work one could hardly expect otherwise. But such a necessarily onesided setting readily gives rise to confusion. For without difficulty one could demonstrate this or that quality, or even a number of them, in the opposite type. For example, there are empiricists who are dogmatic, religious, idealistic, intellectualistic, and rationalistic; there are also ideologists who are materialistic, pessimistic, deterministic, and irreligious. Even were one to show that such expressions designate very complex matters in which many diverse nuances are in question, the possibility of confusion would not be remedied.

Taken individually, James' expressions are too *broad:* only in their totality do they give an approximate picture of the typical contrast, without thereby bringing it to a simple formula. In general, James' types are a valuable supplement to the picture of the types we have gained from other sources. James was the first to indicate, with a certain distinctness, the extraordinary importance of temperament in the shaping of philosophical thinking, and for this great credit is due. For the aim of his pragmatic conception was to reconcile the antagonisms of philosophical views resulting from temperamental differences.

Pragmatism, as we know, is a wide-spread philosophical current, originating in the English philosophy (F. C. S. Schiller, of Oxford), which assigns a value to "truth" that is restricted to its practical efficacy and usefulness, quite unconcerned about its contestability from this or that standpoint. It is characteristic that James should introduce his presentation of this philosophical view with just this very contrast of types, thus practically establishing the necessity of a pragmatic point of view. So the drama, which was already given us by the early medieval psychology, is repeated. At that time the opposition was worded: nominalism versus realism; and it was Abélard who attempted the reconciliation in his sermonism or conceptualism. But, since the understanding of that day was entirely wanting in a psychological point of view, his attempted solution turned out to be correspondingly one-sided in its purely logical and intellectual bias. James takes a deeper grasp; he conceives the opposition psychologically, and, accordingly, attempts a pragmatic solution. It would, however, be unwise to cherish any illusions concerning the value of this solution; pragmatism is but a makeshift, which may claim to be valid only so long as no further sources are discovered that could add fresh elements to the shaping of philosophical view-points, other than the possibilities of cognition which are shaped and coloured by temperament.

Bergson certainly has pointed to intuition and the possibility of an intuitive method. But it admittedly remains merely an *indication*. A *proof* of the method is lacking and will not be so easily forthcoming, although Bergson may point to his concepts of "élan vital" and "durée créatrice" as the results of intuition. Apart from this intuitively conceived basic view, which derives its psychological justification from the fact that, even in antiquity, particularly with neo-platonism, it was already a thoroughly familiar combination of ideas, the Bergson method is intellectual and not intuitive. Nietzsche made use of the intuitive source in an incomparably greater measure, and by so doing was able to free himself from the purely intellectual in the shaping of his philosophical ideas; but he did this in such a way, and to such a degree, that his intuitionism went far beyond the limits of a *philosophical* system, and led him to an artistic creation, *i.e.* to something which, for the most part, is inaccessible to philosophical criticism. I refer naturally to the *Zarathustra*, and not to the collection of philosophical aphorisms, which offer themselves in the first place to philosophical criticism by very reason of their prevailingly intellectualistic method. If, therefore, one may speak at all of an "intuitive method," Nietzsche's *Zarathustra* has, in my opinion, furnished the best example of it; moreover, it has strikingly demonstrated the possibility of a nonintellectualistic, though none the less philosophical comprehension of the problem. Schopenhauer and Hegel appear to be the forerunners of the Nietzschean intuitionism, the former on account of the *feeling-intuition* which lends such a decisive colouring to his views, and the latter by virtue of the *conceptual-intuition* underlying his whole system. With these two fore-runners—if one may use such an expression—intuition ranked below the intellect, but with Nietzsche it ranked above it.

The opposition between the two 'truths' demands a pragmatic attitude, if one desires to do any sort of justice to the other standpoint. Yet, indispensable though the pragmatic method may be, it presupposes too great a resignation, thus becoming almost unavoidably bound up with a lack of creativeness. But the solution of the conflict of the opposites can proceed neither from a logico-intellectual compromise as in conceptualism, nor from a pragmatic estimation of the practical value of logically irreconcilable views, but simply and solely from the positive creation which receives the opposites into itself as necessary elements of co-ordination, just as a co-ordinated muscular movement always involves the innervation of antagonistic muscle groups.

Pragmatism, therefore, can only be a transitional attitude that shall prepare the way for creation by the elimination of prejudice. This new way, which pragmatism prepares, and Bergson indicates, German philosophy— not, of course, the academic schools—has, in my view, already trodden: it was Nietzsche, with a violence peculiarly his own, who burst open this closed door. His creation leads far beyond the unsatisfying formula of the pragmatic solution, and it has accomplished this just as fundamentally, as the pragmatic recognition of the living value of a truth transcends the arid one-sidedness of the unconscious conceptualism of the post-Abélardian philosophy—and still there are heights to be scaled.

CHAPTER IX

THE TYPE-PROBLEM IN BIOGRAPHY

As one might almost expect, the province of *biography* also yields its contribution to the problem of psychological types. Chiefly we have to thank the natural science method of Wilhelm Ostwald[1], who was able, by means of a biographical comparison of certain outstanding natural scientists, to establish a typical psychological antithesis, which he termed the *classic and romantic types*[2]. "While the former", says Ostwald, "is characterized by the well-rounded perfection of each individual achievement, and at the same time by a rather withdrawn nature whose personal effect upon his environment is but slight, the romanticist stands out by reason of the very opposite characters. His quality lies not so much in the perfecting of individual work as in the variety and telling originality of numerous achievements that follow each other in rapid succession; in addition, the effect he exercises upon his contemporaries is, as a rule, immediate and impressive . . . It must also be pointed out that the rapidity of mental reaction is the decisive criterion of the particular type to which the scientist belongs. Pioneers who possess great reactive rapidity are the 'romantics', while those with slower mental reactions are the 'classics' (pp. 44 ff.). The classic produces slowly, as a rule, only bringing forth the ripest fruit of his mind relatively late in life" (p. 89). A never-failing characteristic of the classic type, according to Ostwald, is the "absolute need to stand without error

[1] Ostwald, *Grosse Männer*, iii, iv (Leipzig, 1910); [2] *l.c.*, p. 44.

or blemish in the public eye" (p. 94). "As a compensation for his lack of personal influence, the classic type is assured an all the more potent effect with his writings" (p. 100).

This effect, however, seems also to be beset with limitations, as the following case, quoted by Ostwald from the biography of Helmholtz, testifies. A propos Helmholtz's mathematical researches concerning the effect of induction-shocks, Du Bois-Raymond writes to the scientist: "You should devote yourself—and please don't take this amiss—much more carefully to the problem of how to abstract yourself from your own standpoint of science, so that you may understand the standpoint of one who, as yet, knows nothing about the matter, or what it is you want to discuss." To which Helmholtz replies: "And as to the paper, I really took great pains this time in the presentation of my material, and I imagined that, at last, I might be satisfied with it." Whereat Ostwald observes: "He is quite oblivious of the problem from the reader's point of view, because, true to his 'classic' type, he *is writing for himself, i.e.* he presents the material in a way that seems to him indisputable, while the rest do not matter at all." What Du Bois-Raymond writes in the same letter to Helmholtz is extremely characteristic: "I have read both the treatise and the summary several times without understanding what you have actually done, or the way you did it. Finally, I myself discovered your method, and I am now gradually beginning to understand your presentation."

For the classic type this case is true to the life, for he seldom or never succeeds "in kindling souls of like nature with his own" (p. 100), a thoroughly typical event, which shows that the influence ascribed to him through writing is, as a rule, largely posthumous, *i.e.* it appears only in the subsequent discovery of his writings, as in the case of Robert Mayer. Moreover, his writings often seem to lack any convincing, inspiring, or directly personal appeal, since, ultimately, writing is just as much a personal expression as conversation or lecturing. The influence the classic type transmits through writing depends not so much, therefore, upon the externally stimulating qualities of his writings as upon the circumstance that these are all that finally remain of him, and that only from these can the man's actual achievement subsequently be reconstructed. For it seems to be a fact, which is also alluded to in Ostwald's description, that the classic seldom communicates what he is doing and the way he does it, but only what he arrives at, quite regardless of the fact that his public possesses no inkling of his route. It would seem that his way and method of work are of less importance to the classic just because they are most intimately linked up with his personality, which is something he always keeps in the background.

Ostwald compares his two types with the four ancient temperaments (p 372) with special reference to the peculiarity of slow or rapid reactions, which in his view seems to be fundamental. The slow reaction corresponds with the phlegmatic and the melancholic temperaments, the quick reaction with the sanguine and the choleric. He regards the sanguine and the phlegmatic as the normal middle types, whereas the choleric and the melancholic seem to him morbid exaggerations of the basic character.

If one glances through the biographies of Humphry Davy and Liebig upon the one hand, and of Robert Mayer and Faraday upon the other, one cannot but perceive that the former are both distinctly "romantic" and sanguinely-choleric, while the latter are just as clearly "classic" and phlegmatically-melancholic. This observation of Ostwald's seems to me entirely convincing, since the four antique temperaments were most probably constructed from the same principle of experience as that upon which Ostwald has also established the classic and romantic types. The four temperaments are obviously differentiated from the standpoint of affectivity, *i.e.* the manifest affective reactions. This classification is, however, *superficial* from the psychological standpoint, for it judges exclusively from the outer appearance. According to this ancient division, the man whose behaviour is outwardly peaceful and inconspicuous belongs to the phlegmatic temperament. He passes as 'phlegmatic', and is, thereupon, classified among the phlegmatics. But, in reality, he may conceivably be all this yet no 'phlegmatic', but on the contrary a deeply sensitive, even passionate, nature, in whom emotion pursues the inward course, wherewith the intensest inner excitement expresses itself through the greatest outward calm.

Jordan's type-conception takes this fact into account. He judges not merely from the surface impression, but from a rather deeper grasp of human nature. Ostwald's fundamental marks of distinction, like the antique temperamental divisions, depend chiefly upon the external impression. His romantic type is characterized by the presence of a *quick outward reaction*. Whereas the classic type reacts just as quickly maybe, but *within*.

As one reads the Ostwald biographies, one sees at once that the romantic type corresponds with the extravert, while the classic with the introvert. Humphry Davy and Liebig are perfect examples of the extraverted type, just as Robert Mayer and Faraday are model introverts. The outward reaction is characteristic of the extravert, just as the inner reaction distinguishes the introvert. The extravert has no especial difficulty in his personal manifestations; he asserts his presence almost involuntarily, because in obedience to his whole nature he strives to transvey himself into the object. He easily gives himself to the world about him, and in a form necessarily comprehensible and, therefore, acceptable to his world. The form is, as a rule, pleasing, but, in any case, intelligible, even when it is unpleasing. For, as a result of his quick reaction and discharge, both valuable and worthless contents will be transveyed into the object, winning manners hand-in-hand with forbidding thoughts and affects. But from this quick unloading and transference there is less elaboration of his contents, which are, therefore, easy to understand; so that, even from the mere fleeting apposition of immediate expressions, a shifting succession of images is produced which clearly present to the public eye the ways and means by which the investigator has attained his result.

The introvert, on the other hand, who reacts almost entirely within, does not, as a rule, divest himself of his reactions. (Affect-explosions excepted). He suppresses his reactions, which, however, can be just as quick as those of the extravert. They do not play on the surface—hence the introvert may easily give the impression of slowness. Since immediate reactions are always strongly personal, the extravert cannot choose but exhibit his personality. The introvert, on the other hand, hides his personality, because he suppresses his immediate reactions. 'Feeling-into' is not his aim, nor the transference of his contents into the object, but rather abstraction from the object. Hence, instead of immediately divesting himself of his reactions, he prefers to make a long internal elaboration of them, before finally bringing forth a prepared result. His constant effort is to free his result, as far as possible, from personal elements, to present it clearly differentiated from every personal relation. His contents, the matured fruit of prolonged inner labour, emerge into the outer world in the most completely abstracted and depersonalized form. Accordingly, they are also difficult to understand, because the public lacks all knowledge of the preliminary steps, or the kind of route by which the investigator reaches his result. A personal relation to his public is also lacking, because the introvert in suppressing himself shrouds his personality from the public eye. But often enough it is just the personal relationship which brings about the understanding that was denied to mere intellectual apprehension. This circumstance must constantly be borne in mind when judgment is made upon an introvert's development. As a rule, one is ill-informed about the introvert; because his real self is not visible. His incapacity for immediate outward reactions occludes his personality. Hence, to the public eye, his life provides ample scope for the play of phantastic interpretations and projections, should he ever chance—by virtue of his achievements—to become the object of general interest.

The observation of Ostwald that "*early mental maturity* is characteristic of the romantic*"*, needs, therefore, to be somewhat modified. The romantic is certainly able to display his prematurity, but the 'classic', although perhaps equally mature, may conceal his products within himself, not designedly of course, but from an inability for immediate expression. As a result of deficient differentiation of feeling, the introvert exhibits a certain awkwardness, a real infantilism in the personal relation, *i.e.* in that element which the Englishman calls 'personality'. His personal manifestations are so uncertain and vague, and he himself is so sensitive in this respect, that he dares to reveal himself to his circle only with what, in his own eyes, is an apparently finished product. He also prefers to let his product speak for him, instead of personally interceding on its behalf.

The natural result of such an attitude means a considerably delayed appearance upon the world's stage;

so frequently is this so, that the introvert might easily be described as *late in maturing*. Such a superficial judgment, however, wholly ignores the fact that the infantilism of the seemingly early matured and outwardly differentiated extravert is simply within, in his relation to his inner world. In the early matured extravert this fact is only subsequently revealed, in some moral immaturity, for instance, or, as is so often the case, in an astonishing infantilism of thought.

As a rule, the romantic has more favourable opportunities for development and growth than the classic, a fact which Ostwald justly observes. He makes a visible and convincing appearance before his public, allowing his personal importance to be recognized immediately through his external reactions. In this way many valuable relations are quickly established, which enrich his work and give *breadth* (p. 374) to its development.

The classic, on the other hand, remains hidden; his lack of personal relations limits any extension of his sphere of work, but thereby his activity gains in *depth* and his labour has lasting value.

Both types possess *enthusiasm*, but, while that which fills the extravert's heart overflows from his mouth, the introvert's lips are sealed by the enthusiasm that moves him within. Kindling no flame of enthusiasm in the world about him, he even lacks a circle of colleagues of equal calibre. Even had he, too, the impelling desire to impart his knowledge, his laconic expression, as also the mystified lack of comprehension it produces in his public, would deter him from further communications; for it very frequently happens that no one believes he has anything extraordinary to give. His expression, his 'personality' appear commonplace to the superficial judgment, while not infrequently the romantic immediately appears 'interesting' and understands the art of encouraging this impression by every sort of means, whether permissible or not. This differentiated capacity for expression provides a suitable background for impressive ideas, besides being an accommodating assistance in helping the deficient understanding of his public over the interstices of his thinking.

Ostwald's emphasis upon the successful and brilliant academic activities of the romantic is, therefore, entirely expressive of this type. The *romantic feels himself into his pupils* and knows the right word at the right moment. But the classic is held to his own thoughts and problems, and thus is blind to his pupils' difficulties in understanding. Speaking of the classic Helmholtz, Ostwald remarks (p. 377):

" In spite of his prodigious learning, comprehensive experience, and richly creative mind, he was never a good teacher: his reactions never came instantaneously, but only after a certain lapse of time. Confronted by a pupil's question in the laboratory, he would promise to think it over, and only after several days would he bring the answer; this turned out to be so remote from the situation of the pupil that only in the rarest cases was it possible for the latter to discover any connection between the difficulty he had felt and the well-rounded theory of a general problem subsequently expounded by the teacher. Thus, not only was the immediate help lacking upon which every beginner very largely relies, but also that guidance commensurate with the pupil's personality by which he may gradually develop from the natural dependence of the beginner to the complete mastery of his chosen branch of science. All such defects have their immediate source in the inability of the teacher to react directly as the need of the pupil presents itself, his reactions demanding so much time for their expected and desired operation that their very effect is lost."

Ostwald's explanation of this as the result of the slowness of the introvert's reaction seems to me inadequate. There is no sort of proof that Helmholtz possessed a low reactive rapidity. He merely reacted inwardly rather than outwardly. Because the pupil was not felt-into, as it were, the latter's need was dark to him. His attitude is wholly bent upon his thoughts; hence instead of the personal wish of the pupil, he reacts to the thoughts the pupil's question has excited in himself, and this he does so rapidly and fundamentally that he at once divines a further connection which, at the moment, he is incapable of appraising and rendering back in an abstract and finely elaborated form. This is not because his thinking is too slow, but because it is objectively impossible to seize in a moment the entire dimensions of the problem divined and give it a ready formula. Naturally, not observing that the pupil has no inkling of such a problem he firmly believes he has an important problem to deal with, and not merely an extremely simple and, to him, trivial piece of advice which could be given in a moment, if only he could allow himself to see what the pupil was waiting for to enable him to get on with his work. But as an introvert he has not felt-into the other's psychology; he has only felt-into his own theoretical problems, his inner world, where he goes on spinning the threads of the theoretical problem taken from the pupil—threads which are certainly germane to the problem but not to the pupil's momentary need. Naturally, from the academic standpoint, this peculiar attitude of the introverted teacher is very unsuitable, quite apart from the unfavourable personal impression it engenders. He gives an impression of slowness, singularity, even thick-headedness; on which account he is very often under-estimated, not only by the larger public but also by his own smaller circle of colleagues, until one day his work and ideas are eventually followed up, elaborated, and translated by later investigators.

Gauss, the mathematician, had such a distaste for teaching that he informed each individual student who reported himself that, in all probability, his course of lectures would not take place, hoping by this means to unburden himself of the necessity of giving them. That teaching was so painful to him, as Ostwald justly observes, lay in the "necessity of pronouncing definite scientific results in his lectures without having previously established and elaborated every detail of the text. To be obliged to communicate his results to others without such elaboration may have felt to him as though he were exhibiting himself before strangers in his night-shirt" (p. 380). With this observation Ostwald touches a very essential point, namely the above-mentioned disinclination of the introvert, for any part of himself, other than quite impersonal communications, to reach the surrounding world.

Ostwald emphasizes the fact that, as a rule, the romantic is compelled to bring his career to a close at a comparatively early stage on account of increasing exhaustion. He is also disposed to attribute this fact to his greater reactive rapidity. Since this concept of mental reactive rapidity is, in my view, still remote from the region of scientific fact, and since no proof is, as yet, forthcoming, neither is it susceptible of proof that the external reaction takes place more rapidly than the internal, it seems to me that the earlier exhaustion of the extraverted discoverer must be essentially related to the external reaction peculiar to his type. He begins to publish very early, becomes rapidly famous, and soon develops an intensive activity, both academically and as a publicist; he cultivates personal relationships among a very wide circle of friends and acquaintances and, in addition to all this, he takes an unusual interest in the development of his pupils. The introverted pioneer begins to publish later; his works succeed one another at longer intervals, and are mostly sparing in expression; repetitions of a theme are avoided except where something entirely new can be brought into them. The pithy and laconic style of his scientific communications, which frequently omit all information concerning the way he has traversed or the material elaborated, hinders any general understanding or acceptance of his works; and so he remains unknown. His distaste for teaching does not bring him pupils; he is so little known that any relations with a larger circle of acquaintances is precluded; as a rule, therefore, he lives a retired life, not from necessity merely but also from choice. Thus he escapes the danger of spending himself too lavishly. His inner reactions lead him constantly back to the circumscribed tracts of his research activities; these in themselves are very exacting, proving as time goes on so deeply exhausting as to permit of no incidental expenditure of energy on behalf of acquaintances or pupils. There is the additional circumstance that the manifest success of the romantic is also a vitalizing and invigorating factor, but this is very often denied the classic, so that he is forced to seek his only satisfaction in the perfecting of his work of research. In the light of these considerations, the relatively premature exhaustion of the romantic genius seems to me to depend more upon the *external reaction* than upon the higher reactive rapidity.

Ostwald does not regard his type division as absolute, in the sense that every investigator can be shown forthwith to belong to one or other type. He is, however, of the opinion "that the really great men" can generally be included quite definitely in one or other end-group, while the "average people" much more frequently represent the middle position in respect to reactive rapidity (pp. 372 ff.).

In conclusion, I would like to observe that the Ostwald biographies contain material which though partial, has a very valuable bearing on the psychology of the types, and strikingly exhibits the coincidence of the romantic with the extraverted type, and the classic with the introverted.

CHAPTER X

GENERAL DESCRIPTION OF THE TYPES

A. INTRODUCTION

IN the following pages I shall attempt a general description of the types, and my first concern must be with the two general types I have termed introverted and extraverted. But, in addition, I shall also try to give a certain characterization of those special types whose particularity is due to the fact that his most differentiated function plays the principal rôle in an individual's adaptation or orientation to life. The former I would term *general attitude types*, since they are distinguished by the direction of general interest or libido movement, while the latter I would call *function-types*.

The general-attitude types, as I have pointed out more than once, are differentiated by their particular attitude to the object. The introvert's attitude to the object is an abstracting one; at bottom, he is always facing the problem of how libido can be withdrawn from the object, as though an attempted ascendancy on the part of the object had to be continually frustrated. The extravert, on the contrary, maintains a positive relation to the object. To such an extent does he affirm its importance that his subjective attitude is continually being orientated by, and related to the object. Au fond, the object can never have sufficient value; for him, therefore, its importance must always be paramount.

The two types are so essentially different, presenting so striking a contrast, that their existence, even to the uninitiated in psychological matters becomes an obvious fact, when once attention has been drawn to it. Who does not know those taciturn, impenetrable, often shy natures, who form such a vivid contrast to these other open, sociable, serene maybe, or at least friendly and accessible characters, who are on good terms with all the world, or, even when disagreeing with it, still hold a relation to it by which they and it are mutually affected.

Naturally, at first, one is inclined to regard such differences as mere individual idiosyncrasies. But anyone with the opportunity of gaining a fundamental knowledge of many men will soon discover that such a far-reaching contrast does not merely concern the individual case, but is a question of typical attitudes, with a universality far greater than a limited psychological experience would at first assume. In reality, as the preceding chapters will have shown, it is a question of a fundamental opposition; at times clear and at times obscure, but always emerging whenever we are dealing with individuals whose personality is in any way pronounced. Such men are found not only among the educated classes, but in every rank of society; with equal distinctness, therefore, our types can be demonstrated among labourers and peasants as among the most differentiated members of a nation. Furthermore, these types over-ride the distinctions of sex, since one finds the same contrasts amongst women of all classes. Such a universal distribution could hardly arise at the instigation of consciousness, *i.e.* as the result of a conscious and deliberate choice of attitude. If this were the case, a definite level of society, linked together by a similar education and environment and, therefore, correspondingly localized, would surely have a majority representation of such an attitude. But the actual facts are just the reverse, for the types have, apparently, quite a random distribution.

In the same family one child is introverted, and another extraverted.

Since, in the light of these facts, the attitude-type, regarded as a general phenomenon having an apparently random distribution, can be no affair of conscious judgment or intention, its existence must be due to some unconscious, instinctive cause. The contrast of types, therefore, as a universal psychological phenomenon, must in some way or other have its biological precursor.

The relation between subject and object, considered biologically, is always a *relation of adaptation*, since every relation between subject and object presupposes mutually modifying effects from either side. These modifications constitute the adaptation. The typical attitudes to the object, therefore, are adaptation processes. Nature knows two fundamentally different ways of adaptation, which determine the further existence of the living organism; the one is by increased fertility, accompanied by a relatively small degree of defensive power and individual conservation; the other is by individual equipment of manifold means of self-protection, coupled with a relatively insignificant fertility. This biological contrast seems not merely to be the analogue, but also the general foundation of our two psychological modes of adaptation. At this point a mere general indication must suffice; on the one hand, I need only point to the peculiarity of the extravert, which constantly urges him to spend and propagate himself in every way, and, on the other, to the tendency of the introvert to defend himself against external claims, to conserve himself from any expenditure of energy directly related to the object, thus consolidating for himself the most secure and impregnable position.

Blake's intuition did not err when he described the two forms as the "prolific" and the "devouring"[1]. As is

[1] William Blake, *Marriage of Heaven and Hell*.

shown by the general biological example, both forms are current and successful after their kind; this is equally true of the typical attitudes. What the one brings about by a multiplicity of relations, the other gains by monopoly.

The fact that often in their earliest years children display an unmistakable typical attitude forces us to assume that it cannot possibly be the struggle for existence, as it is generally understood, which constitutes the compelling factor in favour of a definite attitude. We might, however, demur, and indeed with cogency, that even the tiny infant, the very babe at the breast, has already an unconscious psychological adaptation to perform, inasmuch as the special character of the maternal influence leads to specific reactions in the child. This argument, though appealing to incontestable facts, has none the less to yield before the equally unarguable fact that two children of the same mother may at a very early age exhibit opposite types, without the smallest accompanying change in the attitude of the mother Although nothing would induce me to underestimate the well-nigh incalculable importance of parental influence, this experience compels me to conclude that the decisive factor must be looked for in the disposition of the child The fact that, in spite of the greatest possible similarity of external conditions, one child will assume this type while another that, must, of course, in the last resort be ascribed to individual disposition. Naturally in saying this I only refer to those cases which occur under normal conditions. Under abnormal conditions, *i.e.* when there is an extreme and, therefore, abnormal attitude in the mother, the children can also be coerced into a relatively similar attitude; but this entails a violation of their individual disposition, which quite possibly would have assumed another type if no abnormal and disturbing external influence had intervened. As a rule, whenever such a falsification of type takes place as a result of external influence, the individual becomes neurotic later, and a cure can successfully be sought only in a development of that attitude which corresponds with the individual's natural way.

As regards the particular disposition, I know not what to say, except that there are clearly individuals who have either a greater readiness and capacity for one way, or for whom it is more congenial to adapt to that way rather than the other. In the last analysis it may well be that physiological causes, inaccessible to our knowledge, play a part in this. That this may be the case seems to me not improbable, in view of one's experience that a reversal of type often proves exceedingly harmful to the physiological well-being of the organism, often provoking an acute state of exhaustion.

B. The Extraverted Type

In our descriptions of this and the following type it will be necessary, in the interest of lucid and comprehensive presentation, to discriminate between the conscious and unconscious psychology. Let us first lend our minds to a description of the *phenomena of consciousness*.

(1) THE GENERAL ATTITUDE OF CONSCIOUSNESS

Everyone is, admittedly, orientated by the data with which the outer world provides him; yet we see that this may be the case in a way that is only relatively decisive. Because it is cold out of doors, one man is persuaded to wear his overcoat, another from a desire to become hardened finds this unnecessary; one man admires the new tenor because all the world admires him, another withholds his approbation not because he dislikes him but because in his view the subject of general admiration is not thereby proved to be admirable; one submits to a given state of affairs because his experience argues nothing else to be possible, another is convinced that, although it has repeated itself a thousand times in the same way, the thousand and first will be different. The former is orientated by the objective data; the latter reserves a view, which is, as it were, interposed between himself and the objective fact. Now, when the orientation to the object and to objective facts is so predominant that the most frequent and essential decisions and actions are determined, not by subjective values but by objective relations, one speaks of an extraverted attitude. When this is habitual, one speaks of an extraverted type. If a man so thinks, feels, and acts, in a word so *lives*, as to correspond *directly* with objective conditions and their claims, whether in a good sense or ill, he is extraverted. His life makes it perfectly clear that it is the objective rather than the subjective value which plays the greater rôle as the determining factor of his consciousness. He naturally has subjective values, but their determining power has less importance than the external objective conditions. Never, therefore, does he expect to find any absolute factors in his own inner life, since the only ones he knows are outside himself. Epimetheus-like, his inner life succumbs to the external necessity, not of course without a struggle; which, however, always ends in favour of the objective determinant. His entire consciousness looks outwards to the world, because the important and decisive determination always comes to him from without. But it comes to him from without, only because that is where he expects it. All the distinguishing characteristics of his psychology, in so far as they do not arise from the priority of one definite psychological function or from individual peculiarities, have their origin in this basic attitude. *Interest* and *attention* follow objective happenings and, primarily, those of the immediate environment. Not only persons, but things, seize and rivet his interest. His *actions*, therefore, are also governed by the influence of persons and things. They are directly related to objective data and determinations, and are, as it were, exhaustively explainable on these grounds. Extraverted action is recognizably related to objective conditions. In so far as it is not purely reactive to environmental stimuli, its character is constantly applicable to the actual circumstances, and it finds adequate and appropriate play within the limits of the objective situation. It has no serious tendency to transcend these bounds. The same holds good for interest: objective occurrences have a well-nigh inexhaustible charm, so that in the normal course the extravert's interest makes no other claims.

The moral laws which govern his action coincide with the corresponding claims of society, *i.e.* with the generally valid moral view-point. If the generally valid view were different, the subjective moral guiding line would also be different, without the general psychological habitus being in any way changed. It might almost seem, although it is by no means the case, that this rigid determination by objective factors would involve an altogether ideal and complete adaptation to general conditions of life. An *accommodation* to objective data, such as we have described, must, of course, seem a complete adaptation to the extraverted view, since from this standpoint no other criterion exists. But from a higher point of view, it is by no means granted that the standpoint of objectively given facts is the normal one under all circumstances. Objective conditions may be either temporarily or locally abnormal. An individual who is accommodated to such conditions certainly conforms to the abnormal style of his surroundings, but, in relation to the universally valid laws of life, he is, in common with his milieu, in an abnormal position. The individual may, however, thrive in such surroundings, but only to the point when he, together with his whole milieu, is destroyed for transgressing the universal laws of life. He must inevitably participate in this downfall with the same completeness as he was previously adjusted to the objectively valid situation. He is adjusted, but not adapted, since adaptation demands more than a mere frictionless participation in the momentary conditions of the immediate environment. (Once more I would point to Spitteler's Epimetheus). Adaptation demands an observance of laws far more universal in their application than purely local and temporary conditions. Mere adjustment is the limitation of the normal extraverted type. On the one hand, the extravert owes his normality to his ability to fit into existing conditions with relative ease. He naturally pretends to nothing more than the satisfaction of existing objective possibilities, applying himself, for instance, to the calling which offers sound prospective possibilities in the actual situation in time and place. He tries to do or to make just what his milieu momentarily needs and expects from him, and abstains from every innovation that is not entirely obvious, or that in any way exceeds the expectation of those around him. But on the other hand, his normality must also depend essentially upon whether the extravert takes into account the actuality of his subjective needs and requirements; and this is just his weak point, for the tendency of his type has such a strong outward direction that even the most obvious of all subjective facts, namely the condition of his own body, may quite easily receive inadequate consideration. The body is not sufficiently objective or 'external,' so that the satisfaction of simple elementary requirements which are indispensable to physical well-being are no longer given their place. The body accordingly suffers, to say nothing of the soul. Although, as a rule, the extravert takes small note of this latter circumstance, his intimate domestic circle perceives it all the more keenly. His loss of equilibrium is perceived by himself only when abnormal bodily sensations make themselves felt.

These tangible facts he cannot ignore. It is natural he should regard them as concrete and 'objective', since for his mentality there exists only this and nothing more —in himself. In others he at once sees "imagination" at work. A too extraverted attitude may actually become so regardless of the subject that the latter is entirely sacrificed to so-called objective claims; to the demands, for instance, of a continually extending business, because orders lie claiming one's attention or because profitable possibilities are constantly being opened up which must instantly be seized.

This is the extravert's danger; he becomes caught up in objects, wholly losing himself in their toils. The functional (nervous) or actual physical disorders which result from this state have a compensatory significance, forcing the subject to an involuntary self-restriction. Should the symptoms be functional, their peculiar formation may symbolically express the psychological situation; a singer, for instance, whose fame quickly reaches a dangerous pitch tempting him to a disproportionate outlay of energy, is suddenly robbed of his high tones by a nervous inhibition. A man of very modest beginnings rapidly reaches a social position of great influence and wide prospects, when suddenly he is overtaken by a psychogenic state, with all the symptoms of mountain-sickness. Again, a man on the point of marrying an idolized woman of doubtful character, whose value he extravagantly over-estimates, is seized with a spasm of the œsophagus, which forces him to a regimen of two cups of milk in the day, demanding his three-hourly attention. All visits to his fiancée are thus effectually stopped, and no choice is left to him but to busy himself with his bodily nourishment. A man who through his own energy and enterprise has built up a vast business, entailing an intolerable burden of work, is afflicted by nervous attacks of thirst, as a result of which he speedily falls a victim to hysterical alcoholism.

Hysteria is, in my view, by far the most frequent neurosis with the extraverted type. The classical example of hysteria is always characterized by an exaggerated rapport with the members of his circle, and a frankly imitatory accommodation to surrounding conditions. A constant tendency to appeal for interest and to produce impressions upon his milieu is a basic trait of the hysterical nature. A correlate to this is his proverbial suggestibility, his pliability to another person's influence. Unmistakable extraversion comes out in the communicativeness of the hysteric, which occasionally leads to the divulging of purely phantastic contents; whence arises the reproach of the hysterical lie.

To begin with, the 'hysterical' character is an exaggeration of the normal attitude; it is then complicated by compensatory reactions from the side of the unconscious, which manifests its opposition to the extravagant extraversion in the form of physical disorders, whereupon an introversion of psychic energy becomes unavoidable. Through this reaction of the unconscious, another category of symptoms arises which have a more introverted character. A morbid intensification of phantasy activity belongs primarily to this category. From this general characterization of the extraverted attitude, let us now turn to a description of the modifications, which the basic psychological functions undergo as a result of this attitude.

(II) THE ATTITUDE OF THE UNCONSCIOUS

It may perhaps seem odd that I should speak of an 'attitude of the unconscious'. As I have already sufficiently indicated, I regard the relation of the unconscious to the conscious as compensatory. The unconscious, according to this view, has as good a claim to an 'attitude' as the conscious.

In the foregoing section I emphasized the tendency to a certain one-sidedness in the extraverted attitude, due to the controlling power of the objective factor in the course of psychic events. The extraverted type is constantly tempted to give himself away (apparently) in favour of the object, and to assimilate his subject to the object. I have referred in detail to the ultimate consequences of this exaggeration of the extraverted attitude, viz. to the injurious suppression of the subjective factor. It is only to be expected, therefore, that a psychic compensation of the conscious extraverted attitude will lay especial weight upon the subjective factor, *i.e.* we shall have to prove a strong egocentric tendency in the unconscious. Practical experience actually furnishes this proof. I do not wish to enter into a casuistical survey at this point, so must refer my readers to the ensuing sections, where I shall attempt to present the characteristic attitude of the unconscious from the angle of each function-type. In this section we are merely concerned with the compensation of a general extraverted attitude; I shall, therefore, confine myself to an equally general characterization of the compensating attitude of the unconscious.

The attitude of the unconscious as an effective complement to the conscious extraverted attitude has a definitely introverting character. It focusses libido upon the subjective factor, *i.e.* all those needs and claims which are stifled or repressed by a too extraverted conscious attitude. It may be readily gathered from what has been said in the previous section that a purely objective orientation does violence to a multitude of subjective emotions, intentions, needs, and desires, since it robs them of the energy which is their natural right. Man is not a machine that one can reconstruct, as occasion demands, upon other lines and for quite other ends, in the hope that it will then proceed to function, in a totally different way, just as normally as before. Man bears his age-long history with him; in his very structure is written the history of mankind.

The historical factor represents a vital need, to which a wise economy must respond. Somehow the past must become vocal, and participate in the present. Complete assimilation to the object, therefore, encounters the protest of the suppressed minority, elements belonging to the past and existing from the beginning. From this quite general consideration it may be understood why it is that the unconscious claims of the extraverted type have an essentially primitive, infantile, and egoistical character. When Freud says that the unconscious is "only able to wish", this observation contains a large measure of truth for the unconscious of the extraverted type. Adjustment and assimilation to objective data prevent inadequate subjective impulses from reaching consciousness. These tendencies (thoughts, wishes, affects, needs, feelings, etc.) take on a regressive character corresponding with the degree of their repression, *i.e.* the less they are recognized, the more infantile and archaic they become. The conscious attitude robs them of their relatively disposable energy-charge, only leaving them the energy of which it cannot deprive them. This remainder, which still possesses a potency not to be under-estimated, can be described only as primeval instinct. Instinct can never be rooted out from an individual by any arbitrary measures; it requires the slow, organic transformation of many generations to effect a radical change, for instinct is the energic expression of a definite organic foundation.

Thus with every repressed tendency a considerable sum of energy ultimately remains. This sum corresponds with the potency of the instinct and guards its effectiveness, notwithstanding the deprivation of energy which made it unconscious. The measure of extraversion in the conscious attitude entails a like degree of infantilism and archaism in the attitude of the unconscious. The egoism which so often characterizes the extravert's unconscious attitude goes far beyond mere childish selfishness; it even verges upon the wicked and brutal. It is here we find in fullest bloom that incest-wish described by Freud. It is self-evident that these things are entirely unconscious, remaining altogether hidden from the eyes of the uninitiated observer so long as the extraversion of the conscious attitude does not reach an extreme stage. But wherever an exaggeration of the conscious standpoint takes place, the unconscious also comes to light in a symptomatic form, *i.e.* the unconscious egoism, infantilism, and archaism lose their original compensatory characters, and appear in more or less open opposition to the conscious attitude. This process begins in the form of an absurd exaggeration of the conscious standpoint, which is aimed at a further repression of the unconscious, but usually ends in a reductio ad absurdum of the conscious attitude, *i.e.* a collapse. The catastrophe may be an objective one, since the objective aims gradually become falsified by the subjective. I remember the case of a printer who, starting as a mere employé, worked his way up through two decades of hard struggle, till at last he was the independent possessor of a very extensive business. The more the business extended, the more it increased its hold upon him, until gradually every other interest was allowed to become merged in it. At length he was completely enmeshed in its toils, and, as we shall soon see, this surrender eventually proved his ruin. As a sort of compensation to his exclusive interest in the business, certain memories of his childhood came to life. As a child he had taken great delight in painting and drawing. But, instead of renewing this capacity for its own sake as a balancing side-interest, he canalized it into his business and began to conceive 'artistic' elaborations of his products. His phantasies unfortunately materialized: he actually began to produce after his own primitive and infantile taste, with the result that after a very few years his business went to pieces. He acted in obedience to one of our 'civilized ideals', which enjoins the energetic man to concentrate everything upon the one end in view. But he went too far, and merely fell a victim to the power of his subjective infantile claims.

But the catastrophic solution may also be subjective, *i.e.* in the form of a nervous collapse. Such a solution always comes about as a result of the unconscious counter-influence, which can ultimately paralyse conscious action. In which case the claims of the unconscious force themselves categorically upon consciousness, thus creating a calamitous cleavage which generally reveals itself in two ways: either the subject no longer knows what he really wants and nothing any longer interests him, or he wants too much at once and has too keen an interest—but in impossible things. The suppression of infantile and primitive claims, which is often necessary on "civilized" grounds, easily leads to neurosis, or to the misuse of narcotics such as alcohol, morphine, cocaine, etc. In more extreme cases the cleavage ends in suicide.

It is a salient peculiarity of unconscious tendencies that, just in so far as they are deprived of their energy by a *lack of conscious recognition*, they assume a correspondingly destructive character, and as soon as this happens their compensatory function ceases. They cease to have a compensatory effect as soon as they reach a depth or stratum that corresponds with a level of culture absolutely incompatible with our own. From this moment the unconscious tendencies form a block, which is opposed to the conscious attitude in every respect; such a block inevitably leads to open conflict.

In a general way, the compensating attitude of the unconscious finds expression in the process of psychic equilibrium. A normal extraverted attitude does not, of course, mean that the individual behaves invariably in accordance with the extraverted schema. Even in the same individual many psychological happenings may be observed, in which the mechanism of introversion is concerned. A habitus can be called extraverted only when the mechanism of extraversion predominates. In such a case the most highly differentiated function has a constantly extraverted application, while the inferior functions are found in the service of introversion, *i.e.* the more valued function, because the more conscious, is more completely subordinated to conscious control and purpose, whilst the less conscious, in other words, the partly unconscious inferior functions are subjected to conscious free choice in a much smaller degree.

The superior function is always the expression of the conscious personality, its aim, its will, and its achievement, whilst the inferior functions belong to the things that happen to one. Not that they merely beget blunders, *e.g.* lapsus linguæ or lapsus calami, but they may also breed half or three-quarter resolves, since the inferior functions also possess a slight degree of consciousness. The extraverted feeling type is a classical example of this, for he enjoys an excellent feeling rapport with his entourage, yet occasionally opinions of an incomparable tactlessness will just happen to him. These opinions have their source in his inferior and subconscious thinking, which is only partly subject to control and is insufficiently related to the object; to a large extent, therefore, it can operate without consideration or responsibility.

In the extraverted attitude the inferior functions always reveal a highly subjective determination with pronounced egocentricity and personal bias, thus demonstrating their close connection with the unconscious. Through their agency the unconscious is continually coming to light. On no account should we imagine that the unconscious lies permanently buried under so many overlying strata that it can only be uncovered, so to speak, by a laborious process of excavation. On the contrary, there is a constant influx of the unconscious into the conscious psychological process; at times this reaches such a pitch that the observer can decide only with difficulty which character-traits are to be ascribed to the conscious, and which to the unconscious personality. This difficulty occurs mainly with persons whose habit of expression errs rather on the side of profuseness. Naturally it depends very largely also upon the attitude of the observer, whether he lays hold of the conscious or the unconscious character of a personality. Speaking generally a judging observer will tend to seize the conscious character, while a perceptive observer will be influenced more by the unconscious character, since judgment is chiefly interested in the conscious motivation of the psychic process, while perception tends to register the mere happening. But in so far as we apply perception and judgment in equal measure, it may easily happen that a personality appears to us as both introverted and extraverted, so that we cannot at once decide to which attitude the superior function belongs. In such cases only a thorough analysis of the function qualities can help us to a sound opinion. During the analysis we must observe which function is placed under the control and motivation of consciousness, and which functions have an accidental and spontaneous character. The former is always more highly differentiated than the latter, which also possess many infantile and primitive qualities. Occasionally the former function gives the impression of normality, while the latter have something abnormal or pathological about them.

(III) THE PECULIARITIES OF THE BASIC PSYCHOLOGICAL FUNCTIONS IN THE EXTRAVERTED ATTITUDE

1. Thinking

As a result of the general attitude of extraversion, thinking is orientated by the object and objective data. This orientation of thinking produces a noticeable peculiarity.

Thinking in general is fed from two sources, firstly from subjective and in the last resort unconscious roots, and secondly from objective data transmitted through sense perceptions.

Extraverted thinking is conditioned in a larger measure by these latter factors than by the former. Judgment always presupposes a criterion; for the extraverted judgment, the valid and determining criterion is the standard taken from objective conditions, no matter whether this be directly represented by an objectively perceptible fact, or expressed in an objective idea; for an objective idea, even when subjectively sanctioned, is equally external and objective in origin. Extraverted thinking, therefore, need not necessarily be a merely concretistic thinking— it may equally well be a purely ideal thinking, if, for instance, it can be shown that the ideas with which it is engaged are to a great extent borrowed from without, *i.e.* are transmitted by tradition and education. The criterion of judgment, therefore, as to whether or no a thinking is extraverted, hangs directly upon the question: by which standard is its judgment governed—is it furnished from without, or is its origin subjective? A further criterion is afforded by the direction of the thinker's conclusion, namely, whether or no the thinking has a preferential direction outwards. It is no proof of its extraverted nature that it is preoccupied with concrete objects, since I may be engaging my thoughts with a concrete object, either because I am abstracting my thought from it or because I am concretizing my thought with it. Even if I engage my thinking with concrete things, and to that extent could be described as extraverted, it yet remains both questionable and characteristic as regards the direction my thinking will take; namely, whether in its further course it leads back again to objective data, external facts, and generally accepted ideas, or not. So far as the practical thinking of the merchant, the engineer, or the natural science pioneer is concerned, the objective direction is at once manifest. But in the case of a philosopher it is open to doubt, whenever the course of his thinking is directed towards ideas. In such a case, before deciding, we must further enquire whether these ideas are mere abstractions from objective experience, in which case they would merely represent higher collective concepts, comprising a sum of objective facts; or whether (if they are clearly not abstractions from immediate experience) they may not be derived from tradition or borrowed from the intellectual atmosphere of the time. In the latter event, such ideas must also belong to the category of objective data, in which case this thinking should also be called extraverted.

Although I do not propose to present the nature of introverted thinking at this point, reserving it for a later section, it is, however, essential that I should make a few statements about it before going further. For if one considers strictly what I have just said concerning extraverted thinking, one might easily conclude that such a statement includes everything that is generally understood as thinking. It might indeed be argued that a thinking whose aim is concerned neither with objective facts nor with general ideas scarcely merits the name 'thinking'. I am fully aware of the fact that the thought of our age, in common with its most eminent representatives, knows and acknowledges only the extraverted type of thinking. This is partly due to the fact that all thinking which attains visible form upon the world's surface, whether as science, philosophy, or even art, either proceeds direct from objects or flows into general ideas. On either ground, although not always completely evident it at least appears essentially intelligible, and therefore relatively valid. In this sense it might be said that the extraverted intellect, *i.e.* the mind that is orientated by objective data, is actually the only one recognized.

There is also, however—and now I come to the question of the introverted intellect—an entirely different kind of thinking, to which the term "thinking" can hardly be denied: it is a kind that is neither orientated by the immediate objective experience nor is it concerned with general and objectively derived ideas. I reach this other kind of thinking in the following way. When my thoughts are engaged with a concrete object or general idea in such a way that the course of my thinking eventually leads me back again to my object, this intellectual process is not the only psychic proceeding taking place in me at the moment. I will disregard all those possible sensations and feelings which become noticeable as a more or less disturbing accompaniment to my train of thought, merely emphasizing the fact that this very thinking process which proceeds from objective data and strives again towards the object stands also in a constant relation to the subject. This relation is a conditio sine qua non, without which no thinking process whatsoever could take place. Even though my thinking process is directed, as far as possible, towards objective data, nevertheless it is *my* subjective process, and it can neither escape the subjective admixture nor yet dispense with it. Although I try my utmost to give a completely objective direction to my train of thought, even then I cannot exclude the parallel subjective process with its all-embracing participation, without extinguishing the very spark of life from my thought. This parallel subjective process has a natural tendency, only relatively avoidable, to subjectify objective facts, *i.e.* to assimilate them to the subject.

Whenever the chief value is given to the subjective process, that other kind of thinking arises which stands opposed to extraverted thinking, namely, that purely subjective orientation of thought which I have termed introverted. A thinking arises from this other orientation that is neither determined by objective facts nor directed towards objective data—a thinking, therefore, that proceeds from subjective data and is directed towards subjective ideas or facts of a subjective character. I do not wish to enter more fully into this kind of thinking here; I have merely established its existence for the purpose of giving a necessary complement to the extraverted thinking process, whose nature is thus brought to a clearer focus.

When the objective orientation receives a certain predominance, the thinking is extraverted. This circumstance changes nothing as regards the logic of thought—it merely determines that difference between thinkers which James regards as a matter of temperament. The orientation towards the object, as already explained, makes no essential change in the thinking function; only its appearance is altered. Since it is governed by objective data, it has the appearance of being captivated by the object, as though without the external orientation it simply could not exist. Almost it seems as though it were a sequela of external facts, or as though it could reach its highest point only when chiming in with some generally valid idea. It seems constantly to be affected by objective data, drawing only those conclusions which substantially agree with these. Thus it gives one the impression of a certain lack of freedom, of occasional short-sightedness, in spite of every kind of adroitness within the objectively circumscribed area. What I am now describing is merely the impression this sort of thinking makes upon the observer, who must himself already have a different standpoint, or it would be quite impossible for him to observe the phenomenon of extraverted thinking. As a result of his different standpoint he merely sees its aspect, not its nature; whereas the man who himself possesses this type of thinking is able to seize its nature, while its aspect escapes him. Judgment made upon appearance only cannot be fair to the essence of the thing—hence the result is depreciatory. But essentially this thinking is no less fruitful and creative than introverted thinking, only its powers are in the service of other ends. This difference is perceived most clearly when extraverted thinking is engaged upon material, which is specifically an object of the subjectively orientated thinking. This happens, for instance, when a subjective conviction is interpreted analytically from objective facts or is regarded as a product or derivative of objective ideas. But, for our 'scientifically' orientated consciousness, the difference between the two modes of thinking becomes still more obvious when the subjectively orientated thinking makes an attempt to bring objective data into connections not objectively given, *i.e.* to subordinate them to a subjective idea. Either senses the other as an encroachment, and hence a sort of shadow effect is produced, wherein either type reveals to the other its least favourable aspect. The subjectively orientated thinking then appears

GENERAL DESCRIPTION OF TYPES

quite arbitrary, while the extraverted thinking seems to have an incommensurability that is altogether dull and banal. Thus the two standpoints are incessantly at war.

Such a conflict, we might think, could be easily adjusted if only we clearly discriminated objects of a subjective from those of an objective nature. Unfortunately, however, such a discrimination is a matter of impossibility, although not a few have attempted it. Even if such a separation were possible, it would be a very disastrous proceeding, since in themselves both orientations are one-sided, with a definitely restricted validity; hence they both require this mutual correction. Thought is at once sterilized, whenever thinking is brought, to any great extent, under the influence of objective data, since it becomes degraded into a mere appendage of objective facts; in which case, it is no longer able to free itself from objective data for the purpose of establishing an abstract idea. The process of thought is reduced to mere 'reflection', not in the sense of 'meditation', but in the sense of a mere imitation that makes no essential affirmation beyond what was already visibly and immediately present in the objective data. Such a thinking-process leads naturally and directly back to the objective fact, but never beyond it; not once, therefore, can it lead to the coupling of experience with an objective idea. And, vice versa, when this thinking has an objective idea for its object, it is quite unable to grasp the practical individual experience, but persists in a more or less tautological position. The materialistic mentality presents a magnificent example of this.

When, as the result of a reinforced objective determination, extraverted thinking is subordinated to objective data, it entirely loses itself, on the one hand, in the individual experience, and proceeds to amass an accumulation of undigested empirical material. The oppressive mass of more or less disconnected individual experiences produces a state of intellectual dissociation, which, on the other hand, usually demands a psychological compensation. This must consist in an idea, just as simple as it is universal, which shall give coherence to the heaped-up but intrinsically disconnected whole, or at least it should provide an inkling of such a connection. Such ideas as "matter" or "energy" are suitable for this purpose. But, whenever thinking primarily depends not so much upon external facts as upon an accepted or second-hand idea, the very poverty of the idea provokes a compensation in the form of a still more impressive accumulation of facts, which assume a one-sided grouping in keeping with the relatively restricted and sterile point of view; whereupon many valuable and sensible aspects of things automatically go by the board. The vertiginous abundance of the so-called scientific literature of to-day owes a deplorably high percentage of its existence to this misorientation.

2. The Extraverted Thinking Type

It is a fact of experience that all the basic psychological functions seldom or never have the same strength or grade of development in one and the same individual. As a rule, one or other function predominates, in both strength and development. When *supremacy* among the psychological functions is given to thinking, *i.e.* when the life of an individual is mainly ruled by reflective thinking so that every important action proceeds from intellectually considered motives, or when there is at least a tendency to conform to such motives, we may fairly call this a *thinking type*. Such a type can be either introverted or extraverted. We will first discuss the *extraverted thinking type*.

In accordance with his definition, we must picture a man whose constant aim—in so far, of course, as he is a pure type—is to bring his total life-activities into relation with intellectual conclusions, which in the last resort are always orientated by objective data, whether objective facts or generally valid ideas. This type of man gives the deciding voice—not merely for himself alone but also on behalf of his entourage—either to the actual objective reality or to its objectively orientated, intellectual formula. By this formula are good and evil measured, and beauty and ugliness determined. All is right that corresponds with this formula; all is wrong that contradicts it; and everything that is neutral to it is purely accidental. Because this formula seems to correspond with the meaning of the world, it also becomes a world-law whose realization must be achieved at all times and seasons, both individually and collectively. Just as the extraverted thinking type subordinates himself to his formula, so, for its own good, must his entourage also obey it, since the man who refuses to obey is wrong—he is resisting the world-law, and is, therefore, unreasonable, immoral, and without a conscience. His moral code forbids him to tolerate exceptions; his ideal must, under all circumstances, be realized; for in his eyes it is the purest conceivable formulation of objective reality, and, therefore, must also be generally valid truth, quite indispensable for the salvation of man. This is not from any great love for his neighbour, but from a higher standpoint of justice and truth. Everything in his own nature that appears to invalidate this formula is mere imperfection, an accidental miss-fire, something to be eliminated on the next occasion, or, in the event of further failure, then clearly a sickness.

If tolerance for the sick, the suffering, or the deranged should chance to be an ingredient in the formula, special provisions will be devised for humane societies, hospitals, prisons, colonies, etc., or at least extensive plans for such projects. For the actual execution of these schemes the motives of justice and truth do not, as a rule, suffice; they still devolve upon real Christian charity, which has more to do with feeling than with any intellectual formula. 'One really should' or 'one must' figure largely in this programme. If the formula is wide enough, this type may play a very useful rôle in social life, either as a reformer or a ventilator of public wrongs or a purifier of the public conscience, or as the propagator of important innovations. But the more rigid the formula, the more does he develop into a grumbler, a crafty reasoner, and a self-righteous critic, who would like to impress both himself and others into one schema.

We have now outlined two extreme figures, between which terminals the majority of these types may be graduated.

In accordance with the nature of the extraverted attitude, the influence and activities of such personalities are all the more favourable and beneficent, the further one goes from the centre. Their best aspect is to be found at the periphery of their sphere of influence. The further we penetrate into their own province, the more do the unfavourable results of their tyranny impress us Another life still pulses at the periphery, where the truth of the formula can be sensed as an estimable adjunct to the rest. But the further we probe into the special sphere where the formula operates, the more do we find life ebbing away from all that fails to coincide with its dictates. Usually it is the nearest relatives who have to taste the most disagreeable results of an extraverted formula, since they are the first to be unmercifully blessed with it. But above all the subject himself is the one who suffers most —which brings us to the other side of the psychology of this type.

The fact that an intellectual formula never has been and never will be discovered which could embrace the abundant possibilities of life in a fitting expression must lead—where such a formula is accepted—to an inhibition, or total exclusion, of other highly important forms and activities of life. In the first place, all those vital forms dependent upon feeling will become repressed in such a type, as, for instance, æsthetic activities, taste, artistic sense, the art of friendship, etc. Irrational forms such as religious experiences, passions and the like, are often obliterated even to the point of complete unconsciousness. These, conditionally quite important, forms of life have to support an existence that is largely unconscious. Doubtless there are exceptional men who are able to sacrifice their entire life to one definite formula; but for most of us a permanent life of such exclusiveness is impossible. Sooner or later—in accordance with outer circumstances and inner gifts—the forms of life repressed by the intellectual attitude become indirectly perceptible, through a gradual disturbance of the conscious conduct of life. Whenever disturbances of this kind reach a definite intensity, one speaks of a neurosis. In most cases, however, it does not go so far, because the individual instinctively allows himself some preventive extenuations of his formula, worded, of course, in a suitable and reasonable way. In this way a safety-valve is created.

The relative or total unconsciousness of such tendencies or functions as are excluded from any participation in the conscious attitude keeps them in a relatively undeveloped state. As compared with the conscious function they are inferior. To the extent that they are unconscious, they become merged with the remaining contents of the unconscious, from which they acquire a bizarre character. To the extent that they are conscious, they only play a secondary rôle, although one of considerable importance for the whole psychological picture.

Since feelings are the first to oppose and contradict

the rigid intellectual formula, they are affected first by this conscious inhibition, and upon them the most intense repression falls. No function can be entirely eliminated—it can only be greatly distorted. In so far as feelings allow themselves to be arbitrarily shaped and subordinated, they have to support the intellectual conscious attitude and adapt themselves to its aims. Only to a certain degree, however, is this possible; a part of the feeling remains insubordinate, and therefore must be repressed. Should the repression succeed, it disappears from consciousness and proceeds to unfold a subconscious activity, which runs counter to conscious aims, even producing effects whose causation is a complete enigma to the individual. For example, conscious altruism, often of an extremely high order, may be crossed by a secret self-seeking, of which the individual is wholly unaware, and which impresses intrinsically unselfish actions with the stamp of selfishness. Purely ethical aims may lead the individual into critical situations, which sometimes have more than a semblance of being decided by quite other than ethical motives. There are guardians of public morals or voluntary rescue-workers who suddenly find themselves in deplorably compromising situations, or in dire need of rescue. Their resolve to save often leads them to employ means which only tend to precipitate what they most desire to avoid. There are extraverted idealists, whose desire to advance the salvation of man is so consuming that they will not shrink from any lying and dishonest means in the pursuit of their ideal. There are a few painful examples in science where investigators of the highest esteem, from a profound conviction of the truth and general validity of their formula, have not scrupled to falsify evidence in favour of their ideal. This is sanctioned by the formula; the end justifieth the means. Only an inferior feeling-function, operating seductively and unconsciously, could bring about such aberrations in otherwise reputable men.

The inferiority of feeling in this type manifests itself also in other ways. In so far as it corresponds with the dominating positive formula, the conscious attitude becomes more or less impersonal, often, indeed, to such a degree that a very considerable wrong is done to personal interests. When the conscious attitude is extreme, all personal considerations recede from view, even those which concern the individual's own person. His health is neglected, his social position deteriorates, often the most vital interests of his family are violated—they are wronged morally and financially, even their bodily health is made to suffer—all in the service of the ideal. At all events personal sympathy with others must be impaired, unless they too chance to be in the service of the same formula. Hence it not infrequently happens that his immediate family circle, his own children for instance, only know such a father as a cruel tyrant, whilst the outer world resounds with the fame of his humanity. Not so much in spite of as because of the highly impersonal character of the conscious attitude, the unconscious feelings are highly personal and oversensitive, giving rise to certain secret prejudices, as, for instance, a decided readiness to misconstrue any objective opposition to his formula as personal ill-will, or a constant tendency to make negative suppositions regarding the qualities of others in order to invalidate their arguments beforehand—in defence, naturally, of his own susceptibility. As a result of this unconscious sensitiveness, his expression and tone frequently becomes sharp, pointed, aggressive, and insinuations multiply. The feelings have an untimely and halting character, which is always a mark of the inferior function. Hence arises a pronounced tendency to resentment. However generous the individual sacrifice to the intellectual goal may be, the feelings are correspondingly petty, suspicious, crossgrained, and conservative. Everything new that is not already contained in the formula is viewed through a veil of unconscious hatred, and is judged accordingly. It happened only in the middle of last century that a certain physician, famed for his humanitarianism, threatened to dismiss an assistant for daring to use a thermometer, because the formula decreed that fever shall be recognized by the pulse. There are, of course, a host of similar examples.

Thinking which in other respects may be altogether blameless becomes all the more subtly and prejudicially affected, the more feelings are repressed. An intellectual standpoint, which, perhaps on account of its actual intrinsic value, might justifiably claim general recognition, undergoes a characteristic alteration through the influence of this unconscious personal sensitiveness; it becomes rigidly dogmatic. The personal self-assertion is transferred to the intellectual standpoint. Truth is no longer left to work her natural effect, but through an identification with the subject she is treated like a sensitive darling whom an evil-minded critic has wronged. The critic is demolished, if possible with personal invective, and no argument is too gross to be used against him. Truth must be trotted out, until finally it begins to dawn upon the public that it is not so much really a question of truth as of her personal procreator.

The dogmatism of the intellectual standpoint, however, occasionally undergoes still further peculiar modifications from the unconscious admixture of unconscious personal feelings; these changes are less a question of feeling, in the stricter sense, than of contamination from other unconscious factors which become blended with the repressed feeling in the unconscious. Although reason itself offers proof, that every intellectual formula can be no more than a partial truth, and can never lay claim, therefore, to autocratic authority; in practice, the formula obtains so great an ascendancy that, beside it, every other standpoint and possibility recedes into the background. It replaces all the more general, less defined, hence the more modest and truthful, views of life. It even takes the place of that general view of life which we call religion. Thus the formula becomes a religion, although in essentials it has not the smallest connection with anything religious. Therewith it also gains the essentially religious character of absoluteness. It becomes, as it were, an intellectual superstition. But now all those psychological tendencies that suffer under its repression become grouped together in the unconscious, and form a counter-position, giving rise to paroxysms of doubt. As a defence against doubt, the conscious attitude grows fanatical. For fanaticism, after all, is merely overcompensated doubt. Ultimately this development leads to an exaggerated defence of the conscious position, and to the gradual formation of an absolutely antithetic unconscious position; for example, an extreme irrationality develops, in opposition to the conscious rationalism, or it becomes highly archaic and superstitious, in opposition to a conscious standpoint imbued with modern science. This fatal opposition is the source of those narrow-minded and ridiculous views, familiar to the historians of science, into which many praiseworthy pioneers have ultimately blundered. It not infrequently happens in a man of this type that the side of the unconscious becomes embodied in a woman.

In my experience, this type, which is doubtless familiar to my readers, is chiefly found among men, since thinking tends to be a much more dominant function in men than in women. As a rule, when thinking achieves the mastery in women, it is, in my experience, a kind of thinking which results from a prevailingly *intuitive* activity of mind.

The thought of the extraverted thinking type is *positive*, i.e. it produces. It either leads to new facts or to general conceptions of disparate experimental material. Its judgment is generally *synthetic*. Even when it analyses, it constructs, because it is always advancing beyond the analysis to a new combination, a further conception which re-unites the analysed material in a new way or adds something further to the given material. In general, therefore, we may describe this kind of judgment as *predicative*. It is, in any case, characteristic that it is never absolutely depreciatory or destructive, but always substitutes a fresh value for one that is demolished. This quality is due to the fact that thought is the main channel into which a thinking-type's energy flows. Life steadily advancing shows itself in the man's thinking, so that his ideas maintain a progressive, creative character. His thinking neither stagnates, nor is it in the least regressive. Such qualities cling only to a thinking that is not given priority in consciousness. In this event it is relatively unimportant, and also lacks the character of a positive vital activity. It follows in the wake of other functions, it becomes Epimethean, it has an 'esprit de l'escalier' quality, contenting itself with constant ponderings and broodings upon things past and gone, in an effort to analyse and digest them. Where the creative element, as in this case, inhabits another function, thinking no longer progresses: it stagnates. Its judgment takes on a decided *inherency-character*, i.e. it entirely confines itself to the range of the given material, nowhere overstepping it. It is contented with a more or less abstract statement, and fails to impart any value to the experimental material that was not already there.

The inherency-judgment of such extraverted thinking is objectively orientated, *i.e.* its conclusion always expresses the objective importance of experience. Hence, not only does it remain under the orientating influence of objective data, but it actually rests within the charmed circle of the individual experience, about which it affirms nothing that was not already given by it. We may easily observe this thinking in those people who cannot refrain from tacking on to an impression or experience some rational and doubtless very valid remark, which, however, in no way adventures beyond the given orbit of the experience. At bottom, such a remark merely says 'I have understood it —I can reconstruct it.' But there the matter also ends. At its very highest, such a judgment signifies merely the placing of an experience in an objective setting, whereby the experience is at once recognized as belonging to the frame.

But whenever a function other than thinking possesses priority in consciousness to any marked degree, in so far as thinking is conscious at all and not directly dependent upon the dominant function, it assumes a *negative* character. In so far as it is subordinated to the dominant function, it may actually wear a positive aspect, but a narrower scrutiny will easily prove that it simply mimics the dominant function, supporting it with arguments that unmistakably contradict the laws of logic proper to thinking. Such a thinking, therefore, ceases to have any interest for our present discussion. Our concern is rather with the constitution of that thinking which cannot be subordinated to the dominance of another function, but remains true to its own principle. To observe and investigate this thinking in itself is not easy, since, in the concrete case, it is more or less constantly repressed by the conscious attitude. Hence, in the majority of cases, it first must be retrieved from the background of consciousness, unless in some unguarded moment it should chance to come accidentally to the surface. As a rule, it must be enticed with some such questions as 'Now what do you *really* think?' or, again, 'What is your private view about the matter?' Or perhaps one may even have to use a little cunning, framing the question something like this: 'What do you imagine, then, that *I* really think about the matter?' This latter form should be chosen when the real thinking is unconscious and, therefore, projected. The thinking that is enticed to the surface in this way has characteristic qualities; it was these I had in mind just now when I described it as *negative*. Its habitual mode is best characterized by the two words 'nothing but'. Goethe personified this thinking in the figure of Mephistopheles. It shows a most distinct tendency to trace back the object of its judgment to some banality or other, thus stripping it of its own independent significance. This happens simply because it is represented as being dependent upon some other commonplace thing. Wherever a conflict, apparently essential in nature, arises between two men, negative thinking mutters 'Cherchez la femme'. When a man champions or advocates a cause, negative thinking makes no inquiry as to the importance of the thing, but merely asks 'How much does he make by it?' The dictum ascribed to Moleschott: "Der Mensch ist, was er isst" ("Man is what he eats") also belongs to this collection, as do many more aphorisms and opinions which I need not enumerate.

The destructive quality of this thinking as well as its occasional and limited usefulness, hardly need further elucidation. But there still exists another form of negative thinking, which at first glance perhaps would scarcely be recognized as such: I refer to the *theosophical* thinking which is to-day rapidly spreading in every quarter of the globe, presumably as a reaction phenomenon to the materialism of the epoch now receding. Theosophical thinking has an air that is not in the least reductive, since it exalts everything to transcendental and world-embracing ideas. A dream, for instance, is no longer a modest dream, but an experience upon 'another plane'. The hitherto inexplicable fact of telepathy is very simply explained by 'vibrations' which pass from one man to another. An ordinary nervous trouble is quite simply accounted for by the fact that something has collided with the astral body. Certain anthropological peculiarities of the dwellers on the Atlantic seaboard are easily explained by the submerging of Atlantis, and so on. We have merely to open a theosophical book to be overwhelmed by the realization that everything is already explained, and that 'spiritual science' has left no enigmas of life unsolved. But, fundamentally, this sort of thinking is just as negative as materialistic thinking. When the latter conceives psychology as chemical changes taking place in the cell-ganglia, or as the extrusion and withdrawal of cell-processes, or as an internal secretion, in essence this is just as superstitious as theosophy. The only difference lies in the fact that materialism reduces all phenomena to our current physiological notions, while theosophy brings everything into the concepts of Indian metaphysics. When we trace the dream to an overloaded stomach, the dream is not thereby explained, and when we explain telepathy as 'vibrations', we have said just as little. Since, what are 'vibrations'? Not only are both methods of explanation quite impotent—they are actually destructive, because by interposing their seeming explanations they withdraw interest from the problem, diverting it in the former case to the stomach, and in the latter to imaginary vibrations, thus preventing any serious investigation of the problem. Either kind of thinking is both sterile and sterilizing. Their negative quality consists in this: it is a method of thought that is indescribably cheap; there is a real poverty of productive and creative energy. It is a thinking taken in tow by other functions.

3. Feeling

Feeling in the extraverted attitude is orientated by objective data, *i.e.* the object is the indispensable determinant of the kind of feeling. It agrees with objective values. If one has always known feeling as a subjective fact, the nature of extraverted feeling will not immediately be understood, since it has freed itself as fully as possible from the subjective factor, and has, instead, become wholly subordinated to the influence of the object. Even where it seems to show a certain independence of the quality of the concrete object, it is none the less under the spell of traditional or generally valid standards of some sort. I may feel constrained, for instance, to use the predicate 'beautiful' or 'good', not because I find the object 'beautiful' or 'good' from my own subjective feeling, but because it is *fitting* and politic so to do; and fitting it certainly is, inasmuch as a contrary opinion would disturb the general feeling situation. A feeling-judgment such as this is in no way a simulation or a lie—it is merely an act of accommodation. A picture, for instance, may be termed beautiful, because a picture that is hung in a drawing-room and bearing a well-known signature is generally assumed to be beautiful, or because the predicate 'ugly' might offend the family of the fortunate possessor, or because there is a benevolent intention on the part of the visitor to create a pleasant feeling-atmosphere, to which end everything must be felt as agreeable. Such feelings are governed by the standard of the objective determinants. As such they are genuine, and represent the total visible feeling-function.

In precisely the same way as extraverted thinking strives to rid itself of subjective influences, extraverted feeling has also to undergo a certain process of differentiation, before it is finally denuded of every subjective trimming. The *valuations* resulting from the act of feeling either correspond directly with objective values or at least chime in with certain traditional and generally known standards of value. This kind of feeling is very largely responsible for the fact that so many people flock to the theatre, to concerts, or to Church, and what is more, with correctly adjusted positive feelings. Fashions, too, owe their existence to it, and, what is far more valuable, the whole positive and wide-spread support of social, philanthropic, and such like cultural enterprises. In such matters, extraverted feeling proves itself a creative factor. Without this feeling, for instance, a beautiful and harmonious sociability would be unthinkable. So far extraverted feeling is just as beneficent and rationally effective as extraverted thinking. But this salutary effect is lost as soon as the object gains an exaggerated influence. For, when this happens, extraverted feeling draws the personality too much into the object, *i.e.* the object assimilates the person, whereupon the personal character of the feeling, which constitutes its principal charm, is lost. Feeling then becomes cold, material, untrustworthy. It betrays a secret aim, or at least arouses the suspicion of it in an impartial observer. No longer does it make that welcome and refreshing impression the invariable accompaniment of genuine feeling; instead, one scents a pose or affectation, although the egocentric motive may be entirely unconscious.

Such overstressed, extraverted feeling certainly fulfils æsthetic expectations, but no longer does it speak to the heart; it merely appeals to the senses, or—worse still—to the reason. Doubtless it can provide æsthetic padding for a situation, but there it stops, and beyond that its effect is nil. It has become sterile. Should this process go further, a strangely contradictory dissociation of feeling develops; every object is seized upon with feeling-valuations, and numerous relationships are made which are inherently and mutually incompatible. Since such aberrations would be quite impossible if a sufficiently emphasized subject were present, the last vestige of a real personal standpoint also becomes suppressed. The subject becomes so swallowed up in individual feeling processes that to the observer it seems as though there were no longer a subject of feeling but merely a feeling process. In such a condition feeling has entirely forfeited its original human warmth, it gives an impression of pose, inconstancy, unreliability, and in the worst cases appears definitely hysterical.

4. The Extraverted Feeling-Type

In so far as feeling is, incontestably, a more obvious peculiarity of feminine psychology than thinking, the most pronounced feeling-types are also to be found among women. When extraverted feeling possesses the priority we speak of an extraverted feeling-type. Examples of this type that I can call to mind are, almost without exception, women. She is a woman who follows the guiding-line of her feeling. As the result of education her feeling has become developed into an adjusted function, subject to conscious control. Except in extreme cases, feeling has a personal character, in spite of the fact that the subjective factor may be already, to a large extent, repressed. The personality appears to be adjusted in relation to objective conditions. Her feelings correspond with objective situations and general values. Nowhere is this more clearly revealed than in the so-called 'love-choice'; the 'suitable' man is loved, not another one; he is suitable not so much because he fully accords with the fundamental character of the woman— as a rule she is quite uninformed about this—but because he meticulously corresponds in standing, age, capacity, height, and family respectability with every reasonable requirement. Such a formulation might, of course, be easily rejected as ironical or depreciatory, were I not fully convinced that the love-feeling of this type of woman completely corresponds with her choice. It is genuine, and not merely intelligently manufactured. Such 'reasonable' marriages exist without number, and they are by no means the worst. Such women are good comrades to their husbands and excellent mothers, so long as husbands or children possess the conventional psychic constitution. One can feel 'correctly', however, only when feeling is disturbed by nothing else. But nothing disturbs feeling so much as thinking. It is at once intelligible, therefore, that this type should repress thinking as much as possible. This does not mean to say that such a woman does not think at all; on the contrary, she may even think a great deal and very ably, but her thinking is never sui generis; it is, in fact, an Epimethean appendage to her feeling. What she cannot feel, she cannot consciously think. 'But I can't think what I don't feel', such a type said to me once in indignant tones. As far as feeling permits, she can think very well, but every conclusion, however logical, that might lead to a disturbance of feeling is rejected from the outset. It is simply not thought. And thus everything that corresponds with objective valuations is good: these things are loved or treasured; the rest seems merely to exist in a world apart.

But a change comes over the picture when the importance of the object reaches a still higher level. As already explained above, such an assimilation of subject to object then occurs as almost completely to engulf the subject of feeling. Feeling loses its personal character— it becomes feeling per se; it almost seems as though the personality were wholly dissolved in the feeling of the moment. Now, since in actual life situations constantly and successively alternate, in which the feeling-tones released are not only different but are actually mutually contrasting, the personality inevitably becomes dissipated in just so many different feelings. Apparently, he is this one moment, and something completely different the next—apparently, I repeat, for in reality such a manifold personality is altogether impossible. The basis of the ego always remains identical with itself, and, therefore, appears definitely opposed to the changing states of feeling. Accordingly the observer senses the display of feeling not so much as a personal expression of the feeling-subject as an alteration of his ego, a mood, in other words. Corresponding with the degree of dissociation between the ego and the momentary state of feeling, signs of disunion with the self will become more or less evident, *i.e.* the original compensatory attitude of the unconscious becomes a manifest opposition. This reveals itself, in the first instance, in extravagant demonstrations of feeling, in loud and obtrusive feeling predicates, which leave one, however, somewhat incredulous. They ring hollow; they are not convincing. On the contrary, they at once give one an inkling of a resistance that is being overcompensated, and one begins to wonder whether such a feeling-judgment might not just as well be entirely different. In fact, in a very short time it actually *is* different. Only a very slight alteration in the situation is needed to provoke forthwith an entirely contrary estimation of the selfsame object. The result of such an experience is that the observer is unable to take either judgment at all seriously. He begins to reserve his own opinion. But since, with this type, it is a matter of the greatest moment to establish an intensive feeling rapport with his environment, redoubled efforts are now required to overcome this reserve. Thus, in the manner of the circulus vitiosus, the situation goes from bad to worse. The more the feeling relation with the object becomes overstressed, the nearer the unconscious opposition approaches the surface.

We have already seen that the extraverted feeling type, as a rule, represses his thinking, just because thinking is the function most liable to disturb feeling. Similarly, when thinking seeks to arrive at pure results of any kind, its first act is to exclude feeling, since nothing is calculated to harass and falsify thinking so much as feeling-values. Thinking, therefore, in so far as it is an independent function, is repressed in the extraverted feeling type. Its repression, as I observed before, is complete only in so far as its inexorable logic forces it to conclusions that are incompatible with feeling. It is suffered to exist as the servant of feeling, or more accurately its slave. Its backbone is broken; it may not operate on its own account, in accordance with its own laws. Now, since a logic exists producing inexorably right conclusions, this must happen somewhere, although beyond the bounds of consciousness, *i.e.* in the unconscious. Pre-eminently, therefore, the unconscious content of this type is a particular kind of thinking. It is an infantile, archaic, and negative thinking.

So long as conscious feeling preserves the personal character, or, in other words, so long as the personality does not become swallowed up by successive states of feeling, this unconscious thinking remains compensatory. But as soon as the personality is dissociated, becoming dispersed in mutually contradictory states of feeling, the identity of the ego is lost, and the subject becomes unconscious. But, because of the subject's lapse into the unconscious, it becomes associated with the unconscious thinking - function, therewith assisting the unconscious thought to occasional consciousness. The stronger the conscious feeling relation, and therefore, the more 'depersonalized,' it becomes, the stronger grows the unconscious opposition. This reveals itself in the fact that unconscious ideas centre round just the most valued objects, which are thus pitilessly stripped of their value. That thinking which always thinks in the 'nothing but' style is in its right place here, since it destroys the ascendancy of the feeling that is chained to the object.

Unconscious thought reaches the surface in the form of irruptions, often of an obsessing nature, the general character of which is always negative and depreciatory. Women of this type have moments when the most hideous thoughts fasten upon the very objects most valued by their feelings. This negative thinking avails itself of every infantile prejudice or parallel that is calculated to breed doubt in the feeling-value, and it tows every primitive instinct along with it, in the effort to make 'a nothing but' interpretation of the feeling. At this point, it is perhaps in the nature of a side-remark to observe that the collective unconscious, *i.e.* the totality of the primordial images, also becomes enlisted in the same manner, and from the elaboration and development of these images there dawns the possibility of a regeneration of the attitude upon another basis.

Hysteria, with the characteristic infantile sexuality of its unconscious world of ideas, is the principal form of neurosis with this type.

5. Recapitulation of Extraverted Rational Types

I term the two preceding types rational or judging types because they are characterized by the supremacy of the reasoning and the judging functions. It is a general distinguishing mark of both types that their life is, to a

GENERAL DESCRIPTION OF TYPES 453

large extent, subordinated to reasoning judgment. But we must not overlook the point, whether by 'reasoning' we are referring to the standpoint of the individual's subjective psychology, or to the standpoint of the observer, who perceives and judges from without. For such an observer could easily arrive at an opposite judgment, especially if he has a merely intuitive apprehension of the behaviour of the observed, and judges accordingly. In its totality, the life of this type is never dependent upon reasoning judgment alone; it is influenced in almost equal degree by unconscious irrationality. If observation is restricted to behaviour, without any concern for the domestic interior of the individual's consciousness, one may get an even stronger impression of the irrational and accidental character of certain unconscious manifestations in the individual's behaviour than of the reasonableness of his conscious purposes and motivations. I, therefore, base my judgment upon what the individual feels to be his conscious psychology. But I am prepared to grant that we may equally well entertain a precisely opposite conception of such a psychology, and present it accordingly. I am also convinced that, had I myself chanced to possess a different individual psychology, I should have described the rational types in the reversed way, from the standpoint of the unconscious—as irrational, therefore. This circumstance aggravates the difficulty of a lucid presentation of psychological matters to a degree not to be underestimated, and immeasurably increases the possibility of misunderstandings. The discussions which develop from these misunderstandings are, as a rule, quite hopeless, since the real issue is never joined, each side speaking, as it were, in a different tongue. Such experience is merely one reason the more for basing my presentation upon the subjective conscious psychology of the individual, since there, at least, one has a definite objective footing, which completely drops away the moment we try to ground psychological principles upon the unconscious. For the observed, in this case, could undertake no kind of co-operation, because there is nothing of which he is not more informed than his own unconscious. The judgment would entirely devolve upon the observer—a certain guarantee that its basis would be his own individual psychology, which would infallibly be imposed upon the observed. To my mind, this is the case in the psychologies both of Freud and of Adler. The individual is completely at the mercy of the arbitrary discretion of his observing critic—which can never be the case when the conscious psychology of the observed is accepted as the basis. After all, he is the only competent judge, since he alone knows his own motives.

The reasonableness that characterizes the conscious management of life in both these types, involves a conscious exclusion of the accidental and non-rational. Reasoning judgment, in such a psychology, represents a power that coerces the untidy and accidental things of life into definite forms; such at least is its aim. Thus, on the one hand, a definite choice is made among the possibilities of life, since only the rational choice is consciously accepted; but, on the other hand, the independence and influence of those psychic functions which perceive life's happenings are essentially restricted. This limitation of sensation and intuition is, of course, not absolute. These functions exist, for they are universal; but their products are subject to the choice of the reasoning judgment. It is not the absolute strength of sensation, for instance, which turns the scales in the motivation of action, but judgment. Thus, in a certain sense, the perceiving-functions share the same fate as feeling in the case of the first type, or thinking in that of the second. They are relatively repressed, and therefore in an inferior state of differentiation. This circumstance gives a particular stamp to the unconscious of both our types; what such men do consciously and intentionally accords with reason (*their* reason of course), but what happens to them corresponds either with infantile, primitive sensations, or with similarly archaic intuitions. I will try to make clear what I mean by these latter concepts in the sections that follow. At all events, that which happens to this type is irrational (from their own standpoint of course). Now, since there are vast numbers of men whose lives consist in what happens to them more than in actions resulting from reasoned intention, it might conceivably happen, that such a man, after careful analysis, would describe both our types as irrational. We must grant him, however, that only too often a man's unconscious makes a far stronger impression upon one than his conscious, and that his actions often have considerably more weight and meaning than his reasoned motivations.

The rationality of both types is orientated objectively, and depends upon objective data. Their reasonableness corresponds with what passes as reasonable from the collective standpoint. Subjectively they consider nothing rational save what is generally considered as such. But reason is also very largely subjective and individual. In our case this share is repressed—increasingly so, in fact, the more the significance of the object is exalted. Both the subject and subjective reason, therefore, are always threatened with repression; and, when it descends, they fall under the tyranny of the unconscious, which in this case possesses most unpleasant qualities. We have already spoken of its thinking. But, in addition, there are primitive sensations, which reveal themselves in compulsive forms, as, for instance, an abnormal compulsive pleasure-seeking in every conceivable direction; there are also primitive intuitions, which can become a positive torture to the individuals concerned, not to mention their entourage. Everything disagreeable and painful, everything disgusting, ugly, and evil is scented out or suspected, and these as a rule only correspond with half-truths, than which nothing is more calculated to create misunderstandings of the most poisonous kind. The powerful influence of the opposing unconscious contents necessarily brings about a frequent interruption of the rational conscious government, namely, a striking subservience to the element of chance, so that, either by virtue of their sensational value or unconscious significance, accidental happenings acquire a compelling influence.

6. Sensation

Sensation, in the extraverted attitude, is most definitely conditioned by the object. As sense-perception, sensation is naturally dependent upon the object. But, just as naturally, it is also dependent upon the subject; hence, there is also a subjective sensation, which after its kind is entirely different from the objective. In the extraverted attitude this subjective share of sensation, in so far as its conscious application is concerned, is either inhibited or repressed. As an irrational function, sensation is equally repressed, whenever a rational function, *e.g.* thinking or feeling, possesses the priority, *i.e.* it can be said to have a conscious function, only in so far as the rational attitude of consciousness permits accidental perceptions to become conscious contents; in short, realizes them. The function of sense is, of course, absolute in the stricter sense; for example, everything is seen or heard to the farthest physiological possibility, but not everything attains that threshold value which a perception must possess in order to be also apperceived. It is a different matter when sensation itself possesses priority, instead of merely seconding another function. In this case, no element of objective sensation is excluded and nothing repressed (with the exception of the subjective share already mentioned). Sensation has a preferential objective determination, and those objects which release the strongest sensation are decisive for the individual's psychology. The result of this is a pronounced *sensuous hold* to the object. Sensation, therefore, is a vital function, equipped with the potentest vital instinct. In so far as objects release sensations, they matter; and, in so far as it lies within the power of sensation, they are also fully accepted into consciousness, whether compatible with reasoned judgment or not. As a function its sole criterion of value is the strength of the sensation as conditioned by its objective qualities. Accordingly, all objective processes, in so far as they release sensations at all, make their appearance in consciousness. It is, however, only concrete, sensuously perceived objects or processes which excite sensations in the extraverted attitude; exclusively those, in fact, which everyone in all times and places would sense as concrete. Hence, the orientation of such an individual corresponds with purely concrete reality. The judging, rational functions are subordinated to the concrete facts of sensation, and, accordingly, possess the qualities of inferior differentiation, *i.e.* they are marked by a certain negativity, with infantile and archaic tendencies. The function most affected by the repression, is, naturally, the one standing opposite to sensation, viz. intuition, the function of unconscious perception.

7. The Extraverted Sensation Type

No other human type can equal the extraverted sensation-type in realism. His sense for objective facts is extraordinarily developed. His life is an accumulation of actual experience with concrete objects, and the more pronounced he is, the less use does he make of his experience. In certain cases the events of his life hardly deserve the name 'experience'. He knows no better use for this sensed 'experience' than to make it serve as a guide to fresh sensations; anything in the least 'new' that comes within his circle of interest is forthwith turned to a sensational account and is made to serve this end. In so far as one is disposed to regard a highly developed sense for sheer actuality as very reasonable, will such men be esteemed rational. In reality, however, this is by no means the case, since they are equally subject to the sensation of irrational, chance happenings, as they are to rational behaviour.

Such a type—the majority are men apparently—does not, of course, believe himself to be 'subject' to sensation. He would be much more inclined to ridicule this view as altogether inconclusive, since, from his standpoint, sensation is the concrete manifestation of life—it is simply the fulness of actual living. His aim is concrete enjoyment, and his morality is similarly orientated. For true enjoyment has its own special morality, its own moderation and lawfulness, its own unselfishness and devotedness. It by no means follows that he is just sensual or gross, for he may differentiate his sensation to the finest pitch of æsthetic purity without being the least unfaithful, even in his most abstract sensations, to his principle of objective sensation. Wulfen's *Cicerone des rücksichtlosen Lebensgenusses* is the unvarnished confession of a type of this sort. From this point of view the book seems to me worth reading.

Upon the lower levels this is the man of tangible reality, with little tendency either for reflection or commanding purpose. To sense the object, to have and if possible to enjoy sensations, is his constant motive. He is by no means unlovable; on the contrary, he frequently has a charming and lively capacity for enjoyment; he is sometimes a jolly fellow, and often a refined æsthete.

In the former case, the great problems of life hinge upon a good or indifferent dinner; in the latter, they are questions of good taste. When he 'senses', everything essential has been said and done. Nothing can be more than concrete and actual; conjectures that transcend or go beyond the concrete are only permitted on condition that they enhance sensation. This need not be in any way a pleasurable reinforcement, since this type is not a common voluptuary; he merely desires the strongest sensation, and this, by his very nature, he can receive only from without. What comes from within seems to him morbid and objectionable. In so far as he thinks and feels, he always reduces down to objective foundations, *i.e.* to influences coming from the object, quite unperturbed by the most violent departures from logic. Tangible reality, under any conditions, makes him breathe again. In this respect he is unexpectedly credulous. He will, without hesitation, relate an obvious psychogenic symptom to the falling barometer, while the existence of a psychic conflict seems to him a fantastic abnormality. His love is incontestably rooted in the manifest attractions of the object. In so far as he is normal, he is conspicuously adjusted to positive reality—conspicuously, because his adjustment is always visible. His ideal is the actual; in this respect he is considerate. He has no ideals related to ideas—he has, therefore, no sort of ground for maintaining a hostile attitude towards the reality of things and facts. This expresses itself in all the externals of his life. He dresses well, according to his circumstances; he keeps a good table for his friends, who are either made comfortable or at least given to understand that his fastidious taste is obliged to impose certain claims upon his entourage. He even convinces one that certain sacrifices are decidedly worth while for the sake of style.

But the more sensation predominates, so that the

sensing subject disappears behind the sensation, the more unsatisfactory does this type become. Either he develops into a crude pleasure-seeker or he becomes an unscrupulous, designing sybarite. Although the object is entirely indispensable to him, yet, as something existing in and through itself, it is none the less depreciated. It is ruthlessly violated and essentially ignored, since now its sole use is to stimulate sensation. The hold upon the object is pushed to the utmost limit. The unconscious is, accordingly, forced out of its métier as a compensatory function and driven into open opposition. But, above all, the repressed intuitions begin to assert themselves in the form of projections upon the object. The strangest conjectures arise; in the case of a sexual object, jealous phantasies and anxiety-states play a great rôle. More acute cases develop every sort of phobia, and especially compulsive symptoms. The pathological contents have a remarkable air of unreality, with a frequent moral or religious colouring. A pettifogging captiousness often develops, or an absurdly scrupulous morality coupled with a primitive, superstitious and 'magical' religiosity, harking back to abstruse rites. All these things have their source in the repressed inferior functions, which, in such cases, stand in harsh opposition to the conscious standpoint; they wear, in fact, an aspect that is all the more striking because they appear to rest upon the most absurd suppositions, in complete contrast to the conscious sense of reality. The whole culture of thought and feeling seems, in this second personality, to be twisted into a morbid primitiveness; reason is hair-splitting sophistry—morality is dreary moralizing and palpable Pharisaism—religion is absurd superstition—intuition, the noblest of human gifts, is a mere personal subtlety, a sniffing into every corner: instead of searching the horizon, it recedes to the narrowest gauge of human meanness.

GENERAL DESCRIPTION OF TYPES 461

The specially compulsive character of the neurotic symptoms represent the unconscious counterweight to the laisser aller morality of a purely sensational attitude, which, from the standpoint of rational judgment, accepts without discrimination, everything that happens. Although this lack of basic principles in the sensation-type does not argue an absolute lawlessness and lack of restraint, it at least deprives him of the quite essential restraining power of judgment. Rational judgment represents a conscious coercion, which the rational type appears to impose upon himself of his own free will. This compulsion overtakes the sensation-type from the unconscious. Moreover, the rational type's link to the object, from the very existence of a judgment, never means such an unconditioned relation as that which the sensation-type has with the object. When his attitude reaches an abnormal one-sidedness, he is in danger of falling just as deeply into the arms of the unconscious as he consciously clings to the object. When he becomes neurotic, he is much harder to treat in the rational way, because the functions to which the physician must appeal are in a relatively undifferentiated state; hence little or no trust can be placed in them. Special means of bringing emotional pressure to bear are often needed to make him at all conscious.

8. Intuition

Intuition as the function of unconscious perception is wholly directed upon outer objects in the extraverted attitude. Because, in the main, intuition is an unconscious process, the conscious apprehension of its nature is a very difficult matter. In consciousness, the intuitive function is represented by a certain attitude of expectation, a perceptive and penetrating vision, wherein only the subsequent result can prove, in every case, how much was 'perceived-into', and how much actually lay in the object.

Just as sensation, when given the priority, is not a mere reactive process of no further importance for the object, but is almost an action which seizes and shapes the object, so it is with intuition, which is by no means a mere perception, or awareness, but an active, creative process that builds into the object just as much as it takes out. But, because this process extracts the perception unconsciously, it also produces an unconscious effect in the object. The primary function of intuition is to transmit mere images, or perceptions of relations and conditions, which could be gained by the other functions, either not at all, or only by very roundabout ways. Such images have the value of definite discernments, and have a decisive bearing upon action, whenever intuition is given the chief weight; in which case, psychic adaptation is based almost exclusively upon intuition. Thinking, feeling, and sensation are relatively repressed; of these, sensation is the one principally affected, because, as the conscious function of sense, it offers the greatest obstacle to intuition. Sensation disturbs intuition's clear, unbiassed, naïve awareness with its importunate sensuous stimuli; for these direct the glance upon the physical superficies, hence upon the very things round and beyond which intuition tries to peer. But since intuition, in the extraverted attitude, has a prevailingly objective orientation, it actually comes very near to sensation; indeed, the expectant attitude towards outer objects may, with almost equal probability, avail itself of sensation. Hence, for intuition really to become paramount, sensation must to a large extent be suppressed. I am now speaking of sensation as the simple and direct sense-reaction, an almost definite physiological and psychic datum. This must be expressly established beforehand, because, if I ask the intuitive how he is orientated, he will speak of things which are quite indistinguishable from sense-perceptions. Frequently he will even make use of the term 'sensation'. He actually has sensations, but he is not guided by them per se, merely using them as directing-points for his distant vision. They are selected by unconscious expectation. Not the strongest sensation, in the physiological sense, obtains the crucial value, but any sensation whatsoever whose value happens to become considerably enhanced by reason of the intuitive's unconscious attitude. In this way it may eventually attain the leading position, appearing to the intuitive's consciousness indistinguishable from a pure sensation. But actually it is not so.

Just as extraverted sensation strives to reach the highest pitch of actuality, because only thus can the appearance of a complete life be created, so intuition tries to encompass the greatest *possibilities*, since only through the awareness of possibilities is *intuition* fully satisfied. Intuition seeks to discover possibilities in the objective situation; hence as a mere tributary function (viz. when not in the position of priority) it is also the instrument which, in the presence of a hopelessly blocked situation, works automatically towards the issue, which no other function could discover. Where intuition has the priority, every ordinary situation in life seems like a closed room, which intuition has to open. It is constantly seeking outlets and fresh possibilities in external life. In a very short time every actual situation becomes a prison to the intuitive; it burdens him like a chain, prompting a compelling need for solution. At times objects would seem to have an almost exaggerated value, should they chance to represent the idea of a severance or release that might lead to the discovery of a new possibility. Yet no sooner have they performed their office, serving intuition as a ladder or a bridge, than they appear to have no further value, and are discarded as mere burdensome appendages. A fact is acknowledged only in so far as it opens up fresh possibilities of advancing beyond it and of releasing the individual from its operation. Emerging possibilities are compelling motives from which intuition cannot escape and to which all else must be sacrificed.

9. The Extraverted Intuitive Type

Whenever intuition predominates, a particular and unmistakable psychology presents itself. Because intuition is orientated by the object, a decided dependence upon external situations is discernible, but it has an altogether different character from the dependence of the sensational type. The intuitive is never to be found among the generally recognized reality values, but he is always present where possibilities exist. He has a keen nose for things in the bud pregnant with future promise. He can never exist in stable, long-established conditions of generally acknowledged though limited value: because his eye is constantly ranging for new possibilities, stable conditions have an air of impending suffocation. He seizes hold of new objects and new ways with eager intensity, sometimes with extraordinary enthusiasm, only to abandon them cold-bloodedly, without regard and apparently without remembrance, as soon as their range becomes clearly defined and a promise of any considerable future development no longer clings to them. As long as a possibility exists, the intuitive is bound to it with thongs of fate. It is as though his whole life went out into the new situation. One gets the impression, which he himself shares, that he has just reached the definitive turning point in his life, and that from now on nothing else can seriously engage his thought and feeling. However reasonable and opportune it may be, and although every conceivable argument speaks in favour of stability, a day will come when nothing will deter him from regarding as a prison, the self-same situation that seemed to promise him freedom and deliverance, and from acting accordingly. Neither reason nor feeling can restrain or discourage him from a new possibility, even though it may run counter to convictions hitherto unquestioned. Thinking and feeling, the indispensable components of conviction, are, with him, inferior functions, possessing no decisive weight; hence they lack the power to offer any lasting resistance to the force of intuition. And yet these are the only functions that are capable of creating any effectual compensation to the supremacy of intuition, since they can provide the intuitive with that *judgment* in which his type is altogether lacking. The morality of the intuitive is governed neither by intellect nor by feeling; he has his own characteristic morality, which consists in a loyalty to his intuitive view of things and a voluntary submission to its authority. Consideration for the welfare of his neighbours is weak. No solid argument hinges upon their well-being any more than upon his own. Neither can we detect in him any great respect for his neighbour's convictions and customs; in fact, he is not infrequently put down as an immoral and ruthless adventurer. Since his intuition is largely concerned with outer objects, scenting out external possibilities, he readily applies himself to callings wherein he may expand his abilities in many directions. Merchants, contractors, speculators, agents, politicians, etc., commonly belong to this type.

Apparently this type is more prone to favour women than men; in which case, however, the intuitive activity reveals itself not so much in the professional as in the social sphere. Such women understand the art of utilizing every social opportunity; they establish right social connections; they seek out lovers with possibilities only to abandon everything again for the sake of a new possibility.

It is at once clear, both from the standpoint of political economy and on grounds of general culture, that such a type is uncommonly important. If well-intentioned, with an orientation to life not purely egoistical, he may render exceptional service as the promoter, if not the initiator of every kind of promising enterprise. He is the natural advocate of every minority that holds the seed of future promise. Because of his capacity, when orientated more towards men than things, to make an intuitive diagnosis of their abilities and range of usefulness, he can also 'make' men. His capacity to inspire his fellow-men with courage, or to kindle enthusiasm for something new, is unrivalled, although he may have forsworn it by the morrow. The more powerful and vivid his intuition, the more is his subject fused and blended with the divined possibility. He animates it; he presents it in plastic shape and with convincing fire; he almost embodies it. It is not a mere histrionic display, but a fate.

This attitude has immense dangers—all too easily the intuitive may squander his life. He spends himself animating men and things, spreading around him an abundance of life—a life, however, which others live, not he. Were he able to rest with the actual thing, he would gather the fruit of his labours; yet all too soon must he be running after some fresh possibility, quitting his newly planted field, while others reap the harvest. In the end he goes empty away. But when the intuitive lets things reach such a pitch, he also has the unconscious against him. The unconscious of the intuitive has a certain similarity with that of the sensation-type. Thinking and feeling, being relatively repressed, produce infantile and archaic thoughts and feelings in the unconscious, which may be compared with those of the countertype. They likewise come to the surface in the form of intensive projections, and are just as absurd as those of the sensation-type, only to my mind they lack the other's mystical character; they are chiefly concerned with quasi-actual things, in the nature of sexual, financial, and other hazards, as, for instance, suspicions of approaching illness. This difference appears to be due to a repression of the sensations of actual things. These latter usually command attention in the shape of a sudden entanglement with a most unsuitable woman, or, in the case of a woman, with a thoroughly unsuitable man; and this is simply the result of their unwitting contact with the sphere of archaic sensations. But its consequence is an unconsciously compelling tie to an object of incontestable futility. Such an event is already a compulsive symptom, which is also thoroughly characteristic of this type. In common with the sensation-type, he claims a similar freedom and exemption from all restraint, since he suffers no submission of his decisions to rational judgment, relying entirely upon the perception of chance possibilities. He rids himself of the restrictions of reason, only to fall a victim to unconscious neurotic compulsions in the form of oversubtle, negative reasoning, hair-splitting dialectics, and a compulsive tie to the sensation of the object. His conscious attitude, both to the sensation and the sensed object, is one of sovereign superiority and disregard. Not that he means to be inconsiderate or superior —he simply does not see the object that everyone else sees; his oblivion is similar to that of the sensation-type—only, with the latter, the soul of the object is missed. For this oblivion the object sooner or later takes revenge in the form of hypochondriacal, compulsive ideas, phobias, and every imaginable kind of absurd bodily sensation.

10. Recapitulation of Extraverted Irrational Types

I call the two preceding types *irrational* for reasons already referred to; namely, because their commissions and omissions are based not upon reasoned judgment but upon the absolute intensity of perception. Their perception is concerned with simple happenings, where no selection has been exercised by the judgment. In this respect both the latter types have a considerable superiority over the two judging types. The objective occurrence is both law-determined and accidental. In so far as it is law-determined, it is accessible to reason; in so far as it is accidental, it is not. One might reverse it and say that we apply the term law-determined to the occurrence appearing so to our reason, and where its regularity escapes us we call it accidental. The postulate of a universal lawfulness remains a postulate of reason only; in no sense is it a postulate of our functions of perception. Since these are in no way grounded upon the principle of reason and its postulates, they are, of their very nature, irrational. Hence my term 'irrational' corresponds with the nature of the perception-types. But merely because they subordinate judgment to perception, it would be quite incorrect to regard these types as unreasonable. They are merely in a high degree *empirical;* they are grounded exclusively upon experience, so exclusively, in fact, that as a rule, their judgment cannot keep pace with their experience. But the functions of judgment are none the less present, although they eke out a largely unconscious existence. But, since the unconscious, in spite of its separation from the conscious subject, is always reappearing on the scene, the actual life of the irrational types exhibits striking judgments and acts of choice, which take the form of apparent sophistries, cold-hearted criticisms, and an apparently purposeful selection of persons and situations. These traits have a rather infantile, or even primitive, stamp; at times they are astonishingly naïve, but at times also inconsiderate, crude, or outrageous. To the rationally orientated mind, the real character of such people might well appear rationalistic and purposeful in the bad sense. But this judgment would be valid only for their unconscious, and, therefore, quite incorrect for their conscious psychology, which is entirely orientated by perception, and because of its irrational nature is quite unintelligible to the rational judgment. Finally, it may even appear to a rationally orientated mind that such an assemblage of accidentals, hardly deserves the name 'psychology.' The irrational type balances this contemptuous judgment with an equally poor impression of the rational; for he sees him as something only half alive, whose only aim in life consists in fastening the fetters of reason upon everything living, and wringing his own neck with criticisms. Naturally, these are gross extremes; but they occur.

From the standpoint of the rational type, the irrational might easily be represented as a rational of inferior quality; namely, when he is apprehended in the light of what happens to him. For what happens to him is not the accidental—in that he is master—but, in its stead, he is overtaken by rational judgment and rational aims. This fact is hardly comprehensible to the rational mind, but its unthinkableness merely equals the astonishment of the irrational, when he discovers someone who can set the ideas of reason above the living and actual event. Such a thing seems scarcely credible to him. It is, as a rule, quite hopeless to look to him for any recognition of principles in this direction, since a rational understanding is just as unknown and, in fact, tiresome to him as the idea of making a contract, without mutual discussion and obligations, appears unthinkable to the rational type.

This point brings me to the problem of the psychic relation between the representatives of the different types. Following the terminology of the French school of hypnotists, the psychic relation among the more modern psychiatrists is termed 'rapport'. Rapport chiefly consists in a *feeling of actual accord*, in spite of recognised differences. In fact, the recognition of existing differences, in so far as they are common to both, is already a rapport, a feeling of accord. If we make this feeling conscious to a rather high degree in an actual case, we discover that it has not merely the quality of a feeling that cannot be analysed further, but it also has the nature of an insight or cognitional content, representing the point of agreement in a conceptual form. This rational presentation is exclusively valid for the rational types; it by no means applies to the irrational, whose rapport is based not at all upon judgment but upon the parallelism of actual living events. His feeling of accord is the common perception of a sensation or intuition. The rational would say that rapport with the irrational depends purely upon chance. If, by some accident, the objective situations are exactly in tune, something like a human relationship takes place, but nobody can tell what will be either its validity or its duration. To the rational type it is often a very bitter thought that the relationship will last only just so long as external circumstances accidentally produce a mutual interest. This does not occur to him as being especially human, whereas it is precisely in this situation that the irrational sees a humanity of quite singular beauty. Accordingly each regards the other as a man destitute of relationships, upon whom no reliance can be placed, and with whom one can never get on decent terms. Such a result, however, is reached only when one consciously tries to make some estimate of the nature of one's relationships with one's fellow-men. Although a psychological conscientiousness of this kind is by no means usual, yet it frequently happens that, notwithstanding an absolute difference of standpoint, a kind of rapport does take place, and in the following way. The one assumes with unspoken projection that the other is, in all essential points, of the same opinion as himself, while the other divines or senses an objective community of interest, of which, however, the former has no conscious inkling and whose existence he would at once dispute, just as it would never occur to the latter that his relationship must rest upon a common point-of-view. A rapport of this kind is by far the most frequent; it rests upon projection, which is the source of many subsequent misunderstandings.

Psychic relationship, in the extraverted attitude, is always regulated by objective factors and outer determinants. What a man is within has never any decisive significance. For our present-day culture the extraverted attitude is the governing principle in the problem of human relationship; naturally, the introverted principle occurs, but it is still the exception, and has to appeal to the tolerance of the age.

C. THE INTROVERTED TYPE

(I) THE GENERAL ATTITUDE OF CONSCIOUSNESS

As I have already explained in section A (I) of the present chapter, the introverted is distinguished from the extraverted type by the fact that, unlike the latter, who is prevailingly orientated by the object and objective data, he is governed by subjective factors. In the section alluded to I mentioned, inter alia, that the introvert interposes a subjective view between the perception of the object and his own action, which prevents the action from assuming a character that corresponds with the objective situation. Naturally, this is a special case, mentioned by way of example, and merely intended to serve as a simple illustration. But now we must go in quest of more general formulations.

Introverted consciousness doubtless views the external conditions, but it selects the subjective determinants as the decisive ones. The type is guided, therefore, by that factor of perception and cognition which represents the receiving subjective disposition to the sense stimulus. Two persons, for example, see the same object, but they never see it in such a way as to receive two identically similar images of it. Quite apart from the differences in the personal equation and mere organic acuteness, there often exists a radical difference, both in kind and degree, in the psychic assimilation of the perceived image. Whereas the extraverted type refers pre-eminently to that which reaches him from the object, the introvert principally relies upon that which the outer impression constellates in the subject. In an individual case of apperception, the difference may, of course, be very delicate, but in the total psychological economy it is extremely noticeable, especially in the form of a *reservation of the ego*. Although it is anticipating somewhat, I consider that point of view which inclines, with Weininger, to describe this attitude as philautic, or with other writers, as autoerotic, egocentric, subjective, or egoistic, to be both misleading in principle and definitely depreciatory. It corresponds with the normal bias of the extraverted attitude against the nature of the introvert. We must not forget—although extraverted opinion is only too prone to do so—that all perception and cognition is not purely objective: it is also subjectively conditioned. The world exists not merely in itself, but also as it appears to me. Indeed, at bottom, we have absolutely no criterion that could help us to form a judgment of a world whose nature was unassimilable by the subject. If we were to ignore the subjective factor, it would mean a complete denial of the great doubt as to the possibility of absolute cognition. And this would mean a rechute into that stale and hollow positivism which disfigured the beginning of our epoch—an attitude of intellectual arrogance that is invariably accompanied by a crudeness of feeling, and an essential violation of life, as stupid as it is presumptuous. Through an overvaluation of the objective powers of cognition, we repress the importance of the subjective factor, which simply means the denial of the subject. But what is the subject? The subject is man—we are the subject. Only a sick mind could forget that cognition must have a subject, for there exists no knowledge and, therefore, for us, no world where 'I know' has not been said, although with this statement one has already expressed the subjective limitation of all knowledge.

The same holds good for all the psychic functions: they have a subject which is just as indispensable as the object. It is characteristic of our present extraverted valuation that the word 'subjective' occasionally rings almost like a reproach or blemish; but in every case the epithet 'merely subjective' means a dangerous weapon of offence, destined for that daring head, that is not unceasingly convinced of the unconditioned superiority of the object. We must, therefore, be quite clear as to what meaning the term 'subjective' carries in this investigation. As the subjective factor, then, I understand that psychological action or reaction which, when merged with the effect of the object, makes a new psychic fact. Now, in so far as the subjective factor, since oldest times and among all peoples, remains in a very large measure identical with itself—since elementary perceptions and cognitions are almost universally the same—it is a reality that is just as firmly established as the outer object. If this were not so, any sort of permanent and essentially changeless reality would be altogether inconceivable, and any understanding with posterity would be a matter of impossibility. Thus far, therefore, the subjective factor is something that is just as much a fact as the extent of the sea and the radius of the earth. Thus far, also, the subjective factor claims the whole value of a world-determining power which can never, under any circumstances, be excluded from our calculations. It is the other world-law, and the man who is based upon it has a foundation just as secure, permanent, and valid, as the man who relies upon the object. But, just as the object and objective data remain by no means always the same, inasmuch as they are both perishable and subject to chance, the subjective factor is similarly liable to variability and individual hazard. Hence its value is also merely relative. The excessive development of the introverted standpoint in consciousness, for instance, does not lead to a better or sounder application of the subjective factor, but to an artificial subjectification of consciousness, which can hardly escape the reproach 'merely subjective'. For, as a countertendency to this morbid subjectification, there ensues a desubjectification of consciousness in the form of an exaggerated extraverted attitude which richly deserves Weininger's description "misautic". Inasmuch as the introverted attitude is based upon a universally present, extremely real, and absolutely indispensable condition of psychological adaptation, such expressions as 'philautic', 'egocentric', and the like are both objectionable and out of place, since they foster the prejudice that it is invariably a question of the beloved ego. Nothing could be more absurd than such an assumption. Yet one is continually meeting it when examining the judgments of the extravert upon the introvert. Not, of course, that I wish to ascribe such an error to individual extraverts; it is rather the present generally accepted extraverted view which is by no means restricted to the extraverted type; for it finds just as many representatives in the ranks of the other type, albeit very much against its own interest. The reproach of being untrue to his own kind is justly levelled at the latter, whereas, this, at least, can never be charged against the former.

The introverted attitude is normally governed by the psychological structure, theoretically determined by heredity, but which to the subject is an ever present subjective factor. This must not be assumed, however, to be simply identical with the subject's ego, an assumption that is certainly implied in the above mentioned designations of Weininger; it is rather the psychological structure of the subject that precedes any development of the ego. The really fundamental subject, the Self, is far more comprehensive than the ego, because the former also embraces the unconscious, while the latter is essentially the focal point of consciousness. Were the ego identical with the Self, it would be unthinkable that we should be able to appear in dreams in entirely different forms and with entirely different meanings. But it is a characteristic peculiarity of the introvert, which, moreover, is as much in keeping with his own inclination as with the general bias, that he tends to confuse his ego with the Self, and to exalt his ego to the position of subject of the psychological process, thus effecting that morbid subjectification of consciousness, mentioned above, which so alienates him from the object.

The psychological structure is the same. Semon has termed it 'mneme'[1], whereas I call it the '*collective unconscious*'. The individual Self is a portion, or excerpt, or representative, of something universally present in all living creatures, and, therefore, a correspondingly graduated kind of psychological process, which is born anew in every creature. Since earliest times, the inborn manner of *acting*

[1] Semon, *Mneme*, translated by Louis Simon (London: Allen & Unwin).

has been called *instinct*, and for this manner of psychic apprehension of the object I have proposed the term *archetype*. I may assume that what is understood by instinct is familiar to everyone. It is another matter with the archetype. This term embraces the same idea as is contained in 'primordial image' (an expression borrowed from Jakob Burckhardt), and as such I have described it in Chapter xi of this book. I must here refer the reader to that chapter, in particular to the definition of 'image'.

The archetype is a symbolical formula, which always begins to function whenever there are no conscious ideas present, or when such as are present are impossible upon intrinsic or extrinsic grounds. The contents of the collective unconscious are represented in consciousness in the form of pronounced tendencies, or definite ways of looking at things. They are generally regarded by the individual as being determined by the object—incorrectly, at bottom—since they have their source in the unconscious structure of the psyche, and are only released by the operation of the object. These subjective tendencies and ideas are stronger than the objective influence; because their psychic value is higher, they are superimposed upon all impressions. Thus, just as it seems incomprehensible to the introvert that the object should always be decisive, it remains just as enigmatic to the extravert how a subjective standpoint can be superior to the objective situation. He reaches the unavoidable conclusion that the introvert is either a conceited egoist or a fantastic doctrinaire. Recently he seems to have reached the conclusion that the introvert is constantly influenced by an unconscious power-complex. The introvert unquestionably exposes himself to this prejudice; for it cannot be denied that his definite and highly generalized mode of expression, which apparently excludes every other view from the outset, lends a certain countenance to this extraverted opinion. Furthermore, the very decisiveness and inflexibility of the subjective judgment, which is superordinated to all objective data, is alone sufficient to create the impression of a strong ego-centricity. The introvert usually lacks the right argument in presence of this prejudice; for he is just as unaware of the unconscious, though thoroughly sound presuppositions of his subjective judgment, as he is of his subjective perceptions. In harmony with the style of the times, he looks without, instead of behind his own consciousness for the answer. Should he become neurotic, it is the sign of a more or less complete unconscious identity of the ego with the Self, whereupon the importance of the Self is reduced to nil, while the ego becomes inflated beyond reason. The undeniable, world-determining power of the subjective factor then becomes concentrated in the ego, developing an immoderate power claim and a downright foolish egocentricity. Every psychology which reduces the nature of man to unconscious power instinct springs from this foundation. For example, Nietzsche's many faults in taste owe their existence to this subjectification of consciousness.

(II) THE UNCONSCIOUS ATTITUDE

The superior position of the subjective factor in consciousness involves an inferiority of the objective factor. The object is not given that importance which should really belong to it. Just as it plays too great a rôle in the extraverted attitude, it has too little to say in the introverted. To the extent that the introvert's consciousness is subjectified, thus bestowing undue importance upon the ego, the object is placed in a position which in time becomes quite untenable. The object is a factor of undeniable power, while the ego is something very restricted and transitory. It would be a very different matter if the Self opposed the object. Self and world are commensurable factors; hence a normal introverted attitude is just as valid, and has as good a right to existence, as a normal extraverted attitude. But, if the ego has usurped the claims of the subject, a compensation naturally develops under the guise of an unconscious reinforcement of the influence of the object. Such a change eventually commands attention, for often, in spite of a positively convulsive attempt to ensure the superiority of the ego, the object and objective data develop an overwhelming influence, which is all the more invincible because it seizes upon the individual unawares, thus effecting an irresistible invasion of consciousness. As a result of the ego's defective relation to the object — for a will to command is not adaptation—a compensatory relation to the object develops in the unconscious, which makes itself felt in consciousness as an unconditional and irrepressible tie to the object. The more the ego seeks to secure every possible liberty, independence, superiority, and freedom from obligations, the deeper does it fall into the slavery of objective facts. The subject's freedom of mind is chained to an ignominious financial dependence, his unconcernedness of action suffers now and again, a distressing collapse in the face of public opinion, his moral superiority gets swamped in inferior relationships, and his desire to dominate ends in a pitiful craving to be loved. The chief concern of the unconscious in such a case is the relation to the object, and it affects this in a way that is calculated to bring both the power illusion and the superiority phantasy to utter ruin. The object assumes terrifying dimensions, in spite of conscious depreciation. Detachment from, and command of, the object are, in consequence, pursued by the ego still more violently. Finally, the ego surrounds itself by a regular system of safeguards (Adler has ably depicted these) which shall at least preserve the illusion of superiority. But, therewith, the introvert severs himself completely from the object, and either squanders his energy in defensive measures or makes fruitless attempts to impose his power upon the object and successfully assert himself. But these efforts are constantly being frustrated by the overwhelming impressions he receives from the object. It continually imposes itself upon him against his will; it provokes in him the most disagreeable and obstinate affects, persecuting him at every step. An immense, inner struggle is constantly required of him, in order to 'keep going.' Hence *psychoasthenia* is his typical form of neurosis, a malady which is characterized on the one hand by an extreme sensitiveness, and on the other by a great liability to exhaustion and chronic fatigue.

An analysis of the personal unconscious yields an abundance of power phantasies coupled with fear of the dangerously animated objects, to which, as a matter of fact, the introvert easily falls a victim. For a peculiar cowardliness develops from this fear of the object; he shrinks from making either himself or his opinion effective, always dreading an intensified influence on the part of the object. He is terrified of impressive affects in others, and is hardly ever free from the dread of falling under hostile influence. For objects possess terrifying and powerful qualities for him—qualities which he cannot consciously discern in them, but which, through his unconscious perception, he cannot choose but believe in. Since his conscious relation to the object is relatively repressed, its exit is by way of the unconscious, where it becomes loaded with the qualities of the unconscious. These qualities are primarily infantile and archaic. His relation to the object, therefore, becomes correspondingly primitive, taking on all those peculiarities which characterize the primitive object-relationship. Now it seems as though objects possessed magical powers. Strange, new objects excite fear and distrust, as though concealing unknown dangers; objects long rooted and blessed by tradition are attached to his soul as by invisible threads; every change has a disturbing, if not actually dangerous aspect, since its apparent implication is a magical animation of the object. A lonely island where only what is permitted to move moves, becomes an ideal. *Auch Einer*, the novel by F. Th. Vischer, gives a rich insight into this side of the introvert's psychology, and at the same time shows the underlying symbolism of the collective unconscious, which in this description of types I am leaving on one side, since it is a universal phenomenon with no especial connection with types.

(III) PECULIARITIES OF THE BASIC PSYCHOLOGICAL FUNCTIONS IN THE INTROVERTED ATTITUDE

1. Thinking

When describing extraverted thinking, I gave a brief characterization of introverted thinking, to which at this stage I must make further reference. Introverted thinking is primarily orientated by the subjective factor. At the least, this subjective factor is represented by a subjective feeling of direction, which, in the last resort, determines judgment. Occasionally, it is a more or less finished image, which to some extent, serves as a standard. This thinking may be conceived either with concrete or with abstract factors, but always at the decisive points it is orientated by subjective data. Hence, it does not lead from concrete experience back again into objective things, but always to the subjective content. External facts are not the aim and origin of this thinking, although the introvert would often like to make it so appear. It begins in the subject, and returns to the subject, although it may undertake the widest flights into the territory of the real and the actual. Hence, in the statement of new facts, its chief value is indirect, because new views rather than the perception of new facts are its main concern. It formulates questions and creates theories; it opens up prospects and yields insight, but in the presence of facts it exhibits a reserved demeanour. As illustrative examples they have their value, but they must not prevail. Facts are collected as evidence or examples for a theory, but never for their own sake. Should this latter ever occur, it is done only as a compliment to the extraverted style. For this kind of thinking facts are of secondary importance; what, apparently, is of absolutely paramount importance is the development and presentation of the subjective idea, that primordial symbolical image standing more or less darkly before the inner vision. Its aim, therefore, is never concerned with an intellectual reconstruction of concrete actuality, but with the shaping of that dim image into a resplendent idea. Its desire is to reach reality; its goal is to see how external facts fit into, and fulfil, the framework of the idea; its actual creative power is proved by the fact that this thinking can also create that idea which, though not present in the external facts, is yet the most suitable, abstract expression of them. Its task is accomplished when the idea it has fashioned seems to emerge so inevitably from the external facts that they actually prove its validity.

But just as little as it is given to extraverted thinking to wrest a really sound inductive idea from concrete facts or ever to create new ones, does it lie in the power of introverted thinking to translate its original image into an idea adequately adapted to the facts. For, as in the former case the purely empirical heaping together of facts paralyses thought and smothers their meaning, so in the latter case introverted thinking shows a dangerous tendency to coerce facts into the shape of its image, or by ignoring them altogether, to unfold its phantasy image in freedom. In such a case, it will be impossible for the presented idea to deny its origin from the dim archaic image. There will cling to it a certain mythological character that we are prone to interpret as 'originality', or in more pronounced cases as mere whimsicality; since its archaic character is not transparent as such to specialists unfamiliar with mythological motives. The subjective force of conviction inherent in such an idea is usually very great; its power too is the more convincing, the less it is influenced by contact with outer facts. Although to the man who advocates the idea, it may well seem that his scanty store of facts were the actual ground and source of the truth and validity of his idea, yet such is not the case, for the idea derives its convincing power from its unconscious archetype, which, as such, has universal validity and everlasting truth. Its truth, however, is so universal and symbolic, that it must first enter into the recognized and recognizable knowledge of the time, before it can become a practical truth of any real value to life. What sort of a causality would it be, for instance, that never became perceptible in practical causes and practical results?

This thinking easily loses itself in the immense truth of the subjective factor. It creates theories for the sake of theories, apparently with a view to real or at least possible facts, yet always with a distinct tendency to go over from the world of ideas into mere imagery. Accordingly many intuitions of possibilities appear on the scene, none of which however achieve any reality, until finally images are produced which no longer express anything externally real, being 'merely' symbols of the simply unknowable. It is now merely a mystical thinking and quite as unfruitful as that empirical thinking whose sole operation is within the framework of objective facts.

Whereas the latter sinks to the level of a mere presentation of facts, the former evaporates into a representation of the unknowable, which is even beyond everything that could be expressed in an image. The presentation of facts has a certain incontestable truth, because the subjective factor is excluded and the facts speak for themselves. Similarly, the representing of the unknowable has also an immediate, subjective, and convincing power, because it is demonstrable from its own existence. The former says 'Est, ergo est' ('It is; therefore it is'); while the latter says 'Cogito, ergo cogito' ('I think; therefore I think'). In the last analysis, introverted thinking arrives at the evidence of its own subjective being, while extraverted thinking is driven to the evidence of its complete identity with the objective fact. For, while the extravert really denies himself in his complete dispersion among objects, the introvert, by ridding himself of each and every content, has to content himself with his mere existence. In both cases the further development of life is crowded out of the domain of thought into the region of other psychic functions which had hitherto existed in relative unconsciousness. The extraordinary impoverishment of introverted thinking in relation to objective facts finds compensation in an abundance of unconscious facts. Whenever consciousness, wedded to the function of thought, confines itself within the smallest and emptiest circle possible—though seeming to contain the plenitude of divinity—unconscious phantasy becomes proportionately enriched by a multitude of archaically formed facts, a veritable pandemonium of magical and irrational factors, wearing the particular aspect that accords with the nature of that function which shall next relieve the thought-function as the representative of life. If this should be the intuitive function, the 'other side' will be viewed with the eyes of a Kubin or a Meyrink. If it is the feeling-function, there arise quite unheard of and fantastic feeling-relations, coupled with feeling-judgments of a quite contradictory and unintelligible character. If the sensation-function, then the senses discover some new and never-before experienced possibility, both within and without the body. A closer investigation of such changes can easily demonstrate the reappearance of primitive psychology with all its characteristic features. Naturally, the thing experienced is not merely primitive but also symbolic; in fact, the older and more primeval it appears, the more does it represent the future truth: since everything ancient in our unconscious means the coming possibility.

Under ordinary circumstances, not even the transition to the 'other side' succeeds — still less the redeeming journey through the unconscious. The passage across is chiefly prevented by conscious resistance to any subjection of the ego to the unconscious reality and to the determining reality of the unconscious object. The condition is a dissociation—in other words, a neurosis having the character of an inner wastage with increasing brain-exhaustion—a psychoasthenia, in fact.

2. The Introverted Thinking Type

Just as Darwin might possibly represent the normal extraverted thinking type, so we might point to Kant as a counter-example of the normal introverted thinking type. The former speaks with facts; the latter appeals to the subjective factor. Darwin ranges over the wide fields of objective facts, while Kant restricts himself to a critique of knowledge in general. But suppose a Cuvier be contrasted with a Nietzsche: the antithesis becomes even sharper.

The introverted thinking type is characterized by a priority of the thinking I have just described. Like his extraverted parallel, he is decisively influenced by ideas; these, however, have their origin, not in the objective data but in the subjective foundation. Like the extravert, he too will follow his ideas, but in the reverse direction: inwardly not outwardly. Intensity is his aim, not extensity. In these fundamental characters he differs markedly, indeed quite unmistakably from his extraverted parallel. Like every introverted type, he is almost completely lacking in that which distinguishes his counter type, namely, the intensive relatedness to the object. In the case of a human object, the man has a distinct feeling that he matters only in a negative way, *i.e.*, in milder instances he is merely conscious of being superfluous, but with a more extreme type he feels himself warded off as something definitely disturbing. This negative relation to the object—indifference, and even aversion—characterizes every introvert; it also makes a description of the introverted type in general extremely difficult. With him, everything tends to disappear and get concealed. His judgment appears cold, obstinate, arbitrary, and inconsiderate, simply because he is related less to the object than the subject. One can feel nothing in it that might possibly confer a higher value upon the object; it always seems to go beyond the object, leaving behind it a flavour of a certain subjective superiority. Courtesy, amiability, and friendliness may be present, but often with a particular quality suggesting a certain uneasiness, which betrays an ulterior aim, namely, the disarming of an opponent, who must at all costs be pacified and set at ease lest he prove a disturbing element. In no sense, of course, is he an opponent, but, if at all sensitive, he will feel somewhat repelled, perhaps even depreciated. Invariably the object has to submit to a certain neglect; in worse cases it is even surrounded with quite unnecessary measures of precaution. Thus it happens that this type tends to disappear behind a cloud of misunderstanding, which only thickens the more he attempts to assume, by way of compensation and with the help of his inferior functions, a certain mask of urbanity, which often presents a most vivid contrast to his real nature. Although in the extension of his world of ideas he shrinks from no risk, however daring, and never even considers the possibility that such a world might also be dangerous, revolutionary, heretical, and wounding to feeling, he is none the less a prey to the liveliest anxiety, should it ever chance to become objectively real. That goes against the grain. When the time comes for him to transplant his ideas into the world, his is by no means the air of an anxious mother solicitous for her children's welfare; he merely exposes them, and is often extremely annoyed when they fail to thrive on their own account. The decided lack he usually displays in practical ability, and his aversion from any sort of réclame assist in this attitude. If to his eyes his product appears subjectively correct and true, it must also be so in practice, and others have simply got to bow to its truth. Hardly ever will he go out of his way to win anyone's appreciation of it, especially if it be anyone of influence. And, when he brings himself to do so, he is usually so extremely maladroit that he merely achieves the opposite of his purpose. In his own special province, there are usually awkward experiences with his colleagues, since he never knows how to win their favour; as a rule he only succeeds in showing them how entirely superfluous they are to him. In the pursuit of his ideas he is generally stubborn, head-strong, and quite unamenable to influence. His suggestibility to personal influences is in strange contrast to this. An object has only to be recognized as apparently innocuous for such a type to become extremely accessible to really inferior elements. They lay hold of him from the unconscious. He lets himself be brutalized and exploited in the most ignominious way, if only he can be left undisturbed in the pursuit of his ideas. He simply does not see when he is being plundered behind his back and wronged in practical ways: this is because his relation to the object is such a secondary matter that he is left without a guide in the purely objective valuation of his product. In thinking out his problems to the utmost of his ability, he also complicates them, and constantly becomes entangled in every possible scruple. However clear to himself the inner structure of his thoughts may be, he is not in the least clear where and how they link up with the world of reality. Only with difficulty can he persuade himself to admit that what is clear to him may not be equally clear to everyone. His style is usually loaded and complicated by all sorts of accessories, qualifications, saving clauses, doubts, etc., which spring from his exacting scrupulousness. His work goes slowly and with difficulty. Either he is taciturn or he falls among people who cannot understand him; whereupon he proceeds to gather further proof of the unfathomable stupidity of man. If he should ever chance to be understood, he is credulously liable to overestimate. Ambitious women have only to understand how advantage may be taken of his uncritical attitude towards the object to make an easy prey of him; or he may develop into a misanthropic bachelor with a childlike heart. Then, too, his outward appearance is often gauche, as if he were painfully anxious to escape observation; or he may show a remarkable unconcern, an almost childlike naïveté. In his own particular field of work he provokes violent contradiction, with which he has no notion how to deal, unless by chance he is seduced by his primitive affects into biting and fruitless polemics. By his wider circle he is counted inconsiderate and domineering. But the better one knows him, the more favourable one's judgment becomes, and his nearest friends are well aware how to value his intimacy. To people who judge him from afar he appears prickly, inaccessible, haughty; frequently he may even seem soured as a result of his anti-social prejudices. He has little influence as a personal teacher, since the mentality of his pupils is strange to him. Besides, teaching has, at bottom, little interest for him, except when it accidentally provides him with a theoretical problem. He is a poor teacher, because while teaching his thought is engaged with the actual material, and will not be satisfied with its mere presentation.

With the intensification of his type, his convictions become all the more rigid and unbending. Foreign influences are eliminated; he becomes more unsympathetic to his peripheral world, and therefore more dependent upon his intimates. His expression becomes more personal and inconsiderate and his ideas more profound, but they can no longer be adequately expressed in the material at hand. This lack is replaced by emotivity and susceptibility. The foreign influence, brusquely declined from without, reaches him from within, from the side of the unconscious, and he is obliged to collect evidence against it and against things in general which to outsiders seems quite superfluous. Through the subjectification of consciousness occasioned by his defective relationship to the object, what secretly concerns his own *person* now seems to him of chief importance. And he begins to confound his subjective truth with his own person. Not that he will attempt to press anyone personally with his convictions, but he will break out with venomous and personal retorts against every criticism, however just. Thus in every respect his isolation gradually increases. His originally fertilizing ideas become destructive, because poisoned by a kind of sediment of bitterness. His struggle against the influences emanating from the unconscious increases with his external isolation, until gradually this begins to cripple him. A still greater isolation must surely protect him from the unconscious influences, but as a rule this only takes him deeper into the conflict which is destroying him within.

The thinking of the introverted type is positive and synthetic in the development of those ideas which in ever increasing measure approach the eternal validity of the primordial images. But, when their connection with objective experience begins to fade, they become mythological and untrue for the present situation. Hence this thinking holds value only for its contemporaries, just so long as it also stands in visible and understandable connection with the known facts of the time. But, when thinking becomes mythological, its irrelevancy grows until finally it gets lost in itself. The relatively unconscious functions of feeling, intuition, and sensation, which counterbalance introverted thinking, are inferior in quality and have a primitive, extraverted character, to which all the troublesome objective influences this type is subject to must be ascribed. The various measures of self-defence, the curious protective obstacles with which such people are wont to surround themselves, are sufficiently familiar, and I may, therefore, spare myself a description of them. They all serve as a defence against 'magical' influences; a vague dread of the other sex also belongs to this category.

3. Feeling

Introverted feeling is determined principally by the subjective factor. This means that the feeling-judgment differs quite as essentially from extraverted feeling as does the introversion of thinking from extraversion. It is unquestionably difficult to give an intellectual presentation of the introverted feeling process, or even an approximate description of it, although the peculiar character of this kind of feeling simply stands out as soon as one becomes aware of it at all. Since it is primarily controlled by subjective pre-conditions, and is only secondarily concerned with the object, this feeling appears much less upon the surface and is, as a rule, misunderstood. It is a feeling which apparently depreciates the object; hence it usually becomes noticeable in its negative manifestations. The existence of a positive feeling can be inferred only indirectly, as it were. Its aim is not so much to accommodate to the objective fact as to stand above it, since its whole unconscious effort is to give reality to the underlying images. It is, as it were, continually seeking an image which has no existence in reality, but of which it has had a sort of previous vision. From objects that can never fit in with its aim it seems to glide unheedingly away. It strives after an inner intensity, to which at the most, objects contribute only an accessory stimulus. The depths of this feeling can only be divined—they can never be clearly comprehended. It makes men silent and difficult of access; with the sensitiveness of the mimosa, it shrinks from the brutality of the object, in order to expand into the depths of the subject. It puts forward negative feeling-judgments or assumes an air of profound indifference, as a measure of self-defence.

Primordial images are, of course, just as much idea as feeling. Thus, basic ideas such as God, freedom, immortality are just as much feeling-values as they are significant as ideas. Everything, therefore, that has been said of the introverted thinking refers equally to introverted feeling, only here everything is felt while there it was thought. But the fact that thoughts can generally be expressed more intelligibly than feelings demands a more than ordinary descriptive or artistic capacity before the real wealth of this feeling can be even approximately presented or communicated to the outer world. Whereas subjective thinking, on account of its unrelatedness, finds great difficulty in arousing an adequate understanding, the same, though in perhaps even higher degree, holds good for subjective feeling. In order to communicate with others it has to find an external form which is not only fitted to absorb the subjective feeling in a satisfying expression, but which must also convey it to one's fellow-man in such a way that a parallel process takes place in him. Thanks to the relatively great internal (as well as external) similarity of the human being, this effect can actually be achieved, although a form acceptable to feeling is extremely difficult to find, so long as it is still mainly orientated by the fathomless store of primordial images. But, when it becomes falsified by an egocentric attitude, it at once grows unsympathetic, since then its major concern is still with the ego. Such a case never fails to create an impression of sentimental self-love, with its constant effort to arouse interest and even morbid self-admiration. Just as the subjectified consciousness of the introverted thinker, striving after an abstraction of abstractions, only attains a supreme intensity of a thought-process in itself quite empty, so the intensification of egocentric feeling only leads to a contentless passionateness, which merely feels itself. This is the mystical, ecstatic stage, which prepares the way over into the extraverted functions repressed by feeling. Just as introverted thinking is pitted against a primitive feeling, to which objects attach themselves with magical force, so introverted feeling is counterbalanced by a primitive thinking, whose concretism and slavery to facts passes all bounds. Continually emancipating itself from the relation to the object, this feeling creates a freedom, both of action and of conscience, that is only answerable to the subject, and that may even renounce all traditional values. But so much the more does unconscious thinking fall a victim to the power of objective facts.

4. The Introverted Feeling Type

It is principally among women that I have found the priority of introverted feeling. The proverb 'Still waters run deep' is very true of such women. They are mostly silent, inaccessible, and hard to understand; often they hide behind a childish or banal mask, and not infrequently their temperament is melancholic. They neither shine nor reveal themselves. Since they submit the control of their lives to their subjectively orientated feeling, their true motives generally remain concealed. Their outward demeanour is harmonious and inconspicuous; they reveal a delightful repose, a sympathetic parallelism, which has no desire to affect others, either to impress, influence, or change them in any way. Should this outer side be somewhat emphasized, a suspicion of neglectfulness and coldness may easily obtrude itself, which not seldom increases to a real indifference for the comfort and well-being of others. One distinctly feels the movement of feeling away from the object. With the normal type, however, such an event only occurs when the object has in some way too strong an effect. The harmonious feeling atmosphere rules only so long as the object moves upon its own way with a moderate feeling intensity, and makes no attempt to cross the other's path. There is little effort to accompany the real emotions of the object, which tend to be damped and rebuffed, or to put it more aptly, are 'cooled off' by a negative feeling-judgment. Although one may find a constant readiness for a peaceful and harmonious companionship, the unfamiliar object is shown no touch of amiability, no gleam of responding warmth, but is met by a manner of apparent indifference or repelling coldness

One may even be made to feel the superfluousness of one's own existence. In the presence of something that might carry one away or arouse enthusiasm, this type observes a benevolent neutrality, tempered with an occasional trace of superiority and criticism that soon takes the wind out of the sails of a sensitive object. But a stormy emotion will be brusquely rejected with murderous coldness, unless it happens to catch the subject from the side of the unconscious, *i.e.* unless, through the animation of some primordial image, feeling is, as it were, taken captive. In which event such a woman simply feels a momentary laming, invariably producing, in due course, a still more violent resistance, which reaches the object in his most vulnerable spot. The relation to the object is, as far as possible, kept in a secure and tranquil middle state of feeling, where passion and its intemperateness are resolutely proscribed. Expression of feeling, therefore, remains niggardly and, when once aware of it at all, the object has a permanent sense of his undervaluation. Such, however, is not always the case, since very often the deficit remains unconscious; whereupon the unconscious feeling-claims gradually produce symptoms which compel a more serious attention.

A superficial judgment might well be betrayed, by a rather cold and reserved demeanour, into denying all feeling to this type. Such a view, however, would be quite false; the truth is, her feelings are intensive rather than extensive. They develop into the depth. Whereas, for instance, an extensive feeling of sympathy can express itself in both word and deed at the right place, thus quickly ridding itself of its impression, an intensive sympathy, because shut off from every means of expression, gains a passionate depth that embraces the misery of a world and is simply benumbed. It may possibly make an extravagant irruption, leading to some staggering act of an almost heroic character, to which, however, neither the object nor the subject can find a right relation. To the outer world, or to the blind eyes of the extravert, this sympathy looks like coldness, for it does nothing visibly, and an extraverted consciousness is unable to believe in invisible forces.

Such misunderstanding is a characteristic occurrence in the life of this type, and is commonly registered as a most weighty argument against any deeper feeling relation with the object. But the underlying, real object of this feeling is only dimly divined by the normal type. It may possibly express its aim and content in a concealed religiosity anxiously shielded from profane eyes, or in intimate poetic forms equally safeguarded from surprise; not without a secret ambition to bring about some superiority over the object by such means. Women often express much of it in their children, letting their passionateness flow secretly into them.

Although in the normal type, the tendency, above alluded to, to overpower or coerce the object once openly and visibly with the thing secretly felt, rarely plays a disturbing rôle, and never leads to a serious attempt in this direction, some trace of it, none the less, leaks through into the personal effect upon the object, in the form of a domineering influence often difficult to define. It is sensed as a sort of stifling or oppressive feeling which holds the immediate circle under a spell. It gives a woman of this type a certain mysterious power that may prove terribly fascinating to the extraverted man, for it touches his unconscious. This power is derived from the deeply felt, unconscious images; consciousness, however, readily refers it to the ego, whereupon the influence becomes debased into personal tyranny. But, wherever the unconscious subject is identified with the ego, the mysterious power of the intensive feeling is also transformed into banal and arrogant ambition, vanity, and petty tyranny. This produces a type of woman most regrettably distinguished by her unscrupulous ambition and mischievous cruelty. But this change in the picture leads also to neurosis.

So long as the ego feels itself housed, as it were, beneath the heights of the unconscious subject, and feeling reveals something higher and mightier than the ego, the type is normal. The unconscious thinking is certainly archaic, yet its reductions may prove extremely helpful in compensating the occasional inclinations to exalt the ego into the subject. But, whenever this does take place by dint of complete suppression of the unconscious reductive thinking-products, the unconscious thinking goes over into opposition and becomes projected into objects. Whereupon the now egocentric subject comes to feel the power and importance of the depreciated object. Consciousness begins to feel 'what others think'. Naturally, others are thinking all sorts of baseness, scheming evil, and contriving all sorts of plots, secret intrigues, etc. To prevent this, the subject must also begin to carry out preventive intrigues, to suspect and sound others, to make subtle combinations. Assailed by rumours, he must make convulsive efforts to convert, if possible, a threatened inferiority into a superiority. Innumerable secret rivalries develop, and in these embittered struggles not only will no base or evil means be disdained, but even virtues will be misused and tampered with in order to play the trump card. Such a development must lead to exhaustion. The form of neurosis is neurasthenic rather than hysterical; in the case of women we often find severe collateral physical states, as for instance anæmia and its sequelæ.

5. Recapitulation of Introverted Rational Types

Both the foregoing types are rational, since they are founded upon reasoning, judging functions. Reasoning judgment is based not merely upon objective, but also upon subjective, data. But the predominance of one or other factor, conditioned by a psychic disposition often existing from early youth, deflects the reasoning function. For a judgment to be really reasonable it should have equal reference to both the objective and the subjective factors, and be able to do justice to both. This, however, would be an ideal case, and would presuppose a uniform development of both extraversion and introversion. But either movement excludes the other, and, so long as this dilemma persists, they cannot possibly exist side by side, but at the most successively. Under ordinary circumstances, therefore, an ideal reason is impossible. A rational type has always a typical reasonal variation. Thus, the introverted rational types unquestionably have a reasoning judgment, only it is a judgment whose leading note is subjective. The laws of logic are not necessarily deflected, since its onesidedness lies in the premise. The premise is the predominance of the subjective factor existing beneath every conclusion and colouring every judgment. Its superior value as compared with the objective factor is self-evident from the beginning. As already stated, it is not just a question of value bestowed, but of a natural disposition existing before all rational valuation. Hence, to the introvert rational judgment necessarily appears to have many nuances which differentiate it from that of the extravert. Thus, to the introvert, to mention the most general instance, that chain of reasoning which leads to the subjective factor appears rather more reasonable than that which leads to the object. This difference, which in the individual case is practically insignificant, indeed almost unnoticeable, effects unbridgeable oppositions in the gross; these are the more irritating, the less we are aware of the minimal standpoint displacement produced by the psychological premise in the individual case A capital error regularly creeps in here, for one labours to prove a fallacy in the conclusion, instead of realizing the difference of the psychological premise. Such a realization is a difficult matter for every rational type, since it undermines the apparent, absolute validity of his own principle, and delivers him over to its antithesis, which certainly amounts to a catastrophe.

Almost more even than the extraverted is the introverted type subject to misunderstanding: not so much because the extravert is a more merciless or critical adversary, than he himself can easily be, but because the style of the epoch in which he himself participates is against him. Not in relation to the extraverted type, but as against our general occidental world-philosophy, he finds himself in the minority, not of course numerically, but from the evidence of his own feeling. In so far as he is a convinced participator in the general style, he undermines his own foundations, since the present style, with its almost exclusive acknowledgment of the visible and the tangible, is opposed to his principle. Because of its invisibility, he is obliged to depreciate the subjective factor, and to force himself to join in the extraverted overvaluation of the object. He himself sets the subjective factor at too low a value, and his feelings of inferiority are his chastisement for this sin. Little wonder, therefore, that it is precisely our epoch, and particularly those movements which are somewhat ahead of the time, that reveal the subjective factor in every kind of exaggerated, crude and grotesque form of expression. I refer to the art of the present day.

The undervaluation of his own principle makes the introvert egotistical, and forces upon him the psychology of the oppressed. The more egotistical he becomes, the stronger his impression grows that these others, who are apparently able, without qualms, to conform with the present style, are the oppressors against whom he must guard and

R

protect himself. He does not usually perceive that he commits his capital mistake in not depending upon the subjective factor with that same loyalty and devotion with which the extravert follows the object. By the undervaluation of his own principle, his penchant towards egoism becomes unavoidable, which, of course, richly deserves the prejudice of the extravert. Were he only to remain true to his own principle, the judgment of 'egoist' would be radically false; for the justification of his attitude would be established by its general efficacy, and all misunderstandings dissipated.

6. Sensation

Sensation, which in obedience to its whole nature is concerned with the object and the objective stimulus, also undergoes a considerable modification in the introverted attitude. It, too, has a subjective factor, for beside the object sensed there stands a sensing subject, who contributes his subjective disposition to the objective stimulus. In the introverted attitude sensation is definitely based upon the subjective portion of perception. What is meant by this finds its best illustration in the reproduction of objects in art. When, for instance, several painters undertake to paint one and the same landscape, with a sincere attempt to reproduce it faithfully, each painting will none the less differ from the rest, not merely by virtue of a more or less developed ability, but chiefly because of a different vision; there will even appear in some of the paintings a decided psychic variation, both in general mood and in treatment of colour and form. Such qualities betray a more or less influential co-operation of the subjective factor. The subjective factor of sensation is essentially the same as in the other functions already spoken of. It is an unconscious disposition, which alters the sense-perception at its very source, thus depriving it of the character of a purely objective influence. In this case, sensation is related primarily to the subject, and only secondarily to the object. How extraordinarily strong the subjective factor can be is shown most clearly in art. The ascendancy of the subjective factor occasionally achieves a complete suppression of the mere influence of the object; but none the less sensation remains sensation, although it has come to be a perception of the subjective factor, and the effect of the object has sunk to the level of a mere stimulant. Introverted sensation develops in accordance with this subjective direction. A true sense-perception certainly exists, but it always looks as though objects were not so much forcing their way into the subject in their own right as that the subject were seeing things quite differently, or saw quite other things than the rest of mankind. As a matter of fact, the subject perceives the same things as everybody else, only he never stops at the purely objective effect, but concerns himself with the subjective perception released by the objective stimulus. Subjective perception differs remarkably from the objective. It is either not found at all in the object, or, at most, merely suggested by it; it can, however, be similar to the sensation of other men, although not immediately derived from the objective behaviour of things. It does not impress one as a mere product of consciousness—it is too genuine for that. But it makes a definite psychic impression, since elements of a higher psychic order are perceptible to it. This order, however, does not coincide with the contents of consciousness. It is concerned with presuppositions, or dispositions of the collective unconscious, with mythological images, with primal possibilities of ideas. The character of significance and meaning clings to subjective perception. It says more than the mere image of the object, though naturally only to him for whom the subjective factor has some meaning. To another, a reproduced subjective impression seems to suffer from the defect of possessing insufficient similarity with the object; it seems, therefore, to have failed in its purpose. Subjective sensation apprehends the background of the physical world rather than its surface. The decisive thing is not the reality of the object, but the reality of the subjective factor, *i.e.* the primordial images, which in their totality represent a psychic mirror-world. It is a mirror, however, with the peculiar capacity of representing the present contents of consciousness not in their known and customary form but in a certain sense sub specie aeternitatis, somewhat as a million-year old consciousness might see them. Such a consciousness would see the becoming and the passing of things beside their present and momentary existence, and not only that, but at the same time it would also see that Other, which was before their becoming and will be after their passing hence. To this consciousness the present moment is improbable. This is, of course, only a simile, of which, however, I had need to give some sort of illustration of the peculiar nature of introverted sensation. Introverted sensation conveys an image whose effect is not so much to reproduce the object as to throw over it a wrapping whose lustre is derived from age-old subjective experience and the still unborn future event. Thus, mere sense impression develops into the depth of the meaningful, while extraverted sensation seizes only the momentary and manifest existence of things.

7. The Introverted Sensation Type

The priority of introverted sensation produces a definite type, which is characterized by certain peculiarities. It is an irrational type, inasmuch as its selection among occurrences is not primarily rational, but is guided rather by what just happens. Whereas, the extraverted sensation-type is determined by the intensity of the objective influence, the introverted type is orientated by the intensity of the subjective sensation-constituent released by the objective stimulus. Obviously, therefore, no sort of proportional relation exists between object and sensation, but something that is apparently quite irregular and arbitrary. Judging from without, therefore, it is practically impossible to foretell what will make an impression and what will not. If there were present a capacity and readiness for expression in any way commensurate with the strength of sensation, the irrationality of this type would be extremely evident. This is the case, for instance, when the individual is a creative artist. But, since this is the exception, it usually happens that the characteristic introverted difficulty of expression also conceals his irrationality. On the contrary, he may actually stand out by the very calmness and passivity of his demeanour, or by his rational self-control. This peculiarity, which often leads the superficial judgment astray, is really due to his unrelatedness to objects. Normally the object is not consciously depreciated in the least, but its stimulus is removed from it, because it is immediately replaced by a subjective reaction, which is no longer related to the reality of the object. This, of course, has the same effect as a depreciation of the object. Such a type can easily make one question why one should exist at all; or why objects in general should have any right to existence, since everything essential happens without the object. This doubt may be justified in extreme cases, though not in the normal, since the objective stimulus is indispensable to his sensation, only it produces something different from what was to be surmised from the external state of affairs. Considered from without, it looks as though the effect of the object did not obtrude itself upon the subject. This impression is so far correct inasmuch as a subjective content does, in fact, intervene from the unconscious, thus snatching away the effect of the object. This intervention may be so abrupt that the individual appears to shield himself directly from any possible influence of the object. In any aggravated or well-marked case, such a protective guard is also actually present. Even with only a slight reinforcement of the unconscious, the subjective constituent of sensation becomes so alive that it almost completely obscures the objective influence. The results of this are, on the one hand, a feeling of complete depreciation on the part of the object, and, on the other, an illusory conception of reality on the part of the subject, which in morbid cases may even reach the point of a complete inability to discriminate between the real object and the subjective perception. Although so vital a distinction vanishes completely only in a practically psychotic state, yet long before that point is reached subjective perception may influence thought, feeling, and action to an extreme degree, in spite of the fact that the object is clearly seen in its fullest reality. Whenever the objective influence does succeed in forcing its way into the subject—as the result of particular circumstances of special intensity, or because of a more perfect analogy with the unconscious image—even the normal example of this type is induced to *act* in accordance with his unconscious model. Such action has an illusory quality in relation to objective reality, and therefore has a very odd and strange character. It instantly reveals the anti-real subjectivity of the type. But, where the influence of the object does not entirely succeed, it encounters a benevolent neutrality, disclosing little sympathy, yet constantly striving to reassure and adjust. The too-low is raised a little, the too-high is made a little lower; the enthusiastic is damped, the extravagant restrained; and the unusual brought within the 'correct' formula: all this in order to keep the influence of the object within the necessary bounds. Thus, this type becomes an affliction to his circle, just in so far as his entire harmlessness is no longer above suspicion. But, if the latter should be the case, the individual readily becomes a victim to the aggressiveness and ambitions of others. Such men allow themselves to be abused, for which they usually take vengeance at the most unsuitable occasions with redoubled stubbornness and resistance. When there exists no capacity for artistic expression, all impressions sink into the inner depths, whence they hold consciousness under a spell, removing any possibility it might have had of mastering the fascinating impression by means of conscious expression. Relatively speaking, this type has only archaic possibilities of expression for the disposal of his impressions; thought and feeling are relatively unconscious, and, in so far as they have a certain consciousness, they only serve in the necessary, banal, every-day expressions. Hence as conscious functions, they are wholly unfitted to give any adequate rendering of the subjective perceptions. This type, therefore, is uncommonly inaccessible to an objective understanding; and he fares no better in the understanding of himself.

Above all, his development estranges him from the reality of the object, handing him over to his subjective perceptions, which orientate his consciousness in accordance with an archaic reality, although his deficiency in comparative judgment keeps him wholly unaware of this fact. Actually he moves in a mythological world, where men animals, railways, houses, rivers, and mountains appear partly as benevolent deities and partly as malevolent demons. That thus they appear to him never enters his mind, although their effect upon his judgments and acts can bear no other interpretation. He judges and acts as though he had such powers to deal with; but this begins to strike him only when he discovers that his sensations are totally different from reality. If his tendency is to reason objectively, he will sense this difference as morbid; but if, on the other hand, he remains faithful to his irrationality, and is prepared to grant his sensation reality value, the objective world will appear a mere make-belief and a comedy. Only in extreme cases, however, is this dilemma reached. As a rule, the individual acquiesces in his isolation and in the banality of the reality, which, however, he unconsciously treats archaically.

His unconscious is distinguished chiefly by the repression of intuition, which thereby acquires an extraverted and archaic character. Whereas true extraverted intuition has a characteristic resourcefulness, and a 'good nose' for every possibility in objective reality, this archaic, extraverted intuition has an amazing flair for every ambiguous, gloomy, dirty, and dangerous possibility in the background of reality. In the presence of this intuition the real and conscious intention of the object has no significance; it will peer behind every possible archaic antecedent of such an intention. It possesses, therefore, something dangerous, something actually undermining, which often stands in most vivid contrast to the gentle benevolence of consciousness. So long as the individual is not too aloof from the object, the unconscious intuition effects a wholesome compensation to the rather fantastic and over credulous attitude of consciousness. But as soon as the unconscious becomes antagonistic to consciousness, such intuitions come to the surface and expand their nefarious influence: they force themselves compellingly upon the individual, releasing compulsive ideas about objects of the most perverse kind. The neurosis arising from this sequence of events is usually a compulsion neurosis, in which the hysterical characters recede and are obscured by symptoms of exhaustion.

8. Intuition

Intuition, in the introverted attitude, is directed upon the inner object, a term we might justly apply to the elements of the unconscious. For the relation of inner objects to consciousness is entirely analogous to that of outer objects, although theirs is a psychological and not a physical reality. Inner objects appear to the intuitive perception as subjective images of things, which, though not met with in external experience, really determine the contents of the unconscious, *i.e.* the collective unconscious in the last resort. Naturally, in their per se character, these contents are not accessible to experience, a quality which they have in common with the outer object. For just as outer objects correspond only relatively with our perceptions of them, so the phenomenal forms of the inner object are also relative; products of their (to us) inaccessible essence and of the peculiar nature of the intuitive function. Like sensation, intuition also has its subjective factor, which is suppressed to the farthest limit in the extraverted intuition, but which becomes the decisive factor in the intuition of the introvert. Although this intuition may receive its impetus from outer objects, it is never arrested by the external possibilities, but stays with that factor which the outer object releases within.

Whereas introverted sensation is mainly confined to the perception of particular innervation phenomena by way of the unconscious, and does not go beyond them, intuition represses this side of the subjective factor and perceives the image which has really occasioned the innervation. Supposing, for instance, a man is overtaken by a psychogenic attack of giddiness. Sensation is arrested by the peculiar character of this innervation-disturbance, perceiving all its qualities, its intensity, its transient course, the nature of its origin and disappearance

R*

in their every detail, without raising the smallest inquiry concerning the nature of the thing which produced the disturbance, or advancing anything as to its content. Intuition, on the other hand, receives from the sensation only the impetus to immediate activity; it peers behind the scenes, quickly perceiving the inner image that gave rise to the specific phenomenon, *i.e.* the attack of vertigo, in the present case. It sees the image of a tottering man pierced through the heart by an arrow. This image fascinates the intuitive activity; it is arrested by it, and seeks to explore every detail of it. It holds fast to the vision, observing with the liveliest interest how the picture changes, unfolds further, and finally fades. In this way introverted intuition perceives all the background processes of consciousness with almost the same distinctness as extraverted sensation senses outer objects. For intuition, therefore, the unconscious images attain to the dignity of things or objects. But, because intuition excludes the co-operation of sensation, it obtains either no knowledge at all or at the best a very inadequate awareness of the innervation-disturbances or of the physical effects produced by the unconscious images. Accordingly, the images appear as though detached from the subject, as though existing in themselves without relation to the person. Consequently, in the above-mentioned example, the introverted intuitive, when affected by the giddiness, would not imagine that the perceived image might also in some way refer to himself. Naturally, to one who is rationally orientated, such a thing seems almost unthinkable, but it is none the less a fact, and I have often experienced it in my dealings with this type.

The remarkable indifference of the extraverted intuitive in respect to outer objects is shared by the introverted intuitive in relation to the inner objects. Just as the extraverted intuitive is continually scenting out new possibilities, which he pursues with an equal unconcern both for his own welfare and for that of others, pressing on quite heedless of human considerations, tearing down what has only just been established in his everlasting search for change, so the introverted intuitive moves from image to image, chasing after every possibility in the teeming womb of the unconscious, without establishing any connection between the phenomenon and himself. Just as the world can never become a moral problem for the man who merely senses it, so the world of images is never a moral problem to the intuitive. To the one just as much as to the other, it is an *æsthetic problem*, a question of perception, a 'sensation'. In this way, the consciousness of his own bodily existence fades from the introverted intuitive's view, as does its effect upon others. The extraverted standpoint would say of him: 'Reality has no existence for him; he gives himself up to fruitless phantasies'. A perception of the unconscious images, produced in such inexhaustible abundance by the creative energy of life, is of course fruitless from the standpoint of immediate utility. But, since these images represent possible ways of viewing life, which in given circumstances have the power to provide a new energic potential, this function, which to the outer world is the strangest of all, is as indispensable to the total psychic economy as is the corresponding human type to' the psychic life of a people. Had this type not existed, there would have been no prophets in Israel.

Introverted intuition apprehends the images which arise from the a priori, *i.e.* the inherited foundations of the unconscious mind. These archetypes, whose innermost nature is inaccessible to experience, represent the precipitate of psychic functioning of the whole ancestral line, *i.e.* the heaped-up, or pooled, experiences of organic existence in general, a million times repeated, and condensed into types. Hence, in these archetypes all experiences are represented which since primeval time have happened on this planet. Their archetypal distinctness is the more marked, the more frequently and intensely they have been experienced. The archetype would be—to borrow from Kant—the noumenon of the image which intuition perceives and, in perceiving, creates.

Since the unconscious is not just something that lies there, like a psychic caput mortuum, but is something that coexists and experiences inner transformations which are inherently related to general events, introverted intuition, through its perception of inner processes, gives certain data which may possess supreme importance for the comprehension of general occurrences: it can even foresee new possibilities in more or less clear outline, as well as the event which later actually transpires. Its prophetic prevision is to be explained from its relation to the archetypes which represent the law-determined course of all experienceable things.

9. The Introverted Intuitive Type

The peculiar nature of introverted intuition, when given the priority, also produces a peculiar type of man, viz. the mystical dreamer and seer on the one hand, or the fantastical crank and artist on the other. The latter might be regarded as the normal case, since there is a general tendency of this type to confine himself to the perceptive character of intuition. As a rule, the intuitive stops at perception; perception is his principal problem, and—in the case of a productive artist—the shaping of perception. But the crank contents himself with the intuition by which he himself is shaped and determined. Intensification of intuition naturally often results in an extraordinary aloofness of the individual from tangible reality; he may even become a complete enigma to his own immediate circle.

If an artist, he reveals extraordinary, remote things in his art, which in iridescent profusion embrace both the significant and the banal, the lovely and the grotesque, the whimsical and the sublime. If not an artist, he is frequently an unappreciated genius, a great man 'gone wrong', a sort of wise simpleton, a figure for 'psychological' novels.

Although it is not altogether in the line of the introverted intuitive type to make of perception a moral problem, since a certain reinforcement of the rational functions is required for this, yet even a relatively slight differentiation of judgment would suffice to transfer intuitive perception from the purely æsthetic into the moral sphere. A variety of this type is thus produced which differs essentially from its æsthetic form, although none the less characteristic of the introverted intuitive. The moral problem comes into being when the intuitive tries to relate himself to his vision, when he is no longer satisfied with mere perception and its æsthetic shaping and estimation, but confronts the question: What does this mean for me and for the world? What emerges from this vision in the way of a duty or task, either for me or for the world? The pure intuitive who represses judgment or possesses it only under the spell of perception never meets this question fundamentally, since his only problem is the How of perception. He, therefore, finds the moral problem unintelligible, even absurd, and as far as possible forbids his thoughts to dwell upon the disconcerting vision. It is different with the morally orientated intuitive. He concerns himself with the meaning of his vision; he troubles less about its further æsthetic possibilities than about the possible moral effects which emerge from its intrinsic significance. His judgment allows him to discern, though often only darkly, that he, as a man and as a totality, is in some way inter-related with his vision, that it is something which cannot just be perceived but which also would fain become the life of the subject. Through this realization he feels bound to transform his vision into his own life. But, since he tends to rely exclusively upon his vision, his moral effort becomes one-sided; he makes himself and his life symbolic, adapted, it is true, to the inner and eternal meaning of events, but unadapted to the actual present-day reality. Therewith he also deprives himself of any influence upon it, because he remains unintelligible. His language is not that which is commonly spoken—it becomes too subjective. His argument lacks convincing reason. He can only confess or pronounce His is the 'voice of one crying in the wilderness'.

The introverted intuitive's chief repression falls upon the sensation of the object. His unconscious is characterized by this fact. For we find in his unconscious a compensatory extraverted sensation function of an archaic character. The unconscious personality may, therefore, best be described as an extraverted sensation-type of a rather low and primitive order. Impulsiveness and unrestraint are the characters of this sensation, combined with an extraordinary dependence upon the sense impression. This latter quality is a compensation to the thin upper air of the conscious attitude, giving it a certain weight, so that complete 'sublimation' is prevented. But if, through a forced exaggeration of the conscious attitude, a complete subordination to the inner perception should develop, the unconscious becomes an opposition, giving rise to compulsive sensations whose excessive dependence upon the object is in frank conflict with the conscious attitude. The form of neurosis is a compulsion-neurosis, exhibiting symptoms that are partly hypochondriacal manifestations, partly hypersensibility of the sense organs and partly compulsive ties to definite persons or other objects.

10. Recapitulation of Introverted Irrational Types

The two types just depicted are almost inaccessible to external judgment. Because they are introverted and have in consequence a somewhat meagre capacity or willingness for expression, they offer but a frail handle for a telling criticism. Since their main activity is directed within, nothing is outwardly visible but reserve, secretiveness, lack of sympathy, or uncertainty, and an apparently groundless perplexity. When anything does come to the surface, it usually consists in indirect manifestations of inferior and relatively unconscious functions. Manifestations of such a nature naturally excite a certain environmental prejudice against these types. Accordingly they are mostly underestimated, or at least misunderstood. To the same degree as they fail to understand themselves —because they very largely lack judgment—they are also powerless to understand why they are so constantly undervalued by public opinion. They cannot see that their outward-going expression is, as a matter of fact, also of an inferior character. Their vision is enchanted by the abundance of subjective events. What happens there is so captivating, and of such inexhaustible attraction, that they do not appreciate the fact that their habitual communications to their circle express very little of that real experience in which they themselves are, as it were, caught up. The fragmentary and, as a rule, quite episodic character of their communications make too great a demand upon the understanding and good will of their circle; furthermore, their mode of expression lacks that flowing warmth to the object which alone can have convincing force. On the contrary, these types show very often a brusque, repelling demeanour towards the outer world, although of this they are quite unaware, and have not the least intention of showing it. We shall form a fairer judgment of such men and grant them a greater indulgence, when we begin to realize how hard it is to translate into intelligible language what is perceived within. Yet this indulgence must not be so liberal as to exempt them altogether from the necessity of such expression. This could be only detrimental for such types. Fate itself prepares for them, perhaps even more than for other men, overwhelming external difficulties, which have a very sobering effect upon the intoxication of the inner vision. But frequently only an intense personal need can wring from them a human expression.

From an extraverted and rationalistic standpoint, such types are indeed the most fruitless of men. But, viewed from a higher standpoint, such men are living evidence of the fact that this rich and varied world with its overflowing and intoxicating life is not purely external, but also exists within. These types are admittedly onesided demonstrations of Nature, but they are an educational experience for the man who refuses to be blinded by the intellectual mode of the day. In their own way, men with such an attitude are educators and promoters of culture. Their life teaches more than their words. From their lives, and not the least from what is just their greatest fault, viz. their incommunicability, we may understand one of the greatest errors of our civilization, that is, the superstitious belief in statement and presentation, the immoderate overprizing of instruction by means of word and method. A child certainly allows himself to be impressed by the grand talk of its parents. But is it really imagined that the child is thereby educated? Actually it is the parents' lives that educate the child—what they add thereto by word and gesture at best serves only to confuse him. The same holds good for the teacher. But we have such a belief in method that, if only the method be good, the practice of it seems to hallow the teacher. An inferior man is never a good teacher. But he can conceal his injurious inferiority, which secretly poisons the pupil, behind an excellent method or an equally brilliant intellectual capacity. Naturally the pupil of riper years desires nothing better than the knowledge of useful methods, because he is already defeated by the general attitude, which believes in the victorious method. He has already learnt that the emptiest head, correctly echoing a method, is the best pupil. His whole environment not only urges but exemplifies the doctrine that all success and happiness are external, and that only the right method is needed to attain the haven of one's desires. Or is the life of his religious instructor likely to demonstrate that happiness which radiates from the treasure of the inner vision? The irrational introverted types are certainly no instructors of a more complete humanity. They lack reason and the ethics of reason, but their lives teach the other possibility, in which our civilization is so deplorably wanting.

11. The Principal and Auxiliary Functions

In the foregoing descriptions I have no desire to give my readers the impression that such pure types occur at all frequently in actual practice. They are, as it were, only Galtonesque family-portraits, which sum up in a cumulative image the common and therefore typical characters, stressing these disproportionately, while the individual features are just as disproportionately effaced. Accurate investigation of the individual case consistently reveals the fact that, in conjunction with the most differentiated function, another function of secondary importance, and therefore of inferior differentiation in consciousness, is constantly present, and is a relatively determining factor.

For the sake of clarity let us again recapitulate: The products of all the functions can be conscious, but we speak of the consciousness of a function only when not merely its application is at the disposal of the will, but when at the same time its principle is decisive for the orientation of consciousness. The latter event is true when, for instance, thinking is not a mere esprit de l'escalier, or rumination, but when its decisions possess an absolute validity, so that the logical conclusion in a given case holds good, whether as motive or as guarantee of practical action, without the backing of any further evidence. This absolute sovereignty always belongs, empirically, to one function alone, and *can* belong only to one function, since the equally independent intervention of another function would necessarily yield a different orientation, which would at least partially contradict the first. But, since it is a vital condition for the conscious adaptation-process that constantly clear and unambiguous aims should be in evidence, the presence of a second function of equivalent power is naturally forbidden. This other function, therefore, can have only a secondary importance, a fact which is also established empirically. Its secondary importance consists in the fact that, in a given case, it is not valid in its own right, as is the primary function, as an absolutely reliable and decisive factor, but comes into play more as an auxiliary or complementary function. Naturally only those functions can appear as auxiliary whose nature is not opposed to the leading function. For instance, feeling can never act as the second function by the side of thinking, because its nature stands in too strong a contrast to thinking. Thinking, if it is to be real thinking and true to its own principle, must scrupulously exclude feeling. This, of course, does not exclude the fact that individuals certainly exist in whom thinking and feeling stand upon the same level, whereby both have equal motive power in consciousness. But, in such a case, there is also no question of a differentiated type, but merely of a relatively undeveloped thinking and feeling. Uniform consciousness and unconsciousness of functions is, therefore, a distinguishing mark of a primitive mentality.

Experience shows that the secondary function is always one whose nature is different from, though not antagonistic to, the leading function: thus, for example, thinking, as primary function, can readily pair with intuition as auxiliary, or indeed equally well with sensation, but, as already observed, never with feeling. Neither intuition nor sensation are antagonistic to thinking, *i.e.* they have not to be unconditionally excluded, since they are not, like feeling, of similar nature, though of opposite purpose, to thinking—for as a judging function feeling successfully competes with thinking — but are functions of perception, affording welcome assistance to thought. As soon as they reached the same level of differentiation as thinking, they would cause a change of attitude, which would contradict the tendency of thinking. For they would convert the judging attitude into a perceiving one; whereupon the principle of rationality indispensable to thought would be suppressed in favour of the irrationality of mere perception. Hence the auxiliary function is possible and useful only in so far as it *serves* the leading function, without making any claim to the autonomy of its own principle.

For all the types appearing in practice, the principle holds good that besides the conscious main function there is also a relatively unconscious, auxiliary function which is in every respect different from the nature of the main function. From these combinations well-known pictures arise, the practical intellect for instance paired with sensation, the speculative intellect breaking through with intuition, the artistic intuition which selects and presents its images by means of feeling judgment, the philosophical intuition which, in league with a vigorous intellect, translates its vision into the sphere of comprehensible thought, and so forth.

A grouping of the unconscious functions also takes place in accordance with the relationship of the conscious functions. Thus, for instance, an unconscious intuitive-feeling attitude may correspond with a conscious practical intellect, whereby the function of feeling suffers a relatively stronger inhibition than intuition. This peculiarity, however, is of interest only for one who is concerned with the practical psychological treatment of such cases. But for such a man it is important to know about it. For I have frequently observed the way in which a physician, in the case for instance of an exclusively intellectual subject, will do his utmost to develop the feeling function directly out of the unconscious. This attempt must always come to grief, since it involves too great a violation of the conscious standpoint. Should such a violation succeed, there ensues a really compulsive dependence of the patient upon the physician, a 'transference' which can be amputated only by brutality, because such a violation robs the patient of a standpoint—his physician becomes his standpoint. But the approach to the unconscious and to the most repressed function is disclosed, as it were, of itself, and with more adequate protection of the conscious standpoint, when the way of development is *via* the secondary function—thus in the case of a rational type by way of the irrational function. For this lends the conscious standpoint such a range and prospect over what is possible and imminent that consciousness gains an adequate protection against the destructive effect of the unconscious. Conversely, an irrational type demands a stronger development of the rational auxiliary function represented in consciousness, in order to be sufficiently prepared to receive the impact of the unconscious.

The unconscious functions are in an archaic, animal state. Their symbolical appearances in dreams and phantasies usually represent the battle or coming encounter of two animals or monsters.

CHAPTER XI

DEFINITIONS

IT may perhaps seem superfluous that I should add to my text a chapter dealing solely with definitions. But wide experience warns me that, in psychological work especially, one cannot proceed too cautiously when dealing with concepts and expressions; for nowhere do such lamentable conceptual divergences occur, as in the province of psychology, creating only too frequently the most obstinate misunderstandings. This drawback is due not only to the fact that the science of psychology is still in its infancy; but there is also the difficulty that the material of experience, the object of scientific consideration, cannot be displayed in concrete form, as it were, to the eyes of the reader. The psychological investigator is always finding himself obliged to make use of extensive, and in a sense indirect, description for the presentation of the reality he has observed. Only in so far as elementary facts are accessible to number and measure can there be any question of a direct presentation. But how much of the actual psychology of man can be witnessed and observed as mensurable facts? Such facts do exist, in the realm of psychology; indeed my Association Studies have, I think, demonstrated[1] that highly complicated psychological phenomena are none the less accessible to methods of measure. But anyone who has probed more deeply into the nature of psychology, demanding something more of it than science in the wretchedly prescribed limits of a

[1] Jung, *Studies in Word Association:* transl. by M. D. Eder (London: Heinemann).

natural science method is able to yield, will also have realized that an experimental method will never succeed in doing justice to the nature of the human soul, nor will it ever trace even an approximately faithful picture of the complicated psychic phenomena.

But, when we leave the realm of mensurable facts, we are dependent upon *concepts*, which have now to assume the office of measure and number. That precision which exact measurements lend to the observed fact can be replaced only by the *precision of the concept*. Unfortunately, however, as is only too familiar to every investigator and worker in this field, current psychological concepts are involved in such uncertainty and ambiguity that mutual understanding is almost impossible. One has only to take the concept 'feeling', for instance, and attempt to visualize everything that this idea contains, to get some sort of notion of the variability and ambiguity of psychological concepts. Nevertheless this concept does express something characteristic that is certainly inaccessible to rule and number and yet conceivably existing. One cannot simply resign oneself, as Wundt does in his physiological psychology, to a mere denial of the validity of such facts as essential basic phenomena, whereby they are either replaced by elementary facts or again resolved into such. For by so doing a primary element of psychology is entirely lost.

In order to escape the drawback this overvaluation of the natural science method involves, one is obliged to have recourse to well-defined concepts. But, before we could arrive at such concepts, the collaboration of many would be needed; *i.e.* the *consensus gentium*, so to speak, would have to be invoked. But since this is not within the immediate range of possibility, the individual pioneer must at least strive to give his concepts some fixity and precision; and this is best achieved by so elucidating the meaning of the concepts he employs as to put everyone in a position to see what he means by them.

It is in response to this need that I now propose to discuss my principal psychological concepts in alphabetical order, and I must take this opportunity of requesting the reader to refer to these interpretations in every case of doubt. It must, of course, be understood that with these interpretations and definitions I merely wish to establish the sense in which I myself employ the concepts; far be it from me to affirm that such an application is the only possible one under all circumstances, or even the absolutely correct interpretation.

1. Abstraction, as the word already implies, is the drawing out or isolation of a content (*e.g.* a meaning or general character, etc.) from a connection, containing other elements, whose combination as a totality is something unique or individual, and therefore inaccessible to comparison. Singularity, uniqueness, and incomparability are obstacles to cognition, hence to the cognitive tendency the remaining elements, though felt to be essentially bound up with the content, must appear irrelevant.

Abstraction, therefore, is that form of mental activity which releases the essential content or fact from its connection with irrelevant elements; it distinguishes it from them, or, in other words, *differentiates* it. (*v*. Differentiation). In its wider sense, everything is *abstract* that is separated from its connection with non-appertaining elements.

Abstraction is an activity belonging to psychological functions in general. There is a *thinking* which abstracts, just as there is abstracting *feeling, sensation*, and *intuition*. (*v*. these concepts). Abstracting-thinking brings into relief a content that is distinguished from other irrelevant elements by its intellectual, logical qualities. Abstracting-feeling does the same with a content characterized by

DEFINITIONS

feeling; similarly with sensation and intuition. Hence, not only are there abstract thoughts but also abstract feelings, which latter are defined by Sully as intellectual, æsthetic, and moral[1]. Nahlowsky adds the religious feeling to these. Abstract feelings would, in my view, correspond with the 'higher' or 'ideal' feelings of Nahlowsky[2]. I put abstract feelings on the same line as abstract thoughts. Abstract sensation would be æsthetic as distinguished from sensual sensation (*v.* Sensation), and abstract intuition would be symbolical as opposed to phantastical intuition. (*v.* Phantasy, and Intuition).

In this work, the concept of abstraction is linked up with the idea of the psycho-energic process involved in it. When I assume an abstracting attitude towards an object, I do not let the object affect me in its totality, but I distinguish a portion of it from its connections, at the same time excluding the irrelevant parts. My purpose is to rid myself of the object as a single and unique whole, and to extract only a portion of it. Awareness of the whole undoubtedly takes place, but I do not plunge myself into this awareness; my interest does not flow out into the totality, but withdraws itself from the object as a whole, bringing the abstracted portion into myself, *i.e.* into my conceptual world, which is already prepared or constellated for the purpose of abstracting a part of the object. (It is only by virtue of a subjective constellation of concepts that I possess the power of abstracting from the object). 'Interest' I conceive as that energy = libido (*v.* Libido), which I bestow upon the object as value, or which the object draws from me, even maybe against my will or unknown to myself. I visualize the abstracting process, therefore, as a withdrawal of libido from the object, or as a backflow of value from the object to a

---
[1] Sully, *The Human Mind*, vol. ii, ch. 16.
[2] Nahlowsky, *Das Gefühlsleben*, p. 48.

subjective, abstract content. Thus, for me, abstraction has the meaning of an energic *depreciation of the object*. In other words, abstraction can be expressed as an introverting libido-movement.

I call an *attitude* (*v.* Attitude) *abstracting* when it is both introverting and at the same time assimilates to already prepared abstract contents in the subject a certain essential portion of the object. The more abstract a content, the more *unrepresentable* it is. I adhere to Kant's view, which maintains that a concept is the more abstract, "the more it excludes the differences of things"[1], in the sense that abstraction at its highest level is absolutely removed from the object, thereby attaining the extreme limit of unrepresentability. It is this *abstraction* which I term the *idea* (*v.* Idea). Conversely, an abstraction that still possesses representability or obviousness is a concrete (*v.* Concretism) concept.

2. Affect.—By the term affect we understand a state of feeling characterized by a perceptible bodily innervation on the one hand and a peculiar disturbance of the ideational process on the other[2]. I use emotion as synonymous with affect. I distinguish—in contrast to Bleuler (*v.* Affectivity)—*feeling* from affect, in spite of the fact that no definite demarcation exists, since every feeling, after attaining a certain strength, releases physical innervations, thus becoming an affect. On practical grounds, however, it is advisable to discriminate affect from feeling, since feeling can be a disposable function, whereas affect is usually not so. Similarly, affect is clearly distinguished from feeling by quite perceptible physical innervations, while feeling for the most part lacks them, or their intensity

[1] Kant, *Logic*, § 6.
[2] Cf. Wundt, *Grundzeichnungen der physiolog. Psychologie*, 5te Aufl. III, pp. 209 ff.

is so slight that they can only be demonstrated by the finest instruments, as for example the psycho-galvanic phenomenon[1]. Affect becomes cumulative through the sensation of the physical innervations released by it. This perception gave rise to the James-Lang theory of affect, which would make bodily innervations wholly responsible for affects. As opposed to this extreme view, I regard affect as a psychic feeling-state on the one hand, and as a physiological innervation-state on the other; each of which has a cumulative, reciprocal effect upon the other, *i.e.* a component of sensation is joined to the reinforced feeling, through which the affect is approximated more to sensation (*v.* Sensation), and differentiated essentially from the state of feeling. Pronounced affects, *i.e.* affects accompanied by violent physical innervation, I do not assign to the province of feeling but to the realm of the sensation function (*v.* Function).

3. Affectivity is a concept coined by Bleuler. Affectivity designates and embraces "not only the affects proper, but also the slight feelings or feeling-tones of pain and pleasure."[2] On the one hand, Bleuler distinguishes from affectivity all sensations and other bodily perceptions, and, on the other, such feelings as may be regarded as inner perception-processes (*e.g.* the 'feeling' of certainty or probability)[3] or indistinct thoughts or discernments (pp. 13 ff.).

[1] Féré, *Note sur des modifications de la résistance électrique*, etc. (*Comptes-Rendus de la Société de Biologie*, 1888, pp. 217 ff.)
Veraguth, *Das Psychogalvanische Reflexphämomen* (*Monatsschr. f. Psych. u. Neurol.*, XXI, p. 387)
Jung, *On Psychophysical Relations*, etc. (*Journal of Abnormal Psychology*, i, 247)
Binswanger, *On Psychogalvanic Phenomenon in Assoc. Experiments* (Jung, *Studies in Word Association*, p. 446)
[2] Bleuler, *Affektivität, Suggestibität, Paranoia* (1906), p. 6.
[3] Which in reality are intuitions.

4. Anima—v. Soul.

5. Apperception is a psychic process by which a new content is articulated to similar already-existing contents in such a way as to be understood, apprehended, or clear[1]. We discriminate *active* from *passive* apperception; the former is a process by which the subject of himself, from his own motives, consciously and attentively apprehends a new content and assimilates it to another content standing in readiness; the latter is a process in which a new content from without (through the senses) or from within (from the unconscious) presses through into consciousness, and, to a certain extent, compels attention and apprehension upon itself. In the former case, the accent of activity lies with the ego; in the latter, with the obtruding new content.

6. Archaism: With this term, I designate the *ancient* character of psychic contents and functions. By this I do not mean archaistic, *i.e.* imitated antiquity, as exhibited for instance in the later Roman sculpture or the nineteenth century 'Gothic', but qualities which have the character of *survival*. All those psychological traits can be so described which essentially correspond with the qualities of primitive mentality. It is clear that archaism primarily clings to the phantasies of the unconscious, *i.e.* to such products of unconscious phantasy-activity as reach consciousness. The quality of the image is archaic when it possesses unmistakable mythological parallels[2]. The analogy-associations of unconscious phantasy are archaic, as is their symbolism (*v.* Symbol). The relation of identity with the object (*v.* Identity), or "participation mystique" (*q.v.*) is archaic. Concretism of thought and feeling is

---

[1] Cf. Wundt, *Grundzüge der physiolog. Psychologie*, i, 322.
[2] Cf. Jung, *Psychology of the Unconscious*.

archaic. Compulsion and inability for self-control (being carried away) are also archaic. That condition in which the psychological functions are fused or merged one into the other (*v.* Differentiation) is archaic—the fusion, for instance, of thinking with feeling, feeling with sensation, or feeling with intuition. Furthermore, the coalescence of parts of a function ('audition coloriée'), ambitendency and ambivalency (Bleuler), *i.e.* the state of fusion with its counterpart, *e.g.* positive with negative feeling, is also archaic.

7. **Assimilation** is the absorption or joining up of a new conscious content to already prepared subjective material[1], whereby the similarity of the new content with the waiting subjective material is specially emphasized, even to the prejudice of the independent quality of the new content[2]. Fundamentally, assimilation is a process of apperception (*v.* Apperception), which, however, is distinguished from pure apperception by this element of adjustment to the subjective material. It is in this sense that Wundt says[3]: "This method of acquisition (viz. assimilation) stands out most obviously in representations where the assimilating elements arise through reproduction and the assimilated material through a direct sense-impression. For then the elements of memory-images are transferred, as it were, into the outer object, which is especially the case when the object and the reproduced elements differ so considerably from each other that the completed sense-perception appears as an illusion, deceiving us as to the actual nature of things."

I employ assimilation in a somewhat broader sense, namely as the adjustment of object to subject in general, and with it I contrast *dissimilation*, which represents the

[1] Wundt, *Logic*, i. 20.
[2] Cf. Lipps, *Leitfaden der Psychologie*, 2te Aufl., p. 104.
[3] Wundt, *Grundzüge d. physiolog. Psychol.* iii, 529.

adjustment of subject to object, and a consequent estrangement of the subject from himself in favour of the object, whether it be an external object or a 'psychological' or inner object, as for instance an idea.

8. Attitude (Einstellung): This concept is a relatively recent acquisition to psychology. It originated with Müller and Schumann[1]. Whereas Külpe[2] defines attitude as a predisposition of the sensory or motor centres to a definite stimulation or persistent impulse, Ebbinghaus[3] conceives it in a wider sense as a phenomenon of exercise, introducing an air of the customary into the individual act which deviates from the customary. Our use of the concept proceeds from Ebbinghaus' conception of attitude. For us, *attitude* is a readiness of the psyche to act or to react in a certain direction. It is precisely for the psychology of complex psychic phenomena that the concept is so important, since it provides an expression for that peculiar psychological phenomenon wherein we find certain stimuli exercising a powerful effect on one occasion, while their effect is either weak or wholly absent on another. To have a certain attitude means to be ready for something definite, even though this definite something is unconscious, since having an attitude is synonymous with an a priori direction towards a definite thing, whether this be present in consciousness or not. The state of readiness, which I conceive attitude to be, always consists in the presence of a certain subjective constellation, a definite combination of psychic factors or contents, which will either determine action in this or that definite direction, or will comprehend an external stimulus in this or that definite way. Active apperception (*q.v.*) is impossible without an attitude. An attitude always has an objective; this can be either con-

[1] *Pflügers Archiv*, vol. 45, 37.
[2] *Grundz. d. Psychol.*, p. 44. [3] *Ibid.*, i, 681 ff.

scious or unconscious, since in the act of apperceiving a new content a prepared combination of contents unfailingly emphasizes those qualities or motives which appear to belong to the subjective content. Hence a selection or judgment takes place which excludes the irrelevant. As to what is, and what is not, relevant is decided by the already orientated combination or constellation of contents. Whether the attitude's objective be conscious or unconscious is immaterial to its selective effect, since the choice is already given a priori through the attitude, and therefore follows automatically. It is useful, however, to distinguish between conscious and unconscious, since the presence of two attitudes is extremely frequent, the one conscious and the other unconscious. Which means to say that the conscious has a preparedness of contents different from that of the unconscious. This duality of attitude is particularly evident in neurosis.

There is a certain kinship between the concept of attitude and the apperception concept of Wundt, though with this difference, that the idea of apperception includes the process of relating the already prepared content to the new content to be apperceived, while the concept of attitude relates exclusively to the subjectively prepared content. Apperception is, as it were, the bridge which connects the already present and prepared content with the new content, the attitude being, in a sense, the end-pier or abutment of the bridge upon the one bank, while the new content represents the abutment upon the other bank. Attitude signifies an *expectation*, an expectation always operates selectively—it gives direction. The presence of a strongly toned content in the field of consciousness forms (sometimes together with other contents) a certain constellation which is synonymous with a definite attitude, because such a conscious content favours the perception and apperception of everything similar, and inhibits the dissimilar. It creates an attitude corresponding with it. This automatic phenomenon is an essential cause of the onesidedness of conscious orientation. It would lead to a complete loss of equilibrium if there were no self-regulating, compensatory (*q.v.*) function in the psyche to correct the conscious attitude. Thus in this sense the duality of the attitude is a normal phenomenon, which plays a disturbing rôle only when conscious onesidedness becomes excessive.

As ordinary *attention*, the attitude can be either a relatively unimportant subsidiary phenomenon or a general principle determining the whole psyche. From disposition, environmental influence, education, general experience, or conviction a constellation of contents may be habitually present, continually moulding a certain attitude which may operate even down to the most minute details of life. Every man who has a special sense of the unpleasant side of life will naturally have an attitude of constant readiness for the disagreeable. This excessive conscious attitude is counterbalanced by an unconscious attitude for pleasure The oppressed individual has a conscious attitude that always anticipates oppression; he selects this factor in experience; everywhere he scents it out; and in so doing his unconscious attitude makes for power and superiority.

The total psychology of the individual even in its various basic characters is orientated by the nature of his habitual attitude. In spite of the fact that general psychological laws are operative in every individual, they cannot be said to be characteristic of the individual, since the nature of their operation varies completely in accordance with the nature of the general attitude. The general attitude is always a resultant of all the factors that can have an essential influence upon the psyche, such as inborn disposition, education, milieu-influences, experience of life, insight and convictions gained through differentiation (*q.v.*), collective ideas, etc. Without the absolutely fundamental importance of attitude, there would be no question of the existence of an individual psychology. But the general attitude effects such immense displacements of energy, and so modifies the relations between individual functions, that resultants are produced which frequently bring the validity of general psychological laws into question. In spite of the fact, for instance, that a certain measure of activity is held to be indispensable for the sexual function both on physiological and psychological grounds, individuals certainly exist who, without injury to themselves, *i.e.* without pathological phenomena and without any demonstrable restriction of productive power, can, to a very great extent, dispense with it; while, in other cases, quite insignificant deprivations or disturbances in this region may involve very considerable general consequences. How potent individual differences can be is seen perhaps most clearly in questions of likes and dislikes. Here practically all rules go by the board. What is there, in the last resort, which has not at one time given man pleasure, while at another has caused him pain? Every instinct, every function can be subordinated to other instincts and functions and act as a servant. The ego or power-instinct can make sexuality its serviceable subject, or sexuality make use of the ego. Thinking may over-run everything else, or feeling swallow up thinking and sensation, all in obedience to the attitude.

Au fond, the attitude is an individual phenomenon and is inaccessible to the scientific method of approach. In actual experience, however, certain attitude-types can be discriminated in so far as certain psychic functions can also be differentiated. When a function habitually predominates, a typical attitude is thereby produced. In accordance with the nature of the differentiated function, constellations of contents take place which create a corresponding attitude. Thus there exist a typical thinking, a feeling, a sensational, and an intuitive attitude. Besides these purely psychological attitude-types, whose number might possibly be increased, there are also social types, namely, those for whom a collective idea expresses the brand. They are characterized by the various '-isms'. These collective attitudes are, at all events, very important in certain cases, even outweighing in significance the purely individual attitude.

9. **Collective**: All those psychic contents I term collective which are peculiar not to one individual, but to many, at the same time, *i.e.* either to a society, a people, or to mankind in general. Such contents are the "mystical collective ideas" ("représentations collectives") of the primitive described by Lévy-Bruhl[1]; they include also the *general concepts* of right, the State, religion, science, etc., current among civilized man. It is not only concepts and ways of looking at things, however, which must be termed collective, but also *feelings*. Lévy-Bruhl shows that for the primitives collective ideas also represent collective feelings. By virtue of this collective feeling value he also terms the "représentations collectives", 'mystiques" since these representations are not merely intellectual but also emotional[2]. With civilized peoples, collective feelings are also bound up with certain collective ideas, such for example as the idea of God, justice, fatherland, etc. The collective character does not merely cling to individual psychic elements, it also involves whole functions (*q.v.*). Thus, for instance, thinking can have the character of a wholly collective function, in so far as it possesses a generally valid quality, when, for example, it agrees with the laws of logic. Feeling can also be a

---

[1] Lévy Bruhl, *Les fonctions mentales dans les sociétés inférieures*, pp. 27 ff.   [2] *Ibid.*, pp. 28 ff.

wholly collective function, in so far as it is identical with the general feeling, when, in other words, it corresponds with general expectations or with the general moral consciousness. In the same way, that sensation or manner of sensing, and that intuition, are collective which are peculiar to a large group of men at the same time. The antithesis of collective is *individual* (*q.v.*).

10. Compensation means a *balancing* or *supplementing*. This concept was actually introduced [1] into the psychology of the neuroses by Adler [2]. He understands by it a functional adjustment of the feeling of inferiority by a compensating psychological system, comparable to the compensating development of organs in organic inferiority [3]. Thus Adler says: "For these inferior organs and organ-systems the struggle with the outer world begins with the release from the maternal organism, a struggle which must necessarily break out and declare itself with greater violence than ever occurs in the more normally developed apparatus. At the same time, however, the fœtal character provides an enhanced possibility for compensation and overcompensation, increases the capacity for adaptation to ordinary and extraordinary resistances, and ensures the formation of new and higher forms and achievements." [4] The neurotic's inferiority-feeling, which according to Adler corresponds aetiologically with an organ-inferiority, brings about an "auxiliary construction" [5]; in other words, a compensation, which consists in the setting-up of a fiction to balance the inferiority. The fiction or "fictitious guiding line" is a

[1] Allusions to the theory of compensation, originally inspired by Anton are also to be found in Gross.
[2] Adler, *The Neurotic Constitution*: transl. by Glück and Lind. (London: Kegan Paul & Co.)
[3] Adler, *Studie über Minderwertigkeit von Organen*. 1907.
[4] *The Neurotic Constitution*, p. 7.   [5] *Ibid.*, p. 14.

psychological system which seeks to convert the inferiority into a superiority. This conception gains significance in the undeniable existence—for we have all experienced it—of a compensating function in the sphere of psychological processes. It corresponds with a similar function in the physiological sphere, namely, the self-regulation or self-direction of the living organism.

Whereas Adler restricts his concept of compensation to a mere balancing of the feeling of inferiority, I conceive it as a general functional adjustment, an inherent self-regulation of the psychic apparatus [1]. In this sense, I regard the activity of the unconscious (*q.v.*) as a compensation to the onesidedness of the general attitude produced by the function of consciousness. Psychologists often compare consciousness to the eye: we speak of a visual-field and of a focal point of consciousness. The nature of consciousness is aptly characterized by this simile: only a few contents can attain the highest grade of consciousness at the same time, and only a limited number of contents can be held at the same time in the conscious field. The activity of the conscious is *selective*. Selection demands *direction*. But direction requires the *exclusion of everything irrelevant*. On occasion, therefore, a certain onesidedness of the conscious orientation is inevitable. The contents that are excluded and inhibited by the chosen direction sink into the unconscious, where by virtue of their effective existence they form a definite counterweight against the conscious orientation. The strengthening of this counterposition keeps pace with the intensification of the conscious onesidedness until finally a noticeable tension is produced. This tension involves a certain inhibition of the conscious activity which can assuredly be broken down by increased conscious effort.

[1] Jung, *Collected Papers on Analytical Psychology*, 2nd edn., pp. 278 ff. (London: Baillière)

But as time goes on, the tension becomes so acute that the inhibited unconscious contents begin to break through into consciousness in the form of dreams and spontaneous images. The more onesided the conscious attitude, the more antithetic are the contents arising from the unconscious, so that we may speak of a real opposition between the conscious and the unconscious; in which case, compensation appears in the form of a contrasting function Such a case is extreme. Compensation by the unconscious is, as a rule, not so much a contrast as a levelling up or supplementing of the conscious orientation. In dreams, for instance, the unconscious may supply all those contents which are constellated by the conscious situation, but which are inhibited by conscious selection, although a knowledge of them would be quite indispensable to a complete adaptation.

In the normal condition the compensation is unconscious, *i.e.* it performs an unconscious regulation of conscious activity. In the neurotic state the unconscious appears in such strong contrast to the conscious that compensation is disturbed. The aim of analytical therapy, therefore, is to make the unconscious contents conscious in order that compensation may be re-established.

11. Concretism: By this term I understand a definite peculiarity of *thought* and *feeling* which represents the antithesis to abstraction. The actual meaning of concrete is 'grown together'. A concretely-thought concept is one that has grown together or coalesced with other concepts. Such a concept is not abstract, not isolated, and independently thought, but always impure and related. It is not a differentiated concept, but is still embedded in the sense-conveyed material of perception. Concretistic thinking moves among exclusively concrete concepts and views; it is constantly related to sensation. Similarly concretistic feeling is never free from sensuous relatedness.

Primitive thinking and feeling are exclusively concretistic; they are always related to sensation. The thought of the primitive has no detached independence, but clings to the material phenomenon. The most he can do is to raise it to the level of *analogy*. Primitive feeling is always equally related to the material phenomenon. His thought and feeling depend upon sensation and are only faintly differentiated from it. Concretism, therefore, is an archaism (*q.v.*). The magical influence of the fetish is not experienced as a subjective state of feeling, but sensed as a magical effect. This is the concretism of feeling. The primitive does not experience the idea of divinity as a subjective content, but the sacred tree is the habitat—nay, even the deity himself. This is concretism of thinking. With civilized man, concretism of thought consists in the inability to conceive of anything which differs from the immediately obvious external facts, or in the inability to discriminate subjective feeling from the sense-given object.

Concretism is a concept which falls under the more general concept of "participation mystique" (*q.v.*). Just as "participation mystique" represents a fusion of the individual with outer objects, so concretism represents a mixing-up of thought and feeling with sensation. It is a state of concretism when the object of thinking and feeling is at the same time also an object of sensation. This coalescence prevents a differentiation of thought and feeling, anchoring both functions within the sphere of sensation, *i.e.* sensuous relatedness; accordingly they can never be developed into pure functions, but must always remain the mere retainers of sensation. The result of this is a predominance of the factor of sensation in the psychological orientation. (Concerning the importance of the factor of sensation *v.* Sensation; Types).

The disadvantage of concretism is the subjection of function to sensation. Because sensation is the perception of physiological stimuli, concretism either rivets the function to the sphere of sense or constantly leads it back there. The effect of this is a sensual subjection of the psychological functions, favouring the influence of external facts at the expense of individual psychic autonomy. From the standpoint of the recognition of facts, this orientation is, of course, valuable, but from the standpoint of the interpretation of facts and their relation to the individual it is definitely prejudicial. Concretism produces a state where facts gain the paramount importance, thereby suppressing the individuality and its freedom in favour of the objective process. But since the individual is not only determined by physiological stimuli, but also by factors which may even be opposed to the external fact, concretism effects a projection of these inner factors into the outer fact, thus provoking an almost superstitious overvaluation of mere facts, as is precisely the case with the primitive. A good example of this is seen in Nietzsche, whose concretism of feeling resulted in an excessive valuation of diet; the materialism of Moleschott is a similar instance ("Man is what he eats"). An example of the superstitious overvaluation of facts is also provided by the hypostasizing of the concept of energy in the monism of Ostwald.

12. Consciousness: By consciousness I understand the relatedness of psychic contents to the ego (*v.* Ego) in so far as they are sensed as such by the ego[1]. In so far as relations are not sensed as such by the ego, they are un-

[1] Natorp, *Einleitung in der Psych.*, p. 11. Also Lipps, *Leitfaden der Psych.*, p. 3.

conscious (*q.v.*). Consciousness is the function or activity[1] which maintains the relation of psychic contents with the ego. Consciousness is not identical with *psyche*, since, in my view, psyche represents the totality of all the psychic contents, and these are not necessarily all bound up directly with the ego, *i.e.* related to it in such a way that they take on the quality of consciousness. There exist a great many psychic complexes and these are not all, necessarily, connected with the ego[2].

13. **Constructive**: This concept is used by me in an equivalent sense to *synthetic*, almost in fact as an illustration of the latter concept. Constructive means 'building up'. I employ 'constructive' and 'synthetic', in describing a method that is opposed to the reductive[3]. The constructive method is concerned with the elaboration of unconscious products (dreams, phantasies, etc.). It takes the unconscious product as a basis or starting point, as a *symbolical* (*q.v.*) expression, which, stretching on ahead as it were, represents a coming phase of psychological development[4]. In this connection, Maeder actually speaks of a *prospective function* of the unconscious, which half playfully anticipates the future psychological development[5]. Adler, too, recognises an anticipatory function of the unconscious[6]. It is obvious that the product of the unconscious must not be regarded as a finished thing, a sort of end-product; for in this case it would be dis-

---

[1] Cf. Riehl (*s. Einf. in die Phil.*, 161), who regards consciousness as both " activity " and " process ".

[2] Jung, *The Psychology of Dementia Præcox*.

[3] Jung, *Content of the Psychoses* (*Collected Papers*, 2nd edn., ch. xiii, p. 312)

[4] A detailed example of this is to be found in Jung, *Psych. and Path. of so-called Occult Phenomena* (*Collected Papers*, 2nd edn.)

[5] Maeder, *The Dream Problem* (Monograph Series. Nervous and Mental Disease Pub. Co., New York)

[6] Adler, *The Neurotic Constitution*.

DEFINITIONS

possessed of every practical significance. Even Freud allows the dream a teleological rôle as the "guardian of sleep"[1], although for him its prospective function is essentially restricted to "wishes". The practical character of unconscious tendencies, however, cannot be disputed a priori, if we are to accept the analogy with other psychological or physiological functions. We conceive the product of the unconscious, therefore, as an expression orientated to a goal or purpose, but characterizing the objective in symbolical metaphor[2].

In accordance with this conception, the constructive method of interpretation is not so much concerned with the basic sources underlying the unconscious product, or with the mere raw materials as such, as it is with the aim to raise the symbolical product to a general and comprehensible expression[3]. The free associations of the unconscious product are thus considered with a view to a psychological objective and not from the standpoint of derivation. They are viewed from the angle of future action or inaction; their relation to the conscious situation is thereby scrupulously considered, for with the compensatory conception of the unconscious its activity has an essentially supplementary significance for the conscious situation. Since it is now a question of an anticipatory orientation, the actual relation to the object does not loom so large as in the reductive procedure, which is preoccupied with the actual past relations with the object. It is much more a question of the subjective attitude, in which the object merely signifies a sign of the subjective tendencies. The aim of the constructive method,

---

[1] Freud, *The Interpretation of Dreams*.
[2] Silberer, *Problems of Mysticism and its Symbolism*: transl. by Dr S. E. Jelliffe (London, Kegan Paul & Co.) pp. 149 ff., expresses himself in a similar sense in his formulation of *anagogic* significance.
[3] Jung, *The Psychology of Unconscious Processes* (*Collected Papers*, 2nd Ed.)

therefore, is the production of a meaning from the unconscious product which is definitely related to the subject's future attitude. Since, as a rule, the unconscious has the power of shaping only symbolical expressions, the constructive method seeks to elucidate the symbolically expressed meaning in such a way that a correct indication is supplied to the conscious orientation, whereby the subject may discover that harmony with the unconscious which his future action requires.

Thus, just as no psychological method of interpretation is based exclusively upon the association-material of the analysant, the constructive method also makes use of certain comparative material. And, just as the reductive interpretation employs parallels drawn from biological, physiological, literary, folk-lore, and other sources, the constructive treatment of the intellectual problem is dependent upon philosophical parallels, while the intuitive problem is referred to parallels in mythology and the history of religion.

The constructive method is necessarily *individualistic*, since a future collective attitude is developed only through the individual. The reductive method is, on the contrary, *collective*, since it leads back from the individual case to general basic attitudes or facts. The constructive method can be directly applied also by the subject upon his own material. In this latter case it is an *intuitive* method, devoted to the elucidation of the general meaning of an unconscious product. This elucidation succeeds through an associative (hence not *actively* apperceptive ; *q.v.*) articulation of wider material, which so enriches and deepens the symbolical expression of the unconscious that it eventually attains a degree of clarity through which it can become comprehensible to consciousness. Through this enriching of the symbolical expression it becomes interwoven with more universal associations, and is therewith assimilated:

DEFINITIONS

14. Differentiation means the development of differences, the separation of parts from a whole. In this work I employ the concept chiefly in respect to psychological functions. So long as one function is still so merged with one or more of the other functions—as for example thinking with feeling, or feeling with sensation, etc.—as to be quite unable to appear alone, it is in an *archaic* (*q.v.*) state, and therefore undifferentiated, *i.e.* it is not separated out as a special part from the whole having its own independent existence. An undifferentiated thinking is incapable of thinking apart from other functions, *i.e.* it is constantly mixed up with sensations, feelings, or intuitions; such thinking may, for instance, become blended with sensations and phantasies, as exemplified in the sexualization (Freud) of feeling and thinking in neurosis. The undifferentiated function is also commonly characterized by the qualities of *ambivalency* and *ambitendency*[1], *i.e.* every positive brings with it an equally strong negative, whereby characteristic inhibitions spring up in the application of the undifferentiated function. Such a function suffers also from a fusing together of its individual parts; thus an undifferentiated faculty of sensation, for instance, is impaired through an amalgamation of the separate spheres of sensation ("audition coloriée"), and undifferentiated feeling through confounding hatred with love. Just so far as a function is wholly or mainly unconscious is it also undifferentiated, *i.e.* it is not only fused together in its parts but also merged with other functions.

Differentiation consists in the separation of the selected function from other functions, and in the separation of its individual parts from each other. Without differentia-

---

[1] Bleuler, *Die Negative Suggestibilität* (*Psych. Neur. Wochenschr.*, 1904, 27-28).
Idem, Zur Theorie des Schizophrenen Negativismus (*Psych. Neur Wochenschr.*, 1910, 18-21).
Idem, Lehrbuch der Psychiatrie, pp. 92, 285.

tion direction is impossible, since the direction of a function is dependent upon the isolation and exclusion of the irrelevant. Through fusion with what is irrelevant, direction becomes impossible; only a differentiated function proves itself *capable of direction*.

15. Dissimilation: *v.* **Assimilation.**

16. Ego: By ego, I understand a complex of representations which constitutes the centrum of my field of consciousness and appears to possess a very high degree of continuity and identity. Hence I also speak of an *ego-complex*[1].

The ego-complex is as much a content as it is a condition of consciousness (*q.v.*), since a psychic element is conscious to me just in so far as it is related to my ego-complex. But, inasmuch as the ego is only the centrum of my field of consciousness, it is not identical with the totality of my psyche, being merely a complex among other complexes. Hence I discriminate between the ego and the Self, since the ego is only the subject of my consciousness, while the Self is the subject of my totality: hence it also includes the unconscious psyche. In this sense the Self would be an (ideal) factor which embraces and includes the ego. In unconscious phantasy the Self often appears as a super-ordinated or ideal personality, as Faust in relation to Goethe and Zarathustra to Nietzsche. In the effort of idealization the archaic features of the Self are represented as practically severed from the 'higher' Self, as in the figure of Mephisto with Goethe or in that of Epimetheus with Spitteler. In the Christian psychology the severance is extreme in the figures of Christ and the devil or Anti-christ; while with Nietzsche Zarathustra discovers his shadow in the 'ugliest man'.

[1] Jung, *The Psychology of Dementia Præcox*.

17. **Emotion**—v. Affect.

18. **Enantiodromia** means 'a running counter to'. In the philosophy of Heraclitus[1] this concept is used to designate the play of opposites in the course of events, namely, the view which maintains that everything that exists goes over into its opposite. " From the living comes death, and from the dead, life; from the young, old age; and from the old, youth; from waking, sleep; and from sleep, waking; the stream of creation and decay never stands still."[2] " Construction and destruction, destruction and construction—this is the norm which rules in every circle of natural life from the smallest to the greatest. Just as the cosmos itself emerged from the primal fire, so must it return once more into the same—a double process running its measured course through vast periods, a drama eternally re-enacted."[3]

This is the enantiodromia of Heraclitus in the words of qualified interpreters. There are abundant sayings from the mouth of Heraclitus himself which express the same view. Thus he says:

" Even Nature herself striveth after the opposite, bringing harmony not from like things, but from contrasts."
" When they are born, they prepare to live, and therewith to suffer death."
" For souls it is death to become water, for water death to become earth. From the earth cometh water, and from water soul."
" Everywhere mutual exchange; the All in exchange for fire, and fire in exchange for the All, just as gold for wares and wares for gold."

---

[1] Stobaeus, *Ekl.* i, 58: "εἱμαρμένην δὲ λόγον ἐκ τῆς ἐναντιοδρομίας δημιουργὸν τῶν ὄντων."

[2] Zeller, *History of Greek Philosophy*: transl. by S. F. Alleyne, vol. ii, p. 17 (London: Longmans & Co.)

[3] Gomperz, *Greek Thinkers*, vol. i: transl. by Laurie Magnus, p. 64 (London: Murray, 1901)

In a psychological application of his principle Heraclitus says:

"Let ye never lack riches, O Ephesians, lest your depravity cometh to the light."[1]

I use the term enantiodromia to describe the emergence of the unconscious opposite, with particular relation to its chronological sequence. This characteristic phenomenon occurs almost universally wherever an extreme, onesided tendency dominates the conscious life; for this involves the gradual development of an equally strong, unconscious counterposition, which first becomes manifest in an inhibition of conscious activities, and subsequently leads to an interruption of conscious direction. A good example of enantiodromia is seen in the psychology of Saul of Tarsus and his conversion to Christianity; as also in the story of the conversion of Raymond Lully;[2] in the Christ-identification of the sick Nietzsche with his deification and subsequent hatred of Wagner; in the transformation of Swedenborg from scholar into seer, etc.

19. Extraversion means an outward-turning of the libido (q.v.). With this concept I denote a manifest relatedness of subject to object in the sense of a positive movement of subjective interest towards the object. Everyone in the state of extraversion thinks, feels, and acts in relation to the object, and moreover in a direct and clearly observable fashion, so that no doubt can exist about his positive dependence upon the object. In a sense, therefore, extraversion is an outgoing transference of interest from the subject to the object. If it is an intellectual extraversion, the subject thinks himself into the object; if a feeling extraversion, then the subject feels

---

[1] Diels, *Die Fragmente der Vorsokratiker*, 2te Aufl., i, 79 (1907).
[2] 'Doctor Illuminatus' (1234-1315), who as a soldier was notorious for his debaucheries, but later entirely changed his way of life and became a crusader against the Moslems.

himself into the object. The state of extraversion means a strong, if not exclusive, determination by the object. One should speak of an *active* extraversion when deliberately willed, and of a *passive* extraversion when the object compels it, *i.e.* attracts the interest of the subject of its own accord, even against the latter's intention. Should the state of extraversion become habitual, the *extraverted type* (*v.* Type) appears.

20. **Feeling** (Fühlen): I count feeling among the four basic psychological functions. I am unable to support the psychological school that regards feeling as a secondary phenomenon dependent upon "presentations" or sensations, but in company with Höffding, Wundt, Lehmann, Külpe, Baldwin, and others, I regard it as an independent function sui generis.[1]

Feeling is primarily a process that takes place between the ego and a given content, a process, moreover, that imparts to the content a definite *value* in the sense of acceptance or rejection ('like' or 'dislike'); but it can also appear, as it were, isolated in the form of 'mood', quite apart from the momentary contents of consciousness or momentary sensations. This latter process may be causally related to previous conscious contents, though not necessarily so, since, as psychopathology abundantly proves, it can take origin equally well from unconscious contents. But even the mood, whether it be regarded as a general or only a partial feeling, signifies a valuation; not, however, a valuation of one definite, individual,

---

[1] For the history both of the theory and concept of feeling compare: Wundt, *Grundz. d. Physiolog. Psych. Idem, Grundr. d. Psychol.*, pp. 35 ff.
Nahlowsky, *Das Gefühlsleben in seinen wesentlichen Erscheinungen.*
Ribot, *Psychologie der Gefühle.*
Lehmann, *Die Hauptgesetze des menschlichen Gefühlslebens.*
Villa, *Contemporary Psychology*, transl. by H. Manacorda (1903).

conscious content, but of the whole conscious situation at the moment, and, once again, with special reference to the question of acceptance or rejection.

Feeling, therefore, is an entirely *subjective* process, which may be in every respect independent of external stimuli, although chiming in with every sensation[1]. Even an 'indifferent' sensation possesses a 'feeling tone', namely, that of indifference, which again expresses a certain valuation. Hence feeling is also a kind of *judging*, differing, however, from an intellectual judgment, in that it does not aim at establishing an intellectual connection but is solely concerned with the setting up of a subjective criterion of acceptance or rejection. The valuation by feeling extends to *every* content of consciousness, of whatever kind it may be. When the intensity of feeling is increased an *affect* (v. Affect) results, which is a state of feeling accompanied by appreciable bodily innervations. Feeling is distinguished from affect by the fact that it gives rise to no perceptible physical innervations, *i.e.* just as much or as little as the ordinary thinking process.

Ordinary 'simple' feeling is *concrete* (*q.v.*), *i.e.* it is mixed up with other function-elements, frequently with sensation for instance. In this particular case we might term it *affective*, or (as in this book, for instance) *feeling-sensation*, by which a well-nigh inseparable blending of feeling with sensation elements is to be understood. This characteristic fusion is universally present where feeling is still an undifferentiated function, hence most evidently in the psyche of a neurotic with a differentiated thinking.

Although feeling is an independent function in itself, it may lapse into a state of dependence upon another function, upon thinking, for instance; whereby a feeling is produced which is merely kept as an accompaniment to

---

[1] On the distinction between feeling and sensation compare Wundt *Grunds. d. phys. Psychol.*, i, pp. 350 ff.

thinking, and is not repressed from consciousness only in so far as it fits in with the intellectual associations.

It is important to distinguish *abstract* feeling from ordinary concrete feeling. For, just as the abstract concept (*v.* Thinking) does away with the differences of the things embraced in it, so abstract feeling, by being raised above the differences of the individual feeling-values, establishes a 'mood', or state of feeling, which embraces and therewith abolishes the different individual values. Thus, just as thinking marshals the conscious contents under concepts, feeling arranges them according to their value. The more concrete the feeling, the more subjective and personal the value it confers; but the more abstract it is, the more general and objective is the value it bestows. Just as a completely abstract concept no longer coincides with the individuality and peculiarity of things, only revealing their universality and indistinctness, so too the completely abstract feeling no longer coincides with the individual instant and its feeling quality but only with the totality of all instants and their indistinctness. Accordingly, feeling like thinking is a *rational* function, since, as is shown by experience, values in general are bestowed according to the laws of reason, just as concepts in general are framed after the laws of reason.

Naturally the essence of feeling is not characterized by the foregoing definitions: they only serve to convey its external manifestations. The conceptual capacity of the intellect proves incapable of formulating the real nature of feeling in abstract terms, since thinking belongs to a category quite incommensurable with feeling. In fact, no basic psychological function whatsoever can be completely expressed by any other one. This circumstance is responsible for the fact that no intellectual definition will ever be able to render the specific character of feeling in any adequate measure. The mere fact that feelings are classified adds nothing to the understanding of their nature, because even the most exact classification will be able to yield only that intellectually seizable content to which or with which feelings appear connected, but without thereby apprehending the specific nature of feeling. Thus, however many varying and intellectually seizable classes of contents there may be, just as many feelings can be differentiated, without ever arriving at an exhaustive classification of feelings themselves; because, beyond every possible class of contents accessible to the intellect, there still exist feelings which are beyond intellectual classification. The very idea of a classification is intellectual and therefore incommensurable with the nature of feeling. Hence, we must content ourselves with our attempts to define the limits of the concept.

The nature of a feeling-valuation may be compared with intellectual apperception as an *apperception of value*. An *active* and a *passive* feeling-apperception can be distinguished. The passive feeling-act is characterized by the fact that a content excites or attracts the feeling; it compels a feeling-participation on the part of the subject. The active feeling-act, on the contrary, confers value from the subject—it is a deliberate evaluation of contents in accordance with feeling and not in accordance with intellectual intention. Hence active feeling is a *directed* function, an act of will, as for instance loving as opposed to being in love. This latter state would be *undirected*, passive feeling, as, indeed, the ordinary colloquial term suggests, since it describes the former as activity and the latter as a condition. Undirected feeling is *feeling-intuition*. Thus, in the stricter sense, only the active, directed feeling should be termed *rational* : the passive is definitely *irrational*, since it establishes values without voluntary participation, occasionally even against the subject's intention.

When the total attitude of the individual is orientated

by the function of feeling, we speak of a *feeling-type* (*v.* Type).

21. **Feeling-into** (Einfühlung) is an *introjection* (*q.v.*) of the object into the ego. For the fuller description of the concept of feeling-into, see text of Chapter vii (*v.* also Projection).

22. **Function**: By psychological function I understand a certain form of psychic activity that remains theoretically the same under varying circumstances. From the energic standpoint a function is a phenomenal form of libido (*q.v.*) which theoretically remains constant, in much the same way as physical force can be considered as the form or momentary manifestation of physical energy. I distinguish four basic functions in all, two rational and two irrational— viz. *thinking* and *feeling, sensation* and *intuition*. I can give no a priori reason for selecting just these four as basic functions; I can only point to the fact that this conception has shaped itself out of many years' experience.

I differentiate these functions from one another, because they are neither mutually relatable nor mutually reducible. The principle of thinking, for instance, is absolutely different from the principle of feeling, and so forth. I make a capital distinction between this concept of function and phantasy-activity, or reverie, because, to my mind, phantasying is a peculiar form of activity which can manifest itself in all the four functions.

In my view, both will and attention are entirely secondary psychic phenomena.

23. **Idea**: In this work the concept of idea is sometimes used to designate a certain psychological element intimately connected with what I term *image* (*q.v.*). The image may be either *personal* or *impersonal* in its origin. In the latter case, it is collective and is distinguished by mythological

qualities. I then term it *primordial image*. When, on the contrary, it has no mythological character, *i.e.* lacks the intuitive qualities and is merely collective, I speak of an idea. Accordingly I employ the term idea as something which expresses the meaning of a primordial image that has been abstracted or detached from the concretism of the image. In so far as the idea is an abstraction, it has the appearance of something derived, or developed, from elementary factors, a product of thinking. This is the sense, as something secondary and derived, in which it is regarded by Wundt[1] and many others. Since, however, the idea is merely the formulated meaning of a primordial image in which it was already *symbolically* represented, the essence of the idea is not merely derived, or produced, but, considered psychologically, it has an a priori existence as a given possibility of thought-connections in general. Hence, in accordance with its nature (not with its formulation), the idea is an a priori existing and determining psychological factor. In this sense Plato sees the idea as a primordial image of things, while Kant defines it as the "archetype of the use of the mind"; hence it is a transcendent concept which, as such, transcends the limit of experienceable things[2]. It is a concept demanded by reason, "whose object can never be met with in experience"[3]. Kant says:

" For, although we are bound to say of transcendent reasonal concepts *They are only ideas*, yet are we in no way justified in regarding them as superfluous and unreal. For, although no object can be determined by them, nevertheless fundamentally and unperceived they can serve the mind as canons for its extended and harmonious use, whereby it discerns no object *more acutely* than it would according to its own concepts, yet is guided in this

---

[1] Wundt, *Phil. Stud.*, vii, 13.
[2] *Critique of Pure Reason:* transl. by F. Max Müller (London: Macmillan, 1881).
[3] *Logic*, p. 140.

discernment in a better and broader approach. Not to mention the fact that they may, perhaps, bring about a transition from natural ideas to practical concepts, even providing moral ideas with a certain associative texture of the speculative findings of reason ".[1]

Schopenhauer says:

" By idea I understand every definite and established grade of the objectification of will, in so far as it is a thing-in-itself and, therefore, removed from multiplicity; such grades, moreover, are related to individual things as their eternal forms or prototypes ".[2]

With Schopenhauer, however, the idea is plastic in character, because he conceives it wholly in the sense of what I describe as primordial image; it is, however, indiscernible to the individual, revealing itself only to the "pure Subject of cognition", which is raised above will and individuality (§ 49).

Hegel completely hypostasizes the idea, and gives it the attribute of the only real existence. It is "the concept, the reality of the concept and the one-ness of both ".[3] It is "eternal generation ".[4]

Lasswitz regards the idea as a "law indicating the direction, in which our experience should develop". It is the " most certain and supreme reality ".[5]

With Cohen, the idea is the "self-consciousness of the concept", the "foundation" of being [6].

I do not wish to multiply further evidence to establish the primary nature of the idea. These quotations should sufficiently demonstrate that the idea is conceived also as a fundamental, a priori existent factor. It possesses this latter quality from its antecedent, the' primordial, symbolical image (*q.v.*). Its secondary nature of an abstract

[1] *Critique of Pure Reason*, p. 285.
[2] *World as Will and Idea*, transl. by Haldane and Kemp, vol. i, par. 25 (London: Kegan Paul & Co.)
[3] *Aesthetik*, i, 138. [4] *Logic*, iii, pp. 242 ff. [5] *Wirklichkeit*, pp. 152, 154. [6] *Logik*, pp. 14, 18.

and derived entity it receives from the rational elaboration to which the primordial image is subjected before it is made suitable for rational usage. Inasmuch as the primordial image is a constant autochthonic psychological factor repeating itself in all times and places, we might also, in a certain sense, say the same of the idea, although, on account of its rational nature, it is much more subject to modification by rational elaboration, which in its turn is strongly influenced by time and circumstance. It is this rational elaboration which gives it formulations corresponding with the spirit of the time. A few philosophers, by virtue of its derivation from the primordial image, ascribe a transcendent quality to it; this does not really belong to the idea as I conceive it, but rather to the primordial image, about which a timeless quality clings, established as it is from all time as an integral and inherent constituent of the human mind. Its quality of independence is derived also from the primordial image which was never made and is constantly present, appearing so spontaneously in perception that we might also say it strives independently towards its own realization, since it is sensed by the mind as an actively determining power. Such a view, however, is not general, but presumably a question of attitude (*v.* Chap. vii). The idea is a psychological factor which not only determines thought but, in the form of a practical idea, also conditions feeling. As a general rule, however, I only employ the term idea, either when I am speaking of the determination of thought in a thinking-type, or when denoting the determination of feeling in a feeling-type. On the other hand, it is terminologically correct to speak of determination by the primordial image, when we are dealing with an a priori determination of an undifferentiated function.

The dual nature of the idea, as something that is at the same time both primary and secondary, is responsible for the fact that the expression is occasionally used promiscuously with 'primordial image'. For the introverted attitude the idea is the primum movens; for the extraverted, it is a product.

24. **Identification**: This term connotes a psychological process in which the personality is either partially or totally *dissimilated* (*v.* Assimilation) from itself. Identification is an estrangement of the subject from himself in favour of an object in which the subject is, to a certain extent, disguised. For example, identification with the father practically signifies an adoption of the ways and manners of the father, as though the son were the same as the father and not a separate individual. *Identification* is distinguished from *imitation* by the fact that identification is an *unconscious* imitation, whereas imitation is a conscious copying.

Imitation is an indispensable expedient for the developing personality of youth. It has a beneficial effect so long as it does not merely serve as a means of accommodation, thus hindering the development of a suitable individual method. Similarly, identification may be progressive in so far as the individual way is not yet available. But, whenever a better individual possibility presents itself, identification manifests its pathological character by proving henceforth just as great a hindrance as before it was unwittingly supporting and beneficial. For now it has a dissociating influence, dividing the subject into two mutually estranged personalities. Identification is not always related to persons but also to things (for instance, a spiritual movement, or a business, etc.) and to psychological functions. In fact, the latter case is particularly important (*cf.* Chap. ii.). Identification, in such a case, leads to the formation of a secondary character, whereby the individual is so identified with his most developed function that he is very largely or even wholly removed from his original character-foundation, so that his real individuality goes into the unconscious. This is nearly always the rule with men who possess one differentiated function. It is, in fact, a necessary transitional stage on the way to individuation.

Identification with the parents or nearest members of the family is a normal phenomenon, in so far as it coincides with the a priori or pre-existing *familial identity*. In such a case, it is better not to speak of identification but of identity, a term which corresponds with the actual matter of fact. For identification with members of the family is to be distinguished from identity by the fact, that it is not given as an a priori fact, but arises secondarily only through the following process:—As the individual is developing out of the original familial identity, his process of adaptation and development brings him upon an obstacle which cannot immediately be mastered; a damming-up of libido, accordingly, takes place and gradually seeks a regressive outlet. The regression brings about a revivification of earlier states, among others the state of familial identity. The identification with the members of the family corresponds with this regressive revival of a state of identity which has actually almost been overcome. Every identification with persons takes place in this way. Identification has always a purpose, namely, to obtain an advantage, push aside an obstacle, or solve a task after the manner of another individual.

25. Identity: I use the term identity in the case of a psychological equality. It is always an unconscious phenomenon, since a conscious equality would necessarily involve the consciousness of two similar things—hence immediately presupposing a separation of subject and object, whereby the phenomenon of identity would be already resolved. Psychological identity presupposes its unconsciousness. It is a characteristic of the primitive mentality, and is the actual basis of "participation mystique", which, in reality, is merely a relic of the original psychological non-differentiation of subject and object—hence of the primordial unconscious state. It is, therefore, a characteristic of the early infantile mental condition. Finally, it is also a characteristic of the unconscious content in adult civilized man, which, in so far as it has not become a conscious content, remains permanently in the state of identity with objects. From an *identity* with the parents proceeds the identification (*q.v.*) with them; similarly, the possibility of *projection* and *introjection* (*q.v.*) depends upon identity. Identity is primarily an unconscious equality with the object. It is neither *an assumption of equality* nor an *identification*, but an a priori equality which has never appeared as an object of consciousness. Upon identity is founded the naïve presumption that the psychology of one man is the same as that of another, that the same motive is universally valid, that what is agreeable to me must also be obviously pleasurable for others, and that what is immoral to me must also be immoral for others, and so forth. This state of identity is responsible also for the almost universal desire to correct in others what most demands change in oneself. Upon identity rests the possibility of suggestion and psychic contamination. Identity appears with special distinctness in pathological cases, as for instance in paranoic delusions of 'influencing' and persecution, where the patient's own subjective contents are presumed, as a matter of course, to proceed from others. But identity means also the possibility of a conscious collectivism and a conscious social attitude, which found their loftiest expression in the Christian ideal of brotherly love.

26. Image: When I speak of image in this book, I do not mean the psychic reflection of the external object, but a concept essentially derived from a poetic figure of speech; namely, the *phantasy-image*, a presentation which is only indirectly related to the perception of the external object. This image depends much more upon unconscious phantasy-activity, and as the product of such activity it appears more or less abruptly in consciousness, somewhat in the nature of a vision or hallucination but without possessing the pathological character of similar products occurring in a morbid clinical picture. The image has the psychological character of a phantasy-presentation, and never the quasi-real character of hallucination, *i.e.* it never takes the place of reality, and its character of 'inner' image always distinguishes it from sensuous reality. As a rule, it lacks all projection into space, although in exceptional cases it can also appear to a certain extent externalized.

Such a mode of appearance must be termed *archaic* (*q.v.*) when it is not primarily pathological, though in no way does this do away with its archaic character. Upon the primitive level, *i.e.* in the mentality of the primitives, the inner image is easily projected into space as a visual or auditory hallucination without being a pathological phenomenon.

Although, as a rule, no reality-value belongs to the image, its significance for the psychic life is often thereby enhanced, *i.e.* a greater *psychological* value clings to it, representing an inner 'reality' which occasionally far outweighs the physical importance of 'external' reality. In such a case, the orientation of the individual is concerned less with adaptation to reality than with an adaptation to the inner claims.

The inner image is a complex factor, compounded of the most varied material from the most varied sources.

It is no conglomerate, however, but an integral product, with its own autonomous purpose. The image is a concentrated *expression of the total psychic situation*, not merely, nor even pre-eminently, of unconscious contents pure and simple. It undoubtedly does express the contents of the unconscious, though not the whole of its contents in general, but merely those momentarily constellated. This constellation is the product of the specific activity of the unconscious on the one hand, and of the momentary conscious situation on the other: this always stimulates the activity of associated subliminal material at the same time as it also inhibits the irrelevant. Accordingly the image is equally an expression of the unconscious as of the conscious situation of the moment. The interpretation of its meaning, therefore, can proceed exclusively neither from the unconscious nor from the conscious, but only from their reciprocal relation.

I term the image *primordial*[1] when it possesses an archaic character. I speak of its archaic character when the image is in striking unison with familiar mythological motives. In this case it expresses material primarily derived from the collective unconscious (*q.v.*), while, at the same time, it indicates that the momentary conscious situation is influenced not so much from the side of the personal as from the collective.

A *personal* image has neither archaic character nor collective significance, but expresses contents of the personal unconscious and a personally conditioned, conscious situation.

The primordial image (elsewhere also termed the 'archetype'[2]) is always collective, *i.e.* it is at least common to entire nations or epochs. In all probability

[1] Following an expression used by J. Burckhardt. Cf. also Jung, *Psychology of the Unconscious*, p. 41.
[2] Jung, *Instinct and the Unconscious* (*Journal of Psychology*, vol x, 1).

the most important mythological motives are common to all times and races; I have, in fact, demonstrated a whole series of motives from Grecian mythology in the dreams and phantasies of thoroughbred negroes suffering from mental disorders[1].

The primordial image is a mnemic deposit, an *imprint* ("engramm"—Semon), which has arisen through a condensation of innumerable, similar processes. It is primarily a precipitate or deposit, and therefore a typical basic form of a certain ever-recurring psychic experience. As a mythological motive, therefore, it is a constantly effective and continually recurring expression which is either awakened, or appropriately formulated, by certain psychic experiences. The primordial image, then, is the psychic expression of an anatomically and physiologically determined disposition. If one supports the view that a definite anatomical structure is the product of environmental conditions upon living matter, the primordial image in its constant and universal distribution corresponds with an equally universal and continuous external influence, which must, therefore, have the character of a natural law. In this way, the myth could be related to Nature (as, for instance, the solar myths to the daily rising and setting of the sun, or to the equally obvious seasonal changes). But we should still be left with the question as to why the sun, for instance, with its obvious changes, should not appear frank and unveiled as a content of the myth. The fact that the sun, or the moon, or meteorological processes do, at least, appear allegorized, points, however, to an independent collaboration of the psyche, which in this case can be no mere product or imitation of environmental conditions. Then whence this capacity of the psyche to gain a standpoint outside sense-perception?

---

[1] A remarkable example of an archaic image is quoted in Jung, *Psychol. of the Unconscious*, p. 108.

Whence its capacity for achieving something beyond or different from the verdict of the senses? We are forced to assume, therefore, that the given brain-structure does not owe its particular nature merely to the effect of surrounding conditions, but also and just as much to the peculiar and autonomous quality of living matter, *i.e.* to a fundamental law of life. The given constitution of the organism, therefore, is on the one hand a product of outer conditions, while on the other it is inherently determined by the nature of living matter. Accordingly, the primordial image is just as undoubtedly related to certain manifest, ever-renewing and therefore constantly effective Nature-processes as it is to certain inner determinants of the mental life and to life in general. The organism confronts light with a new formation, the eye, and the psyche meets the process of Nature with a symbolical image, which apprehends the Nature-process just as the eye catches the light. And in the same way as the eye bears witness to the peculiar and independent creative activity of living matter, the primordial image expresses the unique and unconditioned creative power of the mind.

The primordial image, therefore, is a recapitulatory expression of the living process. It gives a co-ordinating meaning both to the sensuous and to the inner mental perceptions, which at first appear without either order or connection; thereby liberating psychic energy from its bondage to sheer uncomprehended perception. But it also links up the energies, released through the perception of stimuli, to a definite meaning, which serves to guide action along the path which corresponds with this meaning. It loosens unavailable, dammed-up energy, since it always refers the mind to Nature, transforming sheer natural instinct into mental forms.

The primordial image is the preliminary stage of the *idea* (*q.v.*) its maternal soil. By detaching from it that concretism which is peculiar and necessary to the primordial image, the reason develops the concept—*i.e.* the idea—which, moreover, is distinguished from every other concept by the fact that it is not only given by experience but is actually inferred as underlying all experience. The idea possesses this quality from the primordial image, which as the expression of a specific cerebral structure also imparts a definite form to every experience.

The degree of psychological efficacy belonging to the primordial image is determined by the attitude of the individual. When the general attitude is introverted as a result of the withdrawal of libido from the outer object, a reinforcement of the inner object or idea naturally takes place. This produces a very intensive development of ideas along the line unconsciously traced out by the primordial image. In this way the primordial image indirectly reaches the surface. The further course of intellectual development leads to the idea, which is merely the primordial image at the stage of intellectual formulation. Only the development of the counter-function can take the idea further, *i.e.* when once the idea is apprehended intellectually, it strives to become effective in life. Hence it attracts feeling, which, however, in such a case is much less differentiated, and therefore more concretistic, than thinking. Thus the feeling is impure, and because undifferentiated, is still fused with the unconscious. Hence the individual is unable to reconcile feeling so-constituted with the idea. In such a case, the primordial image, appearing in *symbolic* form in the inner field of vision, embraces, by virtue of its concrete nature, the feeling existing in an undifferentiated, concrete state; but at the same time, by virtue of its intrinsic significance, it also embraces the idea, of which indeed it is the mother—thus reconciling idea with feeling. Hence the primordial image appears in the rôle of mediator, once again proving its redeeming efficacy, a power it has always possessed in the various religions. What Schopenhauer says of the idea, therefore, I would prefer to apply to the primordial image, since the idea—as I have elsewhere observed under 'Idea'—should not be regarded as something wholly and unconditionally a priori, but also as something derived and developed from antecedents. When, therefore, in the following excerpt I am quoting the words of Schopenhauer, I must ask the reader to replace the word 'idea' in the text by 'primordial image': he will then be able to understand my meaning:[1]

"The idea is never known by the individual as such, but only by the man who is exalted above all willing and above all individuality to the pure Subject of knowledge: thus it is attainable only by the genius, or by the man who has achieved mainly through the works of genius an elevation of his pure gift of cognition into a temper akin to genius: it is, therefore, not absolutely, but only conditionally, communicable, since the idea conceived and reproduced in an artistic creation, for instance, only appeals to every man according to his intellectual powers", etc.
"The idea is unity split up into multiplicity by virtue of the temporal and spatial form of our intuitive apprehension."
"The concept is like an inanimate vehicle, in which the things one deposits lie side by side, but from which no more can be taken out than was put in: the idea, on the contrary, develops within the man who has embraced it conceptions which in relation to its homonymous concept are new: it is like a living, self-developing organism endowed with creative force, bringing forth something that was never put into it."

Schopenhauer clearly discerned that the 'idea', *i.e.* the primordial image according to my definition, cannot be reached in the way that a concept or 'idea' is established ('idea' according to Kant corresponds with a "concept derived from notions"[2]), but that there pertains to it an

---
[1] Schopenhauer, *The World as Will and Idea*, vol. i, § 49.
[2] Kant, *Critique of Pure Reason*.

element quite foreign to the formulating reason, rather like Schopenhauer's "temper akin to genius", which simply means a state of feeling. For one only reaches the primordial image from the idea because of the fact that the way leading to the idea is carried on over the summit of the idea into the counter-function, feeling.

The primordial image has advantage over the clarity of the idea in its vitality. It is a self-living organism, "endowed with creative force"; for the primordial image is an inherited organization of psychic energy, a rooted system, which is not only an expression of the energic process but also a possibility for its operation. In a sense, it characterizes the way in which the energic process from earliest time has always run its unvarying course, while at the same time enabling a perpetual repetition of the law-determined course to take place; since it provides just that character of apprehension or psychic grasp of situations which continually yields a further continuation of life. It is, therefore, the necessary counterpart of *instinct*, which is an appropriate form of action also presupposing a grasp of the momentary situation that is both purposeful and suitable. This apprehension of the given situation is vouchsafed by the a priori existing image. It represents the practicable formula without which the apprehension of a new state of affairs would be impossible.

27. Individual ('unique-being'): The psychological individual is characterized by its peculiar, and in certain respects, unique psychology. The peculiar character of the individual psyche appears less in its elements than in its complex formations.

The psychological individual, or individuality, has an a priori unconscious existence, but it exists consciously only in so far as a consciousness of its peculiar nature is present, *i.e.* in so far as there exists a conscious distinctiveness from other individuals.

The psychic individuality is also given a priori as a correlate of the physical individuality, although, as observed, it is at first unconscious. A conscious process of differentiation (*q.v.*) is required to bring the individuality to consciousness, *i.e.* to raise it out of the state of identity with the object. The identity of the individuality with the object is synonymous with its unconsciousness. There is no psychological individual present if the individuality is unconscious, but merely a collective psychology of consciousness. In such a case, the unconscious individuality appears identical with the object, *i.e.* projected upon the object. The object, in consequence, possesses too great a value and is too powerful a determinant.

28. **Individuality**: By individuality I understand the peculiarity and singularity of the individual in every psychological respect. Everything is individual that is not collective, everything in fact that pertains only to one and not to a larger group of individuals. Individuality can hardly be described as belonging to the psychological elements, but rather to their peculiar and unique grouping and combination (*v.* Individual.)

29. **Individuation**: The concept of individuation plays no small rôle in our psychology. In general, it is the process of forming and specializing the individual nature; in particular, it is the development of the psychological individual as a differentiated being from the general, collective psychology. Individuation, therefore, is a *process of differentiation*, having for its goal the development of the individual personality.

Individuation is, to this extent, a natural necessity, inasmuch as its hindrance, by an extensive or actually exclusive levelling to collective standards, involves a definite injury to individual vital activity. But individuality, both physically and physiologically, is already given; hence it also expresses itself psychologically. An essential check to the individuality, therefore, involves an artificial mutilation. It is at once clear that a social group consisting of deformed individuals cannot for long be a healthy and prosperous institution; since only that society which can preserve its internal union and its collective values, while at the same time granting the greatest possible freedom to the individual, has any prospect of enduring vitality. Since the individual is not only a single, separate being but, by his very existence, also presupposes a collective relationship, the process of individuation must clearly lead to a more intensive and universal collective solidarity, and not to mere *isolation*.

The psychological process of individuation is clearly bound up with the so-called *transcendent function* (*q.v.*), since it alone can provide that individual line of development which would be quite unattainable upon the ways dictated by the collective norm (*v.* Symbol).

Under no circumstances can individuation be the unique goal of psychological education. Before individuation can be taken for a goal, the educational aim of adaptation to the necessary minimum of collective standards must first be attained. A plant which is to be brought to the fullest possible unfolding of its particular character must first of all be able to grow in the soil wherein it is planted.

Individuation always finds itself more or less in opposition to the collective norm, since it means a separation and differentiation from the general, and a building up of the particular; not, however, a particularity especially *sought*, but one with an a priori foundation in the psyche. The opposition to the collective norm, however, is only apparent, since on closer examination the individual standpoint is found to be *differently* orientated, but not *antagonistic* to the collective norm. The individual way can never be actually opposed to the collective norm, because the opposite to the latter could only be a contrary *norm*. But the individual way is never a norm. A norm arises out of the totality of individual ways, and can have a right to existence, and a beneficial effect, only when individual ways, which from time to time have a need to orientate to a norm, are already in existence. A norm serves no purpose when it possesses absolute validity. An actual conflict with the collective norm takes place only when an individual way is raised to a norm, which, moreover, is the fundamental aim of extreme individualism. Such a purpose is, of course, pathological and entirely opposed to life. It has, accordingly, nothing to do with individuation, which, though certainly concerned with the individual by-path, precisely on that account also needs the norm for its orientation towards society, and for the vitally necessary solidarity of the individual with society. Hence individuation leads to a natural appreciation of the collective norm, whereas to an exclusively collective orientation of life the norm becomes increasingly superfluous: whereupon real morality goes to pieces. *The more completely a man's life is moulded and shaped by the collective norm, the greater is his individual immorality.*

Individuation is practically the same as the development of consciousness out of the original *state of identity* (*v.* Identity). Hence it signifies an extension of the sphere of consciousness, an enriching of the conscious psychological life.

30. Inferior Function: This term is used to denote the function that remains in arrear in the process of differentiation. For experience shows that it is hardly possible—owing to the inclemency of general conditions

—for anyone to bring all his psychological functions to simultaneous development. The very conditions of society enforce a man to apply himself first and foremost to the differentiation of that function with which he is either most gifted by Nature, or which provides his most effective means for social success. Very frequently, indeed as a general rule, a man identifies himself more or less completely with the most favoured, hence the most developed, function. It is this circumstance which gives rise to psychological types. But, as a consequence of such a one-sided process of development, one or more functions necessarily remain backward in development. Such functions, therefore, may be fittingly termed 'inferior' in the psychological, though not in the psycho-pathological, sense, since these retarded functions are in no way morbid but merely backward as compared with the more favoured function. As a rule, therefore, the inferior function normally remains conscious, although in neurosis it lapses either partially or principally into the unconscious. For, inasmuch as too great a share of the libido is intercepted by the favoured function, the inferior function undergoes a regressive development, *i.e.* it returns to its earlier archaic state, therewith becoming incompatible with the conscious and favoured function. When a function that should normally be conscious relapses into the unconscious, the specific energy adhering to this function is also delivered over to the unconscious. A natural function, such as feeling, possesses its own inherent energy: it is a definitely organized living system, which, under no circumstances, can be wholly robbed of its energy.

Through the unconscious condition of the inferior function, its energy-remainder is transferred into the unconscious; whereupon the unconscious becomes unnaturally activated. The result of such activity is a production of phantasy at a level corresponding with the archaic, submerged condition, to which the inferior function has now sunk. Hence an analytical release of such a function from the unconscious can take place only by retrieving those same unconscious phantasy-images which have come to life through the activation of the unconscious function. The process of making such phantasies conscious also brings the inferior function to consciousness, thus providing it with a new possibility of development.

31. **Instinct**: When I speak of instinct, whether in this work or elsewhere, I therewith denote what is commonly understood by this word: namely, an impulsion towards certain activities. The impulsion can proceed from an outer or an inner stimulus, which releases the instinctive mechanism either psychically, or through organic roots which lie outside the sphere of psychic causality. Every psychic phenomenon is *instinctive* which proceeds from no cause postulated by the will, but from dynamic impulsion, irrespective of whether such impulsion has its origin directly in organic, therefore extra-psychic, sources, or is essentially conditioned by the energies whose actual release is effected by the purpose of the will—with the qualification, in the latter case, that the resulting product exceeds the effect intended by the will. According to my view, all those psychic processes over whose energies the conscious has no disposal come within the concept of instinct[1]. Thus, according to this view, affects (*q.v.*) belong to the instinctive processes just as much as to the processes of feeling (*v.* Feeling). Psychic processes which, under ordinary circumstances, are functions of the will (thus entirely subject to conscious control), can, in abnormal cases, become instinctive processes through a linking up with unconscious energy. This phenomenon always occurs whenever the conscious

[1] Cf. Jung, *Instinct and the Unconscious* (*Journal of Psychology*, vol. x, 1)

sphere is restricted either by repressions of incompatible contents or where, as a result of fatigue, intoxication, or pathological cerebral processes in general, an "abaissement du niveau mentale" (Janet) takes place—where, in a word, the conscious either does not yet control or no longer commands the most strongly toned processes.

Those processes, which were once conscious in an individual but which have gradually become *automatized*, I might term automatic instead of instinctive processes. Normally, they do not even behave as instincts, since under normal circumstances they never appear as impulsions. They do that only when they receive a tributary of energy which is foreign to them.

32. Intellect: I call *directed thinking* (*q.v.*), intellect.

33. Introjection : This term was introduced by Avenarius[1] to correspond with *projection*. The *transveying* therewith intended, of a subjective content into an object is, however, just as well expressed by the concept of projection. It would, therefore, be as well to retain the term 'projection' for this process. Ferenczi has now defined the concept of introjection as the opposite of 'projection', namely, as an 'indrawing' of the object within the subjective circle of interest, while 'projection' means a translation of subjective contents into the object[2]. "Whereas the paranoic expels from his ego emotions which have become disagreeable, the neurotic helps himself to as large a portion of the outer world as his ego can ingest, and makes this an object of unconscious phantasies." The former mechanism is projection, the latter introjection. Introjection is a sort of "diluting process", an "expansion of the circle of interest". According to Ferenczi, introjection

[1] *Menschl. Weltbegr.*, pp. 25 ff.
[2] Ferenczi, *Introjection and Transference* (*Contributions to Psychoanalysis :* transl. by E. Jones. Boston : R. Badger).

is also a normal process. Psychologically, therefore, it is a process of assimilation (*q.v.*), while projection is a process of dissimilation. Introjection signifies an adjustment of the object to the subject, while projection involves a discrimination of the object from the subject, by means of a subjective content transveyed into the object.

Introjection is an extraverting process, since for this adjustment to the object a 'feeling-into', or possession of, the object is necessary.

A *passive* and an *active* introjection may be discriminated: to the former belong the transference-processes in the treatment of the neuroses and, in general, all cases in which the object exercises an unconditional attraction upon the subject; while 'feeling-into', regarded as a process of adaptation, should belong to the latter form.

34. Introversion means a turning inwards of the libido (*q.v.*), whereby a negative relation of subject to object is expressed. Interest does not move towards the object, but recedes towards the subject. Everyone whose attitude is introverted thinks, feels, and acts in a way that clearly demonstrates that the subject is the chief factor of motivation while the object at most receives only a secondary value. Introversion may possess either a more intellectual or more emotional character, just as it can be characterized by either intuition or sensation. Introversion is *active*, when the subject *wills* a certain seclusion in face of the object; it is *passive* when the subject is unable to restore again to the object the libido which is streaming back from it. When introversion is habitual, one speaks of an *introverted type* (*v.* Type).

35. Intuition (from *intueri* = to look into or upon) is, according to my view, a basic psychological function (*v.* Function). It is that psychological function which transmits perceptions *in an unconscious way*. Everything, whether outer or inner objects or their associations, can be the object of this perception. Intuition has this peculiar quality: it is neither sensation, nor feeling, nor intellectual conclusion, although it may appear in any of these forms. Through intuition any one content is presented as a complete whole, without our being able to explain or discover in what way this content has been arrived at. Intuition is a kind of instinctive apprehension, irrespective of the nature of its contents. Like sensation (*q.v.*) it is an *irrational* (*q.v.*) perceptive function. Its contents, like those of sensation, have the character of being given, in contrast to the 'derived' or 'deduced' character of feeling and thinking contents. Intuitive cognition, therefore, possesses an intrinsic character of certainty and conviction which enabled Spinoza to uphold the 'scientia intuitiva' as the highest form of cognition.[1] Intuition has this quality in common with sensation, whose physical foundation is the ground and origin of its certitude. In the same way, the certainty of intuition depends upon a definite psychic matter of fact, of whose origin and state of readiness, however, the subject was quite unconscious.

Intuition appears either in a *subjective* or an *objective* form: the former is a perception of unconscious psychic facts whose origin is essentially subjective; the latter is a perception of facts which depend upon subliminal perceptions of the object and upon the thoughts and feelings occasioned thereby.

Concrete and *abstract* forms of intuition may be distinguished according to the degree of participation on the part of sensation. Concrete intuition carries perceptions which are concerned with the actuality of things, while abstract intuition transmits the perceptions of ideational associations. Concrete intuition is a reactive process, since

[1] Similarly Bergson.

it follows directly from the given circumstances; whereas abstract intuition, like abstract sensation, necessitates a certain element of direction, an act of will or a purpose.

In common with sensation, intuition is a characteristic of infantile and primitive psychology. As against the strength and sudden appearance of sense-impression it transmits the perception of mythological images, the precursors of *ideas* (*q.v.*).

Intuition maintains a compensatory function to sensation, and, like sensation, it is the maternal soil from which thinking and feeling are developed in the form of rational functions. Intuition is an irrational function, notwithstanding the fact that many intuitions may subsequently be split up into their component elements, whereby their origin and appearance can also be made to harmonize with the laws of reason. Everyone whose general attitude is orientated by the principle of intuition, *i.e.* perception by way of the unconscious, belongs to the *intuitive type*[1] (*v.* Type).

According to the manner in which intuition is employed, whether directed within in the service of cognition and inner perception or without in the service of action and accomplishment, the introverted and extraverted intuitive types can be differentiated.

In abnormal cases a well-marked coalescence with, and an equally great determination by, the contents of the collective unconscious declares itself: this may give the intuitive type an extremely irrational and unintelligible appearance.

36. **Irrational**: As I make use of this term it does not denote something contrary to *reason*, but something outside the province of reason, whose essence, therefore, is not established by reason.

[1] The merit of having discovered the existence of this type is due to Miss M. Moltzer.

T*

Elementary facts belong to this category, *e.g.* that the earth has a moon, that chlorine is an element, that the greatest density of water is found to be 4.0 centigrade. An *accident* is also irrational in spite of the fact that it may sustain a subsequent rational explanation.

The irrational is a factor of existence which may certainly be pushed back indefinitely by an increasingly elaborate and complicated rational explanation, but in so doing the explanation finally becomes so extravagant and overdone that it passes comprehension, thus reaching the limits of rational thought long before it can ever span the whole world with the laws of reason. A completely rational explanation of an actually existing object (not one that is merely postulated) is a Utopian ideal. Only an object that has been postulated can also be completely explained on rational grounds, since it has never contained anything beyond what was postulated by rational thinking. Empirical science also postulates rationally limited objects, since its deliberate exclusion of the accidental allows no consideration of the real object as a whole; hence empirical observation is always limited to that same portion of the object which has been selected for rational consideration. Thus, both thinking and feeling as *directed functions* are rational. When these functions are concerned not with a rationally determined choice of objects, or with the qualities and relations of objects, but with the incidental perceptions which the real object never lacks, they at once lose the quality of direction, and therewith something of their rational character, because they accept the accidental. They begin to be irrational. That thinking or feeling which is directed according to accidental perceptions, and is therefore irrational, is either *intuitive* or *sensational*. Both *intuition* and *sensation* are psychological functions which achieve their functional fulfilment in the *absolute perception* of occurrences in general. Hence, in accordance with their nature, their attitude must be set towards every possibility and what is absolutely accidental; they must, therefore, entirely forgo rational direction. Accordingly I term them irrational functions, in contrast to thinking and feeling, which reach perfection only when in complete accord with the laws of reason.

Although the irrational, as such, can never become the object of a science, nevertheless for a practical psychology it is of the greatest importance that the irrational factor should be correctly appraised. For practical psychology stirs up many problems that altogether elude the rational solution and can be settled only irrationally, *i.e.* they can be solved only in a way that has no correspondence with the laws of reason. An exclusive presumption or expectation that for every conflict there must also exist a possibility of rational adjustment may well prove an insurmountable obstacle to a real solution of an irrational character. (*v.* Rational).

37. **Libido**: In my view, this concept is synonymous with *psychic energy* [1]. Psychic energy is the intensity of the psychic process—its *psychological value*. By this I do not mean to imply any imparted value, whether moral, æsthetic, or intellectual; the psychological value is simply conditioned by its *determining* power, which is manifested in definite psychic operations ('effects'). Neither do I understand libido as a psychic *force*, a misunderstanding that has led many critics astray. I do not hypostasize the concept of energy, but employ it as a concept denoting intensity or value. The question as to whether or no a specific psychic force exists has nothing to do with the concept of libido.

Frequently I employ the expression libido promiscuously

[1] Jung, *The Psychology of the Unconscious*, p. 127. *Idem*, *The Conception and the Genetic Theory of Libido*, Pt. ii, ch. 2, p. 139.

with 'energy'. My justification for calling psychic energy libido has been fully gone into in the works referred to in the footnote.

38. The Objective Plane: When I speak of interpretation upon the objective plane, I am referring to that view of a dream or phantasy by which the persons or conditions appearing therein are referred to objectively real persons or conditions; whereas I speak of the *subjective plane* (q.v.) when the persons and conditions appearing in a dream are referred exclusively to subjective elements. The Freudian view of the dream moves almost exclusively upon the objective level, inasmuch as dream-wishes are interpreted as referring to real objects, or are related to sexual processes which fall within the physiological, and therefore extra-psychological, sphere.

39. Orientation: This term is used to denote the general principle of an attitude (*q.v.*). Every attitude is orientated by a certain point-of-view, no matter whether that point-of-view be conscious or unconscious. A so-called power-attitude is orientated by the view-point of ego-power exerted against oppressive influences and conditions. A thinking attitude is orientated by the principle of logic as its supreme law; a sensational attitude by the sensuous perception of given facts.

40. "Participation Mystique": This term originates with Lévy-Bruhl[1]. It connotes a peculiar kind of psychological connection with the object wherein the subject is unable to differentiate himself clearly from the object to which he is bound by an immediate relation that can only be described as partial identity. This identity is based upon an a priori one-ness of subject and object. "Partici-

[1] Lévy-Bruhl, *Les fonctions mentales dans les sociétés inférieures* (Paris, 1912).

pation mystique", therefore, is a vestigial remainder of this primordial condition. It does not apply to the whole subject-object relation, but only to certain cases in which the phenomenon of this peculiar relatedness appears. It is, of course, a phenomenon that is best observed among the primitives; but it occurs not at all infrequently among civilized men, although not with the same range or intensity. Among civilized peoples it usually happens between persons—and only seldom between a person and thing. In the former case it is a so-called state of transference, in which the object (as a general rule) obtains a sort of magical, *i.e.* unconditional, influence over the subject. In the latter case it is a question of a similar influence on the part of a thing, or else a kind of identification with a thing or the idea of a thing.

41. **Phantasy**: By phantasy I understand two different things, namely, (1) *phantasm* and (2) *Imaginative activity*. In my writings the context always shows which of these meanings is intended. When the term is used to denote *phantasm*, it represents a complex that is distinguished from other complexes by the fact that it corresponds with no actual external state of affairs. Although a phantasm may originally be based upon the memory-images of actual experiences, its content corresponds with no external reality; it is merely the output of the creative psychic activity, a manifestation or product of the combination of psychic elements. In so far as psychic energy can be submitted to voluntary direction, phantasy may also be consciously and deliberately produced, as a whole or at least in part. In the former case, it is merely a combination of conscious elements. But such a case is only an artificial experiment of purely theoretical importance. In actual everyday psychological experience, phantasy is either released by an expectant, intuitive attitude, or appears as an

involuntary irruption of unconscious contents into consciousness.

We must differentiate between *active* and *passive* phantasy. Active phantasies are called forth by intuition, *i.e.* by an attitude directed to the perception of unconscious contents in which the libido immediately invests all the elements emerging from the unconscious, and, by means of association with parallel material, brings them to definition and plastic form. Passive phantasies without any antecedent or accompanying intuitive attitude appear from the outset in plastic form in the presence of a wholly passive attitude on the part of the cognizing subject. Such phantasies belong to the category of psychic "automatismes" (Janet). Naturally these latter can occur only as the result of a relative dissociation of the psyche, since their occurrence presupposes the withdrawal of an essential sum of energy from conscious control with a corresponding activation of unconscious material. Thus the vision of Saul presupposes an unconscious acceptance of Christianity, though the fact had escaped his conscious insight.

It is probable that passive phantasy always springs from an unconscious process antithetically related to consciousness, but one which assembles approximately the same amount of energy as the conscious attitude, whence also its capacity for breaking through the latter's resistance.

Active phantasy, on the contrary, owes its existence not merely to a onesided, intensive, and antithetic unconscious process, but just as much to the propensity of the conscious attitude for taking up the indications or fragments of relatively lightly-toned unconscious associations, and developing them into complete plasticity by association with parallel elements. In the case of active phantasy, then, it is not necessarily a question of a dissociated psychic state, but rather of a positive participation of consciousness.

Whereas the passive form of phantasy not infrequently bears the stamp of morbidity or at least some trace of abnormality, active phantasy belongs to the highest form of psychic activity. For here, in a converging stream, flow the conscious and unconscious personality of the subject into a common and reconciling product. A phantasy thus framed may be the supreme expression of the unity of an individual; it may even create the individual by the consummate expression of its unity. (Cf. Schiller's concept of the "æsthetic disposition"). As a general rule, passive phantasy is never the expression of an individuality that has achieved unity, since, as already observed, it presupposes a considerable degree of dissociation, which in its turn can result only from an equally strong opposition between the conscious and the unconscious. Hence the phantasy that breaks through into consciousness as the result of such a state, can never be the perfected expression of a united individuality, but only the prevailing standpoint of the unconscious personality. The life of St Paul is a good example of this: his conversion to the Christian faith corresponded with an acceptance of the hitherto unconscious standpoint and a repression of his previous anti-Christian point of view which latter soon became noticeable in his hysterical fits. Hence, passive phantasy must always require a conscious *criticism*, if it is not to substantiate the one-sided standpoint of the unconscious antithesis. Whereas active phantasy, as the product, on the one hand of a conscious attitude which is *not* opposed to the unconscious, and, on the other, of unconscious processes which do not maintain an antithetic so much as a compensatory relation to consciousness, does not require this criticism, but merely *understanding*.

As with the dream (which is merely passive phantasy) a *manifest* and a *latent* meaning must be distinguished also in phantasy. The former results from the immediate perception of the phantasy-image, and the immediate statement of the complex represented by the phantasy. Frequently, however, the manifest meaning hardly deserves the name, although it is always far more developed in phantasy than in the dream; probably this arises from the fact that the dream-phantasy usually requires no particular energy wherewith to make an effective opposition to the feeble resistance of the sleeping consciousness; whence it also follows that few antagonistic and only rather slight compensatory tendencies can obtain representation. Waking phantasy, on the other hand, must command a considerable sum of energy in order to overcome the inhibition proceeding from the conscious attitude.

Hence, for this to take place, the unconscious antithesis must already be very important before its entrance into consciousness can become possible. If it consisted only in vague and hardly seizable indications, it would never be able so to divert conscious attention (conscious libido) upon itself as effectually to interrupt the associated continuity of consciousness. Hence the unconscious content is dependent upon a very strong inner connection, which reveals itself in a manifest meaning. The manifest meaning always has the character of a plastic and concrete process, which, on account of its objective unreality, can never satisfy the conscious demand for understanding. Hence another signification, in other words, an *interpretation*, or latent meaning, has to be sought. Although the existence of a latent meaning of phantasy is by no means certain, and although nothing stands in the way of an eventual challenge of the whole possibility of a latent meaning, yet the demand for a satisfying understanding is motive enough for a thorough-going investigation. This investigation of the latent meaning may be purely *causal*, inquiring into the psychological causes of the existence of the phantasy.

DEFINITIONS

Such an interrogation leads, on the one hand, to the more remote causes of the phantasy in the distant past, and, on the other, to the substantiation of the instinctive forces which, from the energic standpoint, must be made accountable for the existence of the phantasy. As is well known, Freud has made a specially intensive elaboration of this method. It is this method of interpretation to which I have applied the term *reductive*. The justification of a reductive view is immediately visible; it is also thoroughly intelligible that this method of interpreting psychological realities contains something which for a certain temperament is sufficiently satisfying to obviate any further claims for deeper understanding. If a man has uttered a cry for help, such a fact is adequately and satisfactorily explained when it is shown that the man in question was in instant danger of life. If a man dreams of a lavishly-spread table, and it is shown that he went to bed hungry, a satisfactory explanation of his dream is provided. Or supposing a man who has repressed his sexuality, in the manner of a medieval saint, has sexual phantasies, this fact is sufficiently explained by a reduction to his repressed sexuality.

If, however, we were to explain the vision of St Peter by dwelling upon the fact that he, "being an-hungered", had received an invitation from the unconscious to eat animals that were "unclean", or that the eating of the unclean beasts merely signified the fulfilment of a forbidden desire—with such an explanation we would still go empty away. Neither would our demand find any fuller satisfaction if, for instance, we were to trace the vision of Saul to his repressed envy of the rôle played by Christ among his fellow-countrymen which brought about his identification with Christ. Both explanations may contain some glimmering of truth, yet they stand in no sort of relation to the real psychology of the two apostles, conditioned as this was by the history and atmosphere of that time.

Such an explanation is both too simple and too cheap. We cannot discuss the history of the world as though it were a problem of physiology or a mere personal 'chronique scandaleuse'. That would be altogether too limited a standpoint. Hence we are compelled very considerably to extend our conception of the latent meaning of phantasy. First of all in its causal aspect, for the psychology of the individual can never be exhaustively explained from himself: a clear recognition is also needed of the way in which his individual psychology is conditioned by contemporary history and circumstances. It is not merely a physiological, biological, or personal problem, but also a question of contemporary history. In fine, no psychological fact can ever be exhaustively explained from its causality alone, since, as a living phenomenon, it is always indissolubly bound up with the continuity of the vital process, so that on the one side it is always something that is, and on the other it is also becoming, and therefore always creative. The psychological moment is Janus-faced—it looks both backwards and forwards. Because it is becoming, it also prepares for the future event. Were this not so, intentions, aims, the setting-up of goals, the forecasting or divining of the future would be psychological impossibilities. If, when a man expresses an opinion, we merely relate this circumstance to the fact that at some previous time someone else has also expressed a view, such an explanation is, practically, quite inadequate; for its real understanding, not merely do we wish to know the cause of his action but also what he intends by it, what are his aims and purposes, what does he hope to achieve by it. And usually, when we also know that, we are willing to rest satisfied. In everyday life, we immediately and quite instinctively insert a purposive standpoint into the explanation; indeed, very often we appraise the purposive point-of-view as the decisive one, completely overlooking the strictly causal motive; clearly, in instinctive recognition of the essentially creative factor of the psyche. If we so act in everyday experience, a scientific psychology must also take this circumstance into account, and not rely exclusively upon the strictly causal standpoint originally taken over from natural science; for it also has to consider the purposive nature of the psychic product.

When we find everyday experience establishing the purposive orientation of the conscious content beyond any sort of doubt, we have absolutely no grounds to assume, in the absence of experience to the contrary, that this may not also be the case with the content of the unconscious. My experience gives me no reason at all to dispute the purposive orientation of unconscious contents; on the contrary, the cases in which a satisfactory interpretation could alone be attained through the introduction of the purposive standpoint are in the majority. Suppose, for example, we were again to consider the vision of Saul, but this time from the angle of the Pauline world mission, and were now to reach the conclusion that Saul, though a conscious persecutor of Christians, had unconsciously adopted the Christian standpoint, that he was finally brought to avow it by the increasing predominance and final irruption of the unconscious standpoint, and that his unconscious personality was constantly striving towards this goal in an instinctive apprehension of the necessity and importance of such an act. To me this seems a more adequate explanation of the real significance of the event than a reductive interpretation to personal motives, albeit these latter doubtless cooperated in one form or another, since the 'all-too-human' is never lacking. Similarly, the indication given in the *Acts of the Apostles* of a purposive interpretation of the vision of St Peter is far more satisfying than a merely physiological and personal conjecture.

To sum up, we may say that phantasy needs to be understood both causally as well as purposively. With the causal explanation it appears as a *symptom* of a physiological or personal condition, the resultant of previous occurrences; whereas, in the purposive interpretation, phantasy appears as a *symbol*, which seeks with the help of existing material a clear and definite goal; it strives, as it were, to distinguish or lay hold of a certain line for the future psychological development. Active phantasy being the principal attribute of the artistic mentality, the artist is not merely a *representer*: he is also a *creator*, hence essentially an *educator*, since his works have the value of symbols that trace out the line of future development.

Whether the actual social validity of the symbol is more general or more restricted depends upon the quality or vital capacity of the creative individuality. The more abnormal the individual, *i.e.* the less his general fitness for life, the more limited will be the common social value of the symbols he produces, although their value may be absolute for the individuality in question. One has no right to dispute the existence of the latent meaning of phantasy, unless we also cling to the view that the general Nature-process contains no satisfying meaning. But natural science has developed the meaning of the Nature-process into the form of natural laws. These, admittedly, are human hypotheses advanced in explanation of the Nature-process. But, only in so far as we have ascertained that the proposed law actually coincides with the objective process, are we justified in speaking of a meaning of the natural occurrence. Just so far, therefore, as we have succeeded in demonstrating a law-abiding principle in phantasy, are we also justified in speaking of a meaning of the same. But the disclosed meaning is satisfying, or in other words the demonstrated regularity deserves the name, only when it adequately renders the nature of phantasy.

There is a law-abiding regularity *in* the Nature-process, and also a regularity *of* the Nature-process. It is certainly law-determined and regular that one dreams when one sleeps; but there is no sort of law-determined principle that affirms anything about the nature of the dream. Its nature is a mere condition of the dream. The demonstration of a physiological source of the phantasy is a mere condition of its existence, not a law of its nature. The law of phantasy as a psychological phenomenon can only be a psychological law.

We now come to the second point of our explanation of the concept of phantasy, viz. *imaginative activity*.

Imagination is the reproductive, or creative, activity of the mind generally, though not a special faculty, since it may come into play in all the basic forms of psychic activity, whether thinking, feeling, sensation, or intuition. Phantasy as imaginative activity is, in my view, simply the direct expression of psychic vital activity: it is energy merely appearing in consciousness in the form of images or contents, just as physical energy also reveals itself as a definite physical state wherein sense organs are stimulated in physical ways. For as every physical state—from the energic standpoint—is merely a dynamic system, so, too, a psychic content—regarded energically—is merely a dynamic system appearing in consciousness. Hence from this standpoint one may affirm that phantasy in the form of phantasm is merely a definite sum of libido which cannot appear in consciousness in any other way than in the form of an image. Phantasm is an 'idée-force'. Phantasy as imaginative activity is identical with the course of the energic psychic process.

42. Power-complex: I occasionally use this term as denoting the total complex of all those ideas and strivings whose tendency it is to range the ego above other influences, thus subordinating all such influences to the ego, quite irrespective of whether they have their source in men and objective conditions, or spring from one's own subjective impulses, feelings, and thoughts.

43. Projection signifies the transveying of a subjective process into an object. It is the opposite of introjection (*q.v.*). Accordingly, projection is a process of dissimilation wherein a subjective content is estranged from the subject and, in a sense, incorporated in the object. There are painful, incompatible contents of which the subject unburdens himself by projection, just as there are also positive values which for some reason are uncongenial to the subject; as, for instance, the consequences of self-depreciation. Projection is based upon the archaic identity (*q.v.*) of subject and object, but the term is used only when the necessity has already arisen for resolving the identity with the object. This necessity arises when the identity is disturbing, *i.e.* when, through the absence of the projected content, the process of adaptation is materially prejudiced, so that the restoration of the projected content becomes desirable to the subject. From this moment the hitherto partial identity maintains the character of projection. This expression, therefore, denotes a state of identity which has become noticeable, and, therefore, the object of criticism, whether it be the self-criticism of the subject or the objective criticism of another.

We may discriminate between *passive* and *active* projection. The former is the customary form of every pathological and many normal projections; it springs from no purpose and is a purely automatic occurrence. The latter form is an essential constituent of the act of '*feeling-into*'

Feeling-into (*q.v.*), as a whole, is a process of introjection, since it serves to bring the object into an intimate relation with the subject. In order to establish this relation, the subject detaches a content (a feeling, for instance) from himself; he then transveys it into, therewith animating, the object, which he thus relates to the subjective sphere.

The active form of projection, however, is also an act of judgment which aims at a separation of subject and object. In this case a subjective judgment is detached from the subject as a valid statement of the case, and is transveyed into the object; by so doing the subject distinguishes himself from the object. Accordingly, projection is a process of introversion, since, in contrast to introjection, it leads not to a linking-up and assimilation but to a differentiation and separation of subject from object. Hence it plays a leading part in paranoia, which usually ends in a total isolation of the subject.

44. Rational: The rational is the reasonable, that which accords with reason. I conceive reason as an attitude whose principle is to shape thought, feeling, and action in accordance with objective values. Objective values are established by the average experience of external facts on the one hand, and of inner psychological facts on the other. Such experiences, however, could represent no objective 'value', if 'valued' as such by the subject; for this would already amount to an act of reason. But the reasoning attitude, which permits us to declare as valid objective values in general, is not the work of the individual subject, but the product of human history.

Most objective values—and reason itself among them—
—are firmly established complexes handed down to us through the ages, to the organization of which countless generations have laboured with the same necessity with which the nature of the living organism, in general, reacts

to the average and constantly recurring conditions of the environment, confronting them with corresponding function-complexes—as, for instance, the eye, which so perfectly corresponds with the nature of light. We might, therefore, speak of a pre-existing, metaphysical world-reason, if, as Schopenhauer has already pointed out, the reaction of the living organism that corresponds with average external influence were not the indispensable condition of its existence. Human reason, therefore, is merely the expression of human adaptability to the average occurrence which has gradually become deposited in solidly organized complexes, constituting our objective values. Thus the laws of reason are those laws which rule and designate the average 'correct' or adapted attitude. Everything is rational which harmonizes with these laws, and everything irrational (*q.v.*) which contravenes them.

Thinking and feeling are rational functions in so far as they are decisively influenced by the motive of reflection. They attain their fullest significance when in fullest possible accord with the laws of reason. The irrational functions, on the contrary, are such as aim at pure perception, *e.g.* intuition and sensation; because, as far as possible, they are forced to dispense with the rational (which pre-supposes the exclusion of everything that is outside reason) in order to be able to reach the most complete perception of the whole course of events.

45. Reductive ('leading back'): I employ this expression to denote that method of psychological interpretation which regards the unconscious product not from the symbolic point of view, but merely as a *semiotic* expression, a sort of sign or symptom of an underlying process. Accordingly, the reductive method treats the unconscious product in the sense of a leading-back to the elements and basic processes, irrespective of whether such products are reminiscences of actual events, or whether they arise from elementary processes affecting the psyche. Hence, the reductive method is orientated backwards (in contrast to the constructive method; *q.v.*), whether in the historical sense or in the merely figurative sense of a tracing back of complex and differentiated factors to the general and elementary. The methods both of Freud and of Adler are reductive, since in both cases there is a reduction to elementary processes either of wishing or striving, which in the last resort are infantile or primitive. Hence the unconscious product necessarily acquires the value of a merely figurative or unreal expression, for which the term 'symbol' (*q.v.*) is really not applicable.

The effect of reduction as regards the real significance of the unconscious product is disintegrating, since it is either traced back to its historical antecedents, and so robbed of its intrinsic significance, or it is once again reintegrated into the same elementary process from which it arose.

46. Self:—*v.* Ego.

47. Sensation: According to my conception, this is one of the basic psychological functions (*v.* Function). Wundt also reckons sensation among the elementary psychic phenomena[1].

Sensation, or sensing, is that psychological function which transmits a physical stimulus to perception. It is, therefore, identical with perception. Sensation must be strictly distinguished from feeling, since the latter is an entirely different process, although it may, for instance, be associated with sensation as 'feeling-tone'. Sensation

---

[1] For the history of the concept of sensation compare:
Wundt, *Grundzüge der physiologischen Psychologie*, i, pp. 350 ff.
Dessoir, *Geschichte der neuern deutschen Psychologie*.
Villa, *Einleitung in die Psychologie der Gegenwart*.
v. Hartmann, *Die moderne Psychologie*.

is related not only to the outer stimuli, but also to the inner, *i.e.* to changes in the internal organs.

Primarily, therefore, sensation is *sense-perception*, *i.e.* perception transmitted *via* the sense organs and 'bodily senses' (kinæsthetic, vaso-motor sensation, etc.). On the one hand, it is an element of presentation, since it transmits to the presenting function the perceived image of the outer object; on the other hand, it is an element of feeling, because through the perception of bodily changes it lends the character of affect to feeling, (*v.* Affect). Because sensation transmits physical changes to consciousness, it also represents the physiological impulse. But it is not identical with it, since it is merely a perceptive function.

A distinction must be made between sensuous, or concrete, and abstract sensation. The former includes the forms above alluded to, whereas the latter designates an abstracted kind of sensation, *i.e.* a sensation that is separated from other psychological elements. For concrete sensation never appears as 'pure' sensation, but is always mixed up with presentations, feelings, and thoughts. Abstract sensation, on the contrary, represents a differentiated kind of perception which might be termed 'æsthetic' in so far as it follows its own principle and is as equally detached from every admixture of the differences of the perceived object as from the subjective admixture of feeling and thought, thus raising itself to a degree of purity which is never attained by concrete sensation. The concrete sensation of a flower, for instance, transmits not only the perception of the flower itself, but also an image of the stem, leaves, habitat, etc. It is also directly mingled with the feelings of pleasure or dislike which the sight of it provokes, or with the scent-perceptions simultaneously excited, or with thoughts concerning its botanical classification.

Abstract sensation, on the other hand, immediately picks out the most salient sensuous attribute of the flower, as for instance its brilliant redness, and makes it the sole or at least the principal content of consciousness, entirely detached from all the other admixtures alluded to above. Abstract sensation is mainly suited to the artist. Like every abstraction, it is a product of the differentiation of function: hence there is nothing primordial about it. The primordial form of the function is always concrete, *i.e.* blended (*v.* Archaism, and Concretism). Concrete sensation as such is a reactive phenomenon, while abstract sensation, like every abstraction, is always linked up with the will, *i.e.* the element of direction. The will that is directed towards the abstraction of sensation is both the expression and the activity of the *æsthetic sensational attitude.*

Sensation is a prominent characteristic both in the child and the primitive, in so far as it always predominates over thinking and feeling, though not necessarily over intuition. For I regard sensation as conscious, and intuition as unconscious, perception. For me, sensation and intuition represent a pair of opposites, or two mutually compensating functions, like thinking and feeling. Thinking and feeling as independent functions are developed, both ontogenetically and phylogenetically, from sensation (and equally, of course, from intuition as the necessary counterpart of sensation).

In so far as sensation is an elementary phenomenon, it is something absolutely given, something that, in contrast to thinking and feeling, is not subject to the laws of reason. I therefore term it an *irrational* (*q.v.*) function, although reason contrives to assimilate a great number of sensations into rational associations.

A man whose whole attitude is orientated by the principle of sensation belongs to the sensation type (*v.* Types).

Normal sensations are proportionate, *i.e.* their value approximately corresponds with the intensity of the physical stimulus. Pathological sensations are disproportionate, *i.e.* either abnormally weak or abnormally strong: in the former case they are inhibited, in the latter exaggerated. The inhibition is the result of the predominance of another function; the exaggeration proceeds from an abnormal amalgamation with another function, *e.g.* a blending with a still undifferentiated feeling or thinking function. In such a case, the exaggeration of sensation ceases as soon as the function with which sensation is fused is differentiated in its own right.

The psychology of the neuroses yields extremely illuminating examples of this, where, for instance, a strong *sexualization* (Freud) of other functions very often prevails, *i.e.* a blending of sexual sensation with other functions.

48. **Soul** (*anima*): I have found sufficient cause, in my investigations into the structure of the unconscious, to make a conceptual distinction between the *soul* and the *psyche*. By the psyche I understand the totality of all the psychic processes, both conscious as well as unconscious; whereas by *soul*, I understand a definitely demarcated function-complex that is best characterized as a 'personality'. In order to describe more exactly what I mean by this, I must introduce still remoter points of view—such, in particular, as the phenomena of somnambulism, of character-duplication, of dissociation of personality, the investigation of which is primarily due to French research, and which has enabled us to recognize the possibility of a plurality of personalities in one and the same individual [1].

[1] Azam, *Hypnotisme—Double Conscience*. Paris, 1887.
Morton Prince, *The Dissociation of a Personality*. 1906.
Landmann, *Die Mehrheit geistiger Persönlichkeiten in einem Individuum*. 1894.
Ribot, *Die Persönlichkeit*. 1894.
Flournoy, *Des Indes à la planète Mars*. 1900.
Jung, *On the Psychology and Pathology of so-called Occult Phenomena* (*Collected Papers*, 2nd edn.)

It is at once evident that such a plurality of personalities can never appear in a normal individual; but the possibility of a dissociation of personality which these cases represent must also exist, at least potentially, within the range of normality. And, as a matter of fact, a moderately acute psychological observation can succeed without much difficulty in proving at least the traces of character-splitting in the normal individual. For example, we have only to observe a man rather closely under varying circumstances, to discover that a transition from one milieu to another brings about a striking alteration in his personality, whereby a sharply-outlined and distinctly changed character emerges. The proverbial expression 'angel abroad, and devil at home' is a formulation of the phenomenon of character-splitting derived from everyday experience. A definite milieu demands a definite attitude. Corresponding with the duration or frequency with which such a milieu-attitude is demanded, the more or less habitual it becomes. Great numbers of men of the educated classes are obliged to move in two, for the most part totally different, milieux—viz. in the family and domestic circle and in the world of affairs. These two totally different environments demand two totally different attitudes, which, in proportion to the degree of identification (*q.v.*) of the ego with the momentary attitude, produce a duplication of character. In accordance with social conditions and necessities, the social character is orientated, on the one hand by the expectations or obligations of the social milieu, and on the other by the social aims and efforts of the subject. The domestic character is, as a rule, more the product of the subject's laissez-aller indolence and emotional demands; whence it frequently happens that men who in public life are extremely energetic, bold, obstinate, wilful, and inconsiderate appear good-natured, mild, accommodating, even weak, when at home within the sphere of domesticity. Which, then, is the true character, the real personality? This is a question it is often impossible to answer.

This brief consideration will show that, even in the normal individual, character-splitting is by no means an impossibility. We are, therefore, perfectly justified in treating the question of dissociation of personality also as a problem of normal psychology. According to my view then—to pursue the discussion—the above question should be met with a frank avowal that such a man has no real character at all, *i.e.* he is not *individual* (*q.v.*) but *collective* (*q.v.*), *i.e.* he corresponds with general circumstances and expectations. Were he an individual, he would have but one and the same character with every variation of attitude. It would not be identical with the momentary attitude, neither could it nor would it prevent his individuality from finding expression in one state just as clearly as in another. He is an individual, of course, like every being; but an unconscious one. Through his more or less complete identification with the attitude of the moment, he at least deceives others, and also often himself, as to his real character. He puts on a *mask*, which he knows corresponds with his conscious intentions, while it also meets with the requirements and opinions of his environment, so that first one motive then the other is in the ascendant. This mask, viz. the ad hoc adopted attitude, I have called the *persona*,[1] which was the designation given to the mask worn by the actors of antiquity. A man who is identified with this mask I would call "personal" (as opposed to "individual").

Both the attitudes of the case considered above are collective personalities, which may be simply summed up under the name "persona" or "personae". I have already

[1] Jung, *The Conception of the Unconscious* (*Collected Papers*, 2nd edn., p. 457).

suggested above that the real individuality is different from both. Thus, the persona is a function-complex which has come into existence for reasons of adaptation or necessary convenience, but by no means is it identical with the individuality. The function-complex of the persona is exclusively concerned with the relation to the object.

The relation of the individual to the outer object must be sharply distinguished from the relation to the subject. By the subject I mean those vague, dim stirrings, feelings, thoughts, and sensations which have no demonstrable flow towards the object from the continuity of conscious experience, but well up like a disturbing, inhibiting, or at times beneficent, influence from the dark inner depths, from the background and underground of consciousness which, in their totality, constitute one's perception of the unconscious life. The subject, conceived as the 'inner' object, is the unconscious. There is a relation to the inner object, viz. an inner attitude, just as there is a relation to the outer object, viz. an outer attitude. It is quite intelligible that this inner attitude, by reason of its extremely intimate and inaccessible nature, is far less widely known than the outer attitude, which is immediately perceived by everyone. Nevertheless, the task of making a concept of this inner attitude does not seem to me impossible. All those so-called accidental inhibitions, fancies, moods, vague feelings, and fragments of phantasy, which occasionally harass and disturb the accomplishment of concentrated work, not to mention the repose of the most normal of men, and which evoke rational explanations either in the form of physical causes or reasons of like nature, usually have their origin, not in the reasons ascribed to them by consciousness, but in the perceptions of unconscious processes, which, in fact, they are. Among such phenomena, dreams also naturally belong: these are admittedly liable to be accounted for by such external and superficial causes as indigestion, sleeping on one's back, and the like, in spite of the fact that such explanations never withstand a searching criticism. The attitude of individual men to these things is extremely variable. One man will not allow himself to be disturbed in the smallest degree by his inner processes—he can, as it were, ignore them entirely; while another is in the highest degree subject to them: at the first waking-moment some phantasy or other, or a disagreeable feeling, spoils his temper for the whole day; a vague, unpleasant sensation suggests the idea of a secret malady, or a dream leaves him with a gloomy foreboding, although in other ways he is by no means superstitious. To others, again, these unconscious stirrings have only a very episodic access, or only a certain category of them come to the surface. For one man, perhaps, they have never yet appeared to consciousness as anything worth thinking about, while for another they are a problem of daily brooding. The one values them physiologically, or ascribes them to the conduct of his neighbours; another finds in them a religious revelation.

These entirely different ways of dealing with the stirrings of the unconscious are just as habitual as the attitudes to the outer object. The inner attitude, therefore, corresponds with just as definite a function-complex as the outer attitude. Those cases in which the inner psychic processes appear to be entirely overlooked are lacking a typical inner attitude just as little as those who constantly overlook the outer object and the reality of facts lack a typical outer attitude. The persona of these latter, by no means infrequent, cases has the character of unrelatedness, or at times even a blind inconsiderateness, which frequently yields only to the harshest blows of fate. Not seldom, it is just those individuals whose persona is characterized by a rigid inconsiderateness and absence of relations who possess an attitude to the unconscious processes which suggests a character of extreme susceptibility. As they are inflexible and inaccessible outwardly, so are they weak, flaccid, and determinable in relation to their inner processes. In such cases, therefore, the inner attitude corresponds with an inner personality diametrically opposed and different from the outer. I know a man, for instance, who without pity blindly destroyed the happiness of those nearest to him, and yet he would interrupt his journey when travelling on important business just to enjoy the beauty of a forest scene glimpsed from the carriage window. Cases of this kind are doubtless familiar to everyone; it is needless therefore to enumerate further examples. With the same justification as daily experience furnishes us for speaking of an outer personality are we also justified in assuming the existence of an inner personality. The inner personality is the manner of one's behaviour towards the inner psychic processes; it is the inner attitude, the character, that is turned towards the unconscious. I term the outer attitude, or outer character, the *persona*, the inner attitude I term the *anima*, or *soul*. In the same degree as an attitude is habitual, is it a more or less firmly welded function-complex, with which the ego may be more or less identified. This is plastically expressed in language: of a man who has an habitual attitude towards certain situations, we are accustomed to say: He is quite *another man* when doing this or that. This is a practical demonstration of the independence of the function-complex of an habitual attitude; it is as though another personality had taken possession of the individual, as 'though another spirit had entered into him'. The same autonomy as is so often granted to the outer attitude is also claimed by the soul or inner attitude. One of the most difficult of all educational achievements is this task of changing the outer attitude, or persona. But to change the soul is just as difficult, since its structure tends to be just as firmly welded as is that of the persona.

U

Just as the persona is an entity, which often appears to constitute the whole character of a man, even accompanying him practically without change throughout his entire life, so the soul is also a definitely circumscribed entity, with a character which may prove unalterably firm and independent. Hence, it frequently offers itself to characterization and description.

As regards the character of the soul, my experience confirms the validity of the general principle that it maintains, on the whole, a *complementary* relation to the outer character. Experience teaches us that the soul is wont to contain all those general human qualities the conscious attitude lacks. The tyrant tormented by bad dreams, gloomy forebodings, and inner fears, is a typical figure. Outwardly inconsiderate, harsh, and unapproachable, he is inwardly susceptible to every shadow, and subject to every fancy, as though he were the least independent, and the most impressionable, of men. Thus his soul contains those general human qualities of suggestibility and weakness which are wholly lacking in his outer attitude, or persona. Where the persona is intellectual, the soul is quite certainly sentimental. That the complementary character of the soul is also concerned with the sex-character is a fact which can no longer seriously be doubted. A very feminine woman has a masculine soul, and a very manly man a feminine soul. This opposition is based upon the fact that a man, for instance, is not in all things wholly masculine, but has also certain feminine traits. The more manly his outer attitude, the more will his womanly traits be effaced; these then appear in the soul. This circumstance explains why it is that the very manly men are most subject to characteristic weaknesses; their attitude to the unconscious has a womanly weakness and impressionability. And, vice versa, it is often just the most womanly women who,

DEFINITIONS

in respect of certain inner things, have an extreme intractableness, obstinacy, and wilfulness; which qualities are found in such intensity only in the outer attitude of men. These are manly traits, whose exclusion from the womanly outer attitude makes them qualities of the soul. If, therefore, we speak of the *anima* of a man, we must logically speak of the *animus* of a woman, if we are to give the soul of a woman its right name. Whereas logic and objective reality commonly prevail in the outer attitude of man, or are at least regarded as an ideal, in the case of woman it is feeling. But in the soul the relations are reversed: inwardly it is the man who feels, and the woman who reflects. Hence man's greater liability to total despair, while a woman can always find comfort and hope; hence man is more liable to put an end to himself than woman. However prone a woman may be to fall a victim to social circumstances, as in prostitution for instance, a man is equally delivered over to impulses from the unconscious in the form of alcoholism and other vices.

As regards the general human characters, the character of the soul may be deduced from that of the persona. Everything which should normally be in the outer attitude, but is decidedly wanting there, will invariably be found in the inner attitude. This is a basic rule, which my experience has borne out again and again. But, as regards individual qualities, nothing can be deduced about them in this way. We can be certain only that, when a man is identical with his persona, the individual qualities are associated with the soul. It is this association which gives rise to the symbol, so often appearing in dreams, of the soul's pregnancy; this symbol has its source in the primordial image of the hero-birth. The child that is to be born signifies the individuality, which, though existing, is not yet conscious. Hence in the same way as the persona, which expresses one's adaptation to the milieu, is as a rule strongly influenced and shaped by the milieu, so the soul is just as profoundly moulded by the unconscious and its qualities. Just as the persona, almost necessarily, takes on primitive traits in a primitive milieu, so the soul assumes the archaic characters of the unconscious as well as its prospective, symbolic character. Whence arise the 'pregnant' and 'creative' qualities of the inner attitude. Identity with the persona automatically conditions an unconscious identity with the soul, because, when the subject or ego is not differentiated from the persona, it can have no conscious relation to the processes of the unconscious. Hence it *is* these processes: it is identical with them. The man who is unconditionally his outer rôle therewith delivers himself over unquestioningly to the inner processes, *i.e.* he will even frustrate his outer rôle by absolute inner necessity, reducing it *ad absurdum* (enantiodromia; *q.v.*). A steady holding to the individual line is thereby excluded, and his life runs its course in inevitable opposition. Moreover, in such a case the soul is always projected into a corresponding, real object, with which a relation of almost absolute dependence exists. Every reaction proceeding from this object has an immediate, inwardly arresting effect upon the subject. Tragic ties are frequently formed in this way (*v.* Soul-image).

49. **Soul-Image**: The soul-image is a definite image (*q.v.*) among those produced by the unconscious. Just as the persona, or outer attitude, is represented in dreams by the images of certain persons who possess the outstanding qualities of the persona in especially marked form, so the soul, the inner attitude of the unconscious, is similarly represented by definite persons whose particular qualities correspond with those of the soul. Such an image is called a 'soul-image'. Occasionally these images

are quite unknown or mythological figures. With men the soul, *i.e.* the anima, is usually figured by the unconscious in the person of a woman; with women it is a man. In every case where the individuality is unconscious, and therefore associated with the soul, the soul-image has the character of the same sex. In all those cases in which an identity with the persona (*v.* Soul) is present, and the soul accordingly is unconscious, the soul-image is transferred into a real person. This person is the object of an intense love or an equally intense hatred (possibly even fear). The influence of such a person has the character of something immediate and absolutely compelling, since it always evokes an affective response. The affect depends upon the fact that a real conscious adaptation to the object who represents the soul-image is impossible. Because the objective relation is alike impossible and non-existent, the libido gets dammed up and explodes in a release of affect. Affects always occur where there is a failure of adaptation. A conscious adaptation to the object who represents the soul-image is impossible only when the subject is unconscious of the anima. Were he conscious of it, it could be distinguished from the object, whose immediate effects might then be resolved, since the potency of the object depends upon the projection of the soul-image.

For a man, a woman is best fitted to be the bearer of his soul-image, by virtue of the womanly quality of his soul; similarly a man, in the case of a woman. Wherever an unconditional, or almost magical, relation exists between the sexes, it is always a question of projection of the soul-image. Since such relations are common, just as frequently must the soul be unconscious, *i.e.* great numbers of men must be unaware of how they are related to the inner psychic processes. Because such unconsciousness goes always hand in hand with a correspondingly complete identification with the persona (*v.* Soul), it clearly follows that the latter also must occur very frequently. This accords with reality; for, as a matter of fact, large numbers of men are wholly identified with their outer attitude, and therefore have no conscious relation to their inner processes. But the converse may also happen; namely, where the soul-image is not projected, but remains with the subject; whereupon an identification with the soul is liable to result just in so far as the subject is himself convinced that his manner of behaviour to his inner processes is also his unique and actual character. In such a case, the unconsciousness of the persona results in its projection upon an object, more especially of the same sex, thus providing a foundation for many cases of more or less admitted homosexuality, and of father-transferences in men or mother-transferences in women. Such cases are always persons with defective external adaptation and comparative unrelatedness, because the identification with the soul begets an attitude with a predominant orientation towards the inner processes, whereby the object is deprived of its determining influence.

Whenever the soul-image is projected, an unconditional, affective tie to the object appears. If it is not projected, a relatively unadapted state results, which Freud has partially described as *narcissism*. The projection of the soul-image offers a release from a too great preoccupation with the inner processes, in so far as the behaviour of the object harmonizes with the soul-image. The subject is thus enabled to live his persona, and to develop it further. In the long run, however, the object will scarcely be able to correspond consistently with the soul-image, although many women succeed, by constantly disregarding their own lives, in representing their husband's soul-image for a very considerable time. The biological, feminine instinct assists them in this. A man may unconsciously do the same for his wife, only he is thereby prompted to deeds which, for good or evil, finally exceed his powers. In his case, also, the biological masculine instinct is an assistance.

If the soul-image is not projected, a thoroughly morbid differentiation of the relation to the unconscious gradually develops. The subject is increasingly overwhelmed by unconscious contents, which his defective relation to the object makes him powerless to organize, or to put to any sort of use. Obviously, such contents as these very seriously prejudice the relation to the object. These attitudes only represent, of course, the two extremes, between which the more normal attitudes are to be found. The normal man, as we know, is not distinguished by any special clarity, purity, or depth, in the matter of psychological phenomena, but commonly inclines to a certain indistinctness in such matters. In men with a good-natured and inoffensive outer attitude, the soul-image, as a rule, has a rather malevolent character. A good literary example of this is the dæmonic woman who accompanies Zeus in Spitteler's "Olympischer Frühling." For the idealistic woman, a depraved man is often a bearer of the soul-image; hence the 'salvation phantasy' so frequent in such cases. The same thing often happens with men, where the prostitute is surrounded with the halo of a soul crying for succour.

50. **Subjective Plane**: By interpretation upon the subjective plane, I understand that conception of a dream or phantasy in which the persons or conditions appearing therein are related to subjective factors entirely belonging to the subject's own psyche. It is common knowledge that the image of an object existing in our psyche is never exactly like the object, but at most only similar. Although admittedly brought about through sense-perceptions and their apperception, it is actually the product of processes

inherent in the psyche whose activity the object merely stimulates. Experience shows that the evidence of our senses very largely coincides with the qualities of the object, but our apperception is subject to well-nigh incalculable subjective influences, which render the correct knowledge of a human character extraordinarily difficult. Moreover, such a complex psychic factor as is presented by a human character offers only a very slight field for pure sense perception. Its cognition also demands 'feeling-into', reflection, and intuition. The final judgment that issues from these complex factors is always of very doubtful value; necessarily, therefore, the image we form of a human object is, to a very large extent, subjectively conditioned. Hence, in practical psychology we should be well advised to differentiate the image or *imago* of a man quite definitely from his real existence. Not infrequently as a result of its extremely subjective origin, an imago is actually more an image of a subjective function-complex than of the object itself.

In the analytical treatment of unconscious products, therefore, it is essential that the imago shall not immediately be assumed to be identical with the object; it is wiser to regard it as an image of the subjective relation to the object. This is what is meant by the consideration of a product upon the subjective plane.

The treatment of an unconscious product upon this plane results in the presence of subjective judgments and tendencies of which the bearer is made the object When, therefore, an object-imago appears in an unconscious product, it is not definitely concerned with the real object *per se*, but just as much, possibly even more, with a subjective function-complex (*v.* Soul-image).

The application of meaning upon this plane yields us a comprehensive psychological explanation, not only of dreams but also of literary works, in which the individual figures represent relatively autonomous function-complexes in the psyche of the poet.

51. **Symbol**: The concept of a symbol should, in my view, be strictly differentiated from that of a mere *sign*. *Symbolic* and *semiotic* interpretations are entirely different things. In his book Ferrero[1] does not speak of symbols in the strict sense, but of *signs*. For instance, the old custom of handing over a sod of turf at the sale of a piece of land, might be described as 'symbolic' in the vulgar use of the word; but actually it is purely semiotic in character. The piece of turf is a *sign*, or token, representing the whole estate. The winged wheel worn by the railway employés is not a symbol of the railway, but a sign that distinguishes the personnel of the railway. But the symbol always presupposes that the chosen expression is the best possible description, or formula, of a relatively unknown fact; a fact, however, which is none the less recognized or postulated as existing. Thus, when the winged-wheel badge of the railway employé is explained as a symbol, it is tantamount to saying that the man has to do with an unknown entity whose nature cannot be differently or better expressed than by a winged wheel. Every view which interprets the symbolic expression as an analogous or abbreviated expression of a known thing is *semiotic*. A conception which interprets the symbolic expression as the best possible formulation of a relatively unknown thing which cannot conceivably, therefore, be more clearly or characteristically represented is *symbolic*. A view which interprets the symbolic expression as an intentional transcription or transformation of a known thing is *allegoric*. The explanation of the Cross as a symbol of Divine Love is *semiotic*, since Divine Love describes the fact to be expressed better and more aptly than a cross, which can have

[1] Ferrero, *Les lois psychologiques du symbolisme*, 1895.

many other meanings. Whereas that interpretation of the Cross is symbolic which puts it above all imaginable explanations, regarding it as an expression of an unknown and as yet incomprehensible fact of a mystical or transcendent, *i.e.* psychological character, which simply finds its most striking and appropriate representation in the Cross.

In so far as a symbol is a living thing, it is the expression of a thing not to be characterized in any other or better way. The symbol is alive only in so far as it is pregnant with meaning. But, if its meaning is born out of it, *i.e.* if that expression should be found which formulates the sought, expected, or divined thing still better than the hitherto accepted symbol, then the symbol is *dead*, *i.e.* it possesses only a historical significance. We may still go on speaking of it as a symbol, under the tacit assumption that we are speaking of it as it was before its better expression had been born from it. The way in which St Paul and the early mystical speculators handle the symbol of the Cross shows that for them it was a living symbol which represented the inexpressible in an *unsurpassable way*.

For every esoteric explanation the symbol is dead, since through esoterism it has been brought to a better expression (at least ostensibly), whereupon it merely serves as a conventional sign for associations which are more completely and better known elsewhere. Only for the exoteric standpoint is the symbol always living. An expression that stands for a known thing always remains merely a sign and is never a symbol. It is, therefore, quite impossible to make a living symbol, *i.e.* one that is pregnant with meaning, from known associations. For what is thus manufactured never contains more than was put into it. Every psychic product, in so far as it is the best possible expression at the moment for a fact as yet unknown or only relatively known, may be regarded as a symbol, provided also that we are prepared to accept the expression as designating something that is only divined and not yet clearly conscious.

Inasmuch as every scientific theory contains a hypothesis, and therefore an anticipatory designation of a fact still essentially unknown, it is a symbol. Furthermore, every psychological phenomenon is a symbol when we are willing to assume that it purports, or signifies, something different and still greater, something therefore which is withheld from present knowledge. This assumption is absolutely possible to every consciousness which is orientated to the deeper meaning of things, and to the possibilities such an attitude enfolds. Such an assumption is impossible only for this same consciousness when it has itself contrived an expression, merely to contain or affirm just as much as the purpose of its creation intended, as for example a mathematical term. For another consciousness, however, this restriction does not exist at all. It can also conceive the mathematical term as a symbol of an unknown psychic fact concealed within the purpose of its production, in so far as this fact is demonstrably unknown to the man who created the semiotic expression, and therefore could not be the object of any conscious use.

Whether a thing is a symbol or not depends chiefly upon the attitude of the consciousness considering it; as for instance, a mind that regards the given fact not merely as such but also as an expression of the yet unknown. Hence it is quite possible for a man to produce a fact which does not appear in the least symbolic to himself, although profoundly so to another. The converse is also possible. There are undoubtedly products whose symbolical character not merely depends upon the attitude of the considering consciousness, but manifests itself spontaneously in a symbolical effect upon the regarding subject. Such products are so fashioned that they must forfeit every sort of meaning, unless the symbolical one is conceded them. As a pure actuality, a triangle in which an eye is enclosed is so meaningless that it is impossible for the observer to regard it as mere accidental trifling. Such a figure immediately conjures up a symbolical conception of it. This effect is supported either by a frequent and identical occurrence of the same figure, or by a particularly careful and arresting manner of production which is the actual expression of a particular value placed upon it.

Symbols that are without the spontaneous effect just described are either dead, *i.e.* outstripped by a better formulation, or else products whose symbolical nature depends exclusively upon the attitude of the observing consciousness. This attitude that conceives the given phenomenon as symbolic may be briefly described as the *symbolical attitude*. It is only partially justified by the behaviour of things; for the rest, it is the outcome of a definite view of life endowing the occurrence, whether great or small, with a meaning to which a certain deeper value is given than to pure actuality. This view of things stands opposed to another view, which lays the accent upon pure actuality, and subordinates meaning to facts. For this latter attitude there can be no symbol at all, wherever the symbolism depends exclusively upon the manner of consideration. But even for such an attitude symbols also exist: namely, those that prompt the observer to the conjecture of a hidden meaning. An image of a god with the head of a bull can certainly be explained as a human body with a bull's head. But this explanation could scarcely hold the scales against the symbolic interpretation, since the symbol is too arresting to be entirely overlooked. A symbol that seems to obtrude its symbolical nature need not be alive. Its effect may be wholly restricted, for instance, to the historical or philosophical intellect. It merely arouses intellectual or æsthetic interest. But a symbol really lives only when it is the best and highest possible expression of something divined but not yet known even to the observer. For under these circumstances it provokes unconscious participation. It advances and creates life. As Faust says: "How differently this token works upon me!"

The living symbol shapes and formulates an essential unconscious factor, and the more generally this factor prevails, the more general is the operation of the symbol; for in every soul it touches an associated chord. Since, on the one hand the symbol is the best possible expression of what is still unknown—an expression, moreover, which cannot be surpassed for the given epoch—it must proceed from the most complex and differentiated contemporary mental atmosphere. But since, on the other hand, the living symbol must embrace and contain that which relates a considerable group of men for such an effect to be within its power, it must contain just that which may be common to a large group of men. Hence, this can never be the most highly differentiated or the highest attainable, since only the very few could attain to, or understand it; but it must be something that is still so primitive that its omnipresence stands beyond all doubt. Only when the symbol comprises this something, and brings it to the highest possible expression, has it any general efficacy. Therein consists the potent and, at the same time, redeeming effect of a living, social symbol.

All that I have now said concerning the social symbol holds good for the individual symbol. There are individual psychic products, whose manifest symbolic character at once compels a symbolical conception. For the individual, they possess a similar functional significance as the social symbol for a larger human group. Such products, however, never have an exclusively conscious or unconscious source, but proceed from a uniform co-operation of both. Purely conscious products are no more convincingly symbolic, per se, than purely unconscious products, and vice versa; it devolves, therefore, upon the symbolical attitude of the observing consciousness to endow them with the character of a symbol. But they may equally well be conceived as mere causally conditioned facts, in much the same sense as one might regard the red exanthema of scarlet fever as a 'symbol' of the disease. In such a case, of course, it is correct to speak of a 'symptom', not of a symbol. In my view, therefore, Freud is justified, when, from his standpoint, he speaks of *symptomatic*[1], rather than *symbolical* actions; since, for him, these phenomena are not symbolic in the sense here defined, but are symptomatic signs of a definite and generally known underlying process. There are, of course, neurotics who regard their unconscious products, which are primarily morbid symptoms, as symbols of supreme importance. Generally, however, this is not the case. On the contrary, the neurotic of to-day is only too prone to regard a product that may actually be full of significance, as a 'symptom'.

The fact that there are two distinct and mutually contradictory views, eagerly advocated on either side, concerning the meaning and the meaninglessness of things, can only show that processes clearly exist which express no particular meaning, being in fact mere consequences, or symptoms; while there are other processes which bear within them a hidden meaning, processes which have not merely arisen from something, but also tend to become something, and are therefore symbols. It is left to our judgment and criticism to decide whether the thing we are dealing with is a symptom or a symbol.

The symbol is always a creation of an extremely

[1] Freud, *Psychopathology of Everyday Life.*

complex nature, since data proceeding from every psychic function have entered into its composition. Hence its nature is neither rational nor irrational. It certainly has one side that accords with reason, but it has also another side that is inaccessible to reason; for not only the data of reason, but also the irrational data of pure inner and outer perception, have entered into its nature. The prospective meaning and pregnant significance of the symbol appeals just as strongly to thinking as to feeling, while its peculiar plastic imagery when shaped into sensuous form stimulates sensation just as much as intuition. The living symbol cannot come to birth in an inert or poorly-developed mind, for such a man will rest content with the already existing symbols offered by established tradition. Only the passionate yearning of a highly developed mind, for whom the dictated symbol no longer contains the highest reconciliation in one expression, can create a new symbol. But, inasmuch as the symbol proceeds from his highest and latest mental achievement and must also include the deepest roots of his being, it cannot be a one-sided product of the most highly differentiated mental functions, but must at least have an equal source, in the lowest and most primitive motions of his psyche. For this co-operation of antithetic states to be at all possible, they must both stand side by side in fullest conscious opposition. Such a condition necessarily entails a violent disunion with oneself, even to a point where thesis and antithesis mutually deny each other, while the ego is still forced to recognize its absolute participation in both. But, should there exist a subordination of one part, the symbol will be disproportionately the product of the other, and in corresponding degree will be less a symbol than a symptom, viz. the symptom of a repressed antithesis. But, to the extent in which a symbol is merely a symptom, it also lacks the redeeming effect, since it fails to express the full right to existence of every portion of the psyche, constantly calling to mind the suppression of the antithesis, although consciousness may omit to take this into account.

But, when the opposites are given a complete equality of right, attested to by the ego's unconditioned participation in both thesis and antithesis, a suspension of the will results; for the will can no longer be operative while every motive has an equally strong counter-motive by its side. Since life cannot tolerate suspension, a damming up of vital energy results, which would lead to an insupportable condition from the tension of the opposites did not a new reconciling function arise which could lead above and beyond the opposites. It arises naturally, however, from the regression of the libido effected by its damming up. Since progress is made impossible by the total disunion of the will, the libido streams backwards, the stream flows back as it were to its source, *i.e.* the suspension and inactivity of the conscious brings about an activity of the unconscious where all the differentiated functions have their common, archaic root, and where that promiscuity of contents exists of which the primitive mentality still exhibits numerous remainders.

Through the activity of the unconscious, a content is unearthed which is constellated by thesis and antithesis in equal measure, and is related to both in a compensatory (*q.v.*) relation. Since this content discloses a relation to both thesis and antithesis, it forms a middle territory, upon which the opposites can be reconciled. Suppose, for example, we conceive the opposition to be sensuality versus spirituality; then, by virtue of its wealth of spiritual associations, the mediatory content born from the unconscious offers a welcome expression to the spiritual thesis, and by virtue of its plastic sensuousness it embraces the sensual antithesis. But the ego rent between thesis and antithesis finds in the uniting middle territory its counterpart, its reconciling and unique expression, and eagerly seizes upon it, in order to be delivered from its division. Hence, the energy created by the tension of the opposites flows into the mediatory expression, protecting it against the conflict of the opposites which forthwith begins both about it and within, since both are striving to resolve the new expression in their own specific sense. Spirituality tries to make something spiritual out of the unconscious expression, while sensuality aims at something sensual; the one wishing to create science and art from the new expression, the other sensual experience. The resolution of the unconscious product into either is successful only when the incompletely divided ego clings rather more to one side than the other.

Should one side succeed in resolving the unconscious product, it does not fall alone to that side, but the ego goes with it; whereupon an identification of the ego with the most-favoured function (*v.* Inferior Function) inevitably follows. This results in a subsequent repetition of the process of division upon a higher plane. But if, through the resoluteness of the ego, neither thesis nor antithesis can succeed in resolving the unconscious product, this is sufficient demonstration that the unconscious expression is superior to both sides.

The steadfastness of the ego and the superiority of the mediatory expression over thesis and antithesis are to my mind correlates, each mutually conditioning the other. It would appear at times as though the fixity of the inborn individuality were the decisive factor, at times as though the mediatory expression possessed a superior force prompting the ego to absolute steadfastness. But, in reality, it is quite conceivable that the firmness and certainty of the individuality on the one hand, and the superior force of the mediatory product on the other, are merely tokens of one and the same fact. When the mediatory product is preserved in this way, it fashions a raw product which is for construction, not for dissolution, and which becomes a common object for both thesis and antithesis; thus it becomes a new content that governs the whole attitude, putting an end to the division, and forcing the energy of the opposites into a common channel. The suspension of life is, therewith, abolished, and the individual life can compass a greater range with new energy and new goals.

In its totality I have named the process just described the *transcendent function*, and here I am not using the term 'function' in the sense of a basic function, but rather as a complex-function compounded of other functions, neither with 'transcendent' do I wish to designate any metaphysical quality, but merely the fact that by this function a transition is made possible from the one attitude to the other. The raw material, when elaborated by the thesis and antithesis, which in its process of formation reconciles the opposites, is the living symbol. In the essential rawness of its material, defying time and dissolution, lies its prospective significance, and in the form which its crude material receives through the influence of the opposites, lies its effective power over all the psychic functions.

Indications of the foundations of the symbol-forming process are to be found in the scanty records of the initiation-period experienced by founders of religions, *e.g.* Jesus and Satan, Buddha and Mara, Luther and the Devil, Zwingli and his previous worldly life; also Goethe's conception of the rejuvenation of Faust through the contract with the Devil. Towards the end of Zarathustra we find a striking example of the suppression of the antithesis in the figure of the " ugliest man ".

52. Synthetic: (*v.* Constructive).

DEFINITIONS

53. Thinking: This I regard as one of the four basic psychological functions (v. Function). Thinking is that psychological function which, in accordance with its own laws, brings given presentations into conceptual connection. It is an apperceptive activity and, as such, must be differentiated into *active* and *passive* thought-activity. Active thinking is an act of will, passive thinking an occurrence. In the former case, I submit the representation to a deliberate act of judgment; in the latter case, conceptual connections establish themselves, and judgments are formed which may even contradict my aim— they may lack all harmony with my conscious objective, hence also, for me, any feeling of direction, although by an act of active apperception I may subsequently come to a recognition of their directedness. Active thinking would correspond, therefore, with my idea of directed thinking.[1] Passive thinking was inadequately characterized in my previous work as "phantasying"[2]. To-day I would term it *intuitive* thinking.

To my mind, a simple stringing together of representations, such as is described by certain psychologists as *associative thinking*[3] is not thinking at all, but mere *presentation*. The term 'thinking' should, in my view, be confined to the linking up of representations by means of a concept, where, in other words, an act of judgment prevails, whether such act be the product of one's intention or not.

The faculty of directed thinking, I term *intellect*: the faculty of passive, or undirected, thinking, I term *intellectual intuition*. Furthermore, I describe directed thinking or intellect as the *rational* (q.v.) function, since it arranges the representations under concepts in accordance with the presuppositions of my conscious rational norm. Undirected

---

[1] Jung, *Psychology of the Unconscious*, p. 14.   [2] *Ibid*, p. 19.
[3] James, *Text-book of Psychology*, p. 464 (London: Longmans & Co.).

thinking, or intellectual intuition, on the contrary is, in my view, an *irrational* (*q.v.*) function, since it criticizes and arranges the representations according to norms that are unconscious to me and consequently not appreciated as reasonable. In certain cases, however, I may recognize subsequently that the intuitive act of judgment also corresponds with reason, although it has come about in a way that appears to me irrational.

Thinking that is regulated by feeling, I do not regard as intuitive thinking, but as thought dependent upon feeling; it does not follow its own logical principle, but is subordinated to the principle of feeling. In such thinking the laws of logic are only ostensibly present; in reality they are suspended in favour of the aims of feeling.

54. Transcendent Function.—(*v.* Symbol).

55. Type: A type is a specimen, or example, which reproduces in a characteristic way the character of a species or general class. In the narrower meaning used in this particular work, a type is a characteristic model of a general attitude (*q.v.*) occurring in many individual forms. From a great number of existing or possible attitudes I have, in this particular research, brought four into especial relief; namely, those that are primarily orientated by the four basic psychological functions (*v.* Function) viz. thinking, feeling, intuition, and sensation. In so far as such an attitude is *habitual*, thus lending a certain stamp to the character of the individual, I speak of a psychological type. These types, which are based upon the root-functions and which one can term the thinking, the feeling, the intuitive, and the sensational types, may be divided into two classes according to the quality of the respective basic function: viz. the *rational* and the *irrational*. The thinking and the feeling types

belong to the former. The intuitive and the sensational to the latter, (*v.* Rational; Irrational). A further differentiation into two classes is permitted by the preferential movements of the libido, namely *introversion* and *extraversion* (*q.v.*). All the basic types can belong equally well to the one or the other class, according to the predominance of introversion or extraversion in the general attitude. A thinking type may belong either to the introverted or the extraverted class, and the same holds good for any other type. The differentiation into rational and irrational types is another point of view, and has nothing to do with introversion and extraversion.

In two previous contributions upon the theory of types [1] I did not differentiate the thinking and feeling from the introverted and extraverted types, but identified the thinking type with the introverted, and the feeling with the extraverted. But a more complete investigation of the material has shown me that we must treat the introversion and the extraversion types as superordinated categories to the function types. Such a division, moreover, entirely corresponds with experience, since, for example, there are, undoubtedly two sorts of feeling-types, the attitude of one being orientated more by his feeling-experience, the other more by the object.

56. Unconscious: The concept of the unconscious is for me an *exclusively psychological concept*, and not a philosophical concept in the metaphysical sense. In my view, the unconscious is a psychological boundary-concept, which covers all those psychic contents or processes which are not conscious, *i.e. not related to the ego in a perceptible way.* My justification for speaking of the existence of

[1] Jung, *Contribution à l'étude des types psychologiques* (*Arch. de Psychologie*, T. xvi, p. 152)
Idem, *The Psychology of Unconscious Processes* (*Collected Papers*, 2nd edn., p. 354)

unconscious processes at all is derived purely and solely from experience, and in particular from psychopathological experience, where we have undoubted proof that, in a case of hysterical amnesia, for instance, the ego knows nothing of the existence of extensive psychological complexes, and in the next moment a simple hypnotic procedure is enough to bring the lost contents to complete reproduction.

From thousands of such experiences we may claim a certain justification for speaking of the existence of unconscious psychic contents. The question as to the state in which an unconscious content exists, when not attached to consciousness, is withheld from every possibility of cognition. It is, therefore, quite superfluous to hazard conjectures about it. Conjectures concerning cerebration and the whole physiological process, etc., really belong to such phantasies. It is also quite impossible to specify the range of the unconscious, *i.e.* what contents it embraces. Only experience can decide such questions. We know by experience that conscious contents can become unconscious through loss of their energic value. This is the normal process of 'forgetting'. That these contents do not simply get lost beneath the threshold of consciousness we know from the experience that occasionally, under suitable conditions, they can again emerge from their submersion after a decade or so, *e.g.* in dreams or under hypnosis in the form of cryptamnesia [1], or through the revival of associations with the forgotten content.

Furthermore, experience teaches us that conscious contents can fall beneath the threshold of consciousness through 'intentional forgetting', without a too considerable

---

[1] Cf. Flournoy, *Des Indes à la planète Mars.* 1900.
Idem, *Nouvelles Observations sur un cas de somnambulisme avec glossolalie* (*Arch. de Psychologie*, T. i, p. 101)
Jung, *On the Psych. and Path. of so-called Occult Phenomena* (*Collected Papers*)

depreciation of value—what Freud terms the *repression* of a painful content. A similar effect is produced by the dissociation of the personality, or the disintegration of consciousness, as a result of a violent affect or nervous shock or through the dissolution of the personality in schizophrenia. (Bleuler).

Similarly, we know from experience that sense-perceptions which, either because of their slight intensity or because of the deviation of attention, do not attain to conscious apperception, none the less become psychic contents through unconscious apperception, which again may be demonstrated by hypnosis, for example. The same thing may happen with certain conclusions and other combinations which remain unconscious on account of their too slight energy-content, or because of the deflection of attention. Finally, experience also teaches us that there exist unconscious psychic associations—for instance, mythological images—which have never been the object of consciousness, and hence must proceed wholly from unconscious activity.

To this extent experience gives us certain directing-points for our assumption of the existence of unconscious contents. But it can affirm nothing as to what the unconscious content may possibly be. It is idle to hazard guesses about it, because what the whole unconscious content could be is quite incalculable. What is the furthest limit of a subliminal sense-perception? Is there any sort of measurement either for the extent or the subtlety of unconscious combinations? When is a forgotten content totally effaced? To such questions there is no answer.

Our experience hitherto of the nature of unconscious contents permits us, however, to make a certain general division of them. We can distinguish a *personal* unconscious, which embraces all the acquisitions of the personal existence—hence the forgotten, the repressed, the subliminally perceived, thought and felt. But, in addition to these personal unconscious contents, there exist other contents which do not originate in personal acquisitions but in the inherited possibility of psychic functioning in general, viz. in the inherited brain-structure. These are the mythological associations—those motives and images which can spring anew in every age and clime, without historical tradition or migration. I term these contents the *collective unconscious*. Just as conscious contents are engaged in a definite activity, the unconscious contents —so experience teaches us—are similarly active. Just as certain results or products proceed from conscious psychic activity, there are also products of unconscious activity, as for instance dreams and phantasies. It is vain to speculate upon the share that consciousness takes in dreams. A dream presents itself to us: we do not consciously produce it. Conscious reproduction, or even the perception of it, certainly effects a considerable alteration in it, without, however, doing away with the basic fact of the unconscious source of the productive activity.

The functional relation of the unconscious processes to consciousness we may describe as *compensatory* (*q.v.*), since experience proves that the unconscious process pushes subliminal material to the surface that is constellated by the conscious situation—hence all those contents which could not be lacking in the picture of the conscious situation if everything were conscious. The compensatory function of the unconscious becomes all the more manifest, the more the conscious attitude maintains a one-sided standpoint; this is confirmed by abundant examples in the realm of pathology.

57. **Will**: I regard as will that sum of psychic energy which is disposable to consciousness. In accordance with

this conception, the process of the will would be an energic process that is released by conscious motivation. A psychic process, therefore, which is conditioned by unconscious motivation I would not include under the concept of the will. Will is a psychological phenomenon that owes its existence to culture and moral education, and is, therefore largely lacking in the primitive mentality.

CONCLUSION

IN our age, which has witnessed the 'liberté, égalité, fraternité' achieved by the French Revolution extending into a wide social movement, that not only pulls down or exalts political rights to a general and uniform level but thinks it is able to do away with unhappiness by means of external regulations and social levelling—in such an age it is indeed a thankless task to speak of the complete dissimilarity of the elements which compose the nation. Although it is certainly a fine thing that every man should stand equal before the law, that every man should have his political vote, and that no man through inherited social position and privilege should unjustly over-reach his brother, nevertheless it is distinctly less beautiful when the notion of equality is extended to other provinces of life. A man must needs have a very clouded vision or must regard human society from a very misty distance, to cherish the view that a uniform distribution of happiness can be won through a uniform regulation of life. Such a man must already be somewhat deluded if he can really cling to the notion, for instance, that the same amount of income, or the same external opportunities of life, must possess approximately the same significance for all. But what would such a legislator do with all those for whom life's greatest possibility lies not without, but within? Were he just, he would have to give at least twice as much to one man as to another, since to the one it means much, to the other little. This difficulty of the psychological differences of men, this most necessary factor in providing the vital energy of a human society no social legislation will surmount. It may well serve a useful purpose, therefore, to speak of the heterogeneity of men. These differences involve such different claims to happiness that even the most consummate legislation could never give them approximate satisfaction. No general external form could be devised, however equitable and just it might appear, that would not involve injustice for one or other human type. That, in spite of this fact, every kind of enthusiast—political, social, philosophical and religious—is at work endeavouring to find those general and uniform external conditions which shall signify a more general opportunity for happiness, seems to me to be linked up with a general attitude to life too exclusively orientated by external facts. It is not possible to do more than touch upon this far-reaching question here, since it is not the province of this work to handle such a task. We are here concerned only with the psychological problem; and the fact of the different typical attitudes is a problem of the first order, not only for psychology but also for all those departments of science and life in which human psychology plays a decisive rôle. It is, for instance, an immediately intelligible fact to an ordinary human intelligence that every philosophy, that is not just a mere history of philosophy, depends upon a personal psychological pre-condition. This pre-condition may be of a purely individual nature, and moreover would ordinarily be so regarded, if a true psychological criticism existed at all. Because it has always been taken for granted, we have thereby overlooked the fact that what we regarded as individual prejudice was certainly not so under all circumstances; since the standpoint of the philosopher in question often boasted a very imposing following. His standpoint was acceptable to these men not because they echoed him without thinking, but because it was something they could fully understand and appreciate. Such an understanding would be quite impossible if the standpoint of the philosopher were merely individually determined, for it is quite certain in that case that he would neither be fully understood nor even tolerated. The peculiar character of the standpoint which is understood and appreciated by his following must, therefore, correspond with a typical personal attitude, which in the same or similar form finds many representatives in human society. As a rule, the partisans of either side attack each other merely externally, always seeking out the joints in their opponent's individual armour. Such a dispute, as a rule, bears little fruit. It would be of considerably greater value if the contest were transferred to the psychological realm, whence it actually originates. Such a transposition would soon reveal the fact that many different kinds of psychological attitudes exist, each of which has a right to existence, although necessarily leading to the setting up of incompatible theories. As long as one tries to settle the dispute by forms of external compromise, one merely satisfies the modest claims of shallow minds that have never yet glowed with the passion of a principle. But a real understanding can, in my view, be reached only when the inherent diversity of the psychological pre-conditions is recognised.

It is a fact, which is constantly and overwhelmingly apparent in one's practical work, that a man is well-nigh incapable of comprehending and giving full sanction to any other standpoint than his own. In smaller things a prevailing superficiality, a none too frequent indulgence and tolerance, and an equally rare goodwill, may help to build a bridge over the chasm which lack of understanding makes between man and man. But, in more important matters and especially those wherein the ideal of the type is in question, an understanding seems, as a rule, to be beyond the limits of possibility. Strife and misunderstanding are, assuredly, constant requisites for the tragi-comedy of human life, but it is none the less undeniable that the advance of civilization has led from the right of the strongest to the establishment of laws, and therewith to the creation of a court of justice and a standard of rights which are superordinated above the contending parties.

It is my conviction that a basis for the adjustment of conflicting views could be found in the recognition of types of attitude, not however of the mere existence of such types but also of the fact that every man is so imprisoned in his type that he is simply incapable of a complete understanding of another standpoint, Without a recognition of this far-reaching demand a violation of the other's standpoint is practically inevitable. Just as parties in dispute forgathering before the law refrain from direct violence, and confide their mutual claims to the justice of the law and the impartiality of the judge, so each type, conscious of his own predilection, must abstain from casting indignities, suspicions, and depreciatory valuations upon his opposing type. Through a consideration of the problem of typical attitudes, and the presentation of it in a certain form and outline, I aspire to guide my readers to a contemplation of this picture of the manifold possibilities of viewing life, in the hope that in so doing I may contribute a small share to the knowledge of the almost infinite variations and gradations of individual psychology. No one, I trust, will draw the conclusion from my description of the types that I believe the four or eight types which I describe to be the only ones that might ever occur. That would be a grave misconception, for I have no sort of doubt that the various attitudes one meets with can also be considered and classified from other points of view. Indeed, this actual investigation contains not a few indications of such other possibilities, as, for instance, a division according to the factor of activity. But, whatever may serve as a criterion for the establishment of types, a comparison of various forms of habitual attitudes will invariably lead to the setting up of an equal number of psychological types.

However easy it may be to regard the various existing attitudes from angles other than the one here adopted, it would certainly be difficult to adduce evidence against the existence of psychological types. I have no doubt at all that my opponents will be at some pains to eliminate the question of types from the scientific agenda, since, for every theory of complex psychic processes that makes any pretence to general validity, the type-problem must, to say the least, be a very unwelcome obstacle. Following the analogy of every natural science theory, which also presupposes one and the same fundamental nature, every theory of complex psychic processes presupposes a uniform human psychology. But in the case of psychology there is the peculiar condition that, in the making of its concepts, the psychic process is not merely the object but at the same time also the subject. If, therefore, one assumes, that in every individual case the subject is one and the same, it can also be assumed that the subjective process of the making of concepts is also invariably one and the same. That this is not so, however, is most impressively demonstrated by the very existence of the most diverse views upon the nature of complex psychic processes. Naturally, a new theory is prone to assume that all other views have been wrong, and, as a rule, this is solely due to the fact that the author has a different subjective view from that of his predecessors. He does not reflect that the psychology he sees is *his* psychology, and, in the best case, the psychology of his type. He, therefore, supposes that there can only be one true interpretation of the psychic process which is the object of his investigation, namely that which agrees with his type. All the other views—I might almost say all the seven other views—which, after their kind, are just as true as his, are for him merely errors. In the interest of the validity of his own theory, therefore, he will feel a lively and humanly understandable repugnance to the establishment of types of human psychology, since therewith his conception loses, for instance, seven-eighths of its value as truth. For then, besides his own theory, he would have to regard seven other theories of the same process as equally true, or grant to at least a second theory a value equal to his own.

I am quite convinced that a Nature-process which is largely independent of human psychology, and therefore can only be an object for it, can have but one true explanation. But I am equally convinced that a complex psychic process which cannot be subjected to any objective registering apparatus can necessarily only uphold that explanation which, as subject, it itself produces, *i.e.* the author of the concept can produce only such a concept as corresponds with the psychic process he is endeavouring to explain. But the concept can correspond only when it coincides with the process to be explained in the thinking subject himself. If the process to be explained had neither any sort of existence in the author himself nor any analogy to it, he would be faced by a complete enigma, whose explanation he would have to leave to the man who himself experienced the process. How a vision comes about, I can never bring into experience by any objective apparatus; thus I can explain its origin only as I understand it. In this 'as I understand it', however, there lies the predilection, for at best my explanation proceeds from the way the process of a vision is presented to myself. But who gives me the right to assume that in everyone else the process of the vision has an identical, or even a similar, presentation?

With apparent justice, one will instance the universal homogeneity of human psychology in every age and clime as an argument in favour of this universality of the subjectively conditioned judgment. I am myself so profoundly convinced of this homogeneity of the human psyche that I have actually embraced it in the concept of the collective unconscious, as a universal and homogeneous substratum whose homogeneity extends even into a worldwide identity or similarity of myths and fairy-tales ; so that a negro of the Southern States of America dreams in the motives of Grecian mythology, and a Swiss grocer's apprentice repeats in his psychosis, the vision of an Egyptian Gnostic.

From this fundamental uniformity, however, an equally great dissimilarity of the conscious psyche stands out in all the bolder relief. What immeasurable distances lie between the consciousness of a primitive, a Themistoclean Athenian, and a modern European! What a difference between the consciousness of the learned professor and that of his spouse!! What, in any case, would our world of to-day be like if there existed a uniformity of consciousness? No, the notion of a uniformity of the conscious psyche is an academic chimera, doubtless simplifying the task of a University lecturer when facing his pupils, but shrinking to nothing in the face of reality. Quite apart from the diversity of the individual whose innermost nature is sundered from his neighbour by stellar distances, the types, as classes of individuals, are themselves to a very large extent different one from another, and to the existence of types the diversities of general conceptions must be ascribed.

In order to discover the uniformity of the human psyche I must descend into the very foundations of consciousness. Only there do I find wherein all are alike. When I found a theory upon that which connects all, I explain the psyche from what is its foundation and origin. But, in so doing, my explanation entirely omits that factor which consists in its historical or individual differentiation.

CONCLUSION

With such a theory, I ignore the psychology of the conscious psyche. Therewith I actually deny the whole other side of the psyche, namely, its differentiation from the primordial germinal state. I practically reduce man to his phylogenetic prototype, or I disintegrate him into his elementary processes; and, when I would reconstruct him out of this reduction, in the former case an ape would emerge, and in the latter an accumulation of elementary processes whose interplay would merely yield an aimless and meaningless reciprocal activity.

Doubtless the explanation of the psychic phenomenon upon the basis of homogeneity is not only possible, but also completely justified. But if I wish to develop the picture of the psyche in its completeness, I must keep in mind the fact of the diversity of psyches, since the conscious individual psyche belongs just as much to the general picture of psychology as does its unconscious foundation. Hence, in my construction of concepts, I am equally justified in starting out from the fact of differentiated psyches, and in considering the same process which I previously considered from the angle of its uniformity, although now from the standpoint of differentiation. This naturally leads me to a view that is radically opposed to the former one. Everything which in that view was left out of account as an individual variant here becomes important as a starting-point for further differentiations; and everything which there contained a special value as homogeneous now appears to me worthless, because merely collective. In this view I shall always be on the look-out for the objective aimed at, and never for the source whence things come; whereas in the former view I never troubled myself about the goal, but merely about the origin. I can, therefore, explain one and the same psychic process by two antagonistic and mutually exclusive theories, concerning neither of which am I in a

x

position to maintain that it is wrong, since the rightness of the one is proved by the uniformity of the psyche, while the truth of the other is manifested by its dissimilarity.

But here, both for the lay public and for the scientific world, begins that immense difficulty, which the perusal of my earlier book (*Psychology of the Unconscious*) so aggravated, that, on account of it, many otherwise able minds became utterly confounded (as witnessed by their precarious criticisms). For there I attempted to present in concrete material the one view just as much as the other. But since reality, as we all know, neither consists in nor adheres to theories, there is in both these views, which we are bound to regard as severed, a common living something which, shimmering multi-coloured in the soul, combines and sanctions both. Each is a product of the past and carries a future meaning, and of neither can it be ascertained with certainty whether it be merely the end or holds as well a new beginning. For everyone who thinks there exists but one true explanation of a psychic process, this vitality of the psychic content, which necessitates two opposite theories, is a matter for despair, especially if he should be a lover of simple and uncomplicated truths, incapable maybe of thinking both at the same time.

On the other hand, I am not convinced that, with these two ways of regarding the psyche, the reductive and the constructive as I once called them[1], the possibilities are exhausted. On the contrary, I believe that other equally 'true' explanations of the psychic process can still be advanced, just as many in fact as there are types. Moreover, such explanations will agree just as well, or just as ill, with one another as the types themselves in their personal relations. Should, therefore, the existence of

[1] Jung, *Contents of the Psychoses* (*Collected Papers*).

typical differences of human psyches be granted, and I confess I can see no reason why it should not be granted, the scientific theorist is confronted with the disagreeable dilemma of either allowing severally mutually contradictory theories of the same process to exist side by side, or of making an attempt that is doomed from the outset to found a sect which claims for itself the only correct method and the only true theory. The former possibility encounters not only the above-mentioned extraordinary difficulty of a duplicated and inherently antagonistic thought operation, but also collides with one of the first principles of intellectual morality: 'principia explicandi non sunt multiplicanda—praeter necessitatem'. The necessity of a plurality of explanations, however, in the case of a psychological theory is definitely granted, since, unlike any other natural science theory, the object of psychological explanation is of like nature with the subject: one psychological process has to explain another. This serious difficulty has already driven thinking minds to remarkable subterfuges, as, for instance, the assumption of an 'objective mind' which could stand outside psychology and, hence, be able to regard objectively its own psyche; or the similar assumption, that the intellect is a faculty which can also stand outside itself and regard itself. With these and similar expedients that Archimedean, extra-terrestrial point is to be created by means of which the intellect shall raise itself from its own hinges. I can understand the profound human need for comfort and ease, but I do not understand why truth should bend to this need. I also understand that, æsthetically, it would be far more satisfactory if, instead of the paradox of mutually contradictory explanations, we could reduce the psychic process to the simplest possible, instinctive foundation, and be at rest, or if we could credit it with a metaphysical goal of redemption, and find peace in that hope.

But whatever we strive to fathom with our intellect will end in paradox and relativity, if, indeed, it be honest work and not a mere petitio principii in the service of comfort and convenience. That intellectual apprehension of the psychic process must lead to paradox and relativity is simply unavoidable, for the reason that the intellect is only one among divers psychic functions which Nature intends to serve man in the construction of his objective images. We should not pretend to understand the world only by the intellect; we apprehend it just as much by feeling. Therefore the judgment of the intellect is, at best, only the half of truth, and must, if it be honest, also come to an understanding of its inadequacy.

To deny the existence of types is of little use in face of the fact of their existence. In view of their existence, therefore, every theory of the psychic processes must submit to be valued in its turn as a psychic process, and, moreover, as the expression of an existing and recognized type of human psychology. Only from such typical presentations can the materials be gathered whose *co-operation* shall bring about the possibility of a higher synthesis.

INDEX

A priori categories of thought: 377, 380
" conditions of apprehension: 378
" idea: 378, 379, 380, 385
'Abaissement du niveau mentale': 156, 250, 566
Abegg, Dr, of Zürich: 244
Abélard: 54, 62, 83, 398
Abstract thinking: 376, 377, 379, 380
" thoughts and feelings: 521
Abstracting attitude of oriental religious and art-forms: 364, 365
Abstraction: 64, 339, 340, 342, 358, 520
" as introverted attitude: 362, 363, 365, 368, 369
" attitude of (Worringer): 361, 363, 366, 367
" definition of: 520
" function of: 366, 367, 368
" impulse to: 361
Abstractionist and concrete thinking (Flournoy): 375, 376, 377
Acceptance of evil: 234
Accommodation not true adaptation: 418
Action extraverted: 418
Activation of unconscious images: 292, 293, 294, 296, 300, 301
'Active nature' of Jordan: 185, 188
Active thinking as rational: 611
Activity, factor of in Jordan's descriptions: 185, 188, 195, 206
Acts of the Apostles (vision of St Peter): 579, 580
Adaptation, the observance of universal laws: 419
Adjustment of extravert, his limitation: 419
Adler, psychology of: 309, 454, 478, 531, 532, 536, 585
Adler's 'fictitious guiding line': 369
Adler's interpretation of phantasy: 78-82
Æsthetic animation (Jodl): 359
" devotion, 156
" 'disposition' of Schiller: 148, 153, 154, 160, 161, 575

Æsthetic estimation of the problem by Nietzsche: 177
" sensational attitude: 587
" standpoint: 177, 181
" types as opposed to rational: 181
Æsthetics, problem of typical attitudes in: 358
Æsthetism: 152, 170, 176
Affect, definition of: 522, 544
Affect-explosion occasioned by failure of adaptation: 597
Affective fluctuations: 244
Affective-sensation: 544
Affectivity as Jordan's character criterion: 187, 189, 194
" criterion of (Ostwald): 404
" definition of: 523
Affects as instinctive processes: 565
" pronounced, regarded as sensations: 523, 586
Age of enlightenment: 101, 230, 381
Agni: 251, 252, 258, 259, 260
Agoraphobia, spiritual: 361
Ahasuerus, the Wandering Jew: 331
Allegoric interpretation: 601
Ambitendency: 525, 539
Ambivalency: 525, 539
Ambrosius, St: 286, 287
Amfortas: 269, 270
Amor et visio Dei: 25
Anagogic significance of Silberer: 537
Analogy, primitive thinking on the level of: 534
Analytical therapy, aim of: 533
Ananda or bliss: 150, 308
'Angel abroad and devil at home': 589
Anima as inner attitude or soul: 593-596
" or soul: 273, 524, 593-596
" (soul), definition of: 588, 593
Animus of woman: 595
Anquetil du Perron: 152
Anselm of Canterbury: 54
Anthony, St, biography of: 72
Antinomians: 26
Antiphon of Rhamnus: 40
Antisthenes: 38, 45, 47, 50
Antitactic sect of Gnostics: 26, 312
Anton, 531

Apollo as image of principii individuationis : 173
Apollonian attitude : 180
Apollonian-Dionysian antithesis of Nietzsche : 172
Apperception, active, impossible without attitude : 526
„ as bridge : 527
„ definition of : 524, 525
„ passive and active : 376, 385, 524
„ subject to subjective influences : 600
„ typical differences of : 472
„ unconscious : 615
Approfondissement, introvert's tendency to : 347, 349
Aquinas, Thomas : 58
Archaic function-ways : 370
Archaism, definition of : 524
Archetype . 211, 296, 378, 380, 390, 392, 395, 476, 482, 507, 508, 555
„ as inherited foundation of psyche : 507
„ as instinctive apprehension : 476
„ as law-determined course : 508
„ as pooled experience of organic existence : 507
„ as primordial image : 476
„ as symbolical formula : 476
„ influence of upon objects : 476
„ of woman : 277
„ the noumenon of the image : 508
Archimedean point : 627
Archontici : 26
Aristotle : 53
Arius, heresy of : 30
Arjuna : 243
Artist as creator and educator : 580
Aryaman . 260
Asses feast in *Zarathustra* : 229
Assimilation : 393, 422, 449
„ as process of apperception : 525
„ definition of : 525
„ to object : 422, 423, 525
Association fear (Gross) : 343
Association Studies (Jung) : 518
Associative thinking as mere presentation : 611
Astarte, daughter of Behemoth : 333
Astral and lunar myths : 241
Athanasius, Archbishop of Alexandria : 72

Atharvaveda : 246, 247, 248, 249 259
Atlantis : 445
Atman, or Self : 149, 244, 246, 247, 302
Attention, a secondary psychic phenomenon : 547
„ extraverted : 417
„ in relation to attitude : 528
Attitude, as conscious function : 271
„ as expectation or state of readiness : 527
„ definition of : 526
„ determining efficacy of primordial image : 558
„ duality of, a normal phenomenon : 528
„ habitual as function-complex : 593
„ historical changes of : 229, 230
„ inner and outer : 591, 592
„ inner and outer, as function-complexes : 592
„ of unconscious : 422
„ symbolical : 604
„ the basis of intensity of primary function : 355, 356
„ types : 529, 530
„ underlying sexuality and power, 271, 529
Attitudes, conscious and unconscious : 527
„ general basic : 186, 198, 528, 529, 612
„ typical, formation of . 529, 530
Auch Einer (Vischer) : 369, 480
Audition colorée : 525, 539
Augustine, St : 32, 286, 288
Auto-erotic : 472
'*Automatismes*', psychic (Janet) 574
Automatized processes : 566
Auxiliary construction (Adler) : 531
Avenarius : 566
Azam : 588

Baldwin : 382, 543
Barbarian's danger of one-sidedness : 256
Barbarism : 128, 136, 140, 175, 255, 264, 331
Barlach's *Der tote Tag* : 321, 325
Basic functions : 14, 421, 428, 567, 612
„ instincts, Schiller on the two : 123

Basic Psych. Functions, peculiarities of in extraverted attitude : 428 *et seq.*
" Psych. Functions, peculiarities of in introverted attitude : 480 *et seq.*
Bataks, Religion of the : 304
Beauty as religious ideal with Schiller : 153
Bee, working, sexual deprivation of : 296
Behemoth and his host : 228, 319, 325, 333, 334, 335
" and Leviathan as the two monsters of God : 333, 335
" pact with : 229, 334
Bergaigne on Rita-concept : 258
Bergson : 398, 400, 568
Bernhard, St, prayer of : 273
Berserker rage : 256, 278
Bhagavadgita : 243, 244
Binswanger : 523
Biography, type-problem in : 401 *et seq.*
Biological precursor of types : 414
Bird, as symbol of Epimethean realm : 335
Birth of deliverer equivalent to great catastrophe : 328
"Birth of Tragedy" by Nietzsche : 170, 177, 182
Blake, William : 308, 336, 414
Blessedness, origin and nature of : 308, 311
Bleuler : 143, 522, 523, 525, 539, 615
Blonde beast, cult of : 318
Bodhisattva : 221
Bodhi-tree, the chosen : 222
Borborites : 26
Boring in the worship of Agni : 259
Bostonian tourists (James) : 391
Brahma : 244, 247
Brahman as cosmic life-principle : 248, 249, 251
" as Creator of the world : 245, 247, 254
" as Eternal Truth : 247
" as Gracious One (Vena) : 247
" as life-force : 249, 251
" as process, or irrational factor : 246
" as state of redemption : 245, 246, 247
" as sun : 247, 248
" attainment of : 150, 151, 243, 244
" corresponding with Tao : 265

Brahman essence as psychological state : 248, 249
" identified with Rita : 257, 259
" meaning of the word : 249
" two great monsters of : 254
Brahman-Atman teaching : 149, 150, 151, 242, 245
Brahmanic conception of problem of Opposites : 242 *et seq.*
Brahmans, sacred caste of : 249
'Brain-mythology ' : 353, 380
Brain, newly-born, an ancient instrument : 378
'Breaking through' of Eckehart : 314, 315
Brihadaranyaka-Upanishad : 245 246, 248
Buddha and Mara (symbol-forming process) : 610
" birth of : 221, 222, 320, 331
" fire-sermon of : 364, 366
Buddhism : 242, 272, 306
Budge, Sir Wallis : 290
Burckhardt, Jakob : 476, 555
Bushman and his boy, episode of : 295

Cælestius : 33
Capacity for deviation : 339
Çatapatha-Brahmanam : 251, 252, 253, 258
Catholic authorities : 287
" Church and Luther : 84, 85
Causal investigation of latent meaning : 576, 578, 579
" standpoint taken over from natural science : 579
" thinking and empiricism : 393
Celtic mythology : 288
Chalcedon, council of : 30
'Character as seen in Body and Parentage ' by Jordan : 184
" social and domestic : 589
" -splitting in normal individual : 589, 590
Child as redeeming symbol : 266, 323
" Tao as spiritual state of : 266
" -education, our belief in method : 512
Childhood-complex : 157, 308
Childhood's phantasies : 321
Childlike attitude : 323
" state : 309, 323
Chinese religion : 242, 264, 268
Christ and Anti-Christ : 540

Christ and temptation of the Devil: 70
" as bridegroom: 285
" birth of: 320
" -identification of Nietzsche: 542
Christ's understanding of His kingship phantasy: 70
Christian asceticism: 255
" attempt at solution: 234, 272
" ideal as differentiated function: 231, 232
" passion-theme and fate of jewel: 331
" principle of love: 151
" process, meaning of: 27, 28
" solution: 99
" sphere and phantasy activity: 70
Christianity, traditional: 229, 236, 291, 292
Chthonic craving: 284
Chu-Hi school of China: 268
Church as bride: 285
" schisms of Early: 283, 284, 293
" symbol of in Hermas vision: 283, 293
Churinga rites of Australians: 366
Circulus vitiosus, neurotic: 371, 451
Civilization, advance of: 621
" present state of: 352
Civilizing and cultural genius (Gross): 352
Civitas Dei of St Augustine: 32
Classic and Romantic types (Ostwald): 401, 406
" type as introvert: 404
" type (Ostwald), characters of: 402
Classical solution: 232
'*Cogito ergo cogito*' of mystical thinking: 483
Cognition and necessity of subject: 473
" theory of: 42, 394
Cohen: 549
Collective attitude: 229
" definition of: 530
" psyche: 316, 318, 319, 332
" unconscious: 236, 237, 240, 271, 300, 316, 319, 475, 476, 480, 555, 616, 624
" unconscious, definition of: 616
Colmar manuscript: 287
Compensation, definition of: 531
" disturbed in neurotic state: 533

Compensatory reaction of unconscious: 421, 537
" relation of unconscious to conscious: 422, 616
Complementary relation of soul to outer character: 594, 595, 596
" sex-character of soul: 594
Complex with commanding value: 342
Complexes as ' possessions ': 138
Compulsion as archaic symptom: 525
" -neurosis of introverted intuitive type: 570
" -neurosis of introverted sensation type: 504
Concept, concrete: 522
" developed from primordial image: 558
Concepts, general: 530
" need for precision of: 519
Conceptual-intuition of Hegel: 399
Conceptualism: 63, 66, 398, 399
Conclusion: 618
Concrete thinking, weakness of: 376, 377, 379, 380
Concretism, definition of: 533
" in science: 381
" of thought and feeling, as archaic: 524, 534
Conscience of Epimetheus: 213, 222, 329
Conscious activity, selective: 532
" inner life of introvert: 193
" -unconscious antithesis, development of: 441
Consciousness deepened, as basis for deepening of individuality: 349
" definition of: 535
" shallow extensive and narrow intensive of Gross: 346
Consensus gentium: 57, 58, 519
Constructive, definition of: 536, 585
" method: 83, 312, 313, 536, 537, 538
" method, individualistic: 538
Consubstantiation: 84
Contractive effect (Gross): 341
Co-operation of unconscious: 159
Cosmogonic myth, projection of: 150, 151
Counter-function, development of: 558, 560
Creation, positive, as solution of conflict of opposites: 400
Creative phantasy: 135, 138, 144, 146, 148, 573, 578, 581

Creative psychic activity : 573
„ state, the happy state : 311
Crank, the psychology of the : 508
Crihat, or *saman*=song : 253
Cripple Creek : 391
Criterion of extraverted thinking : 425
Critique of Pure Reason (Kant) : 548, 559
Cross, interpretation of the : 601, 602
Cryptamnesia : 614
Cumont : 288
Cuvier as extraverted thinking type : 484
Cynics : 38, 39, 47
Cyrillian doctrine : 33

Dæmon of Socrates : 182
Dæmoniac possession : 256
Dæmonic effect of soul : 225
Dante's *Divina Commedia* : 273, 299
„ *Inferno* : 236
„ quest of Beatrice : 299
Darwin as extraverted thinking type : 484
Davy, Humphry : 403, 404
De Carne Christi : 21
Definitions : 518 *et seq.*
Dementia Praecox, by Jung : 254
Demiurgos : 117
Demons, as irruptions from unconscious : 138, 139
Dependence upon object : 596, 597, 598
Depersonalization of feeling : 451, 452
De Somniis, of Synesius : 137
Dessoir : 585
Destiny : 262
Destructive character of unconscious archaism : 425, 426
Desubjectification of consciousness : 474
Deus absconditus : 123, 313
Deussen's *Allgemeine Gesch. d. Philos.* : 243 *et seq.*
„ interpretations : 245, 249, 253
Devotion : 156, 157
'Devouring' type of Blake : 336, 414
Diastole as used by Goethe : 11, 179, 252, 263, 313
Diels : 542
Differentiated affectivity of extravert : 198, 199
„ feeling : 125

Differentiation as starting point : 625
„ definition of : 539
„ of function in civilized life : 94, 96
„ of instinct : 296
„ required to bring individuality to consciousness : 561
Diogenes : 39, 50
Dionysian choir : 173
„ expansion or diastole : 179
„ orgies : 174
„ satyr-feasts, as totem feasts : 176
Dionysius the Areopagite : 58
Dionysos : 172, 173, 176, 177
Diotima : 53
Directed function, identification with : 370
„ function, the nature of : 371, 570
Disciple, as incarnation of Brahman : 248
Discrimination necessary between conscious man and his shadow : 203
„ the nature of consciousness : 142, 156
Dissimilation : 393, 394, 395, 525, 540, 551, 582
Dissociation : 484, 574, 575
„ between ego and state of feeling : 450
„ incompatible with united individuality : 575
„ of personality : 588, 590, 615
Divine birth as creation of new symbol : 235
„ birth as psychological fact : 314
„ birth as oft-renewing process (Eckehart) : 313
Divine children, the three : 229, 334, 335
Divine harlot : 234
Docetism : 19, 30, 31
Doctor Illuminatus : 542
Dogmatism governed by idea : 396
„ of extraverted intellectual standpoint : 440
„ versus Scepticism (James) : 396
Dream as 'guardian of sleep' (Freud) : 537
„ law-determined principle of : 581
Dreams and conscious activity : 616
„ and inner attitude : 591

x*

Du Bois-Raymond : 402
Duplication of character : 588, 598
'*Durée Créatrice*' : 246, 265, 398
Dvandva, or pair of opposites : 242
Dyophysitic formula : 30, 31, 33
Dynamis : 23, 173, 307, 311, 316, 318, 327, 328
Dynamistic conceptions of the East : 266

Ebbinghaus, on attitude : 526
Eberschweiler : 338
Ebionites : 30, 31
Ecclesia, figure of : 284
Écrasez l'infâme : 230, 236
Education of man : 155, 156, 159
Ego and consciousness : 535, 536
Ego and its relations : 117
„ and Self : 475, 477, 540
„ and subject, relation of in introverted feeling : 495
„ basis of, always identical with itself : 450
„ defective relation of to object, in introverted attitude : 478
„ definition of : 540
„ development of : 475, 477
„ of introvert, its system of safeguards : 478
„ participation of in thesis and antithesis : 607, 608, 609
„ reservation of : 472
„ resoluteness of (symbol) : 609
'Egocentric' : 472, 474, 477, 495
Egocentricity of morbid introversion : 477, 488, 495, 498
Ego-complex : 540
Einfühlung : 358
Einstellung, or attitude : 526
Élan vital : 398
Eleatic principle : 48
Elijah's ascent into Heaven, medieval illustrations of : 288
Elpore : 224
Émile ou de l'éducation, by Rousseau : 104, 105
Emotion, definition of (*v.* Affect): 541
Empathy : 358
Empirical observation, limitations of : 570
„ thinking : 376, 385, 482
Empiricism and ideologism : 381, 382, 383, 387
„ as pluralistic (James) : 373
„ prevalence of : 381
„ synonymous with sensationalism (James) : 373

Empiricist type (James) : 373
Empiricistic attitude : 393
Enantiodromia, definition of : 541
Enantiodromia of Heraclitus : 123, 228, 333, 541, 596
Encratitic sect of Gnostics : 26, 312
Energetics, laws of : 110
Energic psychic process : 581
Energic value of conscious contents : 143
Energy, concept of : 41, 250, 262, 535, 581
Energy, hypostasizing of : 250, 535, 571
Engrams or archetypes : 211, 296, 556
Enkekalymmenos, the veiled-man fallacy : 44
Enlightenment, age of : 101, 230, 381
Enthusiasm in the two types : 407
Epimeleia : 224, 227
Epimethean attitude : 228, 229, 232, 234, 235, 323, 417, 419
„ quality of inferior function : 442
„ valuation of symbol : 323
Epimetheus and statue of Heracles : 321
„ as extraverted attitude : 207, 222, 228, 419
„ compact of with Behemoth : 228
„ downfall of : 228, 235, 236
„ figure in Goethe's *Pandora* : 224, 225, 226
„ figure of Goethe : 217, 223
„ kingdom of : 222
„ realm of : 333
„ relation of to world : 208, 212, 213, 214, 419
„ reply to angel : 212, 222
„ seeks the jewel : 321
„ the shadow of Spitteler : 540
„ visit to sick Prometheus : 214, 219
Equilibrium, process of psychic : 426
Esoteric explanation of symbol : 602
'*Esprit de l'escalier*' quality of inferior thinking : 442, 514
Esse in anima : 61, 68
'*Est ergo est*' of empiricist : 483
Euclid of Megara : 48
Evangelical movement : 84
Eve : 234
Excessively valued idea : 342
Exodus, Book of : 287

INDEX 635

Exoteric standpoint, symbol alive for : 602
Externalization, laws of (Jodl) : 359
Extraversion, active and passive : 543
,, definition of : 542
,, value of : 198, 202
Extravert and introvert, attitude of vis-a-vis the object : 395, 405, 412
,, archaic thoughts of : 187
,, danger of : 420
,, normality of, its conditions : 419
,, specific psychology of : 203, 341, 404, 405
,, unconscious egoism of : 424
Extraverted attitude and problem of human relationships : 471
,, bias against introverted attitude : 472, 474, 476, 512
,, character of introvert's inferior functions : 489
,, criticism : 197
,, feeling as creative factor : 447
,, feeling, when overstressed in favour of object : 447
,, feeling-judgment as act of accommodation : 446
,, Feeling Type : 448 *et seq.*
,, feeling type, feeling of an adapted function : 448
,, feeling type, love-choice of : 448
,, feeling type, thinking of : 351, 427
,, formula, disagreeable results of : 436-439
,, Intuitive Type : 464 *et seq.*
,, judgment as predicative : 442
,, man of Jordan : 200, 214, 215
,, mentality, dangers of (Gross) : 352, 420
,, Sensation Type : 457 *et seq.*
,, thinking as synthetic : 442
,, thinking, appearance of : 431, 432
,, thinking, concretistic : 377
,, thinking, objective criterion of : 428, 429, 431
,, thinking, peculiarities of : 428, 431
,, Thinking Type, description of : 434 *et seq.*
,, thinking type, impersonal conscious attitude of : 439
,, thinking type, the formula of : 435

Extraverted thinking type, unconscious sensitiveness of : 439
,, Type, general attitude of consciousness of : 416
,, Type, general description of : 416
,, woman of Jordan : 195
Eye as function-complex : 583
,, consciousness compared with : 532, 557

Faculty-psychology (Wundt) : 384
Falsification of type through imitation : 213
Familial identity : 552
Fanaticism as over-compensated doubt : 441
Faraday : 403, 404
Fatalism : 373
Father and Mother divinities : 157
Father-transference : 598
Fathers of the Church : 285, 286, 288, 290, 296
Faust as example of dissociation : 255
,, as the Self of Goethe : 540
,, 'How differently this token works upon me' : 605
,, prayer of, to Virgin Mother : 274
,, rejuvenation of, through pact with Devil : 610
,, solution of problem in : 233, 239, 240
,, the medieval Prometheus : 232, 234
,, transformation of, as figured by Margaret, Helen, etc. : 273
Feeling, a kind of judging : 544
,, a rational function : 545
,, abstract and concrete : 545
,, active, as directed function : 546
,, and affect : 544
,, and thinking, incompatibility of : 514
,, and thinking types as rational : 452
,, as process : 543
'Feeling', concept of : 519
,, criterion of acceptance or rejection : 544
,, definition of : 543
,, dependent upon thinking : 544, 545
,, distinguished from affect : 522

Feeling, disturbance of, from assimilation to object : 449
„ futility of classification : 546
„ inaccessible to intellectual definition : 545
„ in extraverted attitude : 446
„ necessarily represses thinking : 449, 451
Feeling-apperception, active and passive : 546
'Feeling-into' : 64, 156, 393, 567, 582
„ „ and abstraction : 358, 368, 369
„ „ as extraversion : 360, 363
„ „ definition of : 547
Feeling-intuition as undirected feeling : 546
„ „ of Schopenhauer : 399
Feeling-sensation or sensuous feeling : 119, 125, 127, 129, 180, 544
„ -tone as feeling mixed with sensation : 585
„ -type : 547
Féré : 523
Ferenczi : 566
Ferrero : 601
Fetish and churinga, recharging of : 240
„ power of : 302, 366, 534
Fichte : 54, 55
Fictitious guiding-line (Adler) : 369, 531
Fire-sermon of Buddha : 364, 366
Flatus vocis : 37, 59, 65
Flournoy (*Des Indes à la planète Mars*) : 588, 614
„ *une mystique moderne* : 333
„ on James' characters : 375
Forgetting, normal process of : 614
Form and name as two monsters or functions of Brahman : 254
Formative instinct of Schiller : 126, 129
Formula, an intellectual superstition : 441
„ becomes a religion : 441
„ of extraverted thinking type : 435 *et seq.*
„ tyranny of in extraverted thinking type : 435
Fons signatus : 286
France, Anatole : 37
Free-will : 373, 393, 395
Freedom, inner, impossibility of proof of : 394

Freedom of subject, conditions of : 295, 396
„ the feeling of : 395
French Revolution : 100, 103, 230, 618
„ school of hypnotists : 470
Frenzy, the Dionysian state : 172
Freud, incest-wish of : 424
„ his interpretation of phantasy: 78-82, 537, 572, 577, 585
„ on repression of parent-imago ; 157
„ psychology of : 78-82, 454, 537, 539, 584, 585, 598, 606, 614
„ reductive method of : 78, 312, 313, 536, 537, 538, 577, 578, 584
„ his view of symbol : 157
„ wish-view of, true for extravert's unconscious : 423, 424
Frobenius : 325
Function, conscious, nature of : 514
„ definition of : 547
„ main, nature of : 514
„ natural, an organized living system : 564
„ secondary, nature of : 515
„ subjection of, to sensation (concretism) : 535
Function-complex, independence of: 593
Function-engrams : 211, 296, 556
Function-types : 412
Functions, basic : 14, 421, 428, 547, 567, 612
„ combinations of main and auxiliary : 515, 516
„ grouping of unconscious : 516
„ of relation, mind and speech as : 254
„ Principal and Auxiliary : 513 *et seq.*
„ rational and irrational : 570, 571
„ superior and inferior : 87, 324, 370, 426, 427, 563
„ the four basic, selection based upon experience : 547
„ unconscious, their symbolical appearance in dreams : 517
Fundamental laws of human nature: 263

Galtonesque family-portraits, typedescriptions as : 513
Garden enclosed : 285, 286

Gaunilo : 55, 58
Gauss : 409, 410
Geheimnisse (Die) of Goethe : 231, 234
General-attitude types : 412, 414
Genius, civilizing and cultural (Gross) : 352
German ' classics ' . 95
Gilgamesh epic : 256
Gnosis : 234, 256, 289, 290, 291, 292, 298, 299
Gnostic philosophy : 18, 234, 289, 290, 298
Gnostics and their Remains (King) : 289
God and soul essentially the same : 307
„ and Godhead, distinction between (Eckehart) : 315
„ as autonomous complex : 307
„ as collective idea : 139, 530
„ as determining force : 310
„ as function of the soul : 315
„ as highest intensity of life : 307
„ as inner value : 304, 310
„ as psycho-dynamic state : 305
„ as psychological function of man : 300, 304, 310
„ as unconscious content : 306
„ as Universal Self of Toju's philosophy : 268
„ dynamic character of : 301
„ existence of, dependent upon soul (Eckehart) : 311, 315
„ growth of concept of : 318
„ in the Devil's shape : 334
„ individual relationship with : 299
„ orthodox view of : 301
„ psychological significance of : 222, 300
„ relativity of : 300 *et seq.*
„ sickness of : 219, 220
„ subjectification of : 318
God-image : 157, 158, 300
God-imago, source of : 301
God-likeness of introverted attitude towards the idea : 117, 120, 122, 123, 219
„ „ of Prometheus : 219, 220
God-renewal and seasonal phenomena : 241
„ „ symbol of : 240, 241, 320
Goethe and Dante : 298

Goethe and Schiller : 88, 102, 118, 121
Goethe's attempt at solution : 231, 272
„ Faust : 158, 170, 232, 233, 239, 240, 255, 267, 272, 273, 444
„ own type : 215
„ principle of systole and diastole : 11, 179, 252, 313
„ Prometheus : 215, 217
Golden Age : 108
Gomperz, *Greek Thinkers* : 541
„ on inherency and predication : 41, 45, 47, 48, 49
Græco-Roman art, criterion of : 360
Grail, legend of : 269, 270, 290, 298
Grail-symbol, probably derived from Gnosis : 291, 298
Grecian and Christian cultures, comparison of : 92
„ mythology in dreams of negroes : 556, 624
Greek Fathers : 285, 286, 296
„ mistrust of powers of Nature : 171
„ tragedy : 176
Gretchen episode compared with *Pandora* : 233, 234
Gross' hypothesis, summary of : 357
„ Otto : 337, 531
Grosse Männer, by Ostwald : 401
Guardians of the market-place : 330, 332
Guillaume von Champeaux : 54

Hallucination : 554
Harking-back to the primitive : 302, 316
Harnack upon Origen : 24
Hartmann, E. von, philosophy of : 209, 585
Hase's *History of the Church* : 34
Hegel : 55, 60, 399, 549
Heine, on Plato and Aristotle : 9
'-*heit*' and '-*keit*' (Spitteler) : 212, 213, 226
Helen in *Faust* : 233, 234, 273
Hellenism : 91, 170
Helmholtz as teacher : 409
„ biography of : 402, 408
Hephaestus - Athene relationship : 218, 224
Heraclitus : 123, 541, 542
Herbart, on the reason : 383
Hermas : 275, 278, 280, 281, 282, 283

Hermas, vision of: 276, 281, 283, 293, 296
Hero, magical power of: 324
Hero-birth, primordial image of: 595
„ -myth of hero and whale: 325
Heterogeneity of men: 619, 625
Hieronymus, St: 289
Hiphil-Hophal, the high-priest: 329, 332
Historical factor, a vital need: 423
Höffding: 543
Hölderlin's *Patmos*: 326
Holstein-Augustenburg, Duke of, Schiller's letters to: 87
Holy Communion controversy between Luther and Zwingli: 84
„ Communion writing by Radbertus upon: 33
Homer as a naïve poet: 164
Homogeneity of human psyche: 624
Homoiousia: 30
Homoousia: 30
Homosexuality, from projection of persona: 598
Human psychology, as opposed to Nature-process: 623
„ psychology, universal homogeneity of: 623
Hylici: 18, 190
Hymn of the Epimethean priests: 321
„ to Mary, the medieval: 285, 288, 289
Hypatia: 137
Hysteria, the extravert's neurosis: 421, 452
Hysterical amnesia: 614
„ characters: 421

Iakchos, winnowing basket of: 289
Idea, abstract, 376, 377, 389, 392, 394, 396, 522, 547, 551
„ as abstraction: 522
„ as primordial image at stage of intellectual formulation: 558
„ as *primum movens* for introvert: 551
„ as product for extravert: 551
„ as unconscious model: 379, 380, 386, 394, 395, 482
„ definition of: 547
„ dual nature of: 550
„ hierarchical character of: 396
„ related to image: 547

Ideas *ante rem*, 378
„ basic, as much feeling as thought: 181, 490
„ mystical collective: 530
Idealism or ideologism: 387, 389
„ versus Materialism (James): 387, 388, 389, 390
Idealist and Realist, the, of Schiller: 168
Identification backward: 316
„ definition of: 551, 553
„ distinguished from imitation: 551
„ leading to growth of secondary personality: 552
„ purpose of: 552
„ with differentiated function: 127, 128, 551, 552
„ with momentary attitude: 590
Identity, an unconscious equality with object: 553
„ definition of: 552
„ expressed in Christian ideal of love: 553.
„ familial: 552
„ in paranoic delusions: 553
„ original state of: 294, 295, 553, 563, 572, 582
„ responsible for suggestion: 553
„ the basis of '*participation mystique*': 553
„ with *persona*: 595, 596, 597, 598
„ with soul: 596, 598
Ideologism: 381, 382, 387, 389, 394, 395
„ and materialism: 390
Image, an expression of total psychic situation: 555
„ definition of: 554
„ of tottering man pierced by arrow: 506
„ or imago of a man different from his reality: 600
„ personal and primordial: 555
„ personal or impersonal: 547
„ primordial: 149, 250, 265, 267, 269, 271, 272, 277, 378, 384, 476, 481, 490, 500, 548, 550, 555
Images, artistic, philosophical and religious application of: 311, 312
„ value of, for life and happiness: 312
Imagination: 82

Imaginative activity : 573, 581
Imago of object : 600
Immanuel : 327
Imitatio Christi and dissimilation : 394
Imitation a necessary expedient for development : 551
Imprints or engrams : 556
Impulsion as instinct : 566
Indeterminism versus Determinism (James) : 393
Indian religious practice : 250
,, teaching : 149, 151, 153, 242, 263, 302
Individual as against collective : 561, 562, 590
,, definition of : 560
,, degeneration of · 370
,, disposition, factor of : 415, 416
,, nucleus, separability of : 137, 139, 144
,, phantasy repressed by collective symbol : 70
,, psychology, conditioned by contemporary history : 578
,, way can never be opposed to collective norm : 563
,, way, never a norm, 563
Individualism : 133, 272, 318, 563
Individuality, definition of : 561
,, suppression of in concretism : 535
,, when unconscious projected upon objects : 561
Individuation as process of differentiation : 561
, definition of : 561
,, leads to collective solidarity, not *isolation* : 562
,, leads to appreciation of collective norm : 563
,, not unique goal of psychological education : 562
Indra : 247
Infant adaptation : 415
Inferior extraversion : 129
,, function, acceptance of : 99, 110
,, function, analytical release of : 565
,, function, definition of : 563
,, function in extraverted attitude : 427, 428
Inferiority of feeling in extraverted thinking type : 438, 439
,, with contracted consciousness (Gross) : 341

Inferiority with shallow consciousness (Gross) : 341
Inferiority-feeling of Adler : 531
Influence of poets and thinkers : 238
Inherency, principle of : 41, 45, 47, 50
,, character of inferior thinking : 442
Inherited functional disposition of the psyche : 377, 616
Inner object=elements of the unconscious : 505
,, objects : 210, 591
,, personality opposed to outer 593
,, processes, individual variability towards : 592
Inouye, Tetsujiro : 268, 269
Inquisition : 293
Instinct and will : 565
,, as inborn manner of acting : 476, 560
,, definition of : 565
Intellect, definition of : 566, 611
,, inadequacy of : 628
Intellectual formula, limitation of : 436, 437
,, intuition or undirected thinking : 611
,, standpoint betrayed by repressed feeling : 440
Intellectualism versus Sensationalism (James) : 387
Interest as libido bestowed : 521
,, extraverted : 417, 418
Intermediate type of Jordan : 184, 190, 191
Interpretation, causal and purposive : 578, 580
,, or latent meaning of phantasy : 576
,, upon objective plane : 572
,, upon subjective plane : 572, 599 *et seq.*
Introjection, active and passive : 567
,, an extraverting process : 567
,, as feeling-into : 547, 553, 583
,, as process of assimilation : 567
,, definition of : 566
Introversion active and passive : 567
,, and extraversion as biological contrast : 414
,, and extraversion, not characters but mechanisms : 354
,, definition of : 567
,, into unconscious : 147, 149, 150, 156, 309

Introversion of energy into the Self: 145, 147, 149, 304, 309
," state of: 180
Introvert and extravert, comparison of: 199, 202, 205, 404, 405, 406, 483
," general character of: 485, 486, 487
," growing isolation of: 489, 504
," need of, in present day culture: 352
," values of: 193, 203
Introverted and extraverted manner of thinking, opposition of: 386, 483
," and extraverted view of general concepts: 385, 386
," attitude governed by psychological structure: 475
," character of extravert's unconscious: 422
," difficulty of expression: 501
," feeling counterbalanced by primitive thinking: 491
," feeling falsified by egocentric attitude: 491
," feeling intensive rather than extensive: 493
," feeling, peculiarity of: 206
," feeling, tendency to overpower or coerce object: 494
," Feeling Type: 492 *et seq.*
," intellectual, feelings of: 350
," intuitive, from extraverted standpoint: 507
," intuitive, nature of: 505, 506, 507
," Intuitive Type as seer or artist: 508, 509
," Intuitive Type, general description of: 508
," man of Jordan: 144
," mentality: 351, 357, 405, 406, 480
," posture of fear towards the object: 362, 479, 480, 485
," Sensation Type, description of: 500 *et seq.*
," Sensation Type, inaccessible to objective understanding: 503
," thinking: 384, 385, 429, 430, 431, 480
," thinking dependent upon archaic image: 482
," thinking, facts of secondary importance for: 481

Introverted thinking, new views the concern of: 481
," Thinking Type, description of: 484 *et seq.*
," Type, general attitude of consciousness: 471
," Type, general description of: 471 *et seq.*
," woman of Jordan: 191
Introvert's and extravert's relative activity: 410
," apparent egocentricity: 477
," archaic affects: 187
," emotional life: 193, 194
," greater synthetic capacity. 348, 489
," ideal a lonely island: 480
," lack of personal relations: 406, 407, 478
," lack of practical ability: 486
," negative relation to object: 485, 511
," power psychology: 395
," primitive relation to object: 479, 485, 488
," psychology, unconscious attitude of: 477 *et seq.*
," tendency to relativism: 349
," undervaluation of his own principle: 498
," unfavourable personal impression: 409
Intuition an attitude of expectation: 461
," an instinctive apprehension: 568
," an irrational perceptive function: 568
," and sensation maternal soil of rational functions: 568
," compared with sensation in introverted attitude:
," compensating function to sensation: 568
," concrete and abstract: 568
," definition of: 567
," element of: 168, 461
," in extraverted attitude: 461 *et seq.*
," in introverted attitude: 505 *et seq.*
," repressed in sensation type: 457, 460
," seeks to discover possibilities: 463, 464, 465
," subjective and objective: 568
Intuitive and sensation types, similarity of unconscious in: 466

Intuitive attitude : 388
,, cognition possesses character of certainty : 568
,, discernment as shown by Jordan : 189
,, mentality of primitive : 191
,, method of Bergson : 398
,, method of Nietzsche : 399
Intuitive Type : 181, 191, 569
,, ,, thinking and feeling as inferior functions in: 465
Inundation from the unconscious, danger of : 326, 328, 334
Invasion of evil : 235
Irrational, definition of : 569
,, nature of elementary facts: 570
Irrational Types : 468
,, ,, not unreasonable but empirical: 468
,, ,, overtaken by rational judgments : 469
Isaiah : 113, 322, 323, 324, 325, 327, 328
Isis and Osiris : 289, 290
Islands of the Blessed : 55

James himself an ideologist : 390
,, Types, general criticism of : 397
,, Types, characteristic pairs of Opposites in : 382
,, William, on the types : 372 *et seq.*
James-Lang theory of affect : 523
Janet : 156, 566, 574
Janus-faced psychological moment : 578
Jehovah : 285, 333
,, transformation of : 320
Jeremiah : 71
Jerusalem, on the reason : 383
Jesus and Satan (symbol-forming process) : 610
Jew, the wandering : 331
Jewel, fate of : 331
,, nature of in Spitteler's work : 320, 329
,, redeeming nature of : 329, 330, 331
Jews, medieval persecution of : 331
,, the, as symbol of repressed elements : 331
Job, Book of : 333

Jodl : 359
Jordan, as possible introvert : 205
Jordan's description of types : 184, 214, 215, 404
,, impassioned type compared with Gross' sejunctive type : 346
,, types, special description and criticism of : 191
Julian the Apostate's discourse upon King Helios : 99
Julian's discourse upon Mother of the Gods : 17
Juno Ludovisi : 156, 158

Kant : 57, 58, 152, 377, 383, 390, 395, 484, 508, 522, 548, 559
,, as introverted thinking type : 484
,, on nature of the idea : 548
,, on reason, an introverted view : 384
Kant's postulate of God, freedom, and immortality : 395
Keratines, the 'horned-one' fallacy : 44
King, on Gnostic symbolism : 289
Kingdom of Heaven : 266, 305, 309, 310
Klingsor : 269
Kohler : 289
Kore of the mysteries : 288
Krishna : 243
Kubin : 483
Kule, in Barlach's *Der tote Tag* : 321, 325
Kulluka : 242
Külpe : 526, 543
Kundry : 269, 270
Kwei of Tao : 267

Lalitavistara : 221
Lamb, Epimetheus' raging against the : 229, 236
Landmann : 588
Lao-Tse : 83, 149, 151, 264, 268
Lasswitz : 549
Lateran Council : 84
Lehmann : 543
Less-impassioned type of Jordan: 185, 188, 341
'Levelling of ideas ' (Wernicke): 339
Leviathan : 325, 333
Lévy-Bruhl : 106, 165, 365, 530, 572

Libido as psychic energy, not psychic force : 571
,, definition of : 571
,, detachment of, from object : 304
,, detachment of, from both sides : 147, 149
,, splitting of : 29, 256
Libido-concept : 262
,, ,, and Brahman-concept : 249
,, -symbols : 246, 250
Liebig : 403, 404
Likes and dislikes : 529, 543, 544
λίκνον : 289
Lipps : 358, 360, 382, 525, 535
Literary figures, representing function-complexes of author : 601
Living form, Schiller's symbol of : 134, 145, 158, 267, 330
,, symbol : 605
Logos : 54, 83, 256
Loretto, Litany of : 274, 283, 284, 285, 292, 296
' Lost art thou when thou thinkest of danger ' (Nietzsche) : 352
Lotus of Bodhisattva : 221
Lotze : 55
Lully, Raymond, conversion of : 542
Luther : 84

Macbeth : 322
Maeder's prospective function : 536
Magic cauldron of Dagda : 288
Magical powers and the older nationalities : 233
Magna Mater : 290
Mahabharata : 243, 244
Maher-shalal-hash-baz : 327
Man as mere function : 94
Manas as form : 254
,, as psychological function of introversion : 253, 254, 256
,, as serpent-like nous : 256
,, or reason : 252, 253, 256
Manu, Book of : 242
Margaret in *Faust* : 273
Marianus, Doctor, in *Faust* : 274
Marriage of Heaven and Hell (Blake) : 414
Mary the divine harlot : 234
Mask or persona : 590
Mater Gloriosa : 234, 273
Materialism : 210
,, and idealism : 387, 389
,, as extraverted character : 389, 433

Materialistic and theosophical thinking equally negative : 445
,, explanations as superstitious : 445
,, mentality : 433
Mathematical term as symbol : 603
Matter : 289
Maturity, relative, of the two types : 407
Maya : 221
Mayer, Robert : 403, 404
Measure and number, methods of : 518
Mechtild von Magdeburg : 285
Mediatory product, superiority of (symbol) : 609
Medieval Christianity : 176, 285
,, mysticism : 285, 299, 302
,, psychology, problem surviving from : 298
Megara : 39
Megarians : 38
Meister Eckehart : 152, 297, 299, 300, 303, 304, 305, 311, 314, 318, 334
,, Eckehart, on relativity of God : 303, 304, 305, 314, 315
,, Eckehart on soul : 305
Meisterlieder, of Colmar MSS. : 287
Mephisto, personification of negative thinking : 444
,, as archaic elements of Goethe : 540
Mephistopheles, interpretation of : 255, 540
,, the medieval Epimetheus : 232
Messiah or Mediator : 241
Messianic prophecies : 322
Messias in Spitteler myth : 335, 336
' Metaphysical ' signifying ' unconscious ' : 178
Method, constructive, as intuitive : 538
,, over-valuation of : 512, 513
,, reductive and synthetic : 83, 312, 313, 536, 537, 577, 578, 584
Meyrink : 160, 483
Middle disposition of Schiller : 147
Mind and speech, question of precedence : 253
Minerva as soul-figure of Prometheus : 216, 217, 223
Miracle of Hellenic ' will ' : 178
Misautic (Weininger) : 474
Mithraic influence on ecclesiastical art : 288

INDEX 643

Mitra : 251, 258, 260
Mneme (Semon) : 475, 556
Moleschott's dictum : 444, 535
Moltzer, Miss M. : 569
Monism as introverted attitude : 396
„ versus Pluralism (James) : 396
Monophysites : 30
Monsters, the two great, of Brahman : 254, 256
Montanus : 22
Mood : 450, 543, 545
„ as feeling-valuation of conscious situation : 543, 544
Moral problem for introverted intuitive : 509
Morality, extraverted : 418
More-impassioned type of Jordan : 185
Morton Prince : 588
Mosaic morality : 263
Moses' basket of rushes : 286
Mother-dragon, motif of : 325
„ -Earth as source of all power : 302
Mother of God in *Divina Commedia* : 273
„ of the Gods : 117
Mothers, heavenly, in *Faust* : 233
Mother-transference : 598
Mühler and Schumann : 526
Mühler, Max : 248
Muratorian Canon : 275
Mysteries, Grecian : 174, 176, 288
Mystica Vannus Jacchi : 289
Mystical collective ideas (Lévy-Bruhl) : 530
„ thinking of introvert : 482
Mysticism, German : 285, 299
Myth, West African : 267
Mythological world of introverted sensation type : 503
Myths as psychic product : 241, 615
„ astral and lunar : 241

Nahlowsky on higher or ideal feelings : 521, 543
Naïve and sentimental poetry in relation to typical mechanisms : 165
„ attitude : 165
Nakai Toju, the Sage of Omi : 268
Napoleon : 101
Narcissism (Freud) : 598
Natalis solis invicti : 289
Nartorp : 535
Natural beauty as Western criterion of art : 360

Natural-science method, overvaluation of : 519
Naturalism, discussion of : 262, 263, 264
Nature and culture : 113
Nature-process, law-abiding regularity of and in : 581
Necessity for recognition of types of attitude : 621
Negative character of dependent thinking : 443, 444
„ thinking, its destructive character : 444, 452
„ thinking, personified as Mephisto : 444
Negroes' dreams and motives of Grecian mythology : 556, 624
Neo-Platonic views : 117
Nestorian controversy : 33
Nestorius : 33
Neurasthenia as neurosis of introverted feeling type : 495
Neurosis, duality of attitude in : 527
„ from suppression of infantile claims : 425
Nicolaitans : 26
Nietzsche : 37, 93, 122, 123, 161, 170, 237, 261, 298, 352, 399, 400, 477, 484, 535, 542
„ and Schiller, artist nature in : 176
„ as introverted thinking type : 484
„ as advocate of power : 298
Nietzsche's 'Attempt at a Self-criticism' : 177
„ conception of Grecian character : 170
„ intuitionism : 399
„ own type : 182
Nirdvandva : 242, 243, 244, 269
Nominalism and Realism : 37, 63, 65, 349, 374, 398
„ as extraversion : 374
Norm, collective : 562, 563
'Nothing but' style of thinking : 444, 452
Nous, of Gnosis : 256
Novum : 133
Nu or Nut : 289, 290

Obatala and Odudua : 267
Object-animation, as a priori projection : 365
„ -imago : 600
Object, dynamic animation of : 365

Object, influence of, upon thinking: 380
" potency of, depends upon projection of soul-image: 597
" overvaluation of: 309
" unconscious depotentiation of: 366
Objective catastrophe of extravert: 424
" mind, assumption of: 627
" plane, definition of: 572
" values (rational): 583
Objects, inner and outer: 210, 591
Observer, judging and perceptive: 427
Œdipus: 39
Olympian Spring, by Spitteler: 240, 599
Olympus, middle world of: 171, 174
One-sidedness, as sign of barbarism: 255
Ontological proof: 54
Opposition between sensation and thinking: 130
" concept of: 250
Optimism versus Pessimism (James): 389
Optimum of life: 263
Oriental art, impulse of (Worringer): 364
Orientation, definition of: 572
Origen: 23, 38
Organic inferiority, of Adler: 531
Ostwald: 239, 401, 535
Other-world: 218, 222
Overvaluation of instruction by word and method: 512

Paganism: 230, 231, 233
Pagan influence on Christian symbolism: 288, 289, 290
" thinking: 107
Pairs of Opposites, Brahmanic: 242
Pallas Athene: 218
Pandora, box of: 329
" comparison of Goethe's with Spitteler's: 223
" gift of, as symbol: 228, 319
" interlude of Spitteler: 218, 219
" jewel of: 220, 221, 222, 228, 319, 329, 336
" of Goethe: 223, 225, 226, 234
Pandu: 243
· Parables of Christ: 309
Paradisiacal state: 308, 320
Paradiso of Dante: 273

Paradox and relativity, unavoidable end of intellectual effort: 628
Paramatman: 243
Parameshtin: 247
Paranoia: 553, 583
Parent-complex: 157
Parental influence, factor of: 415
Parsifal: 98, 239, 269, 270
" as reconciler of the opposites: 269, 270
'Participation mystique': 106, 120, 165, 279, 316, 365, 366, 524, 534, 553, 572
' " mystique ', definition of: 572
Paschasius Radbertus: 33
Passive thinking, as irrational: 611, 612
Patanjali: 243
Paul, St, and symbol of the Cross: 602
" " conversion of: 575, 577, 578
Paulhan: 213
Pelagian controversy: 32, 33
Pelagius: 33
Perseveration phenomena. 338
Persian religion: 174
Person, introvert's concern with his: 488
Persona: 208, 209, 210, 590, 592, 593, 594, 595
" and soul, relation between: 594, 595, 596
" as collective attitude: 590
" as false self: 268
" as function-complex: 591
" as outer attitude or character: 593
" identification with: 595, 596, 597, 598
" projection of: 598
" represented in dreams: 596
Personal as opposed to individual: 590
" unconscious: 615, 616
Personality: 406, 407
" dissolved in feeling of the moment: 445
Personification of unconscious: 212, 306
" significance of: 254
Pessimism of Schopenhauer: 170
Peter, St, vision of: 577, 580
Phallic symbols: 296
Phantasies as representations of energic transformations: 262
" development of: 312

Phantasm : 573, 581
Phantasy : 69, 75, 154, 312, 378, 554, 573-581
,, active and passive : 574, 575
,, activity, common to all four functions : 547
,, as imaginative activity : 573, 581
,, as symptom or symbol : 580
,, creative, and individuality : 575
,, definition of : 573
,, image : 554
,, latent meaning of not certain : 576, 580
,, law-abiding principle in : 580, 581
,, manifest and latent meaning of : 575, 576, 578, 580
Phantasying not identical with passive thinking : 611
Philautic (Weininger) : 472, 474
Phileros : 227, 229
Philhellenism : 231
Philosopher, and typical personal attitude : 619, 620
Philosophy, English : 398
,, German : 400
,, Modern, the Problem of Types in : 372 *et seq.*
Physiological differences of individuality (Gross) : 346
Pius, brother of Hermas : 278
Plaksa fig-tree : 221
Plato : 38, 40, 44, 45, 47, 50, 53, 216, 378, 548
Play, as dynamic principle of phantasy : 82
Play-instinct of Schiller : 134, 140, 146, 154
Pluralism as extraverted attitude : 396
Plurality of personalities in same individual : 588, 589
Plutarch : 40
Pneumatici : 18, 190
Poimen, or *The Shepherd* : 284, 293
Porphyrius : 23, 52
Positive quality of extraverted thinking : 442
Possession by demons : 278
Powell on primitive thinking : 42
Power and love as incompatibles : 298
Power-attitude : 572
,, -complex, definition of : 582
,, -illusion of introvert : 478

Power-psychology, unconscious basis of : 477
Pragmatism (James) : 390, 397, 398, 400
,, a makeshift : 399, 400
Prajapati : 247, 248, 251, 252, 253, 259
Prana, or breath of life : 248
Pre-condition, psychological : 619, 620
Predication, principle of : 41, 45, 47, 50
Pregnancy of the soul : 595, 596
Primary function of Gross : 338
,, ,, intensity of, due to attitude : 355
Primeval symbol represents future truth : 484
Primitive, and loss of soul : 278
,, idea of God : 301, 302, 304, 310, 316, 534
,, languages (suffix of the thing living) : 365
,, psychology, reappearance of : 484
,, thinking and feeling : 534
,, relation to object : 365
,, spirit, revival of : 230
Primordial image : 149, 250, 265, 267, 269, 271, 272, 277, 378, 384, 476, 481, 490, 500, 548, 550, 555, 556
,, image, a mnemic deposit : 556
,, image, a recapitulatory expression of living-process : 557
,, image, a self-living organism : 560
,, image as compensating factor : 272
,, image as idea and feeling : 490
,, image as psychic mirror world : 500
,, image, definition of : 556, 557
,, image expressing creative power of psyche : 557
,, image, expression of energic process : 560
,, image maternal soil of idea : 557
,, image, nature and function of : 272, 557
,, image necessary counterpart of instinct : 560
,, image reconciling idea with concrete feeling : 558
,, image, rôle of in introverted thinking : 481, 482

Primordial unconscious state : 553
Primum in mundo fecit deus timorem : 361
' *Principia explicandi* ' : 56, 627
Principium individuationis, Apollo the image of : 173
Principle, guiding, irrational nature of : 323, 324
Printer, case of the too-extraverted : 424, 425
Problem of different typical attitudes : 619
Processes with and without symbolic meaning : 606
Procrustean bed : 121, 180
Projection, a process of dissimilation : 567, 582
,, a process of introversion : 583
,, active, an act of judgment : 583
,, definition of (*vide* Introjection) : 566, 582
,, dependent upon identity : 553, 582
,, in paranoia : 583
,, of soul-image : 596, 597, 598
,, passive and active : 582
Projections, nature of : 294, 307, 365, 566, 582
,, of intuitive type : 467
Proktophantasmists : 101
Proletarian philosophy : 50
' Prolific ' and ' devouring ' classification of Blake : 336
Prolific type of Blake : 336, 414
Promethean attitude : 228, 229, 298, 319
Prometheus as introverted attitude : 207, 216, 218, 227
,, comparison of Goethe's with Spitteler's : 215, 217, 218, 223
,, condition of, in unconscious : 219
,, figure of tradition : 216
,, fragment of Goethe : 216, 218, 234
,, intervention of : 335
,, of Goethe as extravert : 226
,, relation to his soul : 208, 210, 214, 216, 217, 218
,, reply to angel : 207, 211
Prophets in Israel (introverted intuitive type) : 507
Prospective function of Maeder : 536
,, meaning of symbols : 536, 607, 610
Protagoras of Plato : 216

Protestantism : 84
Psalms : 283
Psychoasthenia, introvert's neurosis. 479, 484
Psyche and consciousness : 536, 557
,, and soul, distinction between : 588
,, creative factor of : 579
,, definition of : 588
,, independent collaboration of 556
Psychiatric view of Christ's psychology : 71
Psychiatry, type problem in : 337 *et seq.*
Psychic content as dynamic system : 581
,, inertia : 230
,, process, object as well as subject : 622
,, relation between the different types : 470
,, structure : 211
Psychici : 18, 190
Psycho-energic process : 521
,, -galvanic phenomena (Binswanger) : 523
Psychological differences of men : 618
,, types due to identification with superior function : 564
Psychology and methods of measure : 518
,, larger conception of : 75
,, of the oppressed : 497
' Psychology of the unconscious ', difficulty raised by : 626
Psychopathic states : 337
Ptah-tenen, hymn to : 290
Puer Aeternus : 336
Purposive standpoint in relation to phantasy : 578, 579, 580
Pushan=*Savitir*, sun : 248
Pythagoras : 114

Rapport : 470
,, between rational and irrational types : 470, 471
Ratio : 382, 383, 387
,, Schiller's conception of : 133
Rational, definition of : 583
,, explanation as Utopian ideal : 570
,, types judged from their conscious psychology : 453
,, types, limitation of sensation and intuition in : 454

Rational types, subservience to chance of the : 456
,, type, the unconscious of : 455
Rationalism as psychological attitude : 382
,, as monistic (James) : 373
,, logical and feeling : 382
,, synonymous with intellectualism (James) : 373
,, versus Empiricism (James) : 382, 387
Rationalist types (James) : 373
Ratramnus : 34
'Réagibilité' of primary function : 340
Reactive rapidity, criterion of (Ostwald) : 401, 403, 408, 410
Realism : 37, 63, 374
,, as introversion : 374
,, of extraverted sensation type : 457
Reality-adaptation, value of images for : 312
Reason and objective values : 583
,, as capacity to be reasonable : 383
,, as disposition of the will : 383
,, as organ of balance : 280
,, as source of idea (Kant) : 383
,, incapable of creating the symbol : 322
,, laws of : 584
Reasonable judgment refers to objective as well as subjective factors : 496
Rebirth, meaning of : 222
Recapitulation of extraverted irrational types : 468 *et seq.*
,, of extraverted rational types : 452 *et seq.*
,, of introverted irrational types: 511 *et seq.*
,, of introverted rational types : 495 *et seq.*
Reciprocity between thinking and sensation : 132, 133
Reconciliation of Delphic Apollo and Dionysos : 174
,, of differentiated with undifferentiated functions : 223, 231
,, of the opposites : 323, 608
,, of Prometheus and Epimetheus : 227, 236
Reconciling Symbol as Principle of Dynamic Regulation : 257
,, Symbol, Brahmanic conception of : 247

Reconciling Symbol in Chinese philosophy : 264
,, Symbol, Nature of, in Spitteler : 320
,, Symbol, significance of : 234, 320, 608
Redeeming effect of living social symbol : 605, 607, 608
,, factor associated with devastation : 327
,, middle path : 242
,, symbol, effect of : 334
,, symbol, essential qualities of : 324, 326, 327
Reductive, definition of : 584
,, method : 78, 312, 313, 536, 537, 538, 577, 578, 584
,, method as collective : 538
,, thinking of empiricist : 385
'Reflective nature' of Jordan : 185, 188
Reformation, the : 84, 293, 318
Regression converted into progression : 325
,, of libido : 231, 608
Regula fidei : 19, 198
Relativity of God among the primitives : 301, 302
,, of Idea of God in Meister Eckehart : 297 *et seq.*
,, of the Symbol : 272, 300
Relaxed attitude characteristic of extravert : 356
Religion as general attitude : 229
,, Indian and Chinese : 242
,, limitation of James' concept of : 393
,, Western forms of : 241
Religious attitude and feeling : 291, 392
,, character of collective ideas : 271
,, devotion, state of : 156, 157, 159
,, form in Spitteler : 239
,, function as universal psychic constituent : 392
,, symbol, value and meaning of : 158
,, system, effect of upon individual phantasy activity : 70
,, understanding of the problem : 177, 239
Religiousness versus Irreligiousness (James) : 391
Reminiscence-complexes : 157
Rémusat, Charles de : 62, 64, 65

Renaissance : 107, 230
Renunciation of greatest value : 252
'Répresentations Collectives' (Lévy-Brühl) : 530
Repression of feeling, etc., by intellectual formula : 437, 438
„ of feeling, its disastrous results : 438, 439
„ of painful content (Freud) : 615
Retrogressive orientation : 107
Reverie : 547
Rhoda, as soul-image : 275, 276, 277, 278, 280, 293
Ri and Ki, the two world-principles : 268, 269
Ribot : 543, 588
Riehl on consciousness : 536
Rigveda, hymn of : 251
Rita as libido-symbol : 261
„ as source of energy : 260
„ concept of : 151
Rita, meaning of : 257, 258
Rita-concept corresponding with Tao : 264
Ritual-murder notion : 332
Roman auguries : 282
Romantic type (Ostwald) : 401
„ type as extravert : 404
„ type, academic activities of (Ostwald) : 408
„ type, external reaction of : 410, 411
Roscellinus, Johannes : 53
Rosicrucian solution : 231, 234
Rousseau : 104, 112, 113, 127
Ruggieri, Archbishop : 236
Running amok : 256, 278
Ryochi, as individual Self : 268, 269
„ as *summum bonum* : 269
„ paralleled with Brahman as light : 269

Sacred Books of the East : 242 *et seq.*
Sacrifice, necessity of : 309, 313
Sacrificium intellectus : 22, 25
„ *phalli* : 25
Sage of Omi : 268
Salvation - phantasy of idealistic woman : 599
Samadhi : 243
Samskaras : 306
San-tsai, the three chief elements : 267
Saoshyant : 331
Sarepta, widow of : 287

Satyr of Dionysian choir : 173
Saul, interpretation of vision of : 577, 579
„ of Tarsus, example of enantiodromia : 542, 574, 575
Savage *v.* Barbarian
Saviour, birth of : 322, 323, 331
Scepticism, attitude governed by object : 396
Schen of Tao : 267
Schiller and Goethe : 88, 102, 118, 121
„ on Idealist and Realist : 168
„ on naïve and sentimental poetry : 163
„ on reciprocity of the two instincts : 133
„ on 'semblance' : 162
„ on two basic instincts : 123, 140
Schiller's age and world of Greece : 91, 92, 170
„ attitude to Type problem : 83, 207
„ conscious attitude of abstraction : 118, 119
„ 'Golden Age' : 108
„ intellectual concept of Beauty: 111
„ introverted feeling of inferiority : 119
„ letters on *Æsthetic Education of Man* : 87 *et seq.*
„ mediatory state : 161
„ ode *An die Freude* : 179
„ pair of opposites : 115
„ symbol as philosophical concept : 114, 148
„ third instinct : 134, 146
„ transcendental way : 111, 114
„ type : 89
Schiller, F. C. S., of Oxford : 398
Schisms, psychology of : 293
Schizophrenia (Bleuler) : 615
Scholasticism : 52, 62
Schopenhauer : 123, 152, 153, 170, 178, 237, 239, 269, 383, 389, 399, 549, 559, 584
„ on nature of the idea : 549, 559
„ on the reason : 383
Schopenhauer's attitude : 237
Schultz on Tertullian and Origen : 20, 26
Science and religion : 392
„ only one of forms of human thought : 56
'*Scientia intuitiva*' (Spinoza) : 568

Scientific empiricism : 385
" literature, abundance of : 434
" separatism : 381
" theories as symbols : 603
Scotus Erigena : 34
Seasonal analogies of myths : 241
Secondary function (Gross) : 337, 338
" function, criticism of Gross' concept of : 353
" function, effect of personal and milieu influence upon : 354
Seer or disciple, as Brahman : 247, 248
Sejunction (Wernicke) : 342
Sejunctive personality (Gross) : 342, 348
Self and world as commensurable factors : 478
" as a possible aim : 144
" as Brahman : 245, 246, 247
" as opposed to ego : 475, 476, 477, 478
" defined under Ego : 540, 585
" differentiation of, from the opposites : 144
" the individual : 475
" true and false of Toju's teaching : 268
" unity of : 306
Self-divestiture, need of (Worringer) : 368, 369, 371
Self-regulation of living organism : 371, 532
Semblance, Schiller's apologia for : 162
Semiotic as opposed to symbolic : 82, 584, 601
Semon : 475
Sensation, abstract, as directed function : 587
" an irrational function : 456, 587
" and intuition : 587
" as conceived by Schiller : 124, 131
" concrete and abstract : 586
" definition of : 585
" element of : 168, 179, 456, 534, 535, 585
" extraverted : 456
" in introverted attitude : 498 et seq.
" normal and pathological : 587, 588
" repressed in intuitive attitude : 462

Sensation Type : 181, 182, 191, 456, 587
" type, difficulty of rational approach to : 461
Sensation-presentation : 130
Sensational and intuitive attitudes : 388
Sensationalism as empiricism : 387
" as function of sensation (James) : 388
" as reflexive attitude : 388
Sensuality versus spirituality (symbol) : 608, 609
Sensuous instinct of Schiller : 124, 129, 131
" relatedness as concretistic : 534
Sensuousness (*Sinnlichkeit*) as psychological attitude : 388
Sentimental attitude : 166
Sermo of Abélard : 65, 398
Service of Woman and Service of the Soul : 272
Sex, the types uninfluenced by : 413
Sexual function and general attitude : 529
Sexual interpretation of *Parsifal* : 270
Sexuality not the fundamental problem : 270, 271
Sexualization of feeling and, thinking (Freud) : 539, 588
Shadow of the extravert : 203
Shadow-effect of the two kinds of thinking : 432
Shepherd, The, of Hermas : 275
Sign as opposed to symbol : 82, 584, 601
Silberer : 537
Silesius, Angelus, on relativity of God : 317
' *Simulation dans le caractère* ' : 213
Sinister : 282
Socrates' dialogue upon beauty : 53
" Nietzsche's attack upon : 178
Socrates' rationalistic attitude : 182
Somnambulism : 588
Song of Songs : 284, 285, 286, 287, 296, 297
Sophia-Achamoth : 234, 288, 290
Soul and masculine and feminine traits : 594
" as autonomous complex : 305, 306
" as birthplace of God (Eckehart) : 311
" as established character or entity : 594

Soul as function of Godhead (Eckehart) : 315
„ as function of relationship : 209, 210, 279, 306, 310
„ as image of God (Eckehart) : 310
„ as perceptive organ of unconscious : 311
„ as personification of unconscious : 212, 306, 309, 310
„ character of, deducible from persona : 595
„ definition of : 588
„ historical ways of viewing the : 310
„ identification with : 596, 598
„ in league with undifferentiated function : 226
„ loss of : 278, 309
„ Meister Eckehart on the : 305, 315
„ nature of : 211, 212, 273, 305, 310, 329
„ or inner attitude (anima) : 593-596
„ pregnancy of : 595, 596
„ primitive view of : 306, 310
„ projection of : 596, 597
„ prospective symbolic character of : 596
„ psychological view of : 306
„ service of : 272, 279
Soul-image : 276, 277, 283, 310
„ „ as ' vessel of devotion ' : 279, 280
„ „ definition of : 596
„ „ malevolent character of: 599
„ „ projection of : 597
„ „ represented by woman : 597, 598
„ „ when not projected : 599
Soul-stuff or soul-force of the primitive : 365
Spear of Klingsor : 269, 270
Speech (Vac) as extraverting libido movement : 252
Spencer and Gillen on primitive mentality : 42, 316, 366
Spinoza : 568
Spiritualism : 210
Spiritus phantasticus : 137
Spitteler as poet : 236
Spitteler's principle of solution : 272
„ Prometheus and Epimetheus : 207, 240, 319

Spitteler's Prometheus as compared with Goethe's : 215, 217, 218
„ type : 215
Stigmatization of Saints : 393
' Still waters run deep ' (introverted feeling woman) : 492
Stilpon of Megara : 40, 50
Stirner : 93, 237
Stobaeus : 541
Stoic concept, εἱμαρμένη : 32, 261
„ teaching : 280
Sub specie aeternitatis quality of subjective perception : 500
Subject and object relation as relation of adaptation : 414
„ as inner object=the unconscious : 591
„ as only competent judge of his motives : 454
„ extraverted repression of : 423
„ meaning of : 591
Subject-object identification : 294, 295, 553, 563, 572, 582
„ -object identity, as hindrance to collective organization : 295
Subjectification, morbid, of consciousness : 474, 475, 477, 488, 491
Subjective as epithet : 472, 473, 474
„ catastrophe of extravert : 425
„ factor, as firmly established reality : 473, 474
„ factor, importance of : 473
„ factor in introverted psychology : 477
„ factor, its value only relative : 474
„ factor, meaning of the term : 473, 591
„ perception, influence upon thought, feeling, and action: 502
„ perception, nature of : 499-502
„ plane, definition of : 599
„ process inseparable from thought : 431
Subjectively orientated thinking : 431, 432
Subjectivity, anti-real, of introverted sensation type : 502
Sully on abstract feelings : 521
Summum bonum : 269
Sun and Wind as proceeding from Prajapati : 252
„ Brahman as : 247, 248
Sun-goddess : 320

Surya or sun : 248, 251
Swedenborg's transformation : 542
Symbiosis : 132
Symbol a complex creation : 606, 607
,, arising from conscious and unconscious co-operation : 606
,, as effecting transformation of libido : 291, 295, 296, 297, 313
,, as living thing : 602, 605
,, as middleway : 324
,, as reconciling function : 608
,, as value for life : 159, 163, 291, 293, 294, 295, 605
,, definition of : 601 *et seq.*
,, dependent upon attitude of observer : 603
,, dual character of : 141, 162, 266, 607
,, effective nature of : 291, 605
,, efficacy of : 141, 144, 157, 605
,, general, and loss to the individual : 292, 293
,, Goethe's choice of : 231
,, irrational : 267, 322
,, nature of, in Spitteler : 329, 330
,, new : 298, 320, 329, 335
,, of Divine birth : 313
,, of god with bull's head : 604
,, of God-renewal in Spitteler's work : 240, 241, 320
,, of life, as conceived by Sehiller : 134, 148, 158, 267
,, origin of : 144, 146, 158, 291, 293, 295, 296, 605, 606, 607
,, reconciling conscious with unconscious : 326
,, representative of inferior functions : 330
,, social and individual : 605
,, social validity of : 580
Symbols as shaped energies : 311
,, of the great natural mysteries: 314
Symbol-bearers : 225
,, -forming process as biological function : 294
Symbolic determinant of the will : 147
Symbolical attitude : 604
Symptom as distinguished from symbol : 606
,, or symbol (phantasy) : 580
Symptomatic actions (Freud) : 606
Synesius : 137, 139

Synthetic character of introverted thinking : 489
,, defined under Constructive : 536, 610
,, method : 83, 312, 313, 536
,, or constructive : 536
Systole and diastole : 11, 179, 252, 263

Tabula rasa, human mind as : 377
Talbot, P. Amaury : 290
Tao as creative essence : 266
,, as irrational fact : 267
,, as symbol : 266, 267
,, concept of : 151, 264, 268
,, meanings of : 264
,, national religion of : 264
Tao-te-king, of Lao-Tze : 265
Tapas, or self-brooding : 149, 150, 248, 252, 259
Tat twam asi : 149
Taylor : 54
Teacher, inferior man never a good : 513
Temperaments, four ancient : 403, 404
,, human, clash of (James) : 372, 374
Templars, order of : 298
Templum pudoris : 286
Temptations of Christ : 70
Tender and tough-minded as introvert and extravert : 374, 382
Tender-minded and tough-minded (James) : 373, 374, 382
Tense attitude characteristic of introvert : 356
Tension between conscious and unconscious : 532
,, psychic, an expression of libido : 356
Tertium non datur : 52, 133
Tertullian : 19, 288
Tewekkul-Beg, the Mohammedan mystic : 43
Thalamus, or bridal chamber : 286
Thema, '*approfondissement*' of : 341
,, or leading idea of Gross : 338, 339
Theory of cognition : 42, 209
,, of types, Jung's previous contributions upon : 613
Theosophical thinking : 444
Theosophy : 210
Thesis and antithesis in symbol-formation : 607, 608

Thibetan prayer, ' *om mani padme hum* ' : 221
Thin and thick characters of James : 374, 375
Thinking, active or directed : 611
,, an Epimethean appendage to feeling, in extraverted feeling type : 449
,, and feeling as collective functions : 530, 531
,, and feeling, concretistic : 533, 534
,, and feeling types as rational : 452, 570
,, attitude : 572
,, both kinds necessary as mutual correctives : 433
,, definition of : 611
,, dependent upon feeling : 612
,, enticing to the surface : 443
,, in extraverted attitude : 428 *et seq.*
,, in introverted attitude : 480 *et seq.*
,, infantile and negative, of extraverted feeling type : 451
,, passive or intuitive : 611
,, process, relation of, to subject : 430
,, two sources of : 428
,, type : 434
Thomas Aquinas : 58
Thought-activity, active and passive : 611
Thyestian feast : 39
Tibullus : 361
' -tion ' and ' -ness ' (' *-heit* ' and ' *-keit* ') : 212, 213, 226
Tishtrya Lied : 261
Toju, on nature of God : 268
Tondi : 304
Totem animal, assimilation to : 393
Tower of Babel : 283
Tower-symbol, the : 283, 284, 285, 293, 296
Transcendent function : 145, 159, 313, 562, 610, 612
Transference, a feeling-into process : 360, 567
,, state of : 567, 573
,, to object, as extravert's defence : 369
Transformation of attitude : 240, 297
,, of libido : 291, 295, 296, 297

Transubstantiation, problem of : 33, 84
Treasure-symbol : 309
Tree, the chosen : 221
Tristan, of Wagner : 298
Truth identified with extravert and his formula : 440
Tschuang-Tse : 83
Type, definition of : 612
Types described by author not the only possible ones : 621
,, function : 412
,, general-attitude : 412, 414, 529, 530
,, general description of the : 412
,, mutual prejudices of the (James) : 373, 390, 391
,, random distribution of : 413
,, rational and irrational : 612, 613
,, social : 530
Typical conflict of introverted thinking type : 90
Tyrant, psychology of : 594

' Ugliest man ' of Nietzsche : 161, 237, 540, 610
Ugolino : 236
Ular : 268
Unconscious activity : 616
,, and conscious, compensatory relation of : 422
,, and justification of experience : 614
,, apperception : 615
,, as determining factor : 307, 308
,, as historical background of psyche : 211
,, as world of spirits : 310
,, compensatory function of : 616
,, contents, homogeneity of : 624
,, counter-position to intellectual formula : 441, 542
,, definition of : 613
,, embodied in a woman : 441
,, intervention between subject and object : 502
,, not psychic caput mortuum : 508
,, personal and collective : 615, 616
,, product as symbolical expression : 536

Unconscious world of images : 211
Unconsciousness of *anima*, or soul : 597
„ of persona : 598
Undifferentiated function incapable of direction : 540
Uniform human psychology, the assumption of : 622
„ regulation of life, questionable efficacy of : 618
Uniformity of conscious psyche an academic chimera : 624
' Unity of Being ' of Eckehart : 308
Universalia, controversy upon : 37, 38, 52, 62, 374
Universality of the types : 413
Unredeemed elements projected upon the Jews : 332
Upanishad philosophy : 263
Upanishads : 152, 243, 245, 246, 248, 263, 300, 390
Uterus symbolism : 289, 290

Vac as Logos : 256
„ as name : 254
„ as principle of extraversion : 253, 254, 256
„ or speech : 252, 253
Valentinian school, classification of : 190
Varuna : 251, 258, 260
Vas, interpreted as uterus : 286
„ *sapientiæ* . 290
Vase of sin : 289
Vayu, or wind · 248
Vedas : 243, 258
Vedic conception : 242
„ hymns : 258 *et seq.*
Vena, or Gracious One · 247
Veraguth : 523
Vessel of devotion : 279
Vessel symbol, significance of : 291
„ -symbolism : 286, 287, 288, 289, 290, 296
„ symbolism, extra - Biblical origin of : 288 *et seq.*, 296
„ symbolism of Gnosis : 289
Vibrations, theosophical explanation of : 445
Viçvakarman : 253
Villa : 543, 585
Virgin, symbol-attributes of The : 274, 283, 284, 285, 286, 288, 289, 296
„ pregnancy of, as irrational condition : 322

Virgin-worship, a vestige of Paganism : 290, 292, 293, 296
Virginity, symbols of : 286
Vischer, Fr. Th. : 369, 480
Vitality of psychic content, necessitating two opposite theories : 626
Volipresence, concept of : 85
Vulcan : 223

Wagner, Nietzsche's change of attitude to : 542
„ as advocate of love : 298
„ as thinking portion of Faust : 255
Wagner's *Parsifal* ; 98, 269, 292
Wandering Jew, The : 331
Wang-Yang-Ming : 269
Warnecke : 304
Weininger : 472, 474, 475
Wernicke : 339, 342
Western forms of religion : 241
Whale, the invisible, of Behemoth : 335
Will, a secondary psychic phenomenon : 547
„ and instinct : 565
„ as disposable energy : 144
„ as energic process : 617
„ definition of : 616
„ efficacy of : 140, 144, 145
„ lacking in primitive mentality: 617
„ metaphysical, of Schopenhauer : 178, 315
' Will of God ' : 236
Winged-wheel of railway employés : 601
Witch-delusion of Middle Ages : 293
Woman, old, as the Church in Hermas story : 280, 281, 284
„ service of : 272, 292
Wonder-child : 221, 320, 323, 332
Word, magical power of, 59
World an æsthetic not moral problem to perceptive .ypes: 507
„ gaining the : 309
'*World as Will and Idea*' (Schopenhauer) : 549, 559
World-reason, pre-existing : 584
Worringer : 358, 360, 361, 362. 364, 368
Wulfen's *Cicerone d. rücksichtslosen Lebensgenusses* : 458

Wundt: 359, 384, 519, 522, 524, 525, 527, 543, 544, 548, 585
„ on reason, an extraverted empiricistic view: 384
Wuwei, concept of: 268

Yajnavalkya: 246
Yaksha=aspect or dæmon: 254
Yama, or sun: 248
Yang and Yin, Taoistic pair of opposites: 267

Yoga, practice of: 150, 156, 243
Yogasutra, of Patanjali: 243

Zarathustra as the Self of Nietzsche: 540
„ of Nietzsche: 123, 178, 182, 229, 237, 239, 240, 399, 610
Zeller: 541
Zerebrale Sekundärfunktion, of Gross: 337
Zwingli: 84, 85

www.ingramcontent.com/pod-product-compliance
Ingram Content Group UK Ltd.
Pitfield, Milton Keynes, MK11 3LW, UK
UKHW020245240426
12048UKWH00026B/1621